Richard Cruttwell

A General Dictionary of Husbandry

planting, gardening, and the vegetable part of the materia medica - Vol. 2

Richard Cruttwell

A General Dictionary of Husbandry
planting, gardening, and the vegetable part of the materia medica - Vol. 2

ISBN/EAN: 9783337381615

Printed in Europe, USA, Canada, Australia, Japan

Cover: Foto ©Andreas Hilbeck / pixelio.de

More available books at **www.hansebooks.com**

GENERAL DICTIONARY OF HUSBANDRY, PLANTING, GARDENING, AND THE Vegetable Part of the *Materia Medica*;

WITH THE

Deſcription, Uſe, and *Medicinal* Virtues

OF THE SEVERAL

HERBS, FLOWERS, ROOTS, &c.

Selected from the Beſt Authorities,

BY THE

EDITORS of the FARMER's MAGAZINE.

VOLUME II.

BATH: Printed by R. CRUTTWELL;

AND SOLD BY W. GOLDSMITH, No. 24, PATER-NOSTER-ROW, LONDON,

AND BY ALL OTHER BOOKSELLERS.

M DCC LXXIX.

M.

MACE. One of the coverings of nutmeg. *See* NUTMEG.

MACCAW TREE. *See* PALM.

MAD APPLE. *See* APPLE.

MADDER, [*Rubia.*] This is the English name of a plant cultivated with great advantage in several parts of Europe, and lately in England, being a very capital ingredient in the dying business. There are several species of madder, all of which afford a dye. M. Guettard, of the Royal Academy of Sciences, has experienced that the ladies bed-straw, or cheese-rennet, [*gallium*] may be made to yield one; and of this kind is probably the Ray-dechaye, which is used on the coast of Coromandel for dying red. M. Dambourney has not, indeed, as M. Duhamel remarks, hitherto been able to extract a good colour from the gallium: but there yet remains room to hope that he may be more successful in the future experiments which he intends to make on this root.

Mr. Ray mentions and describes four different kinds of gallium or mollugo, bastard madder, which, after the laudable example of our enterprizing neighbours, should likewise afford matter of experiment to those who wish well to this country, and particularly to our dyers.

The azala or izari of Smyrna, perhaps more properly written hazala or lizary (according to the eastern method of pronunciation) which is the sort used by the French dyers at Darnetal and Aubenas, to give cotton that fine carnation colour for which Adrianople is famed, is a true madder. Some species of it grow naturally under hedges and in woods; and the roots of these, when carefully dried, yield as fine a dye as the azala of Smyrna. M. Dambourney has cultivated a species of madder which was found growing wild on the rocks of Oissel in Normandy, and the roots of this plant have yielded him as beautiful a dye as the azala of the east. Mr. Ray describes particularly a wild madder which grows only on St. Vincent's rock near Bristol, but also on the rocks about Biddeford in Devonshire, and in great plenty among the hedges almost all over that county. As Mr. Ray calls this the *Rubia sylvestris Monspessulana major*, and as M. Duhamel suspects M. Dambourney's Oissel madder to be that very species, it surely is a matter of great importance to this nation, and well worth the attention of patriots, to follow M. Dambourney's example in making proper trials of it.

The species most commonly cultivated is the *Rubia tinctorum sativa*, commonly known among us by the general name of madder. It is of this species that the plantations of madder are made in Zealand, and in the neighbourhood of Lisle.

The root of madder is a capital drug used in dying wool, linen, and cotton; and is indispensibly requisite in printing linen and cotton, being the only red dye in general use for that purpose. It was, at the time when the Society for the encouragement of Arts, &c. first engaged in the encouragement of it, wholly imported from Holland: though it had formerly been a staple article of produce in our own country. We pay annually for this root to the Dutch an exceeding great sum; not less, according to calculation, than near three hundred thousand pounds; and, what is still worse, taking the advantage of the necessity we are under to purchase it of them, they have not only advanced the price to an exorbitant rate; but adulterate and sophisticate the madder in so bad a manner, as lays our manufactures, in which it is used, under the greatest difficulties. These manufactures moreover, in which it is absolutely necessary, are of the utmost importance,

importance to us; particularly the printing linen and cotton; which furnishes employment to some thousands of our women and youth, who would otherwise be waste hands, and many of them burthensome to the public. Nothing, therefore, could be more worthy the regard of the society, than the introduction of the culture of madder here; which may tend to the national good so many different ways.

There was however, at first, an almost insurmountable impediment to the culture of madder in England. It consisted in this circumstance, that madder being a crop raised on land, it was subject to pay the tithe in kind: which was in fact so heavy a tax on the produce, as together with the great expence and risk, from the want of a more perfect knowledge of the manner of cultivation, almost entirely discouraged all attempts in a larger way. This obstacle was, nevertheless, removed through the endeavours of the Society, by the obtaining an act of parliament, to change the demand of tythe in kind to a modus, or composition, of five shillings per acre, for a term of years. The society thus, by their interposition in this matter, procured the first opening to that success, which is now likely to attend the attempts, to restore the production of this important article to our country.

The society, the mean time, exerted themselves to incite the public attention and spirit, to undertake the culture of madder by premiums. The first they offered was for the producing twenty pounds weight, the most perfect and best cured. This was obtained in the year 1755. They then, being by this means assured, that a method was known in England of raising and curing good madder, proposed premiums for the largest roots, twenty in number, of one, two, or three years growth: which were accordingly claimed and obtained for each kind, in the year 1758, and again in 1759. Further premiums were given in 1763, 1764, and the following years.

Madder is a plant of very little beauty, it in some degree resembles the common cleavers or goose grass, in its manner of growth. The stalks are numerous, square, and commonly of a reddish colour: they are weak, so that they lie upon the gronnd in their lower part; and in the upper, commonly intangle one with another. The leaves are long and narrow, they stand six at a joint; sometimes more, sometimes fewer, and are disposed like the rays of a star. Their natural colour is a dusky green, but they sometimes, especially toward the lower part of the stalk, grow reddish. The stalk is hairy, but the leaves are more so: their hairyness is not a woolly down like that of some plants, but is short, rough, and hard, so that they prick the hands when touched.

The flowers grow at the tops of the stalks, and small branches; they are small, but very numerous, and of a pale yellow. The seeds follow, which are contained in a kind of round little heads; the root, which is the useful part, is extremely long, and of a beautiful red colour, duskyer on the surface, but very bright within.

The cup in which the flower of madder stands is very small, and stands upon the rudiment of that little roundish fruit in which the seed is to be lodged: it is composed of a single green leaf, hollowed and divided into four little segments at the edge.

The flower is in the same manner formed of a single leaf, a little hollow at the bottom, and divided lightly into four parts at the edge. In the centre of this rise four short filaments, each terminated by a single button or head, from the rudiment of the fruit, which, as it enlarges a little, shews itself to be composed of two parts; there rises a single filament called the style of the flower, this comes up in the midst of the four filaments just named, and is divided into two parts toward the top, each of which has a button to it: this, through certain imperceptible apertures, admits the dust from the heads of the other filaments for the ripening of the seed vessel, which then swells, and becomes a kind of double berry: in each part of which, or each berry, is contained a single seed.

There are two kinds of madder mentioned by those who treat of plants, these are the six-leaved kind we have described, and one which has only four leaves at a joint, but the latter is not worth the farmer's notice.

Madder being one of those plants that roots deep, and the value of which is in the root; the soil for it should be deep and light. This is the principal caution, for it will get nourishment whether the ground be richer or poorer, provided it be not altogether barren. A black mould, such as is common in the fens of England, is very proper; and is the same soil whereon they plant it in Flanders, whence we have our greater supply. A loamy soil that is in some degree rich, and has but little clay in its composition, is also very proper; of a mixture of loam and mould, as is very common in many parts about the edges of the fen countries. A sandy soil will also do well if properly managed.

There is no part of England where this plant would thrive better than in these places, for they have all the advantage of the Flemish grounds, and this further benefit, that they are drier; the Flemish often bursting their roots by their over moisture, or occasioning an expensive manner of dressing to prevent that accident.

Whatever be the soil for madder it must be deep. We have observed it is the nature of the root to extend itself in length, and that no art can bring it to any great thickness; therefore a depth of soil is the most essential point, that it may have room to penetrate. There are usually produced a great many side roots, which spread along just under the surface of the ground. These are the provision of nature, for the nourishment of the stalk and leaves, the great root taking almost all the juices it receives to its own nourishment. Now as the stalks and leaves of this plant are of no use or value, it is idle to provide for the maintaining them in vigour at the expence of the main root. These horizontal shoots never come to any value themselves, and as they only take that nourishment which should supply the main root, the proper course is to destroy them.

This account of the nature of madder, and of the soil that suits it, naturally points out a new method of managing it to advantage; of all the plants that can be raised, none is so perfectly suited to the horse-hoeing husbandry. The soil it requires is such as perfectly suits those implements; the method of horse-hoeing of all other practice, will the most effectually and most essentially cut off the shallow and horizontal roots; and as the main roots are to be encouraged is their growth to the utmost, no method of planting can be so proper as that in rows at a considerable distance from one another. This directs in every article the horse-hoeing husbandry, as the method for raising madder to an excellence, and perhaps such a one as it never reached yet in England. The culture of this profitable and useful species has been recommended frequently and strongly, and has been tried at different times with different success, but always with some profit; we hope therefore that the farmer will be encouraged, from what has been found of the advantages of this crop, in methods less suited to its nature, to try it in the way we are about to propose; in the which it cannot fail of very well answering his care, expence, and trouble; and according to which there is a reasonable prospect of his enriching himself by it in a few years culture.

Madder is to be planted in spring; but the preparation of the ground for it must be undertaken long before. Let the farmer who intends to raise it look carefully out for a field that has a deep light soil, of the nature of either of those kinds we have mentioned. When he has fixed upon the field, in autumn, as soon as the crop is off the ground, let him plough it up deeply and thoroughly. Let him leave it in this condition three months, and then going over it with the plough once again, tear it up to a great depth, and thoroughly break and divide it: let him then leave it to himself till the end of March. Having secured his sets, let him in the last week in March, send in his plough again, set to its greatest depth. As the ground has been twice ploughed before, it will very well give way to this. The sets are now to be taken off from the sides and heads of the old roots, and the ground is to be harrowed even. Then a line is to be drawn along near the edge, as in the planting of liquorice, and the sets are to be let into the ground in the same manner, at a foot distance from one another.

When one row is thus planted, the line is to be removed a foot and half, and another row planted, the sets in this

this not being placed opposite to those in the other, but just over against the middle of the space between.

The line is then to be removed to the distance of five foot, and drawn strait over the ground as before, and a row of the sets are to be planted there; thus there will be a third row at five feet distance from the second, and at six and a half from the first row: the line is then to be moved again one foot and half, and another, being a fourth row, is to be planted opposite the middle distances of the last. Thus the whole ground is to be planted out. The sets are to stand every where at the same distance in the row, as at first ordered; and the whole field will be laid out in double rows, with five feet intervals; the space or partition between one row and another, of each double row, being one foot and a half.

When the sets are all in and lightly covered up, let the planter go over the places, where they stand, with a garden rake, and lay all level.

The beginning of April is a season when showers are seldom wanting; but if it should so happen that there are none, there must be the labour of once watering the sets. The best time for doing it is on the third day after their planting, and when this is done they may be left to nature.

The plants will now quickly appear, and as this is a time when the encreasing warmth of the season, and wet from the showers, sets every thing on growing, weeds will appear among them. As these must be principally seedlings, for we suppose no roots left in the tillage, they will not at once over-run the proper growth, because that is planted with good roots; so that they need not be attacked so soon as ever they appear; but when they have got a little height the hand-hoers must be sent in to clear the partitions of them between row and row, not meddling with those in the five foot intervals, except just on the outside of each row.

This is to be done with care and management, and a great deal depends upon it. The instructions to be given the hoers are these. First to take care of the plants of madder, which being set regularly, and now up at some height, and being very different in their aspect from the weeds, cannot well be mistaken; all this however must be pointed out to them, and they must be strictly cautioned; for the destruction but of a few of the plants where they are set separate, and each intended for a large growth, will be a considerable loss to the owner. This being pointed out to them, they are to be sent in with directions to cut up all weeds in the small partitions, and break the surface of the ground as deep as they readily can with those instruments; then they are to clear away between plant and plant of the madder; and thence advancing to the outside they are to cut up the weeds, and break the ground for about a hoe's breadth all along the rows.

This done, the plants are to be left to themselves three weeks, in which time they will strike very strongly, and the gronnd just above them will be very clear of weeds, from the hoeing; but by this time the middle of the large intervals will be full of weeds of some growth.

The horse-hoe is now to be sent in, and is to cut along the middle of each interval, to as much depth as it can: this will thoroughly root up and destroy that growth of weeds, and break the ground. The weeds will, in great part, be buried, and will become a kind of manure, for weeds that cannot grow soon rot at this season, which is warm and wet; and the ends of some of the longest fibres of the madder roots will be broken off, and new ones will consequently grow in great quantities from them, as is seen in cutting of the fibres of roots in the gardener's way of planting; and there will be a fine quantity of fresh and free earth for these new roots, as also for what farther shoots the others may make; and it will be full of nourishment for them.

We have said that the main downright roots are all that are of value in his madder plants. Now the horizontal or spreading ones, that run under the surface, are to be considered in two distinct lights, as they are larger or as they are smaller, for at one of these times they impoverish, but at the other they feed them; so that at one time they are to be nourished, and at another destroyed.

It is while they are young that they are

are of advantage to the main root. This is their condition in the present instance, and it is therefore we are recommending every method to feed and to encrease them; and on the other hand, we shall soon after take as much pains to destroy them. The part of the madder above ground, now though of some bignesa, is not so large as to demand any vast quantity of nourishment; the root, on the contrary, is pushing downward, and grows the faster the more it is supplied by its fibres, and the less it is drained by the plant above.

This is the case in many instances at the period of growth whereat the madder is at present, but in none more visibly. The first nourishment the new planted roots take in, goes to the pushing some fibres from themselves outward, and a shoot of stalk and leaves upward. This shoot takes up the greater part of the nourishment in the first days, but afterwards it grows slower, and requires a smaller proportion of what is drawn. After this there is a period when the main root is taken care of and supplied, that it may be able to send up nourishment in abundance to the herb, when ripening its flowers and seeds, that being the great purpose of nature in all plants: for this purpose also in madder a number of long horizontal roots grow out every way under the surface.

These horizontal fibres we have named, and for which we are now so carefully providing by the horse-hoe, are in time to become those long horizontal and side roots. At present they are very serviceable, for they draw in nourishment in vast abundance; which being not demanded in that quantity by the plant in its present state, goes according to the design of nature, to the feeding and enlarging the main or downright roots. The present horse-hoeing has vastly encouraged, filled, and encreased them; but the next is to destroy them.

Some time after this horse-hoeing there will be weeds again in the partitions, and between plant and plant, for this is a season that produces them very quickly: the hand-hoers must be sent in again to cut them all up, and the plants of the madder being kept clear, will have a healthy aspect, which is very essential to the good growth of the root, and which they would not have if choaked up with weeds: some weeks after this, when the madder has grown to a considerable size, let the horse-hoe be sent in a second time, with orders to cut much nearer one side, or one row, alternately; by this means all the large horizontal roots on that side will be cut and broken off, and only small ones will grow from the ends of them, which will tend to the service of the main root again.

The hand-hoers at this last time need not hoe the outsides of all the rows, but only alternately of those near which the horse-hoe is not this time to come, for the next hoeing it is to take the others. This instrument could not be brought so near the rows while they were young, for fear of tearing up or burying the plants, but they are too well established now to be in any danger on that head, especially as it is done only on one side; for the horse-hoe is to be carried along the farthest side of the next interval all the way, in the course of this operation; so that it never comes near both sides of the same row.

The plants will immediately after this thrive surprisingly, and advance toward their flowering. There will need no more hand-hoeing, for they will be now of such a size and strength, as to destroy all the weeds about them; and the next horse-hoeing, which will be the last for the summer, will compleat the work for the first season.

This is to be done as soon as the weeds have got some head again in the intervals, for they will rise there tho' they be over-powered in the partitions. The instrument is now to be carried on the other sides of the rows alternately, so that now there will have been a thorough and deep cutting up of the ground, near both sides of every row.

The large horizontal roots, which would impoverish the main roots, and be of no value in themselves' are now broke and cut off on this side also; and the main roots, which are now large and strong, have all the advantage of the nourishment

The flower and seed of madder are wholly useless: and as a plant's running to seed impoverishes the root, this dictates

dictates a new practice in the present case, which is the cutting down the plants just before they are breaking out into flower.

Let this be done with caution, and with moderation. The farmer is not to cut them down close to the ground; it is enough if he stop their running to seed, therefore all he has to do is to cut them off half a foot below the top. This will take off all the flower buds, and yet will leave enough of the plant to draw up a great quantity of sap, and keep nature in her proper course. By this means a vast quantity of rich juice, intended for the perfection of the plant in its ripeness, will go to the main root, for there will be no large side roots to take it up; and the increase in that useful part will be very surprising.

The stalks will shoot out side branches from the part where they were cut off, and from every joint below, and will grow stronger for that cutting, and very bushy. Some of these will make an attempt to flowering, and they may be left to themselves in it. The few flowers that grow upon these shoots are not like the full and universal flowering of the whole growth, they will do neither good nor harm, and are not worth regarding.

The first summer will thus pass, and the plants, not having drawn a vast deal of nourishment upwards, the roots will be greatly strengthened and encreased. This will be the condition of the crop at the autumn of the first season; and all that is to be done is in the same manner to promote the growth of the root, during the rest of the time it is to remain in the ground, which is to the next autumn. A crop of madder, though it remain but eighteen months in the ground, is to be accounted by the farmer as a two years standard, because the preparation of the land takes up the other six. The whole course is this; at autumn the ground is to be taken for it; during the winter it is to be prepared: and in spring it is to be planted: the next autumn the plants have had one summer's growth, and they are to have another, for they must remain through the winter, and the following summer: and the roots must be gathered in autumn following, which is two years from the time of beginning the preparation of the ground.

In the usual way of management, when the roots are taken up at this time for sale, another piece of land is to be sought out for the next crop; but in the method we have proposed by the horsehoeing husbandry, the same piece of ground may raise madder for ever; and will be fitter for it than any other could.

All the winter the ground is to lie perfectly quiet: in spring a fortnight before the plants begin to shoot, the horsehoe should be sent in to cut a deep furrow in the center of every large interval, and the hand-hoers to cut up those weeds that rise in the partitions. After this there will be no more care needful about them, for the growth will be too strong to suffer any annoyance; but the intervals will have weeds, and should be horsehoed just as in the preceding summer, to prevent their farther growth, and to give new supplies of nourishment to the main roots, as well as to cut away and destroy the side or horizontal ones.

This is to be done exactly in the same manner as before mentioned for the first season, and therefore needs not be described more at large here. By this means the crop will proceed as it ought in every respect; and this season the whole care will be over.

In autumn, when the plants wither, is the time to take up the roots; this must be done with care and circumspection, for the more they are broke in the ground, the more of them is lost. The regular method of planting them comes in here to be of great use, for the people employed to take them up know where to look for them one by one, and where they may, and where they may not, work about them.

When they are all taken up they must be cleaned from dirt, and after a quantity of fine sets are separated for a new plantation, they are to be dried for sale. The dyer will be always a ready purchaser, nor need the husbandman fear to overstock the market.

Madder has little or no smell; a sweetish taste, mixed with a little bitterness. The virtues attributed to it are those of a detergent and aperient, whence it has been usually ranked among the opening roots, and recommended in obstructions of the viscera, particularly of the kidneys, in coagulations of the blood from falls or bruises

ses in the jaundice, and beginning dropsies.

It is observable, that this root, taken internally, tinges the urine of a deep red colour; and in the philosophical transactions, we have an account of its producing a like effect upon the bones of animals who had it mixed with their food: all the bones, particularly the more solid ones, were changed both externally and internally, to a deep red; but neither the fleshy or cartilaginous parts suffered any alteration: some of these bones, macerated in water for many weeks together, and afterwards steeped and boiled in spirit of wine, lost none of their colour, nor communicated any tinge to the liquor.

Petty MADDER, [*Asperula.*] A plant growing wild in many woods in England. *See* WOODROOF.

MADS. EARTHWORMS. See

MADWORT. [*Alyssum.*] There are several species of this plant growing naturally in warmer climates, yet will in general bear the cold of ours. They are propagated by slips or seeds; the flowers appear in April or May; are various, white, yellow, &c. and last about three weeks in beauty, if the weather is moderate.

MADNESS, *in a Dog.* There are abundance of prescriptions for the bite of a mad dog; but whether any are good we cannot presume to say. The Ormskirk medicine is much esteemed; but if we might advise, it should be to cut out the part or cauterize it immediately.

Maggot. See Crub. Sheep.

MAHOGANY, [*Cedrus Mahogoni.*] This tree is a native in the warmest parts of America, growing plentifully in the islands of Cuba, Jamaica, and Hispaniola; there are also many of them on the Bahama islands. In Cuba and Jamaica there are trees of a very large size, so as to cut into planks of six feet breadth; but those on the Bahama islands are not so large, though they are frequently four feet diameter, and rise to a great height, notwithstanding they are generally found growing upon the solid rocks, where there is scarce any earth for their nourishment. The wood which has been brought from the Bahama islands has usually passed under the appellation of Madeira wood, but there is no doubt of its being the same wood as the mahogany.

The leaves of this tree are winged like those of the ash, having commonly six or eight pair of pinnæ (or lobes) which are shorter and broader at their base than those of the ash, where they adhere to the midrib by very short footstalks; these lobes are very smooth, having but one vein running through each, which is always on one side, so as to divide them unequally. The entire fruit, before it opens, is of a brown colour; these fruit grow erect upon long footstalks, which closely adhere to the five cornered column, running through the middle of the fruit, and to which the seeds are fastened, lying imbricatim like slates on a house, over each other; so when the fruit is ripe, the outer cover divides at the bottom into five equal parts; and when these fall off, and the seeds are dispersed, the foot-stalk and column remain some months after on the tree.

It is propagated by seeds, which may be easily procured from the Bahama islands, from whence most of the good seeds which have come to England were brought; for most of those which have been sent from Jamaica, although brought in their pods, have not succeeded, whereas those from the Bahama islands have grown as well as if they were immediately taken from the trees; the seeds should be sown in small pots filled with light sandy earth, and plunged into a hot-bed of tanners bark, giving them a gentle watering once a week; if the seeds are good, the plants will appear in a month or five weeks; and when the plants are two inches high, a sufficient number of small pots should be filled with light earth, and plunged into the tan-bed a day or two, that the earth may be warmed before the plants are put into the pots; then the young plants should be shaken out of the pots, and carefully separated, so as not to tear their roots, and each planted in a single pot, being careful to shade them till they have taken fresh root; after which they must be treated in the same manner as other tender plants from the same climate, being careful not to give them much water, especially in winter. If the plants are properly managed, they will make considerable progress.

MAIDEN-HAIR, [*Adianthum.*] The species are 1. *The officinal or true Maiden-hair,* 2. *Canada Maiden-hair.* The first

 sort

ſort is the true Maiden-hair, which is directed to be uſed in medicine; but as it does not grow naturally in England, ſo the Trichomanes is uſually ſubſtituted for it, which is found growing wild in great plenty in ſeveral parts of England. The other is a native of the South of France, Italy, and the Levant. It uſually grows out of the joints of walls, and the fiſſures of rocks, ſo that whoever is inclinable to keep this plant in their gardens, ſhould plant it in pots filled with gravel and lime rubbiſh, in which it will thrive much better than in good earth; but the pots muſt be ſheltered under a frame in winter, otherwiſe the plants are often killed by the froſt.

The ſecond ſort is often preſerved in gardens for the ſake of variety; this ſhould be planted in pots, and treated in the ſame manner as the former; for although it will live through the winter in the open air in moderate ſeaſons, yet in ſevere froſt it is often deſtroyed. This ſort grows naturally in Canada in ſuch quantities, that the French ſend it from thence in package for other goods, and the apothecaries at Paris uſe it for the Maiden-hair, in all their compoſitions in which that is ordered.

Maiden-hair has been greatly celebrated in diſorders of the breaſt, proceeding from a thinneſs and acrimony of the juices; and likewiſe for opening obſtructions of the viſcera, and promoting the expectoration of tough phlegm. But modern practice pays little regard to it; nor is it often to be met with in the ſhops.

Engliſh MAIDEN-HAIR, [*Trichomanes.*] There are three or four varieties of this plant, which grow naturally in Europe; but in America there is a great number of ſpecies, which are remarkably different from each other, as alſo from the European kinds.

Theſe being of the tribe of ferns, or capillary plants, are ſeldom preſerved in gardens. Their roots ſhould be planted in moiſt ſhady places, eſpecially the European ſorts, which commonly grow from between the joints of old walls, and in other very moiſt ſhady ſituations; but thoſe ſorts which are brought from hot countries muſt be planted in pots filled with rubbiſh, and ſtrong earth mixed, and in winter they muſt be ſcreened from hard froſt, to which, if they are expoſed, it will will deſtroy them.

The common ſort in England is generally ſold in the markets for true Maiden-hair, which is a very different plant, and not to be found in England, it being a native of the ſouth of France, and other warm countries, ſo is rarely brought into England.

White MAIDEN-HAIR, [*Ruta Muraria.*] A plant growing out of old walls in many parts of England.

MAIZE, [*Zea.*] *See* GUINEA WHEAT.

MALACCA BEAN. See *Anacadium.*

MALABAR-NUT, [*Juſticia.*] This plant is a native of Ceylon, but hardy enough to live in a green-houſe, in England, without any artificial heat. It riſes here with a ſtrong woody ſtalk to the height of twelve or fourteen feet, ſending out many ſpreading branches, garniſhed with ſpear-ſhaped oval leaves ſix inches long and three inches broad, placed oppoſite. The flowers are produced on ſhort ſpikes at the end of the branches, which are white with ſome dark ſpots, but are not ſucceeded by any ſeeds in England.

It may be propagated by cuttings, which, if planted in pots in June and July, and plunged into a very moderate hot-bed, will take root, but they muſt be ſcreened from the ſun; and if the external air is excluded from them, they will ſucceed better than when it is admitted to them. It may alſo be propagated by laying down the young branches, which will take root in one year, and then ſhould be put each into a ſeparate pot, and placed in the ſhade till they have taken new root; then they may be removed to a ſheltered ſituation during the ſummer, and in the autumn they muſt be houſed, and treated in the ſame way as the orange trees, with only this difference, that theſe require more water.

MALANDERS. This is an external diſorder of a horſe very painful and troubleſome, and very difficult of cure; inſomuch that ſome ſay nothing more is to be attempted than to alleviate the pain; and that it is dangerous to ſtop the diſtemper.

This is a very unhappy error; for there is no degree of the Malanders but may be cured by proper management; and that with perfect ſafety.

This diſeaſe ſhews itſelf on the fore-legs, upon the inner part, juſt againſt the bending of the knee.

It

It is not a knob or ulcer like the farcy, but a hard, dry, flat scab, of which sometimes there is only one great one, sometimes several smaller; and these are cracked and chopped upon the surface, and have stiff hairs like bristles growing upon them.

This is the whole of the disorder: it sometimes is very violent and inveterate, sometimes more slight. When it is very bad it makes the horse halt; and when least it occasions him to go stiff till warmed with exercise.

The general cause of the malanders is bad management. It is the common disorder of horses kept in a slovenly manner, and much more rarely affects those which are managed more carefully.

Those horses are most subject to it which have most hair upon their legs, and they are the most difficult to cure.

One essential difference the farmer is to make in his conduct, for a horse under this disorder, which arises from this consideration, that sometimes the malander is only a soreness in the part, while the horse is otherwise in health; sometimes the blood is corrupt and bad, and in this case the disorder is more violent in its degree, and more difficult to be cured.

When the malander is only the effect of carelessness, and it is upon a horse otherwise healthful, the method to be observed is this. Let him be kept to his usual work and usual food; and let the following wash be made for the part:

"Set on a saucepan with three quarts of water, put to it half a pound of fœnugreek-seed bruised, and a pound of fresh marshmallow root cut in slices. Boil all this till it is like a jelly, strain it off hot, and press it hard out, then add to the thick liquor half a pound of opodeldock ointment."

Make some of this hot morning and night, and dipping flannels in it, wrap them round the leg where the complaint is, as hot as the hand can bear to touch it. Let this be several times repeated; and at the last of all, wet some of the ingredients, which must be saved when the liquor has been pressed out, with some of the liquor hot, and lay them upon one flannel, cover them with another, and wrap the whole round each leg, tying it round so as to keep it on, but not tight.

Let this be done every day twice, as directed, till the hard substances begin to soften; after this once in four and twenty hours will do; and there will thus be a perfect cure.

Before the first dressing let the hair be clip'd round about the place, and the whole part about the Malanders wash'd clean with warm soap suds. Let this be repeated at times during the cure; and after it is perfected, let the legs be kept very clean in this part, for fear of its returning.

In this manner a horse will be cured very easily, and very certainly, that has no taint in his blood: but if there be that added to the outward malady, care must be taken accordingly, by giving inward medicines at the same time.

When this is the case, the owner will perceive it by his habit of body; and by the outward remedy not taking its desired and natural effect; he is then to proceed thus:

Let a pound of crude antimony in powder be mixed with four pounds of flour of brimstone; & let some of this be sprinkled among his food. This is better in such a case than giving it in balls or drenches, for he takes it with his nourishment a little at a time, and often; and accompanying the food in its passage through the Intestines, its virtue goes into the blood, together with the nutritive part of the food.

I have heard many who should know something better than the vulgar, say, that they would not cure a horse of the malanders if they could; for that all that is prudent is to keep him from growing lame with them. They have an old proverb that has misled them from father to son for many generations, which is, "that curing the malanders is shutting up the wolf in the sheep-cot." But they may be sure of this, not only in the present case, but in all others whatever, that there will be no danger of damage in curing any outward disorder, when the blood is at the same time rectified within.

We have shewn the difference already, that when the complaint is only external, outward remedies alone may be trusted, but when the blood is affected, inward things must be given to assist. The danger even of a mistake

take in these cases, is not so great as these persons apprehend; for when the blood is in fault, and no care has been taken to amend it in the cure, the common consequence is only, that it breaks out again.

MALE BALSAM APPLE. *See* APPLE.

MALLOW, [*Malva.*] This is a plant growing common enough in the fields, the leaves are ranked the first of the four emollient herbs: they were formerly of some esteem, in food, for loosening the belly; at present decoctions of them are sometimes employed in dysenteries, heat, and sharpness of urine, and in general for obtunding acrimonious humours: their principal use is in emollient glysters, cataplasms, and fomentations.

There are several species of this plant, exotics, cultivated in the gardens, propagated by seeds.

Bastard MALLOW. *See* BASTARD.

Jew's MALLOW, [*Corchorus.*] There are several species of this plant brought from the East and West Indies and South America, but are all too tender to thrive in England in the open air, therefore their seeds must be sown on a hot-bed in the spring, and when the plants are come up and fit to remove, they should be transplanted on a fresh hot-bed to bring the plants forward. After the plants are rooted in the new hot bed, they must have free air admitted to them every day, for they must not be drawn up weak; and when they have obtained strength, they should be transplanted each into a separate pot, and plunged into a hot-bed, observing to shade them from the sun till they have taken root; in June they should be gradually inured to the open air: part of them may be shaken out of the pots, and planted in a warm border, where, if the season proves warm, they will flower and perfect their seeds; but as these will sometimes fail, so it will be proper to put one or two plants of each sort into pots, which should be placed in a glass-case, where they may be screened from bad weather; and from these good seeds may always be obtained.

Indian MALLOW, [*Urena.*] There are four species of this plant brought from China and the coast of Malabar. They are propagated by seeds in a hot-bed, and require the assistance of a stove to preserve them.

Marsh MALLOW, [*Althæa.*] This plant grows naturally in moist places in divers parts of England, and is frequently used in medicine. It has a perennial root and an annual stalk, which perishes every autumn. The stalks of this plant grow erect to the height of four or five feet; these are garnished with leaves which are hoary and soft to the touch, and placed alternately on the branches; the flowers come out from the wings of the leaves, which are shaped like those of the mallow, but are smaller and of a pale colour. It may be propagated very fast, either by seeds or parting of their roots. When it is propagated by seeds they should be sown in the spring, but if by parting of the roots, the best time is in autumn, when the stalks decay. It will thrive in any soil or situation, but in moist places will grow larger than in dry land.

This plant has the general virtues of an emollient medicine; and proves serviceable in a thin acrimonious state of the juices, and where the natural mucus of the intestines is abraded. It is chiefly recommended in sharp defluxions upon the lungs, hoarseness, dysenteries, and likewise in nephritic and calculous complaints; not, as some have supposed, that this medicine has any peculiar power of dissolving or expelling the calculus; but as by lubricating and relaxing the vessels, it procures a more free and easy passage. Althæa root is sometimes employed externally for softening and maturating hard tumours: chewed, it is said to give ease in difficult dentition of children. There are two other species of this plant brought from Portugal and Hungary, both propagated by seeds.

Rose MALLOW. *See* HOLLYHOCK.

Tree MALLOW, [*Lavatera.*] There are several tall herbaceous flowering annuals and shrubby perennials of this plant, bearing large red, white, and purplish flowers, continuing in bloom from June till August or September.

They are all proper ornaments for any part of the pleasure ground. The annuals particularly have singular beauty, their flowers being large, numerous, and conspicuous, and very proper furniture where large showey plants are required; and are easily and abundantly raised from seed in the open ground.

The

The shrubby kinds are also good furniture for shrubbery compartments, having large, strait, upright, durable stems, terminated by branchy bushy heads, and very large soft foliage, that form a fine variety in assemblage; though their flowers are often hid by their large leaves. These perennial kinds should have a dry soil, otherwise are apt to go off in two or three years; a fresh supply, however, may always be raised from seed in the common ground.

They are propagated abundantly by seed in the open ground in the spring; the annuals in the place where sowed, and the perennials also either where they are to remain, or for transplantation.

Syrian MALLOW, [*Hybiscus.*] This plant is commonly known among nursery-men by the name of Althæa frutex.

Viscous MALLOW, [*Malvaviscus.*] This hath a shrubby stalk, branching ten or twelve feet high, bearing scarlet flowers, succeeded by roundish scarlet viscous berries.

Venice MALLOW, [*Hibiscus Trionum.*] Trionum, Bladder Ketmia, Flower of an hour. This is an annual plant bearing flowers of very short duration, which in hot weather only just open, and then wither away in an hour or two. Its propagation is by seed sown either in autumn or spring in the place where they are to remain, leaving about three of the best plants on the spot.

Yellow MALLOW. *See* INDIAN MALLOW.

MALT. Barley prepared, to fit it for making beer or ale, by stopping it short in the beginning of vegetation.

It is said, that the soil on which barley grows makes a considerable difference in the grain, and that the barley fittest for malt is that which grows on a rich, light, or gravelly soil, and which has been raised from seed brought from a farm of a different soil and situation. The fullest and largest grains of such a crop should be chosen for making malt. It should be heavy and perfectly sound, and such as has not suffered any accident in the field. Its being a little heated in the mow is by some reckoned an advantage, because the grain will be the more equally dried, and will consequently the more equally imbibe water. If it has been so much mow-burnt as to look blackish when broken at the root end, or as Mr. Combrune says, if it has suffered a heat of 120 degrees, it is unfit to make good malt. It is also found by experience, that barley taken immediately from the field does not malt so kindly as that which has been some time in the house, or mow. Special share ould be taken that it be free from the seed of weeds; for these, in the malting, are apt to give the grain a bad taste, which cannot by any means be afterwards got rid of.

By germination, all the principles of barley are put in action. The heat which it undergoes in malting separates and divides its parts; and the viscidity which it before possessed is removed by the looser texture of its oils, and their intimate union with the salt, which gives malt the sweetish taste that distinguishes it from barley.

In order to its being malted, the barley is put into a cistern lined with lead or stone, and covered with water about six inches deep above the barley, to give room for its swelling. All the good grain will sink in the water; but after stirring it, the imperfect or distempered grains will rise to the surface. These should be skimmed off, and given to Poultry or hogs, for they will never make good malt. By the water gaining admittance into the barley, a great quantity of the air is expelled, as appears from the number of bubbles which rise on the surface.

The barley is left in the water two or three days, more or less, in proportion to the heat of the weather and the dryness of the barley. A judgment is formed that grain is fully saturated with water, from its appearing turgid, and easily giving way to an iron rod dropped perpendicularly into it. Or, take a corn from the middle of the cistern, and hold it steadily by the two ends, between the fore-finger and thumb: press it gently, and if it continues firm when so pressed, and the skin does not break, it must soak longer: if it crushes together and feels mellow, and the skin crack, it is watered enough. Nicety in this is a material point, and can be learnt only by experience. If the grain should be suffered to remain too long in water, it would begin to lose part of its sweetness. When it has been steeped sufficiently, the water is drawn off.

The

Barley sometimes appear to have been heated in the Barn or Stack, called Goaf-burnt - and looks so often when only affected by May-weed, but then it has the weed smell - (See May-weed

The water used for this purpose should be that of a clear running stream, or rain water; or if such cannot be had, pond water, provided it be sweet and clean, will do very well; or pump water, which should be rendered soft if it be naturally hard. If the water made use of be any way tainted, it communicates to the malt a taste which it never loses. Mr. Combrune advises the adding of lime to the water in which the barley is steeped: but this seems to be improper, because it appears from Dr. Home's experiments that lime renders water hard.

From the cistern, the barley is laid in a regular heap or couch, where it must remain thirty hours, or till it has contracten a heat. It must then be worked in one or more heaps, and turned every four, six, or eight hours, according as the weather is cold or hot. When it begins to spire, it should be turned every three or four hours, according to the temperature of the air; and as it comes (for so its spiring is commonly termed) the heap must be spread thinner to cool it, lest it be heated too much, and the germination be carried on too fast, by which the oils would be too much consumed. The turning of it must be continued in proportion as it is more or less slow in growth, so that it may be brought tolerably dry to the kiln. When the roots begin to deaden, the couch must be thickened again, and often turned, that the growth of the roots may not revive. At this time, the spire should be near piercing through the outer skin of the barley: for if it grows quite out, the strength of the malt will be too much consumed. After the malt is made thus far, the common practice is to lay it at once on the kiln: but the best way is to gather it all up in one heap, to let it lie in that state twelve hours, and then to turn it every fourth hour, during the space of twenty-four hours.

No person should be suffered to tread on the malt with their shoes, while it is on the floor: because many grains are inevitably bruised thereby, and these, vegetating no longer, afford the roots of the other grains a substance into which they extend their fibres, and are by that means entangled in bunches: and besides this, the bruised corn acquires a degree of putrefaction which taints the liquor made of the malt intermixed therewith. Equal care should also be taken, that the grain be not bruised by any other means.

Mr. Combrune thinks, that the time most proper for malting is when the temperature of the air is such that barley begins naturally to germinate, at which season the thermometer marks from between 32 to 40 degrees. How far that time may be extended, experience alone can determine. The warmer the weather is, the greater must be the disadvantage under which the maſter labours; because the motion of the fluids is then so strong, that the process goes on too quick, and the finer parts are apt to fly off; the consequence of which is, that instead of a sweet, the malt inclines to a bitter taste, the oils being turned rancid. This is so universally experienced, that brewers carefully avoid purchasing what is termed latter-made malt.

The grain thus prepared for drying is spread on the kiln, where, meeting with a greater heat than is suited to vegetation, its farther growth is stopped. It is spread on the kiln three or 4 inches thick, and turned every three or four hours. The laying of it thicker is often attended with inconveniences, among which is particularly its being unequally dried; and therefore that should be avoided. The strength and duration of the fire is different, according as the malt is intended to be dried, pale, amber, or brown. The pale malt requires more leisure and less fire than the amber or brown.

Pale and amber malt are dried with coke or culm, which not emitting any smoke, give the malt a brighter colour, and do not communicate that bad relish which malt has when dried with wood, straw, &c. the smoke of which taints it. Coke is best, because its fire gives a steady and constant heat, whereby the malt is dried uniformly. If wood, or any vegetable fuel be used, it should be extremely well dried, in order that being as free as possible from moisture, it may yield the less smoke.

The size of the malt kiln is generally proportioned to the quantity of malt for which it is intended. Some build their kiln square, and others make it round; but this last is undoubtedly the best form, because the heat of the fire is more equally diffused therein, and the grain is of course more equally dried.

Various

Various substances have been made use of for covering the kiln, such as tiles, plates of tin, and wire: of these, the wire is to be preferred, because it does not contract so great a degree of heat as to parch the grain in contact with it: but for this very reason, hair-cloth is preferable to any other covering; because, when any part of the malt is in immediate contact with a substance more solid than itself, and therefore capable of receiving a proportionably greater degree of heat, the malt in contact with that heated body is parched or burnt, by heat which is not equally diffused through the whole mass, which mass cannot therefore be all equally heated. The hair-cloth is spread upon small wooden rafters, and these are supported by bars of iron laid across the kiln.

An ingenious and attentive malster marked the degree of heat in the malt whilst on the floor: and the result of his observations in this respect is as follows. During the first ten days that the malt was on the floor, the heat in it was between 50 and 60 degrees. During the next three or four days, the heat was increased from 60 to 65 and 67 degrees; and during the last days of its lying there, to 80, 84, and 87, which last was the degree of heat when the malt was put on the kiln. There cannot be any absolute rule as to the difference of heat during the different times in the process of malting, because it must be suited to the heat of the air: at least we have not yet sufficient data whereon to found such a calculation. The heat of the malt on the kiln when fit for pale malt was 120 degrees, and when it was fit for brown the heat was 147.

This intelligent artist's observation, that the malt was fit for what is called pale malt when its heat was at 120 degrees, suggests a caution which should be most carefully attended to, namely, that whatever colour it be intended to give to the malt, the heat at first should always be the same: thus, for example, malt which is dried to the degree of high brown, should first be rendered pale malt, then amber, and so on progressively; not by a sudden increase of the fire, but by a longer continuance thereof. In this manner, the whole body of the grain is equally and gradually dried; whereas a strong and quicker fire would parch, or as it were singe the outside, while the internal parts remain moist: and as that moisture is afterwards evaporated, it must crack the surrounding hardened crust, whereby the grain is again damaged in another respect.

As soon as the malt is dry, it must be removed from the kiln, and spread thin, that it may cool to the temperature of the air. It cannot be supposed, that any of its parts are capable of retaining the fire in such manner as not to suffer it to escape; though some have conceived that they do. In proportion as malts are dried, their particles are more or less separated, and coming in contact with water, they strongly attract from it particles which fill up their interstices. In mashing, this action between the malt and the water generates a small degree of heat, but no way durable; though from hence arose the opinion, that brown malt is full of fire.

Barley may, at a medium, be said to lose by malting one fourth part of its weight, including what is separated from it by the roots being skreened off: but this proportion varies, as it is more or less dried.

The condition of the barley, as to its greenness or ripeness, at the time of its being gathered in, is clearly discernable when it is melted. If it were gathered green, it rather loses than gains in quantity, the malt becomes of a smaller body, appears shrivelled, and is often unkindly hard; whilst, on the contrary, that which was cut at full maturity increases in malting, appears plump, bright, and clear, if properly carried thro' the process, and on being cracked, readily yields that fine mealy substance so much desired by brewers.

Malt which has not had a sufficient time to shoot, so that its plume, or acrospire as the adepts in malting call it, may have reached to the inward skin of the barley, remains charged with too large a quantity of its unattenuated oils. All those parts which have not been put in motion by the act of generation, will, when laid on the kiln to dry, be so hardened, as not to be soluble in water, and consequently will be lost to the strength of the drink.

When malt is suffered to grow too much, or until the spire has shot through the skin of the barley; though all

all that is left be malt, yet as too large a portion of its oils will have been expended in vegetation, the malt will be greatly diminished in proportion to what it ought to have been, & what remains cannot be fit to brew drink for long keeping, because of the loss of the oils.

Malt which has been duly worked on the floor, will, if it has not been sufficiently dried on the kiln, be apt to germinate or sprout afresh; perhaps to conceive so great a heat as to take fire; and should it continue long with a moderate degree of heat, the least evil that can be expected is, that it will grow mouldy and have an ill flavour.

Malt well worked, but over-dried, will be so hardened, or its saponaceous quality will be so destroyed, that it will not imbibe from the air that moisture which is necessary to mellow it, and render it fit for brewing: for when it has been previously softened by the moisture of the air, it mixes more easily & more intimately with the water, and by that means yields a more copious extract, than it would otherwise do.

Malt just, or but lately, taken from the kiln, remains warm a considerable time. Until it becomes as cool as the surrounding air, it does not mellow by the addition of a due quantity of moisture from the air: and the wort made of such malt requires a much longer boiling before it breaks, than that which is made of malt some months old.

The practice of those malsters who sprinkle water on malt newly taken from the kiln, to give it the appearance of having been made a proper time, is highly blameable. It is in fact a downright fraud, practised chiefly because less grain then fills the bushel: but a farther evil is, that if it be not used speedily, it heats, soon grows mouldy, and suffers great damage.

Malt dried on a kiln not sufficiently heated must require a proportionably longer time for it to receive the due effect of the fire, for want of which it will be in the same state as malt not thoroughly dried. If the fire be too quick, or too fierce, instead of gently evaporating the water from the corn, it scorches the outward skin, and separates it from the body of the grain. The malt to which this happens is called blown malt; of which Mr. Combrune observes, that by the internal expansion of its parts, it occupies a larger space than it ought to do. He adds, that if such a fire be continued, it changes some parts of the grain into so brittle a substance, that the malt is said to be glassy. The particles which are thus hardened will not dissolve, or but in small proportion: so that they frequently occasion an almost total want of extract, which, in the phrase of the art, is termed setting the grist.

The goodness of malt may be known by the following marks. Bite a grain of it asunder, and if it tastes mellow and sweet, breaks soft, and is full of flour from one end to the other, it is good. It has a round body, and if upon putting some grains of it in water they swim on the surface, it is good. Barley sinks in water, and malt that is not well made will do the same: but it is to be observed that this is not an invariable proof, because if the malt be broken, or in the least cracked, it will take in water, and sink. Malt that is rightly made will not be hard, but of so mellow a nature, that if drawn over an oak board, across the grain, it will leave a white line upon the board, like a mark of chalk. Its smell also may be consulted; for malt, though otherwise good, may have contracted an ill scent from the fuel, or from the water used in the steeping.

Before malt is ground, it should be freed from the tails and dust, which would otherwise heighten the colour of the wort, render the liquor muddy, and give it a bad taste, which could not afterwards be got rid of. The cylindrical sieve will be of excellent use for this purpose.

The malt must be broken, in order to its communicating its virtue to the water. If it be ground too small, its flour will mix too freely with the water, and cause the wort to run thick. Many are of opinion that the best way is only to crack it, so that none of the grains may come out whole: for the intent is, that the water should draw out an extract, but not be mixed with the mealy part, in the manner of paste or gruel. Some think that malt is better ground by a stone mill, than by a steel one, because the former bruises it, and the latter only cuts the grains.

After the malt is ground, it should lie some time to mellow, in a cool room, where no sun comes. The time

time for this is different, according to its kind. Brown malt may be ground at from three to fourteen days before it is used, in order that the corn, which is rendered uncommonly hard by that degree of drying, may be gradually softened by the moisture in the air; by which means it will become the more soluble in water. The pale malts require only one or two days. After lying thus in the air less mashing suffices, the strength of the malt is more perfectly extracted, and the beer will be considerably stronger than it would be with the same quantity of malt taken directly from the kiln. Care must be taken that it get no damage in lying.

Mr. Combrune observes, that malt imbibes moisture more readily by being ground and exposed for some time to the air, than it does when whole; and that as the dampness thus absorbed by the grain is in reality so much cold water, malt which has been long ground requires to be mashed with hotter water than it would otherwise be necessary to use.

To know whether malt has been mixed with barley unmalted: Take a bowl of water and throw into it a couple of handfuls of the malt; give it a gentle stirring, and the barley which has not been malted will sink to the bottom; the half-malted grains will have one end sunk, being in a vertical position; and the good malt will swim.

Malt Dust. This is an excellent manure sown as a top-dressing on wheat in the spring, especially on harsh, clayey and stubborn soils.

Malt Worm. A cankery sore in the hoof of a horse so called.

MAMMEE. This is a very large tree growing both in Asia and the West-Indies to the height of 60 or 70 feet.

Both these trees in their native soil produce abundance of fine fruit, as large as Catharine peaches, of a yellowish green colour, and said to be of a delicate flavour.

In this country they require to be continued constantly in the stove, so must be kept always in pots, and placed in that conservatory, where they will cause a fine variety all the year with their large splendid foliage.

Their propagation is by seed, which arrives from America, &c. in spring. Sow it in small pots of light rich earth, and plunge them in the bark-bed, where they will soon come up; give gentle waterings, and about August transplant them into separate pots a size larger, plunging them in the bark-bed, and give shade and water till fresh rooted.

MANCHINEEL TREE, [*Hippomane.*] This is a very large tree in its native soil, almost equalling the oak in size; the wood is much esteemed for making of cabinets, book-cases, &c. being very durable and taking a fine polish; it is also said that the worms will not eat it. As these trees abound with a milky caustic juice, they make fires round their trunks before they are felled to burn out their juice, otherwise those who fell them would be in danger of losing their sight, by the juice flying in their eyes: for wherever this falls upon the skin, it will raise blisters, and if it comes upon linen it will immediately turn it black, and on being washed will come in holes. It is also dangerous working of the wood after it is sawed out; for if any of the saw-dust happens to get into the workmen's eyes, it causes inflammations, and the loss of sight for some time; to prevent which, they generally cover their faces with fine lawn during the time they are working the wood.

This tree hath a smooth brownish bark, the trunk divides upwards into many branches, garnished with oblong leaves ending in acute points, slightly sawed on their edges, and are of a lucid green, standing on short foot-stalks. The flowers come out in short spikes at the end of the branches, being of both sexes in the same spike, but having no petals they make but little appearance; these are succeeded by fruit about the size and of the same shape as the golden pippin, turning of a yellow colour when ripe, which has often tempted strangers to eat of them to their cost, for they inflame the mouth and throat to a great degree, causing violent pains in the throat and stomach, which is dangerous unless remedies are timely applied.

The inhabitants of America believe it is dangerous to sit or lie under these trees, and affirm, that the rain or dew which falls from the leaves will raise blisters; but it is very certain that unless the leaves are broken, and the juice of them mix with the rain, it will do no injury.

These plants are preserved in some of the curious gardens in Europe, where they can never be expected to rise to any great height, for they are too tender to live in these northern countries but in stoves; they rise easily from seeds, provided they are good.

MANDRAKE, [*Mandragora.*] This plant grows naturally in Spain, Portugal, Italy, and the Levant, but is preserved here in the gardens of the curious. It hath a long taper root, shaped like a parsnip, which runs three or four feet deep in the ground; it is sometimes single, and at others divided into two or three branches, almost the colour of parsnip, but a little darker; from this arises a circle of leaves, which at first stand erect, but, when grown to their full size, spread open, and lie upon the ground; they are more than a foot in length, and four or five inches broad in the middle, of a dark green colour, and a foetid scent. These rise immediately from the crown of the root, without any foot-stalk; between them come out the flowers, each standing upon a separate foot-stalk about three inches long, which also arise immediately from the root; the flowers are five-cornered, of an herbaceous white colour, spreading open at the top like a primrose, having five hairy stamina, with a globular germen in the center, supporting an awl-shaped style. The germen afterward turns to a globular soft berry lying upon the leaves, which, when fully grown, is as large as a nutmeg, of a yellowish green colour when ripe, full of pulp, in which the kidney-shaped seeds are lodged. It flowers in March, and the seeds are ripe in July.

MANGE. A well-known filthy disease in a horse, which makes him rub against every thing he can lean on, and if other horses that are with him are not removed, they are subject to catch it from him. It is known by the hair staring, and in many places peeling away from the skin, on which a scurf will arise. This disorder is occasioned by over-heats and colds, hard riding, or labour, whereby the blood is corrupted, or by feeding upon unwholsome meat. To cure this disagreeable distemper, we would recommend the following method:

"Take of tobacco stalks half a pound, tobacco dust one pound, black soap half a pound, allum and bay salt each a quarter of a pound, green broom a large handful, and stone lime about the size of a hen's egg; boil all these in two gallons of urine, till half be consumed; when almost cold, stir into it an ounce of flour of brimstone or stone brimstone in powder."

Cut the hair off the mane and tail, and then curry them all over where the distemper is, till the blood is almost ready to start; then take a piece of flannel or woollen cloth, and daub the horse all over with the liquor a little warm, if the weather is not very hot.

This quantity will dress the horse all over twice; the second application may be two days after the first; or if the disorder is very bad, the next day following. This remedy will do for dogs, &c. *See* LEPROSY.

MANGER. A wooden trough in which horses corn is put. Mr. Williamson advises a rack and manger for cows in the following words:

"I would by all means advise every farmer to have a rack and manger for his cows, with a loft over for hay, from whence it may be put down as for horses; and he will find that they will eat with more satisfaction, and make infinitely less waste, than by the common method of laying it on the ground; the manger should be about seven or eight inches from the ground, and always be kept very clean by the cow-boy."

MANGROVE TREE, [*Rhizophora.*] This is a West India tree, of which there are several species, but they will not grow upon land.

MANGROVE GRAPE. See *Seaside* GRAPE.

MANGO TREE, [*Mangifera.*] This plant grows naturally in many parts of India, and has by the Portugueze been trasplanted to the Brazils and other countries, where it grows to a large size; the wood is brittle, the bark rough when old; the leaves are seven or eight inches long, and more than two broad; the flowers are produced in loose panicles at the end of the branches; these are succeeded by large oblong kidney-shaped plumbs.

This fruit, when fully ripe, is greatly esteemed by the persons who reside in the countries where it grows, but in Europe we have only the unripe fruit brought over in pickle; however, the account given of the ripe fruit by those who have tasted it, has excited the curiosity of many persons to procure young plants for their gardens in Europe, but hitherto without effect.

MANDOL, or MANIHET. See CASSADA.

MANNA. The juice of certain trees of the ash kind (growing in Italy and Sicily) either naturally concreted on the plants, or exsiccated and purified by art. There are several sorts of manna in the shops. The larger pieces, called flake manna, are usually preferred; though the smaller grains are equally as good, provided they are white, or of a pale yellow colour, very light, of a sweet not unpleasant taste, and free from any visible impurities. Some people injudiciously prefer the fat honey-like manna to the foregoing: this has either been exposed to a moist air, or damaged by sea or other water. This kind of manna is said to be sometimes counterfeited by a composition of sugar and honey, mixed with a little scammony: there is also a factitious manna, which is white and dry, said to be composed of sugar, manna, and some purgative ingredient, boiled to a proper consistence; this may be distinguished by its weight, solidity, untransparent whiteness, and by its taste, which is different from that of manna.

Manna is a mild, agreeable laxative, and may be given with safety to children and pregnant women: nevertheless, in some particular constitutions, it acts very unkindly, producing flatulencies and distension of the viscera: these inconveniences may be prevented by the addition of any grateful warm aromatic. Manna operates so weakly as not to produce the full effect of a carthartic, unless taken in large doses, and hence it is rarely exhibited in this intention by itself. It may be commodiously dissolved in the purging mineral waters, or joined to the cathartic salts, sena, rhubarb, or the like. Geoffroy recommends accuating it with a few grains of emetic tartar: the mixture is to be divided into several doses, each containing one grain of the emetic tartar: by this management, he says, bilious serum will be plentifully evacuated, without any nausea, gripes, or other inconvenience. It is remarkable, that the efficacy of this drug is greatly promoted, (if the account of Vallisnieri is to be relied on) by a substance which is itself very slow of operation, casia.

MANURE. This term comprises all sorts of dungs, composts, and other materials proper or used for the improvement of lands. See DUNG, COMPOST, &c.

Manure, therefore, is necessary to all soils, to repair them when exhausted by the growth of vegetables, and to cure the defects of soils naturally bad, such as to enrich and fertilize very poor land; to render very strong or stubborn land more light, loose, and pliable; and to render very light, loose, dry soils, more compact and moist: and wet land dryer, &c. Strong moist land is the most improved by light manures, to open and loosen it: very light land by the more heavy and moist sort of manure; and wet land by dry light composts. Some soils require manure annually, others but once in two or three years.

All sorts of horse-dung, neats-dung, hogs-dung, farm-yard mulch, or a mixture of all or any of these together, suits almost all sorts of land; or a compost of any or all of these, and chalk, lime, earth, mud of ponds and ditches, cleansings of streets, ashes, rotten tanner's bark, rotten wood, and saw dust, rotten vegetables, &c. or such of any of these materials as can be had, and formed into a compost-heap to rot together, make a good manure, both for corn and grass-land.

Rotten tanner's-bark alone, or in compost, is good manure for strong, cold, corn-land; and will also suit grass, if applied the beginning of winter, for the rains to wash it into the ground.

Rotten wood, and rotten saw-dust, is very proper for strong land.

Rotten vegetables, such as all sorts of weeds, and the refuse of the kitchen garden, &c. laid in heaps, and if mixed with mud or any earthy substance, and the whole lie to rot, they will make a tolerable good manure for corn-land.

Green fern mowed down and laid in heaps to rot, is also used as manure.

Marle, chalk, lime, &c properly prepared, either alone or in compost, are greatly used in many places as a dressing for corn-land.

Sea-sand and shells, &c. being full of salts, are sometimes used as manure

for

for ſtrong clayey and ſtubborn loamy ſoils.

Sea-weed is likewiſe employed as manure, and being full of ſalts, greatly improves corn-land.

Aſhes of all ſorts prove excellent manure, eſpecially to all ſtrong cold or moiſt land; but coal aſhes are ſuperior to thoſe of wood, or any other kind of vegetables; the farmers in the counties round London have experienced this, and they fetch them from that city by cart and waggon loads, twenty or thirty miles diſtant; for in London they in general uſing coal-fuel, prodigious quantities of aſhes are daily made, and collected in carts and carried to the aſh-hills in the environs of the city; where numbers of people are employed in ſifting them, and ſell the ſiftings by the ſack or load to the farmers for manure; alſo to the brickmakers for tempering their loam or brick-earth.

Bones of animals are alſo uſed as manure for ploughed-land, where they are to be had in due quantities, as about London and other great cities.

Soot is alſo uſed as manure to ſprinkle thinly over corn-land.

Malt-duſt, containing a natural heat and ſweetneſs, proves an eligible manure to moſt ſorts of land, but more particularly to ſtubborn, clayey, and ſour harſh ſoils.

Cleanſing of ſtreets laid in compoſt-heaps with horſe-dung, &c. makes excellent manure both for corn and graſs-ground.

All manure for ploughed or digged land, ſhould be applied at the time the ground is to be tilled, and not ſpread about any long time before it is ploughed in, eſpecially in hot dry weather, which would exhauſt the ſalts, and other enriching particles; obſerving however, where any hard ſubſtances, as marle, chalk, ſhells, &c. are uſed for manure, it is proper to ſpread them abroad ſome conſiderable time, expoſed to the ſun, rains, and froſt, to pulverize, before they are plouhged into the ground.

The manuring graſs-land ſhould generally be performed in autumn, about Michaelmas, or a little before or after, and not in the heat of ſummer, as is often practiſed, whereby the ſun's heat greatly exhauſts its moiſture and goodneſs; but when done in autumn, the rain ſoon waſhes the enriching particles into the ground, to the great benefit of the graſs, and encreaſe of the future crop.

MAPLE TREE, [*Acer.*] The ſpecies are, 1. The greater maple or ſycamore tree; this is a large growing tree, and adapted to encreaſe the variety in our woods and fields. It is very proper, if kept down, for underwood, becauſe it ſhoots very faſt from the ſtool, and makes excellent fuel. There is no tree more proper than this to form large plantations near the ſea; for the ſpray, which is prejudicial to moſt trees, ſeems to have no bad effect upon it. 2. The ſmall or common maple; this does not grow to ſuch a large ſize as the ſycamore, though its timber is of greater value. The timber with us is deemed excellent, and is uſed for ſeveral curious purpoſes, ſuch as muſical inſtruments, inlayings, &c. For the making of turnery ware alſo, ſuch as diſhes, bowls, trays, &c. it is ſuperior to moſt other wood. 3. The Virginia aſh-leaved maple: This is a quick grower, arrives to a large timber-tree, and is admirably adapted to cauſe a beautiful variety in our woods, though is not proper to be planted in expoſed places, the branches being ſubject to ſplit when attacked by violent winds. The leaves are of a pale green colour, moderately large, and fall off pretty early in the autumn. The timber is extremely uſeful for turners; and like the Norway maple, ſerves all the purpoſes of the ſycamore. It is propagated by ſaving the keys, which this tree, though a native of Virginia, perfects in this country. It is alſo propagated by layers, or by planting the cuttings, in a moiſt ſituation, in autumn. 4. The Norway maple with plane-tree leaves: this maple will grow to a great timber-tree, and therefore ſhould be raiſed to encreaſe the variety in our plantations. The leaves are of a ſhining green colour, look beautiful all ſummer, and die to a golden yellow in the autumn. This tree perfects its ſeeds with us; ſo that it may be raiſed in the ſame manner as the ſycamore, from the keys. It may alſo be propagated by layers and by cuttings; which if planted in a moiſt ſoil in the autumn, will grow. 5. The ſcarlet flowering maple of Virginia; of this there are two ſorts, Virginian ſcarlet-flowering maple,

maple, and Sir Charles Wager's maple. Both of these are propagated for the flowers, which are of a scarlet colour, and come out early in the spring. 6. The American sugar maple; this has some resemblance to the Norway maple when the plants are young; but as they grow up the leaves are more deeply divided, and their surfaces less smooth, so that they are easily distinguished From this tree the inhabitants of North-America make a very good sort of sugar, in large quantities, by tapping the trees early in the spring, and boiling the juice, which, by the usual process, is converted into sugar. 7. The mountain maple of America: the body of this tree is slender, and is covere with a whitish bark. It sends forth several red branches, and grows about fifteen feet high. 8. The Italian maple: this is very common in most parts of Italy, but particularly about Rome, where it is one of the largest trees of that country, and is esteemed for the size of the leaves, which are large, affording a great shade: so that these trees are frequently planted by the sides of roads and near habitations. 9. The Montpelier maple; the Montpelier maple grows to about twenty feet high, and is a very beautiful tree. 10. Cretan maple with three entire lobes to the leaves, which are somewhat hairy on their under-side: this grows to about the height of the former. The leaves are downy, composed of three lobes, and grow opposite to each other on long downy foot-stalks. The flowers come out in the spring, and are very seldom succeeded by good seeds in England.

Maple and sycamore are best raised from seed; but as the seeds of the foreign kinds do not ripen in this country, they should be procured from abroad. In a cool and shady part of the seminary let beds of fine mould be marked out about four feet in breadth, and with proper alleys. Upon these let the foreign seeds be regolarly sown, sifting over them about half an inch of the finest mould. When the plants come up, they should be kept clean from weeds, and frequenly watered; and this work must be duly attended to all summer. The spring following, the strongest may be drawn out, and planted in the nursery, in row two feet asunder, and at the distance of a foot from each other in the rows, leaving the others in the seminary to gain strength. The succeeding spring they must receive the same culture; and they may remain in the nursery, with no other trouble than keeping the ground clean from weeds in the summer, digging between the rows in the winter, and taking off all strong and irregular side shoots, till they are planted out for good.

Notwithstanding these are the general laws of raising all the species of maple from foreign seeds, the culture varies with respect to the scarlet flowering kind, when the seeds are gathered at home. This species brings its seeds to maturity the beginning of June in our gardens. They should be then gathered, and after having lain a few days to harden, they should be sown in beds of the finest mould, and covered only a quarter of an inch deep. The beds should be hooped, and covered with mats in scorching weather; but when it is rainy and cloudy, they should always be uncovered. In about a month or six weeks many of the plants will appear; but the far greatest part of them will not come up till the following spring. When the summer-plants first shew themselves, they should hardly ever feel the full beam of the sun. The seeds must be constantly covered with the mats in the day-time, unless cloudy and rainy weather happens, when they should always be uncovered; during the night no mats must be put over the plants, that they may have all the benefit of the refreshing dews, air, and cooling showers. When these latter do not fall, watering must be duly attended to; and this is all the trouble they will require for the first summer in the seed-bed. The summer following they may be exposed to all weather, when they will only require being kept clean from weeds, and watered in dry seasons. The succeeding spring the strongest may be set out in the nursery-way, like the former seedlings.

By layers also all the species of this genus may be propagated; though that method is never practised for the common maple and the sycamore. The young shoots may be laid down in the autumn, winter, or early in the spring. By the autumn following they will have struck root, and become good plants;

when the ſtrongeſt ſhould be ſet out in the places where they are to remain; whilſt the weakeſt may be planted in the nurſery, like the ſeedlings, for a year or two, to gain ſtrength.

Maples raiſed from ſeeds will grow faſter, and arrive at a greater height, than thoſe raiſed from layers; but they will not produce ſuch quantities of flowers; which makes the latter method more eligible for thoſe who want theſe plants for a low ſhrubbery.

By cuttings alſo theſe trees may be propagated: but this method is chiefly practiſed on the aſh-leaved and Norway maples, which more readily take root this way. The cuttings ſhould be the bottom parts of the laſt year's ſhoots: they ſhould be taken off early in October, and planted in rows in a moiſt ſhady place. The ſpring and ſummer following they muſt be duly watered as often as dry weather makes it neceſſary, and be kept clean from weeds. By the autumn they will be fit to remove into the nurſery; though, if the cuttings are not planted too cloſe, they may remain in their ſituation for a year or two longer, and then be ſet out for good, without the trouble of previouſly planting them in the nurſery.

Maples may likewiſe be propagated by budding, grafting, and inarching: but the other methods being more eligible, theſe are never practiſed, except for the variegated ſorts, eſpecially the large broad-leaved kind.

In order to propagate the varieties by budding, let ſome plants of the common ſycamore, one year old, be taken out of the ſeminary, and ſet in the nurſery in rows a yard aſunder, and the plants about a foot and half diſtant from each other in the rows: let the ground be kept clean from weeds all ſummer, and be dug, or as the gardeners call it, turned in, in the winter; and the ſummer following the ſtocks will be of a proper ſize to receive the buds, which ſhould be taken from the moſt beautifully ſtriped branches. The beſt time for this work is Auguſt, becauſe, if it is done earlier, the buds will ſhoot the ſame ſummer; and when this happens, a hard winter will infallibly kill them. Having, therefore, budded your ſtocks the middle or latter end of Auguſt, with the eyes or buds fronting the north, early in October take off the baſs matting, which before this time will have confined the bark and pinched the bud, but not ſo as to hurt it much. Then cut off the ſtock juſt above the bud, and dig the ground between the rows. The ſummer following keep the ground clean from weeds; cut off all natural ſide-buds from the ſtock as they come out; and by autumn, if the land be good, your buds will have ſhot forth, and formed themſelves into trees five or ſix feet high. They may be then removed into the places where they are deſigned to remain; or a few of them only may be drawn out, leaving the others to be trained up for larger ſtandards, to ſerve for planting out in open places, or ſuch other purpoſes as ſhall be wanted.

MANOR. An ancient royalty or lordſhip, with demeſnes, &c.

MARACOCK. Paſſion flower.

MARCHES. The bounds between England and Wales, or England and Scotland.

MARGUERITE. Daiſey.

MARE. The female of the horſe. *See* HORSE.

MARKING *Sheep*. This is done with a marking iron, either of the letters of the owner's name, or of ſome other device, dipped in hot pitch or tar, and clapped on ſome part of the ſheep, to make them be known; ſome mark them with ruddle; but both theſe methods are liable to great objection: the pitch and tar ſpoiling a great deal of wool, and the ruddle waſhing out.

MARJORAM, [*Origanum.*] The ſpecies, 1. Pot or common marjoram. 2. Winter ſweet marjoram. 3. Annual ſweet marjoram. 4. Dittany of Crete. 5. Marjoram of Mount Sipylus. 6. Cretan marjoram. 7. Smyrna marjoram. 8. Egyptian marjoram.

The firſt three ſorts have great merit as culinary aromatics for the kitchen-garden, and may alſo be introduced in the pleaſure-ground, in patches in the open borders to increaſe the variety, and for noſegays, &c. the variegated perennial marjorams in particular have a pretty effect; they are all eaſily raiſed from ſeed in the open ground in ſpring, and the perennial ſorts alſo by dividing the roots; all of which ſorts, both perennials and annuals, when deſigned for the kitchen garden, ſhould generally be diſpoſed in four feet wide beds, the perennials in rows a foot aſunder, where they will abide for years; and the

the annual ſort being always raiſed from ſeed annually, it may either remain where ſowed, or the young plants may be planted out in rows ſix or eight inches diſtant; and when deſigned to have any of the ſorts in the pleaſure gaarden, diſpoſe them about the garden in patches.

The laſt five ſpecies, being exotics from warm countries, require ſhelter here in winter, ſo muſt be potted and placed in the green-houſe collection, or may be preſerved all winter in a common garden-frame, furniſhed with lights to put on in nights and cold weather.

Their different methods of propagation are; The hardy perennial ſpecies by ſeed and by ſlipping the roots; the annual ſort only by ſeed annually; and the five green-houſe kinds principally by ſlips and cuttings.

Sow the ſeed in ſpring, March or April, in any bed or border of light earth, and rake it in with a light hand; they will ſoon come up, and when the ſeedlings are a few inches high, plant them out in moiſt weather, in rows ten or twelve inches diſtant, finally to remain, giving occaſional waterings till freſh rooted.

Autumn is the beſt ſeaſon for parting the roots, though it may alſo be performed ſucceſsfully in ſpring. Having ſome large plants, ſlip or divide the roots into ſlips, each furniſhed with fibres; which plant in rows, as directed for the ſeedlings, giving occaſional waterings, and they will readily grow, and become good buſhy plants by autumn following.

Their general culture is the keeping them clean from weeds; every autumn cut down the decayed ſtalks, looſen the earth between the plants, at the ſame time digging the alleys, ſpread a little of the earth over the ſurface of the beds.

When any are intended for the pleaſure-garden, remove them in autumn or ſpring, with little balls of earth about their roots, and plant them where wanted.

All the green-houſe kinds are propagated by ſlips or cuttings of the young ſhoots in ſpring and ſummer. If you plant them early, let it be in pots, and plunge them in any hot-bed, they will readily take root; but if in ſummer, they may be planted either in pots, or in a ſhady border. In either mode of planting, give water directly, which repeat as occaſion may require in moderate quantities; and if thoſe that are planted in the open air, either in pots, or in the full ground, are covered down with hand-glaſſes, it will facilitate their rooting; but the glaſſes muſt be removed when the plants begin to ſhoot at top. The plants in either way will be rooted the ſame year, and towards autumn may be potted off ſeparately into ſmall pots, and afterwards managed as other hardy green-houſe exotics.

MARLE. Marle is a treaſure to the farmer whereſoever it is found, and there is no country in the world where there is more of it than in England, yet there are few places in which it is known to lie. The induſtry of thoſe who deal in huſbandry has not been in any thing ſo ſlack, as in the ſearching after this valuable commodity.

See Mud.

We ſhall endeavour to awaken them to a ſenſe of their intereſt, by ſhewing its value: and to aſſiſt them in the ſearch after it we ſhall endeavour to make it known to them by ſight and feeling in its ſeveral appearances, for theſe differ greatly. After this, to prevent miſtakes in the application, the ſeveral kinds of marle ſhall be diſtinguiſhed, and the particular kind of land ſhewn, to which each properly belongs.

In order to the huſbandman's finding marles upon his land, he muſt firſt have ſome knowledge of them. The very fineſt kinds have often been thrown up accidentally in digging on other occaſions, and no one has known them. The fields have languiſhed for want of what they contained in their own bowels through the ignorance of their owner.

Marle is of ſeveral kinds, and differs greatly in appearance; but to him who will carry a general knowledge of it in his head, it may be always known in whatever form it is found.

Marle, like other earths, may be pure or foul: for thoſe beds of matter which lie in the earth are ſubject to mixtures as thoſe on the ſurface, tho' not ſo frequently: and the deeper marle lies, the purer it uſually is.

We ſhall firſt then divide the marles into two kinds, the pure and the mixt. The pure marles all agree in their texture; their difference being only in the degree of hardneſs, and in the colour.

Pure

Pure marle is a ſubſtance not unlike fuller's-earth; it is ſoſt and fatty to the touch, it is not tough like clay, nor duſty like ochre, nor ſandy like loam, but is of a tender fine nature, unlike all other ſorts of earths.

When a farmer finds a piece of earth of this kind, whether it be thrown up in digging a well, or by whatever other accident, let its colour be what it will, he may depend upon i' it is a marle. In order to be more confirmed, let him throw a piece of it into a baſon of water, and he will find it ſwell like fuller's-earth, and crumble in the ſame manner of itſelf to pieces. The harder and more compact kinds break ſlower, the ſoft and looſe ones quicker, ſome almoſt immediately. But in whatever manner it happens, this joined to the others is a ſure proof that the earth under examination is a marle, and let him who has fallen by chance upon a piece of it, dig in ſearch of thé treaſure.

Of the pure marles there are four principal kinds, diſtinguiſhed according to their colours. A white, a yellow, a red, a blue, there is alſo a black, but it is leſs common.

Theſe are to be diſtinguiſhed under the name of pure marles of thoſe colours; for there are foul and coarſer kinds of the ſame colours.

There are found in different places marles of theſe ſeveral colours, varying in their texture and hardneſs; but in general, the white or whitiſh are the ſofteſt and lighteſt, and the blue are the firmeſt and heavieſt. For this reaſon the white is generally uſed for paſture grounds, and the blue for corn lands.

This cuſtom however is not to be eſtabliſhed into a law to the farmer; though in thoſe counties where they have choice, they uſe the ſofteſt marles for paſture, becauſe they diſſolve moſt freely: and the harder for ploughed lands, where they are more aſſiſted by tillage. The farmer who has either of theſe kinds, may uſe it indifferently on both occaſions, in this manner.

If it be the blue firm kind, or any of the compact ſorts, let him lay it upon his corn land early in the ſeaſon, that the weather may mellow it before the laſt ploughing: if it be for paſture ground, let him in the ſame manner lay it on in time, ſpreading it thin. If it be the white, or any other of the looſe and crumbly kinds, it need not be laid on either till late, becauſe it breaks and diſſolves almoſt as ſoon as it is expoſed to the weather.

The colour of marle is no certain proof of its compact, or crumbly nature; but in general, the blue is firmeſt, the white ſofteſt, and the red and yellow are of a middle degree between both.

Thoſe already named are the richeſt and fineſt of the marles: and as all mixture debaſes their value, among the other kinds, which we ſhall diſtingiſh by the name of impure or mixed marles, the moſt impure are conſtantly of the leaſt value. Theſe mixed marles differ not only in colour, but in their very nature, according to the ſubſtances which have got in among them. Their colour is no general mark of diſtinction, but they may be very well arranged under ſeparate heads, according to the ſubſtances of which they partake. Theſe being ſand, clay, loam, or ſtone, they may be conſidered as ſandy marles, clayey marles, loamy marles, and ſtony marles: and among theſe laſt are alſo to be comprehended ſome which have at firſt the hardneſs of a ſtone from their own nature and compoſition, though they have not a particle of real ſtone in them.

Many marles alſo, beſide theſe natural earths and ſtony matter, contain great quantities of ſea ſhells which are preſerved in them in a ſingular manner; for inſtead of being petrified, or rendered hard, they are made brittle, and ſeem as if they had been calcined. Theſe ſhells are far from injuring the marle in its improving quality; they on the contrary, are found to encreaſe that virtue.

There are of theſe ſeveral kinds of all the before-mentioned colours, but greyiſh or yellowiſh are the moſt frequent. The ſandy kinds are the richeſt of theſe impure ones; and they are fitteſt for ready uſe, for they break to pieces in the hands eaſier than any others, and crumble the ſooneſt of any with the weather. In a proper application theſe may be accounted of equal value with any, for on clayey lands the very ſand which is contained in them is uſeful.

The loamy marles are the next in value among theſe to the ſandy, for they break eaſily with the weather; but in theſe as the former, a great deal of of the advantage arising from the use of them will depend upon a proper knowledge of their nature, and their use on a right soil.

The clayey and stoney are inferior to the others: but on some lands the former are preferable to those which are more pure: and amongst the stoney kinds there are some, and they even of the hardest, which, when properly mellow'd by the weather, are inferior to none in Richness. Some of these a large hammer would make no impression upon when first dug up, but with frost, rain and sun-shine, they have in six months time crumbled away to powder.

Some of these, when broken with great labour, and laid upon the lands, have for several months appear'd like so many stones scatter'd over the fields, and seem'd to damage rather than improve them: but after one winter there has not been a piece of any one of the lumps so big as a nutmeg to be found: and the land has been kept in heart eight or ten years by that single dressing.

As the considerate husbandman must see the vast value of Marle, it is natural that he should bethink himself of seeking for it on his own grounds; we shall therefore not only encourage, but assist him in the search.

In the first place he has this to tempt him to examine his land in hope of it, that it is frequent in many places where it is not regarded or even known: and that although so little observed, it is a commodity so naturally and generally the produce of England, that there are few pieces of land of any extent in which one kind or other of it may not be found.

If it be too deep indeed, it may not be worth taking up, but that is seldom the case: it is commonly near the surface.

The several kinds and varieties of marle have been so fully described, that the farmer has all the reason in the world to suppose he shall know it at sight: we shall add to these the soils under which it usually lies.

But prior to this, which beginning without any certain information, is a more random kind of search, we would have him examine well both by report and by the appearance of the ground, whether marle has ever before been dug in his Land, or any where near its borders.

If he hear that it has, let him look narrowly after those broad and shallow delves in the ground which have been before mention'd, for they are certainly the places where the pits were. If he can learn no such thing by report, yet let him see if there be any such hollows in the ground, for tho' less certain, still they are an evidence that something has been dug. It may have been gravel, but marle is more likely.

When he has found any such hollows, let him mind the course wherein they run, for that way probably the vein of marle runs also.

If he find only one such, let him first observe how deep it is; for on this depends the nature of his search, since by this he may guess weether the marle lay low or near the surface.

His business is to try all about the place where the hollow is, for marle. If that hollow be very shallow, let him have holes dug the depth of three feet with a spade; if deeper, let him use an augur, such as they bore the ground with on various occasions. Let him bore in a great many places to the depth of six feet; for if the marle lie deeper than that, 'tis hardly worth his digging; but let him examine strictly every thing the augor brings up within this depth. Let him keep in his mind the various kinds of marle, and if any thing come up that has the least appearance or resemblance of any of those several kinds, let him try it by seeing if it moulders away in a bason of water, if it crackles on being put into the fire; and what effect the sun and air take upon it when it has lain two or three nights exposed.

By these means, if there ever have been marle dug there, and the vein of it continues, he will be sure to find where it runs; and he is then to follow the course of it by the augur, and consider where he can open a pit of it the most conveniently for the general use of his land.

But suppose there be not the least sign upon the ground, or the least account from report that marle ever was dug any where thereabouts; yet this should not discourage him from enquiring if there be any; for there is a time for the discovery of every thing.

In this case he must first have recourse to what he can see upon digging any where. If a well be sunk at any time upon or near his land, let him look carefully over all the kinds of earth that are thrown up. Nay, if a pond be dug, let him make the same observations.

Let him examine the sides of ditches new dug or cleaned; and follow the plough with a careful eye, observing if it any where turn up matter different from the soil. For marle often is within the reach of the plough.

If he discover nothing of the nature of marle in all these researches, let him have recourse to the augur, boring in different places, but chiefly in the clayey soils, for under these the marle oftenest lies.

The mellow earth is the next soil that is likely to conceal marle: and after this the loamy earth. It sometimes lies under gravel, but seldom in any great plenty: it very rarely is found under a sandy soil, and then commonly in a thin vein, and at a great depth.

The clayey soil not only oftenest has marle under it, but that which lies under this soil is usually of the finest kind. The Kentish marles generally are covered with a foot or two of tough clay. In general it is the finest, purest, and richest marles the farmer is to expect under a clayey soil.

It has been observed, the fine black mellow earth of the low lands commonly has under it a bed of tough clay. Sometimes it has a think bed of some fine marle, particularly of the reddish kind, in the place of the clay; and very often a vein of marle comes between the clay and the mould.

The former is the best for the farmer; but if the latter presents itself, let him follow with his augur the course of the vein, and he will find it gradually thicken till at last it usually takes the place of the clay. It is here he is to open his marle pit; and he will often fall upon a bed of marle five, six, or seven feet thick, rising within a foot and half of the surface of the ground.

Sometimes the stony marles are found under clay or black mould, but it is more commonly the pure, fatty, and tender sort: as to those found under sandy soils, they are usually one or other of the clayey marles, and, with double expence in digging, are not of half the value.

There are some parts of Suffex where a bed of marle comes up within eight inches of the surface, and when open'd is found to be ten or twelve feet thick, all of some one of the pure and fine kinds: and in Cheshire, and also in Lancashire, where the best marles often lie under the fine black mould, a bed of blue marle has been within a yard of the turf, down to four yards deep, and they were not then got through the vein.

When the farmer has by the methods already described found out a vein of marle, and fix'd upon a convenient part of his land for opening of a pit; let him begin by marking out a tolerable large place for the work; and for a proper way for the carts that are to fetch out the marle. A great deal depends upon all this being well ordered, and now is his time for contrivance.

He is then to employ his labourers to clear away, with pick-axe, spade, and wheel-harrow, all the soil that covers the vein of marle, and when this is done, they are to begin digging it.

The different condition of the marle will now be found, and the necessary accidents of treating it. Where it is of the finest and tenderest kinds, they often work with a kind of hoe, and three hoers will tear up as much as four can fill into the carts.

In the clayey kinds they use spades for digging, and then the diggers must be more than the fillers. Sometimes these are so dry and tough, that the workmen must have water brought to them to wet their spades; and in other places they are so wet, that there must be a pump set up to keep them dry.

When the marle is got into the cart, it is to be shot on the fields; but this in a different manner according to its nature. If it be of the fine soft tender kinds, the best way is to spread it as it is taken out of the cart: but if it be of the stoney or other compact kinds, every load had better be shot separately, and left in a heap for the whole winter, that the frost and air may mellow and break it.

There are very few lands that may not be improved by marle, but some require

quire it more than others; there are also many kinds of marles, as well as many different forts of soils; and the marles of one kind are fit for certain lands, and those of other kinds for others. A strict regard must be had to this, otherwise, as already observed, the land may be spoiled.

In some places they have a way of laying on such a quantity of the marle, that they may be said to add a soil rather than to improve what was there before. This is the practice in some parts of Cheshire, where they will lay fifteen, sixteen, or eighteen hundred load of marle upon one of their acres; they will thus in digging and carriage bestow twelve or fifteen pounds upon marling an acre; and then they will work it with good management twenty or thirty years together.

For the first years they plough very shallow; they don't cut up more than an inch of the soil for fear of burying the marle; so going deeper in the following years. This is a particular practice.

In the first place, the soil which requires marle most of all, and which is the most improved by it, is the sandy. The advantage arising from this practice upon such lands, is beyond the belief of any who have not seen the fact.

The marle which is fit for this land is the clayey kind, and more than all others that brownish or yellowish marle, which looks like real clay in the pit, but is found of so different a nature when examined. This marle, or any one of the clayey kind, laid thick upon a sandy soil, gives it at once a body and a richness. The clay that is in it binding the light soil tolerably together, at the same time that the fatty and enriching earth blends itself with the whole.

This is the application of marle, in which its virtue is most fully seen: for by this means land, that before would yield scarce any thing, has been known to produce suprizing crops; nay, it has been try'd by way of Experiment, to marle one half of a piece of new broke-up ground of this sandy kind, and leave the other in its natural condition; then both being sown with the same seed, the marled part has yielded a plentiful crop, when the other has not ripen'd one ear.

Another great advantage of this practice is, that in years wherein other crops fail, those succeed which are on these grounds even to admiration. Thus when there comes a dropping summer, while a piece of marled sandy soil is in its full vigour, the increase is prodigious. These seasons generally hurt the crop on other lands; but they load these with as much as can stand upon the ground.

But all this time care must be taken that the marle be well suited to the soil; and this is to be done by this rule; the more sandy the ground is, the more clayey the marle must be.

If a rash young husbandman, hearing of the great profit that arises from laying marle on sandy soils, should without any farther thought lay on one of the pure fat and tender marles before described upon a very barren sandy piece of ground, tho' he put on a Cheshire loading, yet the wet would wash it in, and the sand would swallow it up in such a manner, that the whole effect would be lost after all the labour and expence.

Next after the sandy, the soil which receives most advantage from marle is the loamy; and this admits the greatest improvement of all when the sand in its composition bears an over proportion to the clay. Some lands, the soil of which was fitter to make bricks than to yield corn, have been so improved by marle, that the corn has stood like a sward of grass at its first appearance; and has thriven so afterwards, that every stalk has come to a due maturity.

The marle for this kind of land must be the purest and finest that can be had. If the farmer should lay on a clayey, or a sandy marle, he would only increase the proportion of one or other ingredient of the natural land, which already made it barren.

All that renders a loamy earth at all fruitful in its natural state is the quantity of mould that is mix'd in it; now a fine marle is of the nature of that mould, only much richer: it blends among the loam, and the firmness of the loamy soil holds it till it has yielded all its virtue.

Of all the kinds of marle, that which agrees best with a loamy soil, is the blue, pure, and tender marle. After this the best is the yellow: but any marle that is light and free from mixture will anſwer the purpoſe.

The ſtony marles have been try'd in ſome counties upon their loamy ſoils with tolerable good ſucceſs; particularly that ſort they call ſhale marle, laid on a tough loamy ſoil, abounding naturally too much with clay.

This has ſucceeded but poorly at firſt. The firſt year ſcarce at all, the ſecond ſomewhat better, and the third and fourth beſt of all. The pure marle is very much preferable for this ſoil to the ſtony. The farmer may do well to uſe any of the ſtony kinds when he cannot get the other ſort in the neighbourhood, and he will reap conſiderable advantage from it; but when he can have his choice, the pure marle is preferable for this land by many degrees.

Some of theſe ſtony marles, not of the hardeſt kind, have been uſed on ſandy ſoils, but without any great ſucceſs.

The practice of marling lands is founded upon reaſon; and that, as well as experience, will ſhew in what manner it ſhould be done. The pure marles are all fatty; the mix'd kinds are either clayey, ſandy, loamy, or ſtony; now upon conſidering this, the application is eaſy.

After ſandy and loamy ſoils, that which receives moſt advantage from marle is mellow earth: this wants improvement leſs than any other kind, but the proper uſe of marle adds to its fertility; and there is this farther advantage, that there is ſcarce any kind of marle whatſoever but may be uſed to it: but ſtill there are ſome from which it has more benefit than others.

Ploughed land, meadow, & paſture, when they have this mellow earth for their ſoil, equally receive good from marle. As to graſs lands, only the pure marles ſhould be uſed to them, becauſe they waſh in readily, and don't lie about in clots or lumps upon the ground. For plough'd lands of this ſoil, any of all the kinds of marle may be uſed with benefit. If they be of the clayey ſort, they break in with ploughing after a little time; if loamy, they blend ſo much the ſooner; if they be of the ſtoney kind, it takes time for the weather to divide them, but they do very well at laſt; and finally, if they be of the pure, or of the ſandy kind, they break with the firſt dreſſing, and waſh in with the rains immediately.

As to chalkey ſoils, marle is not the manure moſt ſuited to them of all others, becauſe marle is itſelf in ſome degree of a chalkey nature: nevertheleſs, it is to be uſed with prudence to good purpoſe.

Gravelly ſoils have the ſame advantage from marle as the ſandy, and one reaſon of this is, that they always have ſand among the gravel. Theſe let all other manures be waſh'd through them by the firſt rains, but the marles of a proper kind remain in them. They not only enrich thoſe lands by their own mellowneſs, but they give them a firmneſs that will make them hold other dreſſings. Dung laid on a looſe gravelly ſoil is loſt and ſwallow'd up without any benefit, but dung upon ſuch a land that has firſt been dreſſed with marle, takes the ſame effect as upon other ſoils.

In this, as in all the other inſtances, care muſt be taken to ſuit the marle to the ſoil; if a pure marle were uſed, it would be waſhed through quicker than dung; and if a ſandy marle were choſen, the marley part of that mixture would be waſh'd down through the ſoil, and only the ſand that was among it would remain. This could be no improvement to a ſoil already too ſandy.

The proper marle for a gravelly ſoil is the clayey ſort. This is the only kind that is proper; and this never fails of giving the greateſt advantage.

Laſt of all, we come to ſpeak of the clayey ſoils, which are in general ſuppoſed to be improper for marling to a proverb. Every common farmer can repeat what is retailed from one to another through all the common writers on huſbandry, and can tell his ſon,

He that marles Clay,
Throws all away.

And this he thinks he has two ſubſtantial reaſons for believing to be true, becauſe it is verſe; and becauſe it is in print. But let not the reaſonable huſbandman be frighted out of his profits by rhymes.

It may be poſſible enough to throw away coſt and labour by laying an improper ſort of marle upon a clayey ground;

ground; and the ſame may be as truly ſaid of any other. But the buſineſs of the preſent enquiry is the ſuiting the marle to the land; and when that is obſerved, the ſame benefit will follow from the uſe of it on theſe, as on all other ſoils.

Excepting the clayey marles, there is no kind of them but is good on clay grounds. In the firſt place, all the pure marles being well worked in by the plough, blend with the ſoil, and looſen and enrich it. The ſtoney kinds are kept on or near the ſurface till they mellow and break, and the firmneſs of the ground takes in all their benefit: the loamy marles, if there be too much clay in them, are to be rejected as approaching to the nature of the clayey kind, but if otherwiſe, they are excellent, as they approach to the nature of the ſandy ones. Theſe laſt-mentioned are for clayey ſoils the beſt of all, for they conſiſt only of a fine fatty marle and ſand, and they act doubly upon the clay, at once looſening and enriching it. As ſoon as they are laid on, they break and crumble to pieces; for the ſandy marles are the brittleſt of all the kinds; and thus ſeparated, the ſand gets into the clay, and makes way for the marle, which the rains waſh thoroughly in, and which is then detain'd among it to exert the full effect of its fertility.

He therefore that has a clayey ſoil to manure, and can get at a ſandy marle, has it in his power to raiſe his land to many times its original value.

Having taught the practical farmer to know marle when he ſees it, how to ſeek for it on his own grounds, and in what manner to ſuit the kind to the nature of the land; it remains to inſtruct him in the manner of uſing it.

For this is no little article, and in this the experience of others only can be his guide, comparing their ſucceſs one with another: for not only the practice of a particular county may many times miſlead him; but what has been written under the appearance of advice is too often falſe.

As to the quantity that he ſhall lay upon his land, ſo many errors appear on both ſides, that the truth ſeems hard to hit. Some of the Staffordſhire farmers lay on ſo little, that it ſcarce anſwers any purpoſe. Some of theſe are contented to uſe twenty loads to an acre, and then they have complained that what was written of the profit by marle was not true. In Cheſhire, on the contrary, they bury their land under ſuch loads, that they ſeem to ſow their marle and not their ground.

The medium between theſe practices is the right method; and he who would reap all thoſe advantages that have been declared of marle, muſt follow that courſe. The right uſe of marle is not to put it in the place of the ſoil, but to make a mixture of it with the ſoil, ſo as to raiſe a poor land into the condition of one naturally rich: to do this, a due quantity of the marle muſt be employ'd; and to give a general rule, that ſhould be about a hundred loads to an acre.

The beſt way of ſowing marled land is in general under furrow.

The farmer is not to look for the full effect of this the firſt year, but it will laſt as before obſerved: and the continuance will be according to the nature of the ſoil, and the kind of the marle, ſeven, ten, twenty, or even thirty years.

When the farmer ſees his land that has been marled after fair weather look all over white, as if covered with a hoar froſt, he may conclude it will anſwer his beſt expectations. It is a proof that the marle was good in itſelf; that it has been uſed in due quantity; and that it is well mix'd with the land.

Some have delivered this white appearance as a mark that there is marle in any part of the land where it is ſeen; but marle cannot diſcover itſelf in that manner in its natural beds, unleſs they lie almoſt cloſe to the ſurface. It is therefore of little uſe in that reſpect; but on the lands where it has been laid, when there is this appearance, 'tis certain that it is mix'd and mellow'd in the ground.

If the hard and ſtony kinds are uſed, they muſt be laid on early in the ſeaſon: if the clayey a little later; the loamy may be a little later yet than the clayey: the pure marles of all kinds, and the ſandy marles, are to be laid on very late. In this the farmer's diſcretion will direct him after theſe general rules. The proper timing of the laying on this dreſſing regards its effect for the enſuing year; but the harder kinds with the beſt management will not do much ſo ſoon.

The

The last method of laying on the marle is, to shoot the several loads, as they are brought out of the pit, at about equal distances one from another; and then to spread them all. This will occasion the ground to be all cover'd with the same thickness. When it is thus spread, it must be will mix'd with the soil, and all laid smooth and level together: and the quicker this is done from the time that the marle be taken out of the bed, provided it be a pure or a sandy marle, the better; for as these crumble to pieces almost directly, the business is to get them mix'd in the ground at once, that they may begin to break among it, and so perfectly make one body of the whole: for this is the nature of an improvement by marle.

If the field to be marled lie level, the marle is to be spread evenly over it, not thicker in one place than another: but if it lie upon a descent, the best way is to spread the marle half as thick again on the higher part of the field as on the lower, for the rains will wash enough of its best part down to make all equal.

It is impossible to give one and the same direction for all lands, as to the times of marling, and what may be reasonably expected from them, for the nature both of the marle and of the soil make an endless variety; but the farmer will see by his crops when the land needs to be refreshed.

MARCH. The third month of the year;—in which the

Products of the Kitchen-Garden are,

Winter spinage, cabbages sprouts, brocoli, savoys, coleworts, red beets, carrots, parsnips and turnips.

Upon the Hot-beds; cucumbers, asparagus, peas, kidney-beans, purslain, &c. And, on the warm borders, radishes, and young sallet-herbs; as also mint, tansey, tarragon, &c. if planted upon a moderate hot-bed the beginning of February.

Fruits still lasting: Apples, Loan's pearmain, nonpareil, golden russet, winter pearmain, Pile's russet, john apple, pomme d'api, golden pippin, Kentish pippin, Holland pippin, French pippin, Stone pippin, Wheeler's russet, with some others of less note.

Pears: burgamot bugi, winter boncretien, double-flowering Royel d'huyver, bezi de chaumontelle, l' amozelle, union or Doctor Uvedale's St. Germain, Parkinson's warden, cadilliac, with some others.

Plants now in Flower.

Some anemonies, crocuses of several colours, double snow-drop, persian iris, dens canis, crown imperials, spring cyclamen; early, white, blue and starry hyacinths, hepatica's, double pilewort, narcissus's of several sorts; early tulips, violets, primroses, polyanthuses, green-flower'd black hellebore, fennel-leav'd black hellebore, wall-flowers, double daisies, some auricula's, dwarf Portugal navel-wort, with many others of less note.

Hardy Trees and Shrubs now in Flower.

Almond-tree, double flower'd peach, virginian cherry-plumb, mezereons, spurge laurel, laurus-tinus, Spanish travellers joy, cornelian cherry, benjamin tree, and some others.

Plants now in Flower in the Green-house and Stove.

Several sorts of ficoides's; some sorts of aloes, sedum arborescens, chrysanthemums, anemonospermos two or three kinds; germaniums, Aleppo cyclamens, polygala frutescens; the ananas or pine-apple, hermannia two sorts; ilex-leav'd jasmine, Spanish jasmine, with some others.

MARSHY LAND. Marshy land can be made little use of without first draining, therefore that business should be immediately set about by a good husbandman where it is practicable to be done, or where the expences of workmanship would not be more than equal to the profit;——for a farmer above all men should be careful never to buy crops too dear, and on the other hand never let a too great covetousness prevent his applying all necessary expences to the cultivation and improvement of his land.—A farmer from observation will easily comprehend the advantage from draining of marshy land, even from the ditches round his farm, which draw off the water from his land, but are of themselves inadequate to marshes or even springs—we must here have recourse to underground draining—the best materials required for this work, where they can be had at a reasonable price, are stones or brick, laid in such a manner as to give a free passage for the current of of water; and to prevent the earth filling up the interstices, heath should be put over the stones.——If this be found unhandy, bavins or faggots may be used, covered over with heath or even straw; the best kind of wood, perhaps, is holly, but where this cannot be had, oak, alder, &c. may be used. If there be a tolerable descent for the water to run off, the work will be easy enough, but if that should not be the case, ditches must be made sufficient to answer the current of water drawn off. The upper part of the channel should be about 18 inches, and gradually decrease to four at bottom, where the stones are thrown in: if bricks or square stones are placed, they may be rather wider.

Land which was in the marshy or boggy state may, by draining, be made good land.

If it is in such a situation as to be incapable of being drained, it will in general afford a good deal of seed for cows in the summer, but will be improper for sheep.

After the land is drained, it would be an exceeding good method to shave off the upper surface of the land, and dry it like turf, which should be burned on the spot; this operation, which is called burn-baking, would be an excellent manure for the land, and destroy numberless plants which would be mischievous in a state of cultivation;—when this was done, we would recommend a crop of oats, and no fear of having a good one, if not sown too thick; after them a summer fallow for turnips, and then the crops in course as the land may be adapted best for.

This land well managed afterwards will generally turn to very good account, and bear very considerable crops for some years without manure.

If it cannot be burn-baked; a crop of oats will answer very well without, but they will be apt to be very rank in straw and thin in ear.

Beans planted at one ploughing have been known to produce five quarters to an acre; but whatever the first crop may be, we would recommend a fallow the next year; not that the land wants rest, but that it will be necessary to destroy a number of unprofitable plants and weeds which may have taken fast hold of the ground. Chalk and lime will be acceptable to this fresh turned up land, which must of course possess great degree of sourness from its situation; they will correct that sourness, and so do good.

The marsh-lands in Lincolnshire, and many other parts of England, produce a sort of grass, which feeds sheep in a better manner than that of almost any other land, in regard to their size, and the quantity of wool. The sheep about Grimsby, and some other places in this county, produce such lusty wool, or, as they call it, wool of so large a staple, that three or four fleeces usually make a tod of twenty-eight pounds weight. Several hundred loads of this wool are yearly carried from these places to Norfolk, Suffolk, and other parts of the kindom, for the cloth manufacturers. They send this in large packs, which they call pockets, each containing about five and twenty hundred weight.

When marsh-lands lie flat, it is necessary for the owner to keep all the water he can from them. The sea-water in particular is to be kept from them as much as possible; and this is usually done at a very great expence, by high banks and walls.

Two things greatly wanting in these lands, in general, are good shelter for the cattle, and fresh water. The careful farmer may, however, in a great measure obviate these, by digging, in proper places, large ponds to receive the rain water, and by planting trees and hedges in certain places towards the sea, where they may not only afford shelter for the cattle, but keep off the sea breezes, which often will cut off the tops of all the grass in these places, and make it look as if mowed.

These lands fatten cattle the soonest of any, and they preserve sheep from the rot. It would be of great advantage to them, if there were raised, in the middle of every large marsh, banks of earth in a cross, or in the form of two semi-circles, and these planted with trees; these would serve as a shelter for cattle, let the wind blow from what quarter it would, and would soon repay the expences of making.

There are, in different parts of England, very large quantities of land upon the sea-coasts that would be worth taking

king in, though no one has yet thought of doing it. The coasts about Boston, Spalding, and many other parts of Lincolnshire, give frequent instances of this, where the sea falls from the land, so that on the outside of the sea walls, on the owse, where every tide the salt water comes, there grows a great deal of good grass, and the owse is firm to ride upon when the water is upon it.

This owse, when taken in, hardly sinks any thing at all, and they dig the walls from the outside of it, all the earth they are made of being taken from thence, and the sea, in a few tides, filling it up again: and though the sea, at high water, comes only to the foot of the bank, yet once in a year or two, some extraordinary tides go over the banks, though they are ten feet high. These banks are fifty feet broad at the bottom, and three feet at the top; and the common price of making them is three shillings a pole, the earth being all carried in wheel-barrows, and the face towards the sea, where the greatest slope is, being tursed.

MARSH ELDER. *See* GELDER ROSE.

MARSH MALLOW. *See* MALLOW.

MARSH TREFOIL. *See* BUCK-BEAN.

MARTAGON. *See* LILY.

MARVEL *of* PERU, [*Mirabilis.*] There are three species, the common, the long-flowered, and the forked. They all flower in July, continuing in succession until October, very conspicuous and elegant. Having the singularity of being shut all day, and expand towards the evening when the sun declines; hence the inhabitants of the Indies, where they grow naturally, called them Four-o'clock-flowers: their time of opening here, however, depends on the weather, for if cloudy, or that the sun is not very vehement, they often open great part of the day.

The flowers are universally hermaphrodite, and of one funnel-shaped tubular petal, having the lower part a long narrow tube, and the upper spreading.

These plants are naturally perennial in root, which, however, if not preserved here in winter, prove but of one year duration, but if sheltered from frost and wet during the winter season, they will remain alive, and shoot out strongly again in spring: in this country, however, the plants are commonly considered as annuals; because they rise from seed in the spring, and the same year produce flowers and perfect seed: and if left to nature in the open air, totally perish in winter, at the first attack of frost or excessive wet; but, as aforesaid, if in autumn, when the stalks begin to assume a state of decay, the roots are taken up, and preserved in sand in a dry room all winter, and planted again in spring, they shoot out afresh stronger than at first, and sometimes attain four or five feet stature, with very spreading heads; or if plants growing in pots, having the stems cut down in autumn, and the pots placed in a green-house, or garden-frames under glasses, the roots may also be preserved sound, and will shoot out again in spring as above.

The roots generally become large, tuberous, and fleshy, covered with a dark rind.

All the species are of a tender nature, scarcely able to endure the open air here fully day & night, until May or June; that is, they being raised from seed in spring, chiefly in hot-beds under glasses, continued & forwarded there until the beginning of June, then fully exposed in the borders or pots, they become large branchy plants in July and August; and continue flowering until October or November, till prevented by the cold.

They are all elegant furniture for the principal compartments of the pleasure ground, they being both very ornamental in the large branchy growth, closely garnished with leaves, and by flowering so numerously seem as if entirely covered with flowers, in constant plentiful succession from July till the beginning of winter, as aforesaid.

The roots of all these plants are a strong purgative, and, given in a double quantity, operate equal to the true jalap.

The propagation of all the species is by seed in the spring, either in a warm border, or in a hot-bed; but the latter will forward the plants to considerably the earliest and greatest degree of perfection.

MARYGOLD, [*Calendula.*] The species are, 1. the common marygold with great varieties, being all hardy annuals. 2. Cape leafy-stalked violet and white marygold.

marygold. 3. Naked stalked violet and white Ethiopian marygold. 4 Grass leaved low perennial cape marygold. 5. Shrubby cape marygold. The first sort in its common single flowered state is regarded only as a pot-herb, and its flowers are the only parts used; but some of the full double varieties and proliferous kinds demand attention also as ornamental plants for the beauty of their flowers, which will effect an agreeable diversity in the common compartments of the pleasure ground, in assemblage with other hardy annuals.

Likewise the second and third sorts, being hardy annuals, will flower abundantly, and form a good variety in the open borders in the months of June, July, and August.

The fourth and fifth sorts, grass-leaved and shrubby Calendula, producing many flowers in long succession, are also worthy of a place in our gardens: but being impatient of frost, must be kept in pots, to have shelter of a green-house or frame in winter.

All the annual sorts are propagated by sowing the seeds in beds or borders in March or April, either in the places where they are to remain, or for transplanting.

When intended to cultivate the first sort for culinary uses, many either sow the seeds where the plants are to remain, by broad-cast on the surface, and rake them in, or sow them in small shallow drills a foot asunder, covering them half an inch deep, and when the plants in either method have leaves an inch broad, hoe them out to twelve inches distance; or they may be sown thick for transplantation, and when the plants have four or five leaves, plant them out in rows the above distance.

Their flowers being the useful parts, they will be fit for use in constant succession from time to time in dry weather, and, after drying them in the shade, should be put up in paper bags for use.

To propagate the annual kinds in general as flowering plants, sow them either in patches in the borders, &c. where they are to remain, sowing four or five seeds in each patch half an inch deep, but leave only one of the best of the plants in a place; or the plants may be raised in a bed or border, and when they have four or five leaves, transplant them in the order just directed.

They will flower and ripen seeds abundantly from June to the end of October.

The fourth sort is propagated by slipping the heads any time from March till September, planting them in pots, which, if plunged in a hot-bed, or in the common earth, and close covered with a hand-glass, and occasionally shaded and watered, they will readily grow, hardening them gradually to the air.

The shrubby sort is propagated by cuttings of its branches, in pots of light earth, in April, May, or June, plunging them in a moderate hot-bed, or, in default thereof, plunging them to the rims in the common ground, giving shade and water.

African MARYGOLD. *See* AFRICAN MARYGOLD.

Corn MARYGOLD. *See* CORN MARYGOLD.

Fig MARYGOLD. *See* FICOIDES.

French MARYGOLD. *See* AFRICAN MARYGOLD.

Marsh MARYGOLD, [*Caltha.*] This plant grows upon moist boggy land in many parts of England: of this there is a variety with very double flowers, which for its beauty is preserved in gardens, and is propagated by parting of the roots in autumn. It should be planted in a moist soil and a shady situation; and as there are often such places in gardens, where few other plants will thrive, so these may be allowed to have room, and during their season of flowering will afford an agreeable variety.

SYRIAN MARUM, [*Marum Syriacum.*] This is a small shrubby plant, growing spontaneously in Syria, Candy, and other warm climates, and cultivated with us in gardens. The leaves have an aromatic bitterish taste; and, when rubbed betwixt the fingers, a quick pungent smell, which soon affects the head, and occasions sneezing: distilled with water, they yield a very acrid, penetrating essential oil, resembling one obtained by the same means from scurvygrass. These qualities sufficiently point out the uses to which this plant might be applied; at present, it is little otherwise employed than in cephalic snuffs. It is propagated by slips or cuttings.

Common MARUM, *or* MASTIC. This is a pungent aromatic plant, formerly in eſteem as a medicinal, plant but now not much in uſe.

MASH. For horſes, &c. an infuſion of bran, malt, &c. ſteeped, and given as food when they are indiſpoſed.

MAST. *See* BEECH MAST.

MASLIN CORN. Rye and wheat mixed together.

MASTICK TREE, [*Piſtacia.*] This is a pretty evergreen, requiring ſhelter all the winter, is propagated by layers in the ſpring, and they will be well rooted by the following autumn.

MASTICK TREE *of Jamaica.* A ſpecies of the Cornelian cherry.

Indian MASTICK TREE, [*Schinus.*] The ſpecies are, the Peruvian and the Braſilian. Both theſe ſpecies are ſhrubby, durable in root, and top, and retain their leaves the year round; and being natives of hot countries, require ſhelter here of a good green-houſe in winter; or, if ſheltered in a ſtove, two or three winters whilſt young, it will be an advantage to the plants; however, they both ſucceed tolerably with the culture of common green-houſe exotics. They being pretty ever-greens, with finely pinnated leaves, merit a place in the collection of our tender exotics, in which they will effect a good variety; let them, therefore, be cultivated in pots of rich earth, and placed among the plants of the above department.

They are propagated by ſeed obtained from abroad, alſo by layers and cuttings.

Sow the ſeeds in the ſpring, in pots of rich earth, and plunge them in a hot-bed, managing them as other tender ſeedling exotics.

Layers of the young branches in the ſpring will be well rooted in one year; and cuttings of the young ſhoots, planted in ſpring, in pots, and plunged in a hot-bed, will readily emit roots in ſix or eight weeks.

MATFELON. Blue bottle.

MAUDLIN, [*Achillea.*] Yarrow, milfoil.

MAY. The fifth month in the year:—in which the

Products of the Kitchen Garden are,

Radiſhes, ſpinage, ſalleting of all ſorts, cabbage, brown dutch, Sileſia and Imperial lettuces, aſparagus in plenty; early peas and beans, cauliflowers from under bell-glaſſes, young carrots, artichokes, kidney-beans and cucumbers upon hot-beds; purſlain upon warm borders, or on hot-beds, with moſt ſorts of ſpring herbs.

Fruits in Prime, or yet laſting.

Pears: L'Amozelle, or Lord Cheney's green, Parkinſon's warden, burgamot de Pacque, Bezy du Chaumontelle, cadillac, with ſome others.

Apples; golden ruſſet, ſtone pippin, John apple, oaken pin, pomme d'api, winter ruſſet, and ſometimes the nonpareil; May and May-duke cherries; and in a warm ſituation, ſome ſcarlet ſtrawberries; in the forcing frame, maſculine apricots, nutmeg peaches, and ſome early plumbs.

Plants now in Flower.

Late flowering tulips, anemonies, ranunculus's, pinks of ſeveral ſorts; lilly of the valley, double white narciſſus, ſea narciſſus, tuberoſe iris's of ſeveral ſorts; white and yellow aſphodel, pulſatilla's, double rockets, pionies of ſeveral ſorts, corn-flags, yellow and and pompony martagons, Engliſh hyacinths, ſtarry hyacinth, hyacinth of Peru, blue grape hyacinth, feathered hyacinths, bulbous iris, blue aconite or monk's-hood, Tradeſcant's ſpiderwort, ſavoy ſpiderwort, bulbous fiery lily, red day lily, double purple and large blue periwinkle, peach-leaved and nettle-leaved bell-flower, fraxinella white and red, hedyſarum clypeatum, lychnidea Virginiana, double German catchfly, Greek valerian white and blue, double white and red batchelors button, double white mountain ranunculus, double ragged robin, helianthemums ſeveral kinds, jacea's ſeveral ſorts, double feverfew, ſea ragwort, veronica's of ſeveral ſorts, digitalis or fox-glove, two or three ſorts, buphthalmums two or three ſorts, with ſeveral others of leſs note.

Hardy Trees and Shrubs now in Flower.

White, blue, purple and Perſian lilacs, elder roſe, yellow jeſſamine, ſyringa, early white, Italian and common honey-ſuckles, cinquefoil-tree, laburnums, two or three ſorts; bird-cherry, Corniſh-cherry, flowering aſh, horſe-cheſnut, ſcarlet horſe-cheſnut, perfumed cherry, cockſpur hawthorn, double flowering hawthorn, male ciſtus, mallow-tree, Arbor Judæ, cytiſus lunatus, ſcorpion ſena, bladder ſena, cytiſus ſecundus, cluſii, lotus or nettle-

tree

tree, sea buck-thorn, spirea salicis folio, spirea opuli folio, spirea hyperici folio, menthly, cinnamon, damask and burnet-leaved roses, with some others.

Plants now in Flower in the Green-house and Stove.

Several sorts of ficoides's, some geraniums, aloes, oranges, aloe-leaved asphodel, onion-leaved asphodel, African scabious anemonospermos's, salvia Africana flore aureo magno, phlomis's several sorts, polygala Africana, the humble plant, ricinoides folio multifido, lotus argentea Cretica, with some others.

MAYBUSH. Hawthorn.

May LILLY. *See* LILLY *of the Valley.*

May WEED. *See* STINKING CAMOMILE.

MEADOW. The Farmer in his conversation, and writers in their books, divide the natural grass grounds into two kinds, not as differing in the species, but in the place of growth, and the intended use. These they distinguish by the names of meadow and pasture, and generally understand, by that distinction, the grass intended to be cut for hay, and that to be eaten on the ground, but this is an uncertain manner of speaking. By meadow some express the grass of low grounds only, that lie about rivers; and by pasture only such as grows on higher lands; but both these are by the judicious farmer mowed at times, and fed at times, so that all that is properly to be understood by the two words is, that being used together, they express that part of the farmer's land which is not in tillage, and they should be used together, because this variation comprehends all grass ground whatsoever, in distinction from all that which is kept in tilth.

It is a matter of great importance to the farmer, to proportion these two kinds of ground, the tillage and pasturage, one to another. There are many who call themselves farmers near London, and about other great towns, who deal altogether in pasturage; and this they may do without any necessity of tillage; but there is is no such thing as a man's keeping his farm all in tillage, without pasture. His cattle must have food, and his fields for corn in the common way of husbandry, require a great deal of dung for manure.

This brings on the necessity of keeping up a proportion between one kind and the other, for which there is no laying down any general rule; because, according to the nature of his land, and the particular course of husbandry he follows, more or less dung may be wanting.

His experience alone must shew him this, but he will find it easy to make alterations where it is necessary: the laying down a piece of corn land for grass, and the taking up a piece of grass ground for tilth, being, as we have shewn, very easy.

There are particular estates also that answer best in various manners. There are some that are so rich and proper for corn, and that lie so conveniently for dung, that a much greater proportion than the common method may be kept conveniently and profitably in tillage; and there are others naturally favourable to grass, and that lie where there is a great demand for it; and in these the greater part should be kept for pasture.

As we have shewn that the distinction into meadow and pasture is very little settled in its meaning, we shall, to be the better understood by all, speak in general of both under the name of grass ground. The hay from grass grounds that lie low, and are what is most properly called meadows, is generally in larger quantity than that from such as are higher; but this latter, though there is less of it is sweeter.

The abundance of water that often gets into, or upon these low grounds, makes the grass rank; and where they lie in the way of constant wet, they naturally produce very coarse kinds of it. We see rushes grow in barren and wet places, and there are a great many kinds of grass, tho' not enough regarded, that more or less approach to the rushy kind, which greatly diminish the the value of the hay, that comes from the wetter sort of these grounds.

The grass grounds that lie high require assistances from manure, but those which are lower, and in the way of flooding, do not; the overflowing of every river so far imitates that of the Nile, that it always leaves a mud behind it, which serves in the place of manure, and makes the grass spring fresh, as if art had been used to recruit the strength of the ground.

We have named two kinds of grafs grounds, but there is a third yet to be mentioned, which is fuch as are in the reach of falt water, whether by the fides of rivers, near the fea, or of the fea itfelf. Thefe are a great quantity in one part or other of the kingdom, and are capable of being turned to very good account, their management therefore is a material confideration in a work intended for general ufe.

Having premifed thus much concerning the nature and diftinctions of grafs ground in England, we fhall firft confider the three forts feparately, and afterwards the general and particular methods of procuring the richeft produce from each.

Thefe are what the farmer generally expreffes by the term up-land grafs grounds; fome, by way of diftinction from the lower, call them paftures, the other having the name of meadow. Thefe up-land grafs grounds differ in fituation as they lie upon higher or lower rifings, or upon their tops or fides: they alfo vary greatly in their foil, which, tho' it be in general different from that of meadows, yet is alfo very various in kind between one up-land ground and another.

With refpect to their particular fituation, we muft firft obferve, that as a certain degree of expofure is proper for grafs, fo there may be too much; and therefore that thofe rifings which are of a moderate height, are better for grafs than fuch as come under the denomiation of high hills.

The next difference is, that of their lying on the top, or on the fide of a hill; and this is fo great, that it often trebles the value in one above the other: nothing is more frequent than for ground to be wet and boggy on the top of a hill, while it is perfectly fine on the fides all the way down.

Springs naturally rife on hills, and when they are pent in, they break and foak through the very fubftance of the ground, and convert the whole upper part of the furface into a bog.

On the contrary, the fide of a rifing ground that has a gradual defcent, is, of all fituations that can be named, the beft for grafs. In fuch ground there generally is moifture at the bottom, which is very effential to grafs, and there is a way for it to run off, which is equally neceffary.

Grafs will not thrive without water, nor can it be good where there is too much; this is the great article. Where the tops of hills that are any thing high have no fpring, the bleaknefs of the expofure, and the poornefs of the foil, as that is commonly the cafe, render the grafs very weak: it is fweet, but very little of it; and where there are fprings, it is general boggy. The way of getting off the water we have already treated of under the article draining; we here fpeak of the natural condition.

Now the fide of a hill, having foil and moifture, feeds a rich and good grafs, without having fo much wet as to make it rank, or favour the growth of rufhes, or thofe other bad kinds of mixture, which generally depreciate that which grows on the tops of hills, or near rivers.

As to that in meadows, lying low, it is generally a black rich mould, and nothing more favours the growth of fine grafs; but then what thefe grounds gain in foil, they lofe by the abundant moifture.

The up-land paftures, of which we treat here, have all that variety of foils we fee in tilled ground; they are fometimes gravelly, fometimes loamy, in others they are ftony, chalky, or clayey. Of all thefe, the loamy foil, where there is a good proportion of rich earth amongft it, yields the beft grafs; upon clay, it is apt to be coarfe, becaufe of the wet it detains; upon chalk, it is low; upon gravel, it is fweet, but thin; the loam, when of the right condition, yields it juft in the middle way between all thefe, it is plentiful yet fweet, and affords the fineft hay, and the fweeteft and richeft food for cattle.

This will direct the farmer, when he is about to make changes in the proportion of his tillage and pafture, what to keep for grafs, and what to break up.

A foil that is too clayey, is liable to great inconveniencies with refpect to grafs: in winter it detains the wet a long time, and in the fummer it cracks and chaps, and no earth is more perfectly burnt up.

The black mould, fuch as is in the low grounds, yields abundance of fine grafs when it lies dry on the fide of a hill, but then it is commonly infefted in a terrible manner with worms; the loamy foils are lefs fubject to them, and are

are therefore preferable; so that on all accounts, that preference is due to the rich loams, which we have given them in respect to the growth of grass: they are not subject to poach in winter, nor to crack or be burnt up in summer.

All low ground is subject to overflowing, either in a larger way by rivers, or in a smaller by the water coming from the higher grounds in the winter rains; and both these wettings are of great benefit, if proper care be taken to carry off the redundant water; and to prevent the overflowing by rivers at improper times.

The finest part of the mould is washed off by rains from ploughed lands that lie high, and a part of the manure with it, and carried down with the water to the low grass grounds at their bottom; this it is that renders them so fruitful; and in same manner land floods drowning meadows by river sides, have the same effect. The waters of these are thick and yellow, with the richest part of the soil from the adjoining high grounds, and they leave this upon those meadows when they lie upon them to settle, and are then taken off. This renders the grass on these grounds very plentiful, but as there generally remains too much of the moisture behind, it is coarse; there grow weeds, and ill kinds of grass in them, which are not in the sweet pasturage of the up-lands. There is a great deal of difference in the value of those meadows which are liable to be overflowed by accident, and those which are capable of being overflowed at pleasure, but are out of that danger. In the first, the water may come at a wrong time, and often does so to the utter loss of the crop: but, in the other, it never can come but when it is brought, and yet 'tis at all those times, when proper, ready at the husbandman's command.

Such meadows as lie flat on the banks of great rivers, are of the first kind: these are subject to accidental floodings, which may come at very wrong times, and are therefore very precarious and uncertain as to the produce.

Those which lie near lesser streams, and a little higher than the level of their waters, are of the latter kind; they may be overflowed when it will do them good by turning the stream of the water upon them; and these are worth much more than other low grass grounds for this reason; as the others, from their hazardous situation, are worth less.

To those two we may add a third kind of grass grounds, which are of a kind of middle nature between these, and the up-land pastures. These last are such as lie above the level of the water considerably, yet not so much but it may be brought over them by means of wheels or engines: these are expensive, but the benefit very great. We have not the spirit of the Italians in this respect, nor indeed the necessity: they raise water to a surprising height for the overflowing their pastures; and they owe all their verdure to that artificial management.

The meadows that lie on the sides of large rivers, having all the same general soil, which is a rich dark mould, they yield abundance of grass; and they owe their fertility to the overflowing of those rivers.

When grass grounds lie near the borders of great rivers, but so high as not to be flooded accidentally, it will always be worth the farmer's while to have an engine for overflowing them at such times as he shall think proper.

We have shewn what is to be expected from each kind of grass ground with respect to its soil, its situation and its degree of moisture: we now come to consider those accidents to which all grass grounds are liable, and which reduce their value. These are of three principal kinds, the first being from weeds, the second from rubbish of any sort, left on the ground, and the third from ant-hills and mole-hills: these last are the most difficult to be removed, but when mowing is considered, they are of all other annoyances the most obnoxious.

Weeds are of various kinds, and hurtful in different degrees. All plants, not of the grass kind, may be called by this name when among grass, but some are beneficial: the white trefoil, which is a sort of clover; and the red trefoil, which is a wild clover, are both serviceable, and so are several other little plants that rise spontaneously among the grass.

The large weeds are most troublesome, such as thistles, docks, and mallows. These are grubbed up, or drawn with an instrument made for that purpose, called the thistle hook. This

pierce

pierces into the ground, and laying hold of them at some depth, easily pulls the whole root up.

As to accidental rubbish, this must always be picked off. Some will be thrown on by carelessness, and some comes on among the manure; which, though not so easily seen at first, is very plainly to be perceived when the rains have washed the rich part of the dung into the ground.

Women or boys may be sent in to gather up this sort of stuff, which consists of bones, bits of brick, and broken glass; a little trouble takes it off, and saves a great deal of difficulty to the mowers. *See* ANTHILLS.

Dung is an universal manure for grass ground, and the more mellow and rotten it is, the better: most people content themselves with it, and seek no farther; but grass ground of of different soils as well as corn land, admits with advantage the same diversity of manures.

For grass ground of the common kind, where the soil is a fat loam, or a loam with a very large quantity of mellow earth among it, the best of al. manure is old dung and pond mud mixed together. This may be considered as the general manure for these grounds; and the time of laying it on is according to the particular circumstances or use the farmer makes of his land, from September to February.

The most favourable time of all is in the middle of winter, that there may be frost to dissolve and break to pieces the harder parts of the manure, and the rains may wash the whole into the ground at their leisure, while there is no great power of sun to evaporate the virtue of it as it lies spread on the ground.

The way of laying on manure upon grass ground, is to drop it in small heaps at due distance; and first employing labourers to break and spread it well by hand, the owner is afterwards to have it worked over with a bush harrow.

When a piece of grass ground produces moss, and other bad things, but not in such a degree as to require the method of cutting up and burning, the best method is to strew over it twice a year, namely, in October & the beginning of February, a mixture of two parts coal-ashes and one part wood-ashes, wetted with the emptying the pots of the family.

On a piece of grass ground, that is cold, but not very wet, let the husbandman spread a good dressing of pigeon's dung; or of the dung of fowls mixed with earth and coal-ashes. This is to be done at the latter end of February, and being the richest of all manures, it must be spread with the greatest care and attention; it will thus come to the roots of the grass, just as they are about to make their shoot, and will cause twenty blades in many places to grow for one.

There are good grass grounds on the sort of soil quite opposite to what we have been naming, that is, on such a loam as having a great proportion of sand, and little of the binding ingredients in it, is hot, loose, and crumbly. In this case the manure must be varied as the soil varies; and of all that can be recommended, nothing comes near the virtue of any one of those clayey marles we have described under the head of manures; a dressing like this laid on early in winter, becomes quite broken and mouldered by the spring, and will all wash into the earth; the consequence is, that it gives the two qualities wanting firmness and fatness. The quantity of hay may very well be doubled by such a dressing, and the feeding in proportion; and although this be an expensive manure for grass lands in the first laying on, yet it very well answers in the end; for the effect, instead of three or four, which is the common duration of manures, will last ten or twelve years.

In some of the up-land pastures in Derbyshire and Staffordshire, there is a kind of brown earth full of fragments of stone. The proper manure for this is lime.

There is nothing so wrong in the husbandman's whole practice, as the deferring the laying his ground for hay too long: it may be convenient to him to feed upon it; but let him consider what will be the effect of a hot dry summer, and what will be the loss if he be disappointed of his crop. Spring is the season for the grass to make its shoot; and if it be eaten over and over again at that time, and hot dry weather follow, it is deprived of the benefit of rains, and never makes that first shoot tolerably, nor comes to any reasonable

ſonable growth afterwards. For theſe reaſons let the farmer ſuit his ſeveral occaſions, ſo as to be ſure of laying down his ground for the hay in time; and if he loſe ſomething in the advantage of feeding, he may be perfectly aſſured of making himſelf ten-fold returns for it.

As ſoon as the cattle are off let him ſend in women or children to finiſh the clearing of the ground, by picking up the broken boughs of trees that the winter winds may have thrown in upon the graſs, and every other kind of annoyance: this done, let him ſend in a labourer or more, according to the compaſs of ground, and let theſe have orders to break and ſpread all about the dung that may have fallen from the cattle upon it; and alſo to break and ſcatter any freſh mole-hills.

This being done, the expence of which is very little, and the convenience and benefit very great, let him order the ground to be rolled carefully and thoroughly.

The rolling graſs grounds intended for mowing is of great conſequence, as it prepares the ſurface for the ſcythe, and deſtroys the laſt accidents that can happen to it during the preparation for hay.

In the winter months the ſurface of the ground will be rendered here and there unequal, by the treading of cattle, in ſuch places as the wet has moſt affected, and where it has lodged moſt: theſe make the growth of the graſs irregular, and therefore are an injury.

During the firſt approach of ſpring the worms will be at work, and will every damp and mild night throw up abundance of their caſts; theſe alſo are, like the other, nuiſances, though not great ones, and they hinder the right and regular growth of the graſs; if there be moles, or if there be any ants left, they will alſo be at work at the ſame time; and this is a ſeaſon at which all ſhould be ſet right; and the condition of the ground is ſuch that it will eaſily be ſo. The roller will anſwer the purpoſe, for it will take more effect at this time than at any other.

The ground being thus carefully laid for hay, the farmer has no farther care but knowing when to cut it. This he muſt carefully obſerve, for there is a proper time of ripeneſs; and all after, as well as all before that, is ſo much loſs.

There is a time of the year when every plant flowers; and graſs, like others, has its ſeaſon. If we examine in other plants the courſe of nature, we ſhall ſee that, though their leaves ſtand pretty well during the flowering, they wither when they come to ripen the ſeed. The leaves of graſs go to the quantity of hay as well as the ſtalks; and are indeed the beſt part: they are not therefore to be neglected for the ſake of the other. The hay will not have its due quantity till the ſtalks are full grown; but after that time, the leaves will fall ſo faſt into a ſtate of decay, that there will be more loſt by twenty times at the bottom, than there is gained at the top. The price of hay is very conſiderable, but that depends upon its goodneſs; and this upon two articles, the time of cutting, and the manner of making; and upon the former little leſs than on the latter.

The fine green colour of hay is very much valued. This is owing, in a great meaſure, to the making; but then it muſt be in the graſs itſelf, otherwiſe all the care that can be taken in drying it, is all in vain; a proper method of turning will preſerve a colour, but it cannot give it: that muſt be from nature.

This fine colour depends, like the reſt of the good qualities, on the time of mowing, or the degree of ripeneſs of the graſs. When it is juſt in flower, the leaves are freſh and green; but when it is got to ſeed, they grow brown; this is the firſt ſtep toward their decay, and this is the change of colour which no art can recover.

While the graſs is but coming to perfection, it is too green; when it has ſtood too long, it becomes brown; and that fine pale green colour ſo eſteemed in hay, can never be obtained by any art afterwards.

The ſmell of hay is another article of its value, and this, like the reſt, muſt be preſerved by care in the making, but it muſt be entirely owing to the time of cutting.

Hay that has ſtood too long, has the the appearance of ſo much ſtubble, and has no more ſmell; whereas at the time of the graſs flowering, which is its juſt ſtate of perfection, there is one of the pleaſanteſt flavours we know, from the cutting through of the ſtalk, and

and the evaporating of its juice in drying. The colour of the ſtalk fades as well as that of the leaves, after the due ſeaſon is over.

Let the farmer go into his graſs fields from time to time toward the beginning of June, if not prevented ſooner by the full ripeneſs. Let him examine the ſtalks which will be now grown up in height, and ſee how their tops approach toward ripeneſs; he will perceive from time to time the little heads ſwell, and at length there will appear a few white threads. Theſe, in ſome kinds of graſs, only ſhew themſelves on the ſurface of the buttons; and, in others, hang from them a fifth part of an inch. This is the flower of the graſs, and when it appears, the hay-time is near.

He muſt not judge from one or two plants in a hundred, but ſee when the whole field thus gets into bloom; and then he muſt be critical in his examination. The fuller and freſher it is at the top, while the bottom remains perfectly ſound and good, the better; therefore that is to be examined for the final marking of the time. Let the farmer open the graſs with his hands in ſeveral places down to the ground, and obſerve carefully how the lower part looks: as theſe flowery parts, or the top, ripen, the bottom will grow brown. After this the top will get nothing, and the bottom will loſe a great deal, ſo this is the time for the mowing.

The mowers are to be ſent in, and the ground having been thus prepared and levelled for them, they have no excuſe if they do not cut it cloſe. Theſe are a ſort of people, as every one knows who has had any concern with them, who are very apt to ſlight over their work, and ready to ſeize upon any pretence for doing ſo; they have no conſideration that their careleſſneſs is the loſs to the farmer, perhaps of the tenth part of his crop; but let him take care of himſelf. As he has according to theſe directions prepared the ground for them, let him follow them and frequently put them in mind of it, they will thus be brought to do much better than they ever will when left to themſelves; and the addition to the quantity of the hay will very well pay the farmer for his care and attendance.

The buſineſs of hay-making is generally done much better than that of mowing; and if any omiſſion be made in it, it is eaſily ſeen, & there is time to rectify it; but in the mowing, the miſchief is ſcarce to be ſeen, unleſs the ſcythe be followed; and when it is once done, there is no mending of it. The graſs being down, it is to be carefully dried; and in this there is ſo much difference between the practice of the farmers in thoſe parts of the kingdom where huſbandry is moſt improved, and the others, that it ſhould be ſet in the ſtrongeſt light, to render thoſe improvements univerſal.

The graſs being down, it is to be turned and dried, and then it is hay. This is the whole proceſs in a few words, but there muſt go more to the well underſtanding of it.

The great care in this point, is to preſerve the colour. The graſs being cut in the condition we have named, will be of a fine green, and this is to be preſerved; for the farmer may be aſſured, that a loſs of colour is always attended with a loſs of taſte, and loſs of ſmell; and with a certain loſs in the article of price.

To preſerve the colour of the graſs, and give it the full ſweetneſs when it is mowed, it ſhould be let to lie in the ſwarth two days and a half. At the end of this time it is to be ſpread out; this is properly what is called tedding the hay; and thus it is to lie expoſed to the ſun during the remainder of the day. Then it is to be made up in little cocks, which are called graſs cocks, at evening, and ſo left for the night. The next morning, as ſoon as the dew is off the ground, theſe graſs cocks are to be ſpread, and thus the ſide of the graſs that had lain undermoſt, will get dried. In this condition it lies all that day. Toward evening, it is to be cocked up into the ſame little graſs cocks as before.

This is a reaſonable, and an excellent practice, for it at the ſame time gives the hay all the advantage of the air and ſun during the day, and defends it from the dews of the night, which can do little harm when it is gathered up in theſe heaps; though while it lay ſpread upon the ground, they would have greatly interfered with the drying. Sometimes when this caution of cocking up at evening has been omitted, the whole quantity which was very forward in drying the day before, has been

been rendered damp and ſoft, and brought into a worſe condition than at firſt; for the water of the dew is more hurtful to its colour than the natural juices of the graſs. In this condition the ſmell and colour have been greatly impaired, and there has been afterwards no way of recovering them. This is not ſo bad as the practice of the remote farmers, whoſe hay is always brown, and mow-burnt; but it is very much inferior to the true and careful method, and never fails to reduce the price.

In the proper method of hay-making after the tedding, and graſs cocking, ſo far as we have named, the hay is to be ſpread again, and drawn up into a kind of lengths, which they call wind-rows. This is a very good condition for drying, and what is a great advantage alſo, theſe wind-rows are eaſily thrown up into cocks, for they lie conveniently for that purpoſe: thus when the weather is fine, the hay has the full advantage of it, as it lies ſpread out in theſe rows; and if rain come on, the hay-makers can toſs it into cocks in a few minutes, in which condition it will get very little damage, and is ready to be ſpread again to take the advantage of the next fair blaſt.

From theſe wind-rows the hay is to be thrown into large cocks, and in theſe to ſtand through the night, and for ſome time afterwards; but then it is not, though pretty well made, to be carried home directly from the field in this condition. The outſide of one of theſe large cocks will be very dry, while there is moiſture in the middle, and the farmer's buſineſs is to have his hay all alike; not only ſome of the juices of the graſs will remain in that which has been in the innermoſt part of the cock, but it will ſweat a little with lying together: therefore theſe cocks muſt be thrown to pieces, and the whole quantity of the hay once more ſpread upon the ground. If good weather follow, it will thus dry in a very compleat and perfect manner: three hours wind and ſun going farther under theſe circumſtances than a day at another time.

If the weather continue favourable, the buſineſs of hay-making is thus happily finiſhed; but if rain come, the farmer is not to turn the hay that has catched the wet as it lay ſpread, but to let it dry as it lies, which, theſe ſhowers being ſeldom laſting, it will quickly do. On the contrary, if the over-care of the hay-makers ſhould turn the graſs thus nearly dried, and then wetted by accident, to the ground, the damp of the earth would greatly injure it. On the other hand, as the wet is ſlight, and the ſun and air have great power; the top will preſently dry again lying as it is.

After this ſpreading from the cocks, the hay may be thrown together for convenience of loading, and is in perfect good condition to carry in.

Meadow *Rue*, [*Thalictrum*.] There are ſeveral ſpecies of this plant, all hardy perennials, eaſily propagated by parting the roots in autumn, and ſowing the ſeed in the ſpring.

Meadow *Saffron*, [*Colchicum*.] There are three ſpecies, the common autumnal, the mountain Spaniſh, and the variegated eaſtern Meadow Saffron. The firſt grows wild with a purple flower in many rich meadows. They are all hardy, and are propagated by off-ſets of the bulbs, taking them up in June when their flowers decay, and putting them into the ground again in Auguſt.

Meadow *Sweet*, [*Ulmaria*.] This herb is frequent in moiſt meadows, and about the ſides of rivers: it flowers in the beginning of June, and continues in beauty a conſiderable time. The flowers have a very pleaſant flavour, which water extracts from them by infuſion, and elevates in diſtillation.

Meadow *Trefoil*. See Clover.

MEALLY TREE. Wayfaring tree.

MEAK. A hook to cut up peaſe, &c.

MEASLES. This is a common diſorder among hogs, and ſhews itſelf in a redneſs of the eyes, and foulneſs of the ſkin, and in their neglecting their food.

The beſt remedy is this. Keep the hog faſting the whole afternoon and night. Then ſet before him a good meſs of victuals; not large in quantity, but hot and well prepared, and put into it forty grains of ſalt of hartſhorn and two ounces of bole armoniac. It will all go down very well after this faſt; and will make a good beginning of a cure. The ſame method is to be followed every day till he is perfectly recovered, and for a few days after, for fear of returns.

MECHOACAN, [*Mechoacanna.*] The root of an American convolvulus not very unlike jalap, but inferior to it in virtue, and the quantity of reſin it yields.

MEDIC. Lucern.

MEDEOLA. See *African* ASPARAGUS.

MEDLAR, [*Meſpilus.*] A ſpecies of fruit-trees, which may be raiſed by grafting or budding them upon the common white-thorn. This is the uſual way of propagating the American ſorts, which are of the hawthorn kind; but the beſt way to raiſe the other ſorts is from their ſeeds. All medlars will take when they are grafted or budded upon each other. They will alſo take upon ſtocks of pears, or of quinces, and both of theſe will take upon the medlar; ſo that there is a great affinity between them. All the American ſorts will grow twenty feet high, if they are not ſtinted by grafting.

Medlars may alſo be raiſed from their ſeeds, which, if put into the ground in autumn, ſoon after they are ripe, will come up the following ſpring: but if they are not ſet till the next year, they will not ſhoot till the year after.

MELANCHOLY THISTLE, [*Cirſium.*] This plant is preſerved in the gardens for variety, and is propagated by ſowing the ſeeds in the ſpring.

MELILOT, [*Melilotus.*] This grows wild in hedges among corn; and has likewiſe, for medicinal uſes, being cultivated in gardens. The green herb has no remarkable ſmell; when dry, a pretty ſtrong one: the taſte is roughiſh, bitter, and if long chewed, nauſeous. A decoction of this herb has been recommended in inflammations of the abdomen; and a decoction of the flowers in the fluor albus. But modern practice rarely employs it any otherwiſe than in emollient and carminative clyſters, and in fomentations, cataplaſms, and the like; and in theſe not often. It formerly gave name to one of the officinal plaſters, which received from the melilot a green colour, but no particular virtue.

MELON, [*Cucumis.*] Of the melon, there is but one real ſpecies of the plant, but of the fruit there are innumerable varieties, with reſpect to figure, ſize, colour of the rind, and fleſh or pulp.

This fruit, in different varieties, is of various ſizes, from about four to ten or twelve inches in length and diameter, in moſt ſorts ripening externally to a yellowiſh colour, and ſome ripen green, and others white, but have moſtly a reddiſh fleſh or pulp, except one variety, which is green both in rind and pulp, as hereafter deſcribed.

The varieties of moſt eſtimation at preſent in the Engliſh gardens are,

Common Muſk-Melon. A large, oblong-oval, longitudinally-ribbed, and netted-wrought Melon, having a reddiſh tolerably rich flavoured fleſh; and the plants being of the hardier kind, generally ſet a plentiful crop of fruit. This is alſo one of the beſt ſorts of melon for mangoes, for which purpoſe the London gardeners cultivate principally this variety for the ſupply of markets.

Romana-Melon. A roundiſh, moderate-ſized, ribbed, and netted melon, ſomewhat compreſſed at both ends, and with a reddiſh firm fleſh of a fine rich flavour, the plants good bearers, each often ſetting from about five or ſix to eight or ten fruit, and is one of the beſt ſorts, both for an early and general crop.

Cantaleupe, or Armenian Warted Melon. A large, roundiſh, deeply-ribbed melon, a little compreſſed at both ends, and the ſurface full of warted protuberances, and with a reddiſh firm fleſh of a moſt delicious rich flavour, of which there are ſome varieties. Large black carbuncled or black rock cantaleupe melon, being of a blackiſh green colour, having the ſurface covered with high, rugged, ſaxtile protuberances. Large white carbuncled cantaleupe melon. Orange cantaleupe melon. Theſe varieties are the fineſt of the melon kind, with reſpect to the richneſs of flavour of the fruit, and which by the melon-eaters are preferred to all the other ſorts: but the plants being rather more tender, do not ſet fruit ſo freely, nor in ſuch plenty, they often not having more than from one to two or three fruit on a plant, and in a three-light frame ſometimes not more than five or ſix fruit.

This variety derives the term Cantaleupe melon, from Cantaleupe near Roma, the place where it was firſt cultivated in Europe, brought thence from Armenia.

Small Portugal Melon. A ſmalliſh

round melon, having a reddiſh fleſh of a fine muſky flavour, and the plants are plentiful bearers, each often ſetting from eight or ten to twenty fruit, which, however, is more by half than ſhould be left to come to perfection.

Green fleſhed Melon. An oval, moderate-ſized melon, having an even, ſmooth, green rind, and the fleſh or pulp ripening to a greeniſh colour, which is highly flavoured.

Large Green-rinded Melon. A large roundiſh-oval, green, ſmooth-rinded melon, having a reddiſh fleſh.

Black Galloway Melon. A roundiſh oval, middle-ſized, ſlightly-ribbed, dark-green, ſmooth melon, having a reddiſh, rich flavoured fleſh, and the plants excellent bearers, but the ſort not at preſent very plentiful in England. It was brought from Portugal many years ſince by a Lord Galloway.

Netted or Wrought Melon. An oval, middle-ſized, ſcarcely ribbed melon, having the ſurface cloſely wrought with raiſed net-work, and hath a reddiſh fleſh.

White Spaniſh Melon. An oval, ſmalliſh, white, ſmooth-rinded melon, having a reddiſh pulp.

Zatta Melon. A very ſmall, roundiſh, warty-rinded Melon.

Obſerve, that although all the above kinds be only varieties of the ſame ſpecies, yet, by care in cultivating them ſeparate, they may be continued all tolerably permanent.

There are many other intermediate varieties of leſs note, but a few of known good qualities is better than many different ſorts, ſome of which probably not much better than gourds; and of the varieties here ſpecified, the *Romana* and *Cantaleupe* kinds are conſiderably the moſt worthy of attention, as theſe two ſorts ripen to a much higher degree of perfection.

It is an exotic from the hot parts of the world, ſuppoſed principally of Perſia, from which country, however, it was firſt introduced into the different parts of Europe; and conſequently its culture in every part of Britain can be effected only by artificial heat, and conſtant ſhelter of glaſs, &c. till July as at an early ſeaſon they require a temperature of heat almoſt equal to that of our pine-apple ſtoves.

The principal ſeaſon of ripe melons in England, is June, July, and Auguſt; they, however, by different ſowings and plantings, may be obtained from May till October; but they are always in the greateſt perfection in the times before mentioned.

The flowers of the melon are conſequently *monœciaus*, like the cucumber, as being of the ſame genus and claſs, male and female apart on the ſame plant, the males ſtanding immediately on the ſummit of its foot-ſtalk, without any appearance of germen or fruit under it, and the females diſcover the round germen or embrio fruit under its baſe, when not bigger than a pea; obſerving, that the male bloſſoms are by nature deſigned for fertilizing the female flower, as obſerved of the cucumber, ſo muſt not be pulled off until a full crop of fruit is ſet.

With regard to the propagation of the melon, the plants being annual, are raiſed every year from ſeed, ſowed at different times in ſpring, in hot-beds of dung or tanner's bark, under frames and glaſſes, &c. they requiring continual aid of artificial heat and ſhelter, from the time of ſowing until June or July, for they will at no time ſucceed in the natural ground, at leaſt rarely perfect fruit; and each crops require two different hot-beds, that is, to be ſowed in one, and the plants nurſed therein till a month or ſix weeks old, that thay begins to ſhoot runners, then tranſplanted into a ſecond and final hot-bed, to remain to fruit.

The ſeaſon for ſowing is any time from the beginning of January, until the middle of April, according to the conveniencies there may be for their culture, and time the fruit is required in perfection; for the early crops, to be raiſed in January, February, and beginning of March, require very ſubſtantial hot-beds, under conſtant ſhelter of garden frames and lights, until July; but the later crops, ſown in the middle of March, and in April, ſucceed with more moderate hot-beds, and may be ridged out in April and May under hand or bell-glaſſes, or oiled paper frames, and the plants will ſet and ripen their fruit under theſe ſhelters; obſerving, that the early ſowings in January ſometimes produce ripe fruit in May, but come into full bearing in June; and thoſe raiſed in February, and early in March, ripen fruit in June, July, and Auguſt; and ſowings performed any time from about the middle of March till that of April, furnish ripe fruit principally in August and September, and sometimes in October.

Observe, therefore, that, like the cucumbers, crops of melons may be raised in three different ways; under frames and lights, under hand or bell-glasses, and under oiled paper; each of which will be exhibited under a separate head.

The materials principally necessary in their culture are,

Frames and glass lights for early, and hand-glasses, &c. and oiled paper lights, for late crops; and for each crop good mats for covering on nights; all as observed for the cucumbers.

Horse stable dung, a plentiful supply both for making the hot-beds, and for occasional linings, must be in quality, quantity, and preparation, as hinted for cucumbers, and in the article hot-beds.

But sometimes in the melon culture bark hot-beds are employed, or of bark and dung together, which, where tanner's-bark can be easily procured, on account of its regular and durable heat, is a very proper material for hot-beds in the culture of melons, either used alone, or mixed with hot dung.

As to mould, the melon, like the cucumber, will prosper in any rich pliable kitchen-garden earth, prepared some months in a heap; but the favourite and most prosperous soil for the melon is a fine mellow loam, taken from the surface of a pasture field or common, enriching it with about one-third of rotten neat's dung, or thorough rotten dung of old hot-beds, preparing the whole in a heap, and managed as directed under the article Composts; observing, that when it is to be used, not to sift or screen any, only break it well to pieces with the spade.

The situation, or place for making the hot-beds, should be dry, warm, full to the sun, and sheltered, as for cucumbers; likewise observe, not to dig any trench for the early hot-beds, but make them entirely on the surface of the ground, for the reasons there assigned.

It is generally advised to cultivate melons as far as possible distant from cucumbers, lest, by an intercommunication of their *farina*, it should cause a degeneracy; there is apparently some reason in this: however, when we consider that the two plants are real different species, I believe there is no great danger to be apprehended, as in the case of varieties.

The seed, and its kind, being material articles, you should be particularly careful to procure such only as have been saved from the very finest fruit of the respective approved varieties; this, if possible, should be two or three years old, for the reasons observed of the cucumber seed; but when you are obliged to use new seed, it is proper either to hang them in a paper, or phial, in a dry room near the fire, all winter, or in a phial, exposed in a dry window to the sun; or may carry them in your pockets three or four weeks, either of which expedients will dry up much of the watery parts, whereby the plants will be less luxuriant and more fruitful. We receive melon seeds annually from France, Spain, Italy, and other hot countries; but we would caution against depending on these for a principal crop, for not being enured to this climate, the plants from such would be more tender and delicate in their culture, less fruitful, and the fruit often of much less value, than those of seeds saved at home; therefore, only a plant or two of the foreign seeds should be raised at first, just to prove the quality of the fruit.

From the time of sowing the seed to the maturity of the fruit, it is commonly near four months, and sometimes longer; for the plants seldom shew fruit till they have shot several runners, which, from the first appearance of the plants, will be at least six or eight weeks in effecting; from the appearance of the fruit till it is fairly set, a week or fortnight; and from its setting till fully ripe will be about forty days.

The proper quantity of hot-bed in the culture of melons for private use is, that for the smallest family there cannot be less than one three-light frame for the early, and three hand or bell glasses, or three holes under oiled paper, for the late or succession crops, allowing two plants to each light of the frame, the same to each hand-glass, or hole under the paper lights; and supposing each plant, one with another,

to

to produce about three fruit, so that in a three-light frame, and in three holes under hand-glasses, or oiled paper shelters, there will be but about from thirty to forty melons; though of the smaller sorts of melon there will sometimes be from six to ten, or twelve, or more, on a plant; but six or eight is as many as the plants are able to bring to perfection: however, for the supply of a middling family, two three-light frames, and, at least, six hand or bell-glasses, &c. will be necessary to furnish a tolerable supply during the season; and for a large family, four three-light frames, at least, or twelve lights, will be requisite, and double that number of hand-glasses, or holes of plants under paper frames.

We now proceed to the different methods of culture; and first, of their early culture in frames, observe as follows.

The time of year to begin the culture of melons in frames, is January, February, and beginning of March; but when designed to have melons as early as possible, we commonly begin in January, though the beginning of February is a more successful time of sowing to have a good crop; if, however, you begin early in January, it is proper to sow also twice in February and March for succession crops; likewise to be ready in case of accidents to the early plants, or that they should not thrive, as is often the case at a very early season.

The seed may be sowed, and the plants raised, either in a hot-bed of early cucumbers now at work, in the same manner in every respect as for them directed; or, where none is, make a hot-bed for a one-light frame on purpose, observing exactly the same rules with respect to dimensions, making, framing, and earthing the bed, sowing the seed, and other management, as directed for the early cucumbers; likewise, when the plants have been come up three days, that their cotyledons are a little expanded, transplant or prick them into small pots for the convenience of removal, as there directed; but of these, i. e. melons, put only two plants in each pot, plunging them in the bed, and manage them as above till fit to ridge out; for the cucumbers and melons, being nearly of equal temperature, the same degree of heat, air, &c. suits both in this part of their culture; it would therefore be superfluous to trouble the reader with a repetition, since the particulars are fully exhibited under cucumbers.

In this nursery-bed they are to be continued a month or six weeks, till their first runners begin to advance; observing, as their shanks rise in height, to earth them up by degrees with fine mould, till the pots are full, for this will greatly encourage them, and they will come fast into the rough leaf, and begin to form joints and shoot runners.

Observe, when their two or three first rough leaves are fully expanded, and another forming in the centre, appearing like a bud, which part being also the end of an advancing shoot, it should just at this period of its growth be stopped, i. e. cut or pinched off close to the second or third leaf, as advised for the cucumbers, to procure lateral shoots, called runners; for it is from these, or others issuing from them, that we are to expect the fruit; and when these first runners appear, the plants are ready for ridging out into the fruiting hot-bed.

The plants from the time of sowing, till arrived at the above size for ridging-out, take about five or six weeks growth.

The ridging-out, or fruiting hot-bed, should be prepared in due time to receive the plants when arrived to the proper age and size above-mentioned; observing, to prepare fresh hot dung a week or two in a heap, as for the cucumbers, sufficient for one or more three-light frames; let the bed be made entirely on the surface, for the opportunity of lining, carrying it up three feet and half, or four feet high, raising the back or north side three or four inches higher; directly put on the frame and lights, to defend the bed from chilling rains, and to draw up the heat, tilting the glasses behind for the steam to pass away; and in a week, or ten or fifteen days, according to the substance of the bed, its first great heat will abate; then prepare to mould it, and put in the plants, observing the necessary precautions, as for the cucumber beds.

The bed being ready, as above, then wheel in your prepared mould, and lay just under the middle of each light about

about a bushel of it in a heap, for the immediate reception of the plants, forming each heap into a sort of conical hillock about fifteen inches high; and the thus having the hills of earth this height, is proper both that the plants may be near the glasses, which is of importance to early work, and to allow them a good depth of earth; for they should generally have a greater depth of mould than cucumbers, the plants being more impatient of moisture by watering, which is also prejudicial to the prosperity and flavour of the fruit; that, therefore, by allowing a good depth of earth, they will shift much longer without the aid of water: when the hillocks are thus formed, directly earth the other parts of the bed within the frame three inches thick, just to keep down the steam rising immediately from the dung; then shut down the lights, and when the earth is warm put in the plants.

In a day or two the heat of the dung will have sufficiently warmed the hills of earth; then bring the plants in their pots; being two in each, plant one pot of plants, with the balls of earth about their roots, in the middle of each hill, as directed for the cucumbers; and if the mould should appear dry, give a little water towards the outside, being careful not to wet the plants much at this time; and as soon as planted shut down the lights, to draw up the heat about the roots of the plants, but tilt them again in due time, to pass off the steam.

The plants being now ridged out into the fruiting hot-bed, observe, that as the glasses are to be continued constantly on the frames till July, your daily care is to admit fresh air at all opportunities in calm weather, by tilting the lights behind from about half an inch to two, three, or four high, according to the temperature of the heat and steam of the bed, and that of the outward air, which must be also observed occasionally on nights at first ridging-out, if there is a great steam, for this must not be pent up, nor stagnated for want of air; cover the glasses also every night with mats, one or two thick, as shall seem necessary, but never let them hang down all over the sides of the frame and bed, as often done, which would draw up a violent steam, and exclude the air too much from the plants, and draw them up weak and of a yellow colour; give water also occasionally when the earth appears dry: observing, that in the performance of all of the above works in this bed, to follow strictly the same rules as exhibited in the ridging-out bed of early cucumbers; but to keep in mind, that melons, being rather impatient of moisture, must have it more seldom, and less in proportion, than for cucumbers, especially near the main stem and principal roots; for by much moisture these parts are apt to canker and rot, so should be watered mostly at some distance from these principal parts, and never to wet the vine much at an early season; but when there is not less than twelve or fifteen inches depth of earth on the beds, they will not need water oftner than once a fortnight; and sometimes, when the earth is of a loamy nature and depth as above, and pressed down close, that it may the better retain its natural moistness, the plants, after two or three waterings, till they have firmly established their roots, will often succeed without, or, at least, with very little more water; and in which case they generally set their fruit freely, and it ripens to a rich and high flavour; for reduncancy of moisture retards the setting of the fruit; and although, after it is fairly set, occasional waterings will encrease its magnitude, yet much of it greatly debases its flavour and taste; but on the other hand observe, that where the earth of the beds is a light texture, or of but a moderate depth, the plants will all along require occasional waterings, especially in warm sunny weather; let it however be remembered, that when the plants exhibit their first shew of young fruit, no water, or as little as possible, should be given, until the fruit is set as big as walnuts, when, agreeable to the nature and proportion of the earth, and other rules as above mentioned, and as hereafter hinted, use your discretion accordingly in watering.

Examine with care for the first week after ridging out, that the earth of the hills and roots of the plants do not receive too much heat from the violence of the bed; and if there is danger, remove some of the earth around the lower part of each hill; and if any is burned at bottom, add directly some fresh

fresh in its stead, and in a few days or a week the burning quality will subside; then place the removed mould again about the hillocks.

After danger of burning is past, cherish the heat as much as possible, by laying long dry litter around the sides of the bed, to defend it from chilling wet and cold piercing winds.

When the heat begins to decline considerably, be sure to revive it as soon as possible, by adding a substantial lining of hot dung, to the sides of the bed at different times, using the same precaution of earthing the top, &c. to prevent the steam of the linings entering under the bottom, or at any part of the frame; for the rancid steam coming directly from the dung would destroy the plants.

When the fibres of the plants begin to advance through the hills of earth, let some fresh mould be layed in the frame at different times to warm, and by degrees add each parcel around the hills, till the whole bed is gradually molded nearly as high as the top of them; but rather let the top of each hill be about an inch higher, that the main stem and principal roots may be preserved moderately dry, otherwise, being watered, would soak to these principal parts, and cause them to rot, as being very impatient of copious moisture from watering, &c. therefore, according as the mould is occasionally added, observe the afore-mentioned precaution: also to press it down close, that by lying compact it may retain a due moisture in itself the longer, so as the plants will require to be but seldom watered.

As the runners of the plants advance, dispose them with regularity, and when they are three joints long, if no young fruit appears, it is proper to perform a second stopping, by taking off the end of the extreme joint, to promote a more speedy supply of other lateral runners, which, together with others naturally arising from them, will sufficiently spread the bed with vine; and it is from these lateral shoots we may generally expect soon to see plenty of young fruit.

At the first training the vines, as above, if some dry and clean reeds are thinly spread upon the surface of the bed for the vines to run upon, it will preserve all the runners and young fruit from the damp of the earth, as well as prevent the earth and upper fibres of the roots from being dried too fast by the sun; some, for the above purposes, cover the bed all over closely with plane tiles; but this I should think rather excludes the necessary benefit of the sun and air, too much from the earth and roots of the plants.

When the young fruit begins to appear, it is of much importance to support a due temperature of heat in the beds, by occasional linings, &c. do not omit this, because the whole success of having the plants set, a regular and a plentiful crop of fruit depends on a good bottom heat, both to warm the earth sufficiently about the fibres, as well as the internal air of the frame; for these fruit being so extremely tender whilst young, that without a proper heat they set very sparing and straglingly, generally assuming a slow, stunted, and irregular habit of growth; maintain, therefore, the necessary degree of heat, and the fruit will set freely, and swell fast in magnitude.

At this period also of the first appearance of the fruit, I should advise to forbear watering, if possible, till the fruit is set as large as good walnuts, as we above observed; observing, that if the plants are growing in a tolerable depth of soil of a loamy nature, they will shift very well without any during that period, or longer, unless the earth should be very dry indeed, and then let them have it but sparingly; for if any considerable portion of water is given when the fruit is setting, the vine will acquire a glut of sap, and continue shooting with great luxuriancy, which is contrary to the nature of these young fruit, as, being of such a delicate temperature in their infant state, and even during their minor growth, that the exuberant quantity of sap in the branches causes them to turn yellow, and drop off soon after they have blossomed, and sometimes after they have set as large as an egg, and more especially if there is not a due degree of warmth in the beds.

According as the young fruit appears, you will observe it accompanied by abundance of male blossoms; these must not be picked off, as too often practised, their *pulvis antherarum*, or powder of their antheræ, being absolutely necessary for fecundating the female flowers,

flowers, and fertilizing the young fruit; it is therefore of importance not only to retain these flowers, but also, to assist nature, it is proper, in the early crops, to perform the operation of setting, i. e. of applying their antheræ to the stigmata of the female blossoms, using for this purpose such male flowers whose antheræ are duly ripened, and well furnished with *farina*, which you may readily know by previously applying the antheræ gently to the thumb nail, to which some of the *pollen*, if ripened, will adhere; so using one or two males to each female blossom, and it will be found to assist greatly in setting the early fruit.

Air, at this time of blossoming, will also be particularly beneficial in promoting the free setting of the fruit; do not omit therefore to admit it every mild day, in manner before mentioned.

After setting the fruit, observe, that as they are most commonly produced on the lateral runners, issuing from the sides of the main vine, and that exuberancy of sap retards their setting, we would advise, if the plants are rather luxuriant, that, to restrain the sap from flowing too abundantly into the setting fruit, instead of stopping the end of the runner, as often done, rather turn it carefully curve-ways, so that the end may incline towards the main stem, whereby the sap will be directed from the bearing runners, and its course continued principally into the more luxuriant branches; and the sooner this is done the better, which, after the fruit is set, and a little advanced in growth, must be turned again into their former position. Many persons prune off the ends of the bearing runners a joint or two beyond the fruit, in order that the whole nourishment of that branch should be directed to it, to make it more certainly stand; but this has often the contrary effect, since stopping or shortening a branch promotes its drawing a greater quantity of sap, which, as we have above observed, is contrary to setting these fruit; therefore, those branches on which the setting fruit are immediately situated, should not be stopped until the fruit is fairly set, and full as big as a large walnut.

Neither is it proper to stop many of the runners, which would occasion their throwing out numerous shoots, and cause a great confusion of vine.

As the fruit sets, and has attained nearly the size just mentioned, the branches on which they grow, if they were turned towards the main stem, as above advised, should be now reconducted into their former directions, that the sap may now find a freer passage to nourish the fruit.

Likewise, as the fruit sets, lay a piece of clean dry tile under each, to preserve it the better from the moisture of the earth.

The quantity of fruit to be expected to set and arrive to perfection, is from about two or three, to eight or ten upon each plant; but this is according to the sorts; for the Canteleupe Melon sometimes does not set above two or three on a plant; on the other hand, the Romana will sometimes set and ripen eight or ten, and sometimes many more fruit will set than the plants are capable of nourishing; but, when this is the case, they should be thinned; and even of the smaller kinds leave only about six or eight of the most promising fruit upon each plant, and not more than five or six of the larger kinds, and never leave more than one fruit upon the same runner, and that which is nearest the main vine is generally the most eligible to leave, though it is best to fix upon that of the forwardest and handsomest growth.

After a tolerable crop of fruit is set, and they advanced in magnitude, if the earth of the bed is dry, take the first opportunity of a mild day to give a good watering, especially if the bed is kept to a proper heat, which, according to the nature of the earth, and its deepth on the beds, may be afterwards either wholly discontinued, or less or more repeated, as you shall see occasion by the temperature of moistness, or dryness of the earth; observing, in giving water, let it be rather most towards the sides of the bed, so as still to preserve the main stem and principal root always moderately dry.

Continue also to admit air at all opportunities every day when the weather is fine, which is also very beneficial to the free-growth of the young swelling fruit.

Still, likewise, continue to support a due temperature of heat in the bed by occasional linings with the usual care, even till May; for, by maintaining a bottom heat, the fruit will swell freely,

freely, continue a regular growth, and be in a little time surprisingly forwarded in magnitude. In applying the last lining in April, or beginning or middle of May, it is proper to earth it at top equal in depth to that of the bed, and by raising the frame the fibres of the plants will strike into the mould, and receive very great benefit, as will appear from the healthful appearance of the plants, and free growth of the fruit; but observe, this part should be defended from great rains with mats, that the extreme fibres may not receive and convey too much moisture to the vines and fruit, otherwise it would be more adviseable to confine the fibres wholly within the frame.

Shading the plants occasionally from the sun may be necessary in very hot days, when the sun is so powerful as to endanger scorching their leaves, &c. observing the same rules as for the early cucumbers.

As the leaves of the plants grow large, and press against the glasses, continue to raise the frame at bottom three inches; and as, in doing this, the earth next the frame will be disturbed, directly therefore make good all inequalities; and, if the leaves are considerably crouded, it is proper to thin them a little in proportion, so as that the young fruit may receive the necessary benefit of the sun and air.

If, after a due quantity of fruit is fairly set, and advancing in growth, the vine is greatly crowded, it is proper to regulate them, by cutting off close all the small runners, proceeding from the principal fruit-branches, and others, and any luxuriant shoots that support neither bearing runners nor fruit, and such other vine as may appear to be superfluous or unnecessary, cutting them off quite close, which will greatly encourage the free growth, and promote the size of the melons.

In May and June, as the vines of the plants will be advanced to the sides of the frame, if you have a full crop of fruit fairly set, they may be pruned so as to confine them within due compass; or, if you would have as many fruit as possible to succeed each other, they may be suffered to run out from under the frame upon the top of the lining, to produce some late fruit to succeed those already set within the frame, raising the frame high enough at bottom for that purpose towards the middle of June; observing, when the vines are thus trained out, to cover them every night, and all very wet weather, with mats; for the glasses must also still be continued on the frames till the weather is become quite settled and warm towards the end of this, or in next month, (July) and then only taken off a few hours in the warmest time of the day, and always put on at night and in all wet weather.

When the fruit is nearly full grown, no water, or at least very little, should be given; for moisture will considerably retard its ripening, as well as rob it of the richness of its flavour. At this period of growth let each fruit be placed upon a brick, or some flat tiles, placed one upon another, to raise it a little above the leaves, to receive the greater benefit of the sun and air, whereby its flavour and relish will be considerably improved, being careful to turn it every three days, that every part may equally enjoy the benefit of the sun's influence; observing also, at this time, to admit a large portion of fresh air every mild day, by tilting the lights several inches behind, or in front, in very hot weather, which will also contribute very much to the rich flavour of the ripening fruit.

From the setting of the fruit to its maturity, it takes commonly about six or seven weeks, and sometimes more.

The maturity of the fruit is known sometimes by its cracking at the base, as if it would start or recede from the stalk; sometimes by its inclining to a yellow colour; frequently by imparting a fragrant odour; and when the top of the fruit is soft, it is always a sure indication of ripeness; therefore, observing these appearances of maturity, let the fruit be cut at the proper time; for if suffered to remain on the vine a day or two longer, it will lose much of its flavour. Let it be cut in a morning before the sun shines hot to evaporate its rich juices, cutting each fruit with all its stalk, and lay it in a dry but cool airy place till it is wanted for table.

In the latter end of June, and in July, if the weather is dry and warm, the plants may be gradually inured to full air, by shoving the glasses off a few hours in fine dry days; but let them not have much rain, lest it rot the main ſtem of the plants, and it would alſo debaſe the flavour of the fruit; therefore retain the glaſſes ready at the back of the frames, to draw on every night, and in all very wet and boiſterous weather.

The culture of melons under hand or bell-glaſſes is effected by ſowing the ſeed in March or April, in a nurſery hot-bed, under frames and lights, and when the plants are about a month old tranſplant them into ridges or hot-beds, under the above glaſſes, to remain for fruiting; but, in default of frames, the plants might even be raiſed entirely under hand or bell-glaſſes, placed on a hot-bed, ſowing them in April, and tranſplant them into a freſh hot-bed in May, under the ſame ſorts of glaſſes, or oiled paper lights; they will ſometimes come in for a tolerable crop in Auguſt and September; however, the moſt eligible practice is, where poſſible, to ſow and forward the plants in a hot-bed, under frames, pricking the young plants in pots, ſo continuing them in the frame hot-bed till large enough to ridge out, then tranſplant them with balls into the fruiting hot-bed.

The moſt proper period of time for ſowing the above crops is, the third and fourth week in March; but, if poſſible, for the main crops, never be later than the firſt week in April.

And the time for ridging out the plants under theſe glaſſes, is from about the eighteenth or twentieth of April until about the middle of May.

For, it muſt be remembered, that theſe hand-glaſs crops muſt never be raiſed nor ridged out before the above-mentioned times, otherwiſe they will advance too much in growth, and fill the glaſſes before the nature of the ſeaſon admitted of their being trained out, unleſs ſheltered by paper frames, as they muſt not be confined within the ſmall compaſs of theſe glaſſes, longer than the beginning or middle of June, when the weather becomes ſettled and warm; nor ought the principal crops to be ſowed nor ridged out later than the times above ſpecified, becauſe they would not be forward enough to ripen their fruit in perfection before the approach of cold weather in autumn.

The ſeed may be ſown, and the plants raiſed large enough for ridging out, either in the hot-beds of forward melons or cucumbers now at work under frames, or in a ſmall hot-bed made on purpoſe for a one-light box, &c. earthed a few inches deep, ſowing the ſeed either in pots half an inch deep, or in the earth of the bed, drilling it in that depth, ſo managing the ſame as for the ſeedling melons and cucumbers for the frames; prick the plants alſo in pots, when a few days old, two in each pot, as in the frame crops, giving them nearly the ſame culture; and having expanded their two firſt rough leaves, ſtop them at the firſt joint, as there directed; and when a month or five weeks old they will begin to ſhoot runners, and ſhould then be ridged out into the fruiting hot-bed.

Therefore you muſt forecaſt to prepare the dung, and make the ridges or hot-beds in proper time, to be ready to receive the plants at the above period of growth.

The dimenſions of the fruiting hot-bed ſhould be four feet and half wide, and, if made in April, two feet and half, or a yard high; and even if made early in May, two feet and half depth of dung will be requiſite; nor ſhould it be leſs than two feet high, made in any time of that month; and the length in proportion to the number of glaſſes you intend working, allowing them at a yard and half diſtance from centre to centre, in one row along the top of the bed; obſerving, that if the plants are ready for ridging out in April, or beginning of May, the bed ſhould be made entirely above ground, for the opportunity of lining the ſides when the heat declines; or, at this ſeaſon, if the ground be tolerably dry, ſo as there will not be much danger of ſtanding, the bed may be made in a trench, for the advantage of having it retain its heat the longer, making the trench four feet and half wide, and eighteen or twenty inches deep; but obſerving, that in three weeks after the bed is made, the trench muſt be widened a foot and half on each ſide, and to the full depth, to admit of a lining of dung that width and depth to each ſide of the bed; for hot-beds made for theſe plants at either of the above-mentioned times, either on level ground or in a trench, will receive conſiderable benefit by having a lining of hot dung added to each ſide in three or four weeks after making, which will not

only

only throw in a fresh heat, but, by being earthed at top, give an additional width for the roots and vines of the plants to extend; observe likewise, that if more than one range of hot-beds are intended, make them one before another in a parallel direction, allowing a space of four or five feet between, which, if afterwards entirely filled up as high as the ridge with hot dung and earth, will be of great advantage to the plants.

The ridge or ridges being made, then, according to the rules and precautions exhibited in the hand-glass crop of cucumbers, prepare to earth it with the proper compost for the reception of the plants, first marking out with sticks the places for the glasses, in a row along the top of the bed, at a yard and half distance; and then, on each place where the glasses are to stand, lay about a wheel-barrow full of mould in a hill fifteen inches high at least, and wide enough for a hand-glass, for this depth of earth is as necessary here as in the frame crops, covering the other parts of the bed between the bills only three inches deep at present, that the burning steam and heat may have due vent, yet to prevent it from evaporating too suddenly; it is afterwards to be gradually earthed almost as high as the top of each hillock: as soon as the bed is thus earthed set on the glasses, one upon each hill of earth, covering the whole with mats at night, to draw up the heat the sooner, and in a day or two the earth will be warm enough to receive the plants.

When the earth, therefore, under the glasses is properly warmed by the dung, then, having previously watered the pots of plants the day before, that the earth may adhere in a ball about their roots, proceed to plant one pot of two plants under each glass, removing the plants out of the pots with a ball, in the manner directed in the early cucumber hot beds; and, levelling the top of the hillocks broad enough for each glass to stand, make a wide hole in the middle, and plant the ball of plants, giving directly a moderate watering, and put on the glasses, which must remain constantly over the plants, and be covered every night for a month or two, & in all bad weather, with mats.

They being now ridged out, observe, if their removal causes them to flag their leaves at the approach of the sun, it is necessary to indulge them with a moderate shade the first three or four days, when sunny, or till they stand the sun fully without flagging.

Fresh air must also be occasionally admitted in the warmest time of every fine day, by tilting the warm side of the glasses an inch, or a little more or less, according to the heat of the bed & temperature of the weather, having particular attention to shut them down close in due time in the afternoon, or as soon as the weather changes cold, keeping them close on nights; also in all unsavourable weather in the day time, unless there is a very great steam, when, during its continuance, the glasses must not be kept too close; and, if the weather is then cold or windy, the place where they are tilted may be defended with a mat; observing, as the warm weather advances, and the plants make progress in growth, a larger portion of fresh air must be admitted, to harden the runners gradually, in order to be trained out from under the glasses in June.

Cover the glasses and the whole surface of the bed every night with large mats, which must constantly be practised until the beginning or middle of June, or longer, if cold weather renders it necessary.

Likewise, in all heavy or cold rains, at any time, night or day, from the time of ridging out to the maturity of the fruit, particular care should be taken to defend the whole ridge, by a good covering of mats, for much wet would ruin the crop.

Waterings in warm weather once a week or fortnight, in moderate quantities, may be necessary, according to the rules mentioned in the frame crops.

In a week or fortnight after ridging out, when the heat of the bed is become moderate, begin to earth the whole gradually almost as high as the top of the hills on which the plants stand, pressing it down from time to time, that it may retain its moisture the longer, so as the plants may not require much water, raising the whole nearly equal with the summits of the hillocks, preserving the middle of each rather highest, to prevent moisture from soaking to the main stem, &c. as formerly cautioned.

Lining the ridges will be necessary

in about three weeks after they are made; this ought not to be omitted, eſpecially to thoſe made in April, or early in May; and having for this purpoſe a quantity of well prepared hot dung, add to each ſide of the bed a foot and half width at leaſt, and full as high as the dung of the bed, and directly earth it at top to the thickneſs of that on the ridge; and thus, by the addition of the linings, that beſides the advantage of renewing the heat, it widens the bed to about ſeven feet, and forms a fine ſcope for the fibres and vines of the plants; obſerving, if there are two or more ridges ranging parallel, that if the whole ſpace between was afterwards gradually filled up with hot dung and mould, it would prove ſtill more beneficial to the plants.

Having directed ſtopping the plants at the firſt joint to procure lateral runners, if theſe laterals are alſo ſtopt at the third joint they will more ſpeedily furniſh a farther ſupply for bearing, as obſerved of thoſe in the frames.

About the end of May, or beginning of June, the firſt ridged-out plants will have nearly filled the glaſſes with their runners, at which time do not omit indulging them with a large portion of free air at all opportunities, by tilſing the glaſſes every mild day two or three inches high, or in proportion to the temperament of the weather, ſo as to ſtrengthen the runners, and harden them by degrees to the full air, which, in June, when ſo much advanced in growth that they can be no longer contained within the glaſſes, muſt be trained out; the glaſſes muſt then be raiſed three inches on every ſide, on props, as for the cucumbers, and the runners trained out with regularity; but if ſome dry reeds are previouſly ſpread upon the ſurface of the bed, for the vine to run upon, it will preſerve them and the young fruit from the damp of the earth; obſerving, the glaſſes are to remain conſtantly over each hole of plants, to protect the main ſtem and principal roots the better from wet and other inclement weather, but are now to remain day and night ſupported on props, as above: continue alſo the nightly covering of mats for the firſt fortnight, at leaſt, after the plants are trained from under the glaſſes, to protect the tender vines till inured to the full air.

Obſerve, likewiſe, that as melons are rather impatient of copious moiſture, it is adviſeable, after being thus trained out, to protect them with great care from exceſſive rains and cold, at all times, day or night, by proper covering; the moſt effectual means for this purpoſe is, to place oiled paper frames over the ridges, as ſoon as the vines are trained out; however, in default of theſe conveniencies, we would adviſe to arch the bed over with hoops or rods, &c. juſt to the height of the hand-glaſſes; ſo having good thick mats or canvas cloths always ready to draw over the arches, in time of heavy or cold rains, and bluſtering winds, will be found of very conſiderable advantage, ſince a few hours violent rain often injure the plants ſo greatly, that they never after recover, ſo as to produce handſome fruit, nor bring any tolerable crop to perfection.

But when the beds are covered with paper frames, theſe remaining conſtantly on the beds, effectually defend them at all times, and admit a due portion of light, &c. to the plants.

If, however, you uſe only mats or canvas, to cover occaſionally in cold nights and bad weather, let theſe be always taken wholly off betimes every fine morning, or as ſoon in the day as the weather is favourable.

In June and July the plants will ſpread their runners all over the bed, and will ſhew fruit abundantly, at which period of ſhewing fruit very little water ſhould be given, eſpecially if there is a proper depth of earth on the beds, but in very hot & dry weather, after the firſt tolerable ſhew of fruit is fairly ſet, and begin to advance in magnitude, a moderate watering once a week, or ten or twelve days, whilſt the fruit are taking their growth, will encourage them, promote their ſize, and encreaſe the ſubſtance of their fleſh, being careful to apply the water moſtly towards the ſides of the bed to the extreme fibres, ſo as to preſerve the main ſtem and principal roots from receiving too much wet; and be ſure never once to over-water the beds, which might prove of very bad conſequence; but for the greater convenience of watering at this period, a deep drill may be drawn around the outſides of the bed, and the neceſſary ſupply of water poured into theſe drills, whereby the fibres will

will receive its benefit without wetting the leaves, branches, or fruit; but when the fruit is nearly full grown, give as little water as poſſible.

With reſpect to uſeleſs and ſuperfluous or unneceſſary branches or runners, if there be any, it is eligible culture to clear them off occaſionally, to prevent confuſion of vine, and for the proſperity of the fruit, executing it according to the rules laid down for thoſe of the frame plants.

Obſerve alſo the ſame of ſuperfluous fruit, leaving only ſuch a due quantity of the moſt promiſing and beſt-ſituated in each hole, as the plants can be expected to bring to perfection.

During the growth of the fruit, obſerve, that if the ridges are not covered with oiled paper, but only with the hand-glaſſes, &c. and the weather ſhould prove rather unfavourable or wettiſh, and that many of the fruit are ſituated on the advanced vine withoutſide of the glaſſes, it is adviſeable either to move the fruit gently under their own reſpective glaſſes; or rather, where there are any ſpare glaſſes, bring theſe and place over the fruit, contriving each glaſs to cover as many as may be convenient; for it is neceſſary thus to protect theſe fruit from injury of weather, ſupporting each glaſs two or three inches high on props; and this ſhelter of the glaſſes will greatly improve the ſize and flavour of the fruit: but in unfavourable ſeaſons oil'd paper frames are the moſt effectual, becauſe, being the placed all over the ridge, they defend plants alſo, as well as the fruit, both from cold and wet; or, in cold wet ſeaſons, if there are any ſpare garden-frames and lights, theſe might be placed over the ridges, as ſoon as they are at liberty in June, July, or Auguſt, ſo to defend the plants and fruit the remainder of the ſummer, by ſhoving on the lights in all unfavourable weather, day or night.

When the fruit is encreaſed ſomewhat conſiderably in growth, it is proper to turn them every three or four days, that they may ſwell equally, and each ſide have an equal benefit of the ſun.

Their ripening is determinable by the appearance of maturity, mentioned in the early crop, obſerving alſo the ſame rules as there adviſed in cutting them for table.

Melons are alſo fruited in great perfection under oiled paper frames, by placing them over thoſe ridges of plants which are ridged out in April and May, for they will not ſucceed in earlier crops, but for the crops juſt mentioned, they are conſiderably the moſt eligible ſhelters to place over the ridges in the middle or latter end of May, or beginning of June, after the plants have filled the hand-glaſſes, theſe being then previouſly removed entirely away, and the paper frames placed upon the bed; for theſe frames being made of due width and proper length to cover the whole ridge, and the paper being well oiled with linſeed-oil, to render it proof againſt wet, and more pellucid or tranſparent to admit the rays of light and heat in a proper degree, that they are continued conſtantly upon the ridges, whereby the plants are at all times protected from all inclement weather, either wet, wind, cold, or heat, as, although the paper admits the rays of light, &c. yet it, at the ſame time, affords the moſt agreeable ſhade from the ſcorching ſun.

Theſe frames are formed either like the roof of a houſe, or archways, like the tilt of a waggon, four or five feet wide, ten long, and a yard high, framed of thin ſlips of wood and lath, or broad hoops, &c. but thoſe made ridge-faſhion with two ſloping ſides, in the manner of the ridge of a houſe, are rather the moſt eligible form, becauſe on one ſide may be made two pannels, to open with hinges towards each end, and each pannel about two feet wide, being convenient for giving air, and other neceſſary work: in either of the above forms the frames are conſtructed in an open manner, having the ribs or ſpars, a foot or fifteen inches aſunder, or at ſuch diſtances as to admit of paſting the ſheets of paper commodiouſly; but previous to paſting on the paper, draw lines of pack-thread, &c. acroſs corner-ways from rail to rail of the frame, drawing other lines interſecting or croſſing the firſt, theſe being neceſſary for ſupporting the paper the more effectually againſt the power of wet and wind: then having ſome ſtrong printing paper, let it be a little damped, that it may not ſink in hollows after it is fixed on the frame; therefore, as ſoon as it is damped, paſte

it

it on the frame; two large sheets will generally range from bottom to top, pasting it securely to the rafters and rails, and so as the middle of each sheet rests upon the intersections of the pack-thread lines; and when the paper and pasting is thoroughly dry, brush the outside all over lightly with boiled linseed-oil, then suffer the frame to stand in a dry shed till the whole is perfectly well dried before it is used.

But for want of regular made frames, a quantity of hoops or rods might be placed across the ridges of plants archways, sticking both ends into the earth, about one foot asunder, & two high, so drawing lines of pack-thread along from hoop to hoop, both to steady the arches, and help to support the paper; then paste a quantity of strong paper in large pieces about three or four sheets in width, and in length proportionable to that of the ridges they are to cover; then oil them with linseed-oil, and, when thoroughly dry, spread them over the hoop-arches, and secure them by lines drawn from end to end; and that for the admission of air, and doing other necessary work, one side of the paper is readily turned up at bottom as far as convenient.

In respect to the mode of using either of these paper shelters, the plants are previously to be raised in hot-beds, under frames and lights, exactly at the time and manner as directed for the hand-glass crops, and to be ridged out also at the same time and manner there mentioned; observing, that, in default of hand-glasses, these paper frames may be used as soon as the plants are ridged out; but in this case the ridging out should not be performed till May: but the most successful way is, when there are hand-glasses sufficient, to place these glasses over the plants at first ridging out, as directed in the hand-glass culture, managing them in the same way in every respect, till the plants have filled the glasses with their runners; then remove the glasses away, and place over the paper frames.

When these shelters are placed over the plants, free air must be admitted in proportion to the temperature of the season, either by opening the pannels less or more, according to the warmth of each day, or by tilting one side of the frames at bottom, &c. for the article of fresh air must not be omitted at all opportunities, particularly when the plants shew fruit, the air being not only necessary to strengthen the plants, but also to assist in the impregnation of the fruit, for the reasons explained in the early cucumber work; and towards the end of June, when the season is warm, the frames may be raised at bottom about four inches.

It is also necessary to defend the plants over the above shelters with mats every night till towards the middle of June; likewise, occasionally, in all hard rains, day or night.

These paper shelters never last but one season, that is, the paper; but as to the frames, they, with care, will continue useful several years, so must be fresh papered every spring, in proper time to be ready to place over the beds.

Melon plants are generally between three and four months from their first appearance till they produce ripe fruit, and they all the time require the constant aid of artificial heat, which, though they are fruited in great perfection in that of dung, i. e. dung hot-beds, yet those of tanner's bark being considerably of more durable and regular heat, the plants by that aid may still be fruited to greater advantage, and with less trouble, because, if made entirely of new tan, no lining, or but very little, will be necessary, nor is there such danger to be apprehended from steaming or violent heat, as in dung hot-beds; but it must be remembered, that the purchase of the tan renders these kind of hot-beds more expensive than dung, though, if both these materials are obliged to be purchased, and the tan can be obtained within a moderate distance, there is but an inconsiderable difference in the expence.

But, in case of scarcity of new tan for the above purpose, the waste or cast-off bark of the stoves, mixed with a quantity of new, might be used, provided, however, the old tan is not become quite earthy; so mixing one half old to one of new, which will form a moderately strong and durable heat, and will answer for beds made not earlier than the middle of February, or beginning of March.

Or, for the latter crops, beds might be formed entirely of cast-off bark, provided, as above observed, it is not become very earthy, and its fermenting property not quite exhausted; which, if not, when fresh worked up, and formed again into a bed, will renew its heat, though in a moderate degree, therefore should not be used for beds earlier than March or April, and which, if made in a pit formed of post and planking, so as to admit of a substantial lining of hot dung to each side in six weeks or two months after making, would be an addititional advantage to the plants.

Observe, that either the above-mentioned bark-beds for the culture of melons, must be made in some kind of pit, or frame, to confine the bark, which otherwise could not be formed into a bed, or, in default of such a pit, one might be formed of post and planking, of width and length for one or more large three-light frames, and three feet and a half deep, to contain that substance of bark, and may either be sunk half way in the ground, or not so much, according as the soil is dry or wet; but it would be most convenient to have it not sunk more than a foot, for the advantage of adding a lining of hot dung to the sides, if there should be occasion; I would therefore observe, that a planked pit, for the culture of melons, may be rather preferable to brick or stone, because if you shall find it necessary to line the beds, by applying hot dung against the outside of the planking, its heat will readily penetrate sufficiently to recruit the declining heat of the bed; for as the melons are to be planted in the full bed, and not in pots, as practised to pine-apple plants, there is no stirring up the bark to revive the heat, as in stoves, and a lining may probably be necessary to those beds, where cast-off bark is used, or perhaps sometimes one lining to those beds made of new tan, may be of advantage, just when the fruit is setting and taking their first growth; on these considerations, contrive the pit so as to admit of lining the sides almost or quite to the bottom.

The time of year to begin the culture of melons in these sort of hot-beds, is the same as mentioned in dung hot-beds, and the plants should be raised in a nursery-bed as there directed; and when of the proper age and size, as there observed, transplant them into the bark-beds to remain to fruit.

These fruiting-beds should be made a fortnight or three weeks before-hand, to acquire a proper heat in due time for the reception of the plants from the nursery hot-bed, at their proper period of growth. Let the beds be made the full width and length of the pit allotted for them, and three feet at least deep; but if cast-off bark is used, three and a half depth in bark will be requisite. As soon as made, cover the bed with the proper frames and glasses, to defend it from rains; and in about a fortnight it will be arrived to a proper temperature of heat; then earth it at top, as directed for the dung-beds, and the earth being warm, set two plants with their ball of earth entire, just under the middle of each light, give a little water, and manage them according to the former directions.

But if the bed is to be made mostly of cast-off bark, as it will be somewhat of a mouldering texture, and of but moderate heat, instead of earthing it as above observed, you may try the success of planting intirely in the bark, without any earth at all. Let the bed be of the above-mentioned dimentions, and covered with the frames and lights, and in about three weeks it will be warm enough either to receive seed, or plants, first making holes in the middle of the bed, one immediately under the middle of each light, six or eight inches deep, and twelve or fifteen broad, fill them with rotten or finely pounded bark, forming each a little hollow, bason-like, in which either sow seed, and when the plants are a week or two old, thin them to two of the best in each hole, and there let them remain to fruit: or, to make the most of the bed, put in plants raised to a proper age, as in the dung hot-bed culture.

The plants being transplanted into either of the above bark hot-beds, observe the lights are to be kept constantly on, being careful to give the plants a proper share of warm air at all opportunities, as the weather permits, according to the former rules.

It must be remarked, that the plants will not require much water in these hot-beds, as bark continues to support a fine moist heat, of a very agreeable nature to the growth of most sorts of plants, so that the melons will be found to succeed with a very moderate supply

of

of water, and the less the better, both for the continuance of the heat of the beds, as well as for the advantage of plants and fruit.

Should you find the heat of the beds considerably declined when the fruit is setting, or taking its first growth, a good lining of hot dung against the outsides of the pit will be very beneficial.

As to saving melon seed, we need only farther observe here, that it should be saved only from the very finest fruit of the respective varieties, & such as have a firm and highly flavoured flesh; this should be particularly observed when the fruit is served at table, and the right seed properly reserved in its own pulp, and sent to the gardener; which, after laying in the pulp a few days, may be washed out, and all the heavy or good seed which sink in the water are to be preserved, dried, and put up for saving.

It will retain its germinative property ten or twelve years, but when from about three to five years old, is in its best perfection for use.

Water MELON. *See* CITRUL.

MELON *Thistle*, [*Cactus*.] This plant is of a very singular structure, being shaped like a melon, having neither visible stem, branches, nor leaves, but appears like a large, roundish, fleshy mass, or lump, sitting close to the earth, and throwing down roots to a considerable depth. There are two sorts, a larger and a smaller; they are both propagated by seed, but require the assistance of a stove.

MELLET. A dry scab on a horses foot.

MERCURY, [*Mercurialis*.] Male and female French mercury; the leaves. These stand among the five emollient herbs; and in this intention are sometimes made use of in glysters. A syrup made from the leaves, given in the dose of two ounces, is said to prove a mild and useful laxatixe.

There is another sort of mercury growing in woods and hedges, which by some botanic writers, as having the same virtues with the foregoing, and as more palatable, has been lately found possessed of noxious qualities. This may be distinguished from by its being a perennial plant, larger, having its leaves rough, and the stalk not at all branched. The officinal sort is named by Linnæus *mercurialis caule brachiato, foliis glabris*; the poisonous *mercurialis caule simplicissimo, foliis scabris*; it is commonly called dogs mercury.

English MERCURY, [*Bonus Henricus*.] This is met with by road sides, and in uncultivated places. It is ranked among the five emollient herbs, but rarely made use of in practice. The leaves are employed by the common people for healing flesh wounds, cleansing old ulcers, and other like purposes.

Dogs MERCURY. *See* MERCURY.

MET. A strike or bushel.

METHEGLIN. A liquor made with honey and water, or honey and beer fermented together.

MEZERON. *See Spurge* LAUREL.

MEU. *See* SPIGNAL.

METER YARD. A measuring staff.

MICE. Field mice are as numerous as those of the house, and the farmer often finds them as troublesome, and sometimes much more so. There are several species of them; but they are all equally his enemies: all feeding upon his seed-corn and pulse in the same manner: and are all to be destroyed by the same means.

Drier lands are more subject to this kind of vermin than those which lie wet; and of all the kinds of sowing, that under furrow most exposes the seed to them.

In this case, as the furrows will fall somewhat hollow, they afford a shelter to the mice at the time of their committing all their havock.

The farmer seems to contrive for their feasting and safety together in this method; for the corn or other seed lies perfectly exposed to them, and they are not exposed to his eye while they are feeding upon it.

In these lands we have with great concern often traced the path of those devourers, and seen all eaten up, or carried away to some little distance: for under the covert of this manner of tillage they will make their nests and granaries as it were in different places; and the seed shall be found stored up in one of these, that should have covered a great space of ground with its shoot.

The husbandman will by this see a great disadvantage attending that kind of tillage; and he will know in what fields he is most to fear these enemies.

Though

Though his manner of sowing gives the mice an advantage, the other way does not sufficiently secure the corn from them. When it is sown in the common way and harrowed in, it is better covered; and there is a great deal more trouble for them to get at it: but they are very industrious, and in this case will dig after it, and tear up and destroy a great deal.

When it is sown under furrow, they begin with it as soon as it is in the ground; but when it is harrowed in, they wait for its first sprout. This gives the farmer an advantage, because he knows exactly when he is to expect them; and it is a great article of safety to know when to guard against the danger.

The careful husbandman is not in this case to wait till he sees the shoot of his seed; for the mice have very quick eyes, and they will perceive it a day or two before he does: he is therefore to look to his ground a day or two before the time of its being seen covered with the young shoot; and then, as he knows the devourers will be about, he is to prepare for their destruction.

Traps are a very improper method of getting rid of these creatures. There is no way well worth his consideration but poison; and happily for him there are drugs which will answer this purpose of poison to these creatures, which are not literally and strictly poison to ourselves. These he is to use, and they will sufficiently answer his purpose. It would be a disagreeable thing to be meddling with ratsbane; but there is no harm in handling the ingredients he has to use.

In the first place let him consider what fields from their soil are most likely to harbour mice, and in what places he has known them most mischievous. Let him never sow these under furrow, for that takes from him all opportunity of attacking his enemies: they work under ground as it were, and will never come into the way of his poison.

When these fields have been sown otherwise, and harrowed over, the mice must come upon the surface and dig down for the corn, and they will then certainly meet with any thing he lays on the ground for them.

Let him mix up a peck of barley-meal, a pound of powder of white hellebore root, and four ounces of powder of staves-acre; and when these are all mixed together by sifting through a coarse hair sieve, add half a pound of honey, and as much milk as will work the whole into a paste.

Let this be broke into pieces, and scatter'd over the field at the time when the mice are known to be coming. They will eat it greedily, and it is certain death to them. There is nothing in any of the ingredients disagreeable to the taste when thus mixed; and every morsel of it will be devoured. The mice will be kept from digging after the corn; and at the same time killed by the ingredients.

This is the method to be used just at the time of danger; but the farmer who has a field pestered with these vermin, will do well to be thinking at other times also of destroying them.

They live at a small depth under ground, and there breed in abundance. The passage into their nest is by a little round hole, and these are easily seen in dry weather.

On these occasions the farmer should go his rounds with a quantity of the paste before directed: and wherever he sees a hole throw in a piece. A little trouble of this kind taken from time to time in the heat of summer, when the holes are most conspicuous, would utterly root them out.

MIDDING. A dunghill.

MILFOIL, [*Millefolium.*] Milfoil or yarrow. This grows plentifully about the sides of fields, and on dry commons, flowering greatest part of the summer. The leaves have a rough bitterish taste, and a faint aromatic smell. Their virtues are those of a very mild astringent, and as such they stand recommended in hæmorrhagies both internal and external, diarrhœas, debility and laxity of the fibres; and likewise in spasmodic hysterical affections. In these cases, some of the Germans have a very high opinion of this herb, particularly Stahl, who esteems it a very effectual astringent, and in his language, one of the most certain tonics and sedatives. Its virtues are extracted in greatest perfection by proof spirit: water takes up its astringency and bitterness, but little of its aromatic flavour; tinctures made in rectified spirit contain the latter, with little of the former.

The flowers of milfoil are conſiderably ſtronger in aromatic flavour than the leaves; in diſtillation, they yield a ſmall quantity of eſſential oil, of an elegant blue colour.

MIL-DEW. Blights and mill dews have been generally taken to be the ſame thing, which hath begotten much error, and the ways and means uſed for the prevention and cure have miſcarried through the ignorance of the diſeaſe. Mill-dew is quite another thing from blaſting. Mill-dews being cauſed, as ſome ſay, from the condenſation of a fat and moiſt exhalation in a hot and dry ſummer from the bloſſom and vegetables of the earth, and alſo from the earth itſelf, which by the coolneſs and ſerenity of the air is condenſed into a fat glutinous matter, and falls on the earth again, part whereof reſts on the leaves of the oak and other trees, whoſe leaves are ſmooth, and do not eaſily admit the moiſture into them, as the elm or other rougher leaves do, which mill-dews become the principal food of the bees, being of itſelf ſweet, and eaſily convertible into honey.

Other parts thereof reſt on the ears and ſtalks of wheat, beſpotting the ſtalks with a different colour from the natural, being of a glutinous ſubſtance by the heat of the ſun, and ſo binds up the young tender cloſe ears of the wheat, that it prevents the growth and compleating the imperfect grain therein, which occaſioneth it to be very light in harveſt, and to yield a poor lean grain, for which reaſon many reckon the bearded wheat not ſo ſubject to it, as the other, the beards defending the ear from it.

Some think mill-dews to proceed from vapours ariſing from the dung, and ſo falls upon the corn; becauſe lands new dunged are the moſt ſubject to it.

But if, after the mildew falls, a ſhower ſucceeds, or the wind blows ſtiffly, it waſheth or ſhaketh it off, are the only natural remedies againſt this diſtemper.

Some adviſe in the morning, after the mill-dew is fallen, and before the riſing of the ſun, that two men go at ſome convenient diſtance in the furrows, holding a cord ſtretched ſtreight betwixt them, carrying it ſo that it may ſhake off the dew from the tops of the corn, before the heat of the ſun has thickened it.

It is alſo adviſed to ſow wheat in open grounds, where the wind may the better ſhake off the dew, this being looked upon to be the only inconveniency incloſures are ſubject unto, but it is evident that the field lands are not exempted from mill-dews, nor ſmut, where it is more than in incloſed lands.

Some ſay, that lands that have been ſubject to mill-dews many years, have been cured by ſowing of ſoot with, or juſt after, the corn. *See* BLIGHT.

Mr. Miller takes the true cauſe of the mill-dew's appearing moſt upon plants which are expoſed to the eaſt, to proceed from a dry temperature in the air when the wind blows from that point, in which caſe it ſtops the pores of plants, and prevents their perſpiration, whereby their juices are concreted upon the ſurface of their leaves; and that concretion being of a ſweetiſh nature, inſects are incited thereto. Thoſe inſects, finding their proper nutriment, depoſit their eggs, and multiply ſo faſt as to cover the whole ſurfaces of plants, and, by corroding their veſſels, prevent the motion of the ſap. He thinks it very probable, that the excrements of theſe inſects may enter the veſſels of plants; and, by mixing with their juices, may ſpread the infection all over them; for it is obſerveable, that whenever a tree has been greatly infected by this mill-dew, it ſeldom recovers in two or three years, and many times never is entirely clear from it after. But he by no means allows theſe inſects to be the firſt cauſe of this diſtemper, as ſome have miſtakenly imagined. It is obſervable, that mill-dews and blights frequently attack only one ſort of corn, or fruit, and leave the other ſpecies unhurt.

Count Ginanni diſtinguiſhes two principal kinds of mill-dew, one of which ſpots the blades and ſtems of corn, and dries upon them, without ever producing any powder; but penetrates through their outward covering, and entirely dries them up. This is generally of a pale colour, either reddiſh, yellowiſh, purpleiſh, or blackiſh, and ſometimes a variegated mixture of many colours. The other ſpeedily covers the plant with a moiſt and thickiſh ſubſtance, which afterwards becomes dry, and turns into a powder, of one or other of the above-mentioned colours, but moſt commonly reddiſh-dish or yellowish. This, says he, always fades, corrodes, and separates the outer skin from the plant. The former extends to every species of corn; but the latter is almost peculiar to wheat in the blade; though it is sometimes seen upon oats and barley. Some may perhaps reckon, as a third species of mildew, a yellowish substance, or powder, sometimes seen under the membrane of the blades of corn, where it raises blisters, makes many little holes and cracks, and corrodes the fibres; and perhaps they may not be wrong in accounting it such.

He is confident that this distemper is the rubigo of the Latins. *See* HONEY-DEW.

MILK. Milk is a fluid separated from the nutritious juice of bodies, called their chyle; deposited by nature in the breasts or udders of female animals, during their pregnancy, and for the nourishment of their young.

After the young is born, it becomes in greater abundance: and it will be prepared and furnished by nature in that plentiful manner, so long as it is sucked by the young, or any other way drawn at times; but when no use is made of it, the supply ceases; and the milk, as the expression is, dries up of itself.

Milk is very much of the nature of what is called chyle, that is, the nutritious juice separated from our food, and intended for the support and nourishment of our bodies. All our foods tend to the formation of chyle, and the great purpose of nature in their digestion is the furnishing of a sufficient supply of it; for on this restoration and preservation of the fabrick depend.

Chyle is a thin white juice, consisting of the finest and most nourishing part of our food; and milk is, properly speaking, nothing more than a thicker and richer chyle: when the two are compared together, there is found but little difference between them; therefore we may very reasonably conclude, that milk not only is made of chyle, but that it is made by a very natural and easy procedure; for there seems nothing more to have been done than this, that a quantity of chyle has been brought into the glands of the breasts, and there some of its watery parts have been separated from it; and the remainder becoming richer by that means, has been left there ready to be drawn by the mouth of the young, or otherwise, in the form of what we call milk.

When milk is viewed with powerful glasses, it does not look an uniform white liquor, as it appears to the naked eye, but is discovered to consist of two different matters; the one white and rich, which is kept separate in round drops, and the other thin and watry: this last is the more large quantity, and the other drops swim in it.

In the same manner when we make butter and cheese, we force a separation of those parts, which we could not see to be distinct and different in the milk, though this common operation shews they were so: the rich part makes the butter and cheese, and the other runs off poor and watery in the butter milk and the whey.

These three parts are, 1. the oily; 2. the curdy; and 3. the watery. The oily are, as we have seen, the buttery parts; the curdy are the cheesy; and the watery are the wheyey.

Nothing but the force of nature in the body of the animal, could work and blend these perfectly into one rich and nourishing fluid, fit for the tender stomach of the young. We find they are so mixed there; and that they continue mixed in that manner for some time, after the milk is out of the body; but when they have once separated, either naturally or by art, we shall never be able to mix them so again. Butter, cheese, and whey, were all contained in the milk, and nature united them in that manner; but all our chymistry will never be able to mix butter, cheese, and whey, into milk again.

Milk differs extremely in various creatures, according to their diet, their construction of body, and the particular structure of those parts in which it is formed.

The first and great end of nature in the production of milk, we have shewn, was for the nourishment of the young; she knows, or to use more proper words, God, whose immediate and regular care in the guidance of the world is what we call nature, knows best the structure of those young and tender bodies he forms; and he has accordingly provided, in the breasts and udders of their dams, a nourishment suited to them,

Thus in all creatures, milk is, as we have ſhewn, the chyle or nutritive juice of the parent's body, formed into that condition by the ſeparation of its watery parts; but in ſome creatures, more of thoſe watery parts are ſeparated, and in others fewer, according to the ſtructure of thoſe veſſels; and it muſt be according to what we ſee of their food, that in ſome the chyle comes more watry to thoſe glands that ſeparate it, than it does in others: why otherwiſe ſhould it be, that the milk of the cow ſhould be ſo rich, and that of the aſs ſo poor, when both eat the graſs of the ſame paſture.

Let not any be ſurpriſed at the calling aſſes milk poor in compariſon of cows, from an opinion that it muſt be richer, becauſe of the uſe phyſicians make of it to reſtore decayed conſtitutions: it is becauſe it is poorer they prefer it, for the ſtomach in thoſe perſons is not able to bear the richer milk of the cow.

According therefore to what we ſee in nature, it is plain that the different conſtruction of body, and different fabricks of the veſſels formed for ſeparating and preparing milk, occaſion that liquor to be richer in ſome and poorer in others. This is all the real difference between the milk of one creature and that of another: having premiſed this, we ſhall proceed to conſider, ſeparately, thoſe ſeveral kinds that any way come under the farmer's conſideration.

Theſe are principally four; the cows, the aſſes, the goats, and the ſheep: a fifth might be added, for the milk of the mare is uſed in ſome places; but the firſt named kind is the great and principal concern of the farmer, and the ſupport of the dairy.

Nothing can be more rational than the giving ſuch milk as aſſes, and any other kind that can be borne upon the ſtomach, as a reſtorative: for we have ſhewn already, that milk is only chyle under a particular form; therefore, when the ſtomach will bear it, it is nouriſhment ready formed, and fit for immediately mixing with the blood, to anſwer all the purpoſes of life.

This is properly a method of reſtoring nature: it is coming in to her aſſiſtance when ſhe is not able to furniſh nouriſhment, by bringing her that of ſome other animal ready formed, to ſupply the place.

As to the preference of aſſes milk above that of the cow, in the relief of of human kind, the reaſon is ſhewn in nature. Let the milk of our own ſpecies be compared with that of a cow, and that of an aſs; and the aſſes milk will be found to reſemble it much more than the other.

Cows milk is in general by much the richeſt of all the kinds we know, and the moſt profitable: its ſeveral products in butter and cheeſe, being, like its natural condition as milk, preferable to thoſe of all others, not only in quality, but in quantity: two articles which, when they concur, as they do perfectly in this inſtance, conſtitute the higheſt uſe and value to the owner.

The milk of the cow is ſuppoſed to vary according to the colour of the ſkin; but this is an idle obſervation. There is an old ſaying among the farmers, that red cows give the beſt milk; and another, that black cows bring the beſt calves: but we can, from fair trial, and repeated experience, aſſure our readers that there is not in the leaſt truth in either of theſe maxims: he is to look upon them as old wives tales, and no otherwiſe. We have ſeen as much and as good milk from black cows, as ever produced from red; and we may call every butcher to witneſs, that the value of the calf is not in the leaſt dependent upon the colour of the cow. *See* Cow.

Milk appears to be a vegetable juice, with little of an animal nature.

New milk mixes uniformly with common water, the mineral chalybeat waters, wines, and malt liquors that are not acid, weak vinous ſpirits, ſolutions of ſugar, ſoaps, and neutral ſalts; but not with oils expreſſed or diſtilled. Acids, both mineral and vegetable, coagulate it; as alſo do fixt and volatile alcalies, and highly rectified ſpirit of wine: the curd made by acids is reſolved again by alcaline liquors, as that made by alcalies likewiſe is by acids. Neutral ſalts, nitre in particular, preſerve it from coagulating ſpontaneouſly; and likewiſe render it leſs eaſily coagulable by acids.

The human milk is the ſweeteſt of theſe liquors, and that of aſſes next to it: this laſt is the moſt dilute of them all: on ſuffering it to coagulate ſpontaneouſly, the curd ſcarce amounted to two drams from twelve ounces, whilſt that

that of cows milk was five times as much: the coagulum of asses milk, even when made by acids, forms only into fine light flakes which swim in the serum; that of goats milk concretes into more compact masses which sink.

Upon evaporating twelve ounces of	There remained of dry matter drams	From which water extracted a sweet saline substance, amounting, when exsiccated, to drams
Cows milk	13	$1\frac{1}{2}$
Goats milk	$12\frac{1}{2}$	$1\frac{1}{2}$
Human milk	8	6
Asses milk	8	6

The saline substance obtained from asses milk was white, and sweet as sugar; those of the others brown or yellow; and considerably less sweet; that of cows milk, the least sweet of all. It appears therefore, that asses milk contains more serum, and much more of a saccharine saline matter, than those of cows and goats; and that the two latter abound most with unctuous gross matter: hence these are found to be most nutritious, whilst the first proves most effectual as an aperient and detergent.

The inspissated residuum of milk, digested with about as much water as was wasted in the evaporation, yields an elegant kind of whey, more agreeable in taste, and which keeps better, than that made in the common manner. This liquor promotes the natural secretions in general, and if its use is duly continued, does good service in scorbutic, and other disorders, proceeding from thick phlegm and obstructions of the viscera.

There are considerable differences in the milk of the same animal, according to its different aliment. Dioscordeis relates, that the milk of goats, who fed on the scammony plant and spurges, proved cathartic: and examples are given in the *Acta Haffniensia* of bitter milk from the animal having eat wormwood. It is a common observation, that cathartics and spirituous liquors given to a nurse affect the child: and that the milk of animals feeding on green herbs, is much more dilute than when they are fed with dry ones. Hoffman carries this point so far as to direct the ass (the animal, whose milk he in all cases prefers) to be dieted according to the disease which its milk is to be drank for.

MILKING. The best and most commended hours for *Milking* are, indeed, but two in the day; that in the spring and summer, which is the best season for the dairy, is between five and six in the morning, and six and seven in the evening; and though nice and curious housewives have a third hour between them, as between twelve and one o'clock in the afternoon; yet the better experienced allow not thereof, saying, that two good meals of *milk* are ever better than three bad ones. In performing the work itself, the woman must sit on the near side of the cow, gently at first handle and stretch her dugs, and moisten them with milk, that they may yield out the milk the better, and with less pains; neither must she settle herself to milk, nor fix her pail firm to the ground, till she sees the cow stand firm and sure; but be ready, upon any motion of the cow, to save her pail from over-turning: but when she sees all things answerable to her desires, she shall then milk the cow boldly; and desist not to stretch and strain her teats, till not a drop more of milk will come from her, it being the worst point of housewifery imaginable to leave a cow half milked; for besides the loss of the milk, it is the only way to make a cow dry, and utterly unprofitable for the dairy: neither should the milk-maid, while at her work, do any thing rashly or suddenly to affright the cow, or maze her; but as she comes gently, so with all gentleness to depart.

MILK VETCH. Liquorice vetch, wild liquorice.

Bastard MILK VETCH. *See* BASTARD.

MILKWORT. [*Polygala.*] This is a perennial plant, growing wild in many parts of England. There are several species of this plant kept in gardens, which are natives of France, Austria, and America.

MILLET, [*Milium.*] This grain was originally brought from the eastern countries, where it is ftill greatly cultivated, from whence we are furnifhed annually with this grain, which is by many perfons greatly efteemed for puddings, &c.

It muft be fown the beginning of April upon a warm dry foil, but not too thick, becaufe thefe plants divide into feveral branches, and fhould have much room; and when they come up, they fhould be cleared from weeds; after which they will, in a fhort time, get the better of them, and prevent their future growth. In Auguft thefe feeds will ripen, when it muft be cut down and beaten out, as is practifed for other grain; but when it begins to ripen, if it be not protected from birds they will foon devour it.

MILL MOUNTAIN. *See Purging* FLAX.

MILT-PAIN. Is a difeafe in hogs, proceeding from greedinefs of eating mafts, and is known by their reeling and going on one fide; to cure which, give him the juice of wormwood in a little honied water.

MILTING. Is an evil in beafts, arifing from a blow, &c. The figns whereof are, that they will lay themfelves down, rife again prefently, and cannot reft, but fit in pain: The cure is, to take ftone pitch, pound it fmall, and blend the fame with ale, faffron, pepper, and give it him, and walk him a little after it.

MILT-VAST. *See* SPLEENWORT.

MINT, [*Mentha*.] The leaves of mint have a warm, roughifh, fomewhat bitterifh tafte; and a ftrong, not unpleafant, aromatic fmell. Their virtues are thofe of a warm ftomachic and carminative; in lofs of appetite, naufeæ, continual retchings to vomit, and (as Boerhaave expreffes it) almoft paralytic weakneffes of the ftomach, there are few fimples perhaps of equal efficacy. In colicky pains, the gripes to which children are fubject, dycenteries, and other kinds of immoderate fluxes, this plant frequently does good fervice. It likewife proves beneficial to fundry hyfteric cafes, and affords an ufeful cordial in languors and other weakneffes confequent upon delivery. The beft preparations for thefe purpofes are, a ftrong infufion made from the dry leaves in water (which is much fuperior to one from the green herb) or rather a tincture or extract prepared with rectified fpirit. Thefe poffefs the whole virtues of the mint: the effential oil and diftilled water contain only the aromatic part; the expreffed juice only the aftringency and bitternefs, together with the mucilaginous fubftance common to all vegetables.

It is propagated by parting the roots in the fpring, or cuttings, during any of the fummer months.

There are fome people who are very fond of mint fallad in winter and fpring, in order to obtain which, they take up the roots before Chriftmas, and plant them upon a moderate hot-bed clofe together, covering them with fine earth an inch thick, and cover the bed either with mats or frames of glafs. In thefe beds the mint will come up in a month's time, and be foon fit to cut for that purpofe.

When the herb is cut for medicinal ufe, it fhould be done in a very dry feafon, juft when it is in flower; for if it ftand longer, it will be not near fo handfome, nor fo well tafted; and if it be cut when it is wet, it will change black, and be little worth; this fhould be hung up to dry in a fhady place, where it may remain until it be ufed.

Water MINT. [*Mentha Aquatica*.] Horfemint.

Horfe MINT. *See* HORSE MINT.

Pepper-MINT. *See* PEPPERMINT.

Cats MINT. *See* CATMINT.

MISLETOE, [*Vifcus*.] This is a bufhy plant, growing on the trunk and branches of different trees: that met with on the oak is generally preferred, perhaps on account of its being the moft rare. It may, however, be propagated by art on any trees by rubbing the berries againft the bark.

MIST. A meteor, confifting of grofs vapours floating near the furface of the earth.

The bluifh mift, which we fometimes fee on our fields and paftures in a morning, though often innocent, yet has been in fome places found to be the actual caufe of murrain, and other fatal difeafes among the horned cattle.

MITHRIDATE MUSTARD. *See* MUSTARD.

MOAR-LOVRE. A term ufed to exprefs a peculiar diftemperature of corn, generally comprehended under the common term of a blight. In this cafe the earth finks away from the roots of of the corn, and leaves the plant ſtanding in great part above ground with naked roots; theſe being too weak to ſupport the ſtalks, the plants fall, and the ears become light. This is a diſtemperature peculiar to corn growing on light and looſe lands.

The remedy is this: turn a ſhallow furrow againſt the rows, when they are ſtrong enough to bear it, and the mould is fine and dry; the motion of the ſtalks with the wind will draw in this looſe powder, and it will ſpread itſelf equally among all the rows, ſettle about the roots, and cover them.

MOCK ORANGE. A ſpecies of the Syringa.

MOCK PRIVET,] *Phillyrea.*] There are ſeveral ſpecies of this plant which are evergeen ſhrubs, flowering in March. The propagation is by ſeed, ſown in autumn, or by layers in autumn or ſpring.

MOLE. Theſe are miſchievous ſubterraneous animals. We ſee their hills in paſtures, where they work under ground at a ſtrange rate, and are very hurtful; but the damage they do to corn is much greater; and frequently comes upon the farmer quite unexpectedly. He knows that the ants and mice will eat the grain when newly ſowed, and that the ſlugs will deſtroy it when juſt ſhot up; but when theſe times are over, he is at reſt on thoſe heads. On the contrary, there is no time at which the mole may not deſtroy his crop.

This creature, formed for living under ground, preys upon the roots of plants, and is fond, in a particular manner, of thoſe of corn; but beſide the quantity they deſtroy by eating, they damage a vaſt deal more by undermining the ground. It is hardly to be conceived what havock one way or other a ſingle mole will make in a field of corn, or in how little time; one of theſe creatures will burrow through a third part of an acre in a day; and this perhaps at a time when the corn is half grown.

The drieſt lands are the moſt ſubject to theſe animals, but they will get into any; and there is no creature of all the number to whoſe injuries the farmer is expoſed, againſt which it is ſo difficult to guard. There is no foreſeeing when they will come; but it is very important to know of their being in the ground as ſoon as poſſible, in order to ſtop the deſtruction.

The only caution in the farmer's power is to obſerve whether there are any there at the time of plowing; and if there be, he is to uſe every poſſible method of deſtroying them: if not, he is to examine whether the lands neareſt his own every way be infeſted by them, or clear from them.

The freer they are the more likely he is to be clear of them; but there is no certainty from this; for there are times when they will come without any poſſible manner of gueſſing from whence; and they will ſometimes have done irreparable miſchief, before it is diſcovered they are in the place.

The next caution to this, of knowing when to expect them, is the deſtroying them when found. They are a very defenceleſs creature, and not very cunning. Their only ſecurity is the being hid under the ſurface; and they betray themſelves in that retreat by the manner of their working.

The huſbandman, whoſe crop is ſuffering by them, is to look for the tracks where they have gone; and theſe he will eaſily ſee by the different colour of the new turned up earth.

He is to follow the courſe of one of theſe paſſages; when he has got ſight of it, he is to dig croſs holes in it, and to watch the going out or coming back of the mole. And whereever it is caſting, to ſtrike it through with an iron inſtrument made for that purpoſe. The traps for catching them are alſo common, cheap, and of a plain ſtructure. Indeed the deſtruction of this creature is ſo eaſy, and ſo many are ready to undertake it at a trifling price, that the caution we firſt gave is the moſt important; which is, the finding as ſoon as poſſible where they are growing miſchievous.

In ſome places the farmers content themſelves with driving them out of their fields; and this is to be done by ſmoaking them, as other creatures of a leſſer kind are deſtroyed.

To this purpoſe they open their paſſages in ſeveral places, and burn heaps of ſtraw and ſome brimſtone. This will drive the moles out of a corn field ſpeedily enough; but this is not a ſafe or eligible method. It is only sending them out of one's own ground into one's neighbours, who may in the same manner drive them back again. This is only a temporary relief; and there is none wise or effectual but their destruction.

MOLTEN-GREASE. A fat or oily discharge with the dung, which arises from a colliquation, or melting down of the fat of the horse's body, by violent exercise in very hot weather.

It is always attended with a fever, heat, restlessness, starting and trembling, great inward sickness, shortness of breath, and sometimes with the symptoms of a pleurisy. His dung will be extremely greasy, and he will fall into a scouring; his blood will have a thick skin of fat over it when cold, of a white or yellow hue, but chiefly the latter; the congealed part, or sediment, is commonly a mixture of size and grease, which makes it so extremely slippery, that it will not adhere to the fingers, and the small portion of serum feels also slippery and clammy. The horse soon loses his flesh and fat, which probably is dissolved and absorbed into the blood; and those that survive this shock commonly grow hide-bound for a time, their legs swelling both before and behind, and continue in this state till the blood and juices are rectified; and if this is done not effectually, the farcy, or some obstinate surfeit, generally follows very difficult to remove.

In the first place bleed plentifully, and repeat it two or three days successively in smaller quantities; two or three rowels should also be immediately put in, and cooling emollient clysters daily thrown up, to abate the fever, and drain off the greasy matter from the intestines. By the mouth give plenty of warm water, or gruel, with cream of tartar, or nitre, to dilute and attenuate the blood; which in this case is greatly disposed to run into grumes, and endanger a total stagnation.

When the fever is quite gone off, and the horse has recovered his appetite, gentle aloetic purges should be given once a week, for a month or six weeks, in order to bring down the swelled legs; but if the purgative ingredient does not exceed half an ounce, or six drams of fine aloes, it only opens the belly gently; and, with other medicines joined with it, passes into the blood, acts as an alterative, and operates both by urine and perspiration; as will appear by the horse's staling plentifully; and the kindly feel of his skin. To this end give the following, which, repeated for some time, will intirely remove this disorder.

Take of succotrine aloes six drams, of gum-guaiacum powdered half an ounce, of diaphoretic antimony, and powder of myrrh, each two drams: make into a ball with syrup buckthorn.

Or it may be prepared with an ounce of aloes, six drams of diapente, and a spoonful of oil of amber.

These will seldom take a horse from his business above two or three days in a week; neither will he lose his flesh or appetite with them, which cannot be obtained by any other method of purging, and gives this greatly the preference in many cases.

Two ounces of nitre mixed up into a ball with honey, and a dram of camphire, will also be found an excellent medicine for this purpose, as it will powerfully attenuate the blood, and promote the due secretions; to which end it should be given every day for a fortnight or three weeks.

MONOPETALOUS. Formed of one leaf.

MONEYWORT. *See* HERB TWOPENCE.

MONKEY BREAD. *See* SOUR GOURD.

MONKSWOOD. *See* WOLF'S BANE.

Monk's RHUBARB, [*Rumex Alpinus.*] A species of the dock. *See* DOCK.

MOONSEED, [*Menispermum.*] This is a native of North America, which is propagated by layers and parting the roots.

MOON BLIND. *See* BLIND.

MOON WORT. *See* HONESTY.

MOSSES, [*Musci*] The plants of this order.

MOSS *on Trees*, is a distemper of very bad consequence to their increase, and much damages the fruit of the trees of our orchards.

The present remedy is the scraping it off from the body and large branches, by means of a kind of wooden-knife, that will not hurt the bark; or with a piece of rough hair-cloth, which does

very

very well after a soaking rain. But the most effectual cure is, the taking away the cause. This is to be done by draining off all the superfluous moisture from about the roots of the trees, and may be greatly guarded against in the first planting of the trees, by not setting them too deep.

If trees stand too thick in a cold ground, they will always be covered with moss; and the best way to remedy the fault, is to thin them. When the young branches of trees are covered with a long and shaggy moss, it will utterly ruin them; and there is no way to prevent it, but to cut off the branches near the trunk, and even to take off the head of the tree, if necessary, for it will sprout again; and if the cause be in the mean time removed by thinning the plantation, or draining the land, the young shoots will continue clear after this.

If the trees are covered with moss, in consequence of the ground's being too dry, as this will happen from either extreme in the soil, then the proper remedy is, the laying mud from the bottom of a pond or river, pretty thick about the root, opening the ground to some distance and depth to let it in; this will not only cool it, and prevent its giving growth to any great quantity of moss, but it will also prevent the other great mischief which fruit-trees are liable to in dry grounds, which is, the falling off of the fruit too early.

Moss. A name given to moory or boggy gounds, in many parts of England. These sorts of land consist of a turfy surface, below which is a black, moist, spongy earth, which being dug up with spades, almost in the form of bricks, and dried, is what they call peat, and is used as fuel in several parts.

The shortest method of all for the improvement of moss, if the ground be designed only for grass, and its situation be such as admits of it, is this: first drain the moss, and if there be heath upon it, burn that off, and make the surface even. Then make a dam at the lowest part, and a sluice, and work the water upon it through the winter. The mud which comes with the land flood will bring a fine sward upon it in two or three years, and be afterwards a yearly manure; so that it will bear annual cutting, and, besides, be good pasture for cattle, after the sward is become strong enough to bear them.

Mr. Græme found that the improvement of moss may be endangered by draining it too much; for his crops were best where the surface of the water in the surrounding ditches was not above three feet lower than the level of the moss. It will, undoubtedly, be a vast advantage to an improved moss, if the farmer is able to flood it at proper times, by means of a sluice in the lowest part of the surrounding ditch, as mentioned before. This will greatly promote the growth of plants; but should be used with the caution of not letting the water remain too long at a time upon the ground, because, though there will be no danger of its re-converting the soil into a bog so long as there are channels to carry it off, it will be apt to chill, and thereby hurt the plants.

MOOR. *See* Bog and *Marshy Land*.

MOTHER *of* THYME. *See Thyme*.

MOTHERWORT, [*Cardiaca*.] This is common in waste places, and found in flower the greatest part of the summer. The leaves have a bitterish taste, and a strong disagreeable smell: they are supposed to be useful in hysteric disorders, and likewise to promote urine.

MOULD. Earth, soil, loam. The goodness of a mould for the purposes of agriculture and gardening, &c. may be known, according to Mr. Miller, by the sight, smell, and touch. 1. Those moulds that are of a bright chesnut or hazely colour, are counted the best: of this colour are the best loams, and also the best natural earth; and this will be the better yet, if it cut like butter, and does not stick obstinately, but is short, tolerably light, breaking into small clods, is sweet, will be tempered without crusting or chopping in dry weather, or turning to mortar in wet. Next to that the dark grey and russet moulds are accounted the best: but the light and dark ash-coloured the worst, such as is usually found on common heathy ground: the clear tawney is by no means to be approved; but that of a yellowish red colour is the worst of all: this is commonly found in wild and waste

waste parts of the country, and for the most part produces nothing but gofs, furze, and fern, according as their bottoms are more or less of a light and sandy, or of a spewey gravel, or clayey nature. 2. All lands that are good and wholesome, will, after rain, or breaking up by the spade, emit a good smell. 3. By the touch we may discover whether it consists of substances entirely erenaceous, or clammy; or, as it is expressed by Mr. Evelyn, whether it be tender, fatty, detersive, or slippery; or more harsh, gritty, porous, or friable.

MOULDINESS. A term applied to bodies which corrupt in the air, from some hidden principle of humidity therein; and whose corruption shews itself by a certain white down, or lanugo, on their surface, which, viewed through a microscope, appears like a kind of meadow, out of which arises herbs and flowers, some only in the bud, others full blown, and others decayed, each having its root, stalk, and others parts.

MOUSE-EAR. [*Auricula Muris.*] This is a low creeping plant, covered with a kind of blackish hairs. It grows wild in dry pasture grounds, and flowers in June and July. The leaves have a rough subacrid taste: They are recommended as astringents, but practice pays no regard to them.

MOUSEL-SCAB. Is a distemper that sometimes attends sheep and young teggs; and that comes (as shepherds say) where there is great plenty of firrs and gofs, that by eating of the tops and flowers thereof, they prick their lips and mousel, whereby these sorts of scabs are produced; which are healed, by anointing them with fresh-butter; but some take the juice of plantain and fresh grease boiled together, wherewith they anoint them.

MOUND. A bank or fence of earth.

MOW. The pile or collection of corn in the straw, placed in a bay of a barn.

MOW-BURNT. Over-heated in the mow for want of being dry.

MOWING. Cutting down with a scythe, which instrument goes nearer the ground than the reaping hook, and is applied to grass in general, and to barley and oats chiefly.

MUCK. Dirt, rubbish.

MUD, properly so called, is the finest earth, wash'd and worn to a surprizing fineness by the action of water. This is the condition of fine and pure mud: this is such as is drag'd out of the bottoms of rivers, where it has been many years collecting, and where sand and all other foulnesses whatsoever are thoroughly wash'd from it.

Mud, in some of its properties, resembles marle. It is the softest, fattest, and mellowest of all earthy substances after that; and like marle it breaks with the least rains, and crumbles away: so far they are alike, as also in giving great fertility: but marle is a particular substance, and has a lasting quality of enriching land, whereas mud is only mould in a particular form, and its effect is of no great continuance.

The next to the mud of rivers is that of ponds: but this is less pure and fine; it is often clayey, and generally has some mixture of sand.

The last kind to be named is, that mud which is thrown up in the cleansing of ditches. This is the poorest and worst of all: but even the worser sorts are not to be rejected or despised; for they have their particular uses, which the very finest would not answer so well.

The mud of ditches, especially those by road sides, is full of grit and sand blown in with the dust: it is short enough, but wants mellowness.

The first thing the farmer is to do in these matters, is like what he is to do in respect of his marle. He must learn to distinguish these three kinds of mud by the names of river mud, pond mud, and ditch mud; and then consider, from their nature and from experience, what soils each of them will severally suit.

As marle is most used on plough'd lands, mud is most frequently laid on pasture and meadow grounds. But this need not be established as an universal rule. We have seen how marle may be used with advantage on pasture grounds; and mud will also help many corn lands.

Marle is commonly used alone, and mud with other Ingredients; but in some instances marle may be mix'd also; and in several cases mud may be best used alone.

From

From the different nature of the mud it is qualified to anſwer different purpoſes. River mud is proper to give fertility, and nothing elſe: for its richneſs is all its character. Pond mud will enrich, and at the ſame time give a body to the ſoil from the clay it uſually contains; and ditch mud, though it will leſs enrich, will ſerve better than any to break a tough land.

When mud is to be laid on a plow'd land, this is uſually the kind.

From the conſideration of their nature, the farmer will be led to a general notion of their uſe, and the lands to which they are ſuited. Thus the river mud is proper for meadows and paſtures of a mellow ſoil, that want nothing but a recruit of that fine mould, which the ſeveral growths have waſted and drawn forth; pond mud is beſt where the ſoil is too light and crumbly; and ditch mud is preferable to both on a clayey ground.

Mud, eſpecially that out of rivers, has this particular quality, that it mixes in a favourable manner with the finer part of dung. This we have obſerved ſeveral times in meadows. After having given them a ſprinkling of mud and dung mix'd together, and a few ſhowers, falling on the ground, the ſtrawy part has been waſhed clean, and nothing but that remaining the mud and the rich part of the dung being wholly gone down into the land: and the next crop has ſufficiently found their effects.

People who ſtudy the growth of plants, talk greatly of the value of virgin earth, that is, earth on which nothing ever grew. River mud is the neareſt this virgin earth in its nature of any thing whatever.

We adviſe the farmer who has dry paſtures, whether they be of a ſtony, gravelly, or ſandy nature, to uſe this manure preferably to all others; but let him obſerve the following directions:

If the land be entirely of a looſe nature, let him uſe the pond mud, mix'd with rich well-rotted dung; and lay it on in a good round quantity.

If the ſoil be mellow, and only require to be recruited and put in heart, after ſeveral growths that have exhauſted it, let him mix pure river mud with the dung of poultry or ſheep, and ſcatter this lightly over the ground. A very little of this anſwers the purpoſe; and it is beſt to uſe a little at a time, and repeat it often.

If the ſoil be clayey, let him take the mud of ditches, and make a mixture of it with chalk and rotten dung; this, being ſpread tolerably thick, will break and mellow the ground, as well as give it warmth and richneſs.

MUGWORT, [*Artimiſia.*] This plant grows plentifully in fields, hedges, and waſte places, throughout England; and flowers in June. In appearance it ſomewhat reſembles the common wormwood: the difference moſt obvious to the eye is in the flowers, thoſe of wormwood hanging downwards, whilſt the flowers of mugwort ſtand erect. The leaves of this plant have a light aromatic ſmell, and an herbaceous bitteriſh taſte. They are principally celebrated as uterine & antihyſteric: infuſion of them is ſometimes drank, either alone or in conjunction with other ſubſtances, in ſuppreſſions of the menſtrual evacuations. This medicine is certainly a very mild one, and conſiderably leſs hot than moſt others to which theſe virtues are attributed: in ſome parts of this kingdom, mugwort is in common uſe as a pot-herb.

MULBERRY, [*Morus.*] The ſpecies are, 1ſt. The common mulberry, which is cultivated for the delicacy of its fruit. It grows naturally in Perſia, from whence it was firſt brought to the ſouthern parts of Europe, but is now become common in every part of Europe where the winters are not ſevere; for in the northern parts of Sweden theſe trees will not live in the open air; and in ſeveral parts of Germany they are planted againſt walls, and treated in the ſame way as the Peach, and other tender fruits, in this country. 2d. Virginia mulberry, branching like the nettle-tree, having very large leaves. This tree grows to the height of thirty or forty feet. It ſends forth many large branches; and the bark of the young ſhoots is of a blackiſh colour. The leaves are larger than the common mulberry, and rougher, though in other reſpects they ſomewhat reſemble them. It produces plenty of katkins, in ſhape like thoſe of the birch-tree; and the female flowers are ſucceeded

by

by a dark reddish fruit. This is a very scarce plant at present, notwithstanding it bears the severity of our climate extremely well. 3d. Mulberry with a white fruit. This tree will grow to a large size, and is very proper for walks and avenues, or for clumps or standards, either in fields or parks. The leaves are of a clear light green, and the fruit is of a paler colour than any of the other sorts, which makes it take the name of the white mulberry. This tree possesses the peculiar property of breeding no vermin, either when growing or cut down; neither does it harbour any caterpillar, the silk-worm excepted. This species is cultivated for its leaves in France and Italy to feed silk-worms; and, when raised for that use, the tree should not be suffered to grow tall. The leaves should be shorn off together with the tender twigs, which injures the plant much less than pulling them by the hand. This kind should be raised from seeds procured from the south of France or Italy. 4th. Mulberry with a green fruit, whose wood dyes a sulphur colour. Fustick wood. This tree is better known by the title of Fustick, which is given to the wood, than by its fruit, which is of no estimation. It grows naturally in most of the islands in the West-Indies, but more plentifully at Campeachy, where it abounds greatly. This wood is one of the commodities exported from Jamaica, where it grows in greater plenty than in any other of the British islands.——This tree, in the countries where it grows naturally, rises to the height of sixty feet and upward. The bark is of a light brown colour, with some shallow furrows. The wood is firm, solid, and a bright yellow. It sends out many branches on every side, covered with a white bark, and garnished with leaves about four inches long, which are broad at their base, and indented at the footstalk, where they are rounded; but one side is broader than the other, so that they are oblique to the foot-stalk; these diminish gradually, and end in acute points; they are rough like those of the common Mulberry, of a dark green, and stand upon short foot-stalks. Toward the end of the young branches come out short katkins of a pale herbaceous colour; and in other parts of the same branches the fruit is produced, growing upon short foot-stalks. The fruit is as large as a nutmeg, of a roundish form, full of protuberances like the common Mulberry, green within and on the outside, and of a luscious sweet taste when ripe.——This species is too tender to thrive in this country, unless preserved in a warm stove. There are several of the plants now growing in the Chelsea garden, which were raised from seeds sent from Jamaica by William Williams, Esq; with many other curious sorts, which are natives of that island. The seeds of this plant come up freely on a hot-bed; and when the plants are fit to remove, they should be each planted in a separate small pot filled with fresh light earth, and plunged into a hot-bed of tanners' bark, and shaded from the sun till they have taken new root. Let them be treated in the same way as other plants from those hot contries, always keeping them in the tan-bed in the stove, where they will make good progress. These plants retain their leaves great part of the year in the stove. 5th. Mulberry with hand-shaped leaves and prickly fruit. This sort grows naturally in China and Japan, where the inhabitants make paper of the bark. They cultivate the trees for that purpose on the hills and mountains, much after the same manner as Osiers are cultivated here, cutting down the young shoots in autumn for their bark. A few years ago there were several of these trees raised in the garden of his Grace the Duke of Northumberland from seed; and, when removed into the open air, bore the weather without shelter. This plant makes very strong vigorous shoots but seems not to be of tall growth, for it sends out many lateral branches from the root upward. The leaves are large, some of them are entire, others, are deeply cut into three, and some into five lobes, especially while the trees are young, dividing in form of a hand. They are of a dark green, and rough to the touch, but of a pale green, and somewhat hairy on their under side, falling off on the first approach of frost in autumn, as do those of the common Mulberry. The description which Kæmpfer gives of the fruit is, that they are a little larger than pease, surrounded with long pur-

ple

ple hairs, are composed of acini or protuberances, and, when ripe, change to a black purple colour, and are full of sweet juice. 6th. India Mulberry. This kind grows naturally in India, where it becomes a large tree. It hath a soft, thick, yellowish bark, with a milky juice like the Fig, which is astringent. The branches come out on every side, and are garnished with oblong, oval, leaves, standing upon short foot-stalks. Both sides of these leaves are equal, but their edges are unequally sawed. They are rough, of a dark green on their upper side, but pale on their under, standing alternately on the branches. The flowers come out in round heads at the foot-stalks of the leaves on each side the branches; they are of an herbaceous white colour; the male flowers have four stamina; the female flowers are succeeded by roundish fruit, which are first green, afterwards white, and when ripe turn to a dark red colour.—The plants are too tender to live out of a stove in this country. The Mulberry is of the class and order Monoecia Tetrandria, which contains those plants that have male and female flowers at separate distances upon the same plant, the male flowers having four stamina. It is generally observed, that the old Mulberry-trees are not only more fruitful than the young, but their fruit is much larger and better flavoured: so that where there are any of these old trees, it is the best way to propagate from them, and to make choice of those branches which are most fruitful. The usual method of propagating these trees, is by laying down their branches, which will take root in one year, and are then separated from the old trees; but as the most fruitful branches are often so far from the ground as not to be layed, unless by raising of boxes or baskets of earth upon supports for this purpose, so the better way is to propagate them by cuttings, which, if rightly chosen and and skilfully managed, will generally succeed: And in this method there will be no difficulty in having them from trees at a distance, and from the most fruitful branches. These cuttings should be the shoots of the former year, with one joint of the two years wood to their bottom; the cuttings should not be shortened, but planted their full length, leaving two or three buds above ground. The best season for planting them is in March, after the danger of frosts is over. They should be planted in light rich earth, pressing the ground pretty close about them; and if they are covered with glasses, it will forward their putting out roots; but where there is not such conveniency, the ground about them should be covered with moss to prevent its drying; and where this is carefully done, the cuttings will require but little water. If the cuttings succeed well, and make good shoots, they may be transplanted the following spring into the nursery, where they should be regularly trained to stems by fixing down stakes, to which the principal shoots should be fastened; and most of the lateral branches should be closely pruned off, leaving only two or three of the weakest to detain the sap, for the augmentation of the stem; for when they are quite divested of their side-shoots, the sap is mounted to the top, so that the heads of the trees grow too fast for the stems, and become too weighty for their support. After four years growing in the nursery they will be fit to transplant where they are to remain; for these trees are transplanted with greater safety while young, than when they are of a large size.

If the cuttings are planted in a bed fully exposed to the sun, it will be proper to arch the bed over with hoops, that they may be shaded with mats in the heat of the day during the spring, till they have put out roots; after which, the more they are exposed to the sun, the better they will succeed, provided the ground is covered with moss or mulch to prevent its drying; for the sun will harden the shoots, whereby the plants will be in less danger of suffering by the early frosts in autumn; for when these are in a shady situation, they are apt to grow vigorously in summer; and, being replete with moisture, the early frosts in October frequently kill their tops. If the following winter proves severe, they are often killed to their roots, and sometimes are entirely destroyed. Mr. Miller recommends the cuttings to be planted on a hot-bed; and he informs

informs us, that he was led to this improvement by obferving fome fticks of Mulberry-trees which were cut for forks, and thruft into the hot-bed to faften down the vines of cucumbers; which, although they had been cut from the tree a confiderable time, yet many of them put out roots and fhot out branches; fo that when any perfon is in hafte to propagate thefe trees, if the cuttings are planted on a moderate hot-bed, they will take root much fooner than in the common ground.

This tree delights to grow in a light earth, fuch as is in moft of the old kitchen gardens about London; for in fome of thofe gardens there are trees of a very great age, which are very healthy and fruitful, and their fruit is larger and better flavoured than that of younger trees. Dr. Hunter fays, he has never yet feen any of thefe trees which were planted in a very ftiff foil, or on fhallow ground, either upon clay, chalk, or gravel, which have been healthy or fruitful; their ftems and branches are generally covered with mofs, fo that the little fruit which they produce, is fmall, ill tafted, and late before it ripens.

If thefe trees are planted in a fituation where they are defended from the ftrong fouth & north-weft winds, it will preferve their fruit from being blown off; but this fhelter, whether it be trees or buildings, fhould be at fuch a diftance as not to keep off the fun; for where the fruit has not the benefit of his rays to diffipate the morning dews, it will turn mouldy and rot upon the trees.

MULCH. A fort of ftrawey dung, fomewhat moift, and not rooted, and is ufeful in gardening, to protect the rotts of new-planted choice trees or fhrubs from fevere froft in winter and from being dried by the fierce fun or drying winds in fpring & fummer, before they are well rooted; for both of which purpofes, it is fpread evenly on the furface of the ground round the ftem of the tree, as far as the roots extend, about three or four inches thick, but which may be augmented in winter if the feverity of the froft render it neceffary.

MULE. The mule has the good qualities of the afs without its bad ones. It is as patient of fatigue, and as capable of enduring hunger as the afs; but then it is as tractable as the horfe; and is fufficiently fwift of foot for any common fervice. When properly bred it is alfo a very handfome creature: and it is indeed fo well fitted for fo many different fervices, that nothing can be more worth while than raifing them in all places where they will thrive.

The mule is often of the fize of an ordinary horfe, fome fixteen or feventeen hands high. They are very ftrong, and very fure-footed. This is the quality for which they are valued in many parts of Europe, where the roads are mountainous and ftony; they will go with the greateft fafety over thefe, where a horfe would break his neck.

They perform excellently alfo in draught; and will travel many weeks together with fix or feven hundred weight on their backs, without any fign of uncommon fatigue.

The mule is bred from the copulation of an afs and a mare. Thofe for travel and fhew are bred from very large he-affes and Spanifh mares: thefe are tall and ftately, their colour ufually inclining to black, and they are very handfome. But a larger and ftouter kind are bred from the fame affes, and large Flanders mares. Thefe are frequently feventeen hands high; and as large fet as our common coach horfes. They are much ftronger than horfes of the fame fize, and will bear greater hardfhips, and be fed at much lefs expence. At the fame time they are much lefs fubject to diftempers. Thefe are great recommendations of this creature; and may fhew how much it would be to the advantage of the farmer always to have them in his yard.

They are extreamly fit for the faddle, as well as for thefe laborious employments: they are very manageable, and walk and trot very eafy. If it fhould ever become a cuftom to breed them in England, they may be fuited to the fervices for which they are defign'd, by the choice of proper mares, for they take after them. Thofe for the road fhould be bred from light made mares; and thofe for cart, plough, and the like, from the larger bodied and ftouter kinds.

There is a very fubftantial reafon why we fhould breed them in England, which

which is, that such as are bred in colder countries are always better and longer lived than those in hot. As to the objection some have raised of their being vicious, it is a complaint only made where there are but few of them, and those ill taken care of; for where they are common, and are treated in the manner as horses, they are as inoffensive.

Beside the mule already mention'd, which is bred between the ass and the mare, and is a light, beautiful, and lively creature; there is another kind propagated in some places, raised between the horse and the she-ass; but this is an inferior kind.

It has been observ'd, that foals take more after the nature of the female than the male parent; and the same thing is seen very plainly in the breed of mules: those between the ass and the mare, partaking of the nature of the mare, being beautiful, lively and swift; and only inheriting the good qualities of the ass, his patience, strength, and perseverance under fatigue: while on the contrary, those bred from a horse and a she-ass, are of the ass kind, dull, heavy, sluggish, ill-made, and small. There is very little temptation to breed these any where, because the others may be had with as little trouble. Let the husbandman therefore who shall think of breeding mules among his stock, take care that he does not fall into the mistake of supposing that 'tis the same thing, so one parent be of the ass kind, which of the two it is: he here sees the difference.

As the mare is to be suited to the service for which the mule is intended, great care is to be taken to have a proper ass. He should have all the marks of a good one, and above all things he must be large. The fine mules we see, in other parts of Europe, are bred from the tallest asses that can be procured; which they purchase at a vast price, and out of their finest mares. The mare is put into a hollow place rail'd in and the ass has the advantage of higher ground in covering.

We see in this cricumstanec of the mule, the abhorrence of nature to monsters, or animals produced of mix'd breeds. It was believ'd among the antients, that new sorts of savage creatures were every year produced in Africa, from the copulation of different kinds, and the increase of those monsters so produced; but this is an error; and we see in the instance of the mule, that two creatures of a different, tho' like kind, are very difficultly brought to copulate; and that when they are, altho' they produce a creature different from either, as the mule is both from the horse and ass, yet that creature is not able to propagate its kind again.

The pretence that there is any where a sort of mules that produce their own kind one among another, is as false as the new species of monsters in Africa. The horse and ass are difficultly got together, in order to the production of this animal; but when that is done, there is no carrying the power any farther.

The mare is always averse to receive the ass, and in the same manner the she-ass is unwilling to admit the horse to copulation; insomuch that where they breed mules frequently, it is a practice to make the ass colt suck a mare: and the mare foal suck an ass, in order, as is imagin'd, to make them in some degree partake of the nature of either. This has no real effect, but it is named to shew how sensible the breeders of mules are, that those creatures do not go freely and willingly together: and it is certain, that there is not in nature any power of the mules generating its own kind again.

MULLEIN. [*Verbascum.*] This is met with by road sides, in ditches, and amongst rubbish; and flowers in July. It is said to soften tumours, cool inflammations, and ease pains, and is recommended in distempers of the breast, coughs, and spitting of blood. There are many species cultivated in the gardens of the curious.

MURE. The cake of the apples after pressing.

MURRAIN. The murrain is principally caused from a hot dry season of the year, or rather from some general putrefaction of the air, or from the infection of other cattle, from cattle smelling to carrion, and licking of the bones; from foul food, as overflown hay, grass rotted by the long standing of water on it in wet summers; which

sort

fort of food is much better to rot on the ground than to be made ufe of. All thefe things beget an inflammation in the blood, and caufe a fwelling in the throat, which in little time fuffocates the cattle.

The figns of this difeafe are, a hanging down of the head, gum at the eyes as big as your finger, going weakly, ftaggering, the head fwelling very big, the breath fhort, the heart beating, with rattling in the throat; and if you put your hand into his mouth, and find his breath very hot, his tongue fhining, he hath the diftemper very ftrong. If he be taken backward, he will be very ftiff, and his guts rumble very much.

If any of your cattle are infected, fpeedily let both fick and well blood, and drench them. The following receipt we have not had the opportunity to try, but it hath been much recommended:

Take diapente a quarter of an ounce, dialphera, London treacle, mithridate, and rhubarb, of each the quantity of a nut; of faffron a fmall quantity, wormwood, red fage, of each an handful, and two cloves of garlick: boil all together in two pints of beer till it comes to a pint and a half; give it lukewarm, when he is fafting; keep him very warm, and give him a mafh of ground malt, and let him drink warm water a week, & fometimes boiled oats. If you can make him fweat he will do well: if one drink will not do, give him another three days after. Half the proportion will do for a cow.

MUSHROOMS, are, by many perfons, fuppofed to be produced from the putrefaction of the dung, earth, &c. in which they are found, but notwithftanding this notion is pretty generally received amongft the unthinking part of mankind, yet by the curious naturalifts they are efteemed perfect plants, tho' their flowers & feeds have not as yet been perfectly difcovered.

The true Champignon, or Mufhroom, appears at firft of a roundifh form like a button; the upper part of which, as alfo the ftalk, is very white, but being opened, the under part is of a livid flefh colour; but the flefhy part, when broken, is very white: when thefe are fuffered to remain undifturbed, they will grow to a large fize, and explicate themfelves almoft to a flatnefs, and the red part underneath will change to a dark colour.

In order to cultivate them, if you have no beds in your own, or in neighbouring gardens, which produce them, you fhould look abroad in rich paftures during the months of Auguft and September, until you find them (that being the feafon when they are naturally produced;) when you fhould open the ground about the roots of the Mufhrooms, where you will find the earth, very often, full of fmall white knobs, which are the offsets, or young Mufhrooms; thefe fhould be carefully gathered, preferving them in lumps with the earth about them; but as this fpawn cannot be found in the pafture, except at the feafon when Mufhrooms are naturally produced, you may probably find fome in old dunghills, efpecially where there has been much litter amongft it, and the wet hath not penetrated it to rot it; as likewife by fearching old hot-beds it may be often found; for this fpawn has the appearance of a white mould, fhooting out in long ftrings, by which it may be eafily known, wherever it is met with: or this may be procured by mixing fome long dung from the ftable, which has not been thrown on a heap to ferment; which being mixed with ftrong earth, and put under cover to prevent wet getting to it, the more the air is excluded from it, the fooner the fpawn will appear; but this muft not be laid fo clofe together as to heat, for that will deftroy the fpawn: in about two months after the fpawn will appear, efpecially if the heap is clofely covered with old thatch, or fuch litter as hath lain long abroad, fo as not to ferment, then the beds may be prepared to receive the fpawn: thefe beds fhould be made of dung, in which there is good ftore of litter, but this fhould not be thrown on a heap to ferment, that dung, which hath lain fpread abroad for a month or longer, is beft; thefe beds fhould be made on dry ground, and the dung laid upon the furface; the width of thefe beds at bottom fhould be about two feet and a half, or three feet, the length in proportion to the quantity of Mufhrooms defired; then lay the dung about a foot thick, covering it about four inches with strong earth. Upon this lay more dung, about ten inches thick; then another layer of earth, still drawing in the sides of the bed, so as to form it like the ridge of a house, which may be done by three layers of dung and as many of earth. When the bed is finished, it should be covered with litter or old thatch, to keep out wet, as also to prevent its drying; in this situation it may remain eight or ten days, by which time the bed will be in a proper temperature of warmth to receive the spawn; for there should be only a moderate warmth in it, great heat destroying the spawn, as will also wet; therefore when the spawn is found, it should always be kept dry until it is used, for the drier it is, the better it will take the bed. Mr. Miller says, he had a parcel of this spawn, which had laid near the oven of a stove upward of four months, and was become so dry, that he despaired of its success; but never had seen any which produced so soon, nor in so great quantity as this.

The bed being a proper temperature for the spawn, the covering of litter should be taken off, and the sides of the bed smoothed; then a covering of light rich earth, about an inch thick, should be laid all over the bed, but this should not be wet; upon this the spawn should be thrust, laying the lumps two or three inches asunder; then gently cover this with the same light earth, about half an inch thick, and put the covering of litter over the bed, laying it so thick as to keep out wet, and prevent the bed from drying: when these beds are made in the spring or autumn, as the weather is in those seasons temperate, so the spawn will then take much sooner, and the Mushrooms will appear perhaps in a month after making: but those beds which are made in summer, when the season is hot, or in winter, when the weather is cold, are much longer before they produce.

The great skill in managing of these beds is, that of keeping them in a proper temperature of moisture, never suffering them to receive too much wet: during the summer season, the beds may be uncovered to receive gentle showers of rain at proper times; and in long dry seasons the beds should be now and then gently watered, but by no means suffer much wet to come to them; during the winter season they must be kept as dry as possible, and so closely covered as to keep out cold. In frosty or very cold weather, if some warm litter shaken out of a dung heap is laid on, it will promote the growth of the Mushrooms; but this must not be laid next the bed, but a covering of dry litter between the bed and this warm litter; and as often as the litter is found to decay, it should be renewed with fresh; and as the cold increases, the covering should be laid so much thicker. If these things are observed, there may be plenty of Mushrooms produced all the year; and those produced in beds are much better for table than any of those which are gathered in the fields.

A bed thus managed, if the spawn takes kindly, will continue good for several months, and produce great quantities of Mushrooms; from these beds, when they are destroyed, you should take the spawn for a fresh supply, which may be laid up in a dry place until the proper season of using it; which should not be sooner than five or six weeks, that the spawn may have time to dry before it is put into the bed, otherwise it will not succeed well.

Sometimes it happens, that beds thus made do not produce any Mushrooms till they have lain five or six months, so that these beds should not be destroyed, though they should not at first answer expectation; for we have frequently known these to have produced great quantities of Mushrooms afterward, and have continued a long time in perfection.

MUSK, [*Abelmoschus.*] This plant is a native of the West-Indies propagated by seeds sown on a hot-bed, and may be treated as the Amaranth.

MUSK *Hyacinth.* See HYACINTH.

MUSK *Melon.* See MELON.

MUST. New wine or wort before it is fermented.

MUSTARD, [*Sinapis.*] The species are, 1. white mustard; 2. black mustard; 3. Field or Durham mustard. The two first flower in June, and the seeds ripen in July and August; the other flowers in May, and the seeds ripen in June. To save the seed for garden use, sow it on an open spot of ground

ground in March or April, either thinly in drills a foot asunder, or broad-cast all over the surface, and let the plants run up to stalk, and they will furnish ripe seeds in August.

To raise the plants for the seed for Mustard, they should be sowed in the spring, any time in March, in some open situation either in a kitchen-garden, or in the open fields, where large quantities are required for sale; in either case, having digged or ploughed the ground, then sow the seed broadcast all over the surface, and rake or harrow them in lightly, or sow it in shallow drills a foot asunder. They will soon come up, observing, that when the plants have four or more leaves an inch or two broad, those sown in the broad-cast way should be hoed and thinned, leaving them ten or twelve inches asunder, and cut up all weeds, repeating it once or more if necessary; after this the plants will soon spread and cover the ground, and shoot fast up to stalks for flowers and seed, which will ripen in July or August, and the third probably in June, when the stalks should be cut or pulled up, and threshed out for use.

Hedge MUSTARD. *See* HEDGE MUSTARD.

Mithridate MUSTARD, [*Thlaspi.*] A biennial plant that grows among corn, or the sides of dry banks in many parts of England, which dies soon after it has perfected his seeds. There are several species, annuals and biennials, cultivated in botanic gardens. They are propagated from seeds.

Bastard MUSTARD. *See* BASTARD.

Bastard Mithridate MUSTARD. *See* BASTARD.

Treacle MUSTARD. Mithridate mustard. The seeds have an acrid biting taste like the common mustard.

MYROBALANS, [*Myrobalani.*] Dried fruits brought from the East-Indies; their outward part, freed from the stone.

Five kinds of myrobalans were formerly directed as officinals; 1. The yellow; 2. The chebule; 3. The Indian or black; 4. The belliric; 5. The emblic.

All the myrobalans have a low degree of purgative virtue. They have also an astringent quality, discoverable by the taste, from their use among the Indians for tanning leather, and from their striking a black colour with chalybeate solutions; in consequence of this, they are supposed to strengthen the bowels after their operation as a cathartic is over. Nevertheless their purgative virtue is so inconsiderable, that practitioners have for a long time laid them entirely aside in that intention; and the college of Edinburgh, as well as that of London, have now rejected them from the catalogue of officinal simples.

MYRRH, [*Myrrha.*] Is a concrete gummy-resinous juice brought from the East-Indies, in glebes or drops, of various colours and magnitudes. The best sort is of a brown or reddish yellow colour, somewhat transparent; of a lightly pungent, bitter taste, with an aromatic flavour, though not sufficient to prevent its proving nauseous to the palate; and a strong not disagreeable smell. The medical effects of this aromatic bitter are, to warm and strengthen the viscera, and dissolve thick tenacious juices: it frequently occasions a mild diaphoresis, and promotes the fluid secretions in general.

Hence it proves serviceable, in languid cases, diseases arising from a simple inactivity, those female disorders which proceed from a cold, mucous, sluggish indisposition of the humours, suppressions of the uterine discharges, cachectic disorders, and where the lungs and thorax are oppressed by viscid phlegm. Myrrh is likewise supposed in a peculiar manner to resist putrefaction in all parts of the body; and in this light stands recommended in malignant, putrid, and pestilential fevers, and in the small-pox, in which last it is said to accelerate the eruption.

Rectified spirit extracts the fine aromatic flavour and bitterness of this drug, and does not elevate any thing of either in evaporation: the gummy substance left by this menstruum has a disagreeable taste, with scarce any thing of the peculiar flavour of the myrrh: this part dissolves in water, except some impurities which remain. In distillation with water, a considerable quantity of a ponderous essential oil arises, resembling in flavour the original drug. Myrrh is the basis of an officinal tincture, and gives name to a compound tincture, elixir, powder,

der, and troches. It is an ingredient in the aloetic wine or elixir proprietatis, the gum pills, Rufus's pills, stomachic pills, mithridate, theriaca, and theriaca Edinensis.

MYRTLE, [*Myrtus*.] The species are, 1. The common myrtle, the varieties of which are, the broad-leaved Roman, the broad-leaved Dutch, the orange-leaved Spanish, the common upright Italian, Portugal acute-leaved, box-leaved, rosemary-leaved, thyme-leaved, nutmeg, broad-leaved nutmeg, cristated, or cock's-comb, frequently called bird's-nest Myrtle.

They are all beautiful ever-green shrubs of exceeding fragrance; exotics originally of the southern parts of Europe, and of Asia and Africa, and consequently in this country require shelter of a green-house in winter: all of which, though rather of the small-leaved kind, have their foliage closely placed, remain all the year, and are very floriferous in summer; and when there is a collection of the different sorts, they afford an agreeable source of variety with each other; they therefore claim universal esteem as principal green-house plants, especially as they are all so easily raised from cuttings, and of such easy culture, as to be attainable in every garden, where there is any sort of green-house, or garden-frames furnished with glasses for protecting them in winter from frost; but some of the broad-leaved sorts are so hardy as to succeed in the full ground, against a south-wall and other warm exposures all the year, by only allowing them shelter of mats occasionally in severe frosty weather: so that a few of these sorts may be also exhibited in a warm situation in the shrubbery: observing, however, all the sorts are principally to be considered as green-house plants, and a due portion of them must always remain in pots to move to that department in winter.

There are several species of the stove temperature, as natives of the Indies; but there are not more than the four following sorts commonly met with in the English gardens, all of which are beautiful evergreens, with larger leaves then the Common Myrtles and are mostly strong aromatics.

1. Ceylon white-berried Myrtle.

2. Pimento, or Jamaica all-spice tree. This species is wholly an admirable fine aromatic, its leaves are remarkably fine scented; and its fruit is that valuable spice, Jamaica pepper, or all-spice, so called, because it is supposed to partake of the odour and taste of most other spices. The tree grows in great abundance in the island of Jamaica, where its fruit is made a considerable branch of trade; is generally gathered a little before it acquires full growth, and dried in the sun ten or twelve days; it is then packed up ready for exportation to Europe.

3. Diœcious American Myrtle.

4. Brasilian Inodorous Myrtle.

All these five species of Myrtle are exotics of the shrub and tree kind, though in this country, as being confined in pots, the largest of them assume only the growth of moderate shrubs. The first species, Common Myrtle, is considerably the most noted species of the genus in this country; where in most of our green-house collections one or other of the varieties is found in tolerable plenty; but all the varieties of it highly merit notice. The other four species are rare in England, they however are retained in many curious gardens, in the stove collection, more particularly the Pimento, which is a very beautiful odoriferous evergreen, and exhibits a fine variety in the stove at all seasons: in short, all the species, both green-house and stove kinds, have a pretty effect as evergreens, and some of the sorts flower very ornamentally, particularly of the Common Myrtle.

The propagation of the Common Myrtle and varieties is effected abundantly by slips or cuttings, also by layers; but as the former strike freely, it is the most eligible method for raising any considerable quantity, as also the handsomest plants, which may be struck either in natural earth, or by aid of hot-beds, to bring them more forward.

The young shoots, either of the same or former year's growth, of from about two or three to five or six inches long, either slipped or cut off, are the proper parts for planting; and, as above said, may be struck either in natural earth without artificial heat, or by aid of hot-beds; but by the latter you may greatly facilitate the rooting and first effort of growth. By either method the work may be performed any time from March or April until August, though

L 2

though June or July is the moſt common ſeaſon practiſed, eſpecially when intended to uſe the ſhoots of the ſame year, which are generally in prime order in July, and often ſtrike freely that year without aid of hot-beds; the young ſhoots of the former year will alſo often ſtrike tolerably, eſpecially if planted in ſpring or early in ſummer, or by aid of hot-beds may be made to ſtrike root readily at any time in the ſpring or ſummer ſeaſon. By aid of a hot bed, however, all the ſorts, both of one or two years ſhoots may be greatly facilitated in rooting: a dung hot-bed under common frames and lights will do, though a bark hot-bed of a ſtove, &c. is conſiderably the moſt eligible and effectual, and may be readily uſed any time in ſpring and ſummer for this purpoſe; and by which aſſiſtance vaſt numbers of cuttings may be ſtruck with the utmoſt facility in a ſhort time, with but little trouble; and plants thus ſtruck in ſpring or early in ſummer, may be ſo much forwarded as to form pretty little plants the ſame year, and be fit to pot off ſeparately early in autumn. We will, however, exhibit ſeparate directions for both methods, i. e. ſtriking them in natural earth, and by hot-beds.

Firſt, by ſtriking them in natural earth: we noticed above, that the planting might be performed any time from March till Auguſt; obſerve in reſpect to this, that if you would begin in ſpring, or early in ſummer, you muſt chuſe principally the ſhoots of the former year; and if you do not begin planting till June or July, but particularly the latter month, the young ſhoots of the year will be arrived at a proper growth, and will root freely. Obſerve in chuſing the ſhoots, either of the former or ſame year, to chuſe the ſtraight clean growth, of from about two or three to four or five inches length, and as robuſt as poſſible; which diveſt of the lower leaves, two parts in three of their length, they are then ready for planting; then having ſome large wide garden-pots, or rather flat wide earthen pans, ſix inches deep, with holes at bottom to diſcharge the wet, ſuch as are uſed by the ſetting-gardeners about London, who raiſe prodigious quantities of Myrtle annually for the ſupply of the markets; fill the pots or pans with light rich mould, in which plant the ſlips or cuttings, many in each pot or pan, if required, putting them in within an inch of their tops, and about an inch or two aſunder; give directly ſome water to ſettle the earth cloſely about each plant; then either plunge the pots, &c. in a ſhallow garden-frame, and put on the glaſſes, or under oiled paper-frames, or cover each pot or pan cloſe with a low hand-glaſs, which is rather the moſt eligible for facilitating their rooting; in either method, however, obſerve to plunge the pots in the earth, and keep them cloſe covered with the glaſſes, &c. where practicable, to exclude the air, for this will promote the quick emiſſion of roots the ſame ſeaſon; remembering to afford them occaſional ſhade from the mid-day ſun, but if under oiled paper none is wanted; and give plenty of water three or four times a week at leaſt, or oftener in very hot weather; thus they will be rooted in a month or ſix weeks, which will appear by their exhibiting ſigns of growth at top; at which period inure them gradually to the full air, ſtill ſupplying them duly with water during the hot weather, whereby they will ſhoot in height; and thoſe planted early will often branch out laterally a little the ſame year, ſo as to commence pretty little plants by autumn: let them remain in the full air until October, then remove them in their pots or pans into the green-houſe, or under a good garden-frame for the winter, and in ſpring the forwardeſt in growth may be potted off ſeparately in ſmall pots; but if rather ſmall and weak, or but indifferently rooted, let them have another ſummer's growth, and pot them out ſeparately in September or ſpring following, as it ſhall ſeem proper; managing them as other green-houſe ſhrubs of ſimilar temperature, and ſhift them into larger pots annually, or according as they ſhall require.

For want of frames and glaſſes of any ſort to ſtrike the cuttings under, oiled paper-frames may be uſed, which may be obtained at an eaſy expence, and are excellent for ſtriking many ſorts of cuttings; they admit the rays of light and heat ſufficiently, & at the ſame time afford ſuch agreeable ſhade, that no other is required, and which is of ſuch a nature as greatly to promote the rooting of cuttings.

But

But Myrtle cuttings will sometimes strike in the open ground without any coverings; and if planted betimes in summer, either in pots or pans, as above mentioned, and plunged in a shady border, or the slips planted in the earth of such a border of rich earth; and in either method plentifully supplied with moisture, they will often root tolerably the same year, and shoot a little at top; though rarely make so good plants by autumn as those forwarded in the above manner, nor near so strong as those struck in the following method by artificial heat.

By Aid of Hot-beds, either that of dung, under frames and glasses, oiled paper-frames, or in the bark-bed in the stove, &c. but rather the latter; but by either method the rooting and first growth of the slips may be greatly forwarded; a bark-bed in particular in the stove, &c. is the most eligible, and effectual for this purpose, and in which vast numbers of slips or cuttings may be readily struck, at any time from March until August, both in shoots of the former year, and of the same year's growth, from three or four to five or six inches long: and that those struck in spring and early in summer, will form fine young plants for potting off early in the succeeding autumn. However, in default of bark hot-beds, one of dung under glasses may suffice; but if furnished with both, give preference considerably to a bark-bed.

Therefore being furnished with pots, or rather wide pans, as before directed, filled with fine rich earth, take off a quantity of slips or cuttings, the most robust shoots; which if in spring or early in summer, those of the former year must be chosen; and at a more advanced season, those of the same year will be arrived to a proper growth for this purpose: observing for either sort to strip off the under leaves, as before advised; then plant them in the pots or pans, as already exhibited, give a general watering, and directly plunge them in the hot-bed, affording occasional slight shade from the fierce sun, and water them frequently; they will thus root in a fortnight or three weeks, and advance in growth; observing to inure them gradually to the open air, if the temperature of the weather permits, in a sheltered situation; or in a frame, if cold weather; and from thence by degrees expose them fully for the remainder of the summer, in a sheltered place, and supply them duly with water in dry weather. They will be fine plants by September; and, as before observed, those raised early will be then fit to pot off singly into small pots; and the latter plantings will be fit for potting in spring, or autumn following; removing them all to shelter towards the middle or latter end of October.

In striking the cuttings by the above method, if, as soon as they are planted and plunged in the hot-bed, each pot or pan is covered close with a low hand-glass, it will still contribute to facilitate their rooting the more effectually; for being close covered, it will force out roots sooner, and prevent the cuttings from running up weak; observing, however, when they begin to advance at top, to remove the glasses.

By the above methods of artificial heat, in striking Myrtle cuttings, you may make two or three plantings each season, where large quantities are required; the first planting in March or April, of the best last year's shoots; the second early in June, of the succeeding best shoots; or about Midsummer, or soon after, may plant shoots of the year; and in a month or six weeks after, the next best shoots also of the same year will be come forward, and of which may be made another plantation; plunging each planting in the bark-bed, &c. as above; thus may you have three young crops advancing in different stages of growth each year in store-pans; some ready for potting off singly every autumn and spring, whereby a large stock may be always kept up, as is necessary for those who raise them for sale, especially about London, for Covent-garden market, where amazing quantities are brought for sale at all times of the year, which sell from six-pence to half-a-crown per pot, according to the size and goodness of the plants.

Those who propagate large quantities of these plants annually, should always keep some strong bushy plants for furnishing slips or cuttings for this purpose.

Propagation by Layers.——Such plants as are furnished with young bottom branches or shoots situated low

low enough for laying, may be layed in ſpring, in the uſual way; every ſhoot will readily emit roots, and be fit to tranſplant into ſeparate pots in autumn.

By Seed.—Theſe may be ſowed in ſpring, in pots of light mould, plunged in a moderate hot-bed; they will ſoon come up, and, when two or three inches high, pot them off ſeparately in ſmall pots; manage them as the others, and probably as they advance in growth may diſcover ſome new varieties.

With reſpect to the general culture of all theſe ſorts of common Myrtle, they ſucceed in the open air from May until the end of October, when remove them in their pots to the green-houſe, or into a deep garden-frame under glaſſes, allowing air freely in all mild weather, by opening the glaſſes wide; giving water once or twice a week or ten days in winter, and every other day at leaſt in ſummer; and according as they advance in growth, ſhift them into larger pots, as may be neceſſary every year to one or other of them.

In training theſe ſhrubs, obſerve, as they naturally branch out all around, ſo to be feathered quite to the bottom, in a beautiful manner, that if you deſign any ſhall form ſtandards, with buſhy heads for variety, trim off the lower ſhoots gradually ſo as to form a ſtraight clean ſtem, two or three feet high or more, then ſuffer them to branch out every way at top to form a head: but thoſe which are intended to be low and branchy quite to the bottom, ſhould have the lateral ſhoots encouraged nearly in their own way, whereby they will be feathered all the way from bottom to top, and aſſume a more pictureſque appearance.

Let them afterwards for the moſt part aſſume their own natural growth, except when their heads become thin, ſtraggling, and irregular; then ſhorten with a knife ſuch ſhoots as ſhall appear proper, either in order to force out laterals to make good deficiencies, or to form regularity.

Never practiſe clipping theſe ſhrubs with garden-ſhears into globes, pyramids, &c. as ſometimes done; but let all neceſſary trimming be performed be the knife, and that only in caſes of irregularity as above, for they always appear the moſt agreeable when they grow nearly according to nature.

If their heads at any time become very irregular, or thin and ſtubby, by heading down all the branches pretty ſhort in ſpring, and ſhifting them into larger pots of freſh mould, with the ball of earth about their roots, affording plenty of water all ſummer, they will all branch out again numerouſly, and form handſome full heads by the ſucceeding autumn.

Sometimes when Myrtles are become very weak ſtraggling ſhooters, with naked unſightly heads, if headed down, as above, in April or May, turned out of the pots, and plunged in a warm border of rich ſoil, giving plenty of water, they, by ſending their fibres into the freſh earth, often break out with freſh vigour, and become fine full-headed plants by the end of ſummer, when they may be taken up with balls and potted in freſh earth.

As the ſorts in general encreaſe in ſize, ſhift them into larger pots.

The four kinds of Myrtle for the ſtove, are commonly propagated by ſeeds; though, when any are pretty branchy, it may alſo be tried by layers and cuttings.

By Seed.—This is procured from abroad by the dealers, preſerved in ſand, &c. and arrives in ſpring, which ſow as ſoon after it arrives as poſſible, in pots of freſh rich mould, and plunge them in a bark-bed, they will come up the ſame ſeaſon; and, when of two or three inches height, plant out in ſeparate ſmall pots, plunge them alſo in the bark-bed, ſupply them with water, and manage them as other woody plants of ſimilar temperament.

By Layers.—The firſt ſort in particular often branch out low: lay ſome of the young ſhoots in ſpring, by ſlit-laying or wireing, &c. plunging the pots in which they are layed in the tan; they will probably be rooted in one year, though it is frequently two before they ſtrike good root, when pot them off ſeparately.

By Cuttings.—In May or June, cut off ſome ſhort young ſhoots from ſuch of the plants as afford them, plant them in pots of freſh compoſt, plunge them in the bark-bed, and cover them cloſe with a low hand-glaſs, giving due refreſhments of water; they will ſoon take good root, the ſame year, and be fit to plant in ſeparate ſmall pots.

In

In the general management of these sorts, keep them always in the stove, except about a month in the heat of summer, when they may be trusted abroad. Let them shoot nearly in their own way, keeping them, however, to upright stems, and suffer their hands to branch out according to nature, except just reducing very irregular shoots: give frequent waterings in common with other woody plants of the stove department, and shift them occasionally into larger pots.

Dutch MYRTLE, [*Myrica.*] Candleberry Myrtle. This plant grows in the bogs in many parts of England. *See* CANDLEBERRY TREE.

MUM. A kind of liquor much used in Germany; thus made. Take sixty-three gallons of water that hath been boiled to the consumption of a third part, brew it according to art with seven bushels of wheat malt, one bushel of oat meal, and one bushel of ground beans; when it is tunned, let not the hogshead be too full at first; and when it begins to work, put into it, of the inner rind of fir three pounds, tops of fir and birch one pound, carduus benedictus three handfuls, flowers of rosa solis a handful or two, burnet, betony, marjoram, avens, penny-royal, wild-thyme, of each a handful and a half, of elder-flowers two handfuls or more, seeds of cardamom bruised three ounces, barberries bruised one ounce: put the herbs and seeds into the vessel when the liquor hath wrought a while; and after they are added, let the liquor work over the vessel as little as may be; fill it up at last, and when it is stopped, put into the hogshead ten new-laid eggs, unbroken or crack'd, stop it up close, and drink it at two years end.

But our English brewers use cardamom, ginger, and sassafras, which serves instead of the inner rind of fir, also walnut rinds, madder, red sanders, and enula campana; and some make it of strong-beer, and spruce-beer: and where it is designed mostly for its physical virtues, some add water-cresses, brooklime, and wild-parsly, with six handfuls of horse-radish rasped to every hogshead, according to what their inclinations and fancy most lead them.

N.

NAIL. A kind of horny excrescence, upon the ends of the fingers or toes; alſo a well-known ſpike of metal with a ſharp point, and a flat head, uſed to faſten things together.

Nail. In meaſure, the ſixteenth part of a yard.

NARD, [*Nardus.*] There are two ſorts of this plant, the Celtic and the Indian: the Celtic is a root conſiſting of a number of fibres, with the lower part of the ſtalks adhering; theſe laſt are covered with thin yellowiſh ſcales, the remains of the withered leaves. The Indian nard or ſpikenard, is brought from the Eaſt-Indies.

This is a congeries of ſmall fibres iſſuing from one head, and matted cloſe together, ſo as to form a bunch about the ſize of the finger, with ſome ſmall ſtrings at the oppoſite end of the head. The matted fibres (which are the part choſen for medicinal purpoſes) are ſuppoſed by ſome to be the head or ſpike of the plant, by others the root: they ſeem rather to be the remains of the withered ſtalks, or the ribs of the leaves; ſometimes entire leaves and pieces of ſtalks are found among them; we likewiſe now and then meet with a number of theſe bunches iſſuing from one root.

Both the nards have a warm, pungent, bitteriſh taſte; and a ſtrong, not evry agreeable ſmell. They are ſtomachic and carminative; and ſaid to be alexipharmac, diuretic, and emmenagogue: their only uſe at preſent is as ingredients in the mithridate and theriaca.

NASTURTIUM, [*Lepidium.*] Dittander.

Nasturtii *Aquatici.* Water-creſſes. This plant grows wild in rivulets, and the clearer ſtanding waters; its leaves remain green all the year, but are in greateſt perfection in the ſpring. They have a quick pungent ſmell (when rubbed betwixt the fingers) and an acrid taſte. As to their virtues, they are among the milder aperient antiſcorbutics. Hoffman has a mighty opinion of this plant, and recommends it as of ſingular efficacy for accelerating the circulation, ſtrengthening the viſcera, opening obſtructions of the glands, promoting the fluid ſecretions, and purifying the blood and humours; for theſe purpoſes, the expreſſed juice, which contains the peculiar taſte and pungency of the herb, may be taken in doſes of an ounce or two, and continued for a conſiderable time. The juice is an ingredient in the *ſucci ſcorbutici* of the ſhops.

Nasturtii *Hortenſis.* Garden-creſſes. The leaves of garden creſſes make an uſeful ſallad in ſcorbutic habits: in taſte and medical virtues, they are ſimilar to the foregoing, but much weaker. The ſeeds alſo are conſiderably more pungent than the leaves.

NAVE, *of a Wheel*, is that ſhort thick piece in the center of the wheel, which receives the end of the axletree, and in which the ends of the ſpokes are fixed: it is bound at each end with hoops of iron, called the nave-bands. It has likewiſe, in each end of the hole, through which the end of the axletree goes, a ring of iron, called the wiſher, which ſaves the hole of the nave from wearing too big.

NAVEL-GALL. The Navel-gall is ſeated on the top of the ſpine, oppoſite to the navel, from whence it has its name, and is generally cauſed by a bad ſaddle pinching a horſe behind, which, being neglected, turns to a foul fungous excreſcence; and ſometimes, after long continuance, to a

ſinuous

ſinuous and fiſtulous ulcer, ſometimes it looks like a harden'd brown jelly, and ſometimes black and mortifyed. While there is moiſture and ſenſibility in the part, an ointment may be applied of quickſilver and turpentine, *viz.* an ounce of quickſilver to every two ounces of the turpentine, rubbed in a mortar till they be well incorporated, and then ſpread upon hurds or flax: on each ſide of the ſpine, over the ſwelling, may be laid ſmooth dry pledgits of hurds, or bolſters of flaxen cloth, which may be girt round with a ſurſingle. But if the ſore be dead and lifeleſs, a good ſharp razor or knife may be made uſe of to cut it to the quick, and then let it be dreſs'd according to the directions laid down in the cure of wounds, *&c.*

NAVELWORT, [*Cotyledon.*] This plant grows upon old walls, buildings, and rocky places, in many parts of England; it is a biennial plant. There are ſeveral other ſpecies brought from different parts of the world, and cultivated in the gardens, ſome of which require the aſſiſtance of a ſtove.

Shrubby African NAVELWORT, [*Craſſula.*] There are ſeveral ſpecies of this plant, which may be managed like the Sicoides.

Venus's NAVELWORT, [*Cynogloſſum.*] This is an annual plant, with long narrow greyiſh leaves, and white flowers, which grow in looſe panicles. It is propagated by ſeeds ſown in autumn.

Water NAVELWORT, [*Hydrocotyle.*] This plant grows plentifully in moiſt places in moſt parts of England.

NAVEW, [*Rapa.*] This is a ſort of turnep, ſown in ſome of our gardens for culinary uſe: the roots are warmer than the common turnep. The ſeeds have a bitteriſh taſte. accompanied with a faint aromatic flavour: abundance of virtues have been aſcribed to them, as attenuating, detergent, alexipharmac, and others; at preſent, they are of no farther uſe in medicine, than as an ingredient in the theriaca.

NEAT. Cattle of the cow kind.

NEAT-HERD. A cattle-keeper.

NECTARINE. Properly ſo called of nectar the poetical drink of the Gods. This fruit differs from peaches in nothing more than having a ſmooth rind, and the fleſh being firmer; it ſhould have come under the article peaches, but that the writers in gardening have diſtinguiſhed this fruit by the name of nectarine, and we ſhall follow their example, leſt by endeavouring to rectify their miſtakes, we ſhould not be underſtood to the reader. Mr. Miller mentions the following varieties of this fruit:

1. Fairchild's early nectarine. This is one of the earlieſt ripe Nectarines we have; it is a ſmall round fruit, about the ſize of the Nutmeg Peach, of a beautiful red colour, and well flavoured; it ripens the end of July, or the beginning of Auguſt.

2. Elruge Nectarine. The tree has ſawed leaves; the flowers are ſmall; it is a middle-ſized fruit, of a dark red or purple colour next the ſun, but of a pale yellow or greeniſh colour towards the wall; it parts from the ſtone, and has a ſoft melting juice; this ripens in the middle of Auguſt.

3. Newington Nectarine. The tree has ſawed leaves; the flowers are large and open; it is a fair large fruit (when planted on a good ſoil,) of a beautiful red colour next the ſun, but of a bright yellow towards the wall; it has an excellent rich juice; the pulp adheres cloſely to the ſtone, where it is of a deep red colour: this ripens the latter end of Auguſt, and is the beſt flavoured of all the ſorts.

4. Scarlet Nectarine is ſomewhat leſs than the laſt, of a fine red or ſcarlet colour next the ſun, but loſes itſelf in paler red towards the wall: this ripens in the end of Auguſt.

5. Brugnon or Italian Nectarine has ſmooth leaves; the flowers are ſmall; it is a fair large fruit, of a deep red colour next the ſun, but of a ſoft yellow towards the wall; the pulp is firm, of a rich flavour, and cloſely adheres to the ſtone, where it is very red: this ripens in the end of Auguſt.

6. Roman Red Nectarine has ſmooth leaves and large flowers; it is a large fair fruit, of a deep red or purple colour towards the ſun, but has a yellowiſh caſt next the wall; the fleſh is firm, of an excellent flavour, cloſely adhering to the ſtone, where it is very red: this ripens in the end of Auguſt.

7. Murry Nectarine is a middle-ſized fruit, of a dirty red colour on the ſide next the ſun, but of a yellowiſh green towards

towards the wall: the pulp is tolerably well flavoured; this ripens the beginning of September.

8. Golden Nectarine is a fair handsome fruit, of a soft red colour next the sun, but of a bright yellow next the wall; the pulp is very yellow, of a rich flavour, and closely adheres to the stone, where it is of a faint red colour: this ripens the middle of September.

9. Temple's Nectarine is a middle-sized fruit, of a soft red colour next the sun, but of a yellowish green towards the wall; the pulp is melting, of a white colour towards the stone, from which it parts, and has a fine poignant flavour: this ripens the end of September.

10. Peterborough, or late green Nectarine, is a middle-sized fruit, of a pale green colour on the outside next the sun, but of a whitish green towards the wall; the flesh is firm, and, in good seasons, well flavoured: this ripens the middle of October.

There are some persons who pretend to have more sorts than are here set down, but we doubt whether they are different from those here mentioned, there being so near a resemblance between the fruits of this kind, that it requires a very close attention to distinguish them well, especially if the trees grow in different soils and aspects, which many times alters the same fruit so much, as hardly to be distinguished by persons who are very conversant with them; therefore, in order to be thoroughly acquainted with their differences, it is necessary to consider the shape and size of their leaves, the size of their flowers, their manner of shooting, &c. which is many times very helpful in knowing of these fruits.

The culture of this fruit differing in nothing from that of the Peach, we refer the reader to that article, for an ample account of their planting, pruning, &c.

NECTARIUM. From nectar, the fabled drink of the gods; defined by Linnæus to be a part of the *corolla*, or appendage to the petals, appropriated for containing the honey, a species of vegetable salt under a fluid form, that oozes from the plant, and is the principal food of bees and other insects.

Notwithstanding this definition, which seems to consider the nectarium as necessary a part of the *corolla* as the petals, it is certain that all flowers are not provided with this appendage; neither indeed is it essential to fructification.

There is, besides, a manifest impropriety in terming the *nectarium* a part of the *corolla*. Linnæus might, with equal propriety, have termed it a part or appendage of the stamina, calix, or pointal, as the appearance in question is confined to no particular part of the flower, but is as various in point of situation, as of form. The truth is, the term *nectarium* is exceedingly vague; and, if any determinate meaning can be affixed to it, is expressive of all the singularities which are observed in the different parts of flowers.

The tube or lower part of flowers with one petal, Linnæus considers as a true *nectarium*, because it is generally found to contain the sweet liquor formerly mentioned. This liquor Pontedera compares to that called amnios in pregnant animals, which enters the fertile or impregnated seeds: but that this is not at least its sole use, is evident from this circumstance, that the honey or liquor in question is to be found in flowers where there either are no seeds, or those, from the want of male organs, cannot be impregnated. Thus the male flowers of nettle and willow; the female flowers of sea side laurel, and black bryony; the male and female flowers of *clutia*, *higgelaria*, and butcher's broom, all abound with the honey or nectar alluded to.

Dr. Vaillant was of opinion that the *nectarium* was an essential part of the *corolla*; for which reason he distinguished the singular appearances in fennel-flower and columbine, by the name of petals: the coloured leaves, which are now termed the petals, he denominates the flower cup.

That the *nectarium*, however, is frequently distinct from the petals, is evident, both from the well-known examples just mentioned, as likewise from the flowers of monks-hood, hellebore, *isopyrum*, fennel-flower of Crete, barrenwort, grass of Parnassus, chocolate-nut, *cherleria*, and *sauvagesia*.

These general observations being premised, we proceed to take a nearer and more particular view of the princip cipal diversities, both in form and situation, of this striking appendage to the flower.

1. In many flowers, the *nectarium* is shaped like a spur or horn; and that either in flowers of one petal, as valerian, water-milfoil, (*utricularia*) butter-wort, and calves-snout; or in such as have more than one, as lark-spur, violet, fumatory, balsam, and orchis.

2. In the following plants, the *nectarium* is properly a part of the *corolla*, as lying within the substance of the petals: ranunculus, lilly, iris, crown-imperial, water-leaf, mousetail, ananas or pine-apple, dog's-tooth violet, piperidge bush, *vallisneria*, *bermannia*, *uvularia*, and *swertia*.

3. The *nectarium* is frequently placed in a series or row within the petals, though entirely unconnected with their substance. In this situation it often resembles a cup, as in narcissus. A *nectarium* of this kind is said by Linnæus to crown the *corolla*. The following are examples: daffodil, sea daffodil, campion, viscous campion, swallow-wort, *stapelia*, *cynanchum*, *nepenthes*, *cherleria*, balsam-tree, African spiræa, witch hazel, *olax*, and passion-flower.

4. In Indian cress, buckler mustard, Barbadoes cherry, and *monotropa*, the *nectarium* is situated upon, or makes part of the calix.

5. The *nectarium* in bastard flower-fence is seated upon the *antheræ* or tops of the stamina; whence the name *adenanthera*, or glandular anthera, which has been given to this genus of plants. In the following list it is placed upon the filaments: bean caper, bay, fraxinella, marvel of Peru, bell-flower, lead-wort, *roella*, and *commelina*.

6. In hyacinth, flowering rush, stock July-flower, and rocket, the *nectarium* is placed upon the seed-bud.

7. In honey-flower, orpine, buck-wheat, *collinsonia*, *lathræa*, navel-wort, mercury, *clutia*, *kiggelaria*, sea-side laurel, and African spiræa, it is attached to the common receptacle.

Lastly, in ginger, nettle dyer's weed, heart-seed, turmerick, *grewia*, bastard orpine, vanelloe, skrew-tree, and willow, the *nectarium* is of a very singular construction, and cannot properly fall under any of the foregoing heads.

In discriminating the genera, *nectarium* often furnishes an essential character.

Plants which have the *nectarium* distinct from the petals, that is, not lodged within their substance, are affirmed by Linnæus to be generally poisonous. The following are adduced as examples: monk's hood, hellebore, columbine, fennel-flowers, grass of Parnassus, barren-wort, oleander, marvel of Peru, bean caper, succulent swallow wort, fraxinella, and honey-flower.

The term *nectarium*, by which this part of the flower has been distinguished, is the invention of Linnæus, who pretends even to have first recognized the part in question. It is certain, however, that Tournefort, in 1694, observed it in the passion-flower, swallow-wort, and some other plants; and that Vaillant, in 1718, regarded it as a part depending upon the petals, which did not merit any particular appellation. Needles. See Needle.

NEEZEWORT. Sneezewort.

NENUPHAR. Water lily.

NEP. Catmint. This plant is commonly cultivated in our gardens, and is sometimes also found growing wild in hedges and on dry banks. It is a moderately aromatic plant, of a strong smell, not ill resembling a mixture of mint and pennyroyal; of the virtues of which it likewise participates.

NEPHRITIC WOOD, [*Lignum nephriticum.*] An American wood, brought to us in large compact, ponderous pieces, without knots, of a whitish or pale yellow colour on the outside, and dark-coloured or reddish within: the bark is usually rejected. This wood imparts to water or rectified spirit a deep tincture, appearing, when placed betwixt the eye and the light, of a golden colour, in other situations blue: pieces of another wood are sometimes mixed with it, which give only a yellow colour to water. The nephritic wood has scarce any smell, and very little taste. It stands recommended in difficulty of urine, nephritic complaints, and all disorders of the kidneys and urinary passages; and is said to have this peculiar advantage, that it does not, like the warmer diuretics, heat or offend the parts. Practitioners however have not found these

Needle worms. See Ascarides.

these virtues warranted by experience.

NETTLE, [*Urtica.*] This is a very common plant well known. There are several species brought from different countries cultivated in the gardens; they are easily propagated by seeds or parting the roots.

Dead NETTLE. *See* ARCHANGEL.

Hedge NETTLE. *See* HEDGE NETTLE.

NETTLE *Tree*, [*Celtis.*] The lote tree.

NEWING. Yeast or barm.

NICKING. The operation of nicking a horse, in the manner it is commonly performed by our grooms and farriers, is one of the most cruel and absurd (not to say in many cases dangerous) that ever was invented or practised; though, in itself, it is neither severe or dangerous, and, if properly done, the horse in three or four days will be fit again for his accustomed labour. A safe, easy, and rational method of nicking cannot then fail of proving universally useful and acceptable, to all who are lovers of this so noble and serviceable an animal.

In order to understand the rationale of nicking, it may be necessary to premise, that there are, in very limb, both in the *human* and *brute species*, two different sets of muscles, called, the flexors & extensors, whose actions are diametrically opposite to each other, as the flexors, in their actions, will always serve to bend the limb, and the extensors to straiten or extend it.——Of these, the flexors are by much the strongest, and will always keep the limb in a half-bent state, unless, by any effort of the will, the weaker extensors should be brought into action, and overcome the natural contraction of the bending muscles.——The arm of a man, when asleep, or in a state of rest, is always half bent, and the fingers half closed, but he can at any time, at pleasure, extend it, and bring it strait; but this state of extension may be called, a state of violence; as it cannot, for any length of time, be continued without fatigue and pain, owing to the superior strength, and actions, of the flexor muscles.

Let the same method of reasoning be applied to the effect of the operation of nicking on the tail of the horse; and it will readily appear, why it should raise or cock the tail; and, at the same time, will point out to us what are the best, the easiest, and the safest methods of performing the operation.

The tail of a horse is naturally drawn downwards by the actions of the flexor muscles, and the horse has it in his power to raise or elevate his tail when he voids his excrements or the like; yet this may be considered as a state of violence, and is but of short duration.——But weaken or destroy the action of the muscles, which draw it downwards, and the extending, or elevating muscles, having nothing to counteract or resist them, will exert their own particular action, and draw and pull up the tail.

In the methods at present used in nicking, we may see an instance of the barbarity, and savage cruelty of the farriers and grooms; for, as they never trouble themselves to enquire into the rationale of the operation, they in general act as if they believed that the deeper they cut, and the more they punished the horse by pulling and the like, the more likely will he be to carry a good tail; hence they often cut into the very joint itself, and put the horse to such torture, that fevers, and mortifications, will come on; which often end in death: whereas, when the operation is properly performed, it is not attended with any hazard, and but very little pain; and any gentleman may perform it upon his own horse, without risk or danger; as all that is required is to destroy the action of the muscles which draw down the tail; whence necessarily the extenders, having no power to counteract them, will elevate and lift it up.

When the tail is raised, the two flexor muscles may be seen and felt, near or upon the edges of the under part of the tail, from the base to its extremity: an incision is to be made with a lancet or pen-knife, thro' the skin, at the distance of about an inch or two from the base of the tail; and, the muscle will appear like a red cord, about the thickness of the little finger, which is likewise to be cut through.——Make a second incision, in the same manner, at the distance of about two inches from the first, and when the muscle is cut through, the lower extremity of the divided muscle, will drop, so as to hang near half an

inch

inch out of the first incision.——Make a third, and, if necessary, a fourth incision, in the same manner, on each side the tail: but it is not necessary that the skin, in the middle of the tail be divided, or, that the wounds should communicate from side to side with each other: then with a pair of small pincers, lay hold of the ends of the muscle, as they hang out of the wound, and draw them as far out as may be, then with a knife, or pair of scissars, cut off as much of them, as you can come at.——If an artery should be divided, and the wound bleed much, which will seldom or never happen, if the incisions do not extend too far towards the middle of the tail, a little lint or tow, dipped in flour and bound lightly on, will be sufficient to stop it; but, if there should not be a loss of blood, there will be no occasion for any dressing, or application of any kind, as the wounds will, in a very few days, heal of themselves.——It is the general, and indeed universally received practice, to extend the horse's tail with weights and pullies, for many days after the operation, but what service this can be of, is hard to guess; 'tis true indeed, it is a severe punishment to the poor animal, and may carry an appearance of stretching, and keeping open the wounds, but that it is of no real advantage, is manifest from experience, as instances can be produced of horses, which have never been pulleyed, that carry as good a tail, as any of those who have gone through the whole severity of their racks and pullies: besides, as all that can with any degree of reason be attributed to the pullies is, only to keep the divided extremities of the muscle from coming together to heal and unite again, it will appear obvious to any one that will give himself the liberty to think, that this can never be the case, even when no pulley is used, for when the muscle of the tail is divided, the lower part of it shrinks and contracts it to a full half inch from the incision, at the same time near half an inch being cut off from the upper part, there will be a distance of near or quite an inch, between the extremities of the divided muscle; a space far greater than is necessary to prevent a union again.

In the method above related of performing the operation, it is recommended to make the first incision, at the distance of an inch or two from the base of the tail; but this depends entirely upon the manner in which any one may chuse to have the horse carry his tail; if a very high cock-up tail should be required, the nearer the incision is made to the base of it, the likelier will this effect be to happen, and *vice versa*; or if the tail should be required to turn round, up towards the back, four or five incisions may be made, otherwise three will in general be fully sufficient: — or, if the horse's tail should be required with the point dripping downwards, two incisions will be sufficient, and the first may be made at the distance of near three inches from the setting on of the tail.

NIGHTSHADE, [*Solanum.*] Mr. Miller reckons no less than thirty-one different species of this plant, and under this head the botanists range potatoes, love-apples, egg-plant, and winter-cherry. They may be propagated by seeds or cuttings.

Deadly NIGHTSHADE, [*Solanum Lethale.*] This plant grows wild in shady waste grounds. This and the common night-shade have both been supposed cooling and discutient in external applications, and poisonous when taken internally. Late experience has shewn, that an infusion of half a grain or a grain of the dried leaves of either may be taken with safety, and that in many cases the dose may be increased by degrees to five or six grains: that they generally occasion some considerable evacuation, and sometimes, especially in the larger of the above doses, alarming nervous symptoms, which however cease with the operation of the medicine. It has been expected, that a cautious use of these very active plants would afford relief in some obstinate disorders: but though in some instances they promised great benefit, the general event of these trials has not been very favourable. The Edinburgh college, who retained these plants at the preceding revisal of their Pharmacopœia in the year 1744, have, at the late one in 1756, rejected them both.

Enchanters NIGHTSHADE. See ENCHANTERS.

American NIGHTSHADE, [*Solanoides.*] This plant grows naturally in the West-Indies, and may be propagated by by feeds, but will not bear the cold of England.

NIPPLEWORT, [*Lapsana.*] This is a common weed growing by the fides of foot paths and hedges.

NITRE, [*Nitrum.*] A falt, extracted in Perfia and the Eaft-Indies, from certain earths that lie on the fides of hills; and artificially produced in fome parts of Europe, from animal and vegetable matters rotted together (with the addition of lime and afhes) and expofed for a length of time to the air, without the accefs of which, nitre is never generated: the falt extracted from the earths, &c. by means of water, is purified by colature and cryftallization.

Pure nitre diffolves in about fix times its weight of water, and concretes againin to colourlefs tranfparent cryftals; their figure is that of an hexagonal prifm, terminated by a pyramid of an equal number of fides. It readily melts in the fire; and in contact with fuel deflagrates, with a bright flame and confiderable noife; after the detonation is over, a large quantity of alkaline falt is found remaining. The tafte of nitre is fharp, penetrating, and bitterifh, accompanied with a certain fenfation of coldnefs.

Nitre is a medicine of celebrated ufe in many diforders. Befides the aperient quality of neutral falts in general, it has a manifeftly cooling one, by which it quenches thirft, and abates febrile heats and commotions of the blood: it has one great advantage above the refrigerating medicines of the acid kind, that it does not coagulate the animal juices; blood, which is coagulated by all the mineral acids,and milk, &c. by acids of every kind, are by nitre rendered more dilute, and preferved from coagulation: it neverthelefs fomewhat thickens the thin, ferous, acrimonious humours, and occafions an uniform mixture of them with fuch as are more thick and vifcid; by this means preventing the ill confequences which would otherwife enfue from the former, though it has not, as Juncker fuppofes, any property of really obtunding acrimony. This medicine for the moft part promotes urine; fometimes gently loofens the belly; but in cold phlegmatic habits, very rarely has this effect, though given in large dofes: alvine fluxes, proceeding from too great acrimony of the bile or inflammation of the inteftines, are fuppreffed by it: in choleric and febrile diforders, it generally excites fweat; but in malignant cafes, where the pulfe is low, and the ftrength loft, it retards this falutary evacuation and the eruption of the exanthemata.

Dr. Stahl has written an exprefs treatife upon the medical virtues of nitre; in which he informs us, from his own experience, that this falt added to gargarifms employed in inflamations of the fauces in acute fevers, thickens the falival moifture upon the palate and fauces into the confiftence of a mucus, which keeps them moift for a confiderable time, whereas, if nitre be not added, a fudden drynefs of the mouth immediately enfues: that in nephritic complaints, the prudent ufe of nitre is of more fervice than any of the numerous medicines ufually recommended in that difeafe: that nitre gives great relief in fuppreffion and heat of urine, whether fimple or occafioned by a venereal taint; that it is of great fervice in acute and inflammatory pains of the head, eyes, ears, teeth, &c. in all eryfipelatous affections, whether particular or univerfal, and likewife in chronic deliriums; that in diarrhœæ happening in petechial fevers, nitre mixed with abforbents and diaphoretics, had the beft effects, always putting a ftop to the flux, or rendering the evacuation falutary; that in diarrhœæ happening in the fmall-pox, it had been employed with the like fuccefs, two dofes or three at moft (confifting of two, three, or four grains each, according to the age, &c. of the patient) given at the interval of two or three hours, putting a ftop to the flux, after the bezoardic powders, both with and without opium, had been given without fuccefs. The fame author recommends this falt likewife as a medicine of fingular fervice in choleras attended with great anxieties and heat of the blood; in the flatulent fpafmodic heart-burns familiar to hypochondrical people; and the lofs of appetite, naufea, vomiiing, &c. which gouty perfons are fometimes feized with upon the pains of the feet, &c. fuddenly remitting. In cafes of this laft kind, the ufe of nitre furely requires great

great caution, although the author aſſures us, that no bad conſequences are to be feared from it. Nevertheleſs he obſerves, that in a phthiſis and ulcerous affections, it has been found to be of no ſervice; and that therefore its uſe may be ſuperſeded in theſe complaints. Indeed in diſorders of the lungs in general it is commonly reckoned to be rather hurtful than beneficial.

The uſual doſe of this medicine among us is from two or three grains to a ſcruple; though it may be given with great ſafety, and generally to better advantage, in larger quantities; the only inconvenience is its being apt to ſit uneaſy on the ſtomach. Some have affirmed, that this ſalt loſes half its weight of aqueous moiſture by fuſion, and conſequently that one part of melted nitre is equivalent to two of the cryſtals; but it did not appear, upon ſeveral careful trials, to loſe ſo much as one-twentieth of its weight. The officinal preparations of nitre are a decoction or ſolution in water and troches. A corroſive acid ſpirit is alſo extracted from it. It is employed likewiſe in operations on metallic bodies, for promoting their calcination, or burning out their inflammable matter.

NONE-SO-PRETTY. London pride.

NONESUCH, *or* FLOWER OF BRISTOL. Campion.

NORTHERN ASPECT. Is the leaſt favourable of any in England, as having very little benefit from the ſun, even in the height of ſummer, therefore can be of little uſe, whatever may have been advanced to the contrary: for although many ſorts of fruit-trees will thrive and produce fruit in ſuch poſitions, yet ſuch fruit can be of little worth, ſince they are deprived of the kindly warmth of the ſun to correct their crude juices, and render them well taſted and wholeſome; therefore it is to little purpoſe to plant fruit-trees againſt ſuch walls, except it be for ſuch which are intended for baking, &c. where the fire will ripen, and render thoſe juices wholeſome, which, for want of ſun, could not be performed while growing.

You may alſo plant Morello Cherries, for preſerving; and white and red Currants to come late, after thoſe which are expoſed to the ſun are gone: and if the ſoil be warm and dry, ſome ſorts of ſummer Pears will do tolerably well on ſuch an expoſure, and will continue longer in eating, than if they were more expoſed to the ſun. But you ſhould by no means plant winter Pears in ſuch an aſpect, as hath been practiſed by many ignorant perſons, ſince we find that the beſt ſouth walls, in ſome bad years, are barely warm enough to ripen thoſe fruits.

Duke Cherries planted againſt walls expoſed to the north, will ripen much later in the ſeaſon; and if the ſoil is warm, they will be well flavoured, ſo that hereby this fruit may be continued a month later than is uſual.

NOSEBLEED. Milfoil.

NOVEMBER. The ninth month of the year.

Work to be done this month in the Kitchen Garden.

Continue to ſow Beans and Peas on a warm border, to ſupport thoſe ſown laſt month.

About the middle of this month begin to cut off the leaves of Artichokes cloſe down to the ground, and throw the earth up in ridges about the plants, which will keep out the froſt better than laying long dung over them. In very ſevere weather, however, they will require a covering of ſtraw or litter.

Take up Carrots and Parſnips, and other kitchen roots, this month in a dry day, for winter ſtores. Cut the tops off cloſe, clean them from dirt, and depoſit them in a bed of dry ſand, with the crowns of the roots outwards, over which lay a covering of dry ſtraw.

Potatoes ſhould be laid in a dry room, and in froſty weather covered with ſtraw a foot thick. Examine them frequently, and take out the rotten ones, otherwiſe they will corrupt the whole ſtock.

It is a good method to gather only the outſide leaves of Spinage at this ſeaſon, for the inner ones will grow the larger againſt another gathering.

Prepare hot-beds to raiſe Aſparagus, in the manner above directed for making hot-beds.

Nurſery, Fruit, and Flower Gardens.

Prepare your land for new plantations in February or March.

Stake and tie new planted trees; lay mulch on their roots, and cover the beds of ſeedling exotic plants, in

ſharp

as sharp frosts, with hoops and mats, or totally with peas-straw, &c.

Plants in pots should be plunged into the earth to the rim in a warm situation, when they may be easily covered.

Open the Greenhouse windows in the middle of the day, and water the plants as there shall be need.

Take care to shelter the choicest of your Tulips, Hyacinths, Ranunculus's and Anemonies, from heavy rains, sharp frosts, and snow, which will destroy or greatly injure them; and continue to plant those and other bulbous roots as in October.

Continue to transplant Roses, Syringas, Honeysuckles, and other hardy flowering shrubs; and prune off their irregular branches at the same time; you may also take up their suckers, and place them in the nursery for increase.

Prepare the ground for receiving the more tender plants in the spring. Clear the gravel walks of weeds, moss, and rubbish, and roll them once a week in a dry day; which will keep them in better order than the modish custom of digging them up for the winter.

Trees and Shrubs in flowers

Honeysuckles, laurustinus, mezereon, passion-flower, pyracantha in fruit, roses, strawberry-tree in fruit and flower.

Flowers.

Anemonies, asters, Chinese asters, colchicums, cyclamens, daisies, golden-rods, pansies, polyanthuses, primroses, starworts, stocks, striped lilies in leaf, sunflowers, wallflowers.

NOURISHMENT *of Plants.* *See* Food.

NURSERY. A most useful district of gardening, appropriated for the raising and nursing all sorts of trees, shrubs, and herbaceous plants, to a proper growth, for supplying and recruiting the different gardens, orchards, plantations, &c.

In the Nursery-garden are raised all the different sorts of fruit-trees, and fructiferous shrubs, by the methods directed for each sort under their proper genera, nursing and training them up to a proper size & growth for planting in the garden or orchard, where they are finally to remain to produce their fruit.

Likewise in the Nursery is raised the vast train of forest-trees, hardy ornamental trees, and shrubs in general, both deciduous and ever-greens of all those kinds, and training them up to a proper size for the purposes for which they are designed in the plantations and pleasure ground.

And in the Nursery may also be raised all the sorts of hardy herbaceous plants, both fibrous rooted, bulbous, and tuberous-rooted kinds, for adorning the pleasure-garden, medical use, &c.

All sorts of the above kinds may be readily raised together in the same Nursery in separate compartments.

A Nursery thus furnished with the different sorts of all kinds of trees, shrubs, and herbaceous plants, will prove an inexhaustible source of accommodation both for private and public use.

The raising or propagation of the numerous kinds is performed by various methods, as by seed, suckers, layers, cuttings, slips, off-sets, parting the roots, grafting, budding; each of which methods as directed under their proper heads; and after being raised by either of the above methods, & stationed in Nursery-rows, they are to remain until they have acquired a proper growth for their respective uses, then to be transplanted into the garden, orchard, plantation, &c. where they are designed finally to remain, to effect the several purposes for which they are calculated, either for use, ornament, or variety; observing, that as a recruit of some or other of the various sorts will be required to be drawn off every year, to supply the different gardens and plantations, a fresh supply of young plants should also be raised accordingly every year in the Nursery, of most of the various kinds, so as to have this district always fully stocked with all kinds in several different degrees of growth; some in seed-beds, others transplanted in Nursery-rows; some one year, others two, three, or several years: all of which should be well attended to, both in private and public Nurseries, that there may be a sufficiency of plants of all sorts for furnishing every different department of gardening as they shall be occasionally wanted.

In the public Nursery-gardens they have also convenient green-houses, glass-cases, and stoves, with their proper appendages, for raising the tender exotics from the warmer parts of the world; these departments are always stationed in the warmest and most sunny situation, having their front directly facing the south, to have all possible benefit from the sun's influence; and each principal department having its different appendages as aforesaid, which are smaller departments of frame-work, sashed and glazed, either adjoining to the main ones, or detached: serving as seminaries or nurseries for raising and nursing the various tender plants to a proper growth for furnishing the other larger conservatories.

Thus a Nursery ground, furnishing plants of different temperatures, will prove very valuable, and its various growths will afford the most agreeable source of variety at all seasons, which to many will appear as ornamental and desireable as the most elegant pleasure-ground or flower-garden.

With respect to the proper extent or dimensions of a Nursery, whether for private use, or for public supply, it must be according to the quantity of plants required, or the demand for sale; if for private use, from a quarter or half an acre to five or six may be proper, which must be regulated according to the extent of garden-ground and plantations it is required to supply with the various sorts of plants; and if for a public Nursery, not less than three or four acres of land will be worth occupying as such, and from that to fifteen or twenty acres, or more, may be requisite, according to the demand, though some occupy forty or fifty acres in Nursery-ground.

In the neighbourhood of London, for eight or ten miles round, there are a great number of extensive public Nurseries, most beautifully furnished with a prodigious variety of all sorts of trees, shrubs, and herbaceous plants, of different degrees of growth, for supplying noblemen and gentlemen's gardens and plantations, for some hundreds of miles distant at home and abroad; as also all sorts of seeds. Most of which Nurseries are also furnished with all proper green-houses, glass-cases, stoves, &c. for the raising all kinds of curious tender exotics for public supply.

With regard to soil for a Nursery, the nature and quality of this, without all dispute, requires our particular attention. The Nursery-men generally prefer a loamy soil of a moderately-light temperament, if possible, such as in most of the Nursery-grounds around London: however, a Nursery may be of any fat moderately light land, that is fifteen or eighteen inches depth of good working staple, but if two or three spades deep it will be the greater advantage; and where there is scope of ground to chuse from, always prefer that where there is a good depth, and naturally rich or fat soil, for the soil of a Nursery cannot be too good, notwithstanding what some advance to the contrary; for if soil prove poor and lean, the plants raised thereon will be languid, weak, and stunty; and no remedy, how artful soever, will be able to rectify their constitution, especially all the tree-kinds: whereas those raised in a good fat soil always assume a free growth, and advance with strength and vigour. It is not absolutely requisite, however, that the soil should be exceedingly rich, nor over carefully manured, a medium between the two extremes is best. A good fresh fat soil, such as any good pasture, which having the sward trenched to the bottom, is excellent for the growth of trees; any good fat soil of corn-fields is also extremely proper; or any other good soil of the nature of common garden-earth is also very well adapted for a Nursery.

As to situation; if this be rather somewhat low it will be the better, because it is naturally warmer, and more out of the power of cutting and boisterous winds than a higher situation; though if it happens where some parts of the ground is high and some low, it may be an advantage, the better to suit the nature of the different plants. It is also of singular advantage to have a Nursery-ground full exposed to the sun and free air; and, if possible, where there is the convenience of having water for the occasional watering of seedlings, and some newly transplanted plants.

And as to a Nursery for private use, with regard to its place of situation, respecting the other garden districts; that, where there is room, it may either be be entirely detached, or may be ſomewhat contiguous to the outer boundaries of the ſhrubbery plantations of the pleaſure-ground, and ſo contrived as to lead inſenſibly into it by winding walks, ſo as to appear part of the garden.

A fence round the whole ground is neceſſary: this may either be a hedge and ditch, or a paling; the former is the cheapeſt, and in the end the moſt durable; though in ſome places where hares and rabbits abound, paling fences at firſt are eligible, for preſerving the Nurſeries from the depredations of thoſe animals, which often do great miſchief to the young plants, by barking and cropping them: a good hedge-and-ditch-fence, however, may be made very effectual againſt the inroads of both men and brutes; and the moſt eligible plant for this purpoſe is the haw-thorn.

The ground muſt then be all regularly trenched one or two ſpades deep, according as the natural depth of ſoil will admit, for by no means dig deeper than the natural good ſoil, let it be either one, one and a half, or two ſpades deep.

Then, having trenched the ground, proceed to divide it by walks into quarters, and other compartments; a principal walk ſhould lead directly through the middle of the ground, which may be from five to eight or ten feet wide, according as it ſhall ſeem proper for uſe or ornament, having a broad border on each ſide: another walk ſhould be carried all round next the outward boundary, four or five feet wide, leaving an eight or ten-feet border next the fence all the way; then may divide the internal part by croſs walks, ſo as to form the whole into four, ſix, or eight principal diviſions, which are commonly called quarters.

One or more of the diviſions muſt be allotted for a ſeminary, i. e. for the reception of all ſorts of ſeeds, for raiſing ſeedling plants to furniſh the other parts; therefore divide this ſeminary-ground into four-feet-wide beds, with foot-wide alleys at leaſt between bed and bed: in theſe beds ſhould be ſowed ſeeds, &c. of all ſuch trees, ſhrubs, and herbaceous plants, as are raiſed from ſeed; and which ſeeds conſiſt of the various ſorts of kernels and ſtones of fruit, to raiſe ſtocks for grafting and budding; ſeeds of foreſt-trees, ornamental trees, ſhrubs, &c. and ſeeds of numerous herbaceous perennials, both of the fibrous-rooted and bulbous-rooted tribe. The ſowing ſeaſon is both ſpring and autumn, according to the nature of the different ſorts, which is fully illuſtrated under their proper genera; and when the young tree and ſhrub ſeedling-plants ſo raiſed, are one or two years old, they are to be planted out in Nurſery-rows into the other principal diviſion; but many kinds of herbaceous plants require to be pricked out from the ſeed-beds, when but from two to three or four months old. On the other hand, moſt kinds of bulbous ſeedlings will not be fit for planting out in leſs than one or two years.

Another part of the Nurſery-ground ſhould be allotted for ſtools of various trees and ſhrubs, for the propagation by layers, by which vaſt numbers of plants of different kinds are propagated. Theſe ſtools are ſtrong plants of trees and ſhrubs, planted in rows three or four feet diſtant every way, and ſuch of them as naturally riſe with tall ſtems are, after being planted one year, to be headed down near the ground, to force out many lower ſhoots conveniently ſituated for laying.

The other principal diviſions, therefore, of the Nurſery-ground, is for the reception of the various ſorts of ſeedling-plants from the above ſeminary-quarters; alſo for all others that are raiſed from ſuckers, layers, cuttings, &c. there to be planted in rows from one to two or three feet aſunder, according to their natures: obſerving to allow the tree and ſhrub-kinds treble the diſtance of herbaceous perennials.

Of the tree and ſhrub-kinds ſome are to be planted for ſtocks to graft and bud the ſelect ſorts of fruit-trees upon, and other choice plants, which are uſually propagated by thoſe methods; others are trained up entirely on their own roots without budding and grafting, as in moſt foreſt and other hardy tree-kinds; as alſo almoſt all the ſorts of ſhrubs.

Here

Here they are to remain to have two, three, or ſeveral years growth, according as they ſhall require for the ſeveral purpoſes for which they are deſigned in their future ſituations in the garden, &c. which is directed in their reſpective cultures.

With regard to the manner of performing the various methods of propagation for raiſing the numerous Nurſery-plants, it is fully exhibited under the following heads, in the courſe of this work: *ſowing ſeeds—layers—cuttings—ſuckers—ſlips—off-ſets—parting roots—grafting—inoculation.* And the ſorts that are uſually propagated by either of thoſe methods are pointed out under their ſeveral reſpective heads, with particular directions of the ſeveral ways each method is performed on the different kinds.

The ſeaſon for performing the works of ſowing, planting, &c. is different in different kinds, but autumn and ſpring are the principal ſeaſons.

Some ſorts require to be ſowed in autumn, others not till ſpring, which is particularly explained for the various ſorts undr the articles themſevles.

An d as to planting or tranſplanting, the principal ſeaſon is from October until March, or even until April for tender kinds, eſpecially many of the ever-green tribe; but all hardy trees and ſhrubs may be tranſplanted any time in winter, in open mild weather from October until March, as juſt obſerved; and for the tender kinds of ever-greens, &c. early in autumn, or not till ſettled weather in ſpring, is the proper time to remove theſe ſorts.

But as to hardy herbaceous fibrous-rooted plants, they may be tranſplanted almoſt any time in autumn or ſpring; even many ſorts in ſummer, when planting them out from the ſeminary: obſerving, however, autumn and ſpring are the proper planting-ſeaſons for older or larger plants; and which are alſo the only proper ſeaſons for dividing or ſlipping the roots of all theſe kinds of plants for increaſe.

As for bulbous-rooted kinds, & all ſuch tuberous roots whoſe leaves decay in ſummer, the proper ſeaſon for planting or tranſplanting them is from May or June until the beginning of Auguſt, when their flower-ſtalks decay, which in ſome ſorts happens early and ſome late in the ſummer; but as ſoon as it happens in the different ſorts, is the only proper time to remove all thoſe kinds of plants when neceſſary, as alſo to ſeparate their off-ſets for increaſe; and which may either be planted again directly, or kept out of ground one, two, or ſeveral months, though it is proper to plant the principal part again in autumn, unleſs where any is to be retained for ſale.

Succulent perennials may be tranſplanted almoſt any time from March or April until Auguſt or September, which is the beſt ſeaſon for removing theſe kinds; and moſt kinds of ſucculent cuttings ſucceed beſt when planted in ſummer.

In the diſtribution of all the various ſorts of plants in the Nurſery, let each ſort be ſeparate: the fruit-trees ſhould generally occupy ſpaces by themſelves; the foreſt-trees, &c. ſhould alſo be ſtationed together; all the ſhrub kind ſhould alſo be ranged in ſeparate compartments; allot alſo a place for herbaceous perennials; a warm place ſhould likewiſe be allotted for the tender kinds, and incloſed with yew hedges, or a reed hedge, &c. in which compartments you may ſtation all ſuch plants that are a little tender whilſt young, and require occaſional ſhelter from froſt, yet are not ſo tender as to require to be houſed like green-houſe plants, &c. ſo that in ſuch compartments there may alſo be frames of various ſizes, either to be covered occaſionally with glaſs-lights, or with matts, to contain ſuch of the choicer of the above tender kinds in pots, to be nurſed up a year or two, or longer, with occaſional ſhelter, till hardened gradually to bear the open air fully.

The arrangement of all the ſorts in the open grounds, muſt always be in lines or Nurſery-Rows, to ſtand till it arrives at a proper growth for drawing off for the garden and plantations; placing the fruit-tree ſtocks, &c. for grafting and budding upon, in rows two feet aſunder, if for dwarfs; but ſtandards two feet and a half, and a foot and half in the lines; though after being grafted and budded, they then

commencing fruit-trees, &c. that if they are to stand to grow to any large size, they should be allowed the width of a yard between the rows. Forest-trees should also be placed in rows from two or three feet asunder, and half that distance in the rows; varying the distance both ways according to the time they are to stand; the shrub kind should likewise be arranged in rows about two feet asunder, and fifteen or eighteen inches distant in each line; and as to herbaceous plants, they should generally be disposed in four-feet wide beds, in rows from six to twelve or eighteen inches asunder, according to their nature of growth, and time they are to stand.

By the above arrangement of the various sorts of hardy trees, shrubs, and herbaceous plants, in rows at those small distances in the Nursery, a prodigious number of plants are contained within a narrow compass, which is sufficient room, as they are only to remain a short time; and that by being thus stationed in a little compass, they are more readily kept under a proper regulation for the time they are to remain in this department.

But in the public Nurseries they often plant many kinds of seedling-trees and shrubs in much closer rows at first planting out, than the distances above prescribed, not only in order to husband the ground to the best advantage, but by standing closer, it encourages the stem to shoot more directly upward, and prevents their expanding themselves much any where but at top, as for instance, many sorts of evergreens that are but of slow growth the first year or two, such as the pine-trees, firs, and several others; which the Nursery-gardeners often prick out from the seminary, first into four-feet-wide beds, in rows, length-ways, six inches asunder; and after having one or two years growth here, transplant them in rows a foot asunder; and in a year or two after give them another and final transplantation in the Nursery, in rows two or three feet asunder, as observed above; and by these different transplantings, it will encourage the roots to branch out into many horizontal fibres, and prepare them better for final transplantation, which is the more particularly necessary in several of the pine and fir kinds, and several other ever-greens, as is more fully exhibited under their proper genera.

With respect to the different methods of planting the various sorts of Nursery-plants, after being raised either by seed, layers, cuttings, &c. it is performed in several ways to different sorts; some are pricked out by dibble, others are put in by the spade, either by trenches, slitting-in, trenching, or holing; and some are drilled in by a spade or hoe.

As to most of the tree and shrub-kind, sometimes the young seedling-trees and shrubs are pricked out from the seminary by dibble; sometimes they are put in by the spade in the following methods: first, having set a line to plant by, strike the spade into the ground with its back close to the line, and give another stroke at right angles with it; then set a plant into the crevice made at the second stroke, bring it close up into the first made crevice even with the line, and press the mould close to it with the foot; then proceed to plant another in the same way, and so proceed till all is planted. A second method is for plants with rather larger roots: strike the spade down with its back close to the line, as aforesaid, and then with a spade cut out a narrow trench, close along the line, as practised in planting box edgings, making the side next the line perfectly upright; then placing the plants upright against the back of the trench close to the line, at the proper distances, before mentioned; and as you go on, trim in the earth upon their roots: and when one row is thus planted, tread the earth gently all along close to the plants; and then proceed to plant another row. A second method of planting-out small tree and shrub plants is, having set the line as above, then turning the spade edgeways to the line, cast out the earth of that spit, then a person being ready with plants, set one in the cavity close to the line, and directly taking another such spit, turn the earth in upon the roots of the plant, and then placing another plant into the second cut, cover its roots with the earth of a third spit,

ſpit, and ſo on to the end: but ſometimes, when the roots are any thing larger, holes are made along by the line wide enough to receive the roots freely every way; ſo covering them in, as above, as you go on: obſerving always to preſs the earth gently with the foot cloſe to the roots, and cloſe about the ſtems, to ſettle the plants firmly in their proper poſition.

Herbaceous fibrous-rooted plants are, for the moſt part, planted with a dibble, except when the roots are larger and ſpreading, or ſuch as are removed with balls of earth; then they are more commonly planted by holeing them in with a garden trowel, or ſmall ſpade.

Bulbous and tuberous-rooted plants, ſuch as lilies, tulips, anemonies, ranunculas, &c. are very commonly planted with a dibble, but many ſorts may alſo be drilled in with a hoe. Theſe ſorts are alſo ſometimes planted as follows: rake or trim the earth from off the top of the beds from about three to four or five inches deep, into the alleys, then place the roots in rows upon the ſurface, and immediately cover them with the earth which was drawn off into the alleys for that purpoſe, ſpreading it evenly over every part, ſo as to bury all the roots an equal depth.

But as to the tender kinds of exotic plants they require occaſional ſhelter whilſt young, many of them ſhould be potted, in order for moving to a warm ſituation in winter, or ſome into frames, &c. to have occaſional ſhelter from froſt, by glaſſes or mats, as they ſhall require; hardening them, however, by degrees, to bear the open air fully in the Nurſery they earround.

And the moſt tender kinds, that require the aid of a green-houſe and ſtove, muſt all be potted, and placed among the reſpective plants of thoſe conſervatories.

With reſpect to the management of the various hardy Nurſery-plants;

Thoſe deſigned as ſtocks for fruit-trees ſhould have their ſtems generally cleared from lateral ſhoots, ſo as to form a clean ſtraight ſtem, but never to ſhorten the leading ſhoot, unleſs it be decayed, or become very crooked, in which caſe it may be proper to cut it down low in ſpring, and it will ſhoot out again; training the main ſhoot for a ſtem, with its top entire for the preſent, till grafted or budded; and as to the grafting and budding them, that work is full directed under theſe articles, and their general method of training, whether for dwarfs or ſtandards, is alſo particularly exhibited under thoſe two heads, and in the reſpective genera of the various ſorts.

Foreſt-trees ſhould alſo be encouraged to form ſtraight clean ſtems, by occaſional trimming off the largeſt lateral branches, which will alſo promote the leading top-ſhoot in aſpiring farther in height; always ſuffering that part of each tree to ſhoot at full length, that is not to top it, unleſs, however, where the ſtem divides into forks, to trim off the weakeſt, and leave the ſtraighteſt and ſtrongeſt ſhoot or branch, to ſhoot out at its proper length to form the top, as above.

The different ſorts of ſhrubs may either be ſuffered to branch out in their own natural way, except juſt regulating very irregular growths; or ſome may be trained with ſingle clean ſtems, from about a foot to two or three high, according as you ſhall think proper with reſpect to the ſorts or purpoſes for which you deſign them in the ſhrubbery; but many ſhrubs appear the moſt agreeable when permitted to ſhoot out laterally all the way, ſo as be branchy or feathered to the bottom.

All the fruit-trees, as ſoon as grafted or budded, ſhould have all their different varieties numbered by placing large flat-ſided ſticks at the ends of the rows, for which purpoſe many of the London Nurſery-men uſe the ſpokes of old coach-wheels, or any thing about that ſize of any durable wood, painting or marking the numbers therenn, 1, 2, 3, &c. to different ſticks, entering the numbers in the Nurſery-book, with the name of the varieties to which the number-ſticks are placed; whereby you can always readily have recourſe to the ſorts wanted.

The ſame method may be practiſed to any other trees, ſhrubs, or herbaceous plants, eſpecially the varieties of particular ſorts, when they are numerous, ſuch as in many of the flowery-tribe, as as auriculas, carnations, tulips, anemonies, ranunculas, and the like.

With respect to watering the Nursery-plants; this may be very requisite in dry hot weather in spring and summer, to seed-beds and tender seedling-plants, while young, and when first planted out till they have taken good root; also occasionally to new-layed layers, and newly-planted cuttings, in dry warm weather; but as to hardy trees and shrubs of all sorts, if planted out at the proper time, that is, not too late in spring, no great regard need be paid to watering, for they will generally succeed very well without any: indeed where there is but a few, you may if you please water them a little, if it proves a very dry spring in April and May; but where there are great plantations, it would be an almost insupportable fatigue, and great expence; as in many public Nurseries, where they each winter or spring plant out fifty or sixty thousand trees and shrubs, and in some double those numbers.

Every winter or spring, the ground between the rows of all sorts of transplanted plants in the open Nursery-quarters must be digged; this is particulaly necessary to all the tree and shrub-kind that stand wide enough in rows to admit the spade between; which work is by the Nursery-men called turning-in; the most general season for which is any time from October or November until March, but the sooner it is done the more advantageous it will prove to the plants. The ground is to be digged but one spade deep, proceeding row by row, turning the top of each spit clean to the bottom, that all weeds on the top may be buried a proper depth to rot: this work of turning-in is a most necessary annual operation, both to destroy weeds, and to increase the growth of the young Nursery-plants.

In summer be remarkably attentive to keep all sorts clean from weeds; the seedlings growing close in the seminary-beds must be hand-weeded, except the plants of all sorts that grow in rows wide enough to introduce an hoe: this will prove not only the most expeditious method of destroying weeds, but by loosening the top of the soil, it will prove good culture in promoting the growth of all kinds of plants: always perform this work of hoeing in dry weather, in due time before the weeds grow large, and you may soon go over a large space of ground, either with a large drawing-hoe, or with a scuffling hoe, as you shall find the most convenient.

According as any quarter or compartment of the Nursery-ground is cleared from plants, others must be substituted in their room from the seminary; but the ground should previously be trenched and lie some time fallow, to recruit or recover its former vigour; giving it also the addition of manure, if it shall seem proper; and after being trenched in ridges, and having the repose only of one winter, or summer, or a year at most, it will sufficiently recover its vegetative force, and may be planted afresh.

It will be of advantage to plant the ground with plants of a different kind from those which occupied it before.

The tender or exotic plants of all kinds that require shelter only from frost, whilst young, as we formerly mentioned, and by degrees become hardy enough to live in the open air, should, such of them as are seedlings in the open grounds, have the beds arched over with hoops, or rods, at the approach of winter, in order to be sheltered with mats in severe weather; and those which are in pots, either seedlings or transplanted plants, should be removed in October in their pots to a warm sunny situation, sheltered with hedges, &c. placing some close under the fences facing the sun, where they may have occasional covering of mats in frosty weather; others that are more tender may be placed in frames, to have occasional covering either of glass-lights or mats, &c. from frost; observing of all those sorts here alluded to, that they are gradually to be hardened to the open ground, and need only be covered in frosty weather; at all other times let them remain fully exposed, and by degrees, as they acquire age and strength, inure them to bear the open air fully; so as when they arrive at from two or three to four or five years old, they may be turned out into the open ground. The sorts requiring this treatment are pointed out under their proper heads.

NUT. *See* FILBERT.

Bladder NUT. *See* BLADDER.

Earth NUT. *See* EARTH.

Phyſic NUT. This plant grows naturally in the Weſt-India iſlands, where the ſeeds are uſed as phyſic; it riſes with a ſtalk to the height of 12 or 14 feet.

Piſtachio NUT. *See* *Piſtachio.*

Malabar NUT. *See* MALABAR.

Wall NUT. *See* WALNUT.

NUTMEG, [*Nux Moſchata.*]. The kernel of a roundiſh nut which grows in the Eaſt-Indies. The outſide covering of this fruit is ſoft and fleſhy, like that of a walnut, and ſpontaneouſly opens when the nut grows ripe; immediately under this lies the mace, which forms a kind of reticular covering; through the fiſſures whereof appears a hard woody ſhell that includes the nutmeg. Theſe kernels have long been made uſe of both for medicinal and culinary purpoſes, and deſervedly looked upon as a warm agreeable aromatic. They are ſuppoſed likewiſe to have an aſtringent virtue; and are employed in that intention in diarrhœas and dyſenteries. Their aſtringency is ſaid to be increaſed by torrefaction, but this does not appear to the taſte: this treatment certainly deprives the ſpice of ſome of its finer oil, and therefore renders it leſs efficacious to any good purpoſe; and if we may reaſon from analogy, probably abates of its aſtringency. Nutmegs diſtilled with water, afford a large quantity of eſſential oil, reſembling in flavour the ſpice itſelf; after the diſtillation, an inſipid ſebaceous matter is found ſwimming on the water; the decoction, inſpiſſated, gives an extract of an unctuous, very lightly bitteriſh taſte and with little or no aſtringency. Rectified ſpirit extracts the whole virtue of nutmegs by infuſion, and elevates very little of it in diſtillation: hence the ſpirituous extract poſſeſſes the flavour of the ſpice in an eminent degree.

Nutmegs yield to the preſs (heated) a conſiderable quantity of limpid yellow oil, which in cooling concretes into a ſebaceous conſiſtence. In the ſhops we meet with three ſorts of unctuous ſubſtances, called oil of mace, though really expreſſed from the nutmeg. The beſt is brought from the Eaſt-Indies, in ſtone jars; this is of a thick conſiſtence, of the colour of mace, and an agreeable fragrant ſmell: the ſecond ſort, which is paler coloured and much inferior in quality, comes from Holland in ſolid maſſes, generally flat and of a ſquare figure: the third, which is the worſt of all, and uſually called common oil of mace, is an artificial compoſition of ſerum, palm oil, and the like, flavoured with a little genuine oil of the nutmeg. Theſe oils yield all that part in which their aromatic flavour reſides, in diſtillation, to water, and to pure ſpirit by infuſion: the diſtilled liquor and ſpirituous tincture nearly reſemble in quality thoſe prepared immediately from the nutmeg. The officinal preparations of nutmegs are, a ſpirituous water, eſſential oil, and the nutmegs in ſubſtance roaſted. The nutmeg itſelf is uſed in the compound horſeradiſh water, compound ſpirit of lavender, cordial confection, cardialgic troches, and ſyrup of buckthorn; its eſſential oil, in the volatile aromatic ſpirit, and the expreſſed oil in mithridate and theriaca, ſtomachic and cephalic plaſters and cephalic balſam.

NUX VOMICA. This is the poiſonous ſeed of a plant growing in Malabar. Used to kill Rats

O.

OAK, [*Quercus.*] Botanists and nurserymen reckon a great number of species; but as we write chiefly for the use of the farmer, we shall confine ourselves to the cultivation of the sovereign of the woods.

The oak is a large tree with a rough bark, spreading branches, and large leaves, deeply waved at the edges: the flowers are inconsiderable; they are a kind of brown threads: the fruit is the acorn, standing in a cup, and growing in some trees on a longer, and in others on a shorter foot-stalk; from which difference some have distinguished two kinds of oak. Others have, in the same manner, divided the oak into two kinds, one of which rises more in height, and the other, which they call the wild oak, spreads more into branches. But these are accidental varieties, not distinct kinds.

The oak will grow in almost any soil: this we see in fact, as we find oaks on all kinds of land. We see it on clayey, sandy, and stony ground: but those who have made strict observations declare, that in the clayey soils it obtains most firmness, but in these the growth is slow. The best earth for oak, where there is choice, is a rich loam. This is a sound and commonly a deep soil. Too much wet is an enemy to the oak, so that it should be guarded against; and 'tis principally for this reason that it grows best on somewhat rising grounds, for they are naturally more dry than the absolute flats on which the wet lodges and remains.

When the ground is too moist, the oak puts out most branches, and the trunk is defrauded of its due nourishment; in very dry and exposed places it grows low and stubbed.

The timber in too moist ground is softer, and in these hilly and barren places it is harder than its usual quality, but 'tis there of an uneven grain, and less useful.

The finest oak timber is that which has grown on a firm good soil, rather inclining to clay than any other particular quality, and where there is not too much moisture.

The oak is propagated three ways; first, from seed, or the acorn; second, by raising in a nursery, and then transplanting; and, thridly, by taking up young sets out of the woods, where they have risen from the fallen acorns, and are usually plentiful enough.

Of these methods we altogether prefer that of raising the oak from the acorn, in the place where it is to grow. The oaks from the nursery are commonly twice transplanted to come to their standing place, and this gives them two checks greater or less; and disposes them twice to an unevenness in the growth: as to the sets taken out of woods, they are the worst way of all. Idleness or frugality may tempt those who will not raise, or purchase the young sets out of a nursery, to do this, but these wild ones, having been raised under too much shade, are usually very ill shaped; and as they are planted out into more exposed places, they commonly get an ill growth.

Of raising Oaks by Transplantation.

If any one in spite of these disadvantages will plant the wild sets, the method he is to take is to cut them off close to the ground, with a sharp knife, and by a slanting stroke, as soon as they are planted. This gives the root time to recover some strength, and as it affords a new shoot, that is often better than the original plant. But in this case the disadvantage is plain, for it is evident that it would be better

this

this ſhoot roſe from the root than from a ſtump.

Thoſe who raiſe oaks in a nurſery for tranſplantation muſt obſerve a different method from what is to be followed by ſuch as ſow them where they are to ſtand. They are to proceed thus. Let the acorns be ſhook, as ſoon as fully ripe, from a ſtout branch of a well-growing oak, and immediately ſown in the nurſery, for the air withers them.

They are to be ſet in lines, at two inches aſunder, and about two inches and a half deep in the ground. They will ſhoot the ſucceeding ſpring, and they ſhould be ſuffer'd to ſtand till that time twelvemonth: then they are to be tranſplanted into another part of the nurſery, and ſet at eighteen inches diſtance, in rows three feet aſunder. They are to be watered a little when firſt tranſplanted, but this muſt be carefully done, for too much water is apt to hurt the oak, eſpecially when young.

The oak is a particular tree, and requires, as will as deſerves, a particular care in its management. In many little reſpects the conduct is to be different from that obſerved in the raiſing the generality of trees; and it is to a want of regard to theſe, that ſo many young oaks are loſt more than of other trees.

The young trees thus tranſplanted are to be watered ſometimes in dry ſeaſons, and kept clear from weeds. It is alſo good to dig between the rows: for this, by breaking the ſoil, affords them a greater ſupply of nouriſhment, and at the ſame time it cuts off the ſtraggling or far-ſpreading roots, which will make the young trees bear their next tranſplantation the better.

During the time they ſtand in theſe beds they are to be regulated in their growth, but in this only a little is to be done. They who cut off the head deſtroy the tree, for if there be not a leading ſhoot to conduct the top, the whole will periſh. Neither are many of the ſide branches to be taken off, but only ſuch as tend to too much ſpreading. The planter is to remember that the trunk of the oak is to be his beſt benefit; he muſt therefore cut off ſuch very ſpreading branches, as would draw the ſap away from it and ſtarve it: but it is prudent to leave a competent number of the others, to draw up the ſap. When an oak in this young ſtate is too cloſe pruned, the head is always ſeen to grow over proportioned, and weighs down the tree, and ſpoils its future progreſs.

When the trees have ſtood about four years; that is, when they are between five and ſix years old from the ſowing, they may be conveniently tranſplanted. They are at this time of a pretty ſize and having been thus pruned ſhew well. It is dangerous to move them in the common way, when they are older, for the oak bears removing, when grown to a ſize, worſe than any other tree.

The time for tranſplanting them is juſt before they begin to ſhoot; and it is prudent to chuſe a ſhowery ſeaſon: if no rain fall, they muſt be gently watered, as before directed, and ſtaked up to keep them ſtrait.

This is the method for raiſing oaks by tranſplantation; and when they are wanted for beauty and ornament, as for chumps in parks, and for wilderneſſes in large gardens, this is a very good way, becauſe they may be had of a proper growth from the common nurſeries: or from the owner's own ſtock, raiſed there for other purpoſes. But when oaks are intended for timber; and uſe and value are more ſtudied than ornament; 'tis by much the beſt method to raiſe them from the acorn, in the places where they are always to continue.

Of raiſing Oaks from the Acorn.

When the oak is to be raiſed immediately from the acorn, a different method, and different ſeaſon, are to be obſerved for ſowing.

Let the acorns be gathered when full ripe, from a thriving tree, and immediately ſpread upon the floor of a dry ſhady room; when they have lain a week, frequently turning them, let them be put up in large garden pots, with a quantity of dry ſand, and laid by for the winter.

Early in ſpring let the ground be marked out where the plantation is to be made, and at the diſtance of forty feet every way, let the holes be opened for receiving the ſeed. Theſe are to be dug two ſpit deep, and the earth well broken

broken, four or five acrons ready to put into each, and covered two inches deep, and when they have ſhot, and acquired a litt[illegible]wth, all the plants, except the one beſt in each hole, are to be taken up, and that ſingle plant in each hole is to be nurſed up for ſome years with due care.

The head of theſe young trees is to be ſuffered to grow, and none of the branches are to be cut away, except ſuch as ſpread out too wide, as in the nurſery; and if it happen that in ſpite of the care in the choice of thoſe ſhoots which have been ſuffered to ſtand, any one be uneven; the beſt method is to cut it off at the ground, and wait for a new and better ſhoot.

A plantation of oak thus made, if the ſoil be tolerable, is a fortune for the ſucceſſor in the eſtate; but it is not limited to that; men enter too late upon theſe ſtudies, otherwiſe they might reap the benefit of their plantations themſelves. If a man would begin to plant at eight and twenty, and ſhould live to ſee ſixty-three, there is a ſpace of five and thirty years, which is a time for raiſing even an oak plantation, ſlow as that is in growth, to very conſiderable value, though not to its full price, or nearly to that.

It is not eaſy to give what can be called a middle calculation for the growth of the oak, it differs ſo prodigiouſly in reſpect of the ſoil, ſituation, and other circumſtances. We have ſeen oaks of thirty four years fourteen inches in diamater.

An oak of this bigneſs is but advancing toward the proper time of felling, and towards its value; but if the neceſſities of the owner induce him to ſell theſe, the price of the worſt tree among them would pay for the labour and charge of the plantation.

If the young plants, when they riſe in theſe ſpots, appear almoſt above the ground, or ſtand too high with their roots, the beſt method is to lay up a parcel of fine earth againſt the bottom of that which is the moſt thriving ſhoot. This happens ſometimes from the acorns being not ſet deep enough, and ſometimes from the weather: for after a froſt the mould will riſe, and bear up the young ſhoot with it.

Acorns are not to be buried too deep, eſpecially in a moiſt ſoil, for they often rot: and, on the other hand, they muſt not be ſet too ſhallow: for it not only makes the ſhoot ſtand too high; but frequently the field mice find them out, and devour the hopes of the plantation.

The quantity of ground taken up by this plantation, at forty feet diſtance, is not to be ſuppoſed waſted: for though the oaks will, in their larger growth, require that diſtance, they do not at firſt. For many years aſhes may be raiſed upon the ground between the oaks, for poles, and cut to a great advantge. Underwood of all the ſhrubby or coppice wood kinds may alſo be planted for a time, if the ground be fit for it: or it may be grazed, and will loſe little of its value for many years. Nay, the planting the trees at this diſtance is the only way to preſerve a value in the ground for theſe purpoſes; and when the ſoil is good, it will continue to yield fine paſture.

Of the Uſes of the Oak.

No plantation whatſoever exceeds that of oak, when made in this manner: and to thoſe who will ſuffer it to ſtand a proper time, none equals it in value. By this management the trees will all riſe with a ſingle ſtrait and upright ſtem, and their branches ſpreading every way with a beautiful regularity, make, when cloathed with their large and fair leaves, a beautiful appearance. Their ſhade is preferable to that of any tree whatſoever: their very imperfections and excreſcences, the oak apples, oak cones, and oak grapes, are beautiful; and the air is perfumed and rendered healthy by blowing over them.

Among the excreſcences of the oak, we have not followed the common cuſtom of ranking the herb, called miſletoe; becauſe it is not an excreſcence, but a regular plant, riſing from its own ſeeds, but whoſe place of growth is not the ground, but the bark of ſome tree; and no trees afford it ſo ſeldom as the oak.

Its fruit, which a good and well-grown oak bears annually in vaſt abundance, is an excellent food for Hogs. No fruit feeds them ſo well, it gives their fleſh alſo an excellent taſte. The flavour of the Weſtphalia hams is owing to this food. They are made from wild swine that live in the forests; and it would, doubtless, be an improvement of our hogs flesh intended for that service, if the creature were fed with acorns; which can only be done to advantage by letting them run about.

That they give a flavour to the flesh of such hogs as eat them in abundance, is not to be questioned; for our country people, who are not accustomed to that taste in bacon, always feed their hogs some time with pease after the acorns, to take off the flavour.

The effect of food on creatures in giving a taste to their flesh, is not to be doubted. The Heath-Cock of Germany is not eatable in autumn, except by the peasants, because its flesh tastes so strongly of the Juniper berries he eats at that season; and as to the effect of particular food on hogs, an instance is given in the Phisophical Transactions of the very bones of a pig being tinged red, by its eating madder root at a dyer's.

The hog is the creature that eats acorns most freely and naturally, and is best fed with them; but what nature has meant as food to one animal, may, by proper management, or in necessity, be made food to others; all poultry will eat acorns if broke small, and given them among other food, and nothing fattens them more. They have also been given to oxen, and other cattle, among their dry food; and we read that before the cultivation of land was so well known, they were, in part, the food of mankind.

Their effect in fattening the hog is supported by sufficient experience. A peck of acorns a day, with a little bran, will, it is affirmed, upon good authority, make a healthy hog encrease a pound each day in his weight, for fifty or sixty days together.

The bark of the Oak serves the tanner, and fetches a large price; the dyers also use it: and it has been discovered some years since, that the young branches of the oak cut and ground to pieces in a mill, answer all the purposes of the bark, and that in as great perfection on these occasions.

We have mentioned saw-dust among the articles useful as manures; and experience shews that none is so excellent for that purpose as the dust of the oak: this is natural enough, because the oak is the most firm and solid of all our timber. Those who have tryed the experiment say also, that of the kinds of wood ashes used in dressing of land, the oak claims greatly preference.

All these however are but, as it were, accidental articles of value in the oak, its great worth is in the timber, which in solidity, strength, and soundness, exceeds all our other kinds, and is therefore the most fit for great and lasting uses. Of all kinds of wood yet known in this part of the globe, the oak is in its service the most universal.

Beside its prodigious use in our shipping, it is called for, on a thousand occasions, in buildings, and for instruments. It resists the injuries of weather more than any other wood, which is not a wonder; for even the fire takes effect upon it much slower than on any other timber whatsoever: and some of it is so hard that the best tools will scarce work upon it.

In water-works, where the timber is exposed both to the air and the water, no wood stands like the oak: and no wood is equal to it in the support of burthens. The ebony and some other foreign woods, when they are very hard and firm, cut as difficultly as oak, but if they are tryed in the supporting of burthens, they start and fly under half the weight that a piece of oak of the same size will support with perfect safety.

Even the defects, as they naturally appear of oak, serve to give it strength for certain particular purposes. Thus it is not unusual for an oak trunk to grow a little twisted: this may be discovered through the bark as it is standing, but is very visible when the tree is felled and stripp'd: the trunk of such an oak is useful beyond any other, for the supporting vast weights. Where posts and columns are required for such a purpose, nothing equals it.

In buildings, the straitest, finest, and evenest growing pieces of oak are usually wanted, and they bring their price accordingly; but for engines, where a vast strength is required, the body of one of those stubbed, and rough grained oaks, which are not fit for other purposes, and which are so hard that a tool will scarce pierce them, is superior to any thing.

There is no oak, while sound, that is not fitted for some purpose. Those parts which will not do for greater uses make pales, posts, coopers ware, and laths; all which bring their price to the owner: even the least pieces are worked into the pins and pegs used in tyling, and that way are of value.

Oaks that grow crooked, and firm withal, make what they call knee timber for shipping. The knottiest and roughest peices are fit for piles in water-works; and mill wheels, and spokes for other wheels, are made from the proper pieces.

Beside all the uses of the oak in its various conditions, considered as a timber tree, we are yet to consider it as a part of the coppice wood plantation; and no kind is there more valuable. The oak maintains its character in every condition, and is every where of value.

When the oak is sown among the coppice wood, to be felled with it at twelve or fourteen years growth, it yields excellent poles for hoops. 'Tis usual to make these of ash, and some take hazel; but the preference is due to the oak hoop beyond all degree of comparison: the ash does not exceed the hazel for hoops half so much as oak exceeds the ash. An oak hoop will last out seven of any other timber.

The smaller kinds of poles serve as staves, and the least make our walking sticks. The root of the oak, where it is knotty and firm, has also great beauty when used by the turner or inlayer.

Thus we see that this serviceable and universally useful tree supplies us with materials of all kinds, as timber, from the ribs of a man of war to a walking staff, and from the main beam of a house to the pegs in the tiling; not the least particle of it but is useful. Even such as is fit for nothing else in the coppice oak is good for firing; whether split into billets from the larger pieces, or cut into faggots, it excels other wood. The charcoal that is made of the oak is better than any other.

Of the Growth of Oak Trees.

The growth of the oak is not only vary different on various soils; but it has been found by nice observation, to very exceedingly at different periods on the same place. For instance, an oak has been observed to grow very freely and very well for twenty successive years: at the end of this time it has come to a stop, and has for ten or a dozen years made little progress. From this time it has begun to grow again, and has continued in its usual way increasing visibly in height and thickness.

This, though seeming to arise from some hidden cause in the tree itself, is really owing to the soil. The tree being planted in a good earth, spreads out its roots, and flourishes extreamly well, so long as they remain within the compass of that coat or layer of the ground; but when they have pierced through that, and got into some other starving and poor earth, they receive little nourishment, and the tree comes to a stand. It would continue so all along, were it not that the same roots pushing deeper and farther, find good soil again. Thus in the present instance, the good soil holds the roots twenty years, and affording sufficient nourishment, the tree all that while grows freely. At the end of that time they penetrate into some unfavourable layer; there they are kept twelve years, all which time the tree barely lives, and hardly grows at all; till at the end of this period the roots piercing into another bed of good matter, supply the tree as at first, and it then grows and increases again as it did from the beginning.

It has been observed already, that the oak will grow in any soil, though it thrives differently according to the nature of that earth: but the difference that is made by soils in the speedyness or slowness of the oak is not all: for the very grain of the wood is affected by it.

On barren heaths, where the bottom is stony, the oak is ill-grained and coarse: the grain of that oak which has been raised in sandy soils, is smoother

ſmoother and evener than any: but that which has been fed by a good firm loam, inclining to clayey, is the right ſubſtantial and true grained timber.

Though the oak will grow any where, it will be ſtopped in its growth by the interpoſition of a bed of unſavourable matter in its way; it will therefore be worth the planter's while to bore the earth with an auger where an oak plantation is deſigned to be raiſed: and that the planter may know to what a vaſt ſize and value oaks will grow when the ſoil favours them, not only in condition, but depth, we ſhall give him an account of what bigneſs ſome have ariſen to in England, as ſupported by unqueſtionable authority.

In Workſop Park the Duke of Norfork had an oak which ſpread almoſt three thouſand ſquare yards. Near a thouſand horſe might ſtand under the ſhade of it: Plot, in his Oxfordſhire, tells us of an oak at Clifton, that ſpread eighty-one feet from bough end to bough end, and ſhaded 560 ſquare yards of ground. 'Twas computed five and twenty hundred men might ſtand ſheltered under it. The famous Robur Britanicum in Lord Norrey's park at Ricot, was computed to be able to ſhelter between four and five thouſand men.

The mainmaſt of the old Royal Sovereign was ninety-nine feet long, and near a yard thick, all of one piece of oak; and ſome of the beams of that ſhip were made from another oak near five feet thick, and were forty feet in length.

What muſt be the value of theſe trees is very evident; and there is no reaſon why any man who will take the pains in raiſing his oaks from the acorn upon the ſpot with due care, and ſee that the ſoil be perfectly fit for the growth, may not leave an inheritance of ſuch to his poſterity.

The oak requires leſs lopping than any other tree, whether it be intended for beauty, or for uſe. Nature rarely over-proportions the branches to the trunk; and they ſpread with great beauty, and grow in value with it.

Of the Felling of the Oak.

If it be true that an oak continues growing a hundred years, certainly 'tis beſt not to fell that tree till after the full period of the growth, when it can conveniently be ſuffered to ſtand ſo long; but with a view of advantage, it is idle to think of its ſtanding any longer: for certainly it can never be better than when at a full maturity.

This then is, in general, the beſt time of felling, but no particular period can be limited for each tree; for of thoſe raiſed from acorns of the ſame ſoil, ſome will thrive better than others.

More things enter into the conſideration in the article of felling the oak than any other timber; as the ſeparating of the bark for the tanners, and the like. The beſt ſeaſon is in April, which favours the ſeparation of the bark; it then riſing freely and eaſily.

At this ſeaſon the trees being marked out that are to be felled, the firſt thing to be done is to cut off ſuch arms as may damage the trunk in the fall. The manner of doing this is, by beginning below cloſe to the trunk: when they have thus cut the arm about a ſixth part through, they begin at the top near the trunk alſo, and when they come near meeting the other cutting, the arm falls off without ſplitting.

When the branches that may be hurtful in the fall are thus removed, they are to go to work upon the trunk, cutting it down as near as poſſible to the ground, becauſe the length of the timber is a very great article in its value beſide the adding to its quantity.

When the oak is down, its trunk is to be ſtripped of the bark, which will come off freely at this ſeaſon, becauſe the ſap is full and flowing; as the bark is taken off, ſet it up in ſuch a manner as it may dry beſt. After this take off the bark from the branches that were left on, and ſet up in like manner: when this is done, let the branches be cut off, and then cut it into lengths for ſale.

Of the ſeaſoning Oak, and judging of the Timber.

The wood being thus felled and cut, the next conſideration is the ſeaſoning of it, which is done ſeveral ways; but all of them require time. Green oak is fit for very few purpoſes; and a great deal of its value in many caſes depends upon the ſeaſoning.

The plaineſt and moſt familiar method is to truſt to time only, taking care to prevent accidents in the mean while. Thus let the timber, cut as before directed, be laid up till dry in a careful manner. Let it be taken off the ground at a dry time, and laid up in an airy place, but out of the reach of the sun, and defended from the winds, both which crack it in drying. Let blocks be put between the several pieces, to give passage to the air. If this be omitted, they grow moist and mouldy, or breed toadstools. In this manner time will take a proper effect, the timber will shrink gradually and regularly, and being thus seasoned, it will stand when it is employed in building, or on other occasions.

Another way of seasoning oak timber is by burying it for some time under ground: but this must be done in a dry soil, otherwise it will require more seasoning when it comes out than it did when it was put in.

The best method of all for many purposes, and particularly those which require the best seasoned timber, is that we learned of the Venetians, which is called the water seasoning. This is done by sinking the timber under water; and no way is so good to prevent its splitting. The Venetians keep the timber for their sea service two or three years under water before they use it, and then it stands firmly.

The water seasoning is commonly done in England in this manner. When the oak is cut into boards, or pieces, they sink it under river water for fourteen or fifteen days. Then they take it out, and lay it up carefully to dry in a cool airy place, as directed in piling up the fresh timber; preserving it from winds and sun, but leaving the air free passage amongst it.

Oak that is cleft is not so apt to split and crack as such as is entire: and round pieces are always more ready to crack than such as are squared. These are standing rules, and the workman it to conduct himself in his choice accordingly: pieces that are bored through seldom split. In general, the more the oak is in its natural condition, the more liable it is to split; and the more it has been cut and wrought, the less.

Burning the ends of posts of oak that are to be let into the ground, has been accounted an excellent method to preserve them a long time; and some have carried this practice so far, as to burn the ends so deep as to impair their strength. It is at present much disputed by those who pretend experience on their side, whether this practice be of any use at all. If not, 'tis a great deal of trouble thrown away.

This burning naturally preserves that part of the post from the worms by which it is subject to be gnawed under ground; and the Dutch, to prevent the same accident under water, cover over their piles and ship bottoms with pitch and tar; on which they sprinkle sea sand with powder of sea shells among it, and flakes of iron, such as fly off in the hammering.

In the choice of oak timber, the purchaser should examine the weight and the grain; the heaviest timber in this kind is always the best for purposes that require great strength and soundness, and the smoother and evener the grain, the better for most occasions. Oak is not to be trusted in any nice works, till it has been well seasoned: and that from full-grown trees is preferable to such as has been cut from smaller. But when the tree has stood beyond its time, the wood becomes somewhat brittle; this is the first tendency in oak to decay.

To judge of oak as it stands is an article of great consequence very frequently, and nothing is so difficult: it is a common thing to purchase trees standing; and in oak 'tis of great importance to be able to guess at their value. Were all good, nothing would be so easy; for the question might be answered by measuring, instead of guessing; but nothing is so capable of deceiving as a tree while it stands. There may be many infirmities which 'tis impossible to discover till it is down; and which then greatly lessen the value. Such as may be discovered we shall point out; as also the signs of decay.

In the first place, if the head of the tree be in any part dead, 'tis a shrewd sign that there are more faults in the body: in this case it is a very good method to bore into the trunk with a small piercer made auger fashion, and observe the condition of what it draws out.

If in any tree there be a swelling vein perceived rising above the level of the rest of the tree, and covered by the bark, it is a sign all is not well within. When this vein twists about in the manner of a stalk of ivy, it is worst of all; and seldom is seen but where the heart of the trunk is rotten.

Finally, another very good method of judging is, to open the earth about the roots; and examine in what condition they appear. If they are fresh, sound, and full of juice, it is a sign all is well above; but on the contrary, when many of them are found decayed without any visible cause in the ground; when some of them are rotten, brittle, and mouldy, all is wrong in the body of the tree. This is a part not so much attended to, but a decay here is a more fatal sign than the deadness of a part of the head.

Upon the whole, a great deal is to be judged by the general aspect, and that much more by those who are accustomed to these things than by strangers. There is a look of health in a tree that is perfectly well and sound, which no other perfectly has. And tho' people who should be judges are often deceived, yet it is their want of observation, or their want of knowledge, that often leads them to it. There will be faults which no person whatsoever can discover till they are seen in cutting through the tree; but the greater part of those which debase the value, are not of this kind: they may be guessed at least, if not certainly known, from some one or another of these marks on a careful inspection.

Ever-green OAK, [*Ilex.*] Holly. *See* HOLLY.

OAK *of Jerusalem*, [*Botrys.*] This plant is a native of America, where the seeds are given for worms in children. It is propagated by sowing the seeds in the spring.

OAK *Bark. See* BARK.

OATS, [*Avena.*] The oat is distinguished from other corn, by the grain growing in loose panicles.

There are three principal sorts of it.

1. The common, or manured white.

2. The black oats: which are omitted in Gerard and Parkinson, though in some parts of England they are more sowed than the former.

3. The naked oat: much sowed in Cornwall.

To these we may added two others, very considerable.

4. The red or brown oats; and some, I suppose, reckon these the red and the gray, and all of them comprise the large Poland oat under the name of white; the seed of it being brought from Poland, gave it that name. And as it degenerates here in a few years, it is often brought new from thence. It is apt to shed after rain.

The white oat has undoubtedly the larger kernel, and turns out more meal in the grinding than the black oat; the meal of a bushel of the white being near three pecks from the miln, and that of the black but two pecks; but then the white oat requires richer land, and will not bear cold so well; and as to every other article, but what they call the yield, the black is equal to the white, if not superior in some particulars.

Oats, being a very temperate mild grain, are fit for almost all manner of uses and purposes any sorts of corn can be; and being an hardy grain, it will grow in almost any soil, and that with the least culture of any grain whatsoever, and being very prolific, will all things considered, be found the most profitable of any grain whatsoever (except wheat.)

It is commonly known and observed, what great fatigues and labours the Scotch have frequently gone through, when supported only by a small quantity of oatmeal, which is a manifest proof of the goodness and spirit of that grain that could enable man to go through such toils and labours; and it is very well known, that most of the northern peasants have little else to support them in their hard labours, particularly in that of getting of stone; in which work they have been known to sweat day after day, with no other nourishment but oat cake (bread) and water; and the better of them, with only an addition of a little butter and cheese, and a little whey or butter-milk to drink, seldom tasting flesh meat or any malt liquor whatsoever.

Oats, when malted, make a very pleasant ale, and are frequently used for

for that purpose: and they are used in the kitchen in a thousand particulars, in which the flour is preferred to the flour of all other grains; and there is no pretence to set up any other as equal to it, except wheat, which to be sure is to be preferred before it.

It is also exceeding proper for the feeding of all sorts of fowls, and swine, making the sweetest bacon of all feeds; though it is thought very adviseable to give the swine a few pease, toward the end of their feeding, in order to harden their fat.

The excellency of oats, as the best and most wholesome food for horses, is allowed by all; and that, when they have been kept till they are thoroughly dry, there is no danger of those distempers which commonly attend, and are frequently fatal to those fed on beans.

They are equally useful for the feeding the cow or the ewe, to help them to milk, and to nourish their young; and at the same time will support the ox in his labour, or feed him fat for the slaughter. And the straw is valuable for food for beasts, beyond that of all grain, and when some of the lightest oats are left in it, and only the best threshed out (which is called batting) it is thought very good food for beasts; and packs of hounds, and all other dogs, are commonly fed with oats, when ground down.

As to the soils, it has been mentioned that they will grow on all, and do very well on most, where a crop of corn can be reasonably expected; yet oats certainly do best on the best ground, for which we may appeal to common experience, when they are sown at the first breaking up good ground, or when the ground is well manured for them, which is common in the north; and in the instances before, and which will be mentioned hereafter, also fully confirm the truth of this.

The seed usually allowed for an acre is four Bushels; but in several places, they sow six or more, where the ground is poor, or where such an ill custom has prevailed. In this article of seed, the farmer ought to be careful in getting what is good, and changing it from different sorts of soils as in any kind of grain whatsoever, since he will find it equally beneficia.

Formerly they used not to sow oats till March, but of late years they commonly plow for them at the beginning of February, and sow and harrow them in from the middle of February, and so on; and now apply to them in this particular, the saying, the sooner in the ground the sooner out; and find by experience, that their crops are generally ripe sooner than they formerly were when sowed later.

If the sowing be deferred long, as it sometimes is till April, then it should be well harrowed in; and in some places the wetness of the land almost obliges the farmer to the sowing so late.

Miller mentions oats as a very profitable grain, and that the usual produce is five and twenty bushels; though he has sometimes known more than thirty on an acre. This is a very poor account of the produce of this grain, since four quarters are common on very indifferent ground; and six or seven is no extraordinary crop; and ten quarters are frequently had with only one plowing without any further trouble.

There are three very considerable advantages the oat claims, which no other of the white corns do; nor, indeed, any other sort of grain common amongst us, has any pretence to vie with it in, with the least appearance of reason.

The first is, that it will grow and pay frequently very well on those lands, which will not answer to the sowing any other sort of grain: and this advantage is generally allowed the oat by all who write on this subject; which they have rather carried to an excess in its behalf, when they say, it will grow in all countries, and on all lands; that there is no ground too rich or too poor for it; which cannot be said of any other grain whatsoever. So that in this respect oats have undoubtedly the advantage above all other grain whatsoever.

The next advantage of the oat is, that it is pretty certain to bring a very good crop, on the breaking up any any good meadow or pasture ground.

The third particular advantage of the

the oat is, the benefit ariſing from the goodneſs of the ſtraw for food for cattle; and, tolerable good crops may on a medium be valued at twenty ſhillings per acre, in which no other ſtraw can be compared to it as to the ſweetneſs of it for food; nor indeed is there any other ſtraw but wheat of any value to ſpeak of. And though wheat ſtraw excel it for thatch, yet oat ſtraw will laſt ſeveral years for that uſe; and, on the whole, may juſtly have its ſtraw reckoned amongſt the excellencies belonging to the oat.

There is another advantage it certainly has over the two moſt eſteemed ſorts of grain, wheat and barley, which is, that it is got with leſs plowing, requires not ſo fine a tilth, and not near ſo much manuring in general, as they do to procure an equal reſpective proportionable good crop; all which will be ſaved in the farmers out-goings.

Laſtly, It is ſuperior to all other grain but barley in its capacity of receiving the foreign graſſes to be ſowed with it, from which a great part of the advantage of all the new huſbandry particularly depends.

A late writer gives the oat the preference to barley, in this point, in the following words: "An oat crop is the "propereſt corn of all others, to ſow "any of the graſs ſeeds amongſt, if "the ground is in heart, becauſe the "ſtalks of oats are apt to ſtand ſtiffer "than barley, and thereby the crop of "graſs is in leſs danger of being "ſpoiled."

This author juſtly obſerves, "If the "ground is in heart," ſince the land ſet apart for oats is very ſeldom ſo well manured for oats, when the graſs ſeeds are to be ſown in it, as it is for barley; and, conſequently, a leſs valuable crop of the graſſes is to be expected when the land is in a poorer condition: but the right way of judging is, when they are in the ſame equal condition of goodneſs; and then to ſee, which would anſwer the beſt. But even in this caſe I would not inſiſt on its ſuperiority to barley in this particular, but only ſay it is equal to it: for the oat has other ſufficient advantages above the barley in its particular departments or on lands in which barley cannot ſo well be cultivated.

Of keeping of Oats.

The oat has one farther advantage, that it may be kept the ſecureſt and in the eaſieſt manner of moſt ſorts of grain, if not of all kinds whatſoever.

It is little ſubject to receive damage when houſed in the barn, or placed in a ſtack, on account of the nature of the ſtraw, which is both ſweet and dry, and the leaſt ſubject to be muſty of any ſort.

Oats will alſo keep very well when threſhed, and laid by in the chaff, without farther trouble or care, provided they be not laid by wet, or wet be permitted to come to them, in ſuch a degree as would ſpoil any other corn whatſoever.

But the principal method of ſecuring the product of this grain, where it is uſed as bread, is by firſt grinding it, and making it into meal, and then putting it cloſe down in an ark of wood, where it will keep good many years. This method is ſo well known in the countries where the meal is generally uſed for bread, that there is ſcarce a family but has one of theſe arks kept under lock and key, either in the dwelling-houſe, or in ſome building adjoining to it, or in their barns. In which thoſe who are able, keep a ſufficient ſtock for their families, from time to time; and thoſe who can keep it for a riſing market, often ſell at the ſame proportionable profit as thoſe do who can ſave wheat till it riſes. It is very common to put four hundred pecks of meal into one of theſe arks.

Wild OATS. A ſpecies of oats difficult to be extirpated where they have once taken poſſeſſion; for ripening before harveſt, and ſcattering their ſeed round them, they will remain in the ground till it is ploughed up again, though it be for a whole year, ſome ſay four or five years, and will then come up with the corn. The ſureſt way to deſtroy them is to lay the ground down to clover, and to mow the oats and clover together before the oats are ripe. By some called Drauck.

OCTOBER. The tenth month of the year.

Work to be done this month in the Kitchen Garden.

As October is the only time to crop a garden before winter, omit not any thing ordered now till next month.

Aromatic herbs and ſhrubs, in beds, weed; and ſpread ſome earth over them.

Aſparagus-ſtalks cut down, hoe the weeds, and ſpread earth from the paths on them.

Hotbeds prepare for forcing, and plant (three-year-old plants) for the firſt crop.

Beans, the early Mazagan, muſt be planted on a ſouth border, for the firſt crop.

Boreole, plant out the third crop, and hoe the ground about the others.

Broccoli, plant out the reſt of the fourth crop.

Cabbages, ſown in Auguſt, plant half out in a warm ſituation.

Cabbage Turneps, plant early in the month, and earth up others.

Carrots ſown in July, finiſh hoeing.

Cauliflowers, plant ſix to each glaſs, and the reſt in a frame, or under a ſouth wall.

Celery, plant out the fifth and laſt crop, and earth up the ſecond to blanch.

Coleworts, finiſh planting.

Creſs and Muſtard, ſow on a hotbed.

Endive, tie up to blanch, and plant more.

Eſchalots, Garlick, and Rocambole, plant.

Ground, which is vacant, throw in ridges.

Hoe Borecole, Brocoli, Cabbages, and Cabbage-Turneps, and draw up earth to their ſtems.

Hoe Carrots and Spinach.

Hotbeds prepare for forcing aſparagus.

Lettuces, plant out Cabbage and Brown Dutch on Aſparagus beds, ſome under glaſſes and on hotbeds for forcing.

Mint, plant in pots on a hotbed.

Muſhroom-beds cover well with ſtraw and mats, to defend them from rain.

Onions muſt be well weeded.

Peas, the early hotſpurs, ſow on a ſouth border, near the wall, for a firſt crop. As alſo

Plant Aſparagus on a hotbed, the firſt crop.

Beans, Borecole, Brocoli, Cabbages, Cabbage Turneps, Cauliflowers, Celery, Coleworts, Endive, Eſchalots, Garlick, Lettuces, Mint, Rocambole.

Plant out, to ſtand for ſeed,

Beets, Parſley, Cabbages, Parſneps, Carrots, Turneps.

Pot herbs and ſweet-herbs on beds, weed, ſtir up the earth, and ſpread more over them.

Seeds of all ſorts ſhould be threſhed out, dried, and put into bags.

Sow creſs and muſtard on hotbeds.

Peas on a ſouth border.

Spinach, hoe for the laſt time before winter.

Weeds in every part of the garden muſt be deſtroyed.

Flower Garden and Shrubbery.

Any thing ordered laſt month, if omitted, finiſh early in this.

Auriculas and Carnations remove into ſhelter, and in wet weather cover with mats.

Bulbous roots for forcing, in pots or boxes, plant, and finiſh planting all others.

Evergreens ſtill plant, but early in the month.

Graſs walks, finiſh laying.

Gravel walks, weed, and roll when dry.

Layering of ſhrubs, finiſh, if not done.

Layers and ſuckers take off, if rooted.

Leaves, ſweep up frequently.

Mignonette ſhould be removed under glaſſes, or elſe into a green-houſe, or warm cloſet.

Perennials, finiſh planting.

Plant bulbous roots, of all ſorts, in the beginning of the month, if not done.

Box and Thrift early in the month.

Perennials early in the month.

Shrubs and trees of all ſorts.

Strawberries and Thrift for edging.

Tulips, and all other bulbous roots.

Seedlings in pots, place under a ſouth wall, and weed and earth ſeedlings in beds.

Seeds, gather in the middle of the day.

Shrubberies, finiſh pruning and hoeing.

Shrubs and trees, finiſh planting.

Tulips, finiſh planting early in the month, and all ſorts of bulbous roots.

Turf, finiſh laying early in the month

Weeds ſhould be deſtroyed by hoeing and raking off, or they will take root again.

Trees and Shrubs in Flower.

Althæas, bramble, broom, climber, honeyſuckles, jeſſamin, lauruſtinus, paſſion-

paſſion-flower, roſes, ſtrawberry trees, in fruit and flower.

Flowers.

African marygolds, anemonies, aſters, auriculas, balſams, campanulas, carnations, china-aſters, china-pinks, chryſanthemums, colchiums, cyclamens, daiſies, French-marygolds, golden rods, Guernſey lilies, lupines, marvel of Peru, mignonette, naſturtiums, panſies, pinks, polyanthuſes, primroſes, ſaffron, ſcarlet beans, ſcabiuſes, ſtarworts, ſtocks, ſunflowers, ſweetpeas, ſweet ſultan, tuberoſes, wallflowers, and ſome others.

Fruit Garden and Orchard.

Apples and pears gather in the middle of fine dry days, and plant the trees the end of the month.

Currants, gooſeberries, and raſpberries plant.

Nectarines and peaches plant.

Orchard or fruit-trees intended to be planted ſhould have the ground prepared and the holes digged beforehand.

Plant fruit-trees of all ſorts.

Prune all ſorts of wall-trees and ſtone-fruits.

Strawberry-beds finiſh dreſſing.

Vines prune and plant.

Wall-trees may be pruned and planted.

The Greenhouſe.

Give air very freely in the day-time.

Earth the tops of the pots.

Geraniums take in, early in the month.

Leaves clean well before the plants are ſet in order, and dead ones pick off.

Myrtles may be taken in, towards the end of the month.

Oranges ſhould not remain out this month.

Succulent plants water ſparingly.

Water myrtles, oranges, winter cherries, and all woody plants frequently.

Windows open every fine day.

OFFSETS. Young roots that ſpring and grow from roots that are round, tuberous, or bulbous; alſo the looſe, outward brown ſkins, either in tulips, onions, &c.

OILS. The beards or prickles of barley, &c.

OILY SEED, [*Seſamum.*] See OILY GRAIN.

OLEANDER, [*Nerium.*] Roſe bay. There are ſeveral varieties of this plant, all fine evergreens, and producing large cluſters of fine ornamental flowers; they are exotics, brought from the iſland of Crete, and both the Indies, but are hardy enough to bear the open air in ſummer, and green-houſe in winter. They are propagated by layers, cuttings, and ſuckers.

OLIVE, [*Olea.*] The ſpecies are the European, common olive tree, and the cape box leaved olive. The European riſes with upright ſolid ſtems, branching numerouſly on every ſide, twenty or thirty feet high; ſpear-ſhaped, ſtiff, oppoſite leaves, two or three inches long, and half an inch or more broad; and at the axillas ſmall cluſters of white flowers, ſucceeded by oval fruit.

This ſpecies is the principal ſort cultivated for its fruit; the varieties of which are numerous, varying in ſize, colour, and quality.

It is a native of the ſouthern warm parts of Europe, and is cultivated in great quantities in the ſouth of France, Italy, and Portugal, for the fruit to make olive-oil, which is in ſo great repute, and is tranſported to all parts, to the great advantage of thoſe countries where the trees grow in the open ground: the green fruit is alſo in much eſteem for pickling, of which we may ſee plenty in the ſhops.

The Cape Box-leaved Olive riſes with ſhrubby ſtems, branching numerouſly from the bottom, ſix or ſeven feet high; ſmall, oval, thick, ſtiff ſhining leaves; and at the axillas ſmall cluſters of whitiſh flowers; ſucceeded by ſmall fruit of inferior value.

Theſe plants in this country muſt be kept principally in pots for moving to ſhelter of a green-houſe in winter; for they are too tender to proſper well in the open ground here; though ſometimes they are planted againſt a warm ſouth wall, and ſheltered occaſionally from froſt in winter, by mulching the roots, and matting their tops; whereby they may be preſerved, and will ſometimes produce fruit for pickling; a very ſevere winter, however, often kills or greatly injures their young branches; therefore let the principal part be potted in rich earth, and placed among the green-houſe ſhrubs.

Their propagation here is commonly by layers.

The laying is performed on the young

young branches in spring; give plenty of water all summer, and they will sometimes be rooted fit for potting-off by autumn; but sometimes they require two summers to be rooted effectually: when, however, they are properly rooted, take them off early in autumn, and pot them separately; give water, and place them in the shade till they have taken fresh root; and in October remove them into the green-house, &c.

Those you intend to plant in the open-ground, as before suggested, should be kept in pots, in order to have occasional shelter of a garden-frame two or three years, till they have acquired some size, and are hardened to the full air; then transplant them into a warm border against a wall: mulch their roots in winter, and mat their tops in frosty weather.

Wild OLIVE, [*Oleaster, Elæagnus.*] There are two species, the narrow-leaved, and the thorny; both these trees merit culture, the first for the shrubbery, the second for the stove; their silvery-leaves render them very conspicuous, and effects a delightful variety.

Their propagation is easily effected by layers of their young shoots, also by cuttings, which will be rooted in one year, and may then be transplanted, placing the hardy kinds in the nursery, to have two or three years growth, when they will be fit for the shrubbery.

Wild OLIVE *of Barbadoes*, [*Bontia.*] This plant is greatly cultivated in the gardens at Barbadoes for making of hedges, than which there is not a more proper plant to thrive in those hot countries, it being an evergreen, and of quick growth. We have been informed that from cuttings (planted in the rainy season, when they have immediately taken root) there has been a complete hedge, four or five feet high, in eighteen months. In England it is preserved in stoves. It may be raised from seeds, which should be sown on a hot-bed early in the spring, that the plants may acquire strength before winter. When the plants are come up, they must be transplanted out each into a separate small pot, and plunged into a moderate hot-bed of tanners bark, observing to shade them until they have taken root; after which they must have a large share of air in warm weather, and be often refreshed with water. In winter they must be placed in the stove, where they should have a moderate degree of warmth, and but little water during that season. In summer they may be exposed abroad, in very hot weather, in a sheltered situation. With this management these plants will produce flowers and fruit in three years from seed. They may also be propagated by cuttings, which should be planted in the spring before the plants have begun to shoot. These must be put into pots, and plunged into a moderate hot-bed, observing to shade them until they have taken root, after which they must be treated as hath been directed for the seedling plants. These plants being evergreen, and growing in a pyramidical form, make a pretty variety in the stove amongst other exotic plants.

Spurge OLIVE. *See Spurge* LAUREL.

OLITORY. A kitchen garden.

OLLET. Fuel of any kind.

OMY. Mellow, applied to land.

ONE BERRY, [*Paris.*] Truelove. This plant grows wild in moist shady woods in divers parts of England, but especially in the northern counties, and it is with great difficulty preserved in gardens. The only method to procure it, is to take up the plants from the places where they grow wild, preserving good balls of earth to their roots, and plant them in a shady moist border, where they may remain undisturbed, in which situation they will live some years; but as it is a plant of little beauty, it is rarely preserved in gardens.

ONE BLADE, [*Smilax.*] There are twelve or thirteen species, mostly of a shrubby, climbing growth, some hardy, and some of tender nature, but it is principally some of the hardy kinds that are esteemed for culture in our gardens, having long trailing stalks, some armed with prickles, others are unarmed, and mostly climb by means of cirrhi, or claspers, upon the adjacent trees and bushes, many feet high, which renders them proper furniture for thickets and wilderness quarters, &c. are all exotics from different foreign countries, both in Europe, Asia, and America; consisting of several shrubby, and one herbaceous kind for hardy plantations, and some shrubby sorts for the green house, &c.

The hardy kinds are propagated by slipping the roots, by layers, and by seed.

The tender species may be propagated by layers, and by dividing the roots. Perform the laying in spring on the young shoots, which by autumn or spring following will be fit for potting off separately: and by roots, these being slipped in March or April, and the off sets potted separately, they will soon take root; managing the whole as other woody exotics of the greenhouse.

ONION, [*Cepa.*] The varieties are, Strasburgh or common oval onion, Spanish silver-skinned large flat onion, Spanish red-skinned large flat onion, Portugal great oval onion.

Of these four the Strasburgh is the best for general culture; it is a handsome bulb, generally assuming an oval shape, is of firm growth, and keeps well for winter service.

The Spanish onions are large and flat, the white sort is of mildest flavour. Both the varieties generally turn out very profitable crops, and none excels them for culinary purposes, but they rarely keep so well after Christmas as the Strasburgh or oval onion.

The Portugal onion is a very large handsome bulb, of somewhat oval shape, although they rarely attain the size here as in Portugal, &c. as is obvious by those imported annually, from that kingdom by the orange merchants. If, however, seeds saved in Portugal are sown here, the bulbs will arrive at a much larger size than from seeds saved in England, especially if saved two or three years successively, which will often be so far degenerated, that the bulbs become flat, and not larger than the common onions.

This sort being very mild, is greatly esteemed for sauces, and other uses in cookery.

All these sorts are propagated by seed sown annually; which, for the general crops, the proper season is from about the twentieth of February until the latter end of March, observing however, in cold, wet, stubborn land, it is proper to defer sowing entirely until towards the middle of the last named month. It is likewise to be remarked, that in cases of omission in sowing at the times above-mentioned, it may be performed in moist rich soils, with tolerable success, any time before the 15th of April; but remembering that the crops of the February or March sowing always bulb more freely, and acquire a much larger growth than those sown later.

The proper situation and soil for these crops should be an open exposure, and the land moderately light and rich; chusing however a spot of the best mellow ground in the garden, with the addition, if possible, of a good coat of rotten dung, which should be dug in, one spade deep, observing to preserve a level surface; and while it is fresh stirred, let the seed be sown, which is of particular importance. Do not however sow it when the surface is so wet or moist as to clog to the feet, or rake.

The proper quantity of seed is about an ounce to every rod or pole of ground, but if it is not required to have them thick for culture, two ounces for three rods is sufficient.

Be particularly careful to procure fresh seed; for of that which is more than one year old, not one in fifty will grow.

The seed may either be sown all over the piece or plat of ground, and raked in; or the ground may first be divided into beds of four of five feet, allowing foot-wide alleys between; then sow the seed with a regular spreading cast, and immediately tread the surface over evenly; then pare the alleys an inch or two deep, and cast the earth over the beds, and directly proceed to rake them length-ways, keeping an even hand, and trim off all stones.

The sowing them in beds is certainly the most eligible practice, when it is designed to draw or cull the young onions from time to time, for market or family service, because in such cases a person can stand in the alleys without treading at every turn upon the beds, which renders the surface hard, to the detriment of the crop, as well as unvoidably trampling upon the plants themselves; and it is likewise very convenient to stand in the alleys to weed, thin, or hoe the crop.

It is a common practice in the general culture of onions to sow them thick, to allow for culling or drawing out the superabundant plants by degrees as they are wanted. We, how-

ever,

ever, advise to sow a piece particularly for general culling, exclusive of the main crop, for by a daily thinning out the superfluous plants, there is no avoiding treading upon, disturbing, and loosening the remaining ones, and the plants thereby become of stinted growth.

In fifteen or twenty days after the seed is sown, the plants will appear; and in a month or six weeks after that, they will be three or four inches high, and weeds will be numerous, when they should be cleaned from weeds, and thinned to three or four inches distance. The weeding and thinning should be began in due time, before the weeds branch and spread, which may either be performed by hand or small hoeing; the latter is the most expeditious method, as one man may do as much as three, and is also the most beneficial to the plants, for by stirring the ground about them with the hoe, it will greatly facilitate their growth, as will be obvious in a few days after the operation; a small hoe two inches broad is the proper size; chuse dry weather, cut up all weeds, and where the plants stand close, cut them out to two or three inches distance each way, having regard to leave the strongest and most promising plants.

In a month after run over them again with the hoe, and cut up weeds, and any superfluous plants that escaped you the first time; after this they will require no farther culture than pulling out straggling weeds.

In July the plants will begin to swell greatly at bottom, and in August the bulbs will be fully grown.

Towards the middle of August, therefore, examine the crop in general; when the necks shrink and fall, and the leaves wither, it may be presumed the bulbs are arrived at maturity, and are done growing, and should be pulled up, cleaned, dried, and housed for use: this should be done in dry weather; at the same time hoe and rake a piece of the ground clean, and as you pull the onions, spread them thereon to dry and harden. Here let them lie about a fortnight, turning them every day or two, when, if the weather proves dry, they will be duly prepared for keeping, then take the first opportunity to house them before wet weather prevails. Let the bulbs be first divested of all adhering earth, loose skins, and the grossest parts of the leaves and neck, rejecting all infectious and bruised ones; and carry them into any dry upper room out of the damp, spreading them on the floor not more than a foot thick, but if room to lay them thinner, it will be an advantage.

Being now housed, the closer the room is kept the better, observing to turn them over once in three weeks, and clear out such as have any tendency to infection, which they would soon communicate to others in their neighbourhood, and it would become general.

In the culture of onions it often happens that, through badness of seed, many are disappointed of a crop, by waiting long in expectation of the plants rising, till it has been too late to sow again. In this recourse may be had to transplantation from other gardens, either from a neighbouring one, where there are superfluous crops, or may purchase a bed, or such part of one as is necessary from a market gardener; this should be done in May, or early in June, and if possible in moist weather: having a spot of well-dunged ground prepared, take up the plants with good roots, and plant them in rows six inches distance, and four inches asunder in each row, giving directly a hearty watering.

Repeat the waterings occasionally for a week or fortnight, and the plants will grow freely, and you will not be disappointed; they will form handsome bulbs.

Onions for pickling are in great request. Those proper for that purpose should not be bigger than common round buttons; to procure which in due quantity, some seed should be sown late in a spot of light poor land; about the middle of April is the proper time: sow it moderately thick and the plants need not to be thinned, except they rise in very thick clusters. They will bulb in June and July, and be fit to take up in August.

Right pickling onions sell well in the markets; those that are cleaned and trimmed ready for the pickling tub fetch from eight to twelve shillings per bushel.

In the spring many of the keeping onions

enions will unavoidably grow as they lie in the houſe, theſe may be planted out in rows ſix inches diſtance, and will ſerve to draw up by way of eſcaliions.

Of the Autumn or Michaelmas crop.

This crop is generally ſown in Auguſt, and the plants ariſe before Michaelmas, ſtand the winter, and are intended principally for ſpring ſervice, to draw up for young ſallads, &c. and likewiſe, if the Straſburgh or any other variety of the common onion are ſown, they, if permitted to ſtand, will bulb to a tolerable ſize in June, and ſupply the kitchen or market as headed onions till thoſe of the ſpring crop are bulbed.

But as the common onion is liable to be cut off in ſevere winters, it is neceſſary always at the ſame time to ſow ſome beds of Welch onions, which bid defiance to the moſt rigorous froſt.

We obſerved above, that Auguſt is the ſeaſon for ſowing theſe crops; it is to be remarked, that in warm rich land, from the fifteenth to the twenty-fifth is the proper period; but in cold or poor ground, always ſow in the firſt or ſecond week of that month, obſerving to ſow them in beds four feet wide, with twelve-inch alleys between; do not ſpare ſeed, and tread and rake it in as directed in the ſpring crop.

The plants will appear in a fortnight, and with them numerous weeds, to which early attention muſt be had to clear them out by hand before they begin to ſpread, but the plants of this crop are not now to be thinned.

In November and December however, if they ſtand very thick, ſome of the largeſt may be thinned out occaſionally for uſe.

Of ſaving ſeed of this ſpecies

February is the proper time to plant onions for ſeed, though this is often done in October by thoſe that ſave great quantities for ſale.

For this purpoſe make choice of a due quantity of the largeſt and handſomeſt bulbs, rejecting all blemiſhed ones, and ſuch as have already made any effort to grow, and having made choice of a ſpot of ground well expoſed to the ſun, which being dug, proceed to plant the onions; ſtrain a line, and with a hoe or ſpade open three drills, twelve inches aſunder, and ſix deep, place the bulbs therein nine inches diſtance, and rake the earth over them; meaſure off two feet for an alley, and in that manner proceed to the end; the wide ſpaces of two feet is by way of alley to go between to hoe and clear off weeds, as well as to ſtake and ſupport the ſtalks of the plants when neceſſary.

In June the flower ſtalks will be ſhot their full height, and the flower heads will be formed at top, to ſecure which in erect poſition, drive ſome ſtout ſtakes in the ground along each row, at two yards diſtance, and from ſtake to ſtake faſten double lines of pack-thread, and if theſe are tied together in the intervals between the ſtems of each plant, it will effectually ſecure them.

About the latter end of Auguſt the ſeed will be ripe, which is very diſcoverable by the capſules opening, and black colour of the ſeed; cut the heads in a dry day, and ſpread them upon cloths in the ſun, but remove them under cover at night; and in a week or fortnight beat or rub out the ſeed; clean it out from the rubbiſh, and put it up in bags for uſe.

Good onion ſeed is a very material article to be attended to: it is to be remarked that this ſeed never germinates freely after the firſt year, but notwithſtanding this, ſeeds-men are very apt to mix more than half old ſeed with their new, to the great loſs and diſappointment of many; to try its goodneſs, ſome, before they venture their general crop, ſow a little in a pot, and place it in a moderate hot-bed, or near a fire: but the moſt expeditious method is this; tye about a thimble-full of the ſeed looſely in a piece of linen rag, and put it into a veſſel of boiling water, ſuſpended by a thread; in ten or fifteen miutes pull it out, and if the ſeeds are good, they will in that ſhort ſpace of time be germinated or chipped, perhaps a quarter of an inch in length.

Leek, & other ſeed of ſimilar nature, may be tried by the ſame experiment.

Welch ONIONS. A ſort of onions propagated by gardeners for the uſe of the table in ſpring; they never make any bulb, and are therefore only to be eaten green with ſallads.

They are propagated by ſowing their ſeeds towards the end of July, in beds of a dry but rich ſoil; and in three weeks

weeks after sowing they will appear above ground; when they must be kept very free from weeds. About October all their leaves die away, which has occasioned some to think all the plantation lost, and to dig up the ground for some other use; but if they are suffered to stand, they will shoot up again very strong in January, and from that time will grow very vigorously, resist all weathers, and be fit to draw in March, when they will be extemely green and fine. They are much stronger than any other sort of onions, and have much of the taste of garlic.

Sea ONION. *See* SQUILL.

OPIUM. In the materia medica, is an inspissated juice, partly of the resinous, and partly of the gummy kind, brought to us in cakes from eight ounces to a pound weight. It is very heavy, of a dense texture, and not perfectly dry; but in general, easily receives an impression from the finger: its colour is a brownish yellow, so very dark and dusky that at first sight it appears black: it has a dead and faint smell, and its taste is very bitter and acrid. It is to be chosen moderately firm, and not too soft; its smell and taste should be very strong, and care is to be taken that there is no dirty or stony matter in it.

Opium is the juice of the papaver album, or white poppy, with which the fields of Asia Minor are in many places sown, as ours are with corn. When the heads are near ripening, they wound them with an instrument that has five edges, which on being stuck into the head makes at once five long cuts in it; and from these wounds the opium flows, and is next day taken off by a person who goes round the field, and put up in a vessel, which he carries fastened to his girdle: at the same time that this opium is collected, the opposite side of the poppy head is wounded, and the opium collected from it the next day. They distinguish however the produce of the first wounds from that of the succeeding ones, for the first juice afforded by the plant is greatly superior to what is obtained afterwards. After they have collected the opium, they moisten it with a small quantity of water or honey, and work it a long time upon a flat, hard, and smooth board, with a thick and strong instrument of the same wood, till it becomes of the consistence of pitch; and then work it up with their hands, and form it into cakes or rolls for sale.

Opium at present is in great esteem, and is of one of the most valuable of all the simple medicines: applied externally it is emollient, relaxing and discutient, and greatly promotes suppuration; if long kept upon the skin it takes off the hair, and always occasions an itching in it; sometimes it exulcerates it, and raises little blisters if applied to a tender part. Sometimes, on external application, it allays pain, and even occasions sleep: but it must by no means be applied to the head, especially to the sutures of the skull, for it has been known to have the most terrible effects in this application, and even to bring on death itself.

Opium taken internally, removes melancholy, eases pain and disposes to sleep; in many cases removes hæmorrhages, provokes sweating, and is a provocation to venery; and in general has a greater effect on women and children than on men. A moderate dose is commonly under a grain, though according to the circumstances two grains, or even three may be within the limits of this denomination; but custom will make people bear a dram or more, tho' in this case nature is vitiated, and nothing is to be hence judged in regard to others. If given dissolved, it operates in half an hour; if in a solid form, as in pills, or the like, it is sometimes an hour and a half. Its first effect, in this case, is the making the patient cheerful, as if he had drank moderately of wine, and at the same time bold and above the fear of danger; for which reason the Turks always take it when they are going to battle. A very immoderate dose brings on a sort of drunkenness, much like that occasioned by an immoderate quantity of strong liquors; cheerfulness and loud laughter at first, then a relaxation of limbs, a loss of memory, and lightheadedness; then vertigoes, dimness of the eyes, with a laxity of the cornea and a dilatation of the pupils, a slowness of the pulse, redness of the face, relaxation of the under jaws, swelling of the lips, difficulty

ficulty of breathing, painful erection of the penis, convulsions, cold sweats, and, finally, death. Those who escape are usually relieved by a great number of stools, or profuse sweats. People who have gradually accustomed themselves to an immoderate use of opium, are subject to relaxations and weaknesses of all the parts of the body: they are apt to be faint, idle, and thoughtless; and are generally in a stupid and uncomfortable state, except just after they have taken a fresh dose; in short, they lose their appetite, and grow old before their time.

Prepared opium, commonly called extract of opium, is made by dissolving opium in a sufficient quantity of water with a gentle heat; then straining the solution from the fæces, and evaporating it to the consistence of honey. Tincture of opium, or liquid laudanum, otherwise called the thebaic tincture, is made as follows: take of prepared opium two ounces; of cinnamon and cloves, each one drachm; of white-wine, one pint: infuse them a week without heat, and then filtre it through paper. Quincy observes of this preparation, that the addition of the spices are of no use.

OPODELDOC. A liniment in much esteem for sprains, &c. it is thus made:

Take spirit of rosemary one pint,
Soft soap three ounces,
Camphor one ounce.

The College of London direct hard soap, but soft soap is most generally used.

ORACH, [*Atriplex.*] Arrach. The species are, 1. Pale green, or white garden orach. 2. Broad-leaved, or shrubby orach. 3. Shrubby sea orach. There are several other species, some of which grow naturally in England, but as they are plants of no beauty, they are rarely admitted into gardens.

The first of these plants was formerly cultivated in the kitchen-garden as a culinary herb, being used as spinach, and is now by some persons preferred to it, though in general it is not esteemed amongst the English; but the French at present cultivate this plant for use, as the people in the northern parts of England also do.

The second sort was formerly cultivated in gardens as a shrub, and by some persons were formed into hedges, and constantly sheared to keep thick; but this plant is by no means fit for such purposes on many accounts, for it grows too vigorous; the shoots in one month at the growing season of the year will be two feet long, provided they have a good soil, so that a hedge of this plant cannot be kept in tolerable order, nor will it ever form a thick hedge. But a worse inconvenience attends this plant, for in very hard winters it is often destroyed.

It may be propagated by cuttings, which may be planted in any of the summer months on a shady border; they will soon take root, and be fit to transplant the Michaelmas following, when they should be planted where they are to remain.

The third sort grows wild in divers parts of England, on the sea-side, from whence the plants may be procured; or it may be propagated by cuttings in the same manner as the former sort. This is a low under shrub, seldom rising above two feet and a half, or at most three feet high, but becomes very bushy. This may have a place amongst other low shrubs, and if planted on a poor gravelly soil, will abide several years, and make pretty diversity.

ORANGE TREE, [*Aurantium.*] The species are, the Seville Orange, the China Orange, the Shaddock, or Pumplemoes, the Horned Orange, the Hermaphrodite Orange, the Willow Leaved, and the Dwarf or Nutmeg Orange.

There are many more less material varieties than are here noticed, in the countries where they grow in the open ground; and the varieties, like our apples and pears, may be multiplied by seed without end: but, like other fruit so raised, it is probable there may not be one in a hundred worth notice, so that the approved sorts can only be continued with certainty by budding.

The flowers of all the species and varieties are formed each of five spreading petals, appearing here principally in May or June, and the fruit continue setting in June and July, and ripen the year following.

All the sorts are elegant evergreens of the tree kind, obtaining in England from about five to eight or ten feet stature, forming full and handsome heads, closely garnished with beautiful large leaves the year round, and a profusion of sweet flowers, in spring and early in summer, which, even in this country, are often succeeded by abundance of fruit, sometimes arriving to tolerable perfection; but the chief merit of these trees in England is for ornament, which consists not only in their beautiful foliage, but also in the flowers and fruit, and have this peculiar merit, as to exhibit blossoms, green fruit in different stages of growth, and full-grown ripe yellow fruit, all at the same time; which, together with their large shining green leaves, effect one of the most beautiful contrasts of our gardens, which renders all the sorts very desirable furniture for the green-house collection. Oranges and lemons are generally more fruitful in England than the citron, and the Seville orange most of all, which is the only sort of orange to be depended on for any considerable quantity of flowers and fruit; this tree being hardiest, retains its fruit in winter better than most of the other varieties.

These trees are all natives originally of India, but have been long retained in our gardens as green-house plants; and in the southern parts of Europe, as Portugal, Spain, and Italy, they grow in the open ground like our apple and pear trees, and from which countries vast quantities of the fruit are imported hither annually; but in England the trees must always be continued in pots or tubs, to be housed in winter.

They all succeed in the open air from the beginning of June unto the middle or latter end of October, and the rest of the year must have the shelter of a green-house, and they will prosper in any good garden mould.

They are propagated by seed, budding, and inarching. By seed, i. e. the kernels of the fruit: this method of raising these trees is rarely practised in England, except for stocks, on which to bud the different kinds; for although raising the trees entirely from seed, without budding, is the way to gain new varieties, yet out of numbers so raised, it is probable not a tree of them may produce fruit that possesses any good property, but will be small, crablike, and intolerably sour and harsh: but when any new valuable variety is by this means accidentally obtained, it is continued and multiplied by budding it upon stocks raised from the kernels of any of the sorts; by which practice all the above described varieties are annually increased in our gardens. The method of raising them entirely from seeds, except for stocks, is both tedious and uncertain; therefore in this country it is scarce worth practising, unless a few merely for curiosity.

The raising them, however, from the kernel, either to form trees for new varieties, or for stocks to bud upon, is in this country performed effectually and expeditiously by the aid of a hot-bed, and by this means stocks may be obtained of due size for budding, in two years. The following is the method of raising them:—

Early in spring procure some kernels which may be had plentifully from rotten fruits, or others that are perfectly ripened, observing, that for stocks, the citron, lemon, and Seville orange, as being the freest shooters, are to be preferred, though the citron is the strongest shooter of the three: sow the kernels in March, in pots of rich light earth half an inch deep, and plunge them in a hot-bed of dung or tan, under frame and glasses, giving them air, and frequent sprinklings of water. In two or three weeks the plants will come up, and in six weeks or two months more, they will be advanced four or five inches in height; observing, in the middle or latter end of June, to harden them to the full air, in which let them remain till October, then move them into the green-house to stand till spring. In March or April, proceed to plant them singly in small pots, being careful to shake them out of the seed-pot with their roots entire, and having half filled the other pots with light, rich, loamy compost, place one plant in each pot, filling it up over the roots with the same sort of earth, and let them be directly watered, repeating it occasionally till they are fresh rooted; afterwards treat them as other woody exotics of the green-house, and in a year or two, the largest of those designed for stocks will be fit to bud.

But, to have stocks as forward and fine as possible for budding, as soon as they are potted out as above, plunge them directly in a hot-bed, under a

frame

frame and glaffes, about three or four months, which will draw them up in height with handfome ftems.

A bark-bed would be the moft eligible, made either in a glafs pit, or to be covered with a deep frame and lights; fo plunging the pots to their rims in the bed, giving occafional fhade in the middle of hot funny days, and frefh air daily by tilting one end of the lights more or lefs, as you fhall judge expedient: likewife refrefh them frequently with water, and by the middle or end of July the plants will be advanced fifteen or eighteen inches, or near two feet high, obferving then to harden them by degrees to the full air for the remainder of the fummer; and by being thus forwarded, thofe defigned for ftocks will be in excellent order for budding the year following.

But thefe feedlings may ftill be more forwarded, and a year or two's growth may be gained by forcing them, as above, the firft feafon. This is effected by pricking out the feedlings the firft year they come up, when two or three inches high, in fmall pots, as above, to be plunged either in a bark-bed, or even in a dung hot-bed, covered with old tan eight or ten inches deep for the reception of the pots. The plants are then to be potted fingly, and plunged in the hot-bed, and by the middle or end of July, they will have advanced to twelve or fifteen inches, or perhaps to a foot and a half, or near two feet in height; they muft then be gradually hardened to the full air, by raifing the lights more and more every day, leaving them alfo up on nights, and at laft take them quite off in a cloudy calm day. Let the plants remain fully expofed till October, then move them into the green-houfe for the winter, and many of them will be in due order to receive the buds the next Auguft; and the following is the method:

The operation of budding is performed in Auguft upon ftocks of their own kinds, for all the fpecies and varieties of this genus take freely upon one another, and the budding or inoculation is performed in the common way.

As to the buds for budding them, obferve to procure cuttings only from bearing free-fhooting trees, of the forts you would encreafe; young fhoots, that are round and plump, muft be chofen, and from thefe take the buds in the ufual manner, being careful to infert them in a fmooth part of the ftock, at about fix to ten or fifteen inches from the bottom, one bud in each ftock, tying them with a ligature of bafs.

As foon as the budding is finifhed, it is proper to place the plants in their pots in the green-houfe, or in a glafs-cafe, &c. to defend the buds from wet and drying winds, turning the budded part from the fun: or where there is the convenience of a fpare bark-pit, where the heat of the bark is almoft exhaufted, the pots may be plunged therein two or three weeks, and it will more effectually promote the union of the buds; obferving, in either department, to admit air freely, by opening the front glaffes, and allowing a flight fhade of mats in the middle of fcorching funny days: the pots fhould alfo be fupplied with water every day or two during the hot weather. In three or four weeks the buds will be united with the ftocks, when it is proper to loofen the bandage of each bud, that they may have room to fwell; obferving, however, that the buds will all remain dormant till fpring.

After this there is nothing more required this year but due waterings; only obferving, that in cafe of great rains, it will be proper to retain the plants in the green-houfe for the remainder of the fummer, and until next fpring.

In March following, the heads of all the ftocks muft be cut off flanting clofe behind the infertion of the bud; after this operation the buds will foon begin to fpring, and produce each one fhoot, which probably will obtain from about five or fix, to eight or ten inches in length the fame year. It is proper to obferve, that if the ftocks could have the aid of a bark-bed, there will be a chance of having the buds fhoot a foot and half, or more, by the end of fummer; therefore where there is the convenience of a bark pit, or glafs-cafe, or any deep frame, that can be placed on a bark-bed, &c. we fhould advife by all means to make ufe of fuch conveniencies for forwarding the firft fhoot of the buds; fo that as foon as the ftocks are headed, as above directed, plunge the pots in the hot-bed, and let them enjoy the benefit of air and water, in proportion to the temperature of the bed and weather; likewise occasional shade when the sun is very powerful. Here they may be continued, with the above care, till the end of July, when some of the strongest shooters will be advanced near two feet high; and it is then proper to begin to inure them by degrees to the full air, to harden them against winter, that they may be able to live during that season in the green-house, to which they must be removed in October.

When it is however designed to propagate by inarching, stocks must be raised from seed, as before directed, which, when of due size, are to be placed in their pots, upon a sort of stage, or some erection convenient to the head of the trees you intend to inarch from, observing to fix upon some convenient young shoots, nearly the size of the stocks, for the purpose of inarching; these are to be inarched in the stocks, as they grow on the trees, in April or May, one in each stock, and by the end of August following they will be united to the stock, and may be separated from the parent tree.

But this method of propagating these trees, is rather practised by way of curiosity, to raise a few trees to a bearing state in haste, because, by inarching a young bearing branch, furnished with fruit, into any of their own stocks, in April or May, it will frequently be united by the following August, and the branch so inarched may be separated from its parent plant, and, being firmly attached to the stock, it then commences a new tree, bearing fruit, raised in the short space of four or five months.

By the same rule you may inarch an orange into the branch of a citron or lemon, or all three upon the same tree, for the sake of variety.

But trees raised by this method never grow so large nor handsome as those raised by budding.

The flowers are highly odoriferous, and have been for some time past of great esteem as a perfume: their taste is somewhat warm, accompanied with a degree of bitterness. They yield their flavour by infusion, to rectified spirit, and in distillation both to spirit and water: the bitter matter is dissolved by water, and, on evaporating the decoction, remains entire in the extract. The distilled water was formerly kept in the shops, but on account of the scarcity of the flowers is now laid aside: it is called by foreign writers *aqua nephæ*. An oil distilled from these flowers is brought from Italy under the name of *oleum* or *essentia neroli*.

The outer yellow rind of the fruit is a grateful aromatic bitter, and, in cold phlegmatic constitutions, proves an excellent stomachic and carminative, promoting appetite, warming the habit, and strengthening the tone of the viscera. Orange peel appears to be very considerably warmer than that of lemons, and to abound more with essential oil: to this circumstance therefore due regard ought to be had in the use of these medicines. The flavour of the first is likewise supposed to be less perishable than that of the other, hence the College employ orange peel in the spirituous bitter tincture, which is designed for keeping, whilst in the bitter watery infusion, lemon peel is preferred. A syrup and two distilled waters are for the same reason prepared from the rind of oranges in preference to that of lemons.

The juice of oranges is a grateful acid liquor, of considerable use in febrile or inflammatory distempers, for allaying heat, abating exorbitant commotions of the blood, quenching thirst, and promoting the salutary excretions: it is likewise of great use in scurvies, especially when given in conjunction with the *cochlearia*, *nasturtium*, or other acrid antiscorbutics, as in the *succi scorbutici* of the shops.

Orange Mint, [*Mentha Rubra.*] A species of mint smelling like an orange.

Mock Orange. See *Mock* Orange.

ORCHARD. A garden department, consigned entirely to the growth of standard fruit trees, for furnishing a large supply of the most useful kinds of fruit.

In the orchard you may have as standards all sorts of apple trees, most sorts of pears and plumbs, and all sorts of cherries; which four species are the capital orchard fruits: each of which comprise numerous valuable varieties; but to have a compleat orchard, you may also have quinces, medlars, mulberries, service-trees, filberts, Spanish nuts, barberries; likewise walnuts and chesnuts, which two latter are particularly applicable for the boundaries of orchards,

orchards, to screen the other trees from the insults of impetuous winds and cold blasts. All these trees should be arranged in rows from twenty to thirty feet distance.

But sometimes orchards consist entirely of apple-trees, particularly in the cyder-making countries, where they are cultivated in very great quantities in large fields, and in hedge-rows, for the fruit to make cyder for public supply.

And sometimes whole orchards of very considerable extent are entirely of cherry-trees; but in this case, it is when the fruit is designed for sale in some great city, as London, &c. for the supply of which city, great numbers of cherry-orchards are in some of the adjacent counties, but more particularly in Kent, which is famous for very extensive cherry-orchards; many of which are entirely of that sort called Kentish cherry, as being generally a great bearer; others are stored with all the principal sorts of cultivated cherries, from the earliest to the latest kinds.

A general orchard, however, composed of all the before-mentioned fruit-trees, should consist of a double portion of apple-trees or more, because they are considerably the most useful fruit, and may be continued for use the year round.

The utility of a general orchard, both for private use and for profit, stored with various sorts of fruit-trees, must be very great, as well as afford infinite pleasure from the delightful appearance it makes from early spring till late in autumn: in spring the various trees in blossom are highly ornamental; in summer, the pleasure is heightened by observing the various fruits advancing to perfection; and as the season advances, the mature growth of the various sorts arriving to perfection in regular succession from May or June until the end of October, must afford exceeding delight, as well as great profit.

As to the proper extent of ground for an orchard, this must be proportioned, in some measure, to the extent of land you have to work on, and the quantity of fruit required either for private use, or for public supply: so that an orchard may be from half an acre to twenty or more in extent.

With respect to the situation and aspect for an orchard, we may observe very thriving orchards both in low and high situations, and on declivities and plains, in various aspects or exposures, provided the natural soil is good. We should, however, avoid very low damp situations as much as the nature of the place will admit; for in very wet soils no fruit-trees will prosper, nor the fruit be fine: but a moderately low situation, free from copious wet, may be more eligible than an elevated ground, as being less exposed to tempestuous winds; though a situation having a small declivity is very desirable, especially if its aspect incline towards the east, south-east, or southerly, which are rather more eligible than a westerly aspect; but a north aspect is the worst of all for an orchard, unless particularly compensated by the peculiar temperament or good quality of the soil. We would remark, for the advantage of those that are not accommodated with choice of situation and aspect, that they need not be under any great anxiety, if the soil is but suitable; only observing, if possible, to abandon very low damp situations, for the reason before given them.

As for soil, any common field or pasture that produces good crops of corn, grass, or kitchen garden vegetables, is sutiable for an orchard; if it should prove of a loamy nature, it will be a particular advantage: any soil, however, of a good quality, not too light and dry, or too heavy, stubborn, or wet, but of a medium nature, of a soft pliant temperature, not less than one spade deep of good staple, will be proper for this purpose.

Where, however, the soil is naturally defective, the defects must be rectified as well as possible, by the application of proper manures and composts, and applied either to the whole ground, if but of moderate extent, or to the places where each tree is to stand, for a space of eight or ten feet circumference, working it up with the natural soil of the place.

This application, in extensive orchards, would be a very chargeable operation; therefore those who are at liberty to chuse, should have particular regard to the fixing upon a proper spot, where but little or no foreign aid is requisite.

The preparation of the ground for the reception of the trees, is by trenching,

ing, or if for very confiderable orchards, by deep ploughing; but trench-digging, one or two fpades, as the foil will admit, is the moft eligible, either wholly, or only for the prefent, in the places where the lines of trees are to ftand, a fpace of fix or eight feet wide, all the way in each row, efpecially if it be grafs-ground, and intended to be kept in fward; or if any under-crops are defigned to be raifed, the ground may be wholly trenched at firft; but as to this you may fuit your convenience, obferving in either cafe to trench the ground in the ufual way to the depth of the natural foil; and if in grafs, turn the fward clean to the bottom of each trench, which when rotted, will prove an excellent manure.

In planting orchards, however, on grafs-ground, fome only dig pits for each tree, capacious enough for the reception of the roots, loofening the bottom well, without the labour of digging any other part of the ground: where the ground, however, is trenched either wholly, or fome confiderable width along the place of each row of trees, it will confequently prove of greater advantage in promoting their free growth.

The ground muft be fenced fecurely againft cattle, &c. either with a good ditch and hedge, or with a paling fence, as may be moft convenient.

The beft feafon for planting all the forts of fruit trees is autumn, foon after the fall of the leaf, from about the latter end of October until December; or it may be performed any time in open weather from October until March.

All the forts of fruit trees proper for this department, if not furnifhed with them in your own nurfery, may be had very reafonable at all the public nurfery-grounds; obferving to chufe them principally full ftandards, with ftrait clean ftems, fix feet high, efpecially the apples, pears, plumbs, cherries, and other tree kinds, each with a branchy well-formed head, of from two or three to four or five years growth; and let feveral varieties of each particular fpecies be chofen, that ripen their fruit at different times, from the earlieft to the lateft, according to the nature of the different forts, that there may be a fufficient fupply of every fort regularly during their proper feafon; and of apples and pears in particular, chufe a much greater quantity of the autumnal and late ripening kinds, than the early forts; but the moft of all of apples: for the fummer-ripening fruit is but of fhort duration, being only proper for temporary fervice. The later ripening kinds keep found fome confiderable time for autumnal ufe; and the lateft forts that ripen in October continue in perfection for various ufes all winter, and feveral forts until the feafon of apples come again.

Having made choice of the proper forts, and marked them, let them be taken up with the utmoft care, fo as to preferve all their roots as entire as poffible; and when taken up, prune off any broken or bruifed parts of the roots, and juft tip the ends of the principal roots in general with the knife, on the under fide, with a kind of flope outward.

If the trees have been already headed, or fo trained as to have branched out into regular fhoots to form each a proper head, they muft be planted with the faid heads entire, only retrenching or fhortening any irregular or ill-placed fhoots that take an aukward direction, or run longer than the reft.

The arrangement of the trees in the orchard muft be in rows, each kind feparate, at diftances according to the nature of growth of the different forts; but for the larger growing kinds, fuch as apples, pears, plumbs, cherries, &c. they fhould ftand from twenty-five to thirty or forty feet every way afunder, though twenty-five or thirty feet at moft is a reafonable diftance for all thefe kinds.

Each fpecies and its varieties fhould generally be in rows by themfelves, the better to fuit their refpective modes of growth: though for variety you may have fome rows of apples and pears ranged alternately; likewife plumbs and cherries; and towards the boundaries may have ranges of leffer growth, as quinces, medlars, filberts, &c. and the outer row of all may be walnut-trees, and fome chefnuts, fet pretty clofe, to defend the other trees from violent winds.

Proceed to ftake out the ground according to the above diftances, for making the holes for the reception of the trees; which if made to range every way, will have a very agreeable effect, and

and admit the currency of air, and the influence of the sun, more effectually.

In planting very extensive orchards, some divide the ground into large squares or quarters of different dimensions, with intervals of fifty feet wide between, serving both as walks, and for admitting the air. In different quarters plant different sorts of fruit, as apples in one, pears in another, and plumbs and cherries in others, &c. and thus it may be repeated to as many quarters, for each species and its varieties, as may be convenient.

A wide hole must be dug for each tree, capacious enough to receive all the roots freely every way without touching the sides. When the holes are ready, proceed to planting, one tree to each hole, a person holding the stem erect, whilst another trims in the earth, previously breaking it small, and cast it in equally about all the roots, frequently shaking the tree to cause the mould to settle in close about all the smaller roots and fibres, and so as to raise the tree gradually up, that the crown of the roots may be but two or three inches below the general surface; and when the hole is filled up, tread it gently, first round the outside, then near the stem of the tree, forming the surface a little hollow: and then if on the top of all is laid some inverted turf to the width of the holes, forming it with a sort of circular bank, three or four inches high, it will support the tree, and guard the roots from drying winds and the summer's drought: observing that each tree stands perfectly upright, and that they range exactly in their proper rows.

If the orchard is much exposed to the winds, it may be proper to stake the new-planted trees to support them in their proper position, and secure them from being rocked to and fro by the wind, which would greatly retard their rooting afresh; placing one or two strong tall stakes to each tree; but the most effectual method is to have three stakes to each, placed in a triangle, meeting at top near the head of the tree, wrapping a hay-band round that part of the stem, to prevent its being barked by the stakes or tying; then tie the stakes at top close to the tree, with some proper bandage, bringing it close about the stem and stakes together, over the hay-wrapping, in a proper manner to secure the tree firmly in an erect posture.

The ground of the orchard, between the rows of trees, is very commonly laid down in grass, as being the most convenient for admitting of coming readily at the trees at all times to gather the fruit: but if thought proper, it may be employed for some years either wholly, or in part, for the produce of kitchen vegetables, or for the growth of corn, turnips, potatoes, &c. being careful in digging or ploughing the ground for the reception of these crops, not to go too near to disturb the roots of the trees; likewise not have any strong-growing plants within three feet of each side of the rows of trees: however, after the trees are advanced in growth, and begin to bear any thing considerably, it may be more eligible to lay the ground down intirely in grass, as it will be then more in character of an orchard, and be more convenient for gathering the fruit, and doing any necessary work to the trees; but in any of these ways, every one may suit their inclination or convenience.

If, however, it is laid down in grass, no cattle should be turned in to graze at large, unless the stems of each tree be previously well secured with posts and railing, and wattled with thorn-bushes, especially in young orchards, otherwise they will bark the trees, to their very great injury; nor should large cattle be turned into orchards, where the branches of the trees are low and within their reach.

With regard to the general culture of orchard fruit-trees, observe, that as being standards, their heads should generally be permitted to branch out nearly in their own natural manner, with the branches at full length, without shortening, only on particular occasions, and they will gradually form themselves into large branchy heads, and all the branches soon assume a bearing state; very little pruning of any sort being required to standard fruit-trees, except in particular cases, as above hinted, of superfluous or very irregular growths: as for example, all suckers arising from the root, must constantly be taken off close; likewise divest the stems of all side-branches coming out below the head; and all luxuriant shoots arising in the heart or middle of the tree, or in any part where they

they appear too much crouded, ſhould be pruned off cloſe. If any particular branch of the head ſhould become of long ſtraggling growth, extending beyond all the reſt, it may he ſhortened as you ſhall ſee proper, down to ſome young ſhoot, or lower branch it ſupports, that is of a regular growth, or intirely retrenched as it may ſeem proper to keep up ſome uniformity in the head; and if the head in general become at any time over-crouded with branches, thin out the worſt and moſt irregular growers of the ſuperfluity. All dead wood and cankered parts ſhould alſo be cut off to the live wood.

But remarking, that except in the above caſes, the branches in general of ſtandard fruit trees, in every ſtage of growth, ſhould be ſuffered to ſhoot forth, both in length and branch, laterally in their own way; for as moſt of the ſorts firſt form their fruit-buds, or ſpurs, near the extremity of the branches or ſhoots, if pruning their ends were practiſed, it would not only be cutting off the parts where the fruit would have been produced, but would force out a number of lateral uſeleſs ſhoots, and crowd the tree with ſuperfluous or unneceſſary wood, and greatly retard the branches from forming the above fruit-ſpurs or buds for bearing; and unleſs theſe are formed in plenty; none of the principal tree kinds can ever produce any tolerable crops of fruit; but the trees being ſuffered to take their natural growth, according to the above rules, all the branches and ſhoots will gradually form fruit ſpurs towards their extreme parts, at almoſt every eye or bud.

By the above hints it is obvious that ſtandard fruit-trees require but very little culture in reſpect to pruning; and the leſs they are pruned, except in the before-mentioned caſes, the better they will bear.

Beſides, to attempt at any regular pruning of orchard or other ſtandard fruit-trees, would prove a very tedious as well as unneceſſary work.

When neceſſary, however, to prune any of theſe trees occaſionally in the above caſes, obſerve that the proper ſeaſon for that work is any time from the fall of the leaf until March. Likewiſe obſerve in performing that operation, that ſuch branches as require retrenching ſhould be cut off quite cloſe either to their origin, if neceſſary, or cloſe to any more convenient branch it may ſupport, not leaving any ſtump, and make the cut as even and ſmooth as poſſible.

Orchard trees are ſometimes greatly infeſted with moſs growing all over their branches, but more particularly thoſe trees which are ſituated in very damp ſoils; alſo often in old orchards where the trees ſtand ſo cloſe as to croud one another ſo conſiderably as to exclude the free air: in which caſe of moſſineſs, the trees commonly aſſume a ſtunted unkindly growth, producing but indifferent crops, and the fruit often ſmall and ill-flavoured. The only remedy for this diſaſter, is, to thin out ſome of the branches where thickeſt, to admit the ſun and air more freely, and ſcrape the moſs off from the remainder, with an inſtrument directed below; but where the trees thus infeſted ſtand very cloſe to one another, ſome of them ſhould be cut down to admit a larger portion of air, and the ſun's heat and light; and for the ſame reaſon thin the branches of the remaining trees; then clear the branches in general from the groſſeſt of the moſs; for which purpoſe you ſhould be provided with ſome iron ſcrapers hollowed on the edge, and of three different ſizes to ſuit the different branches, having the edges a little blunted; and with theſe tools ſcrape off the moſs from all the principal branches at leaſt, and of as many of the ſmaller ones as your time will permit, for it is tedious work where there are many trees: after this, if the ground of the orchard, either wholly or but ten or twelve feet width along each row of trees, be dug or deeply ploughed, it will give new vigour to the roots, and which together with the thinning of the trees to admit the ſun and air freely, and the principal branches being diveſted of the moſs, you will find them ſhoot at top with freſh vigour, and the quantity, ſize, and quality of the fruit be greatly augmented in a year or two.

ORCHARD-GRASS. The name of a ſmall, coarſe, but very ſweet graſs. It is of very quick growth, and may poſſibly hereafter be cultivated to advantage.

ORE-WEED. A general name for weeds growing at the bottom of the ſea,

sea, and also on the muddy and rocky parts of the shore.

Sea-weeds are so beneficial a manure, that farmers ought not to grudge the expence of carrying them a few miles. In Devonshire, Cornwall, and other maritime parts of England, these weeds are laid in heaps till they are rotten, and then spread upon the land, about a load to three rods: but this lasts only one year, unless sand, or a stiff earth, according to the quality of the soil intended to be improved, be laid on or mixed with them; and then they become a lasting manure. In some places, these weeds are gathered in heaps, and burnt as soon as they are dry; after which about a bushel of their ashes is laid on upon three rods of ground. But these, like all other ashes, should be mixed with sand, or stiff earth, if you will have the land last good: otherwise they are only an improvement for a year. These ashes are particularly good for grass grounds over-run with moss. Loose sandy soils are likewise peculiarly benefitted by this weed: but, being a sub marine plant, the wind and sun soon exhale its moisture; so that the more speedily it is taken from the shore, where storms often throw it up in great quantities, the better it is. When spread on the ground, and afterwards covered over, it soon dissolves into a salt oily slime, proper to fertilize and bind light soils. This is the most approved way of applying it: though some lay it naked, and fresh from the sea, upon their barley lands, towards the end of March and beginning of April, and have a good crop of corn: but such quantities of rank weeds are apt to shoot up afterwards, that no wholesome plant is to be expected that year.

ORCHIS, *See* DOGSTONES.

ORIGANY, [*Origanum.*] Wild Thyme, or Wild Majoram. This is met with upon dry chalky hills, and in gravelly soils, in several parts of England. It has an agreeable smell, and a pungent taste, warmer than that of the garden marjoram, and much resembling thyme, which it seems to agree with in virtue. An essential oil distilled from it, is kept in the shops.

ORPINE, [*Telephium.*] This is a very thick-leaved juicy plant, not unlike the houseleeks. It has a mucilaginous roughest taste, and hence is recommended as emollient and astringent, but has never been much regarded in practice.

Bastard ORPINE. See BASTARD ORPINE.

ORRIS, [*Iris.*] The roots of this plant, when recent, have a bitter, but acrid, nauseous taste, and taken into the body proves strongly cathartic; and hence the juice is recommended in dropsies, in the dose of three or four scruples. By drying they lose this quality, yet still retain a somewhat pungent, bitterish taste: their smell in this state is of the aromatic kind; those produced in the warmer climates have a very grateful flavour, approaching to that of March violets: hence the use of the Florentine iris in perfumes, and for flavouring liquors: the shops employ it in the white pectoral troches, &c.

OSIER, [*Salix.*] A small kind of willow; which from the patricular uses for which it is raised, requires a different sort of management, and another manner of planting.

The osier very much resembles the willow in its appearance, but that is a smaller tree, its shoots are longer and slenderer, and its leaves also much longer; these are very narrow, and in the best kind are green on the upper side, but whitish, as it were, woolly underneath.

The osier loves a wet and low ground near waters, and nearly upon a level with the water. It thrives no where so well as in marshy places, near the edges of large rivers; or in those little islands that are formed by the breaking of their current; and every way surrounded by the water. The ground for an ozier bed should be a rich black mould; and this is very common in these low and wet situations.

The design in planting the osier is, that it may shoot out a great quantity of fine slender twigs, which are to be cut at a small growth. Therefore there is no occasion for a trunk either of the pollard or timber tree form. This would only exhaust a great deal of the nourishment taken in by the root, and deprive the shoots of it; neither are they so apt to rise straight and fine, unless they begin near the ground.

On this depends the peculiar way of planting the ozier. It is raised in the same manner as the other willows, by truncheons or stakes driven into the ground;

ground; and it is proper always to let a certain quantity of the shoots stand for a due growth for this purpose, when the rest are cut. But as these are not to rise in a trunk, they must not be above four foot in length, and three foot of this must be thrusted into the ground.

They will, by this means, have a fine supply of roots; and beginning to shoot so near the earth, all the nourishment will be carried up into the twigs.

These stakes are to be planted at three foot distance, and they will quickly yield a large profit: the twigs rise numerous from their tops; and being cut down pretty close, in the manner of shrowding pollard trees, they send up a new set of twigs again almost immediately, which quickly grow to their proper size.

The time of cutting osiers is in September; and the advantage that may be made of planting them is very great. Many waste pieces of wet ground might be made to yield a great profit by them.

If stakes or truncheons of a proper bigness cannot be had, more time will be required to raise the ozier bed; but it may be done from smaller sets. These are to be cut four or five foot long, and stuck at the same distances into the ground. They will grow very freely; and when they have stood three years, they are to be cut down within a foot of the ground; and from thence will rise the twigs in great abundance; and they will continue affording a supply of them many years.

The finest and best kind of osier is that here described with long leaves, white underneath; but there are several others that answer the purpose very well. The twigs are of constant and ready sale. The basket-maker's work depends upon them; and there is a great consumption of them among the fishermen. The wheels, as they are called, for catching eels and other fish, are made of them: and baskets, hampers, and the like, of which the consumption is, in a manner, endless and unlimited.

The quick growth of the twigs is a great article in the profit of an osier holt, for they are cut every year; and the heads that bear them grow for a long time more and more bushy at every cutting. So that here is a vast profit to be made with scarce any expence; annually returned and increased every year; and this upon ground fit for nothing else; for the osier will grow and flourish on ground that is so loose and so wet, that it would not afford hold for the root of any other kind of plantation whatsoever.

As the stems of the osiers will decay in time, let the husbandman always take care to have a supply. Nothing is so easy: for 'tis only sticking into the ground some twigs between the stems, which will take their time to root themselves, and grow to a due bigness; and when properly cut, and managed according to the directions already given, or raising an osier ground from sets, will be ready to yield their produce as the old ones begin to decay; and may thus be made to supply their place gradually as they are wanted.

OSLETS. Oslets are little hard substances that arise among the small bones of the knee of the horse, on the inside; they grow out of the gummy substance which fastens those bones together, and derive their origin from a matter like that which produces splents, and like them proceed from the same cause, viz. the straining of a horse while he is young, and before his joints be well knit; and from hence also we may understand the nature of all those hard tumours already treated of, which grow near the joints, whether they be *Spavins*, *Jardons*, *Curbs*, or of any other kind, their chief difference consisting in their situation, being all of them formed of a matter, which, in time, grows hard, yea, even as the bone itself; and this is the reason why they cannot be moved but by things that are of the greatest efficacy. Notwithstanding, if they be discovered before they acquire such a degree of hardness, they may be made to yield to less powerful remedies than what we are sometimes constrained to make use of.

OST. *See* OUST.

OVERFLOWING LAND. This is commonly effected by diverting the streams of rivers, brooks, land-floods, or some part of them, out of their natural channel: but were the streams lie so low as to be incapable of over-flowing the lands, they are made use of to turn such engines as may raise a quantity of water to do it.

When you have got your water up

to

to the highest part of the land that you can bring it to, make a small trench to carry some of the water in, to give you the level the land, keeping of it always as much as you can upon a level, or upon the highest part of the land, so that from the upper part you may be able to water the lower when you will, and by carrying of the level of this small trench you will be directed how to cut on your main trench, which ought to be made big enough to receive the whole stream that you raise, and to be rather broad than deep. At convenient distances according unto the bigness of the stream, and the quantity of the land you are to water, make several small trenches, making your main trench the narrower, proportionable to the number of drains you lead from it; only you must note, that the greatest advantage of over-flowing is, where you can do it frequently, and draw it off quickly; because where water stands long on ground, especially in winter, 'tis apt to breed rushes and weeds; and therefore where any such inconveniency is, draw it off by small trenches.

Some graze their land till Christmas, and some longer; but as soon as 'tis fed bare from Allhallowtide to spring, that the grass is not too high, is the best time for over-flowing, except it prove a dry time in April or May: If it do, it will be of mighty advantage; for in hot weather the grass grows three times as much if moistened, as at another time. Land-floods are best to overflow with in winter, and warm fattening springs in summer, only you must observe to let the water dry in before you water it again; and not to let cattle poach it, and that you water it at night so as that the water may be gone before the heat of the day comes, which is apt to occasion the scorching of it; and to rot the roots of the grass by lying too long on the land. The washing of high ways, towns, or streets, especially of commons, where sheep feed, is a very great improvement of land or trees.

But in some places issue springs whose waters are injurious to land, as such usually are that flow from coal mines, or any sulphurous mineral, because they are of such a brackish, harsh quality, that they kill vegetables, instead of nourishing of them; as too much salt, urine, or dung will do, if not applied in due quantities; yet we cannot but think that even these waters would make a great impeovement, it sparingly used, and in wet times, that a great quantity of other water might mix with them. These waters are commonly of a reddish colour, and leave a reddish sentiment where they run, and are much better when they have run some distance, than at their first breaking out.

Also some sorts of lands will not be improved by watering, except only with land floods, and in summer, when 'tis a very dry time; as your cold clay, and strong land that lies very flat; partly because of its flatness, and that water will not easily penetrate stiff clay; and therefore light dry warm grounds are the most improved by watering.

OVER-REACH. A wound in the fore-heel of a horse, made by the point of the hind-shoe.

When this wound is only slight or superficial, it is, in general, very easily cured, by washing it clean, and applying the wound ointment: but it should be observed, from the nature and manner of the injury, where the blow has been smart, that it differs widely from a common cut; the part here being both torn and bruised, and consequently it requires to be properly digested, in order to lay a good foundation for healing.

For this purpose, after washing out any dirt or gravel with soap-suds, &c. let the wound be digested, by dressing it wirh dossils of lint dipped in an ounce of Venice turpentine, divided with the yolk of an egg, to which half an ounce of tincture of myrrh may be added; over this dressing it would be adviseable to apply the turnip poultice, or that with strong beer grounds and oatmeal, three or four times, or oftner, till the digestion is procured, and then both these dressings may be changed for the precipitate medicines, or the lime-water mixture; observing always to apply the dossils carefully to the bottom, to fill up the sore with the same even to the surface, and to bind all on with a compress and roller: and if any cavities appear that cannot conveniently be dressed to the bottom, they should always be laid open, or no proper foundation for healing can be obtained. The hoof also should be kept supple, or pared away, when the growth of it interrupts this end, as is sometimes the case.

OUST. A kiln, generally applied to that used in drying hops.

It is built with fire-places in the nature of malt-kilns; and at a proper distance over the fire is an hair-cloth strained upon laths; and thereon the hops are laid, and raked even to the depth of about six or seven inches, for the better conveniency of drying them equally; and when they are properly cured on the under side, they are carefully turned; and by that means the upper side becoming the under, the whole shares the fire alike. The person that performs this part is called the dryer, whose business it is to manage the fires.

The fuel commonly made use of is charcoal, for its freeness from smoke, and affording a steady heat. Great nicety is required in this part; a small fire being to be made, at first, that they may heat gradually, and so raised as they dry; that it may be done without scorching; and the fire is to be lowered by degrees, against they are ready to be taken off: the time required is about eight hours.

But as charcoal is very dear, being three or four pounds per load, many people have adopted the method of drying with sea-coal, upon what they call cockle-ousts, which are square iron-boxes, placed upon brick-work, and a flue and chimney in the back part of the building for the smoke to go off. The computation is, that a chaldron of sea-coal, at about twenty-four shillings, will dry a load of hops, and that a load of charcoal will do no more. It is indeed expensive to erect such ousts, as there must be no timber near them; and an iron-beam and iron-laths are to be used, and they covered with plates of tin or iron, properly fastened together.

A gentleman has lately claimed the merit of having invented a new method of drying hops with sea-coal, or any kind of fuel whatever, by means of a moveable iron furnace: it is in form of an horizontal cylinder, stopped at both ends: it lies on an iron carriage, which rolls on four iron-wheels: in the fore-end of the cylinder is the furnace door, and a hollow iron flue runs in a horizontal direction along the upper surface of the cylinder from the back, till it reaches the fore-end of it, when it takes a vertical direction, and is carried as high as is necessary to convey the smoke out of the oust. We cannot pretend to say what are the particular advantages resulting from the use of this rolling furnace, never having seen it at work.

OUT-HOUSES. Are such as belong and are adjoining to dwelling-houses.

OUTLAND. Among the Saxons, was that land that lay beyond the demesnes, and was granted out to tenants, though at the will of the Lord, in like manner as copyhold estates.

OXEN. Oxen should be tall, full bodied, short jointed, and well put together in every part, so that one sees their strength. Their hair should be fine, and lie smooth, for that betokens health, and a good kind.

The strength of the ox is very great, and he has patience to endure fatigue, but he is slow, and must not be put beyond his natural pace. He will not work easily or freely, if this be attempted, and what is worse, fretting & hurrying throws him into distempers.

'Tis but in some particular parts of England they now breed their oxen to labour, but it is very profitable. In these places the husbandman cannot be too much warned against his hurrying them in their employments; for he should consider that they are to be fed as well as worked; and while he makes them thus liable to distempers, he takes them off from one, and makes them incapable of the other.

When oxen are to be trained to labour, they must be first put to work at three years old, but they must be brought to it gently, and, by degrees, in the manner of a young horse; for if they be pushed or worked too hard at this time, they are spoiled for ever.

Great care must be taken to match such well as are to draw together, for otherwise they draw unequally, and spoil both the work and one another.

In this case of matching them, regard must be had to three things; their height, their strength, and their spirit: for some are tall that have not much strength; and others have a great deal of power that are sluggish.

In general they are very tractable and gentle, but regard must be had to their several natures, for they will not

be

be forced out of them by any usage; and they may be greatly injured in the endeavour.

Of all the kinds the pyed Lincolnshire ox is the fittest for labour. He is naturally long-bodied, and till put up to feed, is less fleshy than any of the other good breeds; though he takes to fattening very readily with rest, and a good pasture.

When the young oxen are first put to work, a great deal of care must be taken not to overheat or fatigue them. They must be suffered to rest in the middle of the day in hot weather, and the servant should give them some hay, which will support them in the new fatigue of their labour, much better than grass. They must be well fed during the whole time of their labouring, for they will not do much if they be not kept in spirits by good nourishment; but in this let the husbandman understand moderation; for there is difference between feeding them for strength, and for fattening.

An ox for labour must neither be bare, nor must he be too fat; in the first case he will be weak, and in the other he will be lazy. They should be treated gently, for they do not understand blows and hard usage, and may easier be beaten into sicknesses and disorders, than into labour.

In this way an ox may very well be kept to work seven or eight years, that is, till between ten and eleven years old; and in that time he will do the owner an incredible deal of business, provided he thus understand how to manage him, for it all depends upon that; otherwise he will be as stubborn as an ass, and will not be fit half his time for service,

Sometimes a young ox will prove very stubborn, vicious, and unruly; but this, when enquired into, will be found owing to some bad usage at setting out, for the ox has nothing of that bad disposition in his nature. When this happens, he must be kept hungry; and when he has fasted long enough, he must be made to eat out of the hand: when he is brought to his labour, he must be tied with a rope; and at any time when he grows faulty, he must be cherished, and fed with a mouthful of hay by hand; thus bringing him by soft means to quietness, and a readiness in performing his business; for nothing else will do with this creature.

For the breaking a young ox to the field, no way is so well as to single out one of the tamest of the old ones, that is of its own size; and yoke them together. Let them be put to some slight work, and suffered to do it easily and slowly: they will thus draw equally, and the young beast will become perfectly familiar to it. They will be apt to get into too slow a gait at first, but by degrees they must be spirited to be a little brisker in their pace; and after half a dozen times going out with this quiet beast, the young one must be coupled with an ox of more spirit, that will learn him to go quicker. Thus he is to have his companion changed from time to time, till in the first month or six weeks of his labour, he gets to draw with the briskest of the stock.

This is the only way to get the ox to his speed; for at best it is not great, nor will he be brought to it by force.

The advantages of labouring with oxen are so great, that it is wonderful the practice does not extend farther. The ox of eleven years old, when he is unfit for labour any longer, may be fattened as well as at any time; and in the same manner if he fall lame, or by any other accident be spoiled for labour, at whatever age that happen, he may then be fed up for sale.

In this the ox has a great advantage over the horse, which, when aged, or spoiled by accidents, is good for nothing, and becomes an entire loss, and often a very great one to the farmer.

The food of the horse is also a very expensive article to the husbandman, but that of oxen is cheap. They require no oats. They are very little liable to diseases, whereas one is never secure of a horse at all. But though the ox does not require so expensive food as the horse, yet such as he eats must be good in its kind, and he must not be stinted. He must always have good grass to go to, and good hay in winter, else he will be of little service; for though he must not be fattened in his time of working, yet if he be not kept well fed, and in good spirits, he is worth nothing.

The greatest use of the ox in the way of labour, is that of plowing, and 'tis that for which they are suited by nature. They will work at this in the toughest and heaviest grounds as well as horses, and do as much in a day. They do not serve so well for drawing of carts and waggons; and are not fit to be used much in places where the roads are good.

In most counties the farmer would do well to train up some of his oxen for draught, though it is better not to depend upon them entirely for that service in any. We have shewn for what they are most, and for what they are least fitted. Every farmer has occasion both for carting and plowing; and the horses are in general fittest for the former, and the oxen most profitable for the latter: therefore when there are more teams than one kept, some should be of horses, and others of oxen, proportioning the number of either to the nature of the service, and of the roads and the ground. The Farmer who keeps two teams only, will almost always find it his interest to have one of them of oxen, and the other of horses.

In clayey lands, the oxen are most useful; and in chalky countries the least; the chalk soon spoiling their feet.

It is a custom in some places where oxen are used for draught, to yoke them by the horns, but this is awkward and troublesome. It is left off in many places where it was once used; and ought to be in all. The common way of yoaking them together by the neck and breast is vastly preferable, but harness best of all.

Whenever the farmer comes to a resolution of keeping oxen for labour, let him at the same time provide for a proper supply of them; and see that it be rather too much than too little, for it will always be more to his profit to sell what he does not want, than to buy for his necessary uses. To this end he should rear at least two oxen and two cow calves every year to keep up his stock; and put up his old, or injured beasts to fatten, and supply their places from this breed as occasion requires: for an ox, as before said, whether put off the team forage or injuries, will fatten as well as at any other time, and will bring a good price at market; and afford as good beef as any other that had not been worked.

When the husbandman buys in cattle to fatten, it should be either in spring, or toward the beginning of October. These oxen which are bought in early in spring, will, with proper care, be fat in July, August, or September, according to the goodness of the soil, and the manner of feeding them, and according to the condition wherein they were bought. An ox that is very forward when bought in, and is turned into a very rich pasture, will be fit for market in ten weeks; but there is no need that every ox that is bought for this purpose, should be in this forward way; or that every one should be hastened to a market condition in that hurry. The care of the husbandman in this should be, to suit his endeavours to the nature of his grounds, and to the best demand for the cattle: he may keep on fattening the whole summer months, and answer his purpose better both for the market, and for having the best service out of his land, than if he hastened up all that he bought, or bought only very forward ones.

Those oxen that are bought in about the beginning of October, will in general be fit for sale early in the following spring. There requires some management in this article of the husbandman's business, for without it he may lose by his industry, but with due care he will find a sufficient profit in this way. These cattle being for sale early in spring, will always fetch a good price; but the winter feeding of them may easily run away with what should be his profit.

The method is to forward these in flesh, before the winter sets in hard; and then to take care only to keep them up in flesh during the hard time, with hay or turneps.

They may be thus kept in a condition for market whenever it is worth while to sell them; and be sure of fattening up with great ease very early in spring, to a certain advantage.

Another way of buying cattle in the beginning of October, to great advantage, is to purchase young lean oxen which will pay for their winter keeping by their growth, and be ready to fatten up early in spring, to the fairest and fullest profit.

Another very good time of buying oxen for feeding is in August, or the be-

beginning of September. These should be got forward as soon as may be, by putting them into very rich pastures, and they will be ready for the winter sale.

This is the best method the husbandman can take, who has rich and fine pasture ground; for no other will support the large and valuable breed of these oxen. But he who happens not to have this advantage, is not altogether to decline thus much of the grazing business, which to the other proves so very advantageous.

Therefore he who has but moderately good pasturage, and is inclined to deal this way, should set about in a different manner. Let him buy in a number of young Welch heifers, instead of oxen, in August or September, and put them into the best of his ordinary pasturages. He is to take his chance whether these prove with calf or not, but either way they will answer his purpose.

If they prove with calf his business is to keep them till spring, and then he will sell them to a good advantage, with a calf by their side, for the dairy. If they do not prove with calf they will presently begin to fatten upon his ground, which, though poor, is yet very fine in comparison of what they have been used to, and he will be able to sell them out at a very good account at Christmas or in spring; at both which times meat is dear, and consequently cattle fetch a price.

These heifers will, to the husbandman thus situated, answer, in some measure, the purposes of oxen; and he is not to complain they do not bring altogether such a price; because neither the cattle themselves, nor their keeping, have cost him so much as in the other instance. Such land being cheaper than the rich and fine pasture ground, on which the large oxen may be fattened.

But there is this to be considered, that the advantage will be the greater, in proportion as the farmer has the convenience of hay, or turneps, which are the two foods for winter fattening of cattle; and in proportion to his nearness to some large city, where the demand and the price will answer to the expensive feeding of hay. About great towns they must afford to let a beast eat a couple load of hay in a winter, because the demand is certain and the price good: but this will not do in remote places.

Let the husbandman who buys cattle for fattening, take great care in the choice, for on that will depend a large share of his success. Let him examine their bulk and shape, and the forwardness they are in at the time, and after that proportion the goodness of the pasture to their kind.

Those that are intended to be kept up for a winter, or early spring market, must be turned out in September into the rowens, till the weather become severe by much snow or a very hard frost; and till this time they will not need any fodder.

Upon the coming in of the hard weather they must have some hay regularly every morning and evening, which must be proportioned to what the ground still affords. The more they find there the less they want of the supply; and the less there is, the more hay must be each time given them.

The frosts have an effect upon grass, especially upon the worst sorts, to sweeten it. The sour grass which the cattle had left untouched for a great while, becomes palatable to them after two or three nights good frost, with a large white ryme. They will eat this greedily; and it will make hay the less necessary, till the snow covers it, and they cannot get at it. 'Tis at these times the foddering is to be largest and best; for without a due care they will, in a little time, lose all the advantage they had made in many weeks.

For those oxen that were bought in lean, and are not got into any great degree of flesh by the beginning of the hard season, straw will do instead of hay: and the husbandman must begin with barley straw, and then come to oat straw, both which are very good food to cattle in this condition; and will keep them as they are, and in a readiness for any farther improvement, when it comes upon easy terms.

Toward the end of winter the whole product of the ground that hath been thus fed, will be eaten up, and then the oxen are to be taken into the yard. If the husbandman has oxen in two conditions, (the one that he feeds with hay, the other with straw,) they must be put up separate; and their food must be put up in racks for them.

The

The farmer often complains that his cattle will not eat their fodder, when they are taken up into the yard, though they did freely when it was given them in the field. But this is generally owing to the folly of giving them too much at a time. An ox will often eat heartily and freely out of the crib for a time, till when he had often breathed upon it, what was left became quite diſagreeable to him.

This is a delicacy in the nature of the animal, and nothing can break him of it, but all the inconvenience of it is eaſily prevented, by giving theſe cattle a little at a time, and often. This being, for all reaſons, the beſt way of foddering all cattle in the yard.

Let the huſbandman take care that his yard be well ſheltered, and kept dry. Let there be ſtraw enough ſcattered about it, that his cattle may lie ſweet and warm; this will greatly aſſiſt in keeping them in good caſe; and he need not grudge the expence, for what the ſtraw is worth will be many times over made up to him in dung. Their trampling this litter, with their dung and urine, converts the whole into a very rich manure; and the quantity becomes ſo conſiderable, that it is an article of great conſequence.

When oxen are put to be fattened on land, they may be turned in either alone or with horſes; or they may be put into the paſtures firſt, and the horſes afterwards. Which ever way is uſed, let the huſbandman take care of the time of turning in his oxen. Many think they ought to let the graſs be very well grown before they put them to feed upon it; but they are greatly miſtaken. There is not a greater diſadvantage the farmer can lie under, in this way, than the having his paſtures too high grown before he puts the beaſts into them.

The ox is a nice creature, and does not love a rank graſs. In this caſe they only nip the tops, and the remainder rots upon the ground. When graſs is grown too high, in autumn eſpecially, it becomes ſour, and the cattle will not eat it freely before the froſt has ſweetened it to their taſte.

If it happen the farmer have at this ſeaſon of the year, a paſture ground of tall graſs, the beſt method he can follow is this. Let him firſt turn in his oxen in a proper number, and they will eat off the tops; but as they will meddle with no more of it, when this is done they ſhould be removed out of it. Horſes are then to be turned in, who, not being ſo nice as the ox will eat it down lower; and after theſe he may feed it with ſheep, which will ſtill find a great deal for their purpoſe, that the ox and the horſe had both left.

If the paſtures in the farmer's grounds be all of nearly the ſame kind, and all of a proper graſs for feeding of his oxen, ſtill let him frequently change their place, removing from one of the cloſes to another. This anſwers a double purpoſe; it gives the cattle a variety of food, and it gives every piece of the ground reſt at times to ſhoot afreſh after their eating. Their taſte is ſo nice as to diſtinguiſh the growth where it appears to our eye all the ſame; and therefore they will be pleaſed with removing from one ground to another: and each cloſe will ſhoot up with ſpirit and freſhneſs from their cropping of it, when it is quiet for a little time from the treading of their feet.

Let the huſbandman always purchaſe as large a breed as his ground will maintain; and by this management he will find it ſupport a better ſort than perhaps he might imagine it could, or than it in reality would do, in the hands of a leſs ſkilful perſon. The ſize of the ox is a vaſt article, for it makes great addition both in the fleſh and tallow.

Let the ox have a ſmooth forehead and a deep belly, if he be intended for fattening. The ſtrength of his joints is more the matter when he is firſt deſigned for labour.

In buying oxen for fattening preference is to be given to the young; but if they be ſomewhat older, let the farmer ſee that they are healthful. Let him feed his own breed for ſlaughter, if he uſes their labour till the beſt time of their working is over, as before directed; but let him not bring them in for fattening at that age, without he bargain accordingly.

It is always a good ſign of health that an ox frequently licks himſelf. It is a proof that he is in good humour with himſelf, and in ſpirit; for when they grow ſickly, dull, and droniſh, they utterly neglect themſelves, and their coat becomes rough, and ſtares for want of this little care of their own, which keeps it in order.

Never-

Nevertheleſs, every thing is to be underſtood within the bounds of moderation. This licking of himſelf, which is in general a ſign of health in the ox, may be a diſeaſe. They will ſometimes lick till they cannot eat, for they ſwallow a great many of the hairs they lick off, and they will ſometimes get together into a kind of ball in the ſtomach, which will impair the creature's health. In this caſe the owner muſt, at times, waſh the ox with a ſtrong decoction of worm wood, which is a taſte it abhors; and finding this bitterneſs on the ſkin, it will be cured of licking; as children are weaned by rubbing the nipple with aloes.

Some, for this purpoſe, cover the creature with his own dung, but this is a filthy way. As the licking is always done for cleanlineſs, the ox will often tire himſelf, from day to day, with endeavouring to get this off; or elſe he will utterly neglect himſelf, which will prove of as bad conſequence.

In examining how the ox proceeds in fattening, the ſureſt way is to feel the hindermoſt rib. If all be ſoft and looſe about that, 'tis a proof that the creature is getting into good fleſh. The part behind the ſhoulders in an ox, and the navel of a cow, are the parts to be examined, to know how they encreaſe in tallow. Also at the Rump.

Finally, there is one thing we ſhall recommend to the huſbandman very ſtrongly, from experience, as excellent toward the fattening of cattle, and this is the bleeding of them at proper times. This ſhould be done once at leaſt, and commonly it may be done twice, with great benefit during their feeding.

The method to be obſerved is this: in the cattle bought in ſpring, always to bleed them as ſoon as they are put to paſture, which makes them take to fattening directly. In theſe bought in autumn, follow the ſame method of bleeding, at the time of turning into good paſture; which will not only help their fattening, but prevent diſorders. This is all there is to do with thoſe intended for the winter market; but for ſuch as were bought lean to be kept for growing in winter, and fattened up in ſpring, have them blooded twice, once when they are bought in, and a ſecond time early in ſpring, when they are going into the paſture for fattening.

OX-BOOSE. An ox ſtall, or cow-ſtall, where theſe creatures ſtand in the winter.

OX-HARROWS. Very large harrows, called, in ſome counties, drags.

OX-GANG, or *Ox gate*. A quantity of land meaſuring fifteen acres, being as much ground as a ſingle ox is ſuppoſed to be capable of ploughing in a year.

OX-EYE, [*Buphthalmum*.] There are ſeveral ſpecies of herbaceous and ſhrubby plants, which ornament the pleaſure garden and green-houſe, and are all propagated by ſeeds and cuttings.

OXEYE-DAISY, [*Bellis-Major*.] This plant is frequent in fields, and among corn, flowering in May or June. The leaves have a mucilaginous, ſubſaline, roughiſh taſte. They are ſaid to be detergent, reſolvent, aperient, and alſo moderately aſtringent. Geoffroy relates, that the herb, gathered before the flowers have come forth, and boiled in water, imparts an acrid taſte, penetrating and ſubtile like pepper; and that this decoction is an excellent vulnerary and diuretic.

OX-SLIP. A ſpecies of cowſlip.

P.

PACK-HORSE. A horſe uſed for carrying loads on a ſaddle made for that purpoſe.

PACK-SADDLE. A ſaddle contrived for the carrying of burthens on a horſe's back.

PACK *of Wool*, is ſeventeen ſtone and two pounds, or two hundred and forty pounds weight.

PAD. An eaſy pacing horſe.

PAD. A low ſaddle.

PAD. A road, a path.

PADDLE. An inſtrument to open gutters in a water courſe, to clean the ploughſhare from dirt, weeds, *&c.*

PADDOCK. A ſmall field or incloſure.

PAIGLE. A cowſlip.

PAIL. A wooden veſſel to carry water or milk in.

PAINS, *or watery ſores on the legs and paſterns.* Theſe are cauſed by a ſerous matter oozing through the pores, which is indued with ſuch a ſharpneſs, that it makes the hair fall off from ſeveral parts of the legs and paſterns; ſometimes it looſens the *Coronet* from the hoof; and ſometimes the fleſh appears as if it was disjoined from the bones and ſinews; wherever the matter runs, it ſo hardens the ſkin, that it is apt to break out into cracks and refts, which diſcharge abundance of ſtinking matter, as in the abovementioned caſe. The cure conſiſts chiefly in internals, and in thoſe things that are proper to rectify the blood, as decoctions of boxwood, guajacum and ſaſſafras, &c. or the ſaid woods may be raſped and mixt with his oats, and ſometimes among dry bran. All the medicines preſcribed in the farcin may be made uſe of in this caſe: but if the horſe be inclinable to a dropſy, which may be known by the yielding of the ſwelling, and likewiſe as the fore legs will alſo be affected, and by the other ſigns peculiar to that diſtemper, he muſt then be treated accordingly; mean while the following applications may be made outwardly.

'Take honey, turpentine, and hog's-greaſe, of each a like quantity: melt them over a gentle fire in a glazed pipkin, and add a ſufficient quantity of wheat flour to make it into a poultice.' Or this:

'Take fœnugreek meal, bean flour, linſeed meal, and muſtard ſeed pounded, of each a like quantity. Boil them over a gentle fire, with a ſufficient quantity of ointment of marſh-mallows; into the conſiſtence of a poultice.'

Theſe muſt be applyed warm to the legs and paſterns, to draw out the matter, and bring down the ſwelling. If there be foulneſs, you may take a pound of black ſoap, half a pound of honey, four ounces of burnt allum, two ounces of verdigreaſe in powder, a pint of brandy or ſpirit of wine, with a ſufficient quantity of wheat flour. Let this be ſpread on cloths, and applyed as the former.

As ſoon as the ſwelling is abated, and the moiſture dryed up, it muſt be very convenient to keep the legs and paſterns rolled up with firm bandage, whereby the parts will not only be kept cloſe, but the influx of freſh matter prevented; for the continuance or frequent returns of thoſe watery eruptions brings ſuch a looſeneſs into the legs, that it cauſes a rottenneſs in the fruſh, breeds ſplints; and, ſometimes by rotting the tendons, becomes the cauſe of quitter-bones, foundering, and other diſtempers in the feet.

PAINPISS, *or Strangury.* This diſeaſe happens moſt frequently when there is an obſtruction of the dung hardened and indurated in the ſtraight gut, yet ſometimes it proceeds from another cauſe, and is moſt likely occaſioned by an inflammation of the bladder, or an ulcer in the kidneys; for when there happens to be an ulcer in thoſe parts, the ſharpneſs of the matter proceeding from thence may no doubt cauſe pain, when

when it paſſes into the *Urethra* or piſs-pipe, by abrading and carrying off the *mucus* that ſhould defend that ſenſible part, ſo that a horſe in this caſe muſt piſs in pain; and as this will alſo cauſe an inflammation there, inſtead of piſſing freely, he will often dribble.

An inflammation in thoſe parts, ariſing from any other cauſe, as hard riding, too long a detention of his urine, has generally the ſame effect; but an inflammation of this kind happens the more readily if there be a lentor of the dung.

To remove all ſuch diſorders, it will be neceſſary to give emollient ſoftning clyſters, made of a decoction of mallows, marſh-mallows, mercury, camomile and the like, with a mixture of oils and other ſlippery things, or clyſters made of fat broths; and to make them a little purgative, common treacle or manna may be diſſolved in them, to the quantity of ſix ounces or half a pound.

Half an ounce of *Sal Prunella* or purifyed nitre may be diſſolved in his water for two or three days together, or two ounces of crude tartar may be boiled in it; and among his provender may be mixt the leaves of ſtrawberries, radiſhes and turnip-tops.

But if after hard riding you have reaſon to ſuſpect an inflammation in the kidneys, the bladder, or urinary paſſage, which muſt at the ſame time be accompanied with feveriſh ſymptoms, it will then be very proper to take blood from the neck-vein, and the uſe of the clyſters may be repeated as often as you ſhall ſee occaſion; but if you have reaſon to fear an ulcer in the kidneys, in that caſe all cleanſing balſamic medicines are to be complied with, for which purpoſe we chiefly recommended the following balls.

Take gum benjamin half a pound. Balſam of capivi, Flour of brimſtone, each ſix ounces. Bees wax three ounces. Crude opium one ounce. Honey four ounces. Beat them well together with ſyrup of marſh-mallows, enough to make into balls of two ounces each, one to be given every morning, an hour before his water.

PALATE, *Falling off.* A troubleſome diſorder in oxen, from over driving, &c. rub the palate with pepper and ſalt mixt together.

PALE. A piece of wood ſplit or ſawed, for the purpoſe of fencing, where hedges cannot be made, or are not ſufficiently ſecure.

PALING. Fencing with pales.

PALISADE. A row of handſome pales ſet up by way of ornament or defence. The gardeners uſe this word to denote a row of trees, which bear branches and leaves from the bottom, cut and ſpread in the manner of a garden wall, along the ſide of an alley or the like, ſo as to appear like a wall covered with leaves.

PALM-TREE. There are ſeveral ſpecies of this tree, as the DATE-*tree*, MACAW-*tree*, CABBAGE-*tree*, &c.

PALMETTO. A ſpecies of palm, the leaves of which are uſed as thatch in the Weſt-Indies.

PALMS. The flowers of the willow.

PALSY. This diſorder has been uſually reckoned the ſame with the ſtaggers, but certainly, without any reaſon whatſoever; the former implies the abſence of fever or ſtimulus, the latter, an increaſed degree; in the one, warm cordials will be neceſſary; in the other, emollients and anodynes. Warm ſtimulating embrocations will be very proper. Such as the following:

Take ſpirits of wine and camphor 6 ounces, ſpirits of ſal ammoniac 2 ounces, mix and bathe the part affected night and morning.

Such medicines ſhould be given as will promote the circulation of the blood. Such are the following balls:

Take aſſafœtida ſix ounces, grains of paradiſe in powder two ounces, aloes two ounces, honey to make 6 balls, give one night and morning.

PANIC, [*Panicum.*] A plant reſembling millet in its ſtalks, leaves, and roots; but differing in its ſpikes, or ears, which are about the thickneſs of a man's finger at their baſe, and growing taper toward their points. They are about eight or nine inches long, and cloſely ſet with a ſmall roundiſh grain, ſometimes white, ſometimes red or purple, and ſometimes yellow. It is raiſed and reaped in the ſame manner as millet, but does not require ſo much rain. This plant grows naturally in both the Indies, and is cultivated in many parts of Europe for the food of men. Cakes and bread are made of it in Germany, Italy, and the ſouthern parts of France; but it is not reckoned ſo good nouriſh-

ment

ment as millet: nor is the German sort so much esteemed as the Italian; though the former ripens best in cold countries, where it is frequently sowed in land which will not produce better grain. It thrives most in a dry stiffish soil, such as the sides of hills, and even in stony ground; grows to the height of about four feet, and branches very much; for which reason the horse-hoeing husbandry is by far the fittest for it. The plants, if managed rightly, should stand eighteen inches asunder, in rows three feet apart, that there may be room to hoe the ground between them, and to keep them clear from weeds. When grown pretty tall, they should be supported by stakes, lest the wind break them down; and particular care must be taken to guard against birds when their seeds begin to ripen.

PANNAGE. The food which swine feed upon in woods, as acorns, and the masts of beech. It also signifies the money taken by the King's agistors, for the privilege of feeding hogs in the King's forests.

PANNEL. A low saddle.

PANSIES. Hearts-ease.

PANTING-EVIL. A disorder in cattle, caused by extraordinary labour, over heat, &c. the symptoms are, great faintness and unwillingness to move, sighing, moaning, &c.

Let the beast be kept very quiet and be supported with some ale spiced, and bread sopped in it; or, boil some rosemary, and some wormwood, in some ale, and give the beast to drink.

Give an ounce of Bracken's cordial, every four, six, or, eight hours. Let the food be a little bran and oats, with some very sweet hay.

PANTILES. A peculiar kind of tiles made of clay, moulded and burnt.

PAPAW. A plant of the gourd, or squash kind, growing in the Caribbee Islands, and the warmer parts of America. May be propagated as melons.

PARADISE-APPLE. A kind of apple tree, formerly much esteemed for stocks to graft on.

Grains of PARADISE. This fruit is about the size of a fig, divided internally into three cells, in each of which are contained two rows of small seeds like cardamoms. These seeds are somewhat more grateful, and considerably more pungent, than the common cardamoms, approaching in this respect to pepper, with which they agree also in their pharmaceutical properties: their pungency residing, not in the distilled oil, as that of cardamom seeds does, but in the resin extracted by spirit of wine.

PAREIRA BRAVA. This is the root of an American convolvulus, brought to us from Brazil, in pieces of different sizes, some no bigger than one's finger, others as large as a child's arm: it is crooked, and variously wrinkled on the surface; outwardly of a dark colour, internally of a dull yellowish, and interwoven with woody fibres, so that upon a transverse section, a number of concentric circles appear, crossed with fibres, which run from the center to the circumference: it has no smell; the taste is a little bitterish, blended with a sweetness, like that of liquorice. This root is highly extolled by the Brazilians and Portuguese, in a great variety of diseases, particularly against suppressions of urine, nephritic pains, and the calculus. In the two first, Geoffroy says he has given it with good success, and that the patient was almost instantly relieved by it, a copious discharge of urine succeeding. He likewise observed large quantities of gravel, and even small stones, voided after its use: this effect he attributes not to any lithontriptic power, but to its dissolving the viscid mucus, by which the sabulous matter had been detained. He likewise relates, that he has had frequent experience of the good effects of this root in deterging and healing ulcers of the kidneys and bladder, where the urine came away purulent and mucous, and could not be voided at all without extreme pain; by the use of the *pareira*, the urine soon became clear, and of a due consistence, and was evacuated freely; and by joining to this medicine balsam of Copaiba, the ulcer perfectly healed. The attenuating quality, which he had discovered in this root induced him to make trial of it in other diseases, proceeding from tenacious juices, and in these likewise it fully answered his expectations: in humoral asthmas, where the lungs were stuffed up, and the patient almost suffocated by thick phlegm, an infusion of *pareira*, after many other medicines had proved ineffectual, occasioned a plentiful expectoration, and soon completed a cure: in the jaundice, proceeding

ing from thick bile, it did excellent service; but in another icterical case, where the liver was swelled and hard, this medicine did no good. His dose of the root in substance is from twelve grains to half a dram, in decoction two or three drams.

PARK-LEAVES. St. John's wort.

PARSLEY. The name of a well-known herb, which is cultivated in gardens for culinary purposes, it being more used in the kitchen than any other herb whatsoever; it will tolerably endure cold, but is apt to be destroyed in very severe winters, especially where the land is moist; it is commonly sown in the spring, and sends forth a stalk the year after, which flowers in June or July, and the seeds ripen in August.

The common parsley is, by some skilful people, cultivated in fields for the use of sheep, it being a sovereign remedy to preserve them from the rot, provided they are fed twice a week, for two or three hours each time, with this herb: but hares and rabbits are so fond of it, that they will come from a great distance to feed on it.

Bastard-PARSLEY. *See* BASTARD.

Mountain PARSLEY. Candy carrot.

Macedonian PARSLEY. The seeds of the Macedonian parsley are a strong carminative, it is cultivated by seed, like the common parsley.

Bastard-stone PARSLEY. *See* BASTARD STONE PARSLEY.

PARSNEP, [*Pastinaca.*] The name of a well known root, cultivated in the same manner as carrots. If you intend to save the seeds of this plant, you should make choice of some of the longest, straitest, and largest roots, which should be planted about two feet asunder, in some place where they may be defended from the strong south and west winds; for the stems of these plants commonly grow to a great height, and are subject to be broken by strong winds, if exposed thereto; they should be constantly kept clear from weeds, and if the season should prove very dry, you should give them some water twice a week, which will cause them to produce a great quantity of seeds, which will be much stronger than if they were wholly neglected. Toward the latter end of August, or the beginning of September, the seeds will be ripe; at which time you should carefully cut off the heads, and spread them upon a coarse cloth for two or three days to dry; after which, the seeds should be beaten off, and put up for use; but you should never trust to these seeds after they are a year old, for they will seldom grow beyond that age.

PASSION-FLOWER, [*Passiflora.*] The name of a very beautiful plant, having long slender stalks, which run a great length, and require support; they are covered with a purplish bark, and are furnished at each joint with a digitated leaf, composed of five smooth entire lobes, connected with the stalk by pedicles, about two inches long, having two small leaves embracing the stalks at their base; and from the same point comes out a long tendril, which twists round the neighbouring support; the flowers come out at the same joints as the leaves, supported on footstalks almost three inches long; these flowers have a faint smell, and continue but one day; they come out in July, and there is a diurnal succession till the frost in autumn puts a stop to them.

This plant may be propagated either from seeds, layers, or cuttings; they require a good aspected wall; where they may have height for their shoots to extend, which should be properly trained against it; and in the spring, the plants must be pruned, when all the small weak shoots should be cut off, and the strong ones shortened to about four or five feet long, which will cause them to put out strong shoots for flowering the following summer.

PASTURE-LAND, Is properly such land as being laid down to grass, is kept for the purpose of feeding cattle, not for mowing; but this distinction is not strictly observed, and it most usually means, all lands which have been laid down to grass, whether for mowing, or feeding of cattle. *See* MEADOW. & Laying down land

The following method of improving wet pastures, seems to be the result of experience.

" As I have, says an ingenious husbandman, within a few years, not only had some experience in my own farm, but observed the methods employed by many neighbouring gentlemen and farmers in mending their pastures, I shall communicate a few of my remarks to you on the improvement of wet

wet paſtures; which may prove, perhaps, of ſome little utility, as I ſhall ſpeak of nothing but what I have either performed myſelf, or ſeen hereabouts.

"The particular lands of which I ſpeak are looſe, woodcock, brick-earth ſoils, for about eighteen or twenty inches, and under that, clay to a great depth.

"Some that I have drained myſelf were exactly level, ſo as to be quite poiſoned with the wet, which could not drain of.

"From the beſt obſervations I could make on many experiments, the following is the method which anſwers beſt to improve them. I ſhall alſo give you the expence with us.

"The firſt thing to be done is, to make large, deep ditches round every field, and, if the fields are large, to divide them into ſmaller, of five, ſix, or ſeven acres each, by new ditches; nothing is attended with a more ſudden improvement of all the ground near the borders of the fields, than good ditches.

"I generally make mine ſix feet perpendicular deep, ſeven wide at top, and three at bottom. I never pay for them by the rod (which is cuſtomary) but give two-pence halfpenny per load, of thirty buſhels, for all the clay, &c. that is thrown out of them, and two ſhillings and ſixpence a ſcore loads for filling and ſpreading it.

"Thoſe ditches ſhould be made in ſuch a manner that no water can remain in them, but a deſcent from one to another, to carry it quickly off.

"It may eaſily be imagined how much theſe muſt drain the land, beſides the quantity of manure (clay) which ariſes out of them. Add to this the great convenience of having

ſuch fences about a farm, that the farmer is ſure to find his cattle wherever he turns them, inſtead of their breaking perpetually into his corn or hay fields, which, in multitudes of farms, is ſo often the caſe: it is ſometimes the work of a boy, only to be hunting after hogs and ſheep that go aſtray for want of good fences.

"In the banks of new ditches we always lay white-thorn, fifty roots to a rod (the workmen are allowed ſixpence per hundred for gathering them;) but I always avoid intermixing any thing with it, eſpecially haſel, for in the nut ſeaſon, fences are pulled to pieces for the fruit, by all the boys and girls in the neighbourhood; and oak, aſh, &c. only gives an opportunity to get over the hedge with greater eaſe. Sallow, willow, elder, &c. are to be avoided in the hedge, or by way of hedge-ſtake for the dead hedge, as they grow ſo faſt as quite to overſhadow the quick, and even deſtroy it. After frequent cuttings, to render the plants thick and ſtrong, I keep the quick regularly clipped, which, in a few years, renders the fence impenetrable to man or beaſt, conſidering the largeneſs of the ditch.

"If an old fence is grown bad and thin, or compoſed of improper plants, I never yet obſerved it improved by planting quick in the gaps: the beſt way is, to reverſe the bank, and plant freſh quick.

"One advantage ariſing from good fences is not apparent at firſt ſight. To the diſgrace be it ſpoken of moſt of the gentlemen of large fortunes round Bury, the game is wretchedly deſtroyed by poachers, who take it with night-nets. Theſe vermin, who are generally labourers, ſwarm in every village round me. Their method is this: they take the farmer's horſes out of his fields, and, after their doing a hard day's work, ride them all night, as faſt as they can make them go, over the ſtubbles, to catch the partridges, blundering over every hedge (except ſuch as I have deſcribed) in their way, oftentimes ſtaking the horſes making gaps in the fences, riding over ſtanding corn, clover for ſeed, or any thing that is a cover for birds, and, after damaging the farmer in a moſt ſhameful manner, carry the produce of their infamous labour to many, who, to their great diſhonour, encourage theſe raſcals for their convenience. The money they get is ſpent at the next alehouſe, and inſtead of doing the farmer a good day's work, they are drunk, aſleep, or idle, the whole day.

"Now there are very few farmers horſes that will leap a gate; but moſt will plunge through ſuch hedges as are common hereabouts: none could paſs ſuch ditches as I always make and recommend. A farmer in this pariſh has ſo effectually fenced in his fields with prodigious ditches, that I have heard him declare, that not a ſingle night-

night-netter has been on his grounds on horse-back; and were they to attempt it, they would lose more time in passing one ditch than was necessary to drag some whole farms.

"The pernicious effects, to farmers, of this abominable practice, are notorious, and cry aloud for redress: if they would ease themselves, I know of no way but such ditches as I have described.

"But to return:

"When the ditching is done, the next work is to land-drain the whole fields in such a manner that every part of them may be laid dry. In a pasture of six acres, I did two hundred rods. If there is the last fall in any part, or any place more wet than others, the drains should be cut through them. If the surface is exactly level, the depth of the drains should vary, so that the water may every where have a descent.

"These drains are made here, in general, thirty-two inches deep, twenty inches wide at the top, and four wide at the bottom. They are filled eight inches deep, with either stones or wood; but I shall ever recommend the former, as the most effectual and lasting, to those who are not desirous of saving the difference of the expence. However, I know many fields in this parish and neighbourhood that are drained with wood, and which answer extremely well; and I have been assured that they will last twenty or thirty years. Nay, in some parts of Essex I hear they do it with straw alone; but this must be of service for only a few years: if stone be used, there can be no doubt of its lasting. The labour of the whole is three-pence per rod; sometimes it is done for two-pence halfpenny.

"If with stone of the farmers, a load of thirty bushels will do three rods, which costs one shilling and a halfpenny stubbing and picking; so the expence of a rod is seven-pence, besides carriage of the stone, which is not much: but if he buys his stone, as is much the most probable in this country, we may suppose he must go two miles to fetch it, and give a shilling for eighteen bushels ready picked: the carriage is worth a shilling more, and reckoning the eighteen bushels to do a rod and half (which is near the matter) the stone of it will cost per rod, one shilling and four-pence.

"If bushes are used, a load of forty faggots will cost if he buys them, or be worth if he has them, five shillings, and cost cutting one shilling. They will do ten rods; so that the whole expence of doing a rod with them will be ten-pence, and of stone one shilling and seven-pence.

"The very first year the prodigious advantage of these drains appears, especially if the season proves wet. The grass (or corn if in ploughed fields, for it answers in all) will be fresh, vigorous, and sweet, wherever the pastures are drained.

"I have a field of six acres (mentioned above) which by land-draining, ditching, and manuring, is an exceeding good pasture, and has produced two tuns and ten hundred weight of hay per acre, in a very good year, and generally thirty-five hundred weight per acre; whereas the pastures adjoining are scarce worth the farming, and let but at seven shillings an acre, producing scarce any thing, but a little feed for lean cattle. The soil is the same in both; the six acres, about twelve years ago, being full as bad as the rest.

"To improve such wet land, nothing can be more advantageous than the clay which is thrown out of the ditches. Eighty loads per acre is the quantity I have laid on, and have been told by several sensible farmers (who clay a good deal) that it is a proper covering; but if nothing is mixed with it, ninety-five or one hundred. I know a piece of grass-land greatly improved, on which were spread one hundred and fifty loads.

"My method is to make a large hill of manure, by first laying a quantity of clay regularly on a heap; then placing a thin layer of muck, such as I have, upon it, either my stable or rack-yard dung, or bringing it of any kind in my waggon from Bury; on this layer, another thick one of clay; then the second of dung, and so on; letting the proportion be about twenty loads of dung to fifty of clay. These heaps, after remaining six months without stirring, I mix well together by turning them over, which a workman will do at the rate of eight shillings for one hundred loads. Let it lie six months longer in this state, and then carry it on to the land, paying two ſhillings and ſix-pence per ſcore loads for filling and ſpreading. This I take, from experience, to be by much the beſt way of manuring with clay, as it works and impregnates the ſoil much ſooner than alone.

"Whenever I clay arable land, I do it on clover paſtures, after the crop of corn is off, managing it in the ſame manner as for paſtures. If it is ploughed in directly, it is ſeveral years before it works; but having a winter and ſummer to diſſolve and powder it, it waſhes into the ſoil more equally, and in a properer ſtate for improvement.

"These are the principal points to be obſerved in improving ſuch wet, cold, looſe, paſtures as I have deſcribed: ſome that I have quite changed by theſe means were half over-run with moſs and ruſhes; but draining them thoroughly, and claying them, kills all rubbiſh of this ſort, and preſents the farmer with ſo admirable a view of good paſture for dairy or grazing, where ſo lately nothing could live, as is to be equalled in ſcarce any thing of the kind.

"But as all improvement ceaſes to be ſuch when more money is ſpent in it than the advantages will repay, I ſhall in a few words diſplay how far this is from being the caſe here. I will ſuppoſe two or three fields are improved, amounting in the whole to twenty acres,

	l.	s.	d.
"Sixty loads of clay per acre thrown out of the ditches, twelve hundred loads, at two-pence halfpenny per load —	12	0	0
"I will ſuppoſe ſixty rod of new ditching done, which, before clay is thrown out by the load, will coſt one ſhilling per rod —	3	0	0
"Three thouſand quickſets at ſix-pence per hundred	0	15	0
"Land-draining ſeven hundred rods with buſhes (this is the quantity I have now marked out in a field of twenty acres) at ten-pence per rod	29	3	4
"N. B. I had a great part of my laſt crop of barley killed in this field with the wet: I had therefore a fine opportunity of marking exactly where the drains ſhould be made, which ought, on ſuch occaſions, never to be omitted, were it only for the common water-furrows which are made for every crop. In ſome fields, unleſs ſuch a guide offers, it is very difficult to tell exactly where to make the land-drains.			
"Turning and mixing one thouſand ſix hundred loads of manure — — —	6	8	0
"Filling and ſpreading one thouſand ſix hundred loads, at two ſhillings and ſix-pence per ſcore — —	10	0	0
"I will ſuppoſe that the work may be done the ſooner if the farmer brings one hundred loads of the four hundred of dung from the neareſt town; and as I have not reckoned the horſes and driver for the clay cart, I ſhall not in the bringing the dung: therefore the expences per waggon load will be, the coſt three ſhillings, boy ſix-pence, and turnpike ſix-pence. A waggon load is two tumbrel loads (in this country) ſo fifty loads, at four ſhillings, are —	10	0	0
Total	71	6	4

"This is three pounds eleven ſhillings and three-pence per acre: and ſuppoſing the profit to laſt but twenty years, although the draining and ditching part will laſt twice that time, and the clay five and twenty as good as at firſt; and the farmers hereabouts ſeldom change their farms, if tolerable ones, living in them their lives, and their ſons after them, with leaſes of 17, 21, and 25 years; ſuppoſing twenty years profit, I ſay, the expences will then be, per acre, per annum, three ſhillings and ſix-pence halfpenny.

"So ſmall is the expence divided. But now let us conſider the profit.

"Such land as I have deſcribed never lets here for more than ten ſhillings per acre, by far oftener for eight ſhillings, or eight and ſix-pence; and it is from my own experience, as well

as

as various obſervations, that I aſſert the ſame land, after the improvements, will let to any tenant for ſeventeen, eighteen, and twenty ſhillings per acre.

"I will ſuppoſe it only ſixteen ſhillings, though I am certain that is conſiderably under the mark: he then gains, in point of rent, ſix ſhillings per acre; and the whole calculation is abſurd, if we do not add his whole proportionable profit on the acre: ſuppoſing his profit on it before improvement was a rent, ten ſhillings; afterward, it will undoubtedly be the ſame at leaſt; which adds ſix ſhillings more to the profit; ſo that the whole will be twelve ſhillings per acre per annum, or eight ſhillings and ſix-pence clear, after the improvement is paid.

	£.
"Twelve ſhillings per acre is per annum, for twenty years —	240
"Expences of improvement -	71
"Clear profit —	169

"Or eight pounds nine ſhillings per annum. And if we reckon five per cent. intereſt for the ſeventy one pounds, that is, three pounds eleven ſhillings per annum, which, deducted from eight pounds nine ſhillings, leaves four pounds eighteen ſhillings per annum abſolute profit.

"Thus, I think, I have ſtated the caſe of this improvement clearly; and I muſt repeat it, that I ſpeak from experience. The ſum to be expended on twenty acres will appear large to moſt farmers, whoſe property is not conſiderable; but the proportion holds for a ſingle acre; and thoſe who cannot afford to improve twenty, may three, four, or five; and I make no doubt but ſuch as attempt it will find their account in it greater than I have ſtated it.

"As I have mentioned a tumbrel-load to be thirty buſhels, and a waggon load to be but two tumbrels, I ſhould obſerve that we carry away of muck fifty buſhels at a time in our tumbrels, and ſo agree with our men in proportion to the thirty buſhel loads.

"I have obſerved, that in making new ditches or enlarging old ones, I never pay by the rod, but by the load: however, to thoſe who chuſe the former way, I would recommend that they have them worked by a frame of ſmall ſlit deal, nailed into the exact ſize of the intended ditch, and agree with the workmen to do their work by it: This will prevent diſputes which frequently ariſe."

PATIENCE. A ſpecies of the dock. Monk's Rhubarb.

PEA, [*Piſum.*] The ſpecies are 1. The greater garden pea; 2. the dwarf pea; 3. the roſe or crown pea; 4. the ſea pea; 5. Cape-horn pea; 6. the winged pea.

There is a great variety of garden peaſe now cultivated in England, which are diſtinguiſhed by the gardeners and ſeedſmen, and have their different titles; but as great part of theſe have been ſeminal variations, ſo if they are not very carefully managed, by taking away all thoſe plants which have a tendency to alter before the ſeeds are formed, they will degenerate into their original ſtate; therefore all thoſe perſons who are curious in the choice of their ſeeds, look carefully over thoſe which they deſign for ſeeds at the time when they begin to flower, and draw out all the plants which they diſlike from the other. This is what they call roguing their peas, meaning hereby, the taking out all the bad plants from the good, that the farina of the former may not impregnate the latter; to prevent which, they always do it before the flowers open; by thus diligently drawing out the bad, reſerving thoſe which come earlieſt to flower, they have greatly improved their peaſe of late years, and are conſtantly endeavouring to get forwarder varieties; ſo that it would be to little purpoſe in this place, to attempt giving a particular account of all the varieties now cultivated; therefore we ſhall only mention their titles, by which they are commonly known, placing them according to their time of coming to the table, or gathering for uſe.

The Golden Hotſpur.
The Charlton.
The Reading Hotſpur.
Maſters's Hotſpur.
Eſſex Hotſpur.
The Dwarf Pea.
The Sugar Pea.
Spaniſh Moretto.
Nonpareil.
Sugar Dwarf.
Sickle Pea.
Marrowfat.

Rose, or Crown Pea.
Rouncival Pea.
Grey Pea.
Pig Pea, with some others.

The Sea pea is found wild upon the shore in Sussex, and several other counties in England, and is undoubtedly a different species from the common pea.

The fifth sort hath a biennial root, which continues two years. This was brought from Cape Horn by Lord Anson's cook, when he passed that Cape, where the pease was a great relief to the sailors. It is kept here as a curiosity, but the pease are not so good for eating as the worst sort now cultivated in England; it is a low trailing plant; the leaves have two lobes on each foot-stalk; those below are spear-shaped, and sharply indented on their edges, but the upper leaves are small and arrow pointed. The flowers are blue, each foot-stalk sustaining four or five flowers; the pods are taper, near three inches long, and the seeds are round, about the size of tares.

The sixth sort is annual. This grows naturally among the corn in Sicily, and some parts of Italy, but is here preserved in botanic gardens for the sake of variety. It hath an angular stalk rising near three feet high; the leaves stand upon winged foot-stalks, each sustaining two oblong lobes. The flowers are of a pale yellow colour, shaped like those of the other sorts of pea, but are small, each foot-stalk sustaining one flower; these are succeeded by pods about two inches long, containing five or six roundish seeds, which are a little compressed on their sides. These are by some persons eaten green, but unless they are gathered very young they are coarse, and at best not so good as the common pea. It may be sown and managed in the same way as the garden pea.

We shall now proceed to set down the method of cultivating the several sorts of garden pease, so as to continue them throughout the season.

It is a common practice with the gardeners near London, to raise pease upon hot-beds, to have them very early in the spring; in order to which they sow their pease upon warm borders, under walls or hedges, about the middle of October; and when the plants come up, they draw the earth up gently to their stems with a hoe, the better to protect them from frost. In these places they let them remain until the latter end of January, or the beginning of February, observing to earth them up from time to time as the plants advance in height (for the reason before given;) as also to cover them in very hard frost with pease-haulm, straw, or some other light covering, to preserve them from being destroyed; then, at the time before-mentioned, they make a hot-bed (in proportion to the quantity of pease intended) which must be made of good hot dung, well prepared and properly mixed together, that the heat may not be too great. The ung should be laid from two to three feet thick, according as the beds are made earlier or later in the season; when the dung is equally levelled, then the earth (which should be light and fresh, but not over rich) must be laid thereon about six or eight inches thick, laying it equally all over the bed. This being done, the frames (which should be two feet high on the back side, and about fourteen inches in front) must be put on, and covered with glasses; after which it should remain three or four days, to let the steam of the bed pass off, before you put the plants therein, observing every day to raise the glasses, to give vent for the rising steam to pass off; then, when you find the bed of a moderate temperature for heat, you should, with a trowel or some other instrument, take up the plants as carefully as possible, to preserve the earth to their roots, and plant them into the hot-beds in rows, about two feet asunder, and the plants about an inch distant from each other in the rows, observing to water and shade them until they have taken root; after which you must be careful to give them air at all times when the season is favourable, otherwise they will draw up very weak, and be subject to grow mouldy and decay. You should also draw the earth up to the shanks of the plants as they advance in height, and keep them always clear from weeds. The water they should have must be given them sparingly, for if they are too much watered, it will cause them to grow too rank, and sometimes rot off the plants at their shanks, just above ground. When the weather is very hot, you should cover the glasses

glasses with mats in the heat of the day, to screen them from the violence of the sun, which is then too great for them: but when the plants begin to fruit, they should be watered oftner, and in greater plenty than before; for by that time the plants will have nearly done growing, and the often refreshing them will occasion their producing a greater plenty of fruit.

The sort of pea which is generally used for this purpose, is the dwarf, for all the other sorts ramble too much to be kept in frames. The reason for sowing them in the common ground, and afterwards transplanting them on a hot-bed, is to check their growth, and cause them to bear in less compass; for if the seeds were sown upon a hot-bed, and the plants continued thereon, they would produce such luxuriant plants as are not to be contained in the frames, and would bear but little fruit.

The next sort of pea, which is sown to succeed those on the hot-bed, is the hotspur, of which there are reckoned several varieties; as the Golden hotspur, the Charlton hotspur, the Masters's hotspur, the Reading hotspur, and some others; which are very little differing from each other, except in their early bearing, for which the Golden and Charlton hotspurs are chiefly preferred; though if either of these sorts are cultivated in the same place for three or four years, they are apt to degenerate, and be later in fruiting; for which reason, most curious persons procure their seeds annually from some distant place; and in the choice of these seeds, if they could be obtained from a colder situation and a poorer soil, than that in which they are to be sown, it will be much better than on the contrary, and they will come earlier in the spring.

These must also be sown on warm borders, toward the latter end of October; and when the plants are come up, you should draw the earth up to their shanks in the manner before directed, which should be repeated as the plants advance in height (always observing to do it when the ground is dry) which will greatly protect the stems of the plants against frost; and if the winter should prove very severe, it well be of great service to the plants to cover them with pease-haulm, or some other light covering, which should be constantly taken off in mild weather, and only suffered to remain on during the continuance of the frost; for if they are kept too close, they will draw up very weak and tender, and thereby be liable to be destroyed with the least inclemency of the season.

In the spring, you must carefully clear them from weeds, and draw some fresh earth up to their stems, but do not raise it too high to the plants, lest by burying their leaves you should rot their stems, as is sometimes the case, especially in wet seasons. You should also observe to keep them clean from vermin, which, if permitted to remain amongst the plants, will increase so plentifully, as to devour the greatest part of them. The chief of the vermin which infest pease, are the slugs, which lie all the day in the small hollows of the earth, near the stems of the plants, and in the night-time come out, and make terrible destruction of the pease; and these chiefly abound in wet soils, or where a garden is neglected, and over-run with weeds; therefore you should make the ground clear every way round the pease to destroy their harbours; and afterwards, in a fine mild morning very early, when these vermin are got abroad from their holes, you should slack a quantity of lime, which should be strewn hot over the ground pretty thick, which will destroy the vermin wherever it happens to fall upon them, but will do very little injury to the pease, provided it be not scattered too thick upon them. This is the best method I could ever find to destroy these troublesome vermin.

If this crop of pease succeeds, it will immediately follow those on the hot-bed; but for fear this should miscarry, it will be proper to sow two more crops at about a fortnight or three weeks distance from each other, so that there may be the more chances to succeed. This will be sufficient until the spring of the year, when you may sow several more crops of these pease at a fortnight distance from each other The late sowings will be sufficient to continue the early sort of pease through the season, but it will be proper to have some of the large sort of pease to succeed them for the use of the family in order to which, you should sow ſome of the Spaniſh Morotto, which is a great bearer, and a hardy ſort of pea, about the middle of February, upon a clear open ſpot of ground. Theſe muſt be ſown in rows about four feet aſunder, and the peaſe ſhould be dropped in the drills about an inch diſtance, covering them about two inches deep with earth, being very careful that none of them lie uncovered, which will draw the mice, pigeons, or rooks, to attack the whole ſpot; and it often happens, by this neglect, that a whole plantation is devoured by theſe creatures; whereas, when there are none of the peaſe left in ſight, they do not ſo eaſily find them out.

About a fortnight after this you ſhould ſow another ſpot, either of this ſort, or any other large ſort of Pea, to ſucceed thoſe, and then continue to repeat ſowing once a fortnight, till the middle or latter end of May, only obſerving to allow the Marrowfats, and other very large ſorts of peaſe, at leaſt four feet and a half between row and row; and the roſe pea ſhould be allowed at leaſt eight or ten inches diſtance, plant from plant in the rows; for theſe grow very large, and if they have not room allowed them, they will ſpoil each other by drawing them up very tall, and will produce no fruit.

When theſe plants come up, the earth ſhould be drawn up to their ſhanks (as was before directed,) and the ground kept entirely clear from weeds; and when the plants are grown eight or ten inches high, you ſhould ſtick ſome bruſh-wood into the ground cloſe to the peaſe for them to ramp upon, which will ſupport them from trailing upon the ground, which is very apt to rot the large growing ſorts of peaſe, eſpecially in wet ſeaſons; beſides, by thus ſupporting them, the air can freely paſs between them, which will preſerve the bloſſoms from falling off before their time, and occaſion them to bear much better, than if permitted to lie upon the ground, and there will be room to paſs between the rows to gather the peaſe when they are ripe.

The Dwarf ſorts of peaſe may be ſown much cloſer than thoſe beforementioned, for theſe ſeldom riſe above a foot high, and rarely ſpread above half a foot in width, ſo that theſe need not have more room than two feet row from row, and not above an inch aſunder in the rows. Theſe will produce a good quantity of peaſe, provided the ſeaſon be not over-dry; but they ſeldom continue long in bearing, ſo that they are not ſo proper to ſow for the main crop, when a quantity of peaſe is expected for the table, their chief excellency being for hot-beds, where they will produce a greater quantity of peaſe (provided they are well managed) than if expoſed to the open air, where the heat of the ſun ſoon dries them up.

The Sickle pea is much more common in Holland than in England, it being the ſort moſtly cultivated in that country; but in England they are only propagated by curious gentlemen for their own table, and are rarely brought into the markets. This ſort the birds are very fond of, and if they are not prevented, many times deſtroy the whole crop. This ſhould be planted in rows about two feet and a half aſunder, and be managed as hath been directed for the other ſorts.

Although we have directed the ſowing of the large ſorts of peaſe for the great crop, yet theſe are not ſo ſweet as the early hotſpur peaſe; therefore it will alſo be proper to continue a ſucceſſion of thoſe ſorts through the ſeaſon, in ſmall quantities, to ſupply the beſt table, which may be done by ſowing every fortnight; but all theſe which are ſown late in the ſeaſon ſhould have a ſtrong moiſt ſoil, for in hot light land they will burn up, and come to nothing.

The large growing ſorts may be cultivated for the common uſe of the family, becauſe they will produce in greater quantities than the other, and will endure the drought better, but the early kinds are by far the ſweeter taſted peaſe.

The beſt of all the large kinds is the Marrowfats, which, if gathered young, is a well-taſted pea; and this will continue good through the month of Auguſt, if planted on a ſtrong ſoil.

The Grey and other large Winter peaſe are ſeldom cultivated in gardens, becauſe they require a great deal of room, but are uſually ſown in fields in moſt parts of England. The beſt time for ſowing of theſe is about the beginning of March, when the weather is pretty dry, for if they are put into the ground in a very wet ſeaſon, they are apt to rot, especially if the ground be cold; these should be allowed at least three feet distance row from row, and must be sown very thin in the rows; for if they are sown too thick, the haulm will spread so as to fill the ground, and ramble over each other, which will cause the plants to rot, and prevent their bearing.

The common white pea will do best on light sandy land, or on a rich loose soil. The usual method of sowing these pease is with a broad-cast, and so harrow them in: but it is a much better way to sow them in drills about three feet asunder, for half the quantity of seed will do for an acre, and being set regularly, the ground may be stirred with a hoe to destroy the weeds, and earth up the pease, which will greatly improve them, & the pease may be much easier cut in autumn when they are ripe. The usual time for sowing of these pease is about the middle or latter end of March, on warm land, but on cold ground, they should be sown a fortnight or three weeks later. In the common way of sowing, they allow three bushels or more to an acre, but if they are drilled, one bushel will be full enough.

The green and maple Rouncivals require a stronger soil than the white, and should be sown early in the spring; also the drills should be made at a greater distance from each other, for as these are apt to grow rank, especially in a wet season, they should be set in rows three feet and a half, or four feet asunder; and the ground between the rows should be stirred two or three times with a hoe, which will not only destroy the weeds, but, by earthing up the pease, greatly improve them, and also render the ground better to receive whatever crop is put on it the following season.

The grey pease thrive best on a strong clayey land; these are commonly sown under furrow, but by this method they are all always too thick, and do not come up regular; therefore all these rank-growing plants should be sown in drills, where the seeds will be more equally scattered, and lodged at the same depth in the ground; whereas in the common way, some of the seeds lie twice as deep as others, and are not scattered at equal distances. These may be sown toward the end of February, as they are much hardier than either of the former sorts, but the culture of these should be the same.

The best method to sow these pease is to draw a drill with a hoe by a line about two inches deep, and then scatter the seeds therein; after which, with a rake, you may draw the earth over them, whereby they will be equally covered: this is a very quick method for gardens, but where they are sown in fields, they commonly make a shallow furrow with the plough, and scatter the seeds therein, and then with a harrow they cover them over again. After this, the great trouble is to keep them clear from weeds, and draw the earth up to the plants; this, in such countries where labour is dear, is a great expence to do it by the hand with a hoe; but this may be easily effected with a small plough, which may be drawn through between the rows, which will entirely eradicate the weeds, and by stirring the soil, render it mellow, and greatly promote the growth of the plants.

When any of these sorts are intended for seed, there should be as many rows of them left ungathered, as may be thought necessary to furnish a sufficient quantity of seed; and when the pease are in flower, they should be carefully looked over to draw out all those plants which are not of the right sort, for there will always be some roguish plants (as the gardeners turn them) in every sort, which, if left to mix, will degenerate the kind. These must remain until their pods are changed brown, and begin to split, when you should immediately gather them up, together with the haulm; and if you have not room to stack them till winter, you may thresh them out as soon as they are dry, and put them up in sacks for use; but you must be very careful not to let them remain too long abroad after they are ripe, for if wet should happen, it would rot them, and heat, after a shower of rain, would cause their pods to burst, and cast forth their seeds, so that the greatest part of them would be lost; but it is not adviseable to continue sowing the same seed longer than two years, but rather to exchange their seeds every year, or every two years at least, whereby you may always expect to have them prove right.

PEACH-TREE,

PEACH-TREE, [*Malus Persica.*] The varieties of peaches are very great, and by continuing to raise them from the seed or kernel, they may be multiplied indefinitely. It is to be observed, however, that notwithstanding the number of varieties that may be obtained that way, it is probable not one in twenty is possessed of the proper qualities, as is obvious by the cultivated sorts now known in England; for most of the eminent nursery-men retain no more than from twenty to thirty sorts in their catalogues, which they sell as real good peaches. Some indeed extend them to 40 or 50; but among these there are many of very indifferent qualities, and not worth the space they occupy; and since it is not more expence to cultivate the best than the more indifferent ones, the first only deserve our regard; and as all the sorts require to be trained against walls, the expence of building them is very considerable, and a good aspected wall is too valuable to be filled with any but the capital sorts.

These fruit are divided into two classes, viz. peaches and pavies; the former are distinguishable by the flesh or pulp readily quitting the stone, that of the latter firmly adheres thereto.

Botanists allow only one distinct species of peach-trees; all the different sorts of fruit being varieties of one another, so that the trees of all the varieties bear the particular marks of the original species. Varieties are,

1. The early white nutmeg peach; a very small oblong whitish fruit, ripe in July. 2. Early red nutmeg; a small, roundish, bright red fruit, ripe the end of July. 3. Anne peach; a small, round, & yellowish, white fruit, early in Aug. 5. Small mignon peach; a small, and round fruit, red towards the sun, ripe the middle of August. 5. Great mignon peach; large, round, swelling on one side, and beautifully spotted with red to the sun; middle of August. 6. Early purple peach; large and round; middle of August. 7. Late purple; ripe the middle of September. 8. White magdalen peach; round, middle-sized, whitish, and deeply furrowed on one side; early in August. 9. Red magdalen; a beautiful large, round, red fruit; end of August. 10. Early Newington peach; roundish, middle-sized, and red to the sun; in August. 11. Old late Newington peach; middle of September. 12. Montauban peach; middle-sized, roundish, purple, and cleft on one side; end of August. 13. Belle chevreuse peach; middle-sized, oblong red; end of August. 14. Noblesse; large, roundish, marbled with a purplish red; September. 15. Yellow Alberge peach; middle-sized, longish, yellow-fleshed fruit; middle of August. 16. Belle-garde peach; roundish, and almost wholly of a deep purple colour; beginning of September. 17. Chancellor peach; a large, somewhat oblong, bright red fruit; September. 18. La Teton de Venus, or breast of Venus peach; a pretty large, somewhat longish fruit, deeply divided on one side, both divisions swelling and rounded like a woman's breast, and of a pale red colour on the sunny side; the end of September. 19. Rossana peach; a middle-sized, somewhat oval fruit, purple next the sun; early in September. 20. Persique peach; a fine large, roundish, and somewhat oblong fruit, terminated at top by a small nipple, having the sunny side red, the other pale green; early in October. 21. Admirable peach; a very large, round fruit, beautifully adorned with red next the sun; middle of September. 22. Rambouillet peach; a large, longish, deeply-furrowed fruit, the sunny side beautifully reddened, the other yellow; towards the end of September. 23. La Royale, or royal peach; a large, round, almost wholly red fruit, but deeply reddened next the sun; end of September. 24. Bourdine peach; a large, round, very fine fruit, bright red on the sunny side; ripe beginning or middle of September. 25. Bloody peach; a middle sized, deep red fruit next the sun, and its whole pulp of a blood red colour; late in October. 26. Nivette peach; a very fine, large, longish, deep purple fruit next the sun; middle of September. 27. Portugal peach; a large, round, even peach, generally spotted, and the sunny side elegantly red; end of September. 28. Royal George peach; a middle-sized, round peach, furrowed on one side, of a deep red next the sun, the other part white, spotted with red; early in September. 29. Violet peach; a middle-sized, roundish, oval, violet-coloured peach; the middle of September. 30. Catharine peach; a beautiful, very large,

large, round peach, the funny fide wholly of a fine bright red, the other fide white; ripens in October. 31. Monftrous pavie of Pomponne; an amazingly large and beautiful peach, the fhape round, and often meafures twelve or fourteen inches in circumference; the fide next the fun deeply red, and the other a pale flefh colour; the end of October. 32. Cambray peach; middle fized, longifh, pale-coloured; in October. 33. Sion peach; a large, handfome, round peach, reddifh on the funny fide, the other fide whitifh; ripe end of September. 34. Narbonne peach; a very large peach, of a greenifh colour; ripe in October.

The above thirty-four varieties of peaches are the principal forts of that univerfally admired fruit, known in Great-Britain; and the name here annexed to each variety is that by which they are generally known to all the nurfery-men, who cultivate the trees for fale, to fupply noblemen and gentlemen's gardens.

Many of the above varieties approach fo near to one another in fize, fhape, and colour, that it is fometimes difficult to determine their difference without the ftricteft attention.

We do not pretend to recommend all thefe varieties as real good peaches, but for the fake of thofe who have large extent of walling, have collected all the principal forts to view, with fhort defcriptions of their fizes, fhapes, colours, and times of ripening, which it is prefumed will convey fome idea of the refpective varieties to the unexperienced, and help to direct him in the choice of the forts.

The forts that have the greateft claim to efteem, as the beft and moft beautiful, both in regard to fize, fhape, colour, flavour, and the beft bearers, are the following:

The Anne peach, fmall mignon, great mignon, red Magdalen, belle garde, belle chevruefe, mountauban, admirable, early Newington, late Newington, bourdine, nivette, la royale, purple, teton de Venus, Catharine, and great pavie of Pomponne; the latter chiefly for its prodigious fize and beauty, and, as a pickle, it furpaffes all the other forts.

The two nutmeg peaches, though of fmall fize and indifferent flavour, efpecially the white fort, on account of their early perfection, fhould alfo be allowed a place in the collection.

The bloody peach merits a place more for fingularity, than for the quality of the fruit.

The two Newington peaches, Portugal, Catharine, and monftrous pavie, may be deemed of the pavie tribe, their flefh adhering clofely to the ftone. The old Newington and Catharine are efteemed two of the moft valuable peaches that are cultivated in England.

Peach trees in general will grow 15 or 20 feet high, if they have full fcope; and if trained for ftandards, and permitted to take their natural growth, they form regular heads, but they do not ripen their fruit well on ftandards in this country, they being natives of a much warmer climate; fo that, to effect the ripening of their fruit perfectly, they require the fhelter of a warm wall, to which their branches fhould be regularly trained.

The trees in general flower early in fpring; the flowers come out before the leaves, appearing chiefly on the fhoots laft year, arifing fome fingly, others in pairs, all along the fides of the fhoot, to which they fit clofe; they are formed each of five fmall petals, and many ftamina in the middle, with a fmall round germen, which becomes the peach.

The general propagation of peach-trees is effected by budding them upon plum-ftocks.

But all the fine varieties of thefe fruit were originally obtained from the feed or kernel, and more new varieties may be gained by that means; but the procefs is fomewhat tedious, and often terminates in but trifling fuccefs, in refpect to the quality of the fruit fo obtained; for if you plant the ftones of the fineft forts, it is a thoufand to one, if, out of a great number, you obtain one like the originals, and but few that have any real merit, fo greatly do thefe, and indeed all other fruits, vary from the feed. However, for the fake of experiment, there are many who have curiofity and patience enough to undertake the acquifition of new varieties by the above methods, and think themfelves amply rewarded if they gain one or two new forts that poffefs good qualities in refpect to fize, form, colour, and flavour.

The method of planting the ftones

for

for that purpofe, is, they fhould be planted in autumn, in drills about two or three inches deep, and in fpring following they will come up, and after having one fummer's growth, they fhould, in autumn or fpring following, be tranfplanted in rows in the nurfery, and in a year or two after may be planted againft any fpare wall, pales, or reed fence, and trained as other peach-trees; and when they have fhown fruit, thofe of merit fhould be planted where they are to remain, which you may propagate or encreafe by budding, as hereafter directed.

The only method of propagation, however, to continue, with certainty, the approved or any acquired forts of peaches, is by budding, i. e. inoculation; fince, by inoculating the bud of a tree of any of the kinds, in the ftem or ftock of any fort of peach, almond, or plumb, the bud unites with the faid ftock, the head of which being cut off, the bud fhoots forth, branches out, and becomes a peach-tree, which will produce fruit in fize, fhape, colour, and flavour, exactly the fame as that of the parent tree from whence the bud was taken, and by which means you may multiply any of the forts of peaches, and other fruit trees at pleafure, and with certainty; and befides, trees thus raifed, much fooner attain a bearing ftate than thofe from the kernels.

Peaches, as above hinted, may be budded upon three or four different ftocks, viz. upon thofe raifed from their own kernels, upon the almond, apricot, and plumb.

There is however but one fort of ftock proper for general ufe whereon to bud peaches, which is that of the plumb; the peach, the almond, and apricot ftocks, are often attacked by the gum, and communicate it to the trees juft as they arrive at a ftate of full bearing, and quickly go off; whereas, the plumb ftock being in every refpect hardier, and better fuited to different foils, peaches budded upon them are generally healthful, and of long duration; obferving, however, that experience has proved them to be the moft profperous and durable on one particular fort, which is that of the true mufcle plumb.

The propagation or raifing ftocks from the varieties of plumbs indifferently, as alfo of peaches, almonds, and apricots, may with great eafe be effected by fowing the ftones of the fruit in autumn, in drills two inches deep, and they will rife freely the fpring following; and in October they may be tranfplanted in rows two feet and half diftant, and in the two following fummers, thofe that are intended to form dwarfs, may be inoculated with peach buds.

But in refpect to the real mufcle-plumb ftock, this cannot be obtained in its true ftate from the ftones, for they vary fo greatly when raifed from feed, that not one in a hundred will prove of that fort; therefore, the only method to obtain the true mufcle kind is either by layers in autumn, or by fuckers that are fent up from the roots of peach or plumb trees, that are known to be worked upon that fort of plumb. Thefe fhould be collected in October or November; chufe thofe that are about the fize of a large goofe-quill; cut off any knots of old wood that adhere to their roots, and trim off all fide-branches, and plant them in lines two feet and half diftant, and in the following fummer fome will be fit to bud for dwarfs.

The proper fized ftocks to bud upon to form dwarfs, fhould be about half an inch thick.

But if intended to form half or full ftandards, the ftocks, before they are budded, muft be permitted to form ftems an inch thick at bottom, and four, five, or fix feet in height. The feafon for budding them is Auguft, tho' fome perform that work in June and July; but when budded too early, the buds are apt to fhoot the fame year, which fhoots, being weakly, are either killed in winter, or, if they efcape the froft, they never make great progrefs; therefore, from about the 25th of July to the 25th of Aug. is the proper period for that operation, and the buds will remain dormant till fpring, when they will fhoot forth with vigour.

The method of performing the operation of budding, and every thing relating thereto for thofe and other trees, is fully explained under that article. See *Inoculating*.

We fhall therefore only obferve, that as Peach-trees require to be trained againft walls, &c they fhould be budded principally to form dwarfs, that their

their branches may at firſt come out low, ſo as they may by degrees be trained to occupy every part of the wall, from bottom to top; the ſtocks ſhould therefore be budded within five or ſix inches of the bottom, but where there are high walls to furniſh, it is neceſſary alſo to raiſe half-ſtandards and ſtandards, to occupy the upper part, while the dwarfs are gradually advancing to cover the whole; the ſtocks, to conſtitute ſuch ſtandards, ſhould for half-ſtandards be budded at the height of three or four feet, and for full ſtandards at that of five or ſix, or they may be budded near the ground, and the firſt ſhoot from the bud trained to the above heights to form a ſtem.

Obſerve to inſert only one bud in each ſtock, the heads of which are to remain on entire until ſpring.

In March following, the heads of all the ſtocks are to be cut off ſloping, juſt above where the bud is inſerted.

Soon after this the buds will ſhoot forth, each will produce one ſtrong erect ſhoot, which, by autumn, will probably attain three or four feet in height, and the trees have then acquired their firſt ſtate of formation, which, in October or November, ſhould be tranſplanted in the places where they are finally to remain; and in the ſpring after that, they muſt be headed down to a few eyes, to procure laterals near the place of inoculation, to give the tree its ſuitable form for the wall, and in two or three years they will bear fruit.

With reſpect to ſituation and expoſure, the peach-tree being originally a native of warm climates, is, in ſome reſpects, tender, and will not proſper, at leaſt not bear well, in an open ſituation; ſo that for the general part, require to be trained againſt walls.

The trees themſelves, though hardy enough in reſpect to cold, yet the bloſſom and young fruit are extremely impatient of froſt & cutting winds, which generally reign in this country at early ſpring, when the trees bloom and ſet their fruit: the trees, therefore, ſhould be indulged with the ſhelter of a warm wall, or other ſubſtantial cloſe fence, to which they ſhould be planted cloſe, and their branches regularly trained, which is neceſſary, not only to defend the bloſſom and young fruit the better from the inclemency of the weather, but alſo that they may have all the advantages of the ſun's influence, to accelerate its ripening, as well as to give it colour and flavour, which many ſorts, even with all the aid in our power to give, hardly effect in unfavourable ſeaſons in this country.

The proper aſpected walls, or expoſure for the fine ſorts, is that of a due ſouth; ſome may alſo be planted upon an eaſt aſpected wall, and in favourable ſeaſons the trees will alſo ſometimes ſet and ripen fruit tolerably on a weſtern aſpect. However, where there is walling enough, let the capital ſorts be always planted againſt ſuch walls as enjoy the greateſt degree of the ſouth ſun, as even that aſpect, in ſome ſeaſons, is barely ſufficient to ripen ſome of the late ſorts of theſe fruit, in any part of this iſland.

Such of the forward kinds that you deſire as early as poſſible, ſhould have the warmeſt ſituation on the beſt ſouth wall, which, though ſome are inferior in ſize and flavour, yet when obtained at the earlieſt ſeaſon, they are highly acceptable as a rarity in the deſert.

With reſpect to ſoil, the peach-tree will proſper in any common ſoil of a garden, where it is not leſs than fifteen or eighteen inches depth of proper ſtaple, that is ſuch as is proper for the culture of common kitchen herbage, and where moiſture is not very copious; but if the depth of good ſoil in the fruit-tree borders is two or three feet, it will be the greater advantage.

The breadth of the borders againſt the walls where it is intended to plant theſe trees, ſhould never be leſs than three, but thoſe of ſix or eight feet are the moſt proper width.

If the natural ſoil of the borders is of a moderately light, pliable nature, and of proper depth, it is a happy circumſtance; and if it is of a loamy temperature, it will alſo be a particular advantage, provided however there is ſuch depth of proper ſtaple as above noticed, before you come at gravel, clay, or any other bad ſoil at bottom, when nothing more than common digging is neceſſary; but where there is leſs than that depth, the borders muſt be raiſed with a due portion of good freſh earth and rotten dung, working the whole well together.

Where good rich or pliable loam could be eaſily obtained from the ſurface of some contiguous pasture, common, or other field, and with store of rotten dung, working or blending the whole with the natural soil of the border to the proper depth, it would form a fine compost, and the trees will prosper, and be of long continuance.

But if the soil is naturally stiff and clayey, or of any other stubborn or very moist nature, it may be mellowed by adding dry substances, such as coal ashes, drift sand, road soil, and other similar materials, and plenty of rotten dung, working the whole with the natural soil to the above depth.

Where any one is so happy to possess a soil whose natural goodness renders all foreign assistance unnecessary, no more need be done than digging the borders one or two spades deep, and it is fit for the reception of the trees.

The season for planting is October and November, or even any time in open weather till March, in dry warm soils; but in moist or wet soils, we prefer the spring for that work.

Peach-trees, and, in short, all others that are designed for walls, should be planted in their places of final destination when they are one year old, that is when their heads are of one summer's growth from the bud, and with their said heads entire for the present, that we may have the opportunity of training them from their origin, as it were, and in their proper position in the places where they are finally to remain; for the great art in forming a wall-tree depends entirely upon the due pruning and training the two first years, after making the first shoot or head from the budding.

But if any one is in haste to have his walls covered at once, as it were, with bearing trees, he may be supplied with such at most of the nurseries, which are what the nursery-men call trained trees, which they sell from five to ten shillings per tree, according to the sorts, size, and property of growth. Every one may do as they please, but we always preferred those of one year from the bud; for these reasons, first, that trees of that age sooner and more firmly establish their roots, which is an essential point to keep in view; and secondly, because we would have the tree under our own management from the beginning, which we always found to be of importance.

The distance these trees should be planted from one another is fifteen feet, and if the walls are high, half or full standards may be planted between the dwarfs, to occupy the upper part, while the dwarfs grow up to fill that space; for no part of good walls should be left unoccupied.

The rule is this, if the walls are not above six or eight feet high, plant none but dwarfs, and these at fifteen feet distance; if the walls are nine feet high, half standards, of about three or four feet stem, may be planted between the dwarfs; and if the walls are ten or twelve feet, or more in height, full standards, of six feet stem, should be planted to occupy the upper part; and as the dwarfs are to be the principal residents, way must be made, as their branches gradually advance, by cutting away the lowermost ones of the standards by degrees annually, and at last, in seven, eight, ten, or more years, as you shall see necessary, the standards may be entirely taken away, that the dwarfs may advance, and fill the whole space of walling.

The mode of planting being fixed on, mark out on the walls the distances as above for the trees.

Then, having recourse to the nursery, let the trees be taken up with all their roots as entire as possible, for this is of much importance; the extreme ends of all of which should be tipped, i. e. a little shortened, and those of broken or bruised ones smoothed, preserving the heads entire for the present. Holes or pits are then to be opened, capacious enough to receive the roots freely every way. Place the tree therein, about three inches from the wall, with the bud outward, and then break and trim in the earth regularly between all the roots and small fibres, and tread the whole gently, to fix the whole plant in its proper position; then directly tack the head to the wall, or tye it to a stake, to secure it from the power of boisterous winds till March, when it is to be headed down.

If the ensuing spring or beginning of summer should prove very dry, indulge the trees with moderate waterings once or twice a week, according to the drought and heat of the season, which will encourage them to push out more freely and strong after heading down.

The trees being planted with their

first head from the bud entire, as we advised; the next necessary culture is to perform the operation of heading them down, which is to be done just as they begin to shoot, and the proper time is March.

This work consists in shortening the head, or first main shoot down within five or six eyes of the bud, or place of it's origin, sloping it off on the side next the wall, just above an eye, which is a necessary operation, both to dwarfs, half, and full standards, that are planted against walls; that by stopping its upright direction, it may throw out several lateral shoots from the remaining lower part to the right and left, and constitute the proper foundation for forming a wall-tree, whose first branches should always proceed on both sides, from within six inches of the place of inoculation, whether dwarfs for the lower part, or standards for the middle and top of the wall; and that if the heading down was omitted, the consequence would be, the tree would advance with a naked stem, and leave almost one half of the allotted space of walling unoccupied.

Therefore, pay no regard to the first head from the bud, howsoever large and fine it may appear, but cut it down as above; for the general formation of the tree depends entirely upon the form acquired by this practice, and the two succeeding years pruning.

The trees being thus headed down, they will soon after produce one strong shoot from each remaining eye, observing that such as proceed immediately from the front and back, are to be constantly rubbed off close, but all those that advance from the two sides are to be preserved entire, which, in June, when of due length to admit of laying in, should be nailed close to the wall, continuing them thereto at full length during the summer.

At the fall of the leaf following, proceed to give them their first winter pruning.

This may be done any time from November till March. You are now to examine the number of shoots each tree produced the preceding summer from the effect of heading down, and to prune them accordingly; for example, if there are two shoots, one on each side, they are both to be retained; and to encourage their furnishing a farther supply of branches; shorten them to eight or ten, or if of very strong growth, to twelve or fifteen inches, and nail them horizontally to the wall.

If there are three shoots, the middle one of them is to be cut out close, and shorten the other two as above, and nail one to each side in a horizontal direction; but if the middle shoot of the three be considerably weaker than the other two, it may be retained, and nailed in at full length, which probably will furnish a fruit or two, while the other two are providing a farther necessary supply of wood; but if is it a strong shoot, cut it clean away.

If the tree is furnished with four shoots, two on each side, retain them all, and shorten them from ten to fifteen inches, according to their strength, as above, and nail them equally to the right and left.

And if there are five shoots, and that those on the sides are strong, and the middle one weak, shorten the former as above, and lay them horizontally, and nail in the middle one entire; but if the latter is nearly of equal strength, or stronger than the others, cut it clean out, which, if left, would draw the principal part of the nourishment, and impoverish those of the two sides, which should now be wholly attended to, for the middle will always furnish itself in due time.

One fundamental rule to be observed, is, that your tree, at this period of growth, should, if possible, proceed with shoots of an equal strength and number on each side, and depends principally upon two or four good branches, shortened & trained equally to the right and left, in a nearly horizontal direction, which will not fail in their turn to furnish you with more to occupy the wall upward.

The trees having had their first year's pruning, observe the following rules in their second year's culture.

During summer, all shoots that arise from the upper and under side of the former year's horizontals, are now to be retained and trained entire, and all buds or shoots that proceed immediately from the front and back part of the said horizontals, should be constantly rubbed off, because they cannot be trained consistent with the necessary form and regularity of the tree, having particular regard, however, to reſerve all the regular ſhoots, and train them in at full length; for, except in ſome particular inſtances, the ſhoots muſt not be ſhortened in ſummer, therefore continue them to the wall entire till the winter pruning.

In November, when the leaves are fallen, or any time betwixt that and the beginning of March, you may proceed to the ſecond winter pruning; in performing this, we, for example, will ſuppoſe the tree in the firſt pruning to have been trained with four horizontals, that is, two on each ſide, and that each of theſe produced two or three well-placed ſhoots the preceding ſummer, or as many as to make the tree now poſſeſſed of eight, ten, or twelve branches; now, if theſe ſtand four, five, or ſix on one ſide, and as many on the other, it is a happy uniformity, and all of them are to be retained; and that to procure ſtill a farther ſupply of horizontals, each of the above are now to be ſhortened according to its ſtrength; if they are weakly, cut them to ſix or eight inches, and if of middling growth to ten or twelve, and if very ſtrong ones to about fifteen or eighteen inches, and train them to the wall horizontally, at ſix inches diſtance, obſerving that the oppoſite branches of each ſide range exactly in an equal poſition.

But where it happens that there are an unequal number of ſhoots, as for inſtance, four, five, or ſix on one ſide, and ſeven, eight, or more on the other, and that they are all of tolerable ſtrength; then, to render both ſides nearly equal, ſome of the weakeſt and worſt placed on the fulleſt ſide ſhould be cut out.

Obſerve to proceed as near as poſſible with an equal number and ſtrength of horizontals on both ſides, extending the loweſt branches the longeſt, and if you have now five, ſix, or eight on a ſide, trained at five or ſix inches diſtance, your tree will begin to aſſume a handſome form, and next ſummer you may expect ſome fruit.

Previous to the general pruning, obſerve, that peach and nectarine-trees always produce their fruit upon the one-year old ſhoots; that is, the ſhoots produced each ſummer bear the ſucceeding year, and the ſame individual ſhoots rarely bear but once, nor do they furniſh good bearing wood after the firſt year, ſo that the grand article in pruning, is to procure an annual ſucceſſion of theſe young ſhoots in every part, from the very bottom to the extremity every way of the tree, which are to be obtained principally by ſhortening, in winter pruning, thoſe of every year, whereby they furniſh, at the ſame time, both a proper crop of fruit, and ſupply of bearing wood.

The great art in pruning and training a peach and nectarine tree againſt walls, is to preſerve uniformity in every part from the beginning, having ſtrict regard that both ſides to the right and left advance with equal ſtrength, and number of horizontals, whoſe numbers on each ſide ſhould be equally encreaſed every year, and thoſe trained conſtantly in a nearly horizontal poſition, at five or ſix inches diſtance one above another, till by degrees, they cover the whole ſpace of walling allotted for them, both in breadth and height; for this is very eſſentially to be obſerved.

After the tree is thus formed and conducted to a bearing ſtate, its duration, beauty, and fruitfulneſs depend wholly upon proper pruning every ſummer and winter.

The general ſummer pruning conſiſts in reforming the irregularity of the numerous ſhoots then produced, and training to the wall at full length, in every part, all regularly placed ones, as ſucceſſion-wood for next year's bearing, for the great art is to procure a due ſupply of theſe every ſummer in all parts of the tree.

And the general winter pruning comprehends a general reform among all the branches and ſhoots of all ages, ſizes, and ſituation, ſuch as the retrenching all worn-out and naked branches, as they from time to time occur to make room for thoſe that furniſh the beſt bearing-wood, ſhoots of the preceding ſummer; at the ſame time ſelecting and retaining in every part the beſt of the ſaid ſhoots for next ſummer's bearing, cutting out unneceſſary and irregular ones, and all uſeleſs ſhoots in general, as well as part of the former year's horizontals, to make due room to train the proper uſeful ſhoots; all of which ſhould be ſhortened, to promote their emitting laterals in ſummer for bearing the year after, and the whole then nailed cloſe to the wall in regular order.

The time to begin the ſummer pruning is in May or June. Every one knows that in ſpring a peach-tree abounds with a great number of ſhoots, ariſing from every ſide of the laſt year's horizontals or preſent bearers, probably three times more than are uſeful, or than are wanted, or can poſſibly be trained in without confuſion; you muſt therefore thin them, and eaſe the tree of all that are irregular, and ſuch as are evidently uſeleſs and ſuperfluous, at the ſame time retaining a ſufficiency of the regular ſhoots; that is, two, three, or four of the ſide ones upon each horizontal, to be trained for next year's bearing.

The rule is this: Each of the laſt year's horizontals will probably produce from three to ſix, or more ſhoots, and of theſe, ſome proceed from the upper and under ſides, and ſome from the back and fore parts; thoſe of the former ſituation, viz. from the upper and under ſides, are to be regarded as the only proper regular ſhoots, and are to be principally attended to, retained, and trained in at full length, to prune upon in winter for bearing the ſucceeding year; but thoſe that proceed directly foreright from the front, and thoſe from the back of the horizontals, or from any of the other parts of the tree in that irregular direction, muſt be rubbed off cloſe, becauſe, by their ſituation on the branches, they cannot be trained with due regularity; therefore, that though good of themſelves, they are to be deemed irregular, or uſeleſs ſhoots, and ſhould be every where diſplaced, except in caſes where horizontals furniſh no other, when the beſt placed of them may be retained.

In reſpect to the regular ſhoots above deſcribed, examine, as you go on, their ſituation and number upon each horizontal; if two or more ſhoots riſe from the ſame eye, retain only one of them; and if the tree is but a moderate ſhooter, it is neceſſary to diſburthen it of all that are evidently ſuperfluous, which are ſuch ſhoots as, though good and well placed, yet if there are four, five, or more on a horizontal, where only one or two is apparently neceſſary for next year's bearing, ſome of the weakeſt and worſt placed, or any remarkably luxuriant ones, ſhould be cleared away, retaining however, where practicable, always two of the beſt ſituated and faireſt ſhoots upon the weak, and three or four on each of the middling and ſtrong horizontals, which, though double, or even treble of what will be apparently wanted, it is eligible culture to reſerve enough to chuſe from in winter pruning, training the whole at full length during ſummer.

But where a tree ſhoots very vigorouſly in general, it is adviſeable to reſerve as many of the ſide-ſhoots of each horizontal as there is tolerable room to train at full length, which, by dividing the ſap among many, checks luxuriance, which would probably take place in a ſmaller number; for the natural inclination of theſe ſort of trees ſhould, in ſome degree, be followed.

Another circumſtance to be attended to in thinning & regulating the ſhoots, is to leave one good ſhoot at, or as near the end of each bearing horizontal as poſſible, that it may draw the ſay through the whole branch to the nouriſhment of the fruit.

All weak ſhoots riſing from the old wood muſt be diſplaced, unleſs any regular placed ones appear uſeful to fill a vacancy.

If any remarkably vigorous or luxuriant ſhoot ariſe either from the bearing horizontals, or any of the older branches, examine its ſituation and ſtrength, and conſider whether it is wanted; if it is likely to impoveriſh the neighbouring ſhoots of moderate growth, or that it is not immediately wanted to fill a vacancy, cut it out; but if uſeful, either to fill a vacancy, or to prevent an apparent one, or to exhauſt too abundant ſap, retain it, and pinch it in May or early in June to four or five eyes, and you will procure one middling ſhoot from each eye the ſame year, to train in, to chuſe from in the winter pruning.

All thoſe very rank or luxuriant ſhoots, diſtinguiſhed ſingularly from the generality of the others of the ſame tree, by their extraordinary ſize, green colour, and often redneſs at the tips, ſhould be cut out from every part, unleſs you have no other reſource to fill a vacancy, when ſuch that are duly placed for that purpoſe may be reſerved and pinched as above obſerved.

Attention ſhould aways be had to the

the bottom or lower part of the trees, especially those that are aged; if any strong shoot arise in these parts, you must preserve it carefully to succeed worn-out or naked branches, which are cut away by degrees; and if there is a present vacancy, pinch it early in June to four or five eyes, to furnish lateral shoots the same year, to be ready against the winter pruning.

Where a vacancy or want of wood is discovered, at this time, in any part, and that there is only one shoot where two, three, or more are necessary, shorten or pinch the said shoot to three, four, or five eyes, in May or early in June, and it will afford as many laterals the same year to fill the vacant space.

In the whole operation of summer pruning, observe, that all the regular shoots you judge necessary to retain to prune upon in winter, must be left entire, shortening none now, except in cases of vacancy as above, and all irregular and other useless shoots that are now to be taken out, must be rubbed or cut off as close as possible, leaving no stumps, which would shoot out from every eye, and fill the tree with innumerable useless shoots, and choak up and darken the fruit, and deprive it of the necessary benefit of sun, air, showers, &c. and which would require much time to cut out in the winter pruning.

It is necessary to observe, that if the above operations are begun early in summer, the shoots that are to be displaced may readily be rubbed off with the thumb; but observe, if you delay the work till the wood begins to harden, they will not break off easily without damaging the mother-branch, therefore use the knife, and cut them as close as possible.

After the above regulations, let all the remaining shoots, when of due length, be trained close to the wall unshortened, and as their ends advance, continue to train them still along at full length, and let them remain entire until the winter pruning; for in the common course the shoots must never be shortened in summer.

These are nearly all the directions we have to advance relative to the summer pruning; the utility of which, if the operation is performed in due time, is very great both to the tree and fruit.

Therefore, if the operations are begun in May, only just rub off all the ill-placed buds, that is, foreright ones, and those behind the bearing horizontals, and such others that are evidently useless, as before observed; and in June, when the useful or regular shoots are of proper length, they are easily and expeditiously trained in, for every one points to its proper place; besides, when the work is begun early, it can be performed with considerably more expedition and truth, as the useless buds or shoots may then, with the utmost facility, be rubbed off close with the thumb, without the use of any instrument, and the early operation will contribute very considerably to the size and goodness of the fruit, as well as beauty and duration of the trees.

The work however should never be delayed longer than the beginning of June, or till the shoots have attained due length for training in, and not, as is often the case, wait till they are two or three feet in length, and form such a thicket and confusion, that the most expert pruner would be at a loss to know where to begin to break through such obscurity, to determine what is necessary to be done, which, besides, is highly prejudicial to the prosperity of the fruit, the main object, as well as to the beauty and duration of the tree; and the confusion occasioned by such a thicket of wood and leaves prevents you from cutting close, and the trees become full of disagreeable stumps, producing useless shoots from every eye, which take up much time to remove in the winter pruning; and upon the whole the fruit being hidden, choaked up, and as it were buried behind such a thicket, becomes tender, as is evident from the colour, which is rather white than green, and when thus suddenly laid open to the air, joined to a scorching sun, great part of it withers and drops off, which never happens when the fruit has from the beginning been inured to the weather, by early rubbing off the useless, and training close the useful shoots, so as to give the sun and air free admission; but on the contrary the fruit always excels in size, colour, and flavour.

At this time of laying in, or dressing, that is, June, we recommend the following observation, which could not

not be so discoverable at the earlier dressing, viz.

Where short shoots, of an inch or two in length, appear upon this or the former year's horizontals, or sides of the old wood, and that they apparently will not exceed that length, it is of utility to reserve them, at least till the winter pruning, because they may prove natural fruit-spurs, which, at that season, are distinguishable by having a cluster of blossom buds.

If a vacancy is any where discovered early in summer, you may pinch some of the strongest neighbouring shoots to three or four eyes, and they will furnish you shoots the same year, to chuse from in the winter pruning.

Do not pull off any of the leaves at this time, as often practised, with a view to admit the sun, for these are necessary to the growth, both of the young shoots and fruit, so should never be taken away, unless there is indeed in any part so great a thicket as to darken the fruit considerably, when a little thinning may be necessary; in other cases that work must be dispensed with till the fruit are full grown.

After the trees have been summer-dressed, according to the preceding directions, you must not forget to review them once a fortnight, to rub off any unnecessary or straggling shoots that may arise, which is soon done, and to fasten up any shoot that may start from its place, or project from the wall, as well as to continue the trained shoots in general thereto, as they advance in length.

One thing more, which is necessary to observe in the summer dressing, is the blight which attacks these trees: this disorder is the effect of noxious winds, that occasion the curling up of the leaves, which become thick, clammy, yellowish, red, and scabby; and attacks the ends of the shoots, and proves very injurious both to the young shoots and fruit, and often their destruction; for the blighted leaves exhaust the sap, at the expence of all the other parts of the tree. When your trees are first attacked, there is no other remedy for this accident than to pick off all the curled leaves as soon as discoverable, and also cut off, below the disorder, all the infected part of the shoots, which generally form a rough disagreeable bush or thicket; this enables the sap to push out new shoots lower down, for next year's bearing. So destructive is this infection, that it frequently destroys in a short time the whole leaves of a wall of trees; and when these are gone, the principal part of the fruit soon after follow, which generally withers and drops; as likewise the young wood, for next year's bearing, either dies or becomes stunted. Various other methods have been tried to prevent the spreading of this pestilence, but nothing effectual.

Insects also often prove very injurious to these trees; a fumigating engine lately invented is recommended, in which is burned tobacco, the smoak of which issuing with a perpetual stream, is applied to the trees attacked by the vermin, which infallibly destroys them, without injury to the trees or fruit.

The winter pruning may be executed any time from the fall of the leaf in November, until the beginning of March; for no weather has any particular effect with regard to proving injurious to the new-cut shoots.

This work however should never be delayed till late in spring, because the blossom buds will be so very turgid or swelled, that numbers of them will be unavoidably rubbed off in performing the operation of pruning and nailing; though some wait till this period, that they may better judge of the good or bad buds, and of the wood-buds from those that produce blossom and fruit. This is of some importance, but the sap is generally risen sufficiently in January, or sooner, to swell the buds, to enable you to distinguish them.

As these trees always bear their fruit upon the one-year old wood; that is, the shoots produced each summer bear the fruit the summer following, so that the fruit-buds are principally to be looked for upon these shoots.

Wood-buds are distinguishable by their being long and firm; blossom buds are round, swelling, thick, and soft.

It must be observed that good blossom buds are always double, two at an eye, having a leaf-bud or shoot between them; those that are single, though they sometimes have a leaf-bud, and blow pretty well, never set fruit so freely as the twin blossoms.

Great

Great attention muſt always be had to keep every part of the tree well furniſhed with an annual ſupply of young wood, of the former ſummer, for bearing next year, advancing, as it were, gradually one behind another, from the bottom to the extremity every way; which is eaſily acquired by properly ſelecting, thinning, and ſhortening thoſe of every year, and by cutting out annually ſome of the old horizontals to make room for them. Likewiſe obſerve, that as the bottom of the trees are apt to become naked, be alſo watchful of that part, to retain in proper places an annual ſupply of ſtrong young wood, either to fill an immediate vacancy, or to be trained up gradually to ſupply the place of any naked or worn-out branch, that may happen either there, in the middle or upper part; which are ſuch that ſupport little or no young wood, or produce weak and a ſcanty portion of ſhoots, and ſhould, wherever they appear, be cut down to the great branch from which they proceed, or to any lower ſtrong young ſhoot they ſupport, or any convenient branch ſupporting ſuch ſhoots: and part of the old horizontals muſt be cut out annually, to make room to train in the bearing wood.

Previous to the performing the operation of winter pruning, it is eligible to unnail the greater part of the branches, and all the young ſhoots in general; you then have full liberty to examine the ſtate and ſituation of the whole, as well as to have due command in uſing your knife, and nailing the tree again in regular order, according to the ſituation and ſtrength of the general ſupply of young ſhoots neceſſary to be trained for next ſummer's bearing, &c.

The trees being unnailed as above, you ſhould firſt proceed to examine all the principal branches, and ſee if any are become naked, or worn out. Naked branches are ſuch that, as formerly hinted, have advanced a conſiderable length, and ſupport very little or no good bearing ſhoots, or lateral branches furniſhed with ſuch wood, and ſhould be cut out to their origin, provided there are proper young wood, or horizontals, well furniſhed with ſuch ſhoots, properly ſituated to be trained up to ſupply their places; for way muſt always be made for thoſe branches that furniſh the beſt young wood, both for bearing the following ſummer, and providing a further ſupply of ſhoots for future ſervice. And the worn out branches are eaſily diſtinguiſhed by their uncommonly weak ſhooting, ſo ſhould be cut out as above, to make room to extend thoſe of better growth.

From theſe you paſs to regulate the ſhoots of the year; of which you will find often, on the ſame tree, weak ones, middle-ſized ones, and ſome of very luxuriant growth; thoſe of the middle-ſize are to be principally attended to; obſerving, as noticed in the ſummer pruning, that the proper ſhoots for our preſent purpoſe to train for next ſummer's bearing, are principally thoſe that grow upon the one-year old horizontals, and of which we are now to ſelect and retain the moſt regular placed ones, namely, ſuch as are the moſt properly ſituated for training cloſe and neatly to the wall, which are chiefly thoſe that proceed from the two ſides of the ſaid horizontals, ſo that keeping thoſe in view for training, clear away all the irregular and other uſeleſs ſhoots, as hereunder mentioned.

Suppoſe your tree to be chiefly of moderate growth, and here and there in it ſhoots of ſuperior luxuriance and rankneſs; theſe, where-ever ſituated, muſt be cut out cloſe: but if the tree is in general vigorous or luxuriant, the ſhoots muſt only be thinned in a moderate way, as hereafter directed.

All ſhoots of extreme weakneſs ſhould be cut away, unleſs you ſhall ſee it neceſſary to keep one here and there to fill a vacancy, or as a reſerve in caſe of one the future year, in which latter caſe I would cut them down to an eye or two.

I do not comprehend by weak ſhoots thoſe ſhort ones an inch or two long, which I call natural fruit-ſpurs, and often furniſh excellent fruit. Theſe muſt be retained.

All foreright ſhoots, and ſuch that proceed directly from the back of the branches, and in other irregular directions, that cannot be trained conſiſtent with the uniformity of the tree, and thoſe ariſing from the old wood, are alſo to be cut off cloſe, except in caſes of vacancy, and that there is no other reſource.

Cut away all ſtumps of laſt ſummer, and

and leave none now, cutting every thing close.

During the whole operation of the above reforms, great attention must be observed in selecting and retaining all the well-placed regular side-shoots above described, which must next be regulated according to the following rules.

Having in this manner cleared your tree from worn-out branches, and from luxuriant, irregular, and other bad shoots, there is nothing left but useful branches supporting horizontals, furnished with proper young wood, nearly of equal strength, and you see your work clear; you have nothing now to do but select and retain upon each horizontal a due portion of the best placed of these proper shoots, and retrench the superfluous ones.

Examine therefore the number of proper shoots upon each horizontal, and their strength, keeping in mind, that the middling strong ones are to be principally attended to. We advised in the summer pruning to leave upon each horizontal two, three, or four shoots, according to the strength of the tree in general: now, if your tree is fully trained, no more than one or two, as you shall see necessary, need be left upon each horizontal, except in cases where a tree is very luxuriant, or where there is a very wide space to fill, or a vacancy in its neighbourhood; but if the tree is still in training, you may retain two or more shoots upon each bearer, as you shall judge expedient, to forward the tree to its intended form. But suppose you are upon a still trained tree, or such that are nearly so, and that you judge one of the young shoots on each horizontal sufficient, keeping in view they should be trained about five, six, or seven inches distance; on this consideration you are to select the best of the lowermost of these shoots, unless you shall judge necessary to advance the length of the branch; then chuse the best of the uppermost, observing that whatsoever shoot you fix upon, to cut off the upper part of the horizontal on which it stands, close to the said shoot, or if you leave two or more shoots upon each horizontal, let one be near the upper, and the other near the lower part thereof, on the opposite sides, and cut down the horizontal to the uppermost of the two shoots, so that by cutting away part of each of the former year's horizontal, the remaining part is terminated by a young shoot, which now commences the bearer or horizontal of the ensuing year.

Observe, where two or more shoots arise from the same eye, never leave but one.

Where any shoots rise from the sides of the old wood or main branches, and which you shall judge necessary to retain, either to fill a present vacancy, or to be ready for an apparent one, it may be reserved without shortening down the said branch to it, as is necessary in the one year's horizontals, unless that part of the said branch immediately from the shoot upward is naked, or unfurnished with young wood, in which case take it down to the shoot in question.

Those short shoots or natural spurs, an inch or two long, above observed, may be retained wherever they appear, for they are generally well furnished with blossom buds.

Observe, that many of the principal bearing shoots which you now retain, will have probably put out several small twigs or side shoots; these, being produced late, are generally spongy, besides, being superfluous or unnecessary, must be cut close, leaving only the main shoot.

In cutting out the irregular and superfluous wood in general, cut all close, leaving no stump, which would send out shoots from every eye the ensuing summer, and crowd your tree with useless wood; and any of those short natural spurs of the former year, now devoid of blossom buds, or that exceed two or three inches in length, should now also be cut away close, but especially those that advance directly foreright.

After making these reforms of regulating and thinning, we proceed to consider of shortening the remaining select shoots, the utility of which is obvious; for as these trees always produce their fruit upon the one-year old shoots, the same wood, by proper shortening in winter pruning, furnishes, as well as fruit, lateral shoots the following summer, to bear the fruit the year after that; therefore, to procure an annual supply of young wood in the proper parts, we must not omit ſtopping or ſhortening that of each year in the winter pruning, by which each ſhoot will emit two, three, or more lateral ones the ſucceeding ſummer; whereas, if they were left at full length, the ſap which would have thrown out ſhoots below, would mount to the extremities, and leave the bottom bare, and in a ſhort time all the lower part of the tree would become naked, and furniſhed with bearing wood only towards the extreme parts. The rule of ſhortening is this; if the tree is in health, and of a middling free growth, ſhorten or cut off about one-third of the length of each ſhoot; for inſtance, ſhoots of ten or twelve inches ſhould be ſhortened to ſix or eight; thoſe of about fifteen or eighteen inches ſhorten to eight, ten, or twelve; and ſo in proportion to the length and ſubſtance of the reſpective ſhoots, obſerving, where a tree is weak, or on the decline, and makes weakly ſhoots, to leave the ſhoots thin, and cut them ſhorter in proportion: on the contrary, where a tree is in general a vigorous ſhooter, leave the ſhoots cloſe, and ſhorten them moderately, which by retaining a good deal of wood to divide and exhauſt the great redundancy of ſap, is the only means to reduce a luxuriant tree to a ſtate of moderate growth, and to bear plentifully.

In ſhortening theſe ſhoots, it is of importance to cut them juſt above a wood, or branch-bud, that it may produce a ſhoot for a leader, to draw the ſap through the whole horizontal, the more effectually to nouriſh its reſpective fruit. A wood bud is with facility diſtinguiſhed from a bloſſom-bud; the former is long, narrow, and firm, the bloſſom-buds are roundiſh, thick, ſwelling, and ſoft; ſo that by cutting to a wood bud you are ſure of a leading ſhoot, and the fruit will be well nouriſhed; but where two bloſſom-buds appear on the ſame eye, a wood-bud alſo generally iſſues from between, ſo that if you cannot conveniently cut to a wood-bud, make the cut to a twin bloſſom-bud as above.

Thus much for the general directions to be obſerved in the principal winter pruning, although there are other circumſtances that cannot be conveyed by words, nor judged of but upon the ſpot, which depend chiefly upon practice.

We will however ſubjoin a few other particulars very neceſſary to be obſerved.

In the courſe of practice, you will meet with trees of very different habits of growth; ſome, for inſtance, are weakly, and produce ſmall or weak ſhoots; others, of a middling ſtate, ſhoot freely in every part, but not too vigorous, which is the moſt deſireable ſtate of growth of any; and ſome ſhoot very vigorous in almoſt every part. With reſpect to the former, if the tree makes very weak ſhoots, examine whether the diſeaſe is at the root; if it is, pull it up; if not, preſerve it, and dig in rotten dung, which often recovers theſe ſort of trees, obſerving to keep it thin of wood, and prune the ſhoots ſhort, and even the beſt to five or ſix inches, till it recovers. In the ſecond caſe, the middling ſhooting tree is to be managed as in the general directions. And in the third inſtance, if the tree be remarkably vogorous, and bear little, it ſhould in ſome degree be humoured in its own way; for if you cut out many, and ſhorten conſiderably the remainder of theſe very vigorous ſhoots, where they are general, as is frequently done without mercy, ſuppoſing by that practice to check luxuriance, and ſo continue to prune, and depend entirely upon the ſmalleſt ones, the conſequence is, that by much thinning, and cloſe cutting vigorous trees, they continue to ſhoot ſtill with greater vigour and irregularity for ſeveral years, without being able to gain either form or fruit, till at laſt, by ſevere pruning, they paſs into the oppoſite extreme, become, as it were, tired with acting ineffectually, grow weak & ſickly, and ſhoot no more. On the contrary, by following, in ſome degree, the inclination of the tree, leaving the ſhoots as cloſe as there is any tolerable room to lay them in, and ſhortening them very little, ſome of the ſtrongeſt not at all; and by thus leaving a good deal of wood, and that at a conſiderable length, the ſap is divided, and the luxuriance is checked; and in a year or two your tree will become a moderate ſhooter, and furniſh fine young wood, and bear plentifully.

The trees being pruned, they ſhould be directly nailed to the wall; as you go on, that is, as ſoon as one tree is pruned, let that be nailed before you prune another.

Peach

Peach-trees come into blossom early in spring, when cutting frosts prevail, which, in some seasons, is so severe as to cut off the whole. Not only the blossom is liable to this disaster, but also the young fruit, till they are as large as ordinary cherries, which oblige us to have recourse to all possible means to defend them.

The dangerous time lasts a month or six weeks; various ways have been tried to shield the trees during that period; some cover with large garden mats, which are often found of great use; but where there is much walling, it takes up much time to cover and uncover, as the danger threatens, for they must only be used when there is apparent danger: free air and light must be admitted, so that if the mats are nailed up in an evening when there is an appearance of a cutting frost, they should be removed again in the morning, if the weather is quite mild; but if not, they may be permitted to remain till it is: do not omit however to take them down when the weather changes; and so continue their use only occasionally, till your fruit are as big as large peas at least.

This is the principal expedient in practice to defend these trees, which, after all, sometimes does not secure a quarter of a crop; it however should not be omitted in hazardous times, especially to some of the early and choice sorts.

There is another method which we have sometimes experienced to save a few fruit, when all that were fully exposed were cut off: this is to procure a quantity of cuttings from the branches of evergreen trees, such as those of laurel, yew, spruce-fir, &c. and stick them moderately thick between the branches of the peach-tree, so that the leaves of the cuttings cover the blossom; these should be placed when the blossoms begin to open, not too thick to darken it, and may be permitted to remain until the beginning of May, when the fruit will be set, and past danger. In default of the above cuttings, branches of dried fern may be used.

Neither of these methods of covering, nor indeed any other, can we recommend as generally effectual; but a poor expedient is better than none; they often insure a few fruit, when those that are fully exposed are all destroyed by the frost.

In favourable seasons peach and nectarine-trees sometimes set their fruit very thick in every part, often double or treble the quantity that have room to grow, or the trees capable of nourishing, and frequently the fruit are set only here and there in clusters; in either case they must be thinned, otherwise the fruit will not attain half its common size, and during their growth would thrust one another off; besides, if the trees are overloaded, they would produce but very weakly shoots for next year's bearing, and would be two years before they recovered themselves.

This work should be performed when the fruit have attained nearly the size of small cherries, which will be some time in May, for if you thin them sooner, frosts may destroy the remainder, and you have no resource left.

The rule of thinning is, if the tree is weak the fruit must be left thin, not more than one or two on the larger shoots, and none upon the small ones, which is the only way to insure wood for another year: upon trees of a middling strong growth you should retain but one fruit upon the smaller shoots, and two upon the middling sized ones, and three upon the strong shoots: but the smallest kinds of fruit may be left a little thicker in proportion, and the large sorts should be thinner, i. e. about six inches distant upon each shoot, and the largest of all eight or ten. In performing this work, observe to select and retain the best placed, largest, and fairest fruit, in every part, according to the above rule; and in removing the superabundant ones, be careful not to disturb these. Leave no where two or more upon the same eye, especially if one exceeds the other in size, taking off the smallest, which the other would starve; but if they are of equal size, you may, if it shall seem necessary, leave both of them.

We formerly observed, that it was of utility to preserve a slight coverture of the leaves of the tree, by way of shade to the fruit during their growth, and until they begin to change colour: when they have attained that state of perfection, it is necessary to pinch off a few of the leaves that immediately cover the fruit, to admit the sun to give it colour and flavour.

Do this however regularly, and thin the leaves by degrees, which ſhould be pinched, and not torn off, which would mangle the eyes, and prevent the fruit buds from forming themſelves for next year.

Peach-trees, from the time of heading down to the ſixth or ſeventh year, may be ſaid to be in a ſtate of training, though they frequently begin to bear the ſecond or third year after the operation of heading down; and in five, ſix, or ſeven years will bear pretty plentifully, according to their ſize, for they will not have attained their full growth till they are ten, twelve, or fifteen years old, according to the extent of walling they have to cover, at which age they will be arrived at the beginning of their ultimate ſtate of vigour and perfection of bearing, which they generally acquire between the ſeventh and fifteenth year, and in which they will continue for twenty or thirty years to come; for theſe trees, with due management, will endure fifty or ſixty years, provided no accident happen, ſuch as violent blights, or tainted with gum, or attacked by vermin; ſo that the opinion of ſome, that peach-trees are ſeldom of more than twelve or fifteen years duration, is erroneous, and muſt be given up, for it is owing only to bad management that they do not laſt as long as other fruit-trees.

The trees may be ſaid to be in their third ſtate when they begin to decline through age; but if our general directions in pruning are obſerved, this ſeldom happens until they are upwards of thirty or forty years old, when they ſhould be cheriſhed by leaving only the beſt young ſhoots, and that moderately thin, and which ſhould be pruned ſhorter than the general rules. Make the moſt of ſtrong young wood that riſes from or near the bottom, to ſupply the place of worn-out branches.

When it is obſerved any trees approach near their end, and the bottom of the walls become naked, young trees ſhould be planted in due time in the ſpaces between the old ones to ſucceed them, and as they ſhoot up lop off the lower branches of the old trees, which in four or five years may be taken entirely away; thus you may keep your walls always occupied, without intermiſſion.

It ſometimes happens that the trees do not bear fruit of the approved or deſired ſort, which is often the mortifying circumſtance when purchaſed in ſome nurſeries, and a very cruel one, after all the trouble of training, &c. To remedy this you, in Auguſt, may bud ſome of the young ſhoots of the ſame year, in different parts of the tree, and as theſe advance, cut the other parts away, and in two or three years they will ſpread conſiderably, and bear fruit.

If the gum has attacked any ſhoot of a tree, young or old, cut it off an inch below, to ſtop the communication, and prevent killing the whole ſhoot.

The utility of tillage to theſe trees is very obvious, and ſhould be performed every autumn and ſpring.

Dung, in moderation, is alſo of the utmoſt utility in preſerving due vigour and health in theſe trees, and to promote the ſize of the fruit; let it be perfectly rotten, and added every two or three years, ſpreading it all over the border, and dig it in in the uſual way.

As to cultivating kitchen herbage on the borders, the moderate growing ſorts, ſuch as radiſhes, lettuce, ſmall ſallad herbs, kidney-beans, a few ſmall early mazagan beans, peas, &c. do very little or no injury to the trees.

Peach and nectarine-trees are often planted in forcing-frames and hot-walls, to produce early fruit; the ſorts proper for this are the earlieſt kinds.

There are two varieties of peach-trees that are eſteemed chiefly by way of curioſity and ornament, which we judge it moſt proper to ſpeak of under a ſeparate head. Theſe are, the

Double bloſſomed peach-tree; and Dwarf peach-tree.

The former of theſe has great beauty in its double flowers; it attains the height of common peach-trees, and differs in nothing from them but in the doubleneſs of its flowers, which, like thoſe of the others, are ſucceeded by fruit: the tree make a fine appearance in ornamental plantations.

The dwarf peach riſes but two or three feet high; the ſtem is ſmall, and hath very ſlender branches, which produce ſmall inſipid fruit, the ſize of a nutmeg. It is ſometimes planted in pots, and brought to table with the fruit upon for curioſity, and makes a ſingular appearance.

For

For purpoſes of ornament, any of the ſorts of peach-trees may, with propriety, be admitted as ſtandards in the ſhrubbery, and will make a fine appearance when in bloom; and if they ſtand in a ſheltered ſituation, there will be a chance of having now and then ſome fruit from them: they may either be planted as ſtandard-dwarfs, or as half or common ſtandards.

The propagation of the double bloſſomed and dwarf kind is effected by budding, the ſame as common peach-trees.

The nectarine and peach-trees have been generally conſidered as diſtinct ſpecies, principally by the difference of their fruit; but late diſcoveries has determined otherwiſe, and that they are found to be varieties of one another, but which is the original is not yet agreed on; but certain it is, that there have been inſtances of nectarines growing naturally on peach-trees, accompanied by peaches on the ſame branch; which very ſingular phœnomenon determines them to be varieties of one ſpecies.

Neither the trees, by their manner of growth, the wood, leaves, nor flowers of nectarines and peaches, can with any preciſion be diſtinguiſhed from one another; but the fruit is diſtinguiſhable at ſight in all its ſtages of growth: that of the nectarine hath a ſmooth firm ſkin or rind, and the peach is covered with a ſoft downy matter; the fleſh too or pulp of the nectarine is conſiderably firmer than that of peaches. See NECTARINE.

WOLF-PEACH, [*Lycoperſicon.*] Love-Apple, ſee LOVE-APPLE.

PEACOCK, [*Pavo.*] In ornithology, a genus of birds, of the order of the gallinæ, the characters of which are theſe: there are four toes on each foot, and the head is ornamented with an erect creſt of feathers.

PEARL, [*Margarita.*] in natural hiſtory, a hard, white, ſhining body, uſually roundiſh, found in a teſtacious fiſh reſembling an oyſter.

Pearls, though eſteemed of the number of gems by our jewellers, and highly valued, not only at this time, but in all ages, proceed only from a diſtemper in the creature that produces them, analogous to the bezoars, and other ſtony concretions in ſeveral animals of other kinds; and what the antients imagined to be a drop of dew concreted into a pearl in the body of the pearl-fiſh, which they ſuppoſed roſe from the bottom to the ſurface of the water to receive it, is nothing more than the matter deſtined to form and enlarge the ſhell, burſting from the veſſels deſtined to carry it to the parts of the ſhell it would have formed, and by that means producing theſe little concretions.

The fiſh in which theſe are uſually produced is the Eaſt-India pearl-oyſter, as it is commonly called; it has a very large and broad ſhell of the bivalve-kind, ſometimes meaſuring twelve or fourteen inches over, but thoſe of eight inches are more frequent: it is not very deep; on the outſide it is of a duſky brown, and within of a very beautiful white, with tinges of ſeveral other colours, as expoſed in different directions to the light. Beſides this ſhell, there are many others that are found to produce pearls; as the common oyſter, the muſcle, the pinna marina, and ſeveral others, the pearls of which are often very good, but thoſe of the true Indian burberi, or pearl-oyſter, are in general ſuperior to all. The ſmall or ſeed pearls, alſo called ounce pearls, from their being ſold by the ounce, and not by tale, are vaſtly the moſt numerous and common; but as in diamonds, among the multitudes of ſmall ones, there are ſmaller numbers of larger found, ſo in pearls there are larger and larger kinds; but as they increaſe in ſize, they are proportionably leſs frequent, and this is one reaſon of their great price.

Artificial PEARLS. Are made by reducing ſeed pearls to a paſte, by means of a chemical preparation called mercurial water, making the beads in ſilver moulds, boring them with a hog's briſtle, and drying them in a cloſed glaſs in the ſun.

Beads, in imitation of pearls, are alſo made of wax, and covered with the ſcales of ſeveral kinds of fiſhes.

PEAR-TREE, [*Pyrus.*] There is only one ſpecies of this tree, but it comprehends almoſt endleſs varieties, which furniſh fruit for uſe from the beginning of July until May or June the next year. We ſhall confine ourſelves to a liſt of the moſt valuable, arranged in three claſſes; ſummer-pears, autumn-pears, and winter-pears.

Summer-Pears are such as ripen from the beginning or middle of July until the middle or latter end of September, and continue but a short time in perfection: some of the earliest sorts keep good only a few days before they become mealy and rotten; and very few of the sorts will last much above a fortnight; but by having different varieties the succession may be continued two months or ten weeks, till succeeded by the autumnal sorts, which will continue in eating from the end of September till Christmas.

Little Musk-Pear. A small roundish yellow pear of a musky flavour, valuable for its early perfection: ripe beginning or middle of July.

Green Chissel Pear. A smallish, nearly oblong, light-green pear, melting, very juicy, and agreeably flavoured; ripe the middle or end of July.

Red Muscadelle, or Fairest Supreme. A middle-sized, beautiful, red-striped and yellow pear, somewhat firm, breaking juicy and rich flavoured; ripe the end of July and the beginning of August.

Jargonelle Pear, commonly so called, but is properly Cuisse Madam, or Lady's thigh. A largish, long, pyramidal, russetty-green pear: ripe beginning or middle of August.

Cuisse Madam Pear, commonly so called, but is properly the Jargonelle. A fine large oblong, smooth, yellowish-green pear, sometimes reddened next the sun, having a firm pulp, tolerably juicy, and agreeably relished, though not high flavoured, and is apt to become mealy when full ripe; but being a large handsome fruit, and the tree a remarkably good bearer; it highly merits culture, particularly for the supply of markets; and for which purpose it is greatly cultivated about London: ripe towards the middle of August.

Windsor Pear. A large oblongish pear, swelling considerably towards the crown, of a greenish-yellow colour, having a softish pulp, but soon becomes mealy: ripe middle or end of August.

This sort and the former bear a great resemblance to each other, but this is rather shorter and more swelling towards the crown.

Great Blanquette Pear. A large roundish, yellowish-green, smooth pear, having a soft juicy flesh of a rich flavour: ripe beginning or middle of August.

Little Blanquette Pear. A small, roundish, smooth, yellowish-green pear: ripe middle or end of August.

Early Russelet Pear. A middle sized, oblong, reddish pear, melting, and replete with sugary juice: ripe about the middle of August.

Musk Robine, or Queen's Pear. A small roundish, top-shaped, yellowish-coloured pear, tender, sweet, and musky: ripe middle or end of August.

Red Orange Pear. A middle-sized, globular pear, reddened on the sunny side, the other green, melting and richly flavoured: ripe end of August.

Perfumed Pear. A middling, roundish, deep-red pear, spotted with brown, having a melting perfumed flesh: ripe end of August.

Orange Musk Pear. A large, round, yellow pear, very good if eaten from the tree, as soon as a little ripe: it ripens in the end of August.

August Muscat, or Royal Pear. A largish, globular, whitish-yellow pear, breaking sugary and perfumed, and one of the finest pears of the season: ripe end of August.

Onion Pear. A middle-sized, globular, brown-skinned pear: ripe end of August.

Salviati Pear. A largish, globular, flatted pear, reddish and yellow to the sun, and whitish on the other side, tender and agreeably flavoured: ripe beginning of September.

Red Admirable Pear. A large globular pear, crimson-coloured on the sunny-side: ripe in September.

Summer Bon Chretian, or Good Christian. A fine, large, oblong pear, beautifully reddened next the sun, and whitish on the other side, breaking and highly flavoured: ripe beginning of September.

Rose Water Pear. A middle-sized, globular, brownish red, rough pear, breaking and finely flavoured: ripe middle of September.

Summer Bergamot Pear. A largish, round-flatted, greenish-yellow pear, melting and sugary: ripe middle of September.

Varieties. There are two or three varieties of this sort that differ in size, but are all of the Bergamot shape.

Orange Bergamot Pear. A largish round-

round-flatted, greenish-yellow pear, reddish next the sun, breaking and replete with perfumed juice: ripe towards the end of September.

Other Summer Pears of less note are known by the following names; Catharine Pear,—St. James's Pear—Crawford Pear,—Citron Pear,—Pear Piper,—Brute Pear,—Muskdrone Pear,—Lemon Pear,—Green Musk Pear,——Long stalked Blanquette Pear.

All the kinds of Summer pears ripen on the trees fit for eating, but should be gathered before they are too ripe.

Autumnal Pears.

Autumn pears are such as attain their full growth on the trees from about the middle or end of September till the end of October; and which after being gathered gradually mellow and improve in flavour, and will keep some a month, others six weeks, and some two months or longer; being in eating principally in October, November, and December.

Autumn Bergamot Pear. A middle-sized, roundish, flatted, yellowish-green pear, faintly reddening next the sun, melting, and of a richly perfumed flavour: ripe end of September or beginning of October, continuing good until the end of November.

Swiss Bergamot Pear. A middle-sized, roundish, greenish Pear, finely striped with red, melting and tolerably well flavoured: ripe the end of September, continuing in eating till November.

Great Russelet Pear. A large oblong brown and reddish pear, sometimes spotted, having a tender rich pulp: ripe middle or end of September.

Brown Beurre, or Beurre de Roy Pear. A fine, large, oblong, russetty, brown and greenish pear, very melting, juicy, and sugary, and is one of the finest pears of the autumn: ripe beginning of October, and keeps good till December.

White Beurre Pear. A large, roundish, top-shaped, whitish-yellow pear, melting, very juicy and good: ripe beginning of October, and keeps till November.

Red Beurre Pear. A large, oblong, reddish pear, melting and very fine: ripe beginning of October.

Green Sugar Pear. A middle-sized, top-shaped, smooth, green pear, full of a rich sugary juice; ripe end of October, and keeps good all November.

Monsieur John Pear. A largish, nearly round, swelling, brown pear with a rough skin, having a breaking, delicious pulp: ripe end of October, continuing in perfection all November and part of December.

Cresane Pear. A large, somewhat globular, flatted, greenish-yellow, russetty pear, hollowed at the top, is remarkably tender and sweet, and may be ranked as the finest pear of the season: ripe end of October, keeping good till December.

Swann's-egg pear. A moderately large, egg-shaped, dusky-green pear, brownish next the sun, is very juicy and agreeably flavoured: ripe end of October, continuing in tolerable perfection till near Christmas.

Verte Longue, Long-Green Pear, or Autumn Mouth-water. A large, long, very green pear, is melting and juicy: ripe in October, and continues till December.

Marquis's Pear. A fine large, swelling, flat-topped, greenish-yellow pear, faintly spotted with red, having a tender good pulp; is in eating in November and December.

Grey Good-wife Pear. A middle-sized, roundish, brownish-red pear, moderately tender and well-flavoured: is in eating from the end of October till December.

Rousseline Pear, or Long-stalked, late Autumnal Muscat. A large, oblong, long-stalked pear, reddish on the sunny side, is tender, and of a musky flavour: in eating in the end of October and part of November.

Muscat Fleury Pear. A smallish globular, brownish-red, long-stalked Pear, tender and high-flavoured: in eating from October till December.

Twice flowering Pear-tree. It often produces blossom twice a year, the first in the spring, and the second in autumn, so is preserved in many gardens as a curiosity.

Other less material autumnal pears are—Pesideri Pear.—Dean's Pear.—Vicar's Pear.—Vine Pear.—Autumn Rose Pear.—French Bergamot.——Beurre Bergamot.—Knave's Pear.—Burnt Cat Pear.—Pound Pear, very large.

All the autumn pears should have their full growth on the tree, but not hang till quite ripe, which is the end of September and in October, being their season of full growth.

Winter Pears.

Winter pears arrive to full growth about the end of October and in November, but do not attain maturity for eating until they have lain some considerable time in the house, some a month or six weeks, others two or three months or more, before they ripen, as observed below in their descriptions, so that they succeed one another in perfection generally from about December until May.

By the winter pears being so long acquiring perfection after gathered from the tree, many persons have thought them fit only for culinary uses; but most of the following are very fine eating pears, after having lain the proper time to mellow.

St. Germain Pear. A large long yellowish green, extraordinary fine pear, of the melting sugary kind: in eating from December until February.

Chaumontelle Pear. A large oblong pear, having one side purplish, the other of a whitish-green colour, is melting, of a very rich delicious flavour: in eating from December until March or April.

Martin Sec, or Dry Martin Pear. A large, oblong, russety-reddish pear, is breaking, somewhat dry, but of a fine perfumed flavour: in eating end of November, December, and January.

Colmar Pear. A large swelling, flat-topped, greenish-yellow pear, spotted with yellow; is tender and exceedingly fine flavoured: in eating from December till January or February.

Spanish Bon Chretien. A large pyramidal purple and yellow pear, having many dark spots on the purple side; is a fine winter pear, ready for eating the end of December, continues good near two months.

Virgoleuse Pear. A large, oblong, greenish-yellow pear, sometimes brownish next the sun, is an excellent fruit: in eating from the beginning or middle of December until the end of January.

Dauphine Pear. A middle-sized, roundish, top-shaped, smooth, yellowish-green pear, having a melting, sugary, musky pulp: in eating the end of November, continuing in perfection all December and most part of January.

Winter Verte Longue Pear. A longish, green-coloured, smooth, spotted exceeding good pear: in eating the end of December and January, &c.

Winter Beurre Pear. A smallish, oblong, yellowish, red-spotted, very fine pear; ready for eating in December and January.

Winter Thorn Pear. A large, long, pyramidal whitish-green pear; is melting, and in fine eating from December till February.

Martin Sire, or Lord Martin Pear. A large, roundish, irregularly-swelling, smooth pear, red on one side, the other yellow; is breaking, and of a perfumed flavour: in eating in December and January.

Winter Bergamot Pear. A middle-sized, roundish, greenish-yellow pear: in eating from the end of November until the spring.

Hollond's Bergamot. A large, round, greenish pear, having a tender rich pulp: in eating from January till April.

Winter Bon Chretien. A very large, long pyramidal, yellowish-green pear, having often an uneven surface; is breaking, very juicy, remarkably sweet and rich flavoured, and often proves the best winter pear in the collection: in eating from February till April or May.

German Muscat Pear. A middle-sized, oblong, russety-red pear, having a melting rich pulp: in eating from February till May or longer.

Easter Bergamot Pear. A large, roundish, flat-topped, greenish pear, having many rough spots, is of the breaking kind; and is in eating from February till April or May.

Winter Russelet Pear. A middle-sized, longish pear, red on one side, the other of a greenish-yellow, is melting and agreeably relished: in eating in January, March, &c.

St. Martial Pear. A longish, oblong, smooth pear, one side purple, the other yellow; having a buttery rich flesh: in eating from February till May or June.

Cadillac Pear. A very large, roundish, red and yellow pear, having a hard, sour, pulp, but is excellent for baking and other culinary purposes: in use from November or December till May.

Union Pear, or Uvedale's St. Germain. A large, long, deep-green pear, reddish on one side, having a hard, sour, pulp, but is excellent for baking, &c. in perfection from November or December till May or longer.

Black Pear of Worcester, or Parkinson's Warden. A remarkably large, oblong, dusky brown, rough pear, having a hard austere pulp, but is very fine for culinary uses, from November till March or April.

Double Flowered Pear. The tree produces double flowers succeeded by a large, short, yellowish and red pear, rather hard and austere; but is remarkably fine for baking, &c.

Other less material varieties of winter pears are known by the following names.—Good Lewis, a large, longish pear.—Ambrette, a large roundish pear.—Thick-stalked Pear, a very large roundish fruit.—Amadot, a middle-sized oblong pear.—St. Austin, a middling oblong pear.—Russet of Anjou, large roundish pear.—Chaffery, a large oblong pear.——Iron-coloured Pear, a middle-sized oblong fruit.—Golden Winter Pear, a large globular fruit.—Villain of Anjou, a large roundish pear.——Winter Russeler, a middle-sized longish pear.—Carmelite, a middling roundish pear for kitchen uses.——Winter Citron-shaped Pear, for baking.—Blood Pear, for baking, &c.—English Warden, a large pear for baking and other culinary uses.

There are many other varieties of pears of less account, both of summer, autumn, and winter kinds, that are unnecessary to insert here; and indeed it would be almost impossible to discriminate the various sorts of hard pears, and others of little note, found in the orchards and gardens in country villages and about farm-houses, in different parts of England, &c.

But as the varieties described in the above three lists are of known merit, and are cultivated in most of the nurseries for sale, by the names here prefixed to each kind, consisting of near sixty different sorts, they are more than sufficient to furnish the most extensive garden with a copious variety of pears, almost the year round.

All the varieties of this tree are hardy and will succeed in any common soil of a garden or orchard, both as dwarfs for walls and espaliers, &c. and in standards of all sorts; and in all of which modes of training they will bear plentifully: it is however of importance to allot a good wall and espalier for some of the choicer kinds, both summer, autumnal, and winter pears, in order both to forward the growth of the fruit and to improve its size, beauty, and flavour: a south, east, and westerly wall are the proper exposures, and it is eligible to plant some in each of those aspects, to vary the times of ripening, though most of the summer pears will succeed very well in almost any aspect, and if some are planted also against a north-wall, they will ripen later, and continue the succession of any approved sorts longer in eating; but it is particularly necessary to allow all the fine sorts of winter pears an east or west wall, or a well-exposed espalier, otherwise they will not perfect their fruit kindly in unfavourable seasons; in espaliers however that are well trained, all the sorts of pears attain great perfection, and the espaliers may be arranged round the quarters of the kitchen-garden, or in any other free situation where the soil is of similar quality.

Remarking, that these trees, both against walls and espaliers, should generally be allowed a great deal of room to spread, for by having full scope they will extend their branches more than twenty feet on each side of the stem, and the whole will sometimes form a spread of forty or fifty feet, with height in proportion.

Standards of some sorts of pears are also naturally of a very spreading growth, others grow more upright.

However, in all the methods of training these trees, it is highly requisite to allow them sufficient room to spread to their full extent, and their branches should be suffered to extend themselves always at full length; for pear-trees should never be shortened, except in the first or second year, &c. to obtain a supply of lateral branches to form a more regular spreading head, because as they always bear their blossom and fruit upon short spurs arising from the sides of the branches; first, however, towards the extreme parts, then by degrees all along the sides almost from every eye, that shortening would cut away the first fruitful parts, and thus by stopping their progress of shooting in length it would force out strong shoots from all the eyes, and prevent their forming spurs or fruit-buds; but being trained at full length they shoot moderately, and in two or three years naturally form short

ſhort ſpurs of from about half an inch to an inch or two long, the ſame branch and ſpurs continuing fruitful a great number of years.

But it muſt be obſerved, that pear-trees are generally ſeveral years before they attain any tolerable bearing ſtate, for the branches ſeldom begin to form fruit-ſpurs till they are from about two or three, to four or five years old; at that age, however, they ſometimes begin to bear, but never any general crop till they are eight or ten years old.

Pear-trees are propagated by grafting and budding upon any kinds of pear-ſtocks; alſo occaſionally upon quince-ſtocks, and ſometimes upon white-thorn ſtocks, but pear-ſtocks are greatly preferable to all others for general uſe. See Apple-Trees, Espaliers, Grafting, Pruning, &c.

In the gathering of pears, great regard ſhould be had to the bud which is formed at the bottom of the foot-ſtalk, for the next year's bloſſoms, which, by forcing of the pear before it be mature, is many times ſpoiled; for while the fruit is growing, there is always a bud formed by the ſide of the foot-ſtalk upon the ſame ſpur, for the next year's fruit; ſo that when the pears are ripe, if they are gently turned upward, the foot-ſtalk will readily part from the ſpur, without injuring of the bud.

The ſeaſon for gathering all ſummer pears is juſt as they ripen, for none of theſe will remain good above a day or two after they are taken from the tree; nor will many of the autumn pears keep good above ten days or a fortnight, after they are gathered. But the winter fruits ſhould hang as long upon the trees as the ſeaſon will permit, for they muſt not receive the froſt, which will cauſe them to rot, and render their juices flat and ill-taſted; but if the weather continue mild until the end of October, it will then be a good ſeaſon for gathering them in, which muſt always be done in dry weather, and when the trees are perfectly dry.

In the doing of this you ought carefully to avoid bruiſing them, therefore you ſhould have a broad flat baſket to lay them in as they are gathered; and when they are carried into the ſtore-room, they ſhould be taken out ſingly, and each ſort laid up in a cloſe heap, on a dry place, in order to ſweat, where they may remain for ten days or a fortnight, during which time the windows ſhould be open to admit the air, in order to carry off all the moiſture which is perſpired from the fruit; after this, the pears ſhould be taken ſingly, and wiped dry with a woollen cloth, and then packed up in cloſe baſkets, obſerving to put ſome wheat-ſtraw in the bottoms and round the ſides of the baſkets, to prevent their bruiſing againſt the baſkets. And if ſome thick ſoft paper is laid double or treble all round the baſket, between the ſtraw and the pears, this will prevent the pears from imbibing the muſty taſte which is communicated to them by the ſtraw, when they are contiguous; which taſte often penetrates through the ſkin ſo ſtrongly, that when the fruit is pared the taſte will remain. You ſhould alſo obſerve to put but one ſort of fruit into a baſket, leſt by their different fermentations they ſhould rot each other; but if you have enough of one ſort to fill a baſket which holds two or three buſhels, it will be ſtill better. After you have filled the baſkets, you muſt cover them over with wheat-ſtraw very cloſe, firſt laying a covering of paper two or three times double over the fruit, and faſten them down; then place theſe baſkets in a cloſe room, where they may be kept dry and from froſt; but the leſs air is let into the room, the better the fruit will keep. It will be very neceſſary to fix a label to each baſket, denoting the ſort of fruit therein contained, which will ſave the trouble of opening them, whenever you want to know the ſorts of fruit; beſides, they ought not to be opened before their ſeaſon to be eaten, for the oftner they are opened and expoſed to the air, the worſe they will keep. We doubt not but this will be objected to by many, who imagine fruit cannot be laid too thin; for which reaſon they make ſhelves to diſpoſe them ſingly upon, and are very fond of admitting freſh air, whenever the weather is mild, ſuppoſing it very neceſſary to preſerve the fruit; but the contrary of this is found true, by thoſe perſons who have large ſtocks of fruit laid up in their ſtorehouſes in London, which remain cloſely ſhut up for ſeveral months, in the manner before related; and when theſe are opened, the

fruit

fruit is always found plumper and founder than any of those fruits which were preserved singly upon shelves, whose skins are always shrivelled and dry. For (as Mr. Boyle observes) the air is the cause of putrefaction; and, in order to prove this, that honourable gentleman put fruits of several kinds into glasses where the air was exhausted, in which places they remained found for several months, but, upon bein exposed to the air, rotted in a very short time, which plainly shews the absurdity of the common method now used to preserve fruit.

Earth-Nut PEA. See *Everlasting* PEA.

Heart PEA, [*Cardiospermum.*] A plant of which there are two species growing naturally in both the Indies, where they climb up the shrubs that grow near them; they are tender annuals, and if cultivated in England, must be raised in a hot-bed.

PIGEON-PEA [*Cytisus, Cayan.*] A species of Cytisus growing in the American Islands, and cannot be preserved in England but in a stove.

PEARL-ASHES. A salt made from the ashes of wood.

PEARL-BARLEY, [*Hordeum Perlatum.*] Barley prepared by grinding the shelled barley into little round grains.

PEAT-ASHES, are a most excellent manure for young clover and grass, vetches, and wheat sown dry in the spring of the year. They should be kept dry and entirely free from wet. The following are the observations of a judicious farmer:——

"Peat is found in most low grounds that lie betwixt hills, especially if timber has formerly stood on the spot. It lies at various depths, being often near the surface, and sometimes six, eight, or ten feet deep, having a stratum of black moory earth over it, such as is the soil of many of our low meadows near the banks of rivers: it sometimes even lies under a bed of gravel.

"Peat may be burnt, for the sake of procuring its ashes for manure all the summer season: as soon as it is dug, some of it is mixed in a heap regularly disposed with faggot wood, or other ready burning fuel: after a layer or two of it mixed in this manner, peat alone is piled up to compleat the heap. A heap will consist of from one hundred to a thousand loads.

"After setting fire to it at a proper place, before prepared for the purpose, it is watched in the burning, and the great art is to keep in as much of the smoke as possible, provided that as much vent is left as will nourish and feed the fire.

"Whenever a crack appears, out of which the smoke escapes, the labourer in that place lays on more peat; and if the fire slackens too much within, which may easily be known by the heat on the outside, the workman must run a strong pole into the heap in as many places as is necessary to supply it with a quantity of fresh air. When managed in this manner, the work goes on as it should do. It is to be noticed, that when once the fire is well kindled, the heaviest rain does it no harm whilst it is burning.

"Having pocured a sufficient quantity of ashes, the farmer's next care should be to apply them properly to use; and to do this, he must be made well acquainted with the nature of the manure he is to lay on his land.

"All ashes are of a hot, fiery, caustic nature; they must therefore be used with caution. With respect to peat-ashes, almost the only danger proceeds from laying them on in too great quantities at improper seasons.

"Nothing can be better than peat-ashes for dressing low damp meadows, laying to the quantity of from fifteen to twenty Winchester bushels on an acre: it is best to sow them by hand, as they will then be more regularly spread.

"This work should be done in January or February at latest, that the ashes may be washed in towards the roots of the grass by the first rains that fall in the spring.

"If they were spread more forward in the year, and a speedy rain should not succeed, being hot in their nature, they would be apt to burn up the grass, instead of doing it any service.

"It is to be remembered, that the damper and stiffer the soil, the more peat-ashes should be laid on it; but in grass lands the quantity should never exceed thirty Winchester bushels, and on light warm lands less than half that quantity is fully sufficient.

"On wheat crops these ashes are of the greatest service, but they must be used with the utmost discretion. Were they

every other consideration, the sole view of lessening his expences will, it is imagined, sufficiently induce him to be attentive to this particular.

"When peat is burnt for the sake of its ashes in summer time, it is necessary that some care should be taken to defend them from the too powerful influence of the sun, air, dews, rains, &c. or great part of their virtue would be exhaled and exhausted. If the quantity of ashes procured is not very great, they may be easily put under cover in a barn, cart-lodge, or hovel; but large quantities must necessarily, to avoid expence, be kept abroad; and when this is case, they should be ordered as follows.

"A dry spot of ground must be chosen; and on this the ashes are to be laid in a large heap, as near as possible in the form of a cone standing on its base, the top as sharp pointed as possible: when this is done, let the whole be covered thinly over with a coat of soil, to defend the heap from the weather: the circumjacent earth, provided it is not too light and crumbly, will always serve for this purpose.

"When thus guarded, the heap may very safely be left till January or February, when it is in general the season for spreading it: but, before it is used, it is always best to sift the ashes, that the cinders, stones, and half burnt turf, may be separated from them.

"This may, perchance, by many be esteemed an unnecessary trouble; but experience, which is the best guide, has convinced me, that by this means I can better ascertain the quantity that ought to be sown on the several sorts of land; for the small powdered ashes, being equal in quality, are of course equal in effect; whereas, when there has been any other mixture with them, the effect has often been greater or less than I could have wished. Thus, when I mention the number of bushels I strew on an acre, it is always to be understood of sifted ashes: should any farmer be inclined to try them rough as they are first produced after burning, the quantity to be allowed for an acre must be more in proportion to the mixture of other matter that is in them.

"These peat-ashes are almost, as I have already observed, a general manure suited to every soil. On cold clay they warm the too compact particles, dispose it to ferment, and of course fertilize, and, in fine, not only assist it in disclosing and dispensing its great vegetative powers, but also bring to its aid a considerable proportion of ready prepared aliment for plants.

"On light lands these ashes have a different effect: here the pores are too large to be affected, or farther separated by the salts or sulphur contained in them; but, being closely attached to the surfaces of the large particles, of which this earth is generally composed, this manure disposes them, by means of its salts, to attract the moisture contained in the air; by this operation, the plants, which grow on these porous soils, are prevented from being scorched up and burnt; and if they want, which they generally do, more nourishment than the land is of itself capable of affording, this is readily and abundantly supplied by this useful manure.

"In large farms it is very usual to see all the home-fields rich and well-mended by the yard-dung, &c. whereas the more distant lands are generally poor, impoverished, and out of heart, for want of proper manure being applied in time.

"Whilst the farmers depend almost entirely on the yard-dung, this cannot fail being the case; for dung is of very heavy carriage: they are willing, therefore, to drop it as near home as possible, being in this way able to do a great deal more work in the same space of time: but would they once try the virtue of peat-ashes, all their lands might be alike improved, though at a very considerable distance from the home-stall; for so few of them are required, and they are so light of carriage, that a single tumbril will hold as many as ought, in most cases, to be laid on two acres of land; by which means, when these ashes are used as a dressing for the distant fields, it costs the farmer less in carriage than does that of the stable-dung for his home-fields."

PECK. A measure containing two gallons, or 8 quarts.

PELLITORY, *of the Wall*, [*Parietaria*.] This is a small plant, growing upon old walls; of an herbaceous, subsaline taste, without any smell. It is one of the five emollient herbs, and in this intention is occasionally made

use

use of. It is an ingredient in the nephritic decoction of the Edinburgh pharmacopœia. The expressed juice has been given in the dose of three ounces as a diuretic.

PELLITORY *of Spain*, [*Pyrethrum.*] This plant, though a native of the warm climates, bears the ordinary winters of this; and often flowers successively, from Christmas to May; the roots also grow larger with us than those which the shops are usually supplied with from abroad.

Pellitory root has no sensible smell; its taste is very hot and acrid, but less so than that of arum or dracunculus: the juice expressed from it has scarce any acrimony, nor is the root itself so pungent when fresh as after it has been dried. Water, assisted by heat, extracts some share of its taste, rectified spirit the whole; neither of them elevate any thing in distillation. The principal use of pyrethrum in the present practice is as a masticatory, for promoting the salival flux, and evacuating viscid humours from the head and neighbouring parts; by this means it often relieves the tooth-ach, some kinds of pains of the head, and lethargic complaints.

PELT. By this name is called the dead body of any fowl an hawk hath killed.

PELT-WOOL. Is the wool pulled off the skin or pelt of any dead sheep.

PENNY-EARTH. A term used by the farmers for a hard, loamy, or sandy earth, with a very large quantity of sea shells intermixed in it; some of which being round aad flat, and in some measure resembling pieces of money, have occasioned the earth's being called by this name. It is an earth not easily dug, but is usually undermined with pickaxes, and then falls in large lumps; which, with the frosts, break to pieces, and leave the shells loose. It is prepared by breaking and mixing well with water, and then makes very desirable floors. The Jersey combers comb-pots are also made of it, and the sides and roofs of ovens are plaistered with it; and, being rightly managed, it combines into a flower almost as strong as plaister of Paris.

PENGUIN, [*Karatas.*] Wild ananas. This plant is very common in the West-Indies, where the juice of its fruit is often put into punch, being of a sharp acid flavour. There is also a wine made of the juice of this fruit, which is very strong, but it will not keep good long, so is only for present use. This wine is very intoxicating, and heats the blood, therefore should be drank very sparingly.

In England this plant is preserved as a curiosity, for the fruit seldom arrives to any degree of perfection for use in this country, though it often produces fruit in England, which has ripened pretty well; but if it were to ripen as thoroughly here as in its native country, it will be little valued on account of its great austerity, which will often take the skin off from the mouths and throats of those people who eat it incautiously.

This plant is propagated by seeds, for though there are often suckers sent forth from the old plants, yet they come out from between the leaves, and are so long, slender, and ill-shapen, that if they are planted they seldom make regular plants. These seeds should be sown early in the spring in small pots, and plunged into a hot-bed of tanners bark, where the plants will come up in six weeks. When the plants are strong enough to transplant, they should be carefully taken up, each planted into a separate pot, and plunged into the hot-bed again; when the plants have taken new root, they should have air and water in proportion to the warmth of the season. In this bed the plants may remain till Michaelmas, then they should be removed into the stove and plunged into the bark-bed, where they should be treated in the same manner as the Ananas.

The leaves of this plant are strongly armed with crooked spines, which render it very troublesome to shift or handle them; for the spines catch hold of whatever approaches them by their crooked form, being some bent one way, and others the reverse, so that they catch both ways, and tear the skin or clothes of the persons who handle them, where there is not the greatest care taken to avoid them.

PENNY-ROYAL, [*Pulegium.*] This plant grows spontaneously in several parts of England upon moist commons, and in watery places; trailing upon the ground, and striking roots

roots at the joints. Our markets have been for some time supplied with a garden sort, which is larger than the other, and grows upright: this is called by Mr. Dale *pulegium erectum*.

Pennyroyal is a warm, pungent herb, of the aromatic kind, similar to mint, but more acrid and less agreeable; it has long been held in great esteem, and not undeservedly, as an aperient, and deobstruent, particularly in hysteric complaints, and suppressions of the uterine purgations. For these purposes the distilled water is generally made use of, or what is of equal efficacy, an infusion of the leaves. It is observeable, that both water and rectified spirit extract the virtues of this herb by infusion, and likewise elevate greatest part of them in distillation.

In the shops are kept a simple and spirituous water and essential oil of the plant; this herb is used also in the compound valerian water and troches of myrrh, and its simple water for making the lac ammoniac and the camphorated emulsion.

Harts PENNYROYAL, [*Pulegium erectum.*] This species is met with, though not very often, in our gardens. It is somewhat stronger, yet rather more agreeable, than the foregoing, both in taste and smell.

Marsh PENNYROYAL, Water Navel-wort.

PEONY, [*Paeonia.*] The species are 1. The male. 2. The female. 3. The foreign Peony. 4. The Portugal Peony. 5. Tartarian Peony. They are all annual in stalk, and perennial in root; their propagation is easy by dividing the roots in August or September.

PEPPER, [*Piper.*] The pepper plant is a shrub whose root is small, fibrous, and flexible; it rises into a stem, which requires a tree or a prop to support it. Its wood has the same sort of knots as the vine; and when it is dry, it exactly resembles the vine-branch. The leaves, which have a strong smell and pungent taste, are of an oval shape; but they diminish towards the extremity, and terminate in a point. From the flower-buds, which are white, and are sometimes placed in the middle, and sometimes at the extremity of the branches, are produced small berries resembling those of the currant-tree. Each of these contains between twenty & thirty corns of pepper; they are commonly gathered in October, and exposed to the sun seven or eight days. The fruit, which was green at first, and afterwards red, when stripped of its covering, assumes the appearance it has when we see it. The largest, heaviest, and least shrivelled, is the best.

The pepper-plant flourishes in the islands of Java, Sumatra, and Ceylon, and more particularly on the Malabar coast. It is not sown, but planted; and great nicety is required in the choice of the shoots. It produces no fruit till the end of three years; but bears so plentifully the three succeeding years, that some plants yield between six and seven pounds of pepper. The bark then begins to shrink, and the shrub declines so fast, that in twelve years time it ceases bearing.

The culture of pepper is not difficult; it is sufficient to plant it in a rich soil, and carefully to pull up the weeds that grow in great abundance round its roots, especially the three first years. As the sun is highly necessary to the growth of the pepper plant, when it is ready to bear, the trees that support it must be lopped, to prevent their shade from injuring the fruit. When the season is over, it is proper to crop the head of the plant. Without this precaution, there would be too much wood, and little fruit.

Long PEPPER, [*Piper Longum.*] This is the fruit of a plant growing also in the East-Indies. It is of a cylindrical figure, about an inch and a half in length; the external surface appears composed of numerous minute grains disposed round the fruit in a kind of spiral direction.

Jamaica PEPPER. This is the produce of our own plantations; it is the fruit of a large tree, growing spontaneously in the mountainous parts of Jamaica, called by Sir Hans Sloan, *myrtus arborea, aromatica, foliis laurinis.* The smell of this spice resembles a mixture of cinnamon, cloves and nutmegs: its taste approaches to that of cloves, or a mixture of the three foregoing; whence it has received the name of *all-spice.* The shops have been for some time accustomed to employ this aromatic as a succedaneum to the more costly spices, and from them it has been introduced into our hospitals: the London college have given it a

place

place in their late dispensatory, and direct a simple water to be distilled from it, which possesses the flavour of the pimento in great perfection. It yields a large quantity of pleasant essential oil, which sinks in water; this oil is recommended in the Edinburgh pharmacopœia. Rectified spirit extracts its pungency and flavour, and elevates nothing in distillation.

Guinea PEPPER. Capsicum.

Wall PEPPER, [*Sedum acre.*] This plant grows very common upon old walls, in all parts of England.

Water PEPPER. See *Biting Arsmart.*

Poorman's PEPPER, } See *Dittander.*
PEPPERWORT, }

PEPPERMINT, [*Mentha piperis.*] This species has been lately introduced into practice, and received for the first time in our present pharmacopœia: very few of the botanical or medical writers make mention of it; it grows wild in some parts of England, in moist watery places, but is much less common than the other sorts. The leaves have a more penetrating smell than any of the other mints, and a much warmer, pungent, glowing taste like pepper, sinking as it were into the tongue. The principal use of this herb is in flatulent cholics, languors, and other like disorders: it seems to act as soon as taken, and extends it effects through the whole system, instantly communicating a glowing warmth. Water extracts the whole of the pungency of this herb by infusion, and elevates it in distillation.

PERENNIAL, [*Perennis.*] Perennial, or everlasting plants; plants that are perpetuated by the roots, that is, whether their leaves and stalks decay annually in winter, or always remain, provided the roots of several years duration, they are still perennial plants.

All plants, therefore, with abiding roots, both of the herbaceous tribe in general, and of the shrub and tree kinds, are perennials; though in the general acceptation of the word perennial, it is most commonly applied to herbaceous vegetables with durable roots, more especially those of the flowery kind, which among the gardeners are commonly called simple perennials, particularly the fibrous-rooted tribe; but it is equally applicable to fibrous, tuberous, and bulbous-rooted plants, whose roots are of several years duration: likewise all shrubs and trees of every denomination, as having abiding roots, are also perennial plants.

Perennial plants consist both of deciduous and ever-green kinds; those that cast their leaves &c. in winter are termed deciduous perennials, and those which retain their leaves ever-greens.

Of the herbaceous perennials, however, both of the fibrous-rooted tribe, tuberous and bulbous-rooted kinds, far the greater part have annual stalks, rising in spring and decay in winter; and a great many lose their leaves entirely also in that season, such as the perennial sun-flower, asters, (and numerous other sorts; and many sorts retain their leaves all the year, but not their stalks, exemplified in the auricula, polyanthus, some *campanulas*, pinks, carnations, and many others.

Great number of the herbaceous perennials multiply exceedingly by offsets of the root, by which they are propagated in great abundance.

All the tree and shrub perennials are durable both in root, stem, and branch; but all renew their leaves annually, even the ever-green kinds, although they are in leaf the year round, yet they put forth new leaves every year, to which the old ones gradually give place.

PERIWINKLE, [*Vinca.*] There are three pecies, the narrow, the broad-leaved, and the oval; they are easily propagated by their trailing stalks, which put out roots freely.

PERRY. A vinous liquor made of pears, as cyder is made of apples. *See* CYDER. The best pears for perry, or at least the sorts which have been hitherto deemed the fittest for making this liquour, are so excessively tart and harsh, that no mortal can think of eating them as fruit; for even hungry swine will not eat them, nay, hardly so much as smell to them. Of these the Bosbury pear, the Bareland pear, and the horse pear, are the most esteemed for perry in Worcestershire, and the squash pear, as it is called, in Glocestershire; in both which counties, as well as in some of the adjacent parts, they are planted in the hedge-rows and most common fields.

There is this advantage attending pear trees, that they will thrive on land where apples will not so much as live, and

and that ſome of them grow to ſuch a ſize, that a ſingle pear tree, particularly of the Boſbury and the ſquaſh kind, has frequently been known to yield, in one ſeaſon, from one to four hogſheads of perry. The Boſbury pear is thought to yield the moſt laſting and moſt vinous liquor. The John pear, the Harpy pear, the Drake pear, the Mary pear, the Lullum pear, and ſeveral others of the harſheſt kinds, are eſteemed the beſt for perry, but the redder or more tawney they are, the more they are preferred. Pears, as well as apples, ſhould be full before they are ground.

PERUVIAN BARK. *See* BARK.

ST. PETER's-WORK, [*Aſcyrum.*] This plant has a perennial root with an annual ſtalk; it is of little uſe or beauty.

PETTYWHIN. Furze. Cammock.

PHEASANT's EYE, [*Adonis.*] *See* ADONIS.

PHYSIC *for a Horſe.* There are a great variety of occaſions on which this creature may want purging, and many ſorts of phyſic may anſwer the purpoſe; but before we come to the method of preparing any of theſe, it will be neceſſary to give the farmer proper directions concerning the uſe of ſuch medicines. A horſe muſt be prepared for a purge the day before it is given him, or it will take very little effect; and then it will operate more or leſs, according to the management of him during the time.

The day before a horſe is to be purged, give him a good quantity of water with ſcalded bran in it, and let him have it warm. Keep him quiet, and the next morning, before he has any thing to eat, give him the purge. Any one of the following will anſwer the common purpoſes, with little charge.

1. *A Purge with Aloes.*

Take an ounce and a quarter of horſe-aloes beaten to powder, and a quarter of an ounce of cream of tartar, and half an ounce of powder of anniſeeds, work this up into a conſiſtence, and roll it round into two balls. Rub theſe over with butter, and give them to the horſe; they will, by means of being greaſed, ſlip down very freely; and after them give him a horn of ſmall beer made warm.

The doſe is to be made larger or ſmaller, as the horſe is larger and coarſer fed, or finer limb'd, and managed more delicately. There is as much difference between the conſtitution of a cart-horſe and a racer, as between a drayman and a perſon of quality; and they muſt in all reſpects be treated accordingly, not only in the ſtrength of the doſe, but in the management afterwards: for what ſuits one will be quite improper for the other.

2. *A Purge with Jalap.*

Take powder of aloes an ounce, powder of jalap a quarter of an ounce, and powdered ginger a dram: mix all theſe up with two ounces of freſh butter, and make the whole into a couple of balls, or more; greaſe them on the outſide, and give them to the horſe with ſome warm ale afterwards.

Theſe are two common receipts, but they are often ill proportioned in the quantities; ſomething of this kind ſtands under the name of a purge for horſes in moſt books that treat of theſe things; but the quantity of the anniſeeds is too great, in the common directions for the firſt; and this will make a horſe ſick afterwards; and to the other there are commonly added uſeleſs ingredients. Theſe are approved proportions, and they will anſwer almoſt every occaſion there can be for a horſe's being phyſicked in this way.

Let the balls and the beer be given him early in the morning, and let him then be rid out gently for a quarter of an hour. Then bring him cool in, and let him be ſet up two hours without food.

After this time give him a ſmall quantity of good hay, and a quarter of an hour after that ſome warm water.

An hour after this give him ſome ſcalded bran. He will purge kindly after this manner of management; and after this he ſhould be rid out a little again; then when he is brought in, he ſhould have ſome bran and water warm, with but a ſmall quantity of the water. Then let him be rid out again; in this manner a horſe is to be treated with his purge, and, in general, it will be eaſy to make him work more or leſs at pleaſure, by giving him more or leſs exerciſe, and more or leſs of the bran and water.

If

If the purge has been too violent, and will not ſtop, the following aſtringent drink will always ſtop it.

An Aſtringent Drink.

Boil three pints of ſtale beer, and ſome pieces of cruſt of brown bread: to this put an ounce of whiting, and a quarter of an ounce of diaſcordium, made without honey; if this does not ſtop it in four or five hours, give the ſame quantity of whiting and double the quantity of diaſcordium in only one pint of the beer and bread. This will make him altogether quiet and eaſy, and he will be in his body as uſual.

For a Cold.

This is a diſorder ſo well underſtood, that it cannot be miſtaken, nor does it need any explanation.

Boil in a quart of ale three ounces of freſh liquorice-root, beat very fine into threads. Strain the liquor off, preſſing it hard, and add to it three drams of elecampane powder, one dram of powder of anniſeeds, a quarter of a pint of oil, and a quarter of a pound of honey; mix all well, and give it warm. If it does not take effect the firſt time, let it be repeated three or four times, and it ſeldom fails.

Balls for a Cough of long ſtanding.

Put into a large bowl ſix pounds of wheat meal, mix with it two ounces of powder of anniſeeds, cummin-ſeed one ounce, linſeed three ounces, ſenugreek-ſeed one ounce and a half; ſtir theſe well about, then mix half a pound of liquorice powder, and a quarter of a pound of flour of brimſtone: add theſe to the reſt. Laſtly, add bay-berries and Juniper-berries, powdered, three ounces of each, and the ſame quantity of powder of elecampane.

When all are well ſtirred and mixed together, break ſix eggs, throw away the whites, beat up the yolks with two quarts of mountain wine. Add to this a pound and a half of honey and a pint of ſallad oil. Mix all theſe perfectly well together; then bring in the powder, and work the whole to a paſte. If this ſhould be too ſtiff, a little more wine muſt be added; and, if too ſoft, ſome flour muſt be put in, till the whole be of ſuch a conſiſtence that it will conveniently roll into balls.

Theſe are to be made of the bigneſs of a hen's egg, but round. This rolling them up is only for the convenience of keeping; when they are to be uſed, they are to be diſſolved. Two is the proper quantity for a doſe, and they are to be melted in the creature's water, morning and evening, for fifteen days.

PHYSIC NUT. *See Phyſic* NUT.

PIGEON. It is a great recommendation of any creature to the farmer, that it will be kept at ſmall expence, and this is the caſe with the pigeon, which he ſhould keep; for there are ſome kinds that require a great deal of food and charge: the proper pigeon for the dovecoat, which is the only kind he is to regard, is able the greateſt part of the year to provide for itſelf; and when it requires his aſſiſtance, the food is not of any dear kind.

There are at this time many kinds of pigeons kept in England, by people fond of curioſity, and it has become a ſtudy to procure and raiſe new kinds among thoſe who are called pigeon-ſanciers, as much as to get from abroad, or raiſe from ſeed, new kinds of carnations or auriculas among the floriſts. But with this the induſtrious huſbandman has nothing to do. He is to keep pigeons for their value, not their beauty; and he is to conſider which may be kept with moſt eaſe, which is in his way one of the greateſt of recommendations to any thing.

Not to enter into the nice diſtinctions of the kinds which are of late years become endleſs and innumerable, we may ſay in general that there are two ſorts; the tame, and dovecoat pigeon. The tame pigeon is valued not only for beauty, but for the largeneſs of its body; the common pigeon, which is the kind uſually kept in dovecoats, and thence called the dovecoat pigeon, is ſmaller, and leſs beautiful.

The tame kind generally have but two young ones at a brood; but they make ſome amends for the ſmallneſs of the number by the frequency of their hatching; for, if well fed and tended, they will have young ones every month.

For the choice of theſe the beauty is generally moſt regarded; but there ſhould be care taken to pair them well, and this is the more worth while becauſe they are not apt to ſeperate afterwards.

They muſt be kept clean, for they hate dirt, though they make a great deal of it. But their food is ſo dear, that few but thoſe who know very well how to manage them care to meddle with them. Their beſt food is tares or white peaſe, and they ſhould have beſide this ſome gravel ſcattered about, and clean water at all times: and a great deal of care muſt be taken to preſerve them from vermin, and their eggs from the ſtarlings and other birds, which always haunt the places where they are kept, in order to ſuck them.

In order to the perfect thriving of theſe pigeons, it will be proper, beſide their food, gravel, and water, always to let there be ſome ſalt, clay, or ſome other thing with ſea ſalt in it, for them to peck at their pleaſure

We have ſaid thus much with reſpect to the management of the tame pigeon, for the information of ſuch as may chuſe to breed them, and have not had opportunities of ſeeing it done; and it will be proper to add here, that although the expence and trouble they occaſion, be more than is worth the huſbandman's while in general to give himſelf; yet there is this advantage, that their dung is richer than that of the common pigeon as a manure.

After this ſhort account of the tame, we come to the conſideration and management of the common or dovecoat pigeon, which is a ſubject that demands, and deſerves the huſbandman's utmoſt regard.

The keeping of pigeons is a great advantage to every farmer that may do it; and they bring in a great profit for a very ſmall expence in all places; but they thrive beſt in open countries, becauſe there is uſually moſt corn there, and they feed with leſs danger, the hedges in encloſed places ſheltering people while they ſhoot them.

There are ſome counties where the huſbandmen ſow great quantities of horſe beans and grey peaſe, and in theſe particularly the pigeons feed to a great advantage. Theſe ſorts of pulſe are ſowed earlier than other kinds of grain; and their early feeding upon them makes them healthful and ſtout at thoſe times, and is an occaſion of their breeding earlier than they do elſewhere, which is a conſideration of great importance.

The common blue pigeon is properly the dovecoat breed; and it has the advantage of many other kinds, in that it is hardier, and will live in the worſt winters.

If it be too ſmall for the farmer's purpoſe, he may mend the breed by putting in a few tame pigeons of the moſt common kind, and the leaſt conſpicuous in their colours, that the reſt may the better take to them by finding them more like themſelves; this, however, is to be done with caution, and never without a due conſideration; for though the bigneſs of a pigeon's body is a plain advantage, yet it is very well known in the kinds in general, that the ſmalleſt bodyed are the beſt breeders.

The ringdove has been by ſome introduced into the dovecoat, by ſetting the eggs under a common pigeon; they will in this caſe live, and take the chance among the pigeons; and they have two advantages over them, the one in their largeneſs, and the other in their hardyneſs; for they will endure any weather, and live upon any food.

The huſbandman ſhould have a very careful eye upon the proportion of the ſexes among his pigeons; for there is nothing ſo hurtful as the having too many cocks, eſpecially if they keep the larger or tame kind. It is his buſineſs to keep his dovecoat well ſtock'd; and moſt people who keep them make their conſciences eaſy about deluding away thoſe belonging to their neighbours; but this abundance of cocks thins the dovecoat, for they grow quarrelſome, and will beat others away; till by degrees a very thriving dovecoat ſhall be by this ſingle miſtake reduced to a poor condition.

A very cheap and eaſy way of making a dovecoat is to build the walls with clay mixed with ſtraw, they may be made four feet or more in thickneſs, and while they are wet it is eaſy to cut holes in them with a chiſſel or other inſtrument.

This kind of dovecoat, beſide its cheapneſs, has the advantage of great warmth, and no building agrees better with the pigeons. A dovecoat of this kind, of four yards ſquare in the clear, may be built for about five pounds.

The holes ſhould be made about fourteen

fourteen inches deep, and a little dipping backward. The Rev. Mr. Lawrence who used this method of building his dovecoat says, that the pigeons prospered in it better than in any brick or stone building he had seen.

Of whatever materials the coat be erected, it should be white-washed frequently on the outside. The pigeon, as has been said already, is a cleanly bird: it loves the appearance of neatness; and beside the white colour, renders the building more conspicuous.

As to the food of pigeons, beside the pease, and tares already mentioned, barley is very proper, heartening them very much, and making them lay; and for the same purpose buckwheat is also an excellent as well as cheap food.

For the greatest part of the year, however, the common pigeons in a dovecoat take care of themselves, and need no food from their keeper. There are only two seasons at which it is necessary or proper to feed them. One of these times is the depth of winter, when the ground is covered with snow, or hardened so by frost, that nothing is to be got; and the other is, the middle or latter end of June.

The reason of feeding them in the first of these seasons is obvious; the latter, the farmers, when they speak of this fowl, call benting time. There is a grass called bent grass, the seed of which is ripe about this season, and is the only food of that kind the pigeons can easily get, the pease being not yet ripe. This is a very poor food, and the pigeons at this season usually have many young broods; so that they will be starved if they are left to this poor diet: and the farmer will always find his account in giving them food at this season, as well as at the other. This lasts however but a small time; and the other is only necessary at the severest days of winter; so that the pigeon is at the utmost but a small expence, and that for a very short time.

Beside the food, the breeder of tame pigeons has been advised to give them a lump of salted clay, and the same indulgence must be shewn to these. But as they are more numerous, there is to be a larger allowance. A large heap of clay should be laid near the dovecoat, and the brine of the family continually beaten in among it. Another way is to make a kind of mortar with lime, sand, clay, and salt, which they will peck with great satisfaction. The pigeons themselves have pointed out this method, for they are continually pecking at the joints of walls to get out the mortar. When it is thus made on purpose for them it is best to make it thin, and keep it so by often beating it up with brine.

In some places they lay what is called a salt cat, near the dovecoat. This is a large lump of salt made for the purpose at the salt pans; and is the method commonly taken where there are works in the neighbourhood, but the way of using salt in a mixture with clay is better.

What is found by experience to answer best of all is this. A heap of loam is to be laid near the dovecoat, and beat up to a kind of pap with brine or water; into this is to be thrown a large quantity of bay salt, and a little saltpetre, and with it a shovel full or two of large coarse sand. When brine is used to beat up the loam, less salt is to be used; and when water, there must be the more of it in proportion. And in the same manner, if the loam contain a great deal of sand, the less is to be added to it; and if it contain less, the more is to be given. Where loam is not to be had, clay will do, but then a much larger quantity of sand must be put in; and the best sand for this purpose is large coarse sea sand, which is already impregnated with salt water; or that which is got in screening of gravel.

It is a very singular thing, that the pigeon loves salt in this manner; and its fondness for saltpetre, which is very great, is not so well known; though this might have been discovered by observing the liking this bird has to the mortar in old walls, which contains a salt very nearly allyed to the common saltpetre.

Salt is not only useful in this manner to please the pigeons, when they are in health, but nothing recovers them so readily from sickness. A mixture of bay salt and cummin seed being with them an universal remedy.

A great many contrivances have been published; and many more are handed about among the country people as great secrets, for the making the pigeons love their habitation, and tempting

tempting such straglers from their neighbours as chance to come to the coat to settle in it. Some have advised the use of assafœtida, and others of cummin seed before mentioned for this purpose; but the best method of all others is to keep up constantly such a heap of salted loam as before described; this they love, and they will therefore stay where they can have it in plenty. This contrivance, with the addition of keeping the dovecoat neat and clean, and not suffering them to be disturbed in it, will be sure to keep the stock in good number, and too likely to increase it at the expence of the neighbours.

The profit of pigeons is very considerable, and very certain; for they breed very fast, and there is a constant demand for them. Near great towns it may be worth while to keep some of the large tame kind; because although they cannot be fed but at a large expence, yet their young come so early, and are so fat and fine, that they command a price, which very well returns it; but in the country, the common pigeon is the proper kind; for though the price that the birds fetch is not nearly so great, their number, and small expence of keeping, very well make amends.

PILEWORT, (*Chelidonium minus.*) This is a very small plant, found in moist meadows and by hedge sides: the roots consist of slender fibres, with some little tubercles among them, which are supposed to resemble the hæmorrhoids; from whence it has been concluded, that this root must needs be of wonderful efficacy for the cure of that distemper: to the taste, it is little other than mucilaginous.

PIMENTO. Jamaica pepper.

PIMPERNEL, (*Anagallis.*) Common male and female pimpernel. This is a low plant, in appearance resembling chickweed; but easily distinguishable by its leaves being spotted underneath, and joined immediately to the stalk. The male and female pimpernels differ no otherwise than in the colour of their flowers: they are both found wild in the fields, but the male or red flowered sort is most common.

Both the Pimpernels have an herbaceous, roughish taste, with little or no smell. Many extraordinary virtues have been attributed to them. Geoffroy esteems them cephalic, sudorific, vulnerary, antimaniacal, antepileptic, and alexaterial. Tragus, Caspar, Hoffman, Michaeli, and others, are also very liberal in their praises: one of these gentlemen declares, that he has known numerous instances of the singular efficacy of a decoction and tincture of pimpernel, in maniacal and melancholic deliria. But later practitioners have not been so happy as to meet with the like success. Pimpernel is not unfrequently taken as food; it makes no unpleasant sallad; and in some parts of this kingdom, is a common potherb. A spirituous tincture of it contains nothing valuable: the only preparation that promises any utility, is an extract made with water; or the expressed juice depurated and inspissated.

Water PIMPERNEL, [*Samolus.*] This plant grows wild in swampy places, where the water usually stands in winter, and is seldom preserved in gardens. It is an annual plant, which flowers in June, and the seeds are ripe in August; at which time, whoever hath a mind to cultivate this plant, should sow the seeds on a moist soil, where the plants will come up, and require no farther care but to keep them clear from weeds.

PINE, [*Pinus.*] The species are, 1st, the wild or Scotch pine, or Scotch fir.

This is called by us the Scotch fir, because it grows naturally on the Highlands of Scotland, where the seeds, falling from their cones, come up and propagate themselves without any care. But it is not in Scotland only that these trees thrive naturally; for they grow spontaneously in Denmark, Norway, and Sweden. And though, from the above instances, it would seem that they delighted principally in these northern parts; yet when the plants are properly raised and planted out, no climate comes amiss to them, for they will thrive and grow to be good timber trees in almost any part of the world.—The timber of this tree is what we call deal; is sometimes red, sometimes yellow, but chiefly white.

2. *The Weymouth Pine.* This grows naturally in most parts of North America, where it is called the white pine. It is one of the tallest trees of all the species, often growing a hundred feet high in those countries. The bark of this tree is very smooth and delicate, especpailly

especially when young; the leaves are long and slender, five growing out of each sheath; the branches are pretty closely garnished with them, so make a fine appearance; the cones are long, slender, and very loose, opening with the first warmth of the spring, so that if they are not gathered in winter, the scales open and let out the seeds. The wood of this sort is esteemed for making masts for ships; it is in England titled Lord Weymouth's, or New-England Pine. As the wood of this tree was generally thought of great service to the navy, there was a law made in the ninth of Queen Anne for the preservation of the trees, and to encourage their growth in America; and it is within these forty years that these trees began to be propagated in England in any plenty, though there were some large trees of this sort growing in two or three places long before, particularly at Lord Weymouth's, and Sir Wyndham Knatchbull's in Kent; and it has been chiefly from the seeds of the latter that the much greater number of these trees now in England have been raised; for although there has annually been some of the seeds brought from America, yet these have been few in comparison to the produce of the trees in Kent; and many of the trees which have been raised from the seeds of those now produce plenty of good seeds, particularly the trees in the gardens of his Grace the Duke of Argyle at Whitton, which annually produce large quantities of cones.—This sort and the Scotch Pine are the best worth cultivating of all the kinds for the sake of their wood; the others may be planted for variety in parks, &c. where they make a good appearance in winter, when other trees are destitute of leaves.

3. *The Cultivated Pine-tree*, commonly called *the Stone Pine*. The Stone Pine is a tree of which there should be a few in all plantations of ever-greens. It will grow to a considerable height, and arises with a strait and fair stem, though with a rough bark. The leaves will contribute to the diversifying the scene, as they differ in colour from the other sorts, and are arranged in a different manner. The cones which it bears are monstrously large and turbinated; they strike the eye by their bold appearance when hanging on the trees, and afford pleasure upon being more closely examined, from the beautiful arrangement of their scales. They produce a large kernel as sweet to the taste as an almond, which formerly were kept in the shops and sold for restoratives, but are at present neglected. In Italy, the kernels are served up in deserts at the table, and are thought to be salutary in colds, coughs, and consumptions. Its timber is not quite so valuable as the other sorts. The colour is not the same in all trees; some exhibiting their timber of a very white colour, others are yellower, and smell stronger of turpentine.

4. *The Swamp Pine-tree* This is a very large growing tree, and is highly proper, as its name imports, to be planted in moist places.—The leaves are long, of a delightful green colour; three issue out of each sheath, and adorn the younger branches in great plenty.—Its propagation is the same as the Weymouth Pine; and the planting out, and after management of the trees, should be exactly similar.—It will grow well on all upland and dry grounds; but it chiefly delights in moist places.

5. *The Cembra Pine*. The Cembra Pine is a fine tree; the leaves are very beautiful, being of a lighter green than most of the sorts, and are produced five in a sheath. The leaves are long and narrow; and as they closely ornament the branches all round, they look beautiful, and render the tree on that account very valuable. The cones of this tree also have a good effect; for they are larger than those of the Pineaster, and the squamæ are beautifully arranged. This tree is a native of the Alps, and is well described by Mr. Harte, in his elegant essays on husbandry, under the title of *Apheruousli* Pine. He considers it as a tree likely to thrive with great advantage on our bleak, barren, rocky, and moutainous lands; even near the sea, and in north or north-easterly aspects, where something of this hardy kind is much wanted. The timber is large, and has many uses, especially within doors, or under cover. The bark of the trunk or bole of the tree is not reddish like the bark of the Pine, but of a whitish cast, like that of the Fir. The shell which incloses the kernel is easily cracked, and the kernels are covered with a brown skin which peels off. They are about the size of a common pea, triangular like buck-wheat, and white and soft as a blanched almond,

mond, of an oily agreeable taſte, but leaving in the mouth *that* ſmall degree of aſperity which is peculiar to wild fruits, and not unpleaſing. Theſe kernels ſometimes make a part in a Swiſs deſert. Wainſcotting, flooring, and other joiners work, made with the planks of Aphernouſli, are of a finer grain, and more beautifully variegated than deal, and the ſmell of the wood is more agreeable. From this tree is extracted a white odoriferous reſin. On this occaſion the curious planter may conſult a very ſcarce piece, *De Arboribus Coniferis*, written about 200 years ago, by Pietro Belloni.—In the plantations belonging to Jeremiah Dixon eſq; at Gleddow near Leeds, may be ſeen ſeveral of theſe Pines. They are there called the Gleddow Pine.

6. *The Silver Fir-tree.* This is a noble upright tree. The leaves grow ſingly on the branches, and their ends are ſlightly indented. Their upper ſurface is of a fine ſtrong green colour, and their under has an ornament of two white lines, running lengthways on each ſide the midrib, on account of which ſilvery look this ſort is called the Silver Fir. The cones are large, and grow erect; and when the warm weather comes on, they ſoon ſhed their ſeeds; which ſhould be a caution to gather the cones before that happens.——This tree is common in the mountainous parts of Scotland, and in Norway, and affords the yellow deals. From its yielding pitch, it has obtained the title of *Picea*, or Pitch-tree.

7. *The common Spruce Fir-tree.* The Spruce Fir is a beautiful tree, as well as a valuable one for its timber, producing the white deal. It is a native of Norway and Denmark, where it grows ſpontaneouſly, and is one of the principal productions of their woods. It alſo grows plentifully in the Highlands of Scotland, where it adorns thoſe cloud-capped mountains with a conſtant verdure. The longconed Cornish Fir is a variety of this tree, and differs ſcarcely in any reſpect, except that the leaves and the cones are larger. As gardeners generally receive it as a diſtinct Fir, it may not be amiſs to mention it here; though we own the difference is ſo inconſiderable as to make it hardly worth ſeeking after; and though the cones are rather longer than the other ſort, yet of that alſo the cones are very large, oftentimes near a foot; ſo that they may eaſily paſs the one for the other, as they both hang down alike.

8. The Canada Pine. *Hunter's Evelyn.*

For the cultivation of Pine, ſee FIR.

PINEASTER, (*Pinus Sylveſtris.*) A ſpecies of Pine growing wild on the mountains of Italy.

PINE-APPLE, [*Ananus.*] Of this plant there are ſeveral varieties differing in the ſhapes, ſize, and colour of their fruits. The moſt eſteemed are, 1. Oval ſhaped with white fleſh, or the green pine. 2. Pyramidal, or ſugar-loaf pine-apple, with yellow fleſh. 3. Green Sugar-loaf. 4. Black Antigua or Ripley pine-apple. 5. Shining Green-leaved pine, with ſcarce any ſpines; or the King pine. 6. Granada Pine with marbled leaves. 7. Bogwarp pine, with broad green leaves. 8. Smooth long narrow leaved pine. 9. Gold-ſtriped leaved pine. 10. Silver-ſtriped leaved pine.

Of the above ſorts the two former are chiefly eſteemed, and the latter preferred moſt of all.

The plants are propagated by planting the crowns which grow on the fruit, or the ſuckers which are produced either from the ſides of the plants, or under the fruit, both which have been found equally good; although by ſome perſons the crown is thought preferable to the ſuckers, as ſuppoſing it will produce fruit ſooner than the ſuckers, which is certainly a miſtake.

The ſuckers and crowns muſt be laid to dry in a warm place for four or five days, or more (according to the moiſture of the part which adhered to the old plant or fruit); for if they are immediately planted, they will rot. The certain rule of judging when they are fit to plant, is by obſerving if the bottom is healed over and become hard; for if the ſuckers are drawn off carefully from the old plants, they will have a hard ſkin over the lower part, ſo need not lie ſo long as the crowns, or thoſe whoſe bottoms are moiſt. But whenever a crown is taken from the fruit, or the ſuckers from old plants, they ſhould be immediately diveſted of their bottom leaves, ſo high as to allow depth for their planting; ſo that they may be thoroughly dry and healed in every part, leſt when they receive heat and moiſture they ſhould periſh, which often happens when this method is not obſerved. If theſe ſuckers or crowns

are

are taken off late in the autumn, or during the winter, or early in the ſpring they ſhould be laid in a dry place in the ſtove, for a fortnight or three weeks before they are planted, but in the ſummer ſeaſon they will be fit for planting in a week at fartheſt.

As to the earth in which theſe ſhould be planted, if you have a rich good kitchen garden mould, not too heavy, ſo as to detain the moiſture too long, nor over light and ſandy, it will be very proper for them without any mixture: but where this is wanting, you ſhould procure ſome freſh earth from a good paſture, which ſhould be mixed with about a third part of rotten neats dung, or the dung of an old melon or cucumber bed. Theſe ſhould be mixed ſix or eight months at leaſt before they are uſed, but if it be a year it will be the better; and ſhould be often turned, that their parts may be better united, as alſo the clods well broken. This earth ſhould not be ſcreened very fine, for if you can only clear it of the great ſtones, it will be better for the plants than when it is made too fine. You ſhould always avoid mixing any ſand with the earth, unleſs it be extremely ſtiff, and then it will be neceſſary to have it mixed at leaſt ſix months or a year before it is uſed; and it muſt be frequently turned, that the ſand may be incorporated in the earth ſo as to divide its parts: but you ſhould not put more than a ſixth part of ſand, for too much ſand is very injurious to theſe plants.

In the ſummer ſeaſon, when the weather is warm, theſe plants muſt be frequently watered, but you ſhould not give them large quantities at a time: you muſt alſo be very careful that the moiſture is not detained in the pots by the holes being ſtopped, for that will ſoon deſtroy the plants. If the ſeaſon is warm, they ſhould be watered twice a week, but in a cool ſeaſon once a week is often enough; and during the ſummer ſeaſon you ſhould once a week water them gently all over their leaves, which will waſh the filth from off them, and thereby greatly promote the growth of the plants.

There are ſome perſons who frequently ſhift theſe plants from pot to pot, but this is by no means to be practiſed by thoſe who propoſe to have large well-flavoured fruit; for unleſs the pots be filled with the roots, by the time the plants begin to ſhew their fruit, they commonly produce ſmall fruit, which have generally large crowns on them, therefore the plants will not require to be new potted oftener than twice in a ſeaſon: the firſt time ſhould be about the end of April, when the ſuckers and crowns of the former year's fruit (which remained all the winter in thoſe pots in which they were firſt planted) ſhould be ſhifted into larger pots, that is, thoſe which were in halfpenny, or three-farthing pots, ſhould be put into penny, or at moſt three-halfpenny pots, according to the ſize of the plants; for you muſt be very careful not to over pot them, nothing being more prejudicial to theſe plants. The ſecond time for ſhifting of them is in the beginning of Auguſt, when you ſhould ſhift thoſe which are of a proper ſize for fruiting the following ſpring, into two-penny pots, which are full large enough for any of theſe plants. At each of theſe times of ſhifting the plants, the bark-bed ſhould be ſtirred up, and ſome new bark added, to raiſe the bed up to the height it was at firſt made; and when the pots are plunged again into the bark-bed, the plants ſhould be watered gently all over their leaves, to waſh off the filth, and to ſettle the earth to the roots of the plants. If the bark-bed be well ſtirred, and a quantity of good freſh bark added to the bed, at this latter ſhifting, it will be of great ſervice to the plants, for they may remain in the ſame tan until the beginning of November or ſometimes later, according to the mildneſs of the ſeaſon, and will require but little fire before that time. During the winter ſeaſon, theſe plants will not require to be watered more than once a week, according as you find the earth in the pots too dry; nor ſhould you give them too much at each time, for it is much better to give them a little water often, than to over-water them.

You muſt obſerve never to ſhift thoſe plants which ſhew their fruit into other pots, for if they are removed after the fruit appears, it will ſtop the growth, and thereby cauſe the fruit to be ſmaller, and retard its ripening ſo that many times it will be October or November before the fruit is ripe; therefore you ſhould be very careful to keep the plants in a vigorous growing state, from the first appearance of the fruit; for if they receive a check after this, the the fruit is generally small and ill tasted.

When you have cut off the fruit from the plant whose kind you are desirous to propagate, you should trim the leaves and plunge the pots again into a moderate hot-bed, observing to refresh them frequently with water, which will cause them to put out their suckers in plenty; so that a person may be soon supplied with plants enough, because upon this depends its size and goodness; if he keeps the plants in health.

There is not any thing which can happen to these plants of a more dangerous nature, than to have them attacked by small white insects, which appear at first like a white mildew, but soon after have the appearance of lice: these attack both root and leaves at the same time, and if not destroyed will spread over a whole stove in a short time, and in a few weeks stop the growth of the plants, by sucking out the nutritious juice, so that the leaves will appear yellow and sickly, and have a great number of yellow transparent spots all over them These insects, after they are fully grown, appear like bugs, and adhere so closely to the leaves, as not to be easily washed off, and seem to have no local motion. They were originally brought from America upon the plants which were imported from thence, and probably they are the same insects which have destroyed the sugar canes in some of the Leeward Islands.

The stoves which are erected for preserving of these plants are built in different ways, according to the fancy of the contriver. Some persons build them with upright glasses in front, about four feet high, and sloping glasses over these, which rise about six feet high, so that there is just height enough for a person to walk upright on the back side of the bark-bed. Others make but one slope of glasses, from the top of the stove down to the plate, which lies about six or eight inches above the bark-pit, in the front of the stove, so that in this stove there is no walk made in the front between the bark-pit and the glasses; but the inconveniency of watering the plants, as also of coming near those plants which are placed in the front of the stove to clean them, has, in some measure, brought them into disesteem, so that few persons now build them, though the expence is much less than the other kind of stoves. One of these stoves, about twenty-five feet long in the clear, with the pit for the tan reaching from end to end, and six feet and a half wide, will contain about an hundred plants; so that whoever is desirous to have this fruit, may easily proportion their stove to the quantity of fruit they are willing to have.

But it will also be necessary to have a bark-pit under a deep frame, in order to raise the young plants in summer; for in this bed you should plunge the suckers, when they are taken from the old plants, as also the crowns which come from the fruit, so that this frame will be as a nursery to raise the young plants to supply the stove; but these plants should not remain in these frames longer than till the beginning of November, unless the frame is built with brick-work with flues in it to warm the air, which are very useful, as nurseries, to keep the young plants till they are of a proper size to produce fruit; and the air in this frame may be kept either warmer or cooler than the stove, according as the plants may require, so that the stove may be every autumn filled only with bearing plants, whereby a much greater quantity of fruit may be annually produced, than can be where young and old plants must be crowded into the same stove: but where there are no inconveniencies of this kind, the young plants, about the middle or latter end of October, must be removed into the stove, and being small, may be crowded in among the larger plants; for as they will not grow much during the winter season, so they may be placed very close together. The end of March, where there is no nursery for the young plants, they must be removed out into the hot-bed again, which should be prepared a fortnight before, that the tan may have acquired a proper heat; but you should be careful that the tan be not too hot, for that might scald the fibres of the plants if they are suddenly plunged therein. Therefore if you find the bark too hot, you should not plunge the pots above two or three inches into the tan, letting them remain so until the heat of the

tan

tan is a little abated, when you should plunge the pots down to their rim in the bed. If the nights should continue cold after these plants are removed into the bed, you must carefully cover the glasses with mats, otherwise by coming out of a warm stove they may receive a sudden check, which will greatly retard their growth, which must be carefully avoided; because the sooner the plants are set growing in the spring, the more time they will have to gain strength, in order to produce large fruit the following season.

You should not plunge the pots too close together in this frame, but allow them a proper distance, that the lower part of the plants may increase in bulk, for it is on this that the magnitude of the fruit depends; because when the plants are placed too close, they draw up very tall, but do not obtain strength; so that when they are taken out of the bed, the leaves are not able to support themselves, but all the outward long leaves will fall down, leaving the smaller middle leaves naked, and this sometimes will cause them to rot in the center. You must also observe, when the sun is very warm, to raise the glasses of the hot-bed in the heat of the day with props, in order to let out the steam of the bed, and to admit fresh air; for one neglect of this kind, in a very hot day, may destroy all the plants, or at least so scald them, that they will not get over it in many months. It will be also very proper, in extreme hot weather, to shade the glasses with mats, for the glasses lying so near to the leaves of the plants will occasion a prodigious heat at such times.

There are some persons who regulate the heat of their stoves by thermometers in summer, but at that season this is unnecessary, for the outward air in hot weather is frequently greater than the ananas heat marked on the thermometers, so that the heat of the stoves at that season will be much greater. The use of the thermometer is only in winter, during the time the fires are continued, by which it is easy to judge when to increase or diminish the fires; for at that season the stoves should not be kept to a greater warmth than five or six divisions above ananas, nor suffered to be more than as many divisions below it. When the plants are placed into the tan for the winter season (which should be done about the middle of October) the tan-bed should be renewed, adding two thirds of new tan to one third of the old. If this be well mixed, and the new tan is good, the bed will maintain a proper degree of warmth till February, at which time it will be proper to stir up the bed, and add a load or two of new tan, so as to raise the bed as much as it sunk since the autumn; this will give a fresh heat to the bed, and keep the plants growing, and, as the fruit will now begin to appear, it will be absolutely necessary to keep the plants in a growing state, otherwise the fruit will not be large; for if they receive any check at this time, it will greatly injure them.

In April it will be proper to stir up the tan again, and if the bed has sunk since the last stirring, it will be proper to add some fresh tan to it; this will renew the warmth of the bed and forward the fruit. And if the tan-bed is constantly kept in a good temper, and a sufficient quantity of air admitted every day to the plants, they will succeed much better than in a cool bed kept too close.

Those plants which shew their fruit early in February will ripen about June; some sorts are at least a month or five weeks longer in ripening than others, from the time of the appearance of the fruit: but the season in which the fruit is in greatest perfection, is from the beginning of June to the end of September; though in March, April, and October, this fruit may frequently be seen in pretty good perfection, but then the plants have been in perfect health, otherwise they are seldom well flavoured.

The method of judging when the the fruit is ripe, is by the smell, and from observation; for as the several sorts differ from each other in the colour of their fruit, that will not be any direction when to cut them; for should they remain so long as to become soft to the touch before they are cut, they become flat and dead, as they do also when they are cut long before they are eaten: therefore the surest way to have this fruit in perfection, is to cut it the same day it is eaten; but it must be cut early in the morning, before the ſun has heated the fruit, otherwiſe it will be hot, obſerving to cut the ſtalk as long to the fruit as poſſible, and lay it in a cool, but dry place, preſerving the ſtalk and crown unto it until it is eaten.

Mr. Speechly, gardener to the Duke of Portland, has lately introduced oak leaves into the ſtove inſtead of Bark.

"I preſume, ſays he, that the leaves of the oak abound with the ſame quality as the bark of the tree, therefore the ſooner they are raked up, after they fall from the trees, the better; as that quality will naturally decreaſe during the time they are expoſed to the weather.

"After being raked into heaps, they ſhould immediately be carried to ſome place near the hot-houſe, where they muſt lie to couch. I generally fence them round with ſome charcoal-hurdles, or any thing elſe, to keep them from being blown about the garden in windy weather. In this place we tread them well, and water them, in caſe they happen to have been brought in dry. We make the heap ſix or ſeven feet in thickneſs, covering it over with old matts, or any thing elſe, to prevent the upper leaves from being blown away. In a few days, the heap will come to a ſtrong heat. For the firſt year or two that I uſed theſe leaves, I did not continue them in the heap longer than ten days or a fortnight; but in this I diſcovered a conſiderable inconvenience, as they ſettled ſo much, when got into the hot-houſe, as ſoon to require a ſupply. Taught by experience, I now let them remain in the heap for five or ſix weeks, by which time they are properly prepared for the hot-houſe. In getting them into the pine pits, if they appear dry, we water them again, treading them in layers exceedingly well, till the pits are quite full. We then cover the whole with tan to the thickneſs of two inches, and tread it well till the ſurface becomes ſmooth and even. On this we place the pine-pots in the manner they are to ſtand, beginning with the middle-row firſt, and filling up the ſpaces between the pots with tan. In like manner, we proceed to the next row, till the whole be finiſhed. And this operation is performed in the ſame manner as when tan only is uſed,

"After this, the leaves require no farther trouble the whole ſeaſon through: as they will retain a conſtant and regular heat for twelve months without either ſtirring or turning; and if I may form a judgment from their appearance when taken out, (being always entire and perfect) it is probable they would continue their heat through a ſecond year: but as an annual ſupply of leaves here is eaſily obtained, ſuch a trial, with us, is hardly worth the trouble of making. However, as a ſaving in leaves may be an agreeable object in places where they are leſs plentiful, I was induced to make the following experiments: In 1777, one of the pine-pits was filled with one part of old and two parts of new leaves, well mixed together. And laſt year, (1778) one pit was filled with old and new leaves in equal quantities. In both theſe experiments, I had the ſatisfaction to find the pits, ſo filled, to retain a heat through each ſeaſon, equal to the other pits that were filled entirely with new leaves.

"Laſt year (1778) I alſo uſed a conſiderable quantity of the leaves after they were taken out of the hot-houſe in the early-made hot-beds, and found them to anſwer quite as well as freſh leaves.

"I muſt beg leave to obſerve, that when the leaves are intended to be uſed a ſecond time, it will be proper at the taking them out of the pits, to remove ſome few at the top, as alſo on each ſide, becauſe the leaves at the top and outſide of the pit, approach moſt to a ſtate of decay.

"After this, the pines will have no occaſion to be removed but at the ſtated times of their management, viz. at the ſhifting them in their pots, &c. when, at each time, a little freſh tan ſhould be added to make up the deficiency ariſing from the ſetting of the beds; but this will be inconſiderable, as the leaves do not ſettle much after their long couching. During the two firſt years of my practice, I did not uſe any tan, but plunged the pine-pots in the leaves, and juſt covered the ſurface of the beds, when finiſhed, with a little ſaw-duſt, to give it a neatneſs. This method was attended with one inconvenience: for by the caking of the leaves, they ſhrunk from the ſides of the

the pots, whereby they became expoſed to the air, and at the ſame time the heat of the beds was permitted to eſcape.

"Many powerful reaſons may be given why oak leaves (for having an opportunity of collecting an immenſe quantity of them here, I have not tried any other kinds) are preferable to tanner's bark.

"Firſt, They always heat regularly; for during the whole time that I have uſed them, which is near ten years, I never once knew of their heating with violence; and this is ſo frequently the caſe with tan, that I affirm, and indeed it is well known to every perſon converſant in the management of the hot-houſe, that pines ſuffer more from this one circumſtance than from all other accidents put together, inſects excepted. When this accident happens near the time of their fruiting, the effect is ſoon ſeen in the fruit, which always comes ill-ſhaped and exceedingly ſmall. Sometimes there will be little or no fruit at all; therefore gardeners, who make uſe of tan only for their pines, ſhould be moſt particularly careful to avoid an over-heat at that critical ſeaſon—the time of ſhewing fruit.

"Secondly, the heat of oak-leaves is conſtant; whereas tanner's bark generally turns cold in a very ſhort time after its furious heat is gone off. This obliges the gardener to give the tan frequent turnings in order to promote its heating. Theſe frequent turnings, not to mention the expences, are attended with the worſt conſequences; for by the continual moving of the pots backwards and forwards, the pines are expoſed to the extremes of heat and cold, whereby their growth is conſiderably retarded; whereas, when leaves are uſed, the pines will have no occaſion to be moved but at the times of potting, &c.—The pines have one particular advantage in this undiſturbed ſituation; their roots grow thro' the bottoms of the pots and matt amongſt the leaves in a ſurpriſing manner.—From the vigour of the plants, when in this ſituation, it is highly probable that the leaves, even in this ſtate, afford them an uncommon and agreeable nouriſhment.

"Thirdly, there is a ſaving in point of expence, which is no inconſiderable object in places where tan cannot be had but from a great diſtance, as is the caſe here, the article of carriage amounting to ten ſhillings for each waggon-load. Indeed, this was the principal reaſon that firſt induced me to make trial of leaves.

"My laſt ground of preference is the conſideration that decayed leaves make good manure; whereas rotten tan is experimentally found to be of no value. I have often tried it both on ſand and clay, alſo on wet and dry lands, and never could diſcover, in any of my experiments, that it deſerved the name of a manure; whereas decayed leaves are the richeſt, and, of all others, the moſt ſuitable for a garden. But this muſt only be underſtood of leaves after they have undergone their fermentation, which reduces them to a true vegetable mould, in which we experimentally know that the food of plants is contained—but whether that food be oil, mucilage, or ſalt, or a combination of all three, I leave to philoſophers to determine. This black mould is, of all others, the moſt proper to mix with compoſt earth, and I uſe it in general for pines, and almoſt for all plants that grow in pots: For flowers, it is moſt excellent. The remainder of this vegetable mould may be employed in manuring the quarters of the kitchen-garden, for which purpoſe it is highly uſeful.

"Leaves mixt with dung make excellent hot-beds—and I find that beds, compounded in this manner, preſerve their heat much longer than when made entirely with dung."

He deſcribes the different ſpecies of inſects with accuracy; and the directions he gives for their deſtruction are plain to every underſtanding. It conſiſts in waſhing the pine plants well with the following liquor:

"Take one pound of quickſilver; put it into a glazed veſſel, and pour upon it one gallon of boiling water, which let ſtand till it becomes cold; then pour off the water for uſe. Repeat this on the ſame quickſilver, (for it will retain its power) till a ſufficient number of gallons are provided to fill a veſſel intended for the purpoſe. One in the form of a trough, that will hold eight or ten gallons, is the moſt convenient,

venient, especially for the large-sized plants.

" Then to every gallon of this mercurial water add six ounces of soft green soap, dissolved in a portion of the prepared water. Let the mixture stand till it becomes about milk-warm, which is the degree of warmth it must be kept to during the time of dipping, which operation is performed in the following manner:

" The pine plants being now ready, let them be put into the mixture, in which they should remain, with every part covered, for the space of three minutes; then take them out, first letting the tops decline for the mixture to drain out of their centres. The vessel should be immediately filled with fresh plants, and those taken out set in the open air to dry, with their roots downwards; for by placing them in that position, the mixture will descend and penetrate to the very bottom of the leaves in the centre of the plant, whereby the insects which are concealed there will be totally destroyed.

" It will be proper to do this work in a fine day, and as soon in the forenoon as convenient, that the plants might have time to dry, which they will do in a few hours, and then they must undergo the same operation a second time.

" In the next dipping, one table spoonful of sweet oil should be added to every gallon of the mixture. If the oil and some green soap should be put together, and a little prepared boiling water poured thereon, the oil will most readily incorporate.

" The process of the second operation being exactly the same as the first, a repetition thereof is unnecessary.

" After the second dipping, a spunge should be used to remove any unsightly matter left on the leaves of the plants. They should then be set to dry with their tops downwards, that the mixture may drain from every part; for it is necessary that every part of the plant should be quite dry before it is planted.

" For a twelvemonth after the destruction of the insects, I constantly keep a pound of quicksilver in a glazed vessel, at the bottom of the cistern which contained the water for the use of the hot-house. Whether the quicksilver impregnated the water in such a manner as to be of any real use, I do not pretend to say: however, this I can with truth affirm, that I never saw pine plants grow with greater vigour than those did at that time."

Dwarf PINE. Tree Germander.

Wild PINE APPLE. *See* PENGUIN.

PINK. *See* CARNATION.

PINT. A vessel or measure containing in quantity sixteen ounces; half a quart; the eighth part of a gallon.

PIP. This is a disorder peculiar to young fowls, and generally arises from the want of water. The natural moisture of the mouth in this case hardens upon the end of the tongue into a kind of scale, and this prevents their feeding.

The greatest care is required to observe in time which of them have the disease, for the remedy is easy.

Let some bay salt be melted in a little vinegar, and set ready in a saucer.—Then let the young creatures be taken up and the scale loosened, and then pulled off from the tongue with the fingers. Then wet the end of the tongue two or three times over with the vinegar and salt, and turn the chick loose where he cannot drink for an hour. This will prevent a return.

PIPE. A large vessel for wine, equal to two barrels; half a tun.

PIPE TREE, *(Syringa)* *See* LILAC.

Pudding PIPE TREE. *See* CASSIA.

PIPERIDGE *Bush*. *See* BARBERRY.

PISSING *of Blood*, in Horses. Great care should be taken to observe the quantity of urine made; if there be too much in proportion to the liquor drank, restringents should be made use of, such as the following balls:

Japon Earth, two ounces,
Mithridate,
Diascordium, each one ounce and a half, mix altogether in a pint and a half of forge water, and give it in a morning, repeating every third morning.

If on the other hand, urine is made in quantity, and seems made with difficulty.

Take Marshmallow Roots,
Liquorice Roots, each two ounces, boil in three pints of water to a quart. Dissolve in it two ounces of Nitre, and give for a dose night and morning.

Let a clyster be given, made of a strong

ſtrong decoction of marſhmallows and ſweet oil.

"This diſorder in cows (ſays a writer in the Farmer's Magazine) is often produced by a blow or a ſtrain, and in either caſe is dangerous; perhaps more ſo than if it proceeded from an inward diſorder, as a mortification is much to be feared; whereas an exalted ſtate of the urinous ſalts will ſometimes produce the diſorder, but a blow or ſtrain to produce it muſt not only do an external violence to the muſcles of the loins, (probably to the nerves themſelves) but alſo to the veſſels of the kidnies, and thoſe which go from the kidnies to the bladder; and I have ſeen the whole in a ſtate of mortification, and this from a ſtrain which has not been thought of ſufficient conſequence to require medicines;—but remember, that as your beaſt cannot tell how great the injury is, you are to apply immediate remedies.

Take away ſome blood. If the beaſt be coſtive, give the following emollient clyſter, immediately: Milk gruel, three pints; ſweet oil, half a pint. And afterwards the following anodyne clyſter, twice or thrice a day: Sheep's-head broth, three pints; liquid laudanum, one ounce.

"Of all remedies in diſeaſes of the bladder or kidnies, clyſters are the moſt to be depended on; of which I was informed by an ingenious phyſical friend, who told me that in the moſt violent fits of the gravel, retention of urine, &c. he chiefly depended on anodyne clyſters, which acted as a fomentation to the parts immediately concerned, and gave a more immediate relief than medicines taken by the mouth.

"If the diſorder proceed from a ſtrain or blow, the loins ſhould be bathed with Goulard's vegeto-mineral water, and then covered with cloths. The beaſt ſhould be kept up at houſe, and well ſupplied with warm gruel, or rather the following liquor:

Take two dozen of white poppy heads, ſeeds and all; liquorice, marſhmallow, and couch graſs roots, each half a pound; nitre, and gum arabic, each three ounces, camphor, one ounce and a half; boil in ſix gallons of water-gruel to four, and then add a pound of treacle. Give to the quantity of two gallons daily, a little warm.

"Different as the above preſcription may be to the common method purſued by Cowleeches, I can recommend it not only as rational, but ſucceſsful. Reſtringents are unadviſeable."

PISHAMIN, or PERSIMON, (Dioſpyrus) *See* DATE PLUM TREE.

PITCH TREE. The Fir Tree.

PLANE TREE, (*Platanus*) Of this tree there are only two ſpecies. 1. The true Eaſtern Plane-tree. This kind grows naturally in Aſia, where it becomes very large; the ſtem is tall, erect, and covered with a ſmooth bark, which annually falls off; it ſends out many ſide-branches, which are generally a little crooked at their joints; the bark of the young branches is of a dark brown, inclining to a purple colour; they are garniſhed with leaves placed alternate; their foot-ſtalks are an inch and a half long; the leaves are ſeven inches long & eight broad, deeply cut into five ſegments, and the two outer are ſlightly cut again into two more; theſe ſegments have many acute indentures on their borders, and have each a ſtrong mid-rib, with many lateral veins running to the ſides; the upper ſide of the leaves is of a deep green, and the under ſide pale. The flowers come out upon long foot-ſtalks or ropes hanging downward, each ſuſtaining five or ſix round balls of flowers; the upper, which are the largeſt, are more than four inches in circumference; theſe ſit very cloſe to the foot-ſtalks. The flowers are ſo ſmall as ſcarce to be diſtinguiſhed without glaſſes; they come out a little before the leaves, which is in the beginning of June; and in warm ſummers the ſeeds will ripen late in autumn, and if left upon the trees will remain till ſpring, when the balls fall to pieces, and the briſtly down, which ſurrounds the ſeeds, helps to tranſport them to a great diſtance with the wind.

2. *Occidental or Virginian Plane tree.*

This ſort is naturally produced in moſt parts of North America; it grows to a large ſize, with a ſtraight ſtem of equal girt moſt part of the length; the bark is ſmooth, and annually falls off like that of the other; the branches extend wide on every ſide; the young ones have a browniſh bark, but on the old

old ones it is grey; the foot-ſtalks of the leaves are three inches long; the leaves are ſeven inches long, and ten broad; they are cut into three lobes or angles, and have ſeveral acute indentures on their borders, with three longitudinal midribs, and many ſtrong lateral veins. The leaves are of a light green on their upper ſide, and paler on their under. The flowers grow in round balls like the former, but are ſmaller. The leaves and flowers come out at the ſame time with the former, and the ſeeds ripen in autumn.

The flowers come out late in the ſpring, and are ſo ſmall as ſcarcely to be viſible to the naked eye. The buds of the leaves of the oriental ſort begin to ſwell about the fourteenth of April, and the leaves are generally out by the latter end of the ſame month.

Beſides the two ſpecies already deſcribed there are two varieties: 1. The Spaniſh Plane-tree; 2. The Maple-leaved Plane-tree.

The Spaniſh Plane-tree has larger leaves than either of the other ſorts; they are more divided than thoſe of the Occidental, but not ſo much as the Eaſtern. Some of the leaves are cut into five and others into three lobes; theſe are ſharply indented on the edges, and are of a light green; the foot-ſtalks are ſhort, and covered with a ſhort down. This is by ſome called the Middle Plane-tree, from its leaves being ſhaped between thoſe of the two other ſorts. It grows rather faſter than either of the other kinds.

The Maple-leaved Plane-tree differs from the two genuine ſpecies, in having its leaves not ſo deeply cut as the Eaſtern, nor lobed as the Weſtern kind. The foot-ſtalks of the leaves are much longer than thoſe of the above ſorts, and the upper ſurface of the leaves is rougher.

The Oriental and Spaniſh Plane-trees are propagated from ſeeds, when they can be procured; but whoever enjoys not this convenience, muſt have recourſe to layers. The ground proper for the ſeminary ſhould be moiſt and ſhady, well dug, and raked till the mould is fine; then, in the autumn, ſoon after the ſeeds are ripe, let them be ſcattered over this ground, and the ſeeds raked in, in the ſame manner as turnip-ſeeds. In the ſpring many of the young plants will come up, though you muſt not expect the general crop till the ſecond year; the ſpring after which they may be taken out of the ſeminary, and planted in the nurſery in rows one yard aſunder, and at one foot and a half diſtance in the rows. Here they may remain, with the uſual care of digging between the rows and keeping them clean, till they are of ſufficient ſize to plant out for good.

Where the ſeeds of these trees cannot be procured, layering muſt be the method of propagation. For this purpoſe a ſufficient number muſt be planted out for ſtools on a ſpot of earth double dug. After they have ſtood one year, they ſhould be cut down, in order to make them throw out young wood for layering. The autumn following theſe ſhould be laid in the ground, with a little nick in the joint; and by that time twelvemonths they will be trees of a yard high, with a good root, ready to be planted in the nurſery, where they may be managed as the ſeedlings; and as the ſtools will have ſhot up freſh young wood for a ſecond operation, this treatment may be continued *ad libitum*.

The Occidental Plane-tree is propagated by cuttings; which if they are taken from ſtrong young wood, and planted early in the autumn, in a moiſt good mould, will hardly fail of ſucceeding. They are generally planted thick, and then removed into the nurſery-ground, as the layers of the other ſort: But if a large piece of moiſt ground was ready, the cuttings might be placed at ſuch a diſtance as not to approach too cloſe before they were of a ſufficient ſize to plant out for good; and this would ſave the expence and trouble of a removal. The Oriental Plane-tree will grow from cuttings, but not ſo certainly as this; and whoever has not the convenience of proper ground for the cuttings of either, muſt have recourſe to layers with this tree alſo; which, indeed, is always the ſureſt and moſt effectual method.

Plane-trees delight in a moiſt ſituation, eſpecially the Occidental ſort; where the land is inclined to be dry, and Plane-trees are deſired, the other kinds are to be preferred. But in moiſt places, by the ſides of rivulets, ponds, &c. the Occidental makes ſuch ſurpriſing

prising progress as induces me to think that it might be ranked amongst the Aquatics, without any impropriety.

PLANTAIN, (*Plantago*.) There are two kinds of this plant, the narrow and broad-leaved, both common in fields and by road-sides. The leaves are lightly astringent, and the seeds said to be so; and hence they stand recommended in hæmorrhages, and other cases where medicines of this kind are proper. The leaves bruised a little, are the usual application of the common people to slight flesh wounds.—The Edinburgh college directs an extract to be made from the leaves.

PLANTAIN TREE. See BANANA.

PLANTAIN SHOT. Indian Cane. *See* CANE.

PLANTATIONS. Plantations of trees, &c. greatly embellish and improve estates, as well as ornament the adjacent country; and those formed into woods for timber-trees, prove not only very beneficial to the owners, but may be said to be a public convenience to the country around, to have the opportunity of purchasing wood in the neighbourhood, for the various purposes of buildings, fencings, making all sorts of husbandry implements, as carts, waggons, ploughs, &c. and for innumerable other uses; also for furnishing fuel, a very essential article.

In former ages, this island abounded in natural plantations or forests, which spread themselves over the surface of the country, to a very considerable extent, and were composed of various sorts of lofty trees of prodigious magnitude, all blended promiscuously together, and all of spontaneous growth. Those vast forests were never planted by any human hand, such only have been employed for ages in cutting them down; for in many places there were such a profusion of useless wood, that large tracts were obliged to be cleared by degrees, in order to cultivate the ground for other purposes; which, together with the necessary demands for the timber from time to time for buildings, &c. and that owners of estates, reaping considerable advantage from the sale of their timber, continued by degrees, one generation after another, grubbing up their timber without measure; and few ever planted any in lieu of what they cut down; so that in many parts there is almost a general demolition of woodland, and many considerable estates have scarcely any timber of value left standing, whence comes the present scarcity in many parts of the kingdom.

Every possessor of estates, either of large or moderate extent, will reap great pleasure and advantage in dedicating some share of his land to plantations; for in estates of whatsoever extent, they give grandeur and ornament to the premises, as well as an air of fertility and riches; and those large plantations designed for woods, will, after the first eight or ten years, bring in great profit by a gradual thinning of the underwood, besides leaving a sufficiency of standards to attain full growth: in the mean time the plantations in general will contribute exceedingly to the beauty of the estate; for how delightfully it is for travellers to behold the noble plantations in groves, thickets, clumps, &c. variously disposed in parks, and on the boundaries of spacious lawns, and the like places, formed of a great variety of beautiful trees and shrubs, and to see grand avenues of lofty growth, leading to or from a stately mansion, or some main road, or some adjacent town; and in the out-grounds to observe the Plantations of woodlands, &c. ranging along the sides of hills, plains, and other grounds occasionally; but in estates, how fertile soever the soil, yet it appears naked and barren without a proper share of plantations; on the other hand, when estates are beautifully diversified with plantations, the whole may be said to form a sort of pleasure-garden; especially as in the homeward plantations we may have commodious walks of gravel and sand, both private, shady, and sheltered walks, occasionally disposed in many winding turns in the serpentine way, bordered with hardy shrubs and flowers, which will afford most agreeable walking at almost any season of the year, as in summer they afford a screen from the vehement heat of the sun, and at other times shelter from boisterous winds, and cold piercing blasts; there may be also here and there recesses or places of retirement, leading by private turnings from the principal walks, with gladings or openings of grass-ground in the midst of the most extended parts of the plantations.

No land-holder, therefore, let the extent be almost ever so moderate or consideable, but ought to appropriate a proportionable share to commodious plantations as soon as possible, either for ornament or emolument, or both, where the extent will admit, as there is hardly any estate that does not afford soil and situation proper for the cultivation of all our hardy trees, &c. and in many places often furnish soils improper for grass and corn, yet adapted to the growth of many sorts of trees, which would form good plantations, and secure to the planter and his posterity a future pleasure and revenue of considerable importance.

In short, there is hardly any soil so barren and untractable but what will rear a growth of trees and shrubs of some species or other, both for ornament and advantage; and there is scarcely any kind of tree so bad but may be raised to one or other of those purposes: any very poor ground, or such that lies waste, or at a great distance, cannot be better improved than in plantations; even although a tract of land should be so poor as to rear nothing but a crop of aspen trees, alder, and willows, yet the profits even of these productions will greatly exceed what many may think.

So that there is a great number of examples to encourage, and warrant success in plantations, to reward not only with the pleasure of ornamenting our lands, and that of beholding their growth, but also with profit sufficient to compensate amply for the tract of land occupied, and labour in planting.

But to many persons, the necessary expence attending the making a plantation, and knowing that they must wait several years before the trees have made any considerable progress, or can reap any advantage therefrom, often proves an obstacle in attempting the prosecution of that business; but as to the expence of planting, if you raise the plants in your own grounds, it will not prove near so great as many might imagine, especially as a small spot of seminary or nursery-ground will raise plants enough in three or four years to plant a great many acres of land, both ornamental and woodland; and by the latter, the expence of raising and planting them, together with the loss of time in waiting a few years till the plants attain some growth, will be compensated by the first fall or thinning of the underwood, in eight or ten years after planting; and the stools or roots remaining shoot up again, and afford a lopping every eight or ten years, exclusive of the due portion of standards left at proper distances, to attain full growth for timber, as aforesaid.

One particular precaution in making plantations, is the judicious choice of such trees as are the best adapted to the nature of particular soils, which may vary exceedingly in estates of great extent; however, such trees as we find daily growing by road-sides, hedge-rows, and in any adjacent grounds, are rough sketches of what the land will produce.

As to the sorts of trees and shrubs proper for plantations in general, there is a vast variety, both of the deciduous and ever-green tribes, that will prosper in the open ground in any common soil.

It is of importance, in making any considerable plantation, to chuse principally young plants, of from about two or three to five or ten feet stature, which always prove more successful than older trees; for although some persons, being in haste to have plantations as forward as possible in a few years, transplant tall trees, perhaps twelve or fifteen feet high or more, particularly for ornamental plantations, yet younger growth always take root sooner, and more firmly establish themselves, so as to form considerably the finest plantations at last, and be of longest duration; for although large trees of from ten to twenty feet height, especially of the deciduous kind, may with care be transplanted, so as to grow and probably thrive tolerably for some years, yet trees more than twelve or fifteen feet high often fail, by not rooting firmly like young plants, and after some years standing, have hardly made any shoots, and at last gradually dwindle and perish; therefore large trees should never be employed for plantations only on particular occasions, where a few may be necessary to form

form an immediate ſhade or blind, &c. in ſome particular place; but for general work, be perſuaded to employ chiefly young plants, either of your own raiſing, or purchaſed from the nurſeries. And for timber plantations in particular, ſuch plants ſhould be choſen as are only from about two or three, to five or ſix feet in height.

All the different ſorts of trees and ſhrubs, proper both for ornamental and timber plantations, may be had at all the public nurſeries moderately reaſonable; though perſons, accommodated with ſcope of ground, may eaſily raiſe all the ſorts for their own private uſe: A ſmall nurſery will raiſe trees and ſhrubs enough to plant many acres of land.

Obſerve, that where plantations are intended principally for ornament, as great a variety as poſſible of the different ſorts of hardy trees and ſhrubs ſhould be employed, to afford the greater ſource of entertainment; and ſhould conſiſt both of lofty and middling trees, down to the humbleſt ſhrub; diſpoſing the deciduous and evergreen plants principally in ſeparate compartments; ſometimes arranging the tree-kinds by themſelves; ſome in running irregular plantations, towards the boundaries of ſpacious lawns, parks, paddocks, &c. others in avenues, groves, thickets, and clumps, as aforeſaid, variouſly diſpoſed in different parts; and ſometimes arranging the trees and ſhrubs together, in forming ſhrubberies, wilderneſs, ſhady walks, and wood-works; placing the taller growth backward, and the lower in front; bordering the whole with the moſt beautiful flowering ſhrubs, and ſhowy ever-greens, eſpecially next the principal walks and lawns; obſerving to vary the form of all the ſeveral compartments, ſometimes by bold ſweeps and curves outward and inward, of different dimenſions, other parts in long eaſy bends, irregular projections and breaks, ſo as to diverſify the ſcene in imitation of a natural plantation. Allow all the ſorts proper diſtances, which may be from five or ten to fifteen or twenty feet; for example, the tall trees deſigned for continued plantations may be from ten to fifteen or twenty feet, varying the diſtance in different parts, according as light and ſhade, &c. may be proper; and thoſe in groves may, if open groves, be at fifteen or twenty feet diſtance, and cloſe groves ten or twelve; for thickets, five or ſix feet, or cloſer in particular places, where a very dark ſhade, or thick coverture of wood is required; and in clumps of trees, may allow from five or ten to twenty feet between the trees in each clump, varying the diſtance occaſionally, as alſo the ſorts and numbers of trees in each, from two or three to ten or more: likewiſe the form of the clumps; ſome may be triangular, others quadrangular, pentangular, &c. and ſome in curves, others in ſtraight lines, to cauſe the greater variety. And as to the ſhrubbery clumps, and wilderneſs compartments, where the trees and ſhrubs are employed promiſcuouſly together, they may be planted from five to ten feet diſtant; the taller growth being placed backward eight or ten feet aſunder, placing the lower plants gradually forward according to their gradation of ſtature, to the loweſt in front, as above obſerved, at four or five feet diſtance: and if the trees and ſhrubs of the plantations in general are diſpoſed ſomewhat in the quincunx way, they will appear to the greater advantage.

But when deſigned to form large plantations into woods, &c. compoſed principally of foreſt and timber-trees for profit, particular ſorts muſt be choſen, conſiſting both of deciduous and ever-green trees. Of the deciduous kinds chuſing the oak, elm, aſh, beech, cheſnut, hornbeam, birch, alder, maple, ſycamore, plane-tree, poplar, lime-tree, walnut-tree, wild cherry-tree, mountain-aſh, larch-tree, willow-tree, hazel-tree, &c. and of the ever-greens, the pine-trees, firs, cedar of Lebanon, holly-tree, bay-tree, laurel-tree, yew-tree, ever-green oak, box tree, and ſome others. The particular deſcription and culture of all which ſorts, deciduous and ever-greens, are exhibited in their proper genera. They are all hardy, and will grow in almoſt any common ſoil, rich or poor, and moſtly alſo in dry or moiſt ground, high or low; allotting, however, particular ſorts to very low marſhy ſoils, ſuch as the willow, ſallow, and oſier, poplar, alder, and other aquatics, which will proſper in places that are in a manner covered with water, and are the most proper sorts for the embellishing and improvement of such grounds: all the other sorts will succeed in any other more upland places out of water; observing, with respect to disposition, the deciduous and ever-greens should generally be separate, as observed for the ornamental plantations. But the trees of the same tribe may sometimes be intermixed, and sometimes different sorts in separate divisions or quarters, as oaks in one, elms in another, &c. remarking likewise in timber plantations, that all the trees should be planted pretty close together, i. e. not more than three or four feet distance, in order that they may mutually draw each other up tall, more expeditiously, and to allow for a gradual thinning, as hereafter directed.

In forming woods, however, or plantations of timber-trees, the following hints in respect to planting them are proper to be observed.

Let it therefore be remarked, that there are two methods practised in forming plantations of woodlands; one is by raising the trees from seed at once on the ground where the plantation is intended to be, especially of the deciduous kind, and is effected by sowing the seed in drills, a yard asunder, and the plants always to remain where raised, thinning them gradually: the other method is by previously raising the plants in a nursery, till two or three feet high, then transplanting them into places allotted them, in rows of the above distance, to allow also for gradually thinning.

Either of these two methods may be practised, as shall seem most convenient to the owner; but the former, namely, raising the plants where they are to remain, although it may be more expeditious, and at once get rid of the trouble of transplantation, yet they will require greater attendance for a few years, till the plants have shot up out of the way of weeds; but on the other hand, the trees always remaining where raised, not disturbed by removal, probably may make the greater progress. The latter method, however, of raising the trees first in a nursery, is rather the most commonly practised, as being thought the least troublesome and expensive, with regard to the attendance at first of the young growth. However, every one is at liberty to make the experiment as it suits his convenience.

The preparation of the ground for the final reception of the seed or plants of these plantations, is by deep ploughing and harrowing, upon such ground where the plough can be employed; where this, however, or any other tillage, is not practicable, we must use only young plants from the nursery, making holes, &c. at proper distances, for the reception of each plant: where, however, the ground can be tilled, it will prove very advantageous, performing it previously a year at least before; sowing it with a crop of turneps, or the like: when these come off, well plough and harrow the ground again, for the reception either of the seed or plants the ensuing season.

The most proper season to perform this planting, either by seed or plants, is any time in dry mild weather, from October or November till February, though November and February are rather the most eligible for most kinds of hardy tree seeds: however, where large tracts are to be planted, both methods must be pursued all winter, at every favourable opportunity.

If seed is intended, you must be well provided with seeds of the several deciduous trees in particular, which may be obtained at all the nurseries and eminent seed-shops; then, for its reception, draw furrows or drills about two or three inches deep, and three or four feet asunder, scatter the seed along the middle of the drills, and cover the earth evenly over them, the depth of the drills or furrows, and place scarecrows and traps to guard against the insults of birds and vermin.

But if designed to form the plantation with young plants, previously raised in beds in the nursery by the common method, let the following practice be observed: Chuse always young plants, only from two to three or five or six feet high; and if very large plantations are intended, you may, to save time and trouble, take the plants immediately from the seed-bed, when one or two feet high, without giving them any previous transplantation in the nursery; though where the plantations are but moderate, it is most eligible

eligible to plant them out previously in nursery rows, to have two or three years growth: but for remarkable large plantations, this would be a very great trouble and expence. Being, however, furnished with young plants, they are to be planted in rows, three or four feet asunder, as directed for the seed, and one or two feet apart in the lines: they may be planted either by opening small apertures or holes with the spade for each plant; or, if very small plants, it is sometimes performed by making only a slit or crevice with the spade for each plant; and some open small trenches the whole length, then one inserts the plants whilst another turns in the earth about their roots: some again, in very large tracts, where the situation admits of good ploughing and harrowing to divide and break the earth into small particles, open furrows with a plough, two persons being employed in depositing the trees in the furrows, whilst the plough following immediately with another furrow, covers the roots of the plants with the earth thereof.

The ground where the above plantations are made should be previously fenced all round with a deep ditch, &c. to guard against the encroachments of cattle.

Whilst these plantations are young, they must have some attendance to destroy weeds, which may be expeditiously executed by hoeing between the rows in dry weather, particularly by horse-hoeing; and this care will be needful for two or three years, especially the seedling plantations, till the trees are advanced out of the reach of weeds; after which no farther trouble will be required until the trees are ready for the first fall or thinning, for poles, faggots, &c.

In eight or ten years growth, they will be of a proper size to begin the first fall by a moderate thinning, which will serve for poles and faggot-wood, to pay towards the expence of planting, &c. but begin lopping only part of the plantation the first year; thinning out the weakest and most unpromising growth first; leaving a sufficiency of the most vigorous plants pretty close, to grow up for larger purposes; the year following begin thinning another part, and so continue an annual thinning-fall till got through the whole plantation; cutting each fall down near the ground, leaving the stools to shoot out again, especially of the deciduous kinds, and by that time you have made the last fall, the first will have shot up, and ready to be cut again; so the returns of fallings may be contrived to be every six, seven, eight, or ten years, or more, according to the uses the poles or wood are wanted for; and if larger poles, &c. are wanted, the fall may be only once in fourteen, eighteen, or twenty years, still, at every fall, being careful always to leave enough of the most thriving plants for final standards; leaving them pretty close at first, that they may mutually draw each other up in height; but may be thinned every succeeding fall as they encrease in bulk, and meet, so as to leave a sufficient quantity of the principal trees at proper distances to grow up to timber, which, in their turn, as they become fit for the purposes intended, may also be felled according as there may be a demand for them to the most advantage; having young ones from the stools coming up in proper succession as substitutes, so as the ground may be always occupied.

PLANTING. Planting is the art of inserting plants, seeds, and roots, in the earth, for the purpose of vegetation.

There are various methods of planting in practice for different sorts of plants, seeds, and roots; such as hole planting, trench planting, trenching-in planting, slit or crevice planting, holeing-in planting, drill planting, bedding-in planting, furrow planting, dibble planting, planting with balls of earth about the root, planting in pots, &c. all of which methods of planting are occasionally used by different practitioners in the several branches of gardening, according as the several methods shall seem most eligible for different or particular sorts of plants.

1. *Hole-Planting.*—This is the principal method practised in the final planting of all sorts of trees and shrubs in the full ground, by opening with a spade round holes in the ground, at certain distances, one for the reception of each plant. Each hole should be digged capacious enough to admit all the roots of the tree or shrub freely

every

every way to their full fpread, without touching the fides of the hole, and about one fpade deep, or a little more or lefs, or according to the fize of the roots, fo as, when planted, the uppermoft ones may be only about three inches below the common furface, or about as low as they were before in the ground, which is difcoverable by examining the bottom of the ftem of the tree; though in very moift foils, where the water is apt to ftand, the holes fhould rather be fhallow, fo as the uppermoft roots may ftand full as high as the general level, or higher if it fhall feem neceffary, raifing the ground about them, efpecially in winter planting: let the holes, however, be of a proper width and depth, according to the above rules, loofening the bottom well; and if too deep, it is eafily remedied in the time of planting, by fhaking up the tree as you fhall fee occafion; obferving in digging out each hole, to lay the earth in a heap clofe to the edge, in order to be ready to fill in again: the holes being ready, then, having trimmed the roots, &c. of the trees, place one tree in the middle of the hole, making all its roots fpread equally around, a perfon holding the plant erect by the ftem, whilft another with his fpade cafts in the earth about the roots, taking particular care to break all large clods, and trim in fome of the fineft mould firft all round about the roots in general, fhaking the tree occafionally, to caufe the fine foil to fall in clofe among all the fmall roots and fibres; at the fame time, if the tree ftands too deep, fhake it up gently to the proper height, and having filled in the earth to the top of the hole, tread it gently all round, firft round the outfide to fettle the earth clofe to the extreme roots, continuing the treading gradually towards the ftem, to which tread the mould moderately firm, but no where too hard, only juft to fettle the earth, and fteady the plant in an upright pofition: then pare in all the remaining earth evenly round the tree, to the width of the hole, raifing it fomewhat above the general level of the ground, to allow for fettling, giving it alfo a gentle tread, and finifh it off a little hollow at top, bafon-like, the better to receive and retain the moifture from rains, and occafional waterings in fpring and fummer, particularly to the choicer kinds of trees and fhrubs.

After performing this planting, if in winter, or late in fpring, it may be of advantage to the choicer kinds of trees and fhrubs to mulch them, i. e. to lay fome long mulch at top of all the earth, both to keep out the winter's froft, and prevent the drying winds and drought of fpring and fummer from penetrating to the roots before the trees are well rooted in their new quarters. But fome, inftead of mulch, ufe grafs turfs, turned topfy-turvy, efpecially when planting upon any grafs ground, or any out-plantations where turfs of grafs can be obtained; or in orchards, where the ground is grafs; in which cafe it may be proper to bank fome turfs round the fides and top of each hole, particularly for large trees, which will fteady them more effectually, as well as preferve the moifture, if much dry weather fhould happen the fucceeding fummer.

The above work, however, of mulching or turfing new-planted trees, is not abfolutely neceffary to our common hardy kinds of fruit-trees, foreft-trees, and fhrubs; though it may prove beneficial to all forts, but more particularly to the more tender kinds of wall fruit-trees, and more delicate forts of flowering-fhrubs, choice ever-greens, and fome kinds of herbaceous perennials.

2. *Trench Planting.*—This method is fometimes practifed in the nurfery-way, in putting out feedling and other fmall trees and fhrubs in rows; is alfo ufed for planting box edgings; fometimes likewife for planting fmall hedge-fets, &c. and always in planting *Afparagus*, and is performed by opening a long narrow trench with a fpade, making one fide upright, fo place the plants againft the upright fide, and turn the earth in upon their roots.

3. *Trenching-in Planting.*]——This is alfo fometimes practifed in light pliable-working ground, for planting young trees in the nurfery-way, and fometimes in planting hedge-fets, &c. and is performed by digging along by a line, about one fpade wide, and planting as you go on. The method is this: a line is fet, then having the plants ready, and with your fpade beginning

ginning at one end, and standing sideways to the line, throw out a spit of earth, which forming a small aperture, another person being ready with the plants, he directly deposits one in the opening, whilst the digger proceeds with the digging one spade wide, covers the roots of the plants with the earth of the next spit; and another aperture being thereby also formed, place therein another plant, the digger still proceeding, covers its roots, as before, with the next spit of earth, and so on to the end of the row; placing them at about a foot, or fifteen or eighteen inches asunder, according to the size of the plants; observing, when planting larger trees with more spreading roots, by this method, that instead of digging the trench only one spade wide, two may probably be requisite for the proper reception of the roots; likewise in forming the opening for each plant, make it capacious enough to receive the roots freely, digging the earth over them as above. After having planted one row, either small or large plants, tread the earth evenly along to settle it to the roots, and steady the plants all equally upright.

4. *Slit Planting.*]—This method is performed by making slits or crevices with a spade in the ground, at particular distances, for the reception of small trees and shrub plants. A slit being made for each plant, which are inserted as you go on; and is practised sometimes in the nursery-way, &c. in putting out rows of small plants, suckers, &c. at from about a foot to eighteen inches or two feet high, and that have but small roots; it is also sometimes practised for final planting in out-grounds, where very large tracts of forest-trees are intended, and that they are to be planted out at the above sizes, and by the most expeditious and cheapest method of planting; the following is the method.

A line is set, or a mark made accordingly; then having a quantity of plants ready, for they must be planted as you proceed in making the slits, a man therefore having a good clean spade, he strikes it into the ground with its back close to the line or mark, forms a crevice, taking it out again directly, so as to leave the slit open, gives another stroke at right angles with the first, then the person with the plants inserts one immediately into the second-made crevice, bringing it up close to the first, and directly press the earth close to the plant with the foot; proceeding in the same manner to insert another plant; and so on till all is finished, which is a very expeditious way of putting out small plants, for any considerable plantation.——A man and a boy by this method will plant ten or fifteen hundred, or more in a day.

5. *Hoeing-in Planting.*]——This is sometimes used in the nursery way in light loose ground, also sometimes in planting potatoes, &c. in pliable soils.

The ground being previously digged or trenched, and a line placed, they proceed thus: a person with his spade takes out a small spit of earth, to form a little aperture, in which another person directly deposits a plant, &c. the digger at the same time taking another spit at a little distance, turns the earth thereof into the first hole over the roots, placing directly another plant in this second opening, the digger covers it with the earth of a third, and so on to the end of the row.

6. *Drill Planting.*]—This is by drawing drills with an hoe from two to four or five inches deep, for the reception of seeds and roots, and is a commodious method of planting many sorts of large seeds, such as walnuts, chesnuts, and the like; sometimes also broad beans, but always for kidney-beans, and peas: likewise for planting many sorts of bulbous roots, when to be deposited in beds by themselves.

The drills for all which purposes should be drawn with a hoe, two or three inches deep; though for large kinds of bulbous roots, four or five inches depth will be requisite, covering in the seeds and roots with the earth, always the depth of the drills.

7. *Bedding in Planting.*]——This is frequently practised for planting the choicer kinds of flowering bulbs, such as *Hyacinths*, &c. also for larger seeds of trees, as acorns, large nuts, and other larger kinds of seeds, stones, and kernels, and is performed by drawing the earth from off the tops of the beds some inches depth, then planting the seeds or roots, and covering them over with the earth, drawn off for that purpose; after the following method:

The

The ground muſt be previouſly digged or trenched, raked, and formed into beds three or four feet wide, with alleys between bed and bed; then with a rake or ſpade trim the earth evenly from off the top of the bed into the alleys, from three to four or five inches deep for bulbous roots, and for ſeeds, one or two, according to what they are, and their ſize; then, if for bulbous roots, draw lines along the ſurface of the bed, nine inches diſtance, place the roots bottom downward, along the lines, ſix or eight inches apart, but, if ſeeds, they may be ſcattered promiſcuouſly; and having thus planted one bed, then with the ſpade, let the earth that was drawn off into the alley, be ſpread evenly upon the bed again over the roots or ſeed, &c. being careful to cover all equally the above depth, and to rake the ſurface ſmooth.

This method is much in practice among floriſts for the choicer ſorts of bulbous flowers.

The nurſerymen alſo practiſe this method in planting many of their larger ſeeds, nuts, &c.

8. *Furrow Planting.*]——This is by drawing furrows with a plough, and depoſiting ſets or plants in the furrow, covering them in alſo with the plough, and is ſometimes practiſed for planting potatoe-ſets in fields, and has been practiſed in planting young trees for large tracts of foreſt-tree plantations, where the cheapeſt and moſt expeditious method is required; but this method can be practiſed only in light pliable ground, and is performed thus: A furrow being drawn, one or two perſons are employed in placing the ſets or plants in the furrow, whilſt the plough following immediately with another furrow, turns the earth thereof in upon the roots of the plants.

9. *Dibble Planting.*]——This is the moſt commodious method for planting moſt ſorts of fibrous-rooted ſeedling plants, particularly all the herbaceous tribe; alſo for planting ſlips, off ſets, and cuttings, both of herbaceous and ſhrubby kinds; likewiſe for ſome kinds of ſeeds and roots, ſuch as broad-beans, potatoe-ſets, Jeruſalem artichokes, and horſe-radiſh-ſets, with numerous ſorts of bulbous roots, &c. and is expeditiouſly performed with a dibble or ſetting-ſtick, therewith making a narrow hole in the earth for each plant, inſerting them in each hole, always as you go on; obſerving the following hints:

Having a dibble, or ſetting-ſtick, it is uſed by thruſting it into the earth in a perpendicular deſcent, in depth as the particular plants, &c. may require; directly inſerting the plant, ſeed, or ſet, according as each hole is made, cloſing the hole immediately by a ſtroke of the dibble. So proceed dibbling the holes, and planting as you go on, at particular diſtances and depths, according to the nature of the plants, &c. obſerving, in ſetting any kind of plants, ſlips, cuttings, and the like, having long ſhanks or ſtems, it is proper to make holes a proper depth, to admit them ſome conſiderable way in the ground; for example, cabbage-plants, ſavoys, &c. ſhould be planted down to their leaves; ſlips and cuttings ſhould be inſerted two parts of three, at leaſt, in the ground; being particularly careful, in dibbling-in all ſorts of plants, to cloſe the holes well in every part about the roots, by ſtriking the dibble ſlantways into the ground, ſo as to ſtrike the mould firſt firmly up to the root and fibres, at the ſame time bringing it cloſe to the ſtem; for in dibble planting, many only ſtrike the earth about the neck of the plant, and the lower part of the hole is often left hollow about the roots; but by ſtriking the dibble firſt at the root part, you fix the plant effectually, then a ſtroke of the dibble at the top of the ground finiſhes, by cloſing up every part of the aperture. In this manner continue planting and finiſhing each hole as you go on, perfectly cloſe, that neither the ſun, air, nor penetrating winds, can enter, this being of much importance, but often diſregarded, as we may often ſee the holes that are neceſſarily made in fixing the plants left open, though each hole at the inſertion of its plant, at one ſtroke of the dibble, may be cloſed with the utmoſt facility.

10. *Planting with Balls of Earth about the Roots.*]——This is the removing a plant with a large ball of earth about its roots, ſo as the plant by having its roots firmly attached to the ſurrounding ball of earth, it ſtill, during the operation, continues its growing ſtate without receiving any or but very little check

check from its removal; and is often practised more particularly to the more delicate and choicer kinds of exotics, both trees, shrubs, and herbaceous plants: likewise when intended to remove any sort of tree or plant out of the proper planting season, as very late in the spring, or in summer, it is eligible to transplant it with a good ball of earth, to preserve it more certainly in a state of growth. Observing, some trees and shrubs are more difficult to remove with a ball than most kinds of herbaceous fibrous-rooted plants, tho' many of the tree and shrub kinds, having very fibrey roots, they will also readily rise with good balls.

But when trees or shrubs, with balls to their roots, are intended to be sent to any considerable distance, they should be placed in osier baskets, in order to preserve the cohesion of the ball, having a basket for each tree.—In planting them, if they cannot be readily moved out of the baskets without disturbing the ball of earth, plant basket and all; cut it here and there in the sides, and throw some fine mould close all round so as to join with that of the ball, and give a watering to settle it more effectually close; the roots and fibres will readily make their way through the sides of the basket; besides, the baskets will soon rot, without proving any obstruction to the growth of the plants.

The advantage in planting with balls, either in the full ground, or in pots, is, the root of the plant being enclosed in the ball of earth continues all the while drawing nourishment, and the growth of the plant is not retarded in waiting till it has taken fresh root in its new place, which may be of advantage in many places, particularly all tender plants, some of our choicest ever-greens, and many kinds of herbaceous flower plants.

But planting with balls is not recommended for general practice; for all the hardy tree and shrub kind, it would be needless as well as very expensive and troublesome.

II. *Planting in pots.*]—This is practised to all tender exotics, in order for moving them to shelter occasionally, such as all kinds of green-house and hot-house plants; and it is likewise practised for many sorts of hardy flowering-plants, for the convenience of moving some curious sorts when in flower to occasional shelter from the sun's rays, and excessive rains, in order to preserve their beauty, and prolong the time of their bloom; such as the fine auriculas, carnations, &c.

In planting in pots, it is highly requisite carefully to adapt the sizes to the size and nature of the different plants intended to be potted; if small plants, begin first with small pots, one plant only to each pot, especially if to remain; but according as the different plants advance in growth, shift them into pots one or two sizes larger, which may be requisite to many sorts once a year, to others once in two or three years, according to the nature and increased growth of the respective plants; though to some sorts of annuals it may be necessary once or twice in the course of a season; all of which is generally particularized in the culture of the various sorts. And by thus beginning first with small pots adapted to the size of the plants, it is not only cheaper and more commodious for moving and stowing them in different parts occasionally, till they gradually advance in growth, but by thus shifting them into pots a size larger, it admits of adding fresh earth, which proves highly beneficial to their growth.

Garden pots, for the reception of plants, are of several regular sizes, from two to sixty in a cast, so are distinguished at the pot-houses accordingly, as twos, sixes, twelves, sixteens, twenty-fours, thirty-twos, forty-eights, sixties, or sixty-fours, &c. in each cast; each pot having one or more apertures at bottom to discharge the superfluous moisture. They are sold by the potters at so much per cast, large and small, all of a price; those of only two in a cast the same as those of sixty; and from two shillings to half a crown per cast is the general price.

But, with respect to the particular method of planting in pots in general, the following particulars are necessary to be observed.

Having the pots and mould ready for the reception of the intended plants, observe, previous to planting them, to place some pieces of tile, potsherds, or oyster-shell over each hole at the bottom of the pots, both to prevent the holes being

being clogged and ſtopped with the earth, and the earth from being waſhed out with occaſional watering; alſo to prevent the roots of the plants getting out; then having ſecured the holes, put ſome earth in the bottom of each pot, from two or three to five or ſix inches or more in depth, according to the ſize of the pot, and that of the roots of the plant; this done, inſert the plant in the middle of the pot upon the earth, in an upright poſition, making its roots, if without a ball of earth, ſpread equally every way, directly adding a quantity of fine mould about all the roots and fibres, ſhaking the pot to cauſe the earth to ſettle cloſe thereto; at the ſame time, if the root ſtand too low, ſhake it gently up as you ſhall ſee occaſion; and, having filled the pot with earth, preſs it gently all round with the hand, to ſettle it moderately firm in every part, and to ſteady the upright poſture of the plant, raiſing the earth however within about half an inch, or leſs, of the top of the pot, it will ſettle lower; for ſome void ſpace at top is neceſſary to receive waterings occaſionally: as ſoon as the plant is thus potted, give directly a moderate watering, to ſettle the earth more effectually cloſe about all the roots, and promote their rooting more expeditiouſly in the new earth; repeating the waterings both before and after they have taken root, as occaſion requires.——MAWE.

Obſervations on planting Trees in general.

The firſt thing in the planting of trees is to prepare the ground (according to the different ſorts of trees you intend to plant) before the trees are taken out of the earth; for you ſhould ſuffer them to remain as little time out the ground as poſſible.

In taking up the trees, you ſhould carefully dig away the earth round their roots, ſo as to come at their ſeveral parts to cut them off; for if they are torn out of the ground without care, the roots will be broken and bruiſed very much, to the great injury of the trees. When you have taken them up, the next thing is to prepare them for planting; in doing of which, there are two things to be principally regarded; the one is to prepare the roots, and the other to prune their heads in ſuch a manner, as may be moſt ſerviceable in promoting the future growth of the trees.

And firſt, as to the roots; all the ſmall fibres are to be cut off as near to the place from whence they are produced as may be (excepting ever-greens, and ſuch trees as are to be replanted immediately after they are taken up;) otherwiſe the air will turn all the ſmall roots and fibres black, which, if permitted to remain on when the tree is planted, will grow mouldy and decay, and thereby greatly injure the new fibres which are produced, ſo that many times the trees miſcarry for want of duly obſerving this. After the fibres are cut off, you ſhould prune off all the bruiſed or broken roots ſmooth, otherwiſe they are apt to rot, and diſtemper the trees; you ſhould alſo cut out all irregular roots which croſs each other, and all downright roots (eſpecially in fruit-trees) muſt be cut off; ſo that when the roots are regularly pruned, they may in ſome meaſure reſemble the fingers of a hand when ſpread open; then you ſhould ſhorten the larger roots in proportion to the age and ſtrength of the tree, and alſo the particular ſorts of trees are to be conſidered; for the walnut, mulberry, and ſome other tender-rooted kinds, ſhould not be pruned ſo cloſe, as the more hardy ſorts of fruit or foreſt-trees, which in young fruit-trees, ſuch as, pears, apples, plumbs, peaches, &c. that are one year old from budding or grafting, may be left about eight or nine inches long, but in older trees they muſt be left of a much greater length; but this is to be underſtood of the larger roots only, for the ſmall ones muſt be cut quite out, or pruned very ſhort. Their extreme parts, which are generally very weak, commonly decay after moving, ſo that it is the better way entirely to diſplace them.

The next thing is the pruning of their heads, which muſt be differently performed in different trees, and the deſign of the trees muſt alſo be conſidered; for if they are fruit-trees, and intended for walls or eſpaliers, it is the better way to plant them with the greateſt part of their heads, which ſhould remain on until the ſpring, juſt before the trees begin to ſhoot; when they muſt be cut down to five or ſix eyes, being very careful, in doing of this,

this not to disturb the new roots. But if the trees are designed for standards, you should prune off all the small branches close to the places where they are produced, as also irregular branches which cross each other; and by their motion, when agitated by the wind, rub and bruise their bark, so as to occasion many times great wounds in those places; besides, it makes a disagreeable appearance to the sight, and adds to the closeness of its head, which should be always avoided in fruit-trees, whose branches should be preserved as far distant from each other, as they are usually produced when in a regular way of growth (which is in all sorts of trees proportionable to the size of their leaves and magnitude of their fruit.) But to return: After having displaced these branches, you should also cut off all such parts of branches as have by any accident been broken or wounded; for those will remain a disagreeable sight, and often occasion a disease in the tree. But you should by no means cut off the main leading shoots, as is by too many practised, for those are necessary to attract the sap from the root, and thereby promote the growth of the tree.

Having thus prepared the trees for planting, we must now proceed to the placing them into the ground; but before this, we would advise, if the trees have been long out of the ground, so that the roots are dried, to place them in water eight or ten hours before they are planted, observing to put them in such manner, as that their heads may remain erect, and their roots only immersed therein, which will swell the dried vessels of the roots, and prepare them to imbibe nourishment from the earth. In fixing of them, great regard should be had to the nature of the soil, which, if cold and moist, the trees should be planted very shallow; as also, if it be a hard rock or gravel, it will be much the better way to raise a hill of earth where each tree is to be planted, than to dig into the rock or gravel, and fill it up with earth (as is too often practised,) whereby the trees are planted as it were in a tub, there being but little room for their roots to extend; so that after two or three years growth, when their roots have extended to the sides of the hole, they are stopped by the rock or gravel, so can get no farther, and the trees will decline, and in a few years die. But when they are raised above the surface of the ground, their roots will extend, and find nourishment, though the earth upon the rock or gravel be not three inches thick, as may be frequently observed, where trees are growing upon such soils.

Having thus planted the trees, you should provide a parcel of stakes, which should be driven down by the sides of the trees, and fastened thereto to support them from being blown down, or displaced by the wind, and then lay some mulch upon the surface of the ground about their roots, to prevent the earth from drying.

This is to be understood of standard trees, which cast their leaves; for such as are planted against walls, should have their branches fastened to the wall to prevent the trees from being displaced by the wind, and place their roots about five inches from the wall, inclining their heads thereto; and the spring following, just before they shoot, their heads should be cut down to five or six buds.

As to the watering of all new-planted trees, we should advise it to be done with great moderation, nothing being more injurious to them than over-watering. Examples enough of this kind may have been seen in many parts of England; and by an experiment made by the late Rev. Dr. Hales, in placing the roots of a dwarf Pear-tree in water, the quantity of moisture imbibed decreased very much daily, because the sap-vessels of the roots, like those of the cut-off boughs in the same experiment, were so saturated and clogged with moisture, by standing in water, that more of it could not be drawn up. And this experiment was tried upon a tree, which was full of leaves, and thereby more capable to discharge a large quantity of moisture than such trees as are entirely destitute of leaves; so that it is impossible such trees can thrive, where the moisture is too great about their roots.

The distance which trees should be planted at, must be proportioned to their several kinds, and the several purposes for which they are intended; but fruit-trees, planted either against walls, or for espaliers, should be allowed the following distances: for most sorts of vigorous-shooting pear-trees, thirty-six or forty feet; for apricots, sixteen or eighteen feet; apples, twenty-five or thirty feet; peaches and nectarines, twelve feet; cherries and plumbs, twenty-five feet, according to the goodness of the soil, or the height of the wall.

It is common to hear persons remarking, that from the present spirit of planting, great advantages will accrue to the public by the increase of timber; but whoever is the least skilled in the growth of timber, must know, that little is to be expected from most of the plantations which have lately been made; for there are few persons who have had this in their view when they commenced planters, and of those few scarce any of them have set out right; for there never was any valuable timber produced from trees which were transplanted of any considerable size, nor is any of the timber of the trees which are transplanted young, equal in goodness to that which has grown from the seeds unremoved. Beside, if we consider the sorts of trees which are usually planted, it will be found, that they are not designed for timber; so that upon the whole, it is much to be doubted, whether the late method of planting has not rather been prejudicial to the growth and increase of timber than otherwise.

Most people are so much in a hurry about planting, as not to take time to prepare their ground for the reception of trees, but frequently make holes and stick in the trees, amongst all sorts of rubbish which is growing upon the land: nor has any care been afterward taken to dig the ground, or root out the noxious plants; but the trees have been left to struggle with these bad neighbours, which have had long possession of the ground, and have established themselves so strongly, as not to be easily overcome; therefore what can be expected from such plantations?—This is to be understood of deciduous trees; for the pines and firs, if once well rooted in the ground, will soon get the better of the plants and destroy them.

Every person who proposes to plant, should prepare the ground well beforehand, by trenching or deep ploughing it, and clearing it from the roots of all bad weeds, for by so doing there will be a foundation laid for the future success of the plantation. Also we advise no person to undertake more of this work than he can afterward keep clean, for all plantations of deciduous trees will require this care, at least for seven years after they are made, if they hope to see the trees thrive well. Therefore all small plantations should have the ground annually dug between the trees, and as to those which are large, it should be ploughed between them. This will encourage the roots of the trees to extend themselves, whereby they will find a much greater share of nourishment, and by loosening of the ground, the moisture and air will more easily penetrate to the roots, to the no small advantage of the trees. But besides this operation, it will be absolutely necessary to hoe the ground three or four times in summer, either by hand or the hoe-plough. This will be objected to by many, on account of the expence; but if the first hoeing is performed early in the spring, before the weeds have gotten strength, a great quantity of ground may be gone over in a short time; and if the season is dry when it is performed, the weeds will presently die after they are cut; and if this is repeated before the weeds come up again to any size, it will be found the cheapest and very best husbandry; for if the weeds are suffered to grow till they are large, it will be a much greater expence to root them out and make the ground clean; beside, the weeds will rob the trees of great part of their nourishment. We have sometimes been told, that it is necessary to let the weeds grow among trees in summer, in order to shade their roots, and keep the ground moist; but this has come from persons of no skill. For if weeds are permitted to grow, they will draw away all moisture from the roots of the trees for their own nourishment, so that the trees will be thereby deprived of the kindly dews and gentle showers of rain, which are of great service to young plantations; and these will be entirely drawn away by the weeds, which will prevent their penetrating of the ground, so that it is only the great rains which can descend to the roots of the trees. And whoever has the least doubt of this matter, if they will but try the experiment, by keeping one part of the plantation clean, and suffer the weeds to grow on another, they will soon be convinced of the truth by the growth of the trees. And though this cleaning is attended with an expence, yet the success will overpay this, beside the additional pleasure of seeing the ground always clean.

PLIANT MEALLY TREE. *See* WAYFARING TREE.

PLOUGHING. Ploughs seem to have been invented in the rudest times, and, till very lately, to have had little improvement. What has been done on this head, however, by some ingenious persons within these few years, shews what is practicable; and we hope will lead others to the same useful pursuit.

The first kind of tillage was probably with the spade, and were that as convenient for large quantities of ground, as it is useful where it can be properly employed, no instrument in the world could be compared to it.—But when whole fields came to be turned up and tilled, it was natural to devise some method of saving the labour of men; and consequently, the plough which may be called a kind of spade drawn by horses, was invented.

As this was more and more frequently used, its form became probably a little altered, but improvements have been in nothing so slow: and this instrument, of such universal use, and vast advantage and importance to mankind, is still capable of many more; and it still wants them.

All tillage, it is evident, has its advantage from dividing and breaking the earth into a great many parts. The spade, as it is wrought by the hand of the workman, does this most perfectly, and it is for this reason that gardens are more fertile than fields; but it may not be impossible, if proper persons will set themselves about it, now that they know in what the greatest perfection of tillage consists, to make the plough, by more improvements, equal its effect.

The advantage of the spade over the plough is, that it goes deeper, and divides the land into more particles, and smaller: but the plough, when its structure shall be fully perfected, is certainly capable of this. The four-coultered plough is an excellent contrivance, and shews, that there is nothing impracticable in the thought of forming a plough that shall go deeper, and divide the earth as much or more than the spade.

The ancient plough, according to the best accounts we have of it, had no coulter, nor earth-board, for the share, always going obliquely, served as an earth-board; and the two ears which were the corners of a piece of wood lying under the share, did the office of ground wrests.

This sort of plough is used in Italy, and even in some parts of France at this time. It serves for the turning up of light land, but it would do nothing with our stiff and tough soil in many counties.

This, so far as we know, was the first and original plough, and it is a very plain and simple contrivance. It did the office for which it was intended, in the place where it was invented; but it was not fit for other lands, and other countries, and therefore it was altered.

In those parts of Italy, where the soil is perfectly soft and mellow, this instrument does very well to keep it in tillage; but even in these favourable lands it is very unfit for the bringing them into this condition; for when they have lain in grass, and have any turf upon them, it is very difficult to manage them with it. They are obliged to go two or three times over the land before the turf is all broken.

These ploughs, for want of a coulter to cut the turf, tear it to pieces with great awkwardness and difficulty, but when it is once cut through, the soil being soft and tender, they easily get deeper.

As our soil is very different from that of those countries, our ploughs are necessarily made different, for otherwise they could not cut it. The necessity of a coulter to ours is very plain, because of the thickness to be cut, and that necessity was doubtless the mother of the invention. Our ploughs, when well made, cut off the furrow at the bottom flatwise, and therefore it is as thick on the land side as on the furrow side: but the plough cannot break it off from the whole land at such a thickness,

thickneſs, ſo that there muſt be a coulter to cut it off. By this means the furrow is turned perfectly whole, and no part of the turf of it is broken.—Hence if it lie long without new turning, the graſs from the edges will ſpread, and form a new turf or ſward on the other ſide, which was the bottom of the furrow before turning, but is now become the ſurface of the earth.

If the land be left thus, it will ſoon be greener with graſs than it was before ploughing, and the graſs, ſpreading its roots, will bind it firmly and toughly together; ſo that there will require a great deal of time and labour to bring it into a condition for the ſervice it is intended to anſwer.

This has ſhewn the inſufficiency of the common plough, and from a ſenſe of this, has ariſen the invention of the four-coultered kind, to be deſcribed hereafter. Several others have been deviſed to anſwer the ſame purpoſe, but none ſucceed ſo well.

Of the ſeveral kinds of Ploughs in common uſe in England.

The common plough differs very much in ſhape and form in various places; partly according to the fancy of the people, and partly to the nature of the ground. Some have longer and ſome ſhorter beams; and there are great varieties in the length and form of the ſhare, the coulter, and the handles.

In general, without regarding the cuſtoms of particular places, there is great reaſon to have reſpect to the nature of the ſoil on which it is to be uſed. Thus, in general, the plough that is for ſtiff clay ſhould be long, large, and broad, with a deep head, and ſquare earth-board, ſo that it may turn up a large furrow. The coulter ſhould be long, and very little bending, with a very large wing; and the foot long and broad, ſo as to make a deep furrow. The plough for moderate ſoils ſhould be ſomewhat ſmaller than the former, but broad at the breech; the coulter ſhould be long and more bending, and the ſhare narrow, with a wing coming up to arm and defend the earth-board from wearing. The plough for light ſoils, ſuch as ſandy and the like, ſhould be lighter and ſmaller than any of theſe. The coulter ſhould be more circular and thinner, and the wing not ſo large.

This is a direction contained in a ſmall compaſs, yet it will give the farmer the general rule for his conduct in this reſpect: let him conſider his ſoils under theſe three heads of heavy, moderate, and light, and in this general manner ſuit the bulk and fabric of his plough to them, and he will never make any great errors.

Ploughs are ſometimes made with wheels, and ſometimes without, but in general the wheels are a very great advantage; there are circumſtances in which they are troubleſome, and therefore it is fit they ſhould be in ſome ploughs omitted.

The plough, which, from its great advantage above the others, might be eſteemed the firſt great improvement in England, is the wheel-plough; that from the place where it was firſt uſed has been long called the Hertfordſhire plough. This conſiſts of a beam and handle, a neck, an earth-board, a ſheath, a ſhare, a coulter, a pin, pillow, and wheels.

This Hertfordſhire plough, or common wheel-plough, as it is uſually made, is very ſtrong, and is ſerviceable for moſt uſes: it is very eaſily managed, it follows the horſe lightly, and it ſuits almoſt every kind of land. The greateſt exception to its uſe is in miry clay in winter; becauſe the wheels cut into them, and clog and ſtick when they are work'd at that time of the year. This is fit for that ſort of ground when ſummer fallows are to be ploughed, and when a graſs ground is to be turned up for arable, for it turns the turf very well, and is very fit for uneven ground, and for the drieſt ſummer weather. Some make this plough in the original manner, with the handle ſloping of one ſide, but this renders it troubleſome to hold, or to follow; the remedy was very eaſy, and people, not bigotted to fooliſh cuſtoms, have improved it greatly by making it ſtrait.

This is in a manner the general plough uſed at this time, and it is varied more or leſs, but never much, according to the pleaſure of the owner, or faſhion of the place.

The Eſſex plough, (for the beſt way to diſtinguiſh theſe inſtruments is according to the places where they are uſed)

used) has its earth-board, if the expression may be allowed, made of iron; by this means they make it rounding, and this has a great advantage in the turning of the turf; they generally make it light and fine, and the wheels proportioned. It is in this way very fit for light soils, and rids a great deal of business. We do not mean by calling this the Essex plough, that they use no other in that country; but that is the place where this kind is most used, and seems to have been invented.

The Lincolnshire plough owes its invention and form also to the general nature of the soil of that county. The fen land of that place is light, soft, and mellow, free from stones, and naturally over-grown with weeds and sedge on the surface; for this land they use a plough with a circular turning coulter, and a large sharp share; this is often a foot broad, and quite sharp at the edge. This plough has no wheels. There is a foot at the fore part of the beam, which they set higher or lower with a wedge, and by that means they keep the fore part of the plough from going deeper than they chuse. And they have also wedges for setting the hinder part where the handle joins the beam. The coulter stands in its usual place before the share, and is a round iron wheel, with a sharp edge, that turns upon an axle as the plough moves, and cuts through the roots of the sedge and grass as it goes round, while the broad share cuts the bottom. This would not do on other land, but where the soil is of this free and fine kind, and is thus covered with a tough and tangled matting of roots, it answers the purpose excellently.

The dray or drag plough was at one time, in a manner, universal, and there is no particular place where it can be said to be most in use at this time; for it is retained in some, and rejected in others, according to the sense and spirit of the farmers in adopting improvements. It is a very plain and simple kind; but notwithstanding the advantage the others have over it, on many occasions, this still excels them all for wet clays in the winter ploughings; for having the least workmanship of any, it is the least apt to clog, and having the fewest parts it is fittest for such ground, where nothing is required but going on, and turning up. It is limitted to this use; for on other soils, and at other seasons, it is very much inferior to the other kinds. This plough has no wheels, and it consists of a beam, handle, earth-board, and share, and is set higher or lower, as they find occasion, by wedges at the sheath.

In some counties they have a plough with one wheel; it is a very ill-contrived, and very inconvenient instrument. 'Tis broad in the breech, and therefore it draws very heavily. It is a clumsy and ill-contrived kind, that is growing out of use; and of all the ploughs that have been invented, is the least worth introducing any where.

The largest kind of plough used in England, or perhaps in any part of the world, is that which, in some parts of the county of Cambridge, they use for cutting of drains. This is of the shape of the common plough, and has no wheels: it is very bulky in all its parts, and has two coulters; one of these is fixed in the beam as usual, and the other in a piece of wood, fastened to the beam for that purpose; these both turn inwards, and cut each side of the trench. The share is very broad and flat, and cuts the bottom of the trench. The earth-board is three times as long as in other ploughs, and casts the earth a great way off the trench. This instrument cuts a trench a foot and a half wide at the top, a foot at the bottom, and a foot deep. It is excellent for this purpose on wet lands, saving a great deal of the expence of work in the common way of digging trenches by hand, but it requires a great number of horses to draw it. There is something in the contrivance of this plough, that may be useful farther than in the making of trenches, and it is for that reason proposed here to the farmer's consideration.

Of the uses of the common Plough, and their proper make.

Where there is a hard and firm soil; or where the land is full of flints, sharp stones, and gravel, no plough whatsoever does so well as the two-wheel'd kind, which may be suited to the occasion according to the directions already given, with respect to strength; and where strong clays are to be wrought in summer fallows, no other plough

plough is equal to it. The point of the common plough will fly out every ſtep on theſe occaſions, but this will anſwer very well when the earth is ſo baked and hardened by the ſun, that no other will penetrate. The wheels of this plough ſhould be about twenty inches in diameter, and it will always run beſt if the furrow wheel be made a little larger than the other.

A great advantage of this plough alſo is, that it will work upon uneven ground without levelling, ſo that none is equal to it for the ploughing up of paſtures, where there are mole-hills, and other irregularities. Theſe diſturb the other plough extremely, even the leaſt of them, but this goes through all.

Although the ſingle wheel plough be ſo clumſy and ill-contrived an implement, there is no reaſon why the uſe of a plough with one wheel ſhould be rejected. A very light and ſlender-made plough may be furniſhed with one wheel inſtead of two, and it will anſwer excellently on light ſandy ſoils. It will not be fit for harder work, but, running eaſily, it will ſerve this purpoſe better than any other.

The common two-wheel'd plough is to be drawn with horſes or oxen, two a-breaſt. The heavy plough without wheels, which is uſeful for wet clays, and other very heavy and diſagreeable work, is to be drawn by three, four, or five horſes in length. The great uſe of this is where the ground lies level, and where there are no obſtructions of roots, or the like, for theſe greatly diſturb its operation. The two-wheel plough is preferable in ſuch caſes, notwithſtanding all its inconveniences.

Whichever of theſe ploughs the huſbandman chuſes, let him take care, in the make of it, that it be ſuited to the ſoil upon which he is to uſe it. Let him ſee that it be made larger if it be for deep or ſtrong ſoils, and lighter and ſmaller if for the light and ſhallow ones. When the land is ſtiff and deep, let the coulter be long and ſtrong; in the deepeſt ſoils the coulter muſt go the deepeſt, becauſe the weeds root deepeſt there.

Of whatever form, or whatever degree of ſtrength, let him ſee that the iron work be made true as well as ſound; for on the exactneſs of this part of the inſtrument, depends the going of it true to the pitch at which it is ſet, and its keeping to the line wherein it is placed, without running out on one ſide or the other.

As ſo much depends upon the iron work, it is a very prudent method to have that made firſt, and wrought to a perfect truth, and then to have the wood work made to it: for in the common way of making the iron to the wood work, the Smith is often forced to work wrong in order to ſuit it: in this caſe no art will make the plough go well. Let him take care that the iron work is wrought ſmooth, and rightly tempered; and that it be kept bright and clean in the uſing.

The ſhorter and leſs the plough, the eaſier it is worked; but though this be a recommendation in light ſoils, there is no uſing of ſuch as have not a due weight and ſtrength in tough and heavy work.

Of the improvements of the common Plough.

The regard that has been ſhewn to huſbandry of late years has occaſioned ſeveral improvements of the plough, for particular and alſo for general purpoſes, and ſeveral new forms and kinds have been invented, ſome rather fanciful than advantageous, but others extremely uſeful. There is no part of huſbandry in which more improvement may be made, nor in any in which it will be ſo immediately or certainly uſeful.

A double plough has been invented ſome years ago, and is at this time in uſe in ſome places, by which a double quantity of land is ploughed at a time, one furrow by the ſide of another.— As this requires twice the number of horſes, the expence is nearly equal to the advantage: but this is a hint capable of improvement, for although in tough and deep ſoils it loſes its benefit, from the neceſſity of a double expence, yet certainly in ſome of thoſe light and ſhallow lands we have in Buckinghamſhire, and other places, a double plough might be ſo contrived, as to be drawn by two horſes, and managed by one man; and then certainly the advantage would be double, and the expence the ſame.

There has alſo been a contrivance of a plough that turned up two furrows at once one under another. But it is ſo ſo unwieldy, and difficult of draught, that in its preſent form it will never get into reputation, nor does it deſerve it; but we have ſeen already, what would be the advantage of ploughing deeper than ordinary, and that is enough to ſpirit up ſome who underſtand a little more of the mechanic arts to contrive one upon the ſame plan with more judgment. Doubtleſs it is poſſible to obtain this advantage of deep ploughing with much leſs trouble than attends it in the plough that has hitherto been contrived for that uſe.

We have obſerved, that the digging with the ſpade is a much finer and more excellent tillage than that with the plough; and that the reaſon why our gardens are more fertile than fields of the ſame ſoil and with the ſame manure is, that the ſpade digs deeper, and breaks the particles of earth finer.— Now a plough conſtructed upon this plan, with better judgment in the fabrick of it, would have both thoſe advantages: it would dig full as deep as the ſpade, and might be made to break the earth as much. It is ſurely worth the while of thoſe who have a knowledge in the proper arts, to devote ſome of their ſtudies to this improvement of the plough, which is doubtleſs the moſt uſeful engine in the world; and at preſent very deficient, even in its moſt improved ſtate. The adding breadth to the fin of the dray or foot plough, will at all times make it more and more ſerviceable in damp and ſtiff clayey lands; and in ploughing theſe, the horſes ſhould always go at length, that they may tread leſs of the ground: on the other hand, in light ſoils, the cattle, whether horſes or oxen, ſhould always go a-breaſt, for the double treading is ſerviceable to ſuch land, in the ſame manner with the treading of ſheep when they are folded upon it. In ſtony ground that has graſs of ſome ſtanding upon it, the plough ſhould have a round pointed ſhare, with a fin to cut the roots of the graſs, for the broad fin is apt to jump out of the ground.

In ground that has been wood and has roots remaining; or in other places where there are a great many large roots in the way, it is a very good method they uſe in ſome parts of Staffordſhire, of having an inſtrument of iron, with a ſharp edge, ſet through the beam of the plough, behind the coulter, and through the plough-head. This, at the ſame time that it arms the plough for cutting theſe roots aſunder, if rightly fixed, ſtrengthens the whole frame of it, and makes it able to bear the rough work there often is in theſe places, and which elſe would tear it to pieces: in other places thereabout, they uſe a couple of ſharp wings of iron made faſt to the plough-ſhare, which anſwers the ſame purpoſe, but does not ſo ſtrengthen the plough.

But theſe are all of them improvements, which rather ſhew what may be done, than execute it well in themſelves; they may be conſidered as hints to what is proper, rather than as compleat things: there remains one to be ſpoken of in which the improvement is very great, and is carried to a due degree of perfection; ſo that the farmer has no more to do than to order it to be made according to the deſcription.

This is the four-coultered plough, ſo highly and ſo juſtly extolled by the author of the Horſehoeing Huſbandry.

Of the Wheel Plough.

The foundation of this inſtrument is the common two-wheel'd plough, in its moſt improved condition, from which it differs in the having three additional coulters; ſo that inſtead of one there are four. We ſhall here conſider this wheel plough in its moſt improved ſtate; and hereafter deſcribe the four-coultered plough form'd upon it.

This plough conſiſts of two parts, diſtinguiſhed by the names of the plough-head, and plough-tail. The head has two wheels of about eighteen inches diameter, the ſpindle or axis of theſe is of iron, and paſſes through a box which ſtands croſswiſe of the beam. This ſpindle turns round both in the box and in the wheels. From this box riſe two perpendicular ſtaves, called crow ſtaves; theſe are faſtened into the box, and have each two rows of holes, by means of which the beam of the plough is raiſed or ſunk at pleaſure, in order to increaſe or diminiſh the depth of the furrow. This is done by pinning higher or lower a croſs piece, which is called the pillow, becauſe the plough beam reſts upon it. At the top of the two crow ſtaves is another croſs piece, called the gallows. The crow ſtaves paſs through this by mortiſes, and are pinned into it. From the box of the plough within the ſtaves, there is carried a ſmall frame compoſed of two legs, and a croſs top, to which the links of iron are fixed, by which the plough is drawn; this frame is called the wilds of the plough. In the middle of the box there alſo is a hole into which is let one end of an iron chain, the other end whereof is faſten'd to the middle of the beam, this is called the tow chain, and faſtens the head and tail of the plough together: at the end where it reaches the beam, this has a collar that goes round it, and is faſtened by a ſtake within ſide the box. This ſtake is held up to the left crow-ſtaff by a wyth, which paſſes round it above, and under the end of the gallows below: a piece of cord is ſometimes uſed inſtead of a wyth: any thing that may be tied will do. From the top of this ſtake goes an iron chain, called the bridle chain; this is faſten'd at one end to the top of the ſtake, and at the other to the middle of the beam of the plough, by a pin in the ſame place place where the collar of the tow chain paſſes round it.

This is the ſtructure of the head of the plough, and theſe are its ſeveral parts:

The tail conſiſts of the beam, which is a ſtout and long pole, through which, a little below the pin that holds the bridle chain, and the collar of the tow chain, there paſſes the coulter, a long and ſlender iron inſtrument, which running downward and a little forward, ends near the point of the ſhare. This coulter is fixed in its hole of the beam by a wedge, ſo that it can be raiſed or ſunk at pleaſure; behind are two handles, the one longer and the other ſhorter; the ſhorter of which meets the head of the fore ſheat, where it enters the beam, and is fixed by a pin, and faſtened to the top of the hinder ſheat by another pin. Theſe ſheats are two boards, the hinder one near the extremity of the beam; the other forwarder and more ſlanting, and are both faſtened to the ſhare, which runs flat below. On the other ſide of the plough tail deſcends another flat board, called the drock; to this the ground-wriſt is faſtened, which is a board running nearly parallel with a ſhare. The longer of the two handles is alſo faſtened to the drock, and the earth-board riſes at its bottom. The fore-ſheat is ſupported by a double retch, which paſſes through the beam, and is faſtened by ſcrews and nuts.

This is the four-wheel plough as uſed at preſent in the places where agriculture is moſt underſtood, and beſt practiſed: we ſee it conſiſts of more parts than the two wheeled plough of Hertfordſhire, according to the firſt invention, but there is not one of theſe added parts but is an advantage in either ſtrength or convenience.

Of the four-coulter'd Plough.

The beam of the common two-wheel plough, is uſually eight foot long; the proper length of the beam of the four-coulter'd plough, is ten feet four inches. The beam of the common kind is ſtrait all the way, but that of the four-coultered plough riſes with a bend when it comes toward the wheels, to where it reſts upon the pillow. The beam, ſuppoſing the plough to ſtand upon a level ſurface, would be at the end of the plough-tail only eleven inches and a half from the ground: at the place where the bend begins, which is a little before the firſt coulter, it will be one foot eight inches and a half; and where the beam bears upon the pillow, two feet ten inches. This is the proper make of the beam of the four-coulter'd plough.

The four coulters are thus diſpoſed, meaſuring from the tail or extream end of the beam behind. From this extremity to the back of the firſt coulter, is three feet two inches; this coulter has its point near the ſhare: from the back of the firſt, to the back of the next coulter, is thirteen inches; from thence to the third thirteen inches, and from thence to the fourth the ſame. So that from the end of the beam behind, to the place where it begins to bend upwards, which is a little before the fourth coulter, counting from the tail, is ſeven feet. The length of the additional coulters, particularly of the fourth, or that next the head of the plough, would be a great inconvenience in this machine, but that is prevented by the bending of the beam toward the head. If the beam were ſtraight as in other ploughs, theſe coulters muſt be very long to reach the ground, and they would

would require to be very ſtrong, not to bend, and this would make them expenſive and cumberſome; and at the ſame time their length, if ever ſo well formed, would make them apt to looſen the wedges wherewith they are fixed in the holes. This would make the coulter riſe up out of its work, but by this contrivance of a crooked beam, a moderate length in the coulters ſerve; they do not require any great thickneſs or quantity of iron, and they always work with regularity.

As to the materials, the beam may be made of aſh or oak, according to the nature of the ground whereon it is to be employed; for aſh has the advantage of being light, but the oak is vaſtly ſtronger; ſo that when the work will be very hard, the oak, in ſpite of its weight, is preferable. As to its breadth and thickneſs, they may alſo vary according to the ſoil that is to be tilled; but for moderate ground, the beam at the firſt coulter hole ſhould be five inches deep and four broad.

Giving this as a middling proportion, the ſize of the other parts may be as follows. The fore ſheat, commonly called ſimply the ſheat, ſhould be ſeven inches broad; the retch upon it muſt be of iron, and its left leg muſt ſtand foremoſt, that the edge of its forepart, which is flat, may fit cloſe to the wood of the ſheat. The uſe of this retch is to hold the ſheat up to the beam, which it does by means of nuts and ſcrews. Through the top part of the ſheat there is alſo to be a hole, which is to be a ſmall part within the beam, ſo that a pin being driven into the hole, draws up the ſheat very cloſe to the beam. The elevation of this ſheat is a very great article in the management of every wheel plough. If this make an angle of more than five and forty degrees with the plain ſurface whereon the plough ſtands, that inſtrument will never go well. In the four-coulter plough it ought to make an angle of forty-two or forty-three degrees only.

This ſort of expreſſion will be very well underſtood by thoſe who are uſed to mechanics; but for the ſake of the common farmer, we ſhall ſay all that is meant by it is, that the ſheat is to be a little leſs raiſed in this than it is in a well-going common wheel plough.

The length of the ſhare from the point to the tail, ſhould be three feet nine inches. The fin of the ſhare riſing ſlanting from the point upwards. The point of the ſhare ſhould be three inches and a half long, flat underneath, and round at the top, and this ſhould be of hard ſteel underneath. The edges of the fin alſo ſhould be well ſteeled, and its length proportioned to the nature of the ground.

Behind the fin is placed the ſocket, into which the bottom of the ſheat, before deſcribed, enters; and from the tail of the ſhare is to riſe a ſmall plate of iron, this is to be well rivetted to the ſhare: by this the tail of the ſhare is faſtened to the hinder ſheat. This faſtening is done by an iron pin, with a ſcrew at the end, to which a nut is to be ſcrewed on the inner ſide of the ſheat.

The ſocket is to be a mortiſe of about a foot long, at the upper part two inches deep, and the fore end muſt not be perpendicular, but made ſlanting, conformable to the fore part of the ſheat that enters into it. The upper edge of the fore part of the mortiſe muſt bear againſt the ſheat; and if it be not quite ſo ſlanting as the ſheat, a little of the wood is to be pared off at the edge to make it fit.

The upper ſide of the ſhare ſhould be perfectly ſtrait, but its neck on the under ſide ſhould ſtand a little hollow from the ground. This hollowneſs ſhould be about half an inch in a common plough, but in the four-coultered plough it ſhould not be above a quarter of an inch. So that the ſhare, when it is firſt made ſtanding upon its bottom, bears upon the level ſurface only in three places; theſe are the point, the tail, and the corner of the fin. The hollowneſs of the fin muſt be greater in a ſtony ſoil than in others.

The placing of the ſhare rightly upon the ſheat is the moſt important, and the moſt difficult part of the Ploughright's trade: on this depends the well going of the plough, and for this reaſon; as it is more important in the four coultered plough than in any other, we adviſe the farmer when he has made himſelf a maſter by theſe deſcriptions of the form and ſtructure of this plough, to take care that he employ a ſkilful and an honeſt workman; and if he do not find the plough go well when made,

made, to look there for the occasion of the fault, for in that part is generally the seat of it.

The groundwrist is to be of iron, its length must be two feet five inches, its breadth at the longest end four inches, and is to go somewhat smaller all the way. Its thickness in general is to be three-eighths of an inch; but at the smaller end it is to be much thinner, that it may be capable of bending so, that it can be brought close to the share.

At the smaller end of the groundwrist are to be four holes, through one of which there goes a nail that fastens the groundwrist to the sheat. This passes through a long hole which is made in the side of the socket of the share. The space between the outside of the groundwrist, to the outside of the share, is eleven inches and a half, and this is the width of the lower part of the plough-tail at the ground: at the upper side of the broad end of the groundwrist there are also several holes by which it is nailed to the lower part of the drock; this is long, narrow, and has three holes for the reception of its fastenings.

The earth board has a rising near its end, which takes hold of the end of the sheat to fasten it the more firmly; and near that are two holes by which it is fixed to the sheat; at the other end also there is a hole, by which it is fastened to the drock.

The pin which fastens the earth board to the drock, is to be thicker in the middle than at the end, and this prevents the earth board from coming near the drock. By means of this pin the earth board is also set at a greater or smaller distance from the drock, as there is occasion sometimes to throw off the furrow farther from the plough than at others. It always stands a good deal farther out on the right hand than the groundwrist, and this is one reason why the drock is made crooked, bending outwards in that part.

The long handle of the plough is to be five feet four inches in length, and four inches broad in the widest part. It is to have holes in its lower part for pinning it to the sheat, and another near its upper end, by which it is fastened to the drock.

The length of the short handle is three feet nine inches, and it is to have two holes, both toward its lower end: by the upper hole it is pinned to the hinder sheat, and by the lower to the top of the fore sheat above the beam of the plough.

We come now to describe the placing of the four coulters in the beam of this plough, contrived for their reception; this is the most important article of all: and the greatest point to be obtained is, that the four imaginary planes, described by the edges of the four coulters, as the plough moves forward, be all parallel, or nearly so, for if this be not regarded, they will not enter the ground together.

To make sure of this important point, the holes for the coulters must be made in the beam of the plough in the following manner. The first coulter is to be placed as already directed, the second coulter hole is to be made two inches and a half more on the right hand than the first: the third two inches and a half more on the right hand than the second; and the fourth two inches and a half more on the right hand than the third. This will place the four coulters conformable to the four cuts they are to make in a ten-inch furrow.

Now no beam of a plough is broad enough to hold these holes in this direction, and for that reason a piece of wood is added to the beam of the four-coultered plough to give space for it. This piece is to be very well fastened to the beam, and the second hole is to be made, as will be seen, according to the distance, partly in the piece, and partly in the beam; and the others will be all made entirely in the piece. The piece is best fastened by three good screws with their nuts, and its place is on the right side of the beam. The distance of each hole to the right of the last, must be measured from the middle of one hole to the middle of the other.

The fore part of every hole must incline a little to the left, so that the backs of the coulters may not bear against the left side of the incisions made by the edges. Each hole is to be a mortise of an inch and quarter wide, with its two opposite sides parallel from top to bottom. The length at the top is three inches and a half, and

and at the bottom three inches; and the back of each is not perpendicular, but flanting, and makes the coulter ftand flanting. It is fixed in this mortife by a pole wedge in the fame manner as the coulter is in other ploughs.

The coulter is a kind of iron knife, confifting of two parts; a handle, and blade; the latter having an edge.—— The length of the coulter is to be two feet eight inches, but it will fhorten in wearing; the blade is to be fixteen inches long, with its edge running all the way along it; the handle is to be of the fame length. This is fo long that it will at firft very well ftand up above the beam, but it muft be driven down lower and lower, as the point fhortens by wearing. The handle is to be an inch and feven-eighths broad, and feven-eighths of an inch thick throughout.

The firft coulter in all ploughs fhould be fo placed, that its back fhould bear againft the back of the hole; its right fide above to bear againft the upper edge of the hole, and its left fide to bear againft the lower edge: and for this reafon there always are required at leaft three wedges to hold a coulter in its place. The pole wedge ftands before it, the other two, one on the left fide above, and the other on the right fide underneath: and the hole muft be fo made, that the coulter ftanding thus acrofs it, its point may incline two inches and a half or more toward the left than the point of the fhare, if it were driven down as low as it: but it fhould never be fo low in any plough whatfoever. As to its bearing forwards, the point of the coulter fhould never be before the middle of the point of the fhare. It muft be fet obliquely with refpect to the fhare, and it muft never be fet much more flanting; for if it fhould, it would have greater force to raife up the pole wedge, and would be continually getting loofe.

In the four coultered plough, the three other coulters are to ftand in the fame pofture with this in refpect of the inclination of their points to the left: this is a great advantage to them; for by that means when the fin is raifed up by turning the handles toward the left, their points do not rife out of the ground on the right hand as they otherwife would. With refpect to their pointing forwards, experience fhews, that every one of the three fhould be fet a little more perpendicular than the next behind it; fo that the fourth coulter will ftand neareft to perpendicular of any of them.

None of thefe coulters ought to defcend fo low as the bottom of the fhare, unlefs when the ploughing is very fhallow. It is always fufficient that they cut through the turf, however deep the plough go into the ground.

When the ploughing is to be very fhallow, the fin of the fhare fhould be broad enough to cut off the fourth piece of the furrow.

The nut which ferves for faftening the piece to the beam of the plough, fhould have two oppofite corners turn'd up, by which it may be driven round with a hammer. This has fo great a force, that three of thefe will hold the beam and the piece as firmly together, as if they were one bit of wood. In dry weather the wood will fhrink, and then the nuts are to be driven farther on. The fame caution muft be obferved in other parts of the plough.— Between the nut and the wood there fhould be a thin piece of iron by way of bolfter: this prevents the nut from wearing into the wood; it muft be fomething larger than the nut, and of the thicknefs of a fhilling. Some ufe a piece of leather, but when the nut is to be often fcrewed, iron is much better.

There muft alfo be iron plates upon all the coulter holes, both above and below. Thefe muft be nailed on with nails made for that purpofe.

Inftead of a collar moving round the beam, 'tis much better to have a fquare one with an open end, which fhall faften to it by a couple of crooks.— Thefe muft turn upwards, that they may not lay hold of any thing that fhall be turned up under the plough: the front or clofe-end of this collar is to be a ftrong iron bar, with feveral notches. Two pins are to be driven into the beam of the plough, juft behind the fecond coulter hole, one on each fide: and there is to be another crook, called a (C) from its fhape, which is to go over the clofe end of the collar. Each end of this is a hook, and one of thefe lays hold of the crofs bar of the collar, going into one of its notches; and

and to the other is fixed a link, which holds the tow chain to the collar.

The use of these notches, and this fix'd position of the collar is this; that as the share wears at the point, it always inclines a little to the right; and this is remedied by removing the crook into another notch of the cross bar of the collar, so that the point of the share is thus always kept in a proper direction. The length of each side bar of the collar should be a foot.

We have shewn that the tow chain of the plough is fastened within the box by a staff passed through its first link, as the hook of the collar holds its last. This stake is commonly nailed, to prevent its flying out of its place. And when the plough is to be drawn a little nearer the crow staves, the method is to take in another link of this chain, passing through the stake, and fastening it as before: or it may be done better by taking hold of the crook of the collar, with a second or third link of the chain. This shortening of the chain always draws the point of the share a little to the left.

For drawing of the plough there is fastened to the box an iron machine, called the wilds; this is very like the square collar, only its legs are longer. The cross bar at the top is notched as that of the square collar, but only one leg of the wilds is fixed to this square bar in the making; the other leg is loose, and has a loop through which the other end of the cross bar is put, so that it is fixed on at pleasure. Both these legs of the wilds pass through the box of the plough, and are fastened in behind it by a couple of hooked pins made for that purpose. The holes cut through the box for letting these legs pass, are to be made slanting upwards, so that the fore part of the wilds may be higher than the hinder; otherwise the upper end of the crow staves will lean quite back when the plough is drawn. The use of the notches in the bar of the wilds, is to give the plough a broader or a narrower furrow. A double crook with a link is fixed to this bar, and by this the horses draw. If the cattle are tall, the traces must be long, else they will be apt to raise the wheels off the ground, and overturn the plough.

The legs of the wilds should be eight inches and a half asunder, and their length nineteen inches: the links are to be six inches and a half long. They are to be put into two notches distant from one another, or else one wheel of the plough will advance before the other. When they are moved to the notches on the right hand, it brings the wheels toward the left hand, which gives the greater furrow; and, on the contrary, when they are moved on the notches on the left hand, it gives the plough a less furrow, by bringing the wheels towards the right.

The height of the wheels we have mentioned already, as also the proper method of making one of them higher than the other: their distance should be two feet five inches and a half, as set from one another on the ground.— The crow staves should be one foot eleven inches high from the box of the plough to the gallows that goes across them: these are to stand upright upon the box, and they should be ten inches and a half asunder.

The pillow which crosses the staves below the gallows, is to be pinned up at its end by two small iron pins, and it is convenient to keep these chained to it, that if they chance to drop, they may not be lost.

The height from the ground to the hole in the box where the tow chain passes through, is to be thirteen inches. This brings it to two inches below the holes of the wilds, on the hinder side of the box.

The height of the plough at the place where the other end of the tow chain is fastened to the beam, should be twenty inches from the level ground; and about the middle of the tow chain there should be a swivel, that one end of the chain may turn without the other.

This is the construction of the four coultered plough; and as it is founded upon the two wheeled plough improved to the greatest perfection, the parts of that plough can never be so well understood as in the description here given for their perfect and exact construction. It is very necessary that he who would undertake to make, or to give orders for the making of a four coultered plough, should first thoroughly understand the construction, parts, and composition of a perfect one with a single coulter; and we have by this means

means avoided the repetition of a long and dry detail of the parts.

We have before ſhewn what was the firſt conſtruction of the wheel plough, which was a vaſt improvement upon the inſtruments in huſbandry of that time; and we have here explained its farther advances toward that perfection, which it may be juſtly ſaid to have attained in the four coultered kind.

When the four coultered is made, let it be tried with the ſingle coulter before the others are put on. There may be a fault in the work that cannot be diſcovered, even by a judicious eye, till it is tried; and this may prevent its going as it ought. That plough which will not go well with one coulter, certainly would not with four; but it would be very unjuſt to charge upon the number of the coulters, what is really the fault of ſome part of the ſtructure of the inſtrument itſelf, independent of that addition.

If the plough goes well with one coulter, then put in the other three; there is not much fear but it will alſo go well with them. If it do not, then let the poſition of the three additional coulters be examined; and let it be ſeen in what that differs from the rule, laid down here for that purpoſe. That it differs in ſomething need not be doubted; for of a certainty, if they be rightly diſpoſed according to theſe directions, the plough will go well.

To know whether a plough goes well, examine the furrow: if that be of an equal depth on the right hand and on the left; and if the plough turns it off fairly, it is right. If in the going of the plough, the tail of the ſhare, and the bottom of the drock bear againſt the bottom of the furrow; and if it goes eaſy in the hand of the holder, without preſſing one arm more than the other, the farmer may be aſſured it is a good one. Such a plough will go with four coulters as well as one.

Of the management of a Plough in working.

When the farmer has got his plough well made, let him ſee that he keep it in order; and that he employ a man in the working, who is able to manage it as he ought, and who has honeſty enough to take the neceſſary care and pains. The farmer depends more upon the integrity and knowledge of his ploughman, than on the qualities of any other ſervant whatſoever.

The handles of the plough being made of that length we have ordered, are very uſeful for the proper guiding of that inſtrument; but often the ploughman will cut them ſhorter to favour his idleneſs. When they are ſhortened, he can bear his whole weight upon them, and in a manner ride inſtead of walking. If he ſhould play this idle trick with long handles, his weight would tilt up the fore end of the beam, and raiſe the ſhare out of the ground. The keeping the arms long therefore prevents this negligent trick, and at the ſame time gives him an opportunity of managing the plough to the greateſt advantage.

An awkward ploughman will be continually overſetting the two wheel'd plough; but a careful perſon, who is uſed to the management of it, hardly ever meets with ſuch an accident.— The great danger of over-turning is, at the going out at the land's end, from one furrow to another. But the ſkilful ploughman lifts his plough a little round, and then holds up the crowſtaves with the end of the beam, by preſſing his hand hard againſt the handle, while the plough lies down on one ſide, till the horſes, the wheels, and the body of the plough come nearly to a line in the beginning of the furrow; and then he lifts up the plough and goes on.

Theſe little contrivances are exceedingly uſeful. They are more eaſily ſeen in the practice, than taught by words; but what is here ſaid may ſerve to let the farmer know when his ploughman manages his buſineſs right, and when he does not; and may aſſiſt him in the giving one that is willing directions.

In the four coultered plough there is another inconvenience very likely to happen, but very eaſily remedied: this is, that ſometimes the firſt or left furrow is apt to come through betwixt the firſt coulter and the ſheat, and in this caſe it falls upon the left hand ſide of the plough.

This, though not of the conſequence of many other faults, yet it is worth preventing, and the more as the remedy is eaſy. To this purpoſe let the ſecond coulter ſtand a little higher than

the

the third; and then the second furrow holding the first at its bottom, will carry it over together with itself, and throw it on the right side of the earth-board.

Let us give the farmer one caution farther in this matter; which is, that in this placing the coulter, he never sets it so high that it does not cut the turf through. As to the first coulter, though it should cut but an inch or two within the ground, the share will break off the first furrow in raising it up.

If in the ploughing with this four coultered kind, the coulters become clogged and loaded with pieces of the turf, a boy should go by the side with a forked stick to clean them off from time to time, which is done very easily,

The coulters being disposed exactly as we have described, will have more space between them above than below, so that this clogging will not happen often, and when it does, the cleansing is easily performed. The farmer may always know when he shall have occasion for a boy to follow for this purpose, because it rises not from the fault of the plough, but the nature of the ground. This plough in clear ground goes as free and clean as any; but when there is a great quantity of couch grass on the land, its roots hold the turf together in such a manner, that it rises in pieces, and hangs between. This is the only occasion on which there is a need of such assistance; but if it be not taken care of, the load of clogging matter will fill the spaces between the coulters, and raise up the plough out of its work.

In the common two wheel plough there is a very great inconvenience too frequent, and of very bad consequence, this is, the leaving a great part of the land unturned from the share's point going too much to the left. The consequence of this is, that the work is done irregularly, and often a great part of the ground which is covered by the broken earth, is whole and untouched, and the weeds are found afterwards growing upon it. This is a great fault: it defrauds the farmer of so much of the business he engaged should be done; and there is nothing he ought to look into so carefully.

Sometimes he will find it happen from the imperfection of the plough itself, and then he is to apply to the maker. The well going of a plough principally depends in the placing of the share rightly upon the sheat; and in this case the remedy must be by an amendment in that article. This is the nicest and most difficult part of the ploughwright's business, and is what the farmer is most concerned of all other to see done well: it matters not that the maker can tell him, or shew him it is right as it stands upon the ground, let him try it in some work, and never be satisfied with it till it answers his expectation.

This fault last named, though it sometimes be owing to the make of the plough, yet may also arise only from the folly of the ploughman's setting it wrong: therefore this should be tried first. His fault is the setting it so that the point of the share turns too much to the left: in this case it will always cut crossly, and leave a part of the ground untouched, though covered by that which has been cut, and is thrown over it.

There is no part of his business which the farmer is more under a necessity of following with his own eye than this. His interest is engaged in the well executing of it, though the servants' are not. It is easy to plough too shallow, or too deep. Where there is a full soil, the deeper the plough cuts the better; but where the soil is shallow, and the bottom bad, let there be great care taken that the clay, or whatever other bad matter it may be, shall not be turned up with the soil. He should himself oversee this that his ploughing may give him all the advantage, and avoid all the disadvantage there is in the condition and nature of the ground.

Some choice is to be made in regard to the situation, in the manner, and course of the work. When a land lies upon the descent of a hill, let it never be ploughed strait up and down, but crosswise. This has a double advantage: for the horses are not tired, as they would be with going strait up and down, and the land also will fare a great deal the better.

Of laying Land in ridges.

A great article in the rendering of land

fertile, is the breaking and dividing it into small particles, whether this be done mechanically by the plough, or by fermentation given to it by manures; that this breaking of the soil into small particles is essential to the free growth of plants is very plain, because it is from the smallest particles of this matter that they are nourished, and the breaking of the land in this manner is the only method of giving the roots a free passage between them, in their search of this nourishment.

On this depends the famous system of Horse-hoeing Husbandry. But beside these two articles, of liberty of spreading the roots, and a proper quantity of nourishment, there are two other, without which plants cannot thrive, these are, a due degree of heat and moisture.

Corn, and the other common produce of our ploughed land, demand a moderate degree of each of these, and the farmer is to guide his practice throughout in such manner, as to give them a supply without giving them abundance. It will be asked, can the farmer cause sunshine, or can he call down rain? Neither: nor do we expect impossibilities of him; nothing is more easy than what we require him to do, and the effect shews that it will succeed.

But as he is to communicate to his crop all good, so far as he is able, so he is to defend it from all ill: and as we have shewn how he may give the advantage, it remains that we shew how he may prevent the hurt.

Now one of the greatest misfortunes that can attend a crop is too much wet. This sometimes happens from the particularity of a season; but oftner from the nature of the land. When the first is the case, the farmer's care must be to find methods of carrying the wet off; when the latter, he must employ all his care to provide against it. Land that is too wet will never produce corn well, and to prevent the mischief attending this condition of the ground, has been invented the practice of which we now treat, the laying land in ridges.

This is a particular sort of tillage, and its effect is greater than those seem to understand who employ it. They use it only to keep their lands from being too wet, but it has an effect in regard to the degree of heat, not less than with respect to that of moisture.

We shall see, upon examining this practice and its effects, how well nature has taught people to use it. We see them in the moderate soils that are frequent in Buckinghamshire, and elsewhere, frequently lay four ridges together: in Kent they often lay six, and the lower parts of Essex eight, and in Huntingdonshire, upon their wet and stiff clays, they sow all upon broad lands, raising the middle of the ridges in some places two foot and a half higher than the side furrows. This at once exposes those tough and clammy soils to the sun better than any other method, and drains them of the abundant wet.

The chief design of laying land in ridges is draining of it, and making the corn grow properly dry: but we see that by a proper management it may be made to extend its benefits farther. In this case, of a clayey soil laid in ridges open to the east and west, where the situation is such as to allow it without other damage, the sun acts in a double way upon the soil, not only giving it warmth, when the abundant cold moisture is taken away, but by a gentle calcination of the surface, it reduces that superficial part to a state of greater perfection, and to a kind of manure for the rest.

The natural defects of many lands, otherwise useful and good, are a too great degree of moisture, and a defect of heat. The latter naturally arises from the former; for a quantity of water detained among clay, or any other tough earth, becomes cold, and chills the plants that are laid upon it. The great remedy, in this case, is the laying the land in ridges; and that the careful husbandman may be sure to know when this is required, as well as how to do it, we shall give him the following hints.

The two principal kinds of land, that are liable to be chilled by wet, are those on hills, where there is a bed of clay under the mould; and those in level grounds, which consist of a very deep and very stiff soil.

The occasion of the mischief in these is very obvious, the rains fall upon this ground, and, soaking through the mould

mould, are detained by the clay.—— They cannot enter the clay, and therefore they ſpread themſelves among the mould above; and the mould below ſtopping it in its deſcent, and more water falling above, the whole approaches to the nature of a bog; the ground being ſoft, pappy, and raiſed above the natural level by the water ſpread among it.

When this is the caſe in a very great degree, no method of ploughing can be ſufficiently effectual to remedy it. In this caſe, trenches muſt be cut acroſs with a deſcent, to carry the water off. And they may be filled up with rough ſtones, and covered over with earth again, ſo that all may be wrought as a level ſurface: Reaſon points out this remedy, but it is often too expenſive; and ſuch lands, when too wet and too difficult of remedy, are to be neglected; we therefore have named theſe only to ſhew, that they are not to be attempted by ridging; for nothing diſheartens a huſbandman ſo much, as undertaking what he afterwards finds cannot be done.

When the wet is in a conſiderably large degree, it may be diſcharged by laying the land properly in ridges, tho' not where it is thus very abundant; therefore let the farmer firſt examine carefully, whether the ſtate of the ground will or will not admit a cure; if he thinks it will, this is the manner in which he is to ſet about it:

Let him plough the land in ridges, almoſt croſs-wiſe of the hill, but a little ſlanting; for if they be perfectly carried acroſs, or quite ſtrait down, they will neither way do. When they are thus carried croſs-wiſe, but a little diagonally, their parting furrows lying open, will each ſerve as a drain to the ridge next below it: for when the plough has made the bottom of theſe nearly horizontal furrows a few inches deeper than the ſurface of the clay, the water will naturally and ſecurely run to their ends, without riſing into the mould, provided no part of the furrows be lower than their ends.

Theſe parting furrows and their ridges ſhould always be made a little obliquely; and this obliquity, or ſlanting, ſhould be more or leſs, according to the form and declivity of the hill.

We are to conſider that there are two ways, in which water that falls upon an hill runs off. The one is on the ſurface, and the other is between the mould that makes the ſoil, and the clay that makes the bed under it.—— 'Tis this ſecond courſe, or the running of the water upon the bed of clay, and under the mould, that we are to conſider on theſe occaſions; for on that depends the damage we propoſe to rectify. This is the ſource of what we have directed, as to the diſpoſition of the ridges; and it will be found, on the moſt careful examination, that as only this method of ridging could keep that part of the ſoil dry, ſo there is no direction in which they could run, that will ſo well ſecure the advantage, as the carrying them with this ſlant croſs-wiſe of the hill.

In this caſe the conſideration of laying the ridges eaſt and weſt, muſt give way to this croſs direction, with reſpect to the deſcent of the hill. We have mentioned, under that head, that there were exceptions; this is the principal; and in this, as in all other caſes, the greater convenience is to be conſulted, and the leſſer is to give place to it.

The farmer who ſhall make himſelf perfect maſter of his buſineſs, will often find two things would be right, both of which together are impracticable: he muſt, in this caſe, content himſelf with taking the beſt.

The way of working on this occaſion is to plough the ridges in paces, without throwing any earth into the trenches. In this caſe, the ridges will be plain at the top; and the rain water will ſpeedily run downward to the next trench, and thence to the head land, and ſo out of the field.

Theſe are eaſy and plain directions, and the ſucceſs of them is certain; it not only is plain to reaſon, but is vouched by experience; and yet a great deal of land that might be ſaved by it, is left to produce little or nothing by the common treatment.

Wet land, that lies level, is the ſecond kind of land that is liable to be wet and cold, and that may be greatly mended by the tillage in ridges.—— Sometimes there are ſprings on the hills, that add to the quantity of water which they have from rains, and this makes the cure more difficult: in theſe deep, wet, and ſtiff ſoils that lie on a level,

level, the cauſe is always to be found in the water that falls by rain alone. But this will ſometimes put the land into as bad a condition as if there were ſprings in many places.

When a deep ſtiff ſoil lies flat, and is ploughed ſometimes one way, and ſometimes another by croſs ploughing, it will hold water a long time. By that misfortune the plough is kept out two or three weeks longer than if it were in round ridges. Sometimes its flatneſs keeps it from drying, till the ſeaſon of ploughing and ſowing too are loſt.

The farmers are backward in ploughing the hilly wet grounds in ridges, and more in this. They ſay it prevents the benefit of croſs ploughing, which they count as a great advantage, and they think they loſe a part of their ground by the open furrows, which they otherwiſe fill up with harrows. But theſe are miſtakes and prejudices, of which it becomes us to ſet the practical farmer right; for on ſuch notions, which he receives upon credit, without being at the pains of examining whether they be true or falſe, depend the greateſt part of his diſappointments and loſſes. Croſs ploughing is ſometimes a hurt as well as a benefit to land: this is certain, and any one who is accuſtomed to farming, and will examine what he from time to time ſees, inſtead of taking all things upon truſt, will find it ſo in experience. This, therefore, is an objection ariſing only from prejudice in favour of common practice, and common opinion: the other is entirely an error; for, inſtead of loſing any ground by ridges, it is poſſible to gain ſome. In the moſt ſimple and common practice, none is loſt; and managing wiſely and properly, much may be gained.

Ground is gained for the farmer's purpoſe, when its ſurface is increaſed, and is capable of bearing more corn; and this is plainly practicable in the ploughing in ridges. If in this cuſtom of ploughing, we allow two feet in ſixteen for an empty furrow, ſtill the difference of ſurface between the reſt as it lay flat, and as it is ploughed into ridges, is much greater in his favour, than this proportion is in loſs of quantity. All the ſurface thus raiſed in ridges, is capable of bearing corn, and therefore it is ſo much ground gained to the huſbandman.

It is certain, the ſurface of a field meaſures more in quantity when in ridges, than when flat; and it is equally certain, that all its ſurface, the empty furrows excepted, is capable of bearing corn. This is a ſhort ſtate of the caſe. Theſe empty furrows have been taken into the computation, and the difference is in favour of the land in ridges. No ſophiſtry can get the better of ſo plain a fact; and it is upon this fact, and the evident advantage that wet and cold lands receive from this kind of tillage, that we recommend to the farmer the tilling his ſtiff, cold, moiſt, and flat lands, in this method of ploughing in ridges.

PLUM-TREE, (*Prunus.*) The varieties of the fruit are,

White Primordian, or Jean Hative Plum.——A ſmalliſh, oblong, yellow Plum, with a white bloom; ripe the middle or end of July.

Morocco, or early black Damaſk Plum. A middle-ſized, round, blackiſh fruit, powdered with blue, is well flavoured, and diſcharges the ſtone; ripe end of July.

Little Damaſk Plum.—A ſmall, round, black, well-flavoured plum; ripe beginning of Auguſt.

Great Damaſk Violet Plum.—A moderately large, roundiſh-oval, dark-blue Plum, covered with a violet bloom, is of a rich juicy flavour, and quits the ſtone; ripe in Auguſt.

Queen Claudia Plum, ſometimes called Green-Gage.—A middle-ſized, round, yellowiſh-green Plum, having a firm deep-green pulp, of a fine rich flavour, and quits the ſtone; ripe in September.

Little Queen Claudia Plum.—A ſmall, round, whitiſh-yellow Plum, powdered with white, and parts from the ſtone; ripe end of Auguſt and beginning of September.

Green-Gage Plum.—A middle-ſized, roundiſh, green Plum, ſometimes purpliſh on the ſunny ſide, having a yellowiſh-green firm pulp, of a moſt delicious rich flavour, but does not diſcharge the ſtone freely; is one of our moſt valuable plums, and the tree a great bearer; ripe the end of Auguſt and beginning of September.

Varities.] There are ſeveral varieties of greeniſh Plums, that go by the name of Green-Gages, that are of inferior quality.

Blue Gage Plum.——A middle-size, roundish, blueish Plum, of a rich flavour; ripe beginning or middle of September.

Orleans Plum.——A middle-sized, round, pale-red Plum, often of a whitish-green colour on the side away from the sun; is of but a middling flavour, and quits the stone clean. The tree is of spreading growth, a remarkably great bearer, and very profitable for common use, and for those who supply the markets; ripe end of August and beginning of September.

Drap d'Or, or Cloth of Gold Plum.—A middle-sized, roundish, bright-yellow Plum, spotted with red, of an excellent vinous flavour, and adheres to the stone; ripe beginning or middle of September.

Black Perdigron Plum.——A middle-sized, oval, dark-coloured Plum, powdered with a violet bloom; is of a fine rich flavour; ripe middle or end of August.

Blue Perdigron Plum.—A large, roundish, blueish-coloured Plum, replete with a delicious juice; ripe end of August.

White Perdigron Plum.——A middle-sized, oblong, whitish-yellow fruit, covered with a white bloom; is firm, juicy, rich, and quits the stone; ripe end of August and beginning of September.

Roche Courbon, or Red Diaper Plum.—A middle-size, round, fine red Plum, powdered with a violet bloom, is high flavoured, and adheres to the stone; ripe end of August.

Red Imperial Plum.—A large, oblong-oval, flattish, pale-red Plum, covered with a whitish bloom; is of but a middling relish, and parts from the stone; ripe middle of September.

White Bonum Magnum, Mogul or Egg Plum.—A remarkably large, oblong, egg-shaped, whitish yellow Plum, powdered with a white bloom, having a firm pulp that cleaves to the stone; more esteemed for culinary use, than eating raw: the tree shoots strong, with very large leaves; is a great bearer, and the fruit is the largest of the plum kind; ripe beginning or middle of September.

Red Bonum Magnum, sometimes called the Great Imperial Plum.—A very large oblong, deep-red Plum; not of a rich flavour, but is excellent for preserving and culinary purposes; ripe beginning or middle of September.

Fotheringham Plum.—A large, oblong, fine-red plum, having a fine rich pulp, that quits the stone; ripe end of August and beginning of September.

Brignole Plum.—A largish, oval, yellowish plum, tinged with red next the sun, having a firm, dry, rich pulp, is in much estimation for sweetmeats; ripe in September.

Le Royal Plum.—A large, roundish, light-red, finely-powdered plum, having a juicy sugary pulp, that cleaves to the stone; ripe end of August and in September.

Cheston Plum.—A middle-sized, oval, blackish-blue Plum, powdered with a violet bloom; ripe towards the middle of September.

Wentworth Plum.—A large, oval, yellowish plum, of an acid relish, and separates from the stone; is a good culinary fruit; ripe in September.

Mirabelle Plum.—A small, round, greenish-yellow plum, having a rich pulp, that discharges the stone, and the tree a great bearer; ripe end of August.

Apricot Plum.—A large, round, yellowish plum, having a firm, dry, sweet pulp, that separates from the stone; ripe beginning or middle of September.

St. Catharine Plum.—A large, oblong, oval, yellowish-amber-coloured plum, powdered with a white bloom, having a rich juicy agreeable pulp, adhering close to the stone: ripe end of September.

Imperatrice Plum.——A middle-sized, roundish, dark-red, finely-powdered plum, of an agreeable flavour, the pulp adhering to the stone; ripe beginning of October.

Little Green Damask Plum.—A small, round, greenish Plum, powdered with a whitish bloom, having a green very agreeable pulp, adhering to the stone; ripe middle or end of September.

Pear Plum.—A moderate-size, oval, whitish-yellow plum, of an inferior flavour, esteemed principally for preserving; ripe late in September.

Muscle

Muscle Plum.—A smallish, oblong, flat, dark-red plum, but of an indifferent relish; ripe in September.

Damascene Plum.—A small, roundish, dark-blue plum, of a tolerably agreeable acid relish, both for eating and culinary purposes, and the tree a great bearer; ripe in September.

St. Julian Plum.—A small, round, dark-violet-coloured fruit, covered with a mealy powder, but has little relish; ripe end of September.

Cherry Plum.—A very small, round, cherry-shaped red plum, valued chiefly as a curiosity; and the tree is often planted among flowering shrubs, for the sake of its beautiful bloom in spring, and its cherry-like fruit exhibit a pretty variety in summer; though by its flowering very early, the bloom is often cut off, and seldom succeeded by much fruit.

Thus far is principally all the most noted varieties of this fruit cultivated in the English gardens, and in the nurseries for sale; though there are numerous other varieties, particularly of the common sort, growing in the orchards and hedges of farmers, &c. in different parts of the country; all the sorts being varieties of one species, first obtained from seed, and the approved sorts of them have been multiplied and continued by budding and grafting.

But besides the above varieties of the fruit, there are also the following for ornamental plantations.

Double-blossom Plum-tree——Gold striped-leaved—Silver-striped-leaved—and the stoneless plum.

The two following species. *Bullace-tree* and *Sloe-bush*, grow wild in hedges, but are sometimes cultivated both for variety and use.

The general propagation of Plum-trees is, by grafting and budding, and may also be increased occasionally by layers.

By grafting and budding.—This is performed upon stocks of any sorts of the plum-kind, raised from the stones, sowed in autumn in beds of good earth, about two inches deep, and when the plants are a year old, they being planted out in nursery rows two feet and a half asunder, and having from one to two or three years growth, they will be in fit order to graft or bud with the desired sorts, which is performed in the usual way, either low in the stock for dwarfs, or at several feet height for standards. Observing, that when the first shoots from the graft or bud are one year old, those of the trees designed as dwarfs for walls, &c. should be headed down within five or six inches of the bottom, more particularly of the budded trees, in order to force out laterals from the lower eyes, so as to furnish a proper set of branches, proceeding regularly from the bottom of the tree, to cover every part of the wall and espalier. But as to standards, their first shoots may either be suffered to run and branch in their own way, or headed to a few eyes, if it shall seem necessary, to force out lower laterals to give the head a more regular spreading formation; afterwards, let them all take their own growth.

When the trees thus raised by grafting or budding, are from one to two or three years old, they are of a proper size for final transplanting into the garden, &c. though trees of six or eight years old may be safely transplanted; remarking however, the younger they are planted where they are to remain, the sooner and more firmly they will establish themselves, and form for bearing.

By layers.——This is performed on the young wood, any time from November till March, chusing the last summer's shoots, and lay them by slit-laying; in one year they will be rooted; they must then be separated, and planted in nursery-rows, and trained either for dwarfs or standards, as may be required.

The double blossom plum, the two striped varieties, and stoneless kind, are all propagated by budding or grafting, upon any kinds of plum-stocks, either for dwarfs, or half or full standards.

And the bullace-tree and sloe-bush or black-thorn, are propagated by sowing the berries or stones an inch deep in a bed of common earth in autumn; and the sloe-tree also abundantly by suckers from the root.

Cocoa PLUM, *or American* PLUM, (*Chrysobalanus.*) There are two species; 1. with oval indented leaves, flowers growing in clusters, and a shrubby stalk;—2. with decompounded leaves, whose leaves are oval and entire.——They are both natives of the West-India islands,

iſlands, and the warmer parts of America, and will not thrive in England, unleſs preſerved in ſtoves. They are propagated by ſeeds, which muſt be procured from their native country, and ſown in the ſpring.

Indian Date Plum. *See* Date Plum-tree.

POA GRASS.—Meadow graſs, or that common ſpecies of graſs, which principally forms the green covering of our fields, &c.

POCKET, A large ſort of bag, in which wool or hops are packed up, in order to be ſent from one part of the kingdom to the other.

POCKWOOD. *See* Guaicum.

POD, A term uſed to expreſs a pericarpium, conſiſting of two valves, which open from the baſe to the point, and are ſeparated by a membraneous partition, from which the ſeeds hang by a kind of minute ſtalk.

POISON Tree, (Toxicodendron.) There are ſeveral ſpecies of this plant growing in moſt parts of North America.——Theſe plants are preſerved by the curious in botany, for the ſake of variety; but as there is little beauty in them, there are not many of the ſorts cultivated in England. The wood of theſe trees, when burnt, emits a noxious fume, which will ſuffocate animals when they are ſhut up in a room where it is burnt; an inſtance of this is mentioned in the Philoſophical Tranſactions by Dr. William Sherard, which was communicated to him in a letter from New England, by Mr. Moore, in which he mentions ſome people who had cut ſome of this wood for fuel, which they were burning, and in a ſhort time they loſt the uſe of their limbs, and became ſtupid; ſo that if a neighbour had not accidentally opened the door, and ſeen them in that condition, it is generally believed they would ſoon have periſhed. This ſhould caution people from making uſe of this wood for ſuch purpoſe.

When a perſon is poiſoned by handling this wood, in a few hours he feels an itching pain, which provokes a ſcratching, which is followed by an inflammation and ſwelling. Sometimes a perſon has had his legs poiſoned, which have run with water. Some of the inhabitants of America affirm, they can diſtinguiſh this wood by the touch in the dark, from its extreme coldneſs, which is like ice; but what is mentioned of this poiſonous quality is moſt applicable to a ſort like the aſh.

The juice of the tree is milky, when it firſt iſſues out of the wounded part; but ſoon after it is expoſed to the air, it turns black, and has a very ſtrong fœtid ſcent, and is corroding; on cutting off a ſmall branch from one of theſe ſhrubs, the blade of the knife has been changed black in a moment's time, ſo far as the juice had ſpread over it, which could not be got off without grinding the knife.

Poison Ash, a ſpecies of the poiſon-tree.

Poison Oak, a ſpecies of the poiſon-tree.

Poison Bush. *See* Spurge.

POKE, a ſack or bag.

Hop POLES, the upright poles, or pieces of wood, round which they bind, twiſt, and ſupport themſelves.

POLLARD, a tree that has been frequently polled or lopped, and its top taken off.——Pollards are inferior to coppice trees, in the quantity of wood they yield, and in its value; for the coppice wood is fit for many purpoſes that the ſhrowdings of the pollards can never anſwer, and therefore brings a better price; but on the other hand, pollards are maintained at a ſmaller expence, indeed it may almoſt be ſaid at none at all; for they require no fences; they take up no quantity of ground; and they are in their ſhoots above the reach of cattle.

The moſt frequent and moſt profitable trees for pollards, are, the willow for watery places, the aſh for hedge rows, and the oak for commons. But each of theſe ſituations will ſupport ſeveral others to advantage; and there is ſcarce any tree that may not be brought to a pollard at the owner's pleaſure.

In general, the huſbandman ſhould ſhrowd ſuch trees as are not fit for timber; or any from which he deſires to have a preſent advantage, or which he intends ſhall ſupply his family, or the market, with fuel quickly and readily: for there is no growth ſo ſpeedy as that of the tree which is ſhrowded.

Trees intended for ſhrowding may be raiſed in many places, where it would

would not be worth while to have others, because of the injury they would do the ground: for, as to throwded trees, the farmers may have the benefit of grazing under them, while the tops are growing, so that little produce of the ground, where that is of any considerable value, is lost by their growth: and when their heads are so large that they injure the growth of the grass, they make amends another way, for they then afford shelter for the cattle, the necessity of which is sufficiently known to every grazier.

POLE-EVIL, An abscess near the poll of a horse, formed in the sinuses between the noll bone, and the uppermost vertebræ of the neck.

If it proceeds from blows, bruises, or any external violence, at first bathe the swelling often with hot vinegar; and if the hair be fretted off with an oozing through the skin, make use of two parts of vinegar, and one of spirit of wine; but if there be an itching with heat and inflammation, the safest way is to bleed, and apply poultices with bread, milk, and elder flowers: this method, with the assistance of physic, will frequently disperse the swelling, and prevent this evil.

But when the tumour is critical, and has all the signs of matter, the best method then is to forward it by applying the ripening poultices already taken notice of, till it come to maturity, and burst of itself; or if opened with a knife, great care should be taken to avoid the tendinous ligament, that runs along the neck under the mane: when matter is on both sides, the opening must be made on each side, and the ligament remain undivided.

If the matter flows in great quantities, resembles melted glue, and is of an oily consistence, it will require a second incision, especially if any cavities are discovered by the finger or probe; these should be opened by the knife, the orifices made depending, and the wound dressed with the common digestive of turpentine, honey, and tincture of myrrh, and after digestion with the precipitate ointment; or wash the sore with the following, made hot, and fill up the cavity with tow soaked in it.

Take vinegar, or spirit of wine, half a pint, white vitriol dissolved in spring water, half an ounce, tincture of myrrh, four ounces.

This may be made sharper by adding more vitriol; but if the flesh is very luxuriant, it should first be pared down with a knife before the application; with this wash alone, Mr. Gibson has cured this disorder without any other formality of dressing, washing with it twice a day, and laying over the part a quantity of tow soaked in vinegar, and the white of eggs beat together. This last application will serve instead of a bandage, as it will adhere close to the pole, and come off easy when there is occasion to dress. Some wash with the phagedenic water, and then fill up the abscess with loose dossils of tow soaked in Ægyptiacum and oil of turpentine made hot, and continue this method till the cure is effected.

But the most compendious method of cure, is found by observation to be by scalding, as the farriers term it, and is thus prosecuted when the sore is foul, of a bad disposition, and attended with a profusion of matter.

Take corrosive sublimate, verdigrease in fine powder, and Roman vitriol, of each two drams; green copperas half an ounce; honey or Ægyptiacum two ounces, oil of turpentine and train oil, of each eight ounces; rectified spirit of wine four ounces: mix together in a bottle.

Some make their scalding mixture milder, using red precipitate instead of the sublimate; and white vitriol instead of blue; the following has been successfully used for this purpose, viz. half an ounce of verdigreate, half a pint of train oil, four ounces of oil of turpentine, and two of oil of vitriol.

The manner of scalding is, first to clean the abscess well with a piece of spunge dipped in vinegar; then put a sufficient quantity of the mixture in a ladle with a spout, and when it is made scalding hot, pour it into the abscess, and close the lips together with one or more stitches. This is to remain in several days, and if good matter appears, and not in an over-great quantity, it will do well without any other dressing, but bathing with spirit of wine; if the matter flows in great

abundance

abundance, and of a thin consistence, it must be scalded again, and repeated till the matter lessens and thickens.

These liquid corrosive dressings agree well with horses, whose fibres are stiff and rigid, and whose juices are oily and viscid; in this case they contract the vessels of the tendons on the hind part of the head and upper part of the neck, which are continually spewing out a matter or ichor that can hardly be digested, or the profusion abated without such applications as these.

POLEY, (*Policum.*) There are several species of this plant, natives of France, and the warmer parts of Europe; and from thence brought into the English gardens, and are propagated by setts, cuttings, or slips.

POLYPODY, (*Polypodium.*) Polypody is a capillary plant, growing upon old walls, the trunks of decayed trees, &c. That found upon the oak is generally preferred, though not sensibly different from the others. The roots are long and slender, of a reddish brown colour on the outside, greenish within, full of small tubercles, which are resembled to the feet of an insect; whence the name of the plant: the taste of these roots is sweetish and nauseous.

Polypody has been employed in medicine for many ages; nevertheless its virtues remain as yet to be determined. The ancients held it to be a powerful purger of melancholic humours; by degrees, it came to be looked upon as an evacuator of all humours in general; at length, it was supposed only to gently loosen the belly; and afterwards even this quality was denied it: succeeding physicians declared it to be astringent; of this number is Boerhaave, who esteems it moderately styptic and antiscorbutic. For our own part, we have had no direct experience of it, nor is it employed in practice; it is probable that (as Juncker supposes) the fresh root may loosen the belly, and that it has not this effect when dry.

POLYANTHUS, (*Polyantha.*) The several sorts of Polyanthuses are produced by sowing of seeds, which should be saved from such flowers as have large upright stems, producing many flowers upon a stalk, which are large, beautifully striped, open, flat, and not pin-eyed. From the seeds of such flowers, there is room to hope for a great variety of good sorts, but there should be no ordinary flowers stand near them, lest by the mixing of their farina the seeds should be degenerated.

These seeds should be sown in boxes filled with light rich earth in December, being very careful not to bury the seed too deep, for if it be only slightly covered with earth, it will be sufficient. These boxes should be placed where they may have the benefit of the morning sun until ten of the clock, but must by no means be exposed to the heat of the day, especially when the plants begin to appear, for at that time one whole day's sun will entirely destroy them. In the spring, if the season should prove dry, you must often refresh them with water, and as the heat encreases, you should remove the boxes more in the shade, for the heat is very injurious to them.

By the end of May, these plants will be strong enough to plant out, at which time you should prepare some shady borders, which should be made rich with neats dung, upon which you must set the plants about four inches asunder every way, observing to water them until they have taken root; after which they will require no farther care, but to keep them clear from weeds, until the latter end of August following, when you should prepare some borders, which are exposed to the east, with good light rich earth, into which you must transplant your polyanthuses, placing them six inches asunder equally in rows, observing, if the season prove dry, to water them until they have taken root. In these borders your plants will flower the succeeding spring, at which time you must observe to mark such of them as are fine to preserve, and the rest may be transplanted into wildernesses, and other shady places in the garden, where, although they are not very valuable flowers, they will afford an agreeable variety.

Those which you intend to preserve may be removed soon after they have done flowering, (provided you do not intend to save seeds from them) and may be then transplanted into a fresh border of the like rich earth, allowing them the same distance as before, ob-

serving

serving also to water them, until they have taken root; after which they will require no farther care, but only to keep them clean from weeds, and the following spring they will produce strong flowers, as their roots will be then in full vigour; so that, if the kinds are good, they will be little inferior to a shew of Auriculas.

These roots should be constantly removed and parted every year, and the earth of the border changed, otherwise they will degenerate, and lose the greatest part of their beauty.

If you intend to save seeds, which is the method to obtain a great variety, you must mark such of them, which have good properties. These should be, if possible, separated from all ordinary flowers, for if they stand surrounded with plain-coloured flowers, they will impregnate each other, whereby the seeds of the valuable flowers will not be near so good, as if the plants had been in a separate border, where no ordinary flowers grew; therefore the best way is to take out the roots of such as you do not esteem, as soon as the flowers open, and plant them in another place, that there may be none left in the border but such as you would chuse for seeds.

The flowers of these should not be gathered, except such as are produced singly upon pedicles, leaving all such as grow in large bunches; and if the season should prove dry, you must now and then refresh them with water, which will cause their seeds to be larger, and in greater quantity, than if they were entirely neglected. In June the seed will be ripe, which may be easily known by the pods changing brown, and opening; so that you should at that time look over the plants three times a week, gathering each time such of the seed-vessels as are ripe, which should be laid upon a paper to dry, and may then be put up until the season of sowing.

As the plants which arise from seeds, generally flower much better than offsets, those who would have these flowers in perfection should annually sow their seeds.

POMEGRANATE (*Punica.*) This tree is a native of Spain, Italy, Portugal, &c. but when planted against a warm wall, will often produce fruit in England. There are several varieties, and may be propagated by layers.

POND, a reservoir or receptacle for collecting and preserving water.

The necessity of water, in all pastures, is self-evident; as cattle cannot live without it, and the driving of them far for it is known to be prejudicial to their health, in hot weather, besides being attended with great trouble, and a considerable loss of time. This is so sensibly felt in many parts of England, that people are obliged to dig wells, even to such a depth as, frequently, to require the assistance of a horse to draw up the water. The means of rendering it easily come at must therefore inhance the value of the land where it can be so procured, and it is of very essential consequence to the husbandman.

Where the surface of the ground is sand or gravel, there seldom is occasion to dig deep for water; because such soils generally lie upon marle, or some other rich earth, through which the water cannot descend. Beds of clay are most commonly thicker than those of sand or gravel; and chalk is, too often, the thickest of all. But wherever water is wanting, the farmer should bore through the incumbent earth, if he intends to fit his land for pasture: and if he finds the expence of obtaining it too great, his best way will be to convert the ground, so circumstanced, into arable, or to plant it with timber-trees suited to the nature of the soil.

Wherever water stagnates in a sandy or gravelly soil, the husbandman sees at once at what depth is the surface of the earth which retains it. But in other soils, and when this does not happen, Palladius, and the authors of the *Maison Rustique*, give the following directions how to seek for water, with the greatest probability of success.

Where rushes, reeds, flags, willows, or other aquatic plants grow spontaneously, or where frogs are observed to lie squatted down close to the ground, in order to receive its moisture, there generally is water underneath. Persons who make it their business to find out springs for fountains, cascades, &c. look upon it as an infallible sign of subterranean water, when they see a vapour arise frequently from the same ſpot of ground. Others aſſure, that wherever ſwarms of little flies are ſeen conſtantly flying in the ſame place, and near to the ground, in the morning, after ſun-riſe, there certainly is water under that ſpot. Again, where water is wanted on land apparently dry, let a man, before ſun-riſe, lie down flat on his belly, reſting his chin upon his fiſt placed cloſe to the ground, that his view may be directed quite horizontally, and not riſe too high, and in that ſituation let him look ſtedfaſtly toward the eaſt. If he then ſees a tremulous vapour ariſe from any particular ſpot, let him mark the place, by noticing ſome neighbouring tree, ſhrub, or other indication, and he will find water underneath it. But this experiment is to be made only on ground whoſe ſurface is dry; becauſe other exhalations, from a damp ſurface, would be apt, in this caſe, to miſlead the enquirer.

Another way is thus: Dig a hole three feet wide, and at leaſt five feet deep, and place at the bottom of it, when the ſun is about to ſet, a pan, or baſon, rubbed with oil on the inſide: let the bottom of this veſſel be uppermoſt; cover it with dry hay, fern, or ruſhes, and over that with earth; and if any drops of water are found ſtanding on its inſide the next day, a ſpring is probably not far off. Or, put a new, unbaked, but well dried, earthen veſſel into ſuch a hole, and cover it as before; and if there be water in that place, this veſſel will be found ſoft and wet the next day. Likewiſe, if wool be left all night in a trench of this kind, and water can be ſqueezed out of it the next day, little doubt remains but that plenty of water may be met with there.

The month of Auguſt is generally looked upon as the moſt proper time to ſearch for water; becauſe, as the heat of the preceding ſummer will have warmed the earth to a conſiderable depth, any ſteam ariſing from water reſting on an impervious ſoil underneath, and particularly in hollows on the ſurface of that impervious ſoil, will then be moſt exhaled by this warmth. Now it is this ſteam, or vapour, which produces the before-mentioned ſigns.

By whatever method water is found, the means of coming eaſily at it are the next conſideration. If it be on a plain, there is no other way than digging a well. In doing this, the ſubſtance under the ſand or light ſoil muſt be dug into, to form a reſervoir of water for occaſional wants; and this reſervoir ſhould be made deep and large, in proportion to the quantity wanted. If there were no ſuch reſervoir, the water, after having riſen a little above the impervious body underneath, would glide along its ſurface, as uſual, and very little of it could then be obtained, either by pumps, buckets, or any other way employed to raiſe it. If the well is made in a ſloping ground, and the declivity is ſufficient to give it an horizontal vent, it will be worth the huſbandman's while to dig ſuch a paſſage, and, by means of pipes, or any other conveyance, to carry the water acroſs the light ſoil, through which it would otherwiſe ſink. The greateſt quantity of water will be obtained in this manner, becauſe there will then be a continual ſtream.

If the ſoil is very deep, and its ſurface has inequalities in which rain-water runs in any quantity; this may be collected in ponds made in the loweſt parts of ſuch grounds.

If a body of clay is found near the ſurface, it is worth the farmer's while to bore, that he may know at what depth a bed of ſand or gravel may be met with, for he will be ſure to find plenty of water in this laſt. If this be in a declivity, he need only cut an horizontal paſſage, and the water will flow ſo freely as even to double the value of his land.

Here again the farmer needs not ever to be at a loſs, becauſe it cannot be very difficult to make a pond in a clayey ſoil, which is, of itſelf, retentive of water. But it may, perhaps, be adviſeable, even in this, to cover the bottom of the pond with a coat of gravel, in order to prevent its being poached by cattle, whoſe feet would otherwiſe be apt to ſink deep into the clay.—— Some farmers judiciouſly pave the declivity by which the cattle enter into the pond, and this renders it much more laſting than it would otherwiſe be, and preſerves the water clean.

When ponds are made in a looſe ſoil, much more care is neceſſary. The bottom and ſides there muſt be covered with a thick coat of the tougheſt clay,

from

from a foot to two feet thick, well rammed down. Some have added hair and loam to the outer part of this covering, with a view of rendering it less liable to chap: but a thick coat of gravel is more necessary here, that the feet of the cattle may not pierce through the clay. Perhaps the expence of paving the whole inside of a pond might, in the end, be money well laid out.

The greatest difficulty of finding water is in chalky soils, because these are not, of themselves, very retentive of it, and generally lie in such thick beds, that it is expensive to dig through them. However, it should be tried; and if sand or gravel be found underneath, water may be depended on.—Even here, ponds are easily made, by digging into the chalk, and lining them with a coat of clay, as before directed. If there be a supply of proper manure, such as clay or marle, this situation is well adapted to grain, which loves to stand dry; and as this kind of ground produces more forward crops than clayey or strong soils, it may be sowed early with corn, which will not, in that case, be so apt to be parched up as grass is, by the summer's drought. If a good soil can be made here, a foot deep, it will yield plenty of various sorts of pasture, either roots or grasses, as the farmer shall judge most proper: or it may be planted with different kinds of timber-trees.

POPLAR-TREE, (*Populus.*) A genus of trees, of which botanists enumerate four species, viz. the common white poplar, with large leaves; the common white poplar, with smaller leaves; the common black poplar, and the poplar with trembling leaves, called the aspen-tree. The poplar, whether black or white, may be easily propagated, either by layers, cuttings, or suckers, of which the white kind always produces a great many from the roots. The best season for the transplanting these suckers is in October, when the leaves begin to decay; and they should be removed into a nursery for two or three years, at the end of which time they will have got strength enough to be transplanted into the places where they are to remain.

When they are to be propagated by cuttings, it is best to do that in February, cutting off large truncheons of eight or ten feet long; which, being thrust down a foot deep in the ground, will take root very quickly, and, if the soil be moist, will grow to a considerable size in a few years.

The black poplar is not so easily raised from these large truncheons, but should be planted in cuttings, of about a foot and a half long, planting them a foot deep in the ground. This will grow on almost any soil, but does much better on a moist one than on any other. They are the fittest of all trees for raising a shade quickly, as they will grow fourteen feet in height sometimes in one season, and in four or five years will be large trees.

A considerable advantage may be obtained by planting these trees upon moist boggy soils, where few other trees will thrive: many such places there are in England, which do not, at present, bring in much money to their owners; whereas, if they were planted with these trees, they would, in a very few years, over-purchase the ground, clear of all expence: but there are many persons in England, who think nothing except corn worth cultivating; or, if they plant timber, it must be oak, ash, or elm; and, if their land be not proper for either of these, it is deemed little worth; whereas, if the nature of the soil were examined, and proper sorts of plants adapted to it, there might be a very great advantage made of several large tracts of lands, which at this time lie neglected.

The wood of these trees, especially of the white, is very good to lay for floors, where it will last many years; and, for its exceeding whiteness, is, by many persons, preferred to oak; but, being of a soft contexture, is very subject to take the impression of nails, &c. which renders it less proper for this purpose: it is also very proper for wainscotting of room , being less subject to swell or shrink, than most other sorts of wood: but for turnery-ware, there is no wood equal to this for its exceeding whiteness, so that trays, bowls, and many other utensils, are made of it; and the bellows-makers prefer it for their use; as do also the shoemakers, not only for heels, but also for the soles of shoes: it is also very good to make light carts; the poles are very proper to support vines, hops, &c: and the lopping will afford good fuel, which, in many countries, is much wanted.

POPPY, the name of a plant, of which, several species are cultivated in gardens for the beauty of the flowers. They are all easily propagated by sowing the seeds in autumn. When the young plants come up, they are to be cleared from weeds, and thinned to a proper distance by pulling some up, where they stand too thick; for they never thrive well, if they are to be transplanted. They are to be left, according to their sizes, at six, eight, or ten inches distance.

They are very showy flowers, and make a splendid appearance in gardens, but they are but of a short duration, and are of an offensive smell, which makes them less valued at present than they have been.

Some sow these plants in spring, but it is not so well; because they then have not time to get strength before autumn, when they are to flower; and, for that reason, those sown in spring usually flower weakly.

The heads and stalks of these plants contain a milky juice; which may be collected in considerable quantity, by lightly wounding them when almost ripe: this juice, exposed for a few days to the air, thickens into a stiff tenacious mass, agreeing in quality with the opium brought from abroad. The juices of both the poppies appear to be similar to one another; the only difference is in the quantity afforded, which is generally in proportion to the size of the plants: the larger or white poppy, is the sort cultivated by the preparers of opium in the eastern countries, and for medicinal uses in this.

Poppy heads, boiled in water, impart to the menstruum their narcotic juice, together with the other juices, which they have in common with vegetable matters in general. The liquor strongly pressed out, suffered to settle, clarified with whites of eggs, and evaporated to a due consistence, yields about one-fifth or one sixth the weight of the heads, of extract. This possesses the virtues of opium; but requires to be given in double its dose to answer the same intention, which it is said to perform without occasioning a nausea and giddiness, the usual consequences of the other. A strong decoction of the heads, mixed with as much sugar as is sufficient to reduce it into the consistence of a syrup, becomes fit for keeping in a liquid form; and is the only officinal preparation of the poppy. Both these preparations are very useful ones, though liable to variation in point of strength: nor does this inconvenience seem avoidable by any care in the prescriber, or the operator; since the poppy heads themselves (according to the degree of maturity, and the soil and season of which they are the produce) contain different proportions of the narcotic matter to the other juices of the plant; as has been observed in the Pharmacopœia reformata.

The seeds of the poppy are by many reckoned soporific; Juncker says, they have the same quality with those of henbane, and Herman looks upon them as a good substitute to opium; misled probably by an observation which holds in many plants, that the seeds are more efficacious than the vessels in which they are contained.

The seeds of the poppy have nothing of the narcotic juice which is lodged in their covering, and in the stalks; an oil expressed from them has been used for the same purposes as oil olive, and the seeds themselves taken as food: their taste is sweetish and farinaceous.

Red POPPY *or Red-Weed*. The common wild red poppy is one of the most mischievous weeds the farmers are plagued with among their corn, and it is the most difficult to thoroughly destroy of almost any other. Its seed will lie a long time in land unploughed, without ever shooting; but they will be sure to grow with every crop of corn. Mr. Tull gives an instance of the seeds of this plant being buried four and twenty years in a field of saintfoin, and at the end of that time, the land being ploughed for wheat, they all grew up among the corn, though they had lain dormant so long before.

The flowers of this plant yield upon expression a deep red juice, and impart the same colour by infusion to aqueous liquors. A syrup of them is kept in the

 POT

the shops; this is valued chiefly for its colour; though some expect from it a lightly anodyne virtue.

Horned Poppy. Celandine.

Prickly Poppy. [*Argemone.*] Infernal Fig.

Spatling Poppy. See *Berry-bearing* Chickweed.

Wild Poppy. See *Red* Poppy.

POTATOES. [*Lycopersicon.*] The name of a well-known plant, the roots of which make a very nourishing food.

Mr. Houghton describes the potatoe to be a bacciferous herb, with esculent roots, bearing winged leaves and a belled flower, and says, that, according to his information, which is allowed to be very right in this respect, it was first brought from Virginia, by Sir Walter Raleigh, who, stopping at Ireland, about the year 1623, gave away a number of these roots, which were planted there, and multiplied so exceedingly, that, in the wars which happened afterwards in that country, when all the corn above ground was destroyed, potatoes became the chief support of the people; for the soldiers, unless they had dug up all the ground where they grew, and almost sifted it, could not have extirpated them. The Philosophical Transactions observe likewise, that the Irish were relieved from their last severe famine, which lasted two years, during which all their corn failed, merely by the help of this root. From Ireland it was brought to Lancashire, now famous for its potatoes; and the culture of this plant has, within these last thirty years, been extended to almost every part of England. The rich, who, at first, deemed them fit for none but the meaner sort of people, now esteem them so much, that Mr. Miller thinks the quantity of them which is cultivated around London only, exceeds that of any other part of Europe.

The red-rooted potatoes have purplish flowers, and the white-rooted (for Mr. Miller distinguishes only these two general varieties) bear white flowers.

The potatoe seldom perfects its seeds in England; and if it did, the raising of it from them would be much more tedious and uncertain than propagating it by its roots, as is the general and right method: for these multiply exceedingly, and may be made to yield vast crops, with little cost or labour.

" The Irish husbandman, says Mr. Switzer, after blaming the English for planting this root uncut, because it often contains five or six eyes, or perhaps more, from which the produce of the ensuing year is to spring; and also for not allowing that bulb, or rather the great number of shoots and bulbs that proceed from it, a space of earth sufficient for their nourishment, which is the reason why so many poor, stinted, unserviceable potatoes are dug up in the autumn, relates the practice of his country, which is to chuse middle-sized roots, for the largest are generally eaten, to single out the eyes that seem strongest and most vigorous, and to cut them out in squares of at least half an inch every way: so that one root will sometimes furnish three or four good pieces to set.

" The ground, prepared for planting, is marked out for beds four or five feet wide, with intermediate alleys of two or three feet. It is then trenched, only a single spit deep, and the bottom of the trench, made as in common garden-trenching, is covered with dung, long and short, taken out of a wheelbarrow which stands at the labourer's elbow. The potatoe-eyes, cut as before directed, are placed upon this dung, at about five or six inches asunder; and this trench is filled up with the mould taken out of the next, which is marked by a line at the distance of two or three feet. This trench is again filled with the mould of the next, and so on to the last, which is filled from the alley.

" The use of the dung thus laid at the bottom of the trenches, is not only to make the roots grow single, for not above one root, or at most two, will in this case be produced by each eye, and these will be large and well fed; but it is attended with the farther advantage of making the potatoes run, and spread themselves to a certain determinate depth, which is no small help to their growing large.

" The last thing to be done to them is, in April or May, (for they are planted in February or March) as soon as they begin to rise, to dig the earth out of the alleys as is done for asparagus, and to cover the potatoe bed with it, about five or six inches thick. This

will

will give new life and vigour to the roots, will keep the green from running too much to haulm, and will make the bulbs grow much the larger. By this means the crop of fine large potatoes will be almost the double of what is obtained when they are planted promiscuously in the common way; nor will any farther culture be requisite till they are fit to be dug up; except the pulling out of some of the largest weeds."

Mr. Miller's reasons for disapproving of the planting, either of the small offsets entire, or the eyes cut out of larger roots, are, that though the former generally produce a greater number of roots, these roots are always small; and that the cuttings of the larger roots are apt to rot, especially if wet weather happens soon after they are planted. He therefore recommends, to make choice of the fairest roots for setting, and to allow them a larger space of ground, both between the rows, and between the plants in the rows; and he assures us that he has observed, when this method has been followed, that the roots, in general, have been large the following autumn. M. Duhamel, in his Elements of Agriculture, does not object at all to the planting of the cuttings.

The soil in which this plant thrives best, is a light sandy loam, neither too dry nor over moist, but brought to a fine tilth, and ploughed very deep: for the deeper the earth is loosened, the finer and larger the roots will grow. In the spring, just before the last ploughing, a good quantity of rotten dung should be spread on the ground, and this should be ploughed early in March, if the season be mild; otherwise it had better be deferred until the middle or latter end of that month; for if a hard frost should come on soon after the roots are planted, they may be greatly injured, if not destroyed, thereby; but if they can be planted in the spring, without that danger, the better it will be.

The last ploughing should lay on the ground even, and then furrows should be drawn three feet asunder, and seven or eight inches deep. The roots should be laid at the bottom of these furrows, about a foot and a half asunder, and they should then be covered in with earth.

After all, the ground intended for potatoes is planted in this manner, it must remain in the same state till near the the time when the shoots are expected to appear; then it should be well harrowed both ways, as well to loosen the surface and render it smooth, as to tear up the young weeds which will have begun to grow by that time. If much wet has fallen after the planting, it may have caked the surface of the earth, so as to retard the sprouting of the plants; and this harrowing will, in such case, almost answer the intent of a first hoeing.

I have placed the rows of potatoes at three feet distance, continues Mr. Miller, in order to introduce the hoe-plough between them; because that will greatly improve their roots: for by twice stiring and breaking of the ground between these plants, not only weeds will be destroyed, but the soil will be so loosened, that every shower of rain will penetrate to the roots, and greatly quicken their growth. But these operations should be performed early in the season, before the stems or branches of the plants begin to fall and trail upon the ground: for after that, it cannot be done without injuring the shoots.

If these hoe-ploughings are carefully performed, they will prevent the growth of weeds, till the haulm of the plants cover the ground; and after that there will be little danger of their growing so as to injure the crop; for the haulm will keep them under: but as the horse-hoe can only go between the rows, it will be necessary to make use of the hand-hoe to stir the ground, and destroy the weeds in the rows, between the plants. If this be well done in dry weather, immediately after each of the two horse-hoeings, it will be sufficient to keep the ground clean until the potatoes are fit to be taken up; which will be very soon after the first frost in the autumn has killed the haulm. They should not remain much longer in the earth, lest the roots themselves be frost-bitten, which spoils them. A four or five pronged fork is better to dig them up with, than a spade, because it is less apt to cut them: but the principal

principal thing to be confidered here, is the clearing of the ground thoroughly of them: for if any are left, they will shoot up among the next crop, whatever it be, and do confiderable damage, especially if it be wheat, as is generally the case, sown in the common broad-cast way.

The best way of keeping these roots during the winter, is to lay them up in a dry place in very dry sand, or in fine and perfectly dry earth.

The method of laying dung only at the bottom of the furrows in which the roots are planted, "is a very poor one, (says Mr. Miller) because, where the potatoes begin to push out their roots, they are soon extended beyond the width of these furrows, and the new roots are commonly formed at a distance from the old: so will be out of the reach of this dung, and consequently will receive little benefit from it." But rather the contrary would seem to be the case, according to the Irish husbandman, who, seems to speak from experience, when he says, he had intended expresly to answer this very objection, that "the dung is placed at the bottom of the furrows on purpose to make the roots grow single; and that its being so placed is attended with the farther conveniency of making the potatoes run, and spread themselves at a certain determinate depth, which is no small help to their growing large." Facts must here determine which is right: as they also must in regard to some parts of what Mr. Miller adds in the following words: "As most farmers covet to have a crop of wheat after the potatoes are taken off the ground, so the land will not be so thoroughly dressed in every part, nor so proper for this crop, as when the dung is equally spread, and ploughed in all over the land, nor will the crops of potatoes be so good. I have always observed, where this method of planting the potatoes has been practised, the land has produced a fine crop of wheat afterward, and there has scarce one shoot of the potatoe appeared among the wheat, which I attribute to the farmers planting only the largest roots: for when they have forked them out of the ground the following autumn, there have been six, eight, or ten large roots produced from each, and often many more, and scarce any very small roots; whereas, in such places where the small roots have been planted, there has been a vast number of very small roots produced, many of which were so small, as not to be discovered when the roots were taken up; so have grown the following season, and have greatly injured whatever crop was upon the ground."

Will not a thorough ploughing and good harrowing, after the crop of potatoes has been taken off the ground, intermix the dung laid in the furrows, and the contiguous earth most impregnated thereby, with the rest of the soil; perhaps almost as well as if the dung had been spread equally over the whole field, at the very first? If it will, the presumption seems strong in favour of the Irish method. For certain it is, that the land ought to be well ploughed and harrowed after the potatoes are removed, before it is sown with any other crop; unless the seed for that crop, which generally is wheat, be sprinkled by hand between the rows, as they are dug up, and there covered with the earth then turned over. This is practised in some parts of France: but, as M. Duhamel observes, the grain is so apt to be distributed unequally in this method, that it is better to plough the ground, and sow it, in the regular way.

If the farmer apprehends that his land has not been thoroughly cleared of the potatoes, and is therefore afraid of their damaging his ensuing crop; his best way will be to lay it up very rough against winter; because the frosts of that season are known to kill and rot all potatoes in the ground exposed to them, and it will at the same time be thereby finely prepared for spring corn; especially as it will have been well enriched by the haulm of the potatoes lying upon it.

Though potatoes delight most in a light sandy loam, neither too dry, nor over moist, as was observed before; yet Mr. Maxwell says he has seen them thrive well on ground that seemed to be very bad; even in deep moss, which could not bear horses to plow it, but which is considerably bettered by them; and on coarse heath, where they were succeeded by grain, without more dung than

than was laid on at firſt. Of ſo improving a nature are they, and ſo much is the land enriched by the rotting of their ſtalks among it, and the digging it gets in raiſing them.

Several experiments communicated to M. Duhamel concur to prove the extraordinary increaſe of potatoes cultivated with the horſe-hoe: but as this will always be the conſequence of the new huſbandry, wherever it is properly uſed, I ſhall only borrow from him, on this occaſion, M. de Villier's account of his method of practice, becauſe it is the cleareſt and moſt conciſe:

"There are, ſays he, ſeveral ſorts of potatoes. That which I cultivate is the middle-ſized. It is planted about the end of April, or the beginning of May, and it ripens in October. My beds are five feet wide. I give them two ploughings in the ſpring; at the ſecond of which I half fill the main furrow. Before I plant, I cut a ſmall furrow with the ſingle cultivator, which likewiſe looſens the earth; but if it be moiſt, I put a double ſpring-tree bar to the cultivator, to avoid the poaching of the horſes. I then plant the potatoes a foot aſunder in the row; chooſing for this purpoſe ſuch as are about the ſize of a walnut. They are thruſt in by hand, two or three inches deep; and if the mould does not then cover them ſufficiently of its own accord, a little more is puſhed down upon them.

"A ſlight hand-hoeing can hardly be avoided afterwards, to deſtroy the weeds which ſpring up at the ſame time as the potatoes: but this hoeing need not extend farther than three or four inches on each ſide of the row; becauſe the plough will do the reſt.

"I give the firſt hoe-ploughing in the ſpring, as for wheat; but earlier or later, according to the condition of the ground.

"My ſecond hoe-ploughing is given as ſoon as the plants are tall enough to be earthed up; that is to ſay, when they are eight or ten inches high. I then turn the earth up towards them as much as poſſible.

"As this plant ſpreads greatly, and ſhoots out very faſt, it would be impoſſible to give more than two of theſe hoeings, if one ſhould neglect to take advantage of the time when its leaves and branches do not entirely cover the bed.

"The roots are dug up in October or perhaps ſomewhat earlier or later, according to the ſeaſon, with a ſtrong iron prong; ſhaking and clearing them well from the mould. They are then left to dry for ſome hours, and are afterwards laid in a place where the froſt cannot reach them.

"This fruit, which yields ſurpriſingly, is of great ſervice to feed and fatten cattle, eſpecially when it has been boiled a little. They like it very well raw, after it has been kept a few months above ground: but it is beſt for them after it has been boiled."

The reader is obliged to the ingenious Mr. Irwin for the following account of cultivating potatoes in Ireland, and which we ſhall give in his own words:——

"The potatoe, ſays he, is become a root of ſuch immenſe utility, eſpecially to the poorer ſort, within this century, that too much, methinks, cannot be ſaid towards improving and extending the culture of it.

"In Provence, Dauphiny, Switzerland, and ſeveral other parts of Europe, and even in America, it yields commodious, abundant relief to the more indigent, as being eaſily and plenteouſly propagated in almoſt every kind of ſoil.

"In Ireland particularly it is the principal food of the poor during the greater part of the year, without which, ſince the late unproportionable riſe of lands in that kingdom to the trade of it, they could not well ſubſiſt. And, indeed, it ſeems a particular favour of Providence ſent to them on this account.

"In times, not very remote, lands were cheap there, and the peaſantry, conſequently, lived on nouriſhment ſomewhat more luxurious, and diverſified: their labour alſo was leſs burtheenſome. But now, being obliged to work hard at four-pence and ſix-pence a day, and their rents conſiderably augmented, it will not ſeem ſurpriſing, that this root alone has become the ſtaple of their ſupport, and that they have been the firſt people in Europe, or, perhaps, in the world, that have led the example

example in an extenſive improvement of it. This may naturally be ſuppoſed to ariſe from cloſe-preſſing neceſſity, the moſt cogent and inſpiriting of all motives.

" In truth with much reaſon; for a poor labourer, in that ill-fared country, is driven to ſeek his ſole refuge for ſubſiſtence in this root, from the inexorable impoſition of a hard-hearted landlord, (ſorry I am to have it to ſay, too many of them grind the poor; but hope it will not be long the caſe) who thinks he cannot get too much for his land out of the perſons, or purſes, of his dependents, and who hath ſo inverted the old cuſtoms, that a hewer of wood, and drawer of water, (and many of theſe perhaps deſcendants of former proprietors) can afford himſelf but a miſerable ſcanty platter of potatoes, ſeaſoned with a palatable grain of ſalt, and waſhed down with a draught from the next rivulet, to ſupport the fatigue of thirteen hours (ſtatute quantity) of unceaſing labour, about his ancient manſion-houſe, or in his elegant gardens, well-laid out cloſes, or refreſhing bog-holes.

" The potatoe is a root, a little of which is very filling, quickly appeaſing hunger; but by no means a laſting ſolid nouriſhment for a labourer, as evidently teſtify the ſquallid looks of numbers of the poorer Iriſh; though at the ſame time it is in general wholſome, agreeing with moſt ſtomachs that can vary their food; but, like other productions of the earth, forbid in many caſes by the medicinal tribe.

" There are ſeveral ways of breeding potatoes in Ireland, which partly ariſe from the difference in ſoil, and kinds of ſeed. The different ſoils for this purpoſe in uſe in my neighbourhood, for about twenty years paſt, and which, I believe, are pretty general, are the following, wherein they are abundantly propagated, viz.

" Firſt, On rich clay land without any manure, vulgarly called graſs potatoes.

" When a leaſe is near being expired, that is, during the laſt ſeven years of it, if there be no covenants grounded on the ſtatute againſt waſte, &c. the tenant, finding no hopes of a renewal, ſets conſiderable tracts in this way, where the ſoil will admit of it.

" Secondly, on good ley land well gravelled, (otherwiſe ſanded) which ought to be done a year before planting. But the poorer ſort, who are the chief cultivators of this root, are obliged to ſand and plant at the ſame time, or nearly thereabouts; which is very deſtructive to themſelves, their potatoes not having the proper benefit of the manure; at leaſt one part in three of the return are on this account exceeding ſmall, and are from hence called poreens by them, being a diminutive expreſſion. Whole fields are ſet in this way, (commonly called ſpad lane) in which a conſiderable trade is driven; eſpecially in the provinces of Munſter and Connaught.

" Had it been properly and moderately done, it would be a fine preparation for the increaſe of corn, and the laying down and bringing in, or in other terms the reclaiming of land; but the poor do it ſo negligently, and mangle it ſo intolerably, having but a ſhort temporary uſe in it, beſides paying near double the worth for it, that this manufacture, which might otherwiſe be of conſiderable benefit to Ireland, is, as now carried on, rather the contrary.

" Thirdly, On ground previouſly gravelled (that is, perhaps ſix months before) and dunged at ſetting time. There is but little done in this way, except by the gentry, and renters of land for their private uſe; it being as yet out of reach of the peaſantry, unleſs in a few inſtances.

" Fourthly, On the ley with dung alone. Marle is not in uſe in my neighbourhood, though there is plenty of it in ſeveral parts of it; therefore cannot yet inform you how it would do for the potatoes in that diſtrict. As to potatoes ſet in the ley with dung alone, this manufacture alſo is done, as you may judge, moſtly by the more opulent. I have, however, often ſeen large fields ſet in this way to the public: but it is not of late years ſo much the cuſtom, this ſort of land being commonly kept for grazing: this hurts the land: and any preparation out of the ley for potatoes will, if not previouſly gravelled.

" Fifthly, In arable or ſtubble land, (vulgarly called ſticking or thruſting of potatoes, becauſe they are ſown with a ſtick,

ſtick, pointed at the end, about an inch diameter and two feet long, with the loy, otherwiſe the Iriſh ſpade.) In this method dung is alſo uſed, which ſhall be noticed in its place.

" Theſe are the moſt general methods that now occur to me, or I believe that are in uſe. There are, however, ſome others ariſing from the quality of the ſeed, practiſed only by the curious, in which the plants are put down at nine or twelve inches aſunder every way, in little hillocks, (like the hop plant) as practiſed in ſeveral counties in England; and, if you land them at certain proper ſtated times while vegetation continues, you will have a handſome neſt of large oblong potatoes at every landing.

" I made the experiment of one ſort in my garden; and out of half a dozen potatoes cut into ſeveral pieces, each having an eye, I had, to the beſt of my remembrance, without exaggeration, a quantity equal to twelve Wincheſter buſhels.

" This kind of potatoe is introduced into Ireland but of late years: it is however well known there.

" A potatoe entirely black is alſo in uſe in Fingal, near Dublin, fructifies abundantly, and eats exceeding dry, which principally marks the goodneſs of this root in almoſt every inſtance.

" There are ſeveral kinds of potatoes. Mr. Maxwell, of Arkland in Scotland, a very judicious gentleman, has particularly noticed ſix ſorts, viz. The long red, the round red; the long white, the round white, or Spaniſh potato; the blue, the leather-coat, and an early kind that comes in a month ſooner than the common ſort, though planted at the ſame time.

" This root being greatly manufactured in Ireland, they mix moſt of the better ſorts promiſcuouſly, both for uſe and ſeed.

" I remember, about twenty-five years ago, the large red potatoe, then called the Caſtonian, (perhaps from Caſtile) as alſo the oblong Spaniſh white potatoe, to be chiefly in uſe; but now a leſſer ſort, ſuch as the Munſter or kidney potatoe, of a whitiſh or lightiſh yellow colour, the leather-coat, or round red Cronian potatoe, with a rough thick ſkin, and particularly that ſtiled the Spaniſh white potatoe, are moſtly in uſe.

" All theſe ſorts are cut for ſeed according to the number of eyes on them, and thrive generally well with very little care, ſo that all ſorts being now ſo plenty, and anſwering ſo well, there are (as we may eaſily judge) no over-nice diſtinctions made about them there. The poorer Iriſh, who affect not to plant this root in bottom lands, or wet ſwampy grounds, unleſs hard preſſed for ſoil, are even in this caſe ſeldom attentive about the kind of potatoe they put down, the return being commonly wet, unfit for eating, and only proper for ſeed, which (from my little experience) I think makes but indifferent, though ſown in the beſt prepared upland; for too much moiſture, as well as too much dung, makes a potatoe wet: and plant it when you will, I am apprehenſive it never loſes this quality, which is the worſt it can have, except being rotten, or froſt-bit; nor will any eat ſo well, raiſed from dung, as without.

" As the potatoe thrives in different ſoils, ſo there are different methods of cultivating it: I will therefore now proceed to that moſt generally in uſe in my neighbourhood, (and indeed all over the kingdom) called graſs potatoes or ſpuddane, and by ſome (improperly) conacres, which ſeems to be the natural culture, but doubtleſs not ſo good to make the land ſtand long proof, (notwithſtanding the gravelling) as if artificial manures were added, ſuch as dung, compoſt, lime, &c.; for marle, lime-ſtone, gravel, ſea-ſand, ſhells, &c. I conſider in the claſs of natural manures and the beſt; and providence hath kindly given them in every ſpot, (even in the unpromiſing deſerts of Zara, &c.) had we known how to come at them.

" Land in the ley, (as I ſaid before) and that which requires no manure, the Iriſh ſeek moſt greedily after, ſome of which has not been ploughed perhaps within this century: ſo that you can only juſt diſtinguiſh that it has been tilled, and the tilth generally curved, the old people inclining the plough with the caſual ſhape of the field, ſo as to let the water in the furrow have a drip or fall.

"When a peasant has the good luck to get a bit of such choice ground, (for two or three of them will be concerned in an acre, and few take more than one) he follows the old ridge with his *loy*, or Irish spade, unless compelled by the possessor of the land to make his ridges straight, which he most unwillingly does, and at best but aukwardly, with a rope made of hay or straw, or some of his wife's worst tow; neither of which stretching tight, and often breaking, seldom admit well-looking ridges: these he makes from one end of his ground to the other, the beds being about three, or at most four feet wide, and the furrows, or trenches, about two. When he deposits the seed on his bed, at about four or six inches at most asunder, he divides the turf of his furrow in two equal parts, which he turns alternately in sods on the edge or verge of each bed, the green side on the potatoes, cutting the sods on three sides or angles, leaving that next the bed uncut. This laborious work the poor fellow does surprizingly quick: two more men follow him, one digging the under-stratum, and throwing up on the middle of the bed as much of the earth as he conveniently can with his *loy*: the remainder the third man casts on with his shovel, settling the bed in the form, or manner, in which it is to remain.

"Some cover their potatoes at first (through want of time) with only the sod, and about four or five inches of earth, and finish them perhaps, that is, cast the last covering on them, not for a month, or six weeks after; which possibly may greatly check their growth. Many account this the best way, and it is become common; but I attribute the neglect of not finishing their potatoes (as the term is) in due time, to no want of proper knowledge in the common Irish, but their inability to give the proper attention to their own little affairs, occasioned by the greedy severity of their masters, as before observed.

"Others there are (and many) who, making the furrows unproportionably narrow to the beds, throw up a third spit or stratum, and perhaps not until two months after the first setting.

"This pernicious method may possibly destroy or check the weeds; but certain I am, it will not contribute to the increase or largeness of the root, in the unphysical or over heavy manner in which I have seen it done; because this lower stratum, which is mostly sand, remains on the top of the richest part of the soil, and being thus unmixed with it, prevents it from receiving the proper benefits of the air, &c. besides, too great a covering on the potatoe is highly prejudical to it.

"In other cases, these stratums thrown up, and mixed into a good tilth, would answer wonderfully, mixing well being the life of good tillage. I would therefore in this place recommend to our farmers (who are too penurious of their land) to make their potatoe trenches so wide, as not to require throwing up much of the third or sandy stratum on the last covering, or landing, of their potatoes: and they will find a much greater return, and one half (or more) less of *poreens*, or small potatoes: which is an object highly worthy of their notice. The experiments I have made, I purpose repeating on my return to Ireland, and hope to prove this simple method to exceed that in the hillock, or in the drill way.

"In this manner all ley land is sown with potatoes by the common people, and most others, whether manured or not. If dunged, the dung is laid out as the ridges are to be, but the sand is spread all over the surface. Commonly little boys and girls precede the setters on the ridges, laying down the seedlings or potatoe eyes, which they do very quick, and tolerably well, at the appointed distance. This seems a giddy part of the business, and well suited to their years; but custom makes them perfect in it.

"The next general method is planting potatoes in stubble ground, which is, in the common way above-mentioned, by dunging it well, and sometimes by plowing it in, and then shovelling up the ridges, a man going before, lightly digging them, that there may be a sufficient quantity of mould to cover them; but this the poorer sort cannot well compass to do, and always avoid it when they can get a fresh or ley surface.

 "Nor

" Nor do they ſow them to chuſe, the ſecond year, in the ſame ground, without dung or ſome other artificial manure, (for the natural, ſuch as ſand, marle, &c. would not do) unleſs it be exceeding good.

" Lime, indeed, in this caſe would very probably anſwer, but it is rarely tried.

" There is alſo a cuſtom a good deal in uſe, which is by ſticking or thruſting potatoes in ſtubble land freſh ploughed, which is done in this manner: a man (but ſeldom two) goes on the crown of a narrow ploughed ſet, and ſticks his *ley*, or *Iriſh ſpade*, in it, every here and there, with his right foot, holding it in his left hand, and with it puſhing the ſpade once, and ſometimes twice from him, to make an opening, (which I have ſeen done with a good deal of dexterity) and with the right hand, that contains the ſeed, (a convenient quantity of which he carries in an apron or cloth tied round his middle, ſo as to let the contents be eaſily come at, he throws one, and ſometimes two ſets, or eyes, into the opening which the *loy* makes behind; and on his drawing it away, the looſened earth falls in and covers them: Soon after he dungs the ridges, and covers them up, as in the preceding method, with mould out of the furrows.

" Sometimes alſo they do this work with a ſtick about eighteen inches long, and an inch or ſo diameter, pointed at one end, and ſomewhat curved at the other. By this eaſy means huſband, wife, children, and ſervants,) if they have any) and a friendly neighbour or two, (who may be helped in return) aſſiſt at it for greater expedition, eſpecially when the ſeaſon happens to be advanced.

" In Scotland they do this work ſomewhat differently.

" In Ireland alſo there are many who ſow potatoes after the plough, the ploughman letting the ſets drop in as he goes along; and a harrow matched to the ſame plough, following him cloſe behind, covers them in. There is no great difficulty in this, the land being in tilth. Over all they put dung; but they ſhould mind to give it a light covering, that the ſubſtance of it might impregnate with the adjacent earth, which it would not do, but evaporate by being left expoſed to the air, &c. yet this precaution many are very negligent in.

The other methods, as in the drill, or hillock, or horſe-hoeing way, &c. are little uſed there, except among the more curious; but they being well known in England, it is needleſs to mention them in this place.

" The next thing requiſite is the fencing, which ſhould be done, at fartheſt, before the ſtalk begins to appear; for if the cattle, that are in that ſeaſon greedy for freſh vegetables, get at them, the roots of ſuch as they nip will never come to the ſize they otherwiſe would.

" This is well known in Ireland; and the poor, chiefly I believe from inability, and partly from a ſort of careleſſneſs or rather lazineſs they ſtill inherit (notwithſtanding the mixture of Engliſh and Norman blood, &c.) from their Spaniſh anceſtors, are very remiſs in this reſpect; eſpecially in the chiltern or more fertile parts of the country; where, in moſt matters of huſbandry, they leave too much to chance, relying on the bounty of the ſoil.

" About me, and in many other parts, they very commonly do not put on the firſt covering till about the middle of May; and the ſecond, perhaps, not for a month after; ſo that it is often July before they fence them properly: and where many of them are concerned in a plantation (as is uſually the way) it is moſt troubleſome and difficult to get each man to do his part of the ditching, which commonly is but a ſorry mound of ſods, with ſome buſhes ſodded down on top, to keep out ſheep that ſmell this plant when it riſes, (as cattle do corn) and are very dextrous at getting at it.

" Some of theſe poor people are ſo heedleſs, they never can be brought to make their fences; and then the owner of the ground, in his own defence, is obliged to get it done at an advanced price, and they to pay for it, or their potatoes to remain.

" Many of them, eſpecially in cheap years, leave them on the landlord's hands; and, unleſs a farmer collects himſelf, or has a good ſervant to do it, the rent is not had without immenſe trouble, and ſome of it never. Notwithſtanding

withstanding these difficulties, many farmers have made easy fortunes in this way.

"Thus it happens, at the time they are often finishing the fencing, they ought to be weeding their potatoes.— The weed that mostly annoys them is the Scotch thistle: this should be cut away in June, and if the soil should be so rich as to require a second weeding (which is very often the case) it should be done in August. There will be no other trouble with them till digging time.

"The best time for this work is in the latter end of October, or beginning of November, to avoid the early frosts, which are mortal to them: but if, by bad husbandry, they have been planted late, they should be left longer in the ground, and covered with litter, or haulm, to prevent being lost in this way.

"About Michaelmas, the cattle are let through them, the roots not being then affected by the nipping, or beating down of the stalk: this the peasants know by the colour of it, which becomes a dark brown, losing its verdure; as also by the apple and root.

"The more needy begin to dig them for use in August, though they are not then near so long in ground as they are in England; which demonstrates the excellence and strength of the Irish soil.

"When gentlemen farmers dig their potatoes, they set on a great number of hands at once, two to a ridge: boys and girls gather them promiscuously, big and little, into bags containing about two Winchester bushels; and thus they are carried to the farm-house, and thrown into a room, in one heap, part of which is destroyed by the frost, a great part by the kitchen, also by the hogs, who destroy them much while in the ground, there being hardly any fencing against them; a great part are also stole by the followers, or hangers-on; and the remainder rarely suffices for seed;—of so little value is this estimable root considered in those parts: and yet I have often known them at a very high price, from ten to twenty shillings, and upwards, the big barrel, which is the usual measure in the western parts of Ireland; that is, above two barrels, or eight bushels, Winchester measure.

"Had they such places as Covent-Garden near them the case would be far different: but where there are no convenient and brisk markets, the waste in farms is always great.

"Though, as I remarked before, low or swampy grounds do not answer well for potatoes, yet they sometimes thrive, and are large, the meat being generally scabby, close, wet, and heavy, from the too great impregnation of the water, which renders them unpalatable, and not the best for seed; however, such are chiefly used in this way: yet I have seen them planted in red bogs, which are the wettest and worst; and the bog being previously sanded and dunged, the stalk looked green and healthy, and some of the roots might perchance have eat dry; but those planted in black, or drier bogs, have been found to succeed well.

"There is no culture perhaps, yet known, will better reclaim waste and unprofitable lands, than that of the potatoe. Ireland can well prove the truth of this assertion, in a numberless variety of instances.

"I have seen several tracts of woodland stubbed up, and brought into fine tilth, by means of the potatoe husbandry. America, I believe, can say the same.

"Of late years the hard-hearted sky-farmers, that is, the inferior sort, and even some of our gentlemen-farmers, drive the poor into the mountains, moory grounds, wooded and stony lands, and even into the bogs; and when, by the culture of the potatoe principally, they have reclaimed them, so as to be fit to admit cattle, they are turned out without ceremony. I have in such places seen as fine crops of potatoes, and afterwards flax, and different kinds of corn, as ever I met with any where.

"The mountain and other surfaces, except bog, seldom fail being blessed by nature with limestone, gravel, (which is the commonest) or some other manure, adapted to them; so that it is nothing but hands, money, and a proper limitation of the grazing-farming, that are wanting to make almost the whole kingdom look like a garden,

garden, or like England; I need go no higher with the comparison.

"It is true, in some few counties of Ireland, in particular districts, nature either has not been so bountiful, or the farmers have not found out the internal manures; being obliged to carry sea-sand, and other sorts, many miles; in which, however, they find their account, notwithstanding the impolitically too much limited trade of the kingdom.

"Before I dismiss this subject, it may be proper to observe, that a second crop of potatoes is sometimes taken out of the same land successively; but this is not common, at least about me, though I believe the land is as good as any in the province. On the contrary, the usual way is, after the first crop of potatoes is taken off, if the soil is strong, they immediately sow bere in it, or keep it till the following spring for flax, which requires an equally strong soil: or if the ground be but of a middling good sort, they sow it, just after the potatoes are taken out, with wheat; or keep it till the April following for barley.

"The sky-farmer generally takes the land into his own hands after the first crop of potatoes, and sows it with bere, wheat, or barley, for two or three seasons; after which, if he refreshes it with a summer, or a winter fallow, he sows the same kinds of grain in it for two or three seasons more; then he takes two or three crops of oats; and when it is well impoverished, or drawn (as they call it there) he lets it for several years together, in con-acres, to the poor people for at least one third more than the real value.

"From hence we may judge how much an alteration of method in husbandry is wanting in those parts."

POUND, *Avoirdupois*, contains sixteen ounces. A pound Troy, twelve ounces.

POX. A disorder in hogs. This is a name by which the farmers express a disorder of their swine, that shews itself outwardly in a multitude of pimples and blotches; and keeps the creatures miserable, and makes them pine and waste.

It rises from wet and filth in their sties, and from unwholesome food.

The remedy is this: Make a hot mess for the creature, and give it in an ounce of venice treacle.

After it has taken this, let the whole skin be well cleaned with soap suds, and then wherever the sores and pimples are, use the following ointment. Melt over the fire two pounds of hog's lard, and stir in half a pint of tar. When it is taken off the fire, put to it as much flower of brimstone as will thicken it when cold into a firm ointment. Rub this upon the hog every night for four times, and keep him dry and clean, and it will commonly make a cure in that time.

The farmer must observe, that this disease is infectious; so that he must separate those hogs which have it from the rest, and not put them together again till they have been some time well, and he sees there is no return of the disorder.

PREDIAL TITHES, Are those which are paid of things arising and growing from the ground only, as corn, hay, fruits of trees, and the like.

PRICKS *in a horse's foot*. Whenever this accident happens, we advise the owner to turn his horse immediately to grass, and to apply nothing external to it. If that cannot be done, only rub on the horse's hoof some ointment of elder two or three times a day. All tents are pernicious, and all spirits.

PRICKLY PEAR. *See* INDIAN FIG.

PRICK MADAM. [*Sedum.*] Houseleek.

PRICKWOOD. [*Euonymus.*] This grows very common in hedges in different parts of the kingdom, in some places called Dogwood. The best butchers skewers are made of this wood.

PRIMROSE. [*Primula.*] This plant grows in hedges and woods in almost every part of the kingdom; if transplanted into gardens it loses its beautiful pale colour, and becomes reddish.

Tree, or *Night* PRIMROSE. [*Oenothera.*] There are several species of this plant natives of Virginia and other parts of America, and are propagated by seeds.

PRIVET. [*Ligustrum.*] There are two sorts. 1. The common. 2. The Italian Privet.

The first sort grows common in the hedges in most parts of England, where it rises fifteen or sixteen feet high, with a woody a woody ſtem covered with a ſmooth grey bark, ſending out many lateral branches, garniſhed with ſpear-ſhaped leaves, ending with obtuſe points, and are of a dark green. The flowers are white, and are produced in thick ſpikes at the end of the branches, having a tubular petal cut at the top in four parts, which ſpread open. Theſe are ſucceeded by ſmall, round, black berries, which ripen in the autumn. The leaves of this ſort frequently remain green till after Chriſtmas. There are two varieties of this, one with white, and the other hath yellow variegated leaves; but to preſerve theſe varieties they ſhould be planted in poor land, for if they are in a rich ſoil they will grow vigorous, and ſoon become plain.

The ſecond ſort grows naturally in Italy; this riſes with a ſtronger ſtem than the former, the branches are leſs pliable, and grow more erect; their bark is of a lighter colour, the leaves are much larger, and end in acute points, and are alſo of a brighter green; they continue in verdure till they are thruſt off by the young leaves in the ſpring. The flowers of this are rather larger than thoſe of the common ſort, and are ſeldom ſucceeded by berries in this country.

Both theſe ſorts are cultivated in the nurſeries near London, to furniſh the ſmall gardens and balconies in the city, the firſt being one of the few plants which will thrive in the ſmoke of London; but although they will live ſome years in the cloſe part of the town, yet they ſeldom produce flowers after the firſt year, unleſs it is in ſome open places where there is free air.

The Italian Privet is now generally preferred to the common ſort for planting in gardens, the leaves being larger, and continuing green all the year, render it more valuable; and being ſo hardy as to reſiſt the greateſt cold in this country, it may be planted in any ſituation where the common ſort will thrive.

Mock Privet. [*Phillyrea.*] There are ſeven or eight ſpecies of Mock Privet, all natives of France, Spain, and Italy, but hardy enough to thrive in the open air of England, except the winters are very ſevere. They are all propagated either from ſeeds or layers, but the latter is generally preferred.

PRONG. An implement much uſed in huſbandry, conſiſting of two or three pieces of iron inſerted into a handle for taking up corn, ſtraw, dung, &c.

Prong-*hoe.* A term uſed to expreſs an inſtrument uſed to hoe or break the ground near, and among the roots of plants.

The ordinary contrivance of the hoe in England is very bad, it being only made for ſcraping on the ſurface; but the great uſe of hoeing being to break and open the ground, beſides the killing the weeds, which the antients, and many among us, have thought the only uſe of the hoe, this dull and blunt inſtrument is by no means calculated for the purpoſes it is to ſerve.

The prong-hoe conſiſts of two hooked points of ſix or ſeven inches long, and, when ſtuck into the ground, will ſtir and remove it the ſame depth as the plough does, and thus anſwers both the ends of cutting up the weeds and opening the land. The antient Romans had an inſtrument of this kind, which they called the bidens; but they were afraid of its uſe in their fields and gardens, and only uſed it in their vineyards. The prong-hoe comes into excellent uſe, even in the horſe-hoeing huſbandry; in this the hoe-plough can only come within three or four inches of the rows of corn, turnips, and the like; but this inſtrument may be uſed afterwards, and with it the land may be raiſed and ſtirred, even to the very ſtalk of the plant.

PRUNING. Pruning is an operation of the knife performed upon trees occaſionally, in order both to give them any deſired form, and to retrench or reduce irregular and redundant or ſuperfluous growths, or whatever creates confuſion and diſorder.

But this operation is particularly neceſſary to be practiſed on many ſorts of fruit-trees, more eſpecially the dwarf ſorts, ſuch as all kinds of wall and eſpalier fruit trees; it is alſo neceſſary to be performed occaſionally upon ſtandard trees, both dwarfs and half and full ſtandards, to all of which proper pruning is neceſſary; ſome ſorts annually, as all kinds of wall trees, espaliers, and most other dwarf or trained fruit-trees; to which it is requisite in order to preserve the proper figure, and to keep them within their limited bounds, as well as to promote fruitfulness; but as to common standards whose heads having full scope of growth every way, they require but very little pruning, except just to retrench any occasional redundancy, ill-growing branch, and dead wood. Wall trees and espaliers, however, require a general regulation of pruning twice every year, in summer to retrench the evidently superfluous and ill-placed shoots of the year, and to train in a supply of the most regular ones; and in winter to give a general regulation both to the supply of young wood left in summer and to the old branches where necessary.

For in pruning wall trees and espaliers, it is to be observed, that as these trees having their branches arranged with great regularity to the right and left one above another parallelly, about five or six inches asunder, forming a regular spread, so as the branches of each tree completely cover a certain space of walling, &c. and as the whole spread of branches constantly send forth every year a great number of unnecessary and useless shoots: and each tree being limited to a certain space, an annual pruning is consequently most necessary to retrench the redundancies, and all irregular and bad shoots, to give the proper bearing branches due room, as well as to enable us to confine each tree within its allotted limits, consistent with its regular form.

The first pruning necessary for fruit-trees is when we attempt to give the head its first regular formation, effected by pruning short or heading down in spring all the shoots produced the first year from budding and grafting, that is, the first shoots from the budding, &c. when a year old being generally pruned down in March, within four or five eyes of the bottom, whereby it throws all the sap into the remaining lower buds, and thus, instead of running up to one stem, it pushes forth several strong shoots from the lower part the ensuing summer, so as to fill the allotted space of walling and espalier regularly quite from the bottom; which shoots being trained strait and regular in a spreading manner, each at full length all summer; and in winter or spring following, if a supply of more principal shoots shall seem necessary to form the head more effectually, prune short also these shoots each to four or five eyes, and each of them will throw out the like number of shoots the same year, which according as they advance in length, train at regular distances at full length during the summer as before observed; for the shoots of wall trees should never be shortened in the summer season, for this would cause them to push forth many trifling lateral shoots; though sometimes, in order to fill a vacancy as soon as possible, strong young shoots being pinched early in the season, as in May or beginning of June, to four or five eyes, will throw out several proper shoots the same summer, repeating however the work of pruning short occasionally one or two years, &c. as above, either in general or to particular shoots, as it may seem proper till a proper set of branches are by that means obtained to give the head of the tree a proper formation; afterwards pruning short is to be omitted except occasionally to any particular shoot to fill a vacant space: but some sorts of wall trees require almost a general shortening of their supply of shoots, such as peach, nectarines, &c. which bear only on the young wood; have that of each year shortened, to force out a supply of shoots for future bearing; other sorts of wall-trees and espaliers are not in the general course of pruning to be shortened, such as pears, apples, plums, and cherries, which bear in the old wood from two or three to many years growth.

After the trees are thus furnished with a proper spread of branches trained regularly to the wall and espalier, they will every year throw out many more shoots than are wanted, or can be converted to use, by being some too numerous, others ill placed, and others of a bad growth, all of which must therefore be regulated accordingly by proper pruning; for as the regular figure of the tree, well furnished in every part equally from the bottom to the top of the wall or espalier with proper branches, capable of producing a reasonable quantity of good

good fruit, are the principal objects of pruning; all our operations must be directed to these ends.

We must therefore be careful to ease the trees of every thing that is either superfluous, irregular, or hurtful, by pruning twice every year, a summer and a winter pruning. We call that superfluous which, though good and well placed, yet are more than are wanted or can be properly laid in, and that irregular which is so ill placed as it cannot be trained with regularity to the wall or espalier, such as all fore-right shoots, being such as grow immediately from the front or back of the branches in a fore-right direction, which though good of themselves, yet their situation renders them irregular or unfit for training; and we call that hurtful which is in itself of bad growth, such as all very rank or singularly luxuriant rude shoots; so that the superfluous or redundant growths should be thinned by pruning out all that seem to cause confusion, and the irregular and hurtful rank shoots should be displaced, cutting every thing of all these sorts off quite close to the place from whence they proceed, leaving however a proper supply, more or less, of the regular or best placed side-shoots where necessary, so as to preserve every part well furnished with bearing wood, trained straight and close to the wall or espaliers at equal distances; observing, that some sorts of wall-trees, &c. require a general annual supply of young wood, such as peach and all other trees which bear only on the shoots of a year old; others require only an occasional supply of wood, such as apples, pears, &c. and all other kinds that bear on the old wood from two or three to ten or twenty years old or more, so that the same branches continuing in bearing many years, the trees require only a supply of young shoots now and then to replace any worn-out and dead branches.

For the mystery of pruning consists in being well acquainted with the nature of bearing of the different sorts of trees, and forming an early judgment of the future event of shoots and branches, and many other circumstances, for which some principal rules may be given; but there are particular instances which cannot be judged of but upon the spot, and depend chiefly upon practice and observation.

The nature or mode of bearing of the different sorts of wall and espalier trees, &c. is materially to be considered in pruning.

For example: Peaches, nectarines, apricots, &c. all produce their fruit principally upon the young wood of a year old, that is, the shoots produced this year bear the fruit the year following, and the same of every year's shoots, so that consequently, in all these trees, a general supply of the best regular shoots of each year must be every where preserved at regular distances quite from the very bottom to the extremity of the tree, on every side in such order as to seem coming up regularly one after another, which should be trained principally at full length all summer; but in winter pruning, a general shortening less or more, according to the strength of the different shoots, is necessary, in order to promote their throwing out more effectually a supply of young wood the ensuing summer, in proper places for training in for next year's bearing, the fruit being generally produced all along their sides, immediately from the eyes, they rarely forming any considerable fruit-spurs, as in the apple, pear, &c. but the same shoots both produce the fruit and a supply of shoots at the same time for the succeeding year's bearing.

Vines also produce their fruit always upon the young wood, shoots of the same year arising from the eyes of the last year's wood only, and must therefore have a general supply of the best regular shoots of each year, trained in, which in winter pruning must be shortened to a few eyes, in order to force out shoots from their lower parts only, properly situated to lay in for bearing the following year.

Figs bear also only upon the young wood of a year old, and a general supply of it is therefore necessary every year; but these shoots must at no time be shortened unless the ends are dead, because they always bear principally towards the extreme part of the shoots, which if shortened would take the bearing or fruitful parts away: Besides, these trees for the general part naturally throw out a sufficient supply of shoots every year for future bearing without the precaution of shortening.

And as to apple, pear, plum, and cherry trees, they generally bear principally on spurs arising in the wood of from two or three to ten or twenty years old, the same branches and spurs continuing bearing a great number of years, so that having once procured a proper set of branches, in the manner already directed, to form a spreading head, no farther supply of wood is wanted than only some occasional shoots now and then to supply the place of any worn-out or dead branch as before hinted; the above-mentioned spurs or fruit-buds are short robust shoots, of from about half an inch to one or two inches long, arising naturally in these trees, first towards the extreme parts of the branches of two or three years old, and as the branch increases in length the number of fruit-buds increase likewise accordingly; this, therefore determines, that in the general course of pruning all these kind of trees, their branches that are trained in for bearing must not be pruned or shortened, but trained at full length; for if they were shortened it would divest them of the very parts where fruit-buds would have first appeared, and instead thereof would throw out a number of strong unnecessary wood shoots, from all the remaining eyes: therefore let all the shoots or branches of these trees be trained principally at full length, and as they advance, still continue them entire; thus they will all readily form the afore-mentioned little spurs or fruit-buds from almost every eye; when indeed there is a vacancy, and there is only one shoot where two or three may be requisite, in this case only pruning or shortening is allowable in these trees, to force out the supply required.

In these trees great care is necessary to preserve all the proper fruit-buds or spurs; which are readily distinguished by their short, thick, robust growth, rarely exceeding one or two inches long.

In the general course of pruning all sorts of wall and espalier trees, that when displacing the superfluous and ill-placed woods, &c. always take them off quite close both in the summer and winter pruning, not leaving any spurs or stumps of them an inch or two long, as often done, which fills the tree full of disagreeable stumps, and which pushing out strongly from every eye, crowd the tree with a multitude of unnecessary and irregular shoots, and cause great confusion and obscurity, and exhaust the sap to no purpose, as well as occasion a great deal of labour to retrench them; remember, therefore, that all shoots and branches necessary to be retrenched must be taken off quite close to the place from whence they arise; which in the summer pruning if attended to early, while the shoots are quite young and tender, they may readily be rubbed off quite close with the thumb; but when the shoots become older and woody, as they will not readily break, it must be done with a knife, cutting them as close as possible, and all winter pruning must always be perfomed with a knife.

It should also generally be observed in pruning in summer, that all the necessary supply of regular shoots that are left for training in should never be shortened during this season, unless to particular shoots to fill a vacancy; for by a general shortening in this season, all the shoots so treated would soon push again vigorously from every eye, and run your trees into a perfect thicket of useless wood; therefore all sorts, whether they require shortening in the winter pruning or not, should in the summer dressing, be layed in at full length.

Two seasons of pruning are requisite for all sorts of wall and espalier trees, a summer and a winter pruning.

Summer Pruning.——The summer pruning is a most necessary operation; every one must know that in spring and summer, wall and espalier trees abound with a great number of young shoots that require thinning and other reforms to preserve the beauty of the trees and encourage the fruit, and the sooner it is performed the better; it is therefore adviseable to begin this work in May or early in June, and timely disburthen the trees of all evidently redundant or superfluous growth and ill-placed and bad shoots, which may be performed with considerably more expedition and exactness than when after the trees have shot a considerable length and run into confusion and disorder,

disorder, by their shoots forming a thicket, when it will, in a manner be impossible to see what you are about, besides the disadvantage of choaking up the fruit behind such a thicket of wood and leaves; it is therefore of great importance to perform this operation in the month of May or early in June, or when the same year's shoots are sufficiently formed to enable you to make a proper choice, and tender enough to require no other instrument than the thumb to displace the bad growths and superfluities.

However, at any rate, let the work of summer pruning be began before the trees have so far advanced in shooting as to cause much confusion, which would cost you a great deal of pains, precaution, and perplexity, to penetrate and break through the obscurity to determine what is proper to retrench or what to leave.

In this pruning, we observe above, that a great many more shoots arise from all the principal branches than are wanted, or that can possibly be trained with regularity, or that are well placed or proper for the purpose; our business therefore now is to thin and regulate them, by pruning away the superfluous shoots, and all such as are ill-placed and of bad growth as aforesaid; as to superfluous shoots they are to be considered as such when any tree throws out a redundancy of wood, or much more than what is wanted, or that can be trained in; of these you must now retrench the most irregular placed, weakest, and all such as are evidently not wanted for use, and where two or more shoots any where arise from the same eye, clear all away but one of the best, reserving a sufficiency of the moderately strong and most regular placed side shoots, and always a leading one at the end of every branch, all of which to be trained in to choose from in the winter pruning, leaving more or less in proportion, according to what the trees are, or the mode of bearing before hinted; though in all those trees that bear always on the young wood leave rather more shoots at present than what may appear just necessary, especially of peaches, nectarines, apricots, vines, figs, &c. for it is highly requisite to reserve regular wood enough in the summer to choose out of in winter pruning to lay in for next year's bearing; but as to apples, pears, plums, and cherries, &c. which continue bearing many years on the same branches, should leave only here and there some good shoots towards the lower parts, or in any vacancy till winter, and if then not wanted they are easily retrenched. Ill-placed shoots being such as either grow directly from the front or back of the branches straight foreright, (called foreright shoots) or any other ways so ill placed as not to admit of training with regularity, so must all be cut out quite close; and bad or hurtful growth being considered as any very luxuriant shoots, distinguished from the others by their rank, vigorous shooting, and are like to prove injurious by drawing all the nourishment, and impoverishing the neighbouring ones that are of more moderate growth, should generally be removed, except where any may seem proper to leave to fill a vacant space, in which it may be pinched early to three or four eyes, when it will furnish you with the like number of more moderate shoots to fill the vacancy.

Where, however, a tree is in general inclined to luxuriancy, it is proper to retain as many of the regular shoots as can be commodiously trained in with any regularity, in order to divide and exhaust the too abundant sap which causes the luxuriancy; for by humouring somewhat the natural inclination of luxuriant trees by leaving plenty of branches and these mostly at full length, is the only method by which we can the most readily reduce them to a more moderate state of growth.

Pay particular attention always to the lower parts of your trees, for frequently we shall find proper shoots arising in places necessary to be trained in, either to supply a present or an apparent future vacancy, or as a reserve to replace any decayed, or worn-out, or other bad branch, so that if moderately strong well placed shoots arise in such parts, they are particularly to be regarded at this time; and in winter pruning such of them as are not wanted may be easily cut off.

All weak trifling shoots should now also be taken out, unless any shall appear useful to fill a vacancy, or likely to be of service hereafter.

Observe in this pruning not to disturb the natural fruit-buds or spurs before described.

After having summer pruned and cleared any tree from all useless shoots as above, let all the remaining proper shoots be directly, or as soon as they are long enough, trained in straight and close to the wall or espaliers, and all of them at full length during the summer season, for the reasons before given; not shortening any at this time except as before observed, when there is any great vacancy, when pinching to three or four eyes may be proper; but let all the rest be trained at full length till winter pruning, when they must undergo another regulation and shorten those of such trees as require it, as peach, nectarine, &c.

The work of training in the shoots in this season is, if against walls, both by nailing by means of proper shred and nails, and occasionally by fastening in the smaller shoots with little sticks or twigs stuck between the main branches and the wall; and for espaliers tie them with small oziers, rushes, or bass strings.

Having thus summer dressed and trained your trees, it will be necessary to review them occasionally, in order to reform such branches or shoots as may have started from their places or taken a wrong direction, also that according as any fresh irregular shoots produced since the general dressing may be displaced; and likewise as the already trained shoots advance in length or project from the wall or espalier, they should be trained in close, still continuing them at full length during their summer's growth, for every thing should be kept close and regular all summer, whereby your trees will appear beautiful to the eye, and the fruit will shew itself and attain its due perfection.

For by thus properly summer pruning and training wall and espalier trees early in the summer, you preserve their regularity and prosperity, and by clearing out all the unnecessary and useless growths, training the rest close and regular, the fruit will receive all requisite advantage from the sun, air, rains, &c. and it will of course attain the greater perfection both in size, beauty, and flavour.

Winter Pruning.—In the winter pruning a general regulation must be observed both of the mother branches and the supply of young wood laid in the preceding summer, and the proper time for this work is any time in open weather from the fall of the leaf in November until March.

In performing this work of winter pruning, it is proper to unnail or loosen great part of the branches, particularly of peaches, nectarines, apricots, vines, and such other trees as require an annual supply of young wood.

First look over the principal or mother branches, and examine if any are worn out or not furnished with parts proper for bearing fruit, according to the rules before illustrated, with respect to the nature of bearing of the different sorts of trees; and let such branches be cut down to the great branch from which they proceed, or to any lower shoot or good branch they may support towards their bottom part, leaving these to supply its place; likewise examine if any branches are become too long for the allotted space either at sides or top, and let them be reformed accordingly by shortening them down to some lower shoot or branch properly situated to supply the place, being careful that every branch terminates in a young shoot of some sort for a leader, and not stumped off at the extremity, as is too often practised by unskilful pruners.

From the principal or larger branches pass to the shoots of the year, which were trained up in summer, first cutting out close all foreright and other irregular shoots that may have been omitted in the summer pruning, likewise all very weak shoots, and those of very luxuriant growth, unless it be necessary to keep some to supply a vacant place; then of the remaining regular shoots, you are to select a greater or smaller portion to leave either as a general supply for next year's bearing as in the case for peach, nectarine, apricots, vines, and figs, or only some occasional shoots, as in apple, pear, plum, and cherry trees, to supply the place of any bad or dead branch.

But as peaches, nectarines, apricots, vines, and figs, always bear principally on the year-old wood as before noticed,

noticed, a general supply of young shoots must be left in every part from bottom to top at regular distances, all of which, except the fig, must be more or less shortened according to their situation and strength to encourage their furnishing more readily a proper supply of shoots in spring and summer for next year's bearing, as before observed, leaving the strongest shoots always the longest, as is more fully explained under each of their respective *genera*; but as the figs always bear towards the end of the shoots, they must not be shortened.

And with respect to the apples, pears, plums, cherries, &c. as they continue to bear on the old branches from two or three to many years standing, they only require an occasional supply of young wood, according as the branches become unfit for bearing and want removing, so should accordingly train in here and there in proper places some good regular young shoots towards the lower part, to be coming gradually forward to a bearing state, to be ready to replace worn-out and other useless branches; and what shoots are not now wanted for that purpose cut them out close, not leaving any spur or stump, as every one of these, as we before observed, would push out several strong unnecessary shoots the next spring, to the prejudice both of the trees and fruit; have particular regard to preserve the shoots at the termination of all the already trained branches entire, not however suffer more than one shoot to terminate each branch; preserve also carefully all the proper fruit-spurs; likewise observe, that the supply of young wood occasionally reserved, and the branches in general of these trees, should all be trained in at full length, and continued so in future, as far as the limited space will admit; and according as any extend above the wall or espalier, or any where beyond their proper limits, they should be pruned down with discretion to some convenient bud, or lateral shoot, or lower branch, which train also entire.

In this pruning, as in the summer dressing, it is of importance to have a strict eye to the lower parts of wall trees, &c. to see if there is any present vacancy or any that apparently will soon happen, in which cases, if any good shoot is situated contiguous, it should be trained in either at full length, or shorten it to a few eyes to force out two or more shoots if they shall seem necessary; for precaution should ever be observed in taking care to have betimes a sufficient stock of young wood coming forward to fill up any casual vacancy, and substitute a new set of branches in place of such as are either decayed or stand in need of retrenchment.

Sometimes in wall trees and espaliers there are many large disagreeable barren spurs, consisting both of old worn-out fruit spurs, and of clusters of stumps of shortened shoots projecting considerably from the branches, occasioned by unskilful pruning when retrenching the superabundant and irregular shoots, which instead of being cut out close, are stumped off to an inch or two long, and in the course of a few years, forming numerous barren stumps, as abovesaid, and very little fruit, the trees appear like a stumped hedge; it is therefore, in this season of pruning, adviseable to reform them as well as possible, by cutting all the most disagreeable stumps clean out close to the branches, leaving these at full length, especially of apples, pears, &c. as before advised: and reserve an occasional supply of young wood in different parts; and thus in two or three years you may reduce such trees to a regular figure and a proper state of bearing.

Bad pruning ruins many a good tree, as is observable in numerous gardens, where the wall-trees and espaliers appear as just above described, pruned every year, yet never produce any tolerable crop of fruit.

The reason is, the operation or art of pruning is much more generally practised than understood; different pruners have different ideas of pruning; many proceed upon little or no principle, and often prune all trees alike, and their idea of pruning often consists in retrenching annually most of the young shoots, shortening all the branches of every tree without exception, to the great injury of some sorts, and retarding their bearing; likewise many pruners in retrenching the superfluous and irregular shoots, instead of cutting close, as formerly

observed,

observed, they often stump them off to about one or two inches long; these remaining stumps shoot out again from every eye, and fill the tree with more numerous useless shoots than before, which being also pruned down to stumps of an inch or two long, as above, practising the same every pruning, so as in the course of a few years every branch is loaded with clusters of large rugged barren spurs, formed wholly of the stumps of shortened shoots, occupying the places where fruit-buds might be expected: It is also observable, that many pruners think every branch of all sorts of wall trees whatsoever must, in the annual pruning, undergo the discipline of the knife, so shorten all without distinction or reluctance, often too with so much severity on trees that should not be shortened, as to destroy the very parts where fruit-buds would have been produced, they thinking this general shortening necessary to strengthen the branches, which, however, in many sorts, promotes a too vigorous growth, particularly in trees that produce their fruit on natural spurs, forming themselves gradually all along the sides of the branches, first towards the extreme parts, that shortening not only cuts off these first fruitful parts of the branches, but throws the sap back with so much vigour to the remaining buds, that instead of forming fruit-spurs, almost every bud pushes out luxuriant shoots, and the trees are continually crouded with unnecessary wood, causing a great annual trouble to retrench it, without the pleasure of having a quarter of a crop of fruit; besides the annually cutting out so much strong wood is very prejudicial to some sorts of fruit-trees.

Too severe pruning is very prejudicial to the health of some sorts of stone fruit-trees in particular, causing them to gum and soon decay.

Plums and cherries in particular are often greatly damaged by a too severe discipline of the knife, these trees being very liable to gum by large amputations; it is therefore of importance to attend to these trees well in the summer pruning, to retrench all the superfluous and irregular shoots betimes in the summer while quite young, and pinch others occasionally where wood is wanted to fill vacancies, so as to require but little pruning out of large wood in winter.

But if our former hints in the summer and winter pruning are attended to in retrenching the useless wood every year at the time advised, you will always preserve your trees free from all incumbrance and every part will be regularly filled with bearing wood, and their general management will prove easy.

A general nailing, &c. must every year be performed according as we advance with the pruning.

Therefore it is proper that every tree as soon as pruned be directly nailed to the wall, or if espaliers, tie them to the treilage, observing, that in the winter pruning, as the work of nailing, &c. will require to be performed more or less upon all the branches, we must be careful to train them with great regularity, nailing them along horizontally, as straight and close as possible; never cross any of the branches, but train them distinct and parallel five or six inches asunder, as formerly advised, or in proportion to the size of the leaves and fruit of the different sorts, making the opposite branches of each side arrange equally in the same position.

Thus far is principally all we have to advance respecting the general mode of pruning wall and espalier trees; particulars for each sort being noticed more fully under their proper *genera*; but what we have here advanced under this article of *pruning* is to convey some general hints to unexperienced pruners, though there are many expedients and resources not to be discovered but by repeated practice.

Pruning Standards.

Standard fruit-trees require but very little pruning, for as their branches have full scope to extend themselves every way, they must not be shortened; besides, as our standard fruit-trees consist principally of apples, pears, plums, and cherries, these, as before said, bear fruit on natural spurs arising towards the upper parts of the branches, which, as observed in the wall-tree and espalier pruning, determines that we must not shorten them, nor practise any other pruning than just to reform any great irregularity, &c.

The first occasional pruning, however,

ever neceſſary for ſtandard fruit-trees, is the firſt two years of their growth, in order to form their heads ſomewhat regular, by retrenching any irregular ſhoots, and when deſigned to have them form more regular ſpreading heads, it is cuſtomary to prune the firſt ſhoots when a year old to four or five eyes, in order to force out lateral ſhoots from theſe lower buds the following ſummer, to give the head a proper formation. After this, ſuffer the branches to take their natural growth, except that, if while the trees are young, any very luxuriant ſhoots ramble away conſiderably from all others, and draw moſt of the nouriſhment, it is proper to prune them, either by retrenching entirely very irregular ones, or ſhorten others more or leſs, ſo as to cauſe them to branch out conſiſtent with the requiſite form of the head.

But let it be remarked in general, that except in ſuch caſes of reducing irregularities, let the heads of all kinds of ſtandards always branch away as faſt as poſſible, both in length and laterally, agreeable to their natural mode of growing; and they will naturally furniſh themſelves abundantly with bearing wood.

Obſerve, however, that as in ſtandard trees of ſome years growth, irregularities and diſorder will occaſionally happen, which ſhould be regulated a little by pruning the moſt conſpicuouſly irregular and redundant growths; performing it always in winter.

For inſtance: Where any branch grows right acroſs others, or in any aukward direction, to incommode or cauſe confuſion in the head, it ſhould be retrenched cloſe; likewiſe any branch that rambles conſiderably from all the reſt, ſhould be reduced to order, by cutting it down to ſome convenient lower branch, ſo as to preſerve ſome regularity. Where the head is conſiderably crouded with wood, let the worſt of the redundancy be thinned out as regularly as poſſible, cutting them cloſe to their origin; obſerve likewiſe where any vigorous ſhoots ariſe in the heart of the tree towards the bottom of the old branches, and grow upright and croud the middle of the head, they ſhould be conſtantly retrenched to their very bottom; cut alſo any very cankered parts, and decayed wood, and clear off all ſuckers from the root and ſtem.

Standard trees thus diſburthened from any conſiderable irregularities and confuſion, ſo as all the proper branches have full ſcope to ſpread free and eaſy in their natural manner, they will not fail to repay the trouble in the ſuperior quality of their future fruit.

Pruning Foreſt-Trees, &c.

With reſpect to pruning of foreſt and ornamental trees, flowering ſhrubs, &c. it is very inconſiderable.

Foreſt-trees, &c. muſt be ſuffered to run up as faſt as poſſible, ſo their heads muſt not be ſhortened; all that is neceſſary is, to prune off lateral branches occaſionally from the ſtem, or if while young, any lateral ſhoot of the head is of a very rude rambling growth, and draws all the nouriſhment, it is proper to reduce it as you ſee convenient; but otherwiſe ſuffer the top and all the branches of the head to remain entire, and take their own natural growth; only prune lower ſtragglers occaſionally; obſerving, however, it is very improper to trim up the ſtem too high, as often practiſed to foreſt-trees, as ſcarce to leave any head: never, therefore, trim the ſtem much higher than the full ſpread of the head, for a full head is both ornamental and eſſentially neceſſary to the proſperity of the tree.

And as to the ſhrub kind, they ſhould alſo, for the general part, take their own growth at top; and only prune occaſionally any lower ſtragglers, from the lower part of the ſtem, or any very irregular rambling ſhoot of the head, and all dead wood; but except in theſe caſes, let their heads moſtly ſhoot in their own way, according to their different modes of growth, in which they will appear always the moſt agreeable.

Where, however, it is required to keep ſhrubs low in any particular compartment, you muſt regulate this as you ſhall ſee convenient, either with a knife or garden-ſheers, though knife-pruning is the moſt eligible.

Pruning Implements.

For the purpoſe of general pruning ſeveral implements are neceſſary, ſuch as pruning knives, ſaws, chiſſels, hand-bills, hatchets, &c.

As to pruning-knives, two or three different ſizes are requiſite in order to enable us to prune neatly; a ſtrong one for cutting out larger branches, ſhoots, &c. and a ſmall one for the more exact pruning among the ſmaller branches and ſhoots of peach and nectarine-trees, &c. Theſe knives are generally made curving at the point; they ſhould not be too long, broad, or clumſey, but have rather a ſhortiſh narrow blade, and but very moderately hooked at the point, for when too crooked they are apt to hang in the wood, and not cut clean; it is alſo proper to be furniſhed with a ſtrong thick-backed knife, to uſe by way of a chiſſel occaſionally, in cutting out any hard ſtubborn ſtumps, &c. placing the edge on the wood, and with your nailing hammer ſtrike the back of it, and it will readily cut through even and ſmooth.

Pruning hand-ſaws are proper for cutting out any large branch too thick and ſtubborn for the knife; they ſhould be of moderate ſizes, one of which ſhould be quite ſmall and narrow, in order to introduce it occaſionally between the forks and the branches, to cut to exactneſs.

As ſaws generally leave the cut rough, it is proper to ſmooth it with a knife or a pruning chiſſel.

Pruning chiſſels are neceſſary to uſe occaſionally, both to cut off any thick hard branch or ſtump, and to ſmooth cuts after a ſaw; they ſhould be flat, and from about one to two inches broad; ſometimes large ſtrong chiſſels, fixed on a long pole, are uſed in pruning or lopping branches from the ſtems of high ſtandard foreſt trees, one man holding the chiſſel againſt the branch, while another with a large mallet or beetle ſtrikes the end of the pole.

A hand-bill and hatchet are alſo neceſſary to uſe occaſionally among larger kinds of the ſtandard trees.

All theſe pruning tools in their different ſizes may be had at the cutlery ſhops and ironmongers, alſo of many of the nurſery and ſeedſmen; and as the expence of the whole will be but trifling, every one ſhould furniſh himſelf properly.

PUCCOON. [*Sanguinaria.*] It is a native of moſt of the northern parts of America, where it grows plentifully in the woods; and in the ſpring, before the leaves of the trees come out, the ſurface of the ground is, in many places covered with the flowers, which have ſome reſemblance to our Wood Anemone, but they have ſhort naked pedicles, each ſupporting one flower at the top. Some of theſe flowers will have ten or twelve petals, ſo that they appear to have a double range of leaves, which has occaſioned their being termed double flowers. The roots of this plant are tuberous, and the whole plant has a yellow juice, which the Indians uſe to paint themſelves with.

This plant is hardy enough to live in the open air in England, but it ſhould be planted in a looſe ſoil and a ſheltered ſituation, not too much expoſed to the ſun. It is propagated by the roots, which may be taken up and parted every other year; the beſt time for doing of this is in September, that the roots may have time to ſend out fibres before the hard froſt ſets in. The flowers of this plant appear in April, and when they decay, the green leaves come out, which will continue till Midſummer; then they decay, and the roots remain inactive till the following autumn; ſo that unleſs the roots are marked, it will be pretty difficult to find them, after their leaves decay, for they are of a dirty brown colour on the outſide, ſo are not eaſily diſtinguiſhed from the earth.

PUCK-BALL, a ſpecies of muſhroom, full of duſt.

PULSE, a term applied to all leguminous plants, as beans, peas, tares, &c.

PUMKIN. Gourd.

PURGING. See PHYSIC.

PURGING-NUT. See PHYSIC-NUT.

PURGING-FLAX. See FLAX.

PURGING OILY GRAIN. See OILY GRAIN.

PURSLANE. [*Portulaca.*] This is a ſallad herb propagated from ſeeds, which may be ſown upon beds of light rich earth during any of the ſummer months; but if you intend to have it early in the ſeaſon, it ſhould be ſown upon a hot-bed, for it is too tender to be ſown in the open air before April, and then it muſt be in a warm ſituation. This ſeed is very ſmall, ſo that a little of it will be ſufficient to ſupply a family. There is no other culture which this plant requires, but to keep it clear from weeds, and in dry weather

ther to water it two or three times a week. In warm weather this plant will be fit for use in six weeks after sowing; so that in order to continue a succession of it, you should sow it at three or four different seasons, allowing a fortnight or three weeks between each sowing, which will be sufficient to last the whole summer, while it is proper to be eaten; for being of a very cold nature, it is unsafe to be eaten, except in the heat of summer in England; for which reason it is not to any purpose to sow it upon a hot-bed, since it will come early enough for use in the open air. If the seeds are intended to be saved, a sufficient number of the earliest plants should be eft for this purpose, drawing out all those which are weak, or have small leaves, from among them; and when the seeds are ripe, the plants should be cut up, and spread upon cloths in the sun to dry, and then the seeds may be easily beaten out and sifted, to clear it from the leaves and seed-vessels.

Sea PURSLANE, a species of Orach.

PYRACANTHA. The ever-green hawthorn.

Q.

QUAKING GRASS. [*Gramen Maximum*.] A large species of grass, rising from fourteen inches to two feet high, with loose panicles, shaken by every wind.

QUARTER. A fourth part. A quantity of corn containing eight bushels, or one-fifth of a load.

False QUARTER. A false quarter is a reft or chink in the quarter of the hoof, from top to bottom; it happens generally on the inside, that being the weakest and the thinnest, and proceeds from the dryness of the hoof, but especially when a horse is ridden in dry, sandy, or stony ground, in hot weather, or in frosty weather, when the ways are flinty and hard: It is likewise caused by bad shoeing, and all the other accidents whereby a horse becomes hoof-bound, for the narrowness of the heels and brittleness of the quarters continually expose a horse to all the said accidents.

This accident is both dangerous and painful, for as often as a horse sets his foot to the ground the chink widens, and when he lifts it up, the sharp edges of the divided hoof wound the tender flesh that covers the coffin-bone, which is, for the most part, followed with blood, and it must of course be apt to render a horse lame, as it is very difficult to form a re-union.

The usual method taken to remedy this imperfection is, by cutting off that part of the shoe which lies upon the chink, that it may be wholly uncovered; then with a drawing iron to open the rift to the quick, filling it up in all parts with a rowel of hurds dipt in turpentine, wax, and sheep's suet, molten together, renewing it every day until the seam is filled up; after it is closed in the top, or upper part, it is usual to draw the place betwixt the hoof and the cronet, which, by softening the hoof, and bringing a moisture into it, causes it to grow the faster, and shoot downwards. But there are some who sear the cronet above the crack, without piercing the skin just where the hoof begins; and with another iron sear the chink about the middle of the hoof, which succeeds very well, if care be taken to keep the hoof moist with applications of tar, honey, and grease. Some pour aqua-fortis into the rift when the pain is violent, to deaden the part, making a border of wax on each side to hinder it from spoiling the rest of the hoof; and there are others who prepare a flat piece of wood about an inch in breadth, but at the same time so slender, that it will bend like a hoop, and of a sufficient length to go twice round the hoof; and having first drawn the whole length of the cleft, they apply turpentine, pitch, and suet, molten

molten together, to the ſore, and faſten the hoof with pieces of liſt or filleting. This is a contrivance to anſwer inſtead of bandage, to keep the chink united, and to prevent it from jarring when the foot is moved, which is, indeed, very reaſonable, for the leaſt motion will be apt to diſcompoſe the tender ſubſtance that grows up in the cleſt, and cauſe impoſthumation, which will again open the hoof. But I am of opinion, inſtead of this troubleſome way, the following method will be found more eaſy and ſucceſsful:

Firſt, draw the whole length of the cleſt gently with your drawing iron, then anoint the hoof with tar, honey, and ſuet, molten together as directed, for nothing can be more proper for the hoof, and lay a thin pledgit dipt in the ſame along the cleſt; after this, take of rope-yarn, ſuch as the ſailors uſe, which is no other than hemp moiſtened in melted pitch and tar, and ſpun looſe; apply the yarn all down the hoof, beginning at the cronet, and deſcend downwards, one lay after another, as cloſe as the binding of the hoops of wine-caſks, laying a ſmooth pledgit of flax behind, to keep it from fretting the heel. This ſhould be opened once in three or four days, that the cleſt may be dreſt; and to prevent any inconveniency that can happen by the opening, a thin ſtaple may be alſo contrived with points like horſe-ſhoe nails, caſt off obliquely, to take a ſlender hold, the plate of it croſſing the cleſt where part of the ſhoe is cut off, and the nails coming out on each ſide the cleſt on the upper part, to be rivetted as the other nails. By this method a cleſt in any part of the hoof may eaſily be cured, if the horſe be not very old and diſeaſed.

QUEEN *of the Meadows*. See Meadow-ſweet.

QUICK, or *Quickſet-Hedge*, A general name for all hedges, of whatever ſorts of plants they are compoſed, to diſtinguiſh them from dead hedges; but, in a more confined ſenſe of the word, it is applied to the white or hawthorn, the ſets or young plants of which are raiſed by the nurſery gardeners for ſale.

QUICKBEAM. See SERVICE.

QUINCUNX, A diſpoſition of trees originally formed into a ſquare, conſiſting of five trees, one at each corner, and a fifth in the middle; which diſpoſition often repeated forms a regular grove, and then viewed by an angle of the ſquare or parallelogram, repreſents equal and parallel alleys.

QUINCE-TREE. [*Cydonia*.] The ſpecies are, 1. The Pear Quince. 2. The Apple Quince. 3. The Portugal Quince. And 4. The eatable Quince.

All the ſorts are eaſily propagated either by layers, ſuckers, or cuttings, which muſt be planted in a moiſt ſoil. Thoſe raiſed from ſuckers are ſeldom ſo well rooted as thoſe which are obtained from cuttings or layers, and are ſubject to produce ſuckers again in greater plenty, which is not ſo proper for fruit-bearing trees. The cuttings ſhould be planted early in the autumn on a moiſt border. The ſecond year after they ſhould be removed into a nurſery at three feet diſtance row from row, and one foot aſunder in the rows, where they muſt be managed as was directed for Apples. In two years time theſe trees will be fit to tranſplant, where they are to remain for good, which ſhould be either by the ſide of a ditch, river, or ſome other moiſt place, where they will produce a greater plenty, and much larger fruit than in a dry ſoil; though thoſe in the dry ſoil will be better taſted, and earlier ripe. The trees require very little pruning; the chief thing to be obſerved is, to keep their ſtems clear from ſuckers, and cut off ſuch branches as croſs each other; likewiſe all upright luxuriant ſhoots from the middle of the tree ſhould be taken entirely out, that the head may not be too much crouded with wood, which is of ill conſequence to all ſorts of fruit-trees. If they are propagated by budding, or grafting upon ſtocks raiſed by cuttings, to multiply the beſt ſorts, the trees ſo raiſed will bear fruit much ſooner and be more fruitful, than thoſe which come from ſuckers or layers.

Quince ſtocks are alſo in great eſteem for to graft and bud pears on, which on a moiſt ſoil will greatly improve ſome ſorts, eſpecially thoſe deſigned for walls and eſpaliers: for the trees upon theſe ſtocks do not ſhoot ſo vigorouſly as thoſe upon free ſtocks, and therefore may be kept in leſs compaſs,

paſs, and are ſooner diſpoſed to bear fruit: but hard winter fruits do not ſucceed ſo well upon theſe ſtocks, their fruit being very ſubject to crack, and are commonly ſtony, eſpecially all the breaking pears, but more eſpecially if they are planted in dry ground; therefore theſe ſtocks are only proper for the melting pears, and for a moiſt ſoil. The beſt ſtocks are thoſe which are raiſed from cuttings or layers.

QUIT-RENT, a ſmall rent payable by the tenants of moſt manors, whereby the tenant is quit or free from all other ſervices, and is ſaid to be an acknowledgment of their ſubjection to the lord of the manor.

QUITTOR, an ulcer formed between the hair and hoof, uſually on the inſide quarter of a horſe's foot; it often ariſes from treads and bruiſes, ſometimes from gravel, which by working its way upwards, lodges about the coronet: if it is only ſuperficial, it may be cured with cleanſing dreſſings, bathing the coronet every day with ſpirit of wine, and dreſſing the ſore with precipitate medicine.

But if the matter forms itſelf a lodgment under the hoof, there is no way then to come at the ulcer, but by taking off part of the hoof; and if this be done artfully and well, the cure may be effected without danger.

When the matter happens to be lodged near the quarter, the farrier is ſometimes obliged to take off the quarter of the hoof, and the cure is then for the moſt part but palliative; for when the quarter grows up it leaves a pretty large ſeam, which weakens the foot: This is what is called a falſe quarter, and a horſe with this defect ſeldom gets quite ſound.

If the matter, by its confinement, has rotted the coffin-bone, which is of ſo ſoft and ſpongy a nature, that it ſoon becomes ſo, you muſt enlarge the opening, cut away the rotten fleſh, and apply the actual cautery, or hot iron pointed pyramidically, and dreſs the bone with doſſils of lint, dipped in tincture of myrrh, and the wound with the green, or precipitate ointment. When the ſore is not enlarged by the knife, which is the beſt, and leaſt painful method, pieces of ſublimate are generally applied, which bring out with them cores, or lumps of fleſh: Blue vitriol powdered, and mixed with a few drops of the oil, is uſed alſo for this purpoſe, and is ſaid to act as effectually, and with leſs pain and danger.

R.

RABBIT. The rabbit is a ſmall animal, and may appear of ſmall conſequence to the farmer who breeds other animals of more profit, yet this is very well worth his regarding as a part of his flock. It has the recommendation of the goat, that it will thrive where nothing elſe can live; and the ſame advantage as the hog, in the great increaſe by young.

Both the buck and doe rabbit are eager for copulation, and they muſt not be reſtrained. The does go but a month with young; and as ſoon as they have brought forth they are ready to copulate again. When they run wild they get together in a very little time; and when they are kept tame and ſeparate, they muſt be put together ſoon after the bringing forth, otherwiſe the doe grows ſullen, and will take little or no care of her young ones.

The rabbit is diſtinguiſhed into two kinds, the wild and the tame. Theſe are kept in a diſtinct manner; the wild running looſe, and burrowing themſelves holes in the ground, and the tame being kept in houſes, huts, or boxes.

Both kinds yield a very large profit, though under different management.

The wild rabbit breeds fast and freely in warrens, or other places where there is room and a free air. They will thrive upon the poorest, and barrenest, gravelly, stony, or sandy soils; by stony we mean such as are full of small stones, not the rocky, for in these last they cannot burrow. In these sort of grounds the farmer will find great advantage from the breeding of rabbits, either altogether or occasionally; for in the latter way they improve these barren lands extremely by their dung and urine, and render the worst of them fit for raising good crops of rye; and such as are but a little better, for the other kinds of corn.

The distinction between wild and tame rabbits is not founded in nature, but on our own practice; for the wild kinds may be as well kept tame as the others. They are used to a kind of imprisonment in their holes, and for that reason they bear confinement better than most other creatures.

As to the wild kind there is properly but one breed of them, and all the direction that is needful in the choice is, that such as are taken to begin a stock, be large and big bodied, with a good deep fur that hangs fast upon their backs, and with stout limbs. The husbandman that has waste ground in his hands, that is fenced well, and not with live hedges, should never omit this part of his stock, for the very worst of his ground will do, and the advantage he receives from them will be very great.

A small number is sufficient to be first turned in; for of all creatures useful to mankind, they are the greatest breeders.

Experience shews that the wild rabbit succeeds better in some places than others; the young growing up much quicker, and the flesh being finer and better tasted. The reason of this is to be searched in the soil and the produce; and this may teach the husbandman on which of such grounds as seem proper, it will be most to his benefit to breed them.

In general, the shorter and scantier the grass, the better is the taste of the rabbit. The drier the ground the better they succeed; where there is much water, they never are well-flavoured.

Of all creatures, water is the least necessary to a rabbit, for we see the tame ones will live very well altogether without it, on moist food. Where the soil is driest, the air finest, and the water that there is in the way is running and clear, there the rabbits may reasonably be expected to succeed best. Damp grounds, and standing waters, being the greatest disadvantage to this creature.

The common rabbit will very freely be kept tame; for it has been found, many years since, that those which we usually understand as tame rabbits, will live very well wild, especially the hardier kinds. This is a consideration of some consequence, because there is one of the tame kinds that is, in every respect, better than the common wild one. This is that which is known by the name of the silver-haired rabbit. It will live and thrive as well wild as the common sort; and it is always better tasted and fairer to the eye, so that it brings a larger price. The skin also is of much more value, and the demand for it among the furriers is constant and certain.

For these reasons it is, in many cases, advisable to breed this kind wild instead of the other: but though it often is so, it is not always. This, though as hardy as the other, requires a better supply of food, and is poor, and of little value upon those barren and heathy lands, on which the common wild rabbit succeeds very well.

The proper place for this kind is a park, where they may run at liberty among the deer and other cattle, and where there is good grass, though not rank, upon the ground; the other is the proper kind for the miserablest and poorest lands.

Tame rabbits are distinguished into several kinds, according to their colours and other accidental distinctions; but the differences are not great, nor is there any material point of profit attending the choice of one or the other sort.

The silver-haired rabbit last-named is a very good and profitable kind to be kept tame, because of the advantage of the skin. The Dutch rabbit is a much a much larger kind, and is very good for the table, but the skin is of less value. The most beautiful, when kept cleanly, is the white long-haired rabbit; this is, by some, called the Turkey rabbit, from the place from whence we first had it; and by others the Shagge rabbit, from the length of its hair. This is a very good kind to breed tame also, but if not kept very clean, it is subject to a disorder not unlike what the doctors call the Plica Polonica; the hair growing together in clots and cakes, and this often in such a manner, that blood vessels from the skin run up amongst the clots, and they will bleed on being cut off.

It is not very material which of these, or of the several other kinds that it is the custom to breed at this time, the farmer chooses; for with proper management, any of them will turn to very good account; but whichever sort it be, let him take a more strict and critical care in the choice, than he has been directed to do in those which are to run wild, for a great deal more depends upon it in this kind, than in those. The skin here is of much consequence, and the distinctions in this are nice, and never enough to be regarded in the choice for breed.

In the silver-haired rabbit, for instance, let the husbandman take care to choose his buck of the true kind and colour, for on this, more than on the doe, will depend the value of the breed. Let the fur be thick, deep, smooth, and glossy; and let the ground colour be black, with a moderate quantity of white or silvery hair. It is proper to choose them rather too dark for breeding, because the colour in the young is more apt to grow paler than deeper; and a silver skin that is too dark, always will bring a better price than one that is too light.

In the same manner let the fur of the several other kinds be examined, when they are chosen for breeding; for the rest of the directions already given for the choice of the wild, hold good here; the largest and best shaped being to be fixed upon. In the same manner as these rabbits were first chosen, let them be picked out from time to time for keeping, to preserve the breed; for upon this will depend a great part of the advantage.

The farmer having thus selected his stock of these little animals, is to take his choice of the several methods which are in use for the breeding and keeping of them. These are many, and among them some allow more and some less liberty to the animal; in general, such as allow most freedom, even in this way, and most air, are best; for though the rabbit will bear confinement very well, yet it will thrive best where that is least strict.

Cleanliness also is a very great article in the breeding of these, as well as other creatures, and where the confinement is least strict, there is naturally least foulness. The dung and urine of the rabbit have a very disgreeable and rank smell; and nothing prejudices the creature more than being kept nasty with these about it.

The general way of keeping tame rabbits is in a kind of boxes made for this purpose: others keep them in pits; but it would be a much better way to keep them in buildings made for that purpose. This might be done at a small expence, and would answer very well; for it would be cleanlier and more wholesome than any other way. The boxes are too small, and therefore are apt to grow nasty, and the pits are liable to be damp, which, as we have observed already, is one of the worst things that can happen in a place where rabbits are to breed.

The boxes, for such as prefer them, should be made of thin wainscot, and divided into larger and smaller rooms, two for each rabbit. One of these should be for eating, and the other for lodging and bringing forth the young. That for eating should be the larger, and should have a grate before it for light, and the smaller should be entirely dark. Before both there must be placed a trough with the food; and thus the creature will live, thrive, breed, and fatten: But there wants free air, and it is very difficult to keep them cleanly, so that although this method may do, the others are sure to answer better, when they are managed properly.

These

Those who use this method by boxes, set them one above another, in so many stories, and keep the bucks by themselves, and the does by themselves, unless it be such does as have not bred, and with those they lodge a buck in the same box. The common size of these boxes is two feet long, the same in breadth, and a foot high. It is surprising to see so large a creature as a rabbit live so well as it does in this small compass, but it will always do better when it has more room.

The method of keeping them in pits is preferable, and is thus. A dry soil is to be fixed upon for this purpose, and the pit is to be dug seven foot deep, and of a bigness proportioned to the number intended to be kept in it. This must be walled up on the inside, only leaving spaces for them to make their burrows. A sandy soil, not too destitute of other earth, will answer for the purpose of these pits better than any other. At one end an hollow place is to be made for the buck to rest in, he must be chained to a stump, and have room only to go to the rack where the food is placed in these pits, and thence to his den to rest. At the other parts of the pit, out of the reach of the buck, are to be the places left for the does to make their stops or burrows. The rack is to be placed near the middle of the pit, between the bucks and does, he being on one side by himself, and they on the other.

Three does may very well be kept in the same pit with one buck, and the pit for this purpose should be about ten foot square. Some make them larger, and keep more bucks than one, but it is a better practice to make more of them, only allowing one buck and two or three does to each.

This will naturally appear to those who are not acquainted with these things, a large provision for three or four rabbits, and a great expence for so few small animals; but those who have kept these creatures know that it very well answers the expence. Provided the pit be dry they live more comfortably by much in it, than in the other way of boxes; and the produce is so great that one buck and three does will bring a hundred and fifty, two hundred, or more young ones in a year.

The young are to be left under the care of the dam till they are about a month old, and they are then to be taken from her either for sale or the table; or if there be no demand either of these ways for them, they must be put into some pit, or other place made for that purpose.

The same practice is to be observed in removing the young, if they are kept in boxes, or whatever other way. In whatever manner the old ones are kept, when they have brought forth a second brood, the first is to be taken away, and reared up elsewhere. The common way in this case is, to remove them to other boxes, keeping those of several broods of about the same age together; and thus they are to be treated in the other way, either rearing them in another pit, or in any manner that is convenient, only allowing them some room and air, the more of both the better.

The reason of chaining up the buck rabbit in the pit, and of keeping him in a separate box in the other way, is his mischievous disposition, for he will kill all the young ones. This the does are themselves so sensible of, that they, in their natural wild life, hide the young ones, and close up their holes, that the buck may not find them.

The two great requisites in these pits are warmth and dryness; their depth, unless the ground be very favourable, making them subject both to damp and cold, in either of which cases the rabbits will not breed well.

The most profitable time of their breeding is in the depth of winter; and they will never breed at this season, at least not successfully, unless they be kept dry and warm.

It is from the danger of the cold and damp in pits, and because of the want of air in boxes, some have been led to think of such other methods as may give rabbits the advantage of both in a fit degree, and yet keep them in such an easy and ready way, that they may be always at hand, easily fed, tended, and looked after, in every respect, and yet have warmth and freedom.

To obtain these several advantages, by means of which tame rabbits of the

the beſt kinds would be kept in the greateſt perfection of health and beauty, and to the greateſt advantage of breeding, let the huſbandman erect a building purpoſely for them.

Having choſen his rabbits for breed, let him fix upon a proper ſpot of ground for his edifice, and draw the plan of it of ſuch extent as to contain conveniently the number he ſhall think proper to keep.

Let the ſoil on which he builds this place, be of a dry loamy kind, with a large proportion of ſand in it; for this is the ſort of earth the rabbit loves beſt, and in which it is always moſt healthy.

Let the building be ſquare, and run up of wood in a ſlight but yet in a tight manner; and let there be a kind of cloſet carried up at one end.

In each corner of this ſquare let there be a den made for a buck rabbit, and a ſmall poſt driven in, to which faſten him by a chain, in the ſame manner as in the pit. At ſome ſmall diſtance from the corners let there be racks ſet up for food, which ſhall be within reach of the bucks, and one or two others in the middle.

When the houſe is thus prepared, let the bucks be chained in their places, and the does turned in. They will all live much more comfortably in this houſe than in the pits; and at the times of taking away their young, let them be put into the ſmaller rooms or cloſets, prepared for that purpoſe, where they will thrive and live very comfortably. A building of this kind will coſt little, and the profit ariſing from the rabbits will be much greater than in any other way, becauſe they will breed freely throughout the winter; and neither the old nor the young will be ſubject to diſeaſes. Both the old and the young will be, in this manner alſo, defended better againſt vermin than by any other way whatſoever.

The feeding of the rabbit is an article of great conſequence with regard to its health and increaſe, and it is leſs underſtood than moſt things of the like kind. Some feed them in a manner entirely with wet meat, others almoſt altogether with dry: Now, both theſe methods are wrong. A mixture, or diverſity of food, keeps them better in health and vigour, and occaſions their breeding faſter, and more ſucceſsfully than any other kind.

The dry meat of the rabbit is hay, oats, and bran. Their moiſt or wet food is freſh herbage, or roots, of almoſt any kind, which they will eat with the greateſt eagerneſs, as coleworts, parſley, and others, from the gardens; and ſow-thiſtles, mallows, and the like, from the fields. Now, theſe the huſbandman ſhould give them interchangeably; always obſerving this caution, that when he gives his rabbits dry meat, he muſt ſet them water; and that when they have the freſh or moiſt meat, they have no occaſion for any; the juices of thoſe leaves and herbs ſupplying them with a ſufficient humidity.

It is a common cuſtom with many to cut up the freſh food for their rabbits from under an hedge, taking every kind of herb that offers, ſo it be young, and the rabbits will eat almoſt any; but in this ſome caution is neceſſary, for the herb hemlock is very common under hedges, and it is poiſonous; the rabbit will eat it greedily, but it dies by the effect.

The hay that is given to rabbits muſt be the fineſt, ſweeteſt, and ſhorteſt, that can be got. Nor let any one grudge the expence, for they eat but little, ſo that the amount is ſcarce worth conſideration.

This is the beſt and healthieſt food of all others for rabbits, and ſhould be their ſtandard diet, but about once in five days they ſhould have the freſh herbs, which cool and ſcour them. And by this management they will be kept healthful and vigorous; always ready for breeding, and their young will be luſty, ſtrong, and thriving.

Among the other food of the rabbit ſhould be mentioned grains; this is of a middle nature between the moiſt and dry food, and is a very cheap diet; but it is not wholeſome, and is therefore dearer in the end. The rabbits will ſeem to thrive upon it, but there is no food whatſoever that makes them ſo liable to diſeaſes.

In general, the advantage of their dry meat is, that it prevents diſeaſes; and thoſe who commonly keep them upon freſh and moiſt food, as many do, giving them carrots and other roots among it, would do well to change it for dry meat in wet weather; for moist food is the great cause of these creatures having the rot, and they are most of all subject to this in damp seasons.

RACK. A wooden frame made to hold hay or fodder for cattle.

RADIATED *Flowers*, such as have several semi-floscules round a disk, in form of a radiant star: those which have no such rays, are called *discous* flowers.

RADICLE, that part of the seeds of plants which upon vegetating becomes its root, and is discoverable by the microscope.

RADISH, the name of a well-known vegetable, and which is commonly cultivated in the kitchen-garden for its root.

Radishes are sown in different seasons, according to the time when they are desired for use. Those sown in September will be fit to eat at Christmas, if they are not destroyed by frost: but they must be used whilst very young, for they soon grow hot and sticky. If sown towards the end of October, which is commonly the time of sowing for the earliest crops, they will be fit for the table in the beginning of March. Those sown at Christmas, if the season is mild, and the ground in good order, will, if they escape the frost, be fit for eating about the end of March or beginning of April; and by continuing the sowing once in a fortnight, from the middle of January till the beginning of April, always observing to sow the earliest crop in the warmest and best sheltered situations, and the later ones in a moist soil and open situation, without which they will run up, and grow sticky, before they are fit for use, a regular succession of these roots may be had throughout the season. The tenderest, and mildest to the taste, are those which have been raised in deep, rich, and light mould.

When the radishes are come up, and have got five or six leaves, they must be thinned wherever they stand too close; for otherwise they will run up in tops, and not increase in their roots. Some thin them by hand; but it is much better to use a small hoe, which will stir the ground, destroy the weeds, and promote the growth of the young plants. They may be left about three inches asunder, if they are intended for drawing up small; but six inches will be little enough, if they are to stand till they are pretty large.

The kitchen gardeners about London, who pay great prices for their ground, and therefore are obliged to make it produce as many crops as possible in the year, sow carrot-seed with their early radishes, in order that if the radishes are killed soon after their coming up, as they sometimes are, the carrots may remain; for the seeds of these last generally lie in the ground five or six weeks before they grow, while those of the radishes sprout in about a fortnight; but when both crops succeed, the radishes must be pulled up while very young, or they will weaken the carrots; so that these last will not be able to support themselves after the former are gone.

It is also the constant practice of these industrious and intelligent men, to sow spinach with their latter crop of radishes; for after the radishes are taken off, and the ground has been cleared between the plants of spinach, these last will grow up so prodigiously as to cover the whole space in a fortnight's time: and if this spinach is of the broad-leaved kind, it will be larger and fairer than it usually is when sown alone; because most people are apt to sow it too thick, when they do not mix it with any other crop.

The small topped, the deep red, the scarlet, and the long topped striped radish, are the varieties generally cultivated in kitchen gardens. The small topped is most commonly preferred, because it takes up the least room; but a small spot of ground will furnish, from each sowing, as many radishes of any kind as can be spent in a family while they are good.

The Naples radish, which has a very white, round, small, and sweet root, may be propagated in the same manner as the common sort, excepting that it should not be sown till the beginning of March, and the plants should be allowed a greater distance. It is not very common in this country, and, indeed, its seeds are apt to degenerate here.

The white and the black Spanish radishes

radiſhes will be fit for the table by the end of Auguſt, or the beginning of September, if they are ſown about the middle of July, or a little earlier, and will continue good till the froſt ſpoils them. Theſe ſhould be thinned to a much greater diſtance than any other ſort; for their roots will grow as big as common turnips. If they are drawn out of the ground before a hard froſt comes on, and laid up in dry ſand, in the ſame manner as is practiſed for carrots, they will keep good all the winter.

To ſave the ſeeds of radiſhes, ſome of the ſtraiteſt and beſt-coloured roots ſhould be planted in rows three feet aſunder, and at the diſtance of two feet from each other in the rows, in deep and well dug ground. If the ſeaſon is dry, they muſt be watered from time to time till they have taken róot, after which they require no further care but keeping them clear from weeds; nor need theſe be feared after the branching ſeed-ſtalks of the radiſhes have overſpread the ground, as they will ſoon do, in ſuch a manner as to prevent their farther growth.

In this tranſplanting of the radiſhes, an allowance ſhould always be made for bad ſeaſons, becauſe the very ſame plants will not yield a fourth part of the quantity of ſeeds in dry ſeaſons, that they would do in a moiſt ſeaſon.

When the ſeed begins to ripen, it ſhould be carefully guarded from birds, and when it is ripe (which is known by the pods turning brown) it ſhould be cut, dried in the ſun, threſhed out, and laid up in a place where mice cannot come at it.

Horſe-Radish. See Horse-*Radiſh*.

RAGS. Woollen rags, and the nippings of the pitch-marks upon ſheep, are a ſingularly good manure. The rags ſhould be chopped ſmall, about an inch or two ſquare, and ſcattered on the earth at the ſecond ploughing; for being thereby covered, they will begin to rot by ſeed-time. They imbibe the moiſture of dews and rain, retain it long, and, as Dr. Home obſerves, thereby keep looſe ſoils in a moiſt ſtate. They coſt about fourpence a buſhel at London, from whence many loads are ſent every year to Dunſtable, which is thirty-three miles, where they are laid even on ſtiff lands, juſt after the ſowing of the corn, allowing to the acre four ſacks of ſix buſhels each.

RAGWORT, [*Othonna.*] or, as it is called in Yorkſhire, *Seagrim*, is a very pernicious weed.

The Rev. Mr. Camber, of Eaſt-Newton, has obliged the public with the following obſervations on the growth and deſtruction of ragwort, or ſeagrim.

"This plant," ſays he, "has a ſtalk, in its early ſtate, green; but, as it advances in age, inclining to violet, or purple, eſpecially downwards. Its flowers are both yellow, and thick-ſet, and compoſed each of a number of ſmall-pointed leaves. It runs to ſeed in the latter end of ſummer. The ſmell, both of the ſtalk and leaves, which are jagged, (whence probably it obtains one name) and the flower itſelf, are offenſive to all animals, I think; for I have obſerved that hardly any creatures feed upon it, except almoſt hungered or ſtarved. I have not indeed obſerved whether or no aſſes reject it.

"Like moſt other weeds, it thrives beſt in the beſt ſoils, either natural or artificial; and I took up a plant of it in my orchard, about two years ago, (with the root) which, when in flower, touched my chin, (my height is about five feet eight or nine inches) and its root, which is round, and thick ſet with taws, was much larger than a new-born child's head: but the uſual dimenſions are much leſs than theſe.

"About four years ago, I obſerved the ſpreading of this weed in that part of this eſtate which was in our own hands. I took notice, that neither cows nor horſes eat it; and when I ſmelled it, I ceaſed to wonder that they did not. It was obvious to remark, that a weed ſo bulky as this, and ſo groſs, muſt extract much nouriſhment from the earth, and that it was adviſable to get rid of it as faſt as poſſible. The moſt eaſy method was mowing. I therefore ordered a ſervant to mow theſe weeds in the paſtures as near to the ground as he could: and I hoped that the common mowing in the meadows would be ſufficient to deſtroy them: but I ſoon found my miſtake, for in a very few weeks theſe offenſive ſtrangers shot up again into a stalk and leaf, and even flower, though all in much smaller size than before, but with this disagreeable circumstance, that the root was so far from being injured with the scythe, that for one stalk several arose, and the root seemed to have gained new vigour from the wound.

"I now applied myself to plucking up by the roots these odious inmates, and found new difficulties; for while the ground was dry, as it usually is in the latter end of summer, I found the stalks of such of the seagrims as were longest, and afforded the tightest grasp, either break in plucking, and leave the root in the ground entirely, or at best bring with it only a small part of the root; and when the wet weather came on, and loosened the ground, and made it possible, or even easy, to bring away the whole ball of the root, yet the season of seeding was come on also, and the earliest ripe seeds had dispersed themselves, and produced an assurance of a larger crop for succeeding years than the most careful plucking of the present crop could destroy.

"But if these were the difficulties which attended my attempts to eradicate those seagrims, which had happened not to be mowed, I was much more embarrassed by those which had been; for here it was impossible to get any such fast hold, as to pluck them up with much, or even any root.

"I now applied myself to enquire what gentlemen or farmers were plagued with this weed, and what methods they had tried with success to destroy it.

"I was told by a gentleman in my own neighbourhood, that Sir G. Cayley, bart. of Brompton, near Scarborough, had been plagued with this weed, and had pursued the method of plucking with success.

"Animated by this assurance, I resolved to pursue this method with great attention; and as it seemed to be a work which required great care, both in the choice of season and manner of plucking, I resolved not to depute the work to others, but to endeavour to clear a spot in my cow-pasture with my own hands, that, if my labour succeeded, I might employ others to follow the same method under my own eye in the rest of this pasture.

"Accordingly, in the evenings of the summer, or rather autumn, of 1762, after showers, I applied myself to this work: and by the help of a pair of strong gloves, and a tight grasp, I brought up almost every root, in a space of about two hundred yards square, whole; so that I had good hopes I should see this spot clear in the succeeding summer. It is true, I saw leaves of the species of this weed, and of a very vivid green too, around the plants which I pulled up; but as I reasonably concluded these to be fed by the taws which spread themselves from the main root, so I (methought reasonably) concluded also, that this main root being destroyed, the side taws would die, and consequently these young leaves.

"But how was I disappointed, when, in the summer of 1763, I saw this spot of ground as much over-run with seagrims as any part else of the pasture which had been unpulled!

"Conversing, however, with G. Watson, esq; of New Malton, towards the latter end of summer, on this subject, I was assured by him, that by a repetition of this labour of plucking for some years, he thought he had lessened the number of his seagrims, though they were still numerous. Urged by this example, I had gone through the whole of my pasture, which is about ten acres, and keeps five cows, at the latter end of last summer, of 1763, with the same care as was used to a small part of it in 1762; yet am I not elated with much hope of success; for a little plot before my garden (in which my horses run, and which was managed with still more accuracy on account of the odious appearance of the seagrims from my windows) seems to threaten another considerable crop.

"As I did not confine my enquiries about the method of destroying this hateful weed to any one rank of men, I was told by an honest quaker, a farmer in my neighbourhood, that he had found turning of sheep in winter into his cow-pasture the only effectual method of destroying this hateful weed.

"I thought

"I thought this method very likely to ſucceed: for ſheep are ſuch cloſe eaters, that I have known them deſtroy whole beds of the rankeſt docks, which could not be killed by any other means.

"I have not been able to try this experiment conſiderably; for, as I am raiſing quick fences, both in my meadow and paſture, I keep no ſheep. I have, however, occaſionally admitted ſome of my tenants ſheep into the ſmall plot before my garden this winter; and, upon an accurate examination this morning, I do not entertain any ſanguine hopes of great ſucceſs from this method. I find that many of the young leaves of this weed, now level with the ſurface of the ground, are untouched by the ſheep; and that ſuch others as appear bitten by them, do not ſeem in a dying condition.

"The truth ſeems to me, that ſheep, though they may not have the ſame averſion to this weed as horſes and cows, yet are far from being fond of it; and if any great ſucceſs is to be hoped for from their bite, (which may prepare beds for the water, and ſo decay the root) the ſheep ſhould be folded pretty cloſe upon it, and obliged to eat it near, and at ſuch a ſeaſon that the winter-rains may have time to work its deſtruction. And ſuch a method, if carefully purſued, ſeems to be moſt probable for the extirpation of this pernicious weed.

"If the method of plucking is followed, I would ſubjoin ſome cautions:

"Firſt, In order to prevent the large plants from ſeeding, I would adviſe to cut off all the tops, and the tops only, when the flowers begin to die, that then good hold of the ſtalk may be gotten.

"Secondly, I would defer the plucking till the rains have moiſtened the ground ſufficiently to bring up the whole main root.

"Thirdly, I recommend ſtriking the root ſo brought up againſt the ground, in order to diſperſe the earth which adheres to it, by way of manure.

"Fourthly, I always pile the plants thus pulled up and cleanſed from the earth, that, if the ſeaſon proves favourable, they may be burnt, and the aſhes ariſing from them ſpread on the ground; or if this cannot be conveniently done, (though it is much the better method, and may, with a ſufficient fire, be done when they are ever ſo green) they may be left to rot and manure the ſoil.

"The groſſneſs, and even ſtench, of this weed, is a proof of the great quantity of ſalts it contains; and in the ſame proportion as any plant exhauſts the ground of its ſalts it repays when reduced to manure. There can, however, be no queſtion, but whilſt weeds are left to rot, a great quantity of the ſalts, which by burning would mingle with the ſoil, are carried into the air.

"I ſuppoſe your readers will be curious to know in what manner I account for the ſudden appearance of theſe ſeagrims in vaſt abundance, in this eſtate, where they were hardly ever known before.

"I will give you an account, which I dare ſay, you will eſteem perfectly ſatisfactory. About eight years ago I undertook to improve a piece of ground of about fourteen acres, which was over-run with thorns of both ſorts, brambles, broom, and furze.

"When I had got it cleared of all this traſh, my next buſineſs was to pare the hills off, and pile them, and, after a winter's mellowing, to break and ſpread them with a mixture of lime, and all other kinds of manure which I could collect. As the ſoil was very poor, having been exhauſted by the great quantity of traſh it had nouriſhed for many years, I was not yet ſatisfied, but reſolved to take the advantage of the firſt dry ſummer, to lead out the riches of a pond of about thirty yards long, and half as many broad, which had been occupied by a great number of geeſe, &c. and never thoroughly cleaned during near thirty years. I got through this work, tho' at a great expence, being obliged to employ a conſiderable number of draughts, leſt the rains ſhould make the mud too thin, or the heat bake it too much, the mud being for a conſiderable ſpace a yard perpendicular.

"All this mud I laid on my newly improved ground, except a few cart-loads, which were brought and laid by the wall of a kitchen-garden, to be mingled with the other ſoil.

"I had divided my improved ground,

 reſerving

reserving about four acres for meadow. Behold!, the succeeding year gave me a crop of seagrims both in my new meadow, my new cow-pasture, and the plot of ground in which the mud for my garden had been scattered; and more particularly in those parts where the ground had been broke, either to stub the thorns, &c. or to take away the hills, while the adjoining ground on every side was free from this pernicious weed.

"As I knew little or nothing of this weed, I suffered it to seed before I took any necessary precautions for its destruction. The succeeding year presented me with a much larger crop, and I have been ever since struggling for its extirpation, and have the mortification to see its encroachments on adjoining grounds by the seeds which winds have carried.

"This fact, and another of the same kind, in a piece of ground which I improved since, at some distance from the former, have confirmed me in an opinion, which I before thought very probable, viz. "That all soils are originally impregnated with the seeds of almost all grasses and weeds, (though of some in greater quantities) which only want a proper stirring and manure to awaken them to vegetation, though at the expence of one another, some being suffocated by that process which gives life to the others."

"I will add another striking instance in confirmation of this sentiment, notorious in this neighbourhood.

"A considerable quantity of the park at Gilling was over-run with brakes and moss, and that wretched grass which grows in such company. Lord Fairfax, the owner, finding that he could not have his venison fat as it ought to be, destroyed his park, and applied himself seriously to the improvement of it at a vast expence. In course of time by due tillage he brought this worst part of it to be not only good corn land, but even tolerable, though coarsish, meadow and pasture; yet both of them thick set with seagrims, a weed never seen there till the quantity of lime which his Lordship put into that poor soil had warmed it sufficiently.

"I have only to add, on this subject, that I am persuaded seagrim does more harm in meadow than pasture land; for in the latter it only exhausts the ground on which it stands to no good purpose; but in the former it communicates its disagreeable stench in the sweat to the good hay, and destroys its sweetness. I advise, therefore, that hay-makers be ordered to throw it with their rake-shafts out of the swathe whenever they meet with it." *Museum Rusticum*, vol. v. p. 117.

RAGGED ROBIN. [*Lychnis Flos-cuculi.*] A species of campion common in moist meadows, and by the sides of rivers.

RAMPION, A species of campanula or bell-flower. The crimson rampion is greatly prized by the curious, for the beauty of its rich crimson flowers, which exceed all the flowers we have yet seen in the deepness of its colour; and these commonly when their roots are strong, produce large spikes of these flowers, which continue a long time in beauty, and make a most magnificent shew among other flowers. The time of their flowering is commonly in July or August; and if the autumn proves very favourable, they will sometimes produce good seeds in England. These plants are natives of Virginia and Carolina, where they grow by the sides of rivulets, and make a most beautiful appearance; from whence the seeds are often sent to England. These seeds commonly arrive here in the spring, at which time they should be sown in pots filled with light earth, and but just covered over; for, if the seeds are buried deep, they will not grow. These pots should be placed under a frame, to defend them from the cold, until the season is a little advanced; but they should not be placed on an hot-bed, which will also destroy the seeds.

When the weather is warm, towards the middle of April, these pots should be placed in the open air, in a situation where they may have the morning sun till twelve o'clock, observing to water them constantly in dry weather; and when the plants are come up, and are grown pretty strong, they should be transplanted each into a small pot filled with fresh light earth, and placed in the same situation, observing to water them in dry weather; and,

and, in winter, they ſhould be placed under an hot-bed frame, where they may be ſheltered from ſevere froſts; but, in mild weather, they ſhould be as much expoſed to the open air as poſſible.

The March following theſe plants ſhould be put into larger pots filled with the ſame freſh earth, and placed, as before, to the morning ſun; obſerving to water them in dry weather, which will cauſe them to flower ſtrong the autumn following.

Theſe plants are alſo propagated by parting of their roots; the beſt ſeaſon for which is, either ſoon after they are paſt flower, or in March; obſerving to water and manage them as hath been directed for the ſeedling plants both in winter and ſummer.

RAMSONS, Broad-leaved wild garlick.

RANUNCULUS. There are eight or ten ſpecies of the ranunculus, ſome growing wild in different places; but the moſt beautiful is the Perſian, or Turkey ranunculus, the varieties of which are almoſt numberleſs, but almoſt all flower in April or May.

The beds in which the Perſian ranunculus roots are planted, ſhould be made with freſh light ſandy earth, at leaſt three feet deep; the beſt ſoil for them may be compoſed in this manner, viz. take a quantity of freſh earth from a rich upland paſture, about ſix inches deep, together with the green ſward: this ſhould be laid in heaps to rot for twelve months before it is mixed, obſerving to turn it over very often to ſweeten it, and break the clods; to this you ſhould add a fourth part of very rotten neat's dung, and a proportionable quantity of ſea or drift ſand, according as the earth is lighter or ſtiffer; if it be light, and inclining to a ſand, there ſhould be no ſand added; but if it be an hazel loam, one load of ſand will be ſufficient for eight loads of earth; but if the earth be ſtrong and heavy, the ſand ſhould be added in a greater proportion: this ſhould be mixed ſix or eight months before it is uſed, and you ſhould often turn it over, in order to unite their parts well together, before it is put into the beds.

The depth which this ſhould be laid in the beds muſt be about three feet; this ſhould be below the ſurface, in proportion to the dryneſs or moiſture of the place where they are ſituated; which, in dry ground, ſhould be two feet eight inches below the ſurface, and the beds raiſed four inches above; but in a moiſt place they ſhould be two feet four inches below, and eight above the ground; and, in this caſe, it will be very proper to lay ſome rubbiſh and ſtones at the bottom of each bed, to drain off the moiſture; and if upon this, at the bottom of the beds, ſome very rotten neat's-dung be laid two or three inches thick, the roots will reach this in the ſpring, and the flowers will be fairer. This earth I would by no means adviſe to be ſkreened very fine; only turning it over each time, you ſhould be careful to break the clods, and throw out all large ſtones, which will be ſufficient; for if it is made very fine, when the great rains in winter come on, it will cauſe the earth to bind into one ſolid lump, whereby the moiſture will be detained, and the roots, not being able to extend their tender fibres, will rot.

The beds being thus prepared ſhould lie a fortnight to ſettle, before the roots are planted, that there may be no danger of the earth ſettling unequally after they are planted, which would prejudice the roots by having hollow places in ſome parts of the bed, to which the water would run and lodge, and ſo rot the roots in ſuch places. Then having levelled the earth, laying the ſurface a little rounding, you ſhould mark out the rows by a line, at about ſix inches diſtance each way, ſo that roots may be planted every way in ſtraight lines; then you ſhould open the earth with your fingers at each croſs, where the roots are to be planted, about two inches deep, placing the roots exactly in the middle, with their crowns upright; then with the head of a rake, you ſhould draw the earth upon the ſurface of the bed level, whereby the top of the roots will be about an inch covered with earth, which will be ſufficient at firſt. This work ſhould be done in dry weather, becauſe the earth will then work better than if it were wet; but the ſooner after planting there happens to be rain the better it will be for the roots, for if it ſhould prove dry weather long after, and the earth of the beds be very dry, the roots will be subject to mould and decay; therefore, in such a case, it will be proper to give a little water to the beds, if there should no rain happen in a fortnight's time, which is very rare at this season of the year; so that they will seldom be in danger of suffering that way.

When the roots are thus planted, there will no more be required until towards November, by which time they will begin to heave the ground, and their buds appear; when you should lay a little of the same fresh earth of which the beds were composed about half an inch thick all over the beds, which will greatly defend the crown of the root from the frost: and when you perceive the buds to break through this second covering, if it should prove a very hard frost, it will be very proper to arch the beds over with hoops, and cover them with mats, especially in the spring, when the flower buds will begin to appear; for if they are exposed to too much frost, or blighting winds, at that season, their flowers seldom open fairly, and many times their roots are destroyed; but this happens more frequently to the Persian kinds, which are tenderer, than to those sorts which are pretty hardy; for which reason they are commonly planted in open borders, intermixed with other flowers, though in very hard winters these are apt to suffer where care is not taken to guard off the frost.

In the beginning of March the flower stems will begin to rise, at which time you should carefully clear the beds from weeds, and stir the earth with your fingers between the roots, being very careful not to injure them; this will not only make the beds appear handsome, but also strengthen their flowers. When the flowers are past, and the leaves are withered, you should take up the roots and carefully clear them from the earth, then spread them upon a mat to dry in a shady place, after which they may be put up in bags or boxes, in a dry room until the October following, which is the season for planting them again.

RAPE. [*Rapa.*] Rape or colefeed. This is a produce confined, in a manner, to a few parts of the kingdom, but it might very well be carried to others. We shall shew the profits to the husbandman in general, and if we can tempt him to cultivate the plant, shall not leave him deficient in any article regarding the management.

There is the less reason to wonder that colefeed, so profitable in some parts of the kingdom, is so little raised in others, for this, that the plant itself is less known than any other among the whole number of those cultivated for use. To ask what herb it is that yields this feed, is a question that would puzzle many beside the farmer. Even its name is not commonly known. Colefeed is the name of the feed only, it is also called rapefeed, but this does not lead to the matter: Cole is not the name of any plant, and rape signifies turnip; we shall explain this matter, and before we enter upon the culture shew the farmer what the herb properly is that he is to cultivate.

Colefeed is very well known in Lincolnshire, and some other counties; and rape oil is as well known which is made from it.

The feed is known at the shops, and the plant by the farmers who raise it; but nothing more. In some places the feed is sown among the other kinds of what are called young salleting; but in this case, as the first leaves are only eaten, no more is seen of it.

All the time that this ignorance remains about the form of a very useful plant, it is common, wild on our ditch banks, and there needs nothing more than to shew its feed to the Lincolnshire farmer, for him to say that is it. These are the inaccuracies and errors which so greatly retard the progress of improvements in husbandry. The articles are themselves unknown to those who should be the authors of the amendments.

The price of colefeed, if the farmer chooses to sell it in that condition, is very considerable, reckoning the quantity an acre yields; and if he will be at the trouble of drawing the oil, the method of doing it is very easy, and his profit vastly greater. Nor are these all the advantages he receives from the growth of this plant: it is like

like the dyers weed in this, that it will grow on soils which will not yield any thing else to advantage; and though these are of a very different kind from those peculiar to the dyers weed, that flourishing on the most dry, and this best on marshy grounds; yet there are enough of these last in many parts of the kingdom to shew how advantageous it must be to the nation to render the plant more known, and the culture of it among our farmers more universal.

There is no other name by which we can treat of this intelligibly to the farmer, than this formed from the seed: What herb it is that is thus called in the colesced countries, or what is the plant that yields coleseed, we are about to shew.

There are three kinds of plants, each containing several species, and distinguished by different names, but are very nearly agreeing in their flowers, seed-vessels, and other general circumstances; these are, 1. The Cabbage kind. 2. The Turnip kind. And 3. The Navew kind. The confusion that has been made amongst these has been one occasion of the uncertainty about the coleseed plant.

The root of the turnip kind, and the stalk of the cabbage kind, are what principally distinguish them; as to the navew, it differs very little from the turnip, and that principally in the smallness and length of the root.

The flowers of these are alike, and the seeds of them all resemble one another, and they will all in the same manner yield that oil which we call rape oil; but there is one kind that yields it in greater quantity than the others. This is the wild navew, called Napus Sylvestris, by authors, and this is the proper coleseed plant.

The turnip and cabbage kind we have in our gardens in great variety, and some have for curiosity introduced the garden navew, or Napus Sativus, but it is inferior to the turnip, and therefore but little regarded. The authors who figure and describe the garden navew, figure also the wild kind, and this is what we have on the banks of ditches. We have observed that the navew differs little from the turnip, except in the shape and bigness of the root; and this plant, which otherwise much resembles the turnip kind, yet is properly a navew, because it has a very small root.

Any of these kinds therefore will answer under the farmer's hands; but as the wild navew yields much the finer seed, and much the larger quantity of it, and that is also the richest in oil, so it is best to cultivate that particular kind. This is oftener to be had from Holland than any where else, and we shall inform the purchaser how he is to know it by the eye.

The proper coleseed plant, or wild navew, is four feet high, and of an irregular growth. The root is long, slender, and white; it is of a sweeter taste than the turnip, but with somewhat more warmth. The lower leaves are long, large, deeply divided at the edges, and of a dusky green. One stalk usually rises in the midst of these, sometimes two or more. This is round, smooth, of a pale green colour, and divided into many branches towards the upper part. The leaves upon this stand one by one, not in pairs; they are smaller and narrower than those from the root, and are of a paler colour. The flowers grow at the tops of all the branches, they are small, of a bright yellow, and perfectly resemble those of the turnip: After these come pods which contain the seed. This resembles turnip-seed, but that it is larger and smoother. The common appearance of the plant in summer is with long spikes of pods, and a few flowers at the top of each.

This is the appearance of the wild navew in our fields and on banks. When it is cultivated for coleseed it grows somewhat taller and more branched, otherwise there is no difference; and in good ground the root will be larger and more tender. There is no difference between the wild navew and the garden navew, except that the root of the garden kind is yet tenderer and thicker; but this is principally while it has only the lower leaves, for when it is suffered to run to seed, the root grows sticky in the garden. Indeed there seems no other difference between the garden and the wild navew, but what is made by culture.

The flowers and fructification of the coleseed plant, when nicely examined,

mined, are thus formed. The flowers ſtand in a cup compoſed of four little oval-pointed green leaves, and this does not remain after the flower is faded, as in the dyers weed, but periſhes and falls off with it. The flower is compoſed of four plain narrow yellow leaves, placed croſs-wiſe. Theſe are broadeſt at the ends, and not at all divided; they are of the ſame length as the leaves of the cup. In the center of this flower riſe ſix filaments, four of which are conſiderably longer than the other two; they have ſmall pointed buttons growing on them. In the center of theſe riſes a ſmall upright body, which is the rudiment of the ſeed-veſſel; this has a kind of button at its top, in which there are ſmall openings for receiving the fine duſt out of the heads of the filaments; for in propagating the ſeed, when the leaves and cup of the flower are fallen, this part enlarges, and at length becomes a ſeed-veſſel of a longiſh depreſſed ſhape, divided in the inſide by a membrane, which ſhews itſelf beyond its extremity, and containing ſeveral large, round, bright ſeeds.

This is the conſtruction of the flower and fruit of the coleſeed plant, the proper name of which is wild navew, and which grows naturally wild, not only in England, but in Flanders, and other parts of Europe.

The ſeeds of the natural wild plant may be gathered and ſown; but thoſe from ſuch as have been cultivated raiſe the ſtouteſt plants; theſe therefore the farmer is to chooſe, according to the following marks:— .

When the farmer has procured a quantity of good ſeed, let him pick out the moſt proper piece of ground for the crop. This will depend on the two great articles, ſoil and ſituation; as to the firſt, the richer the land the better; and as to the other, all that is required is, that it lie tolerably dry. There is no part of England where ſo much coleſeed is raiſed as in the fens, but the lands are firſt laid dry that are intended for this purpoſe: In the ſame manner they cultivate it in Flanders and Holland, on ground originally marſhy; but they are at all the neceſſary pains and expence of making them properly dry firſt.

No lands are more proper for coleſeed than ſuch as have been ſubject to overflowings, but they muſt be ſecure from that accident while the crop is upon them: and muſt be properly dry, in order to receive it.

Whether this overflowing have been from land floods, great rivers within reach of the ſea, or the ſea itſelf, it prepares them equally for the crop of coleſeed. Thoſe where ſalt-water has come, are properer than any others; but they require ſomewhat more preparation.

There are parts of Eſſex where the huſbandman might raiſe coleſeed to a very great advantage; and in many places where grounds have been newly recovered from the ſea by banking, &c. coleſeed is an excellent crop.

Every piece of fat rich land is proper for it; and the farmer need not fear to beſtow it upon this ſpecies, for it will yield to his full content.

If he has a piece of ground that is too rank for wheat, or the other uſual growths, let him ſow it with coleſeed: this will yield an extremely rich increaſe, and the land that would not before have done for corn, will, by proper management, be perfectly well prepared for it by this means.

The right ſoil for coleſeed is mellow earth. A ſoft deep black mould, with little other ad-mixture, feeds it better than any other. The plants never grow ſo robuſt, and the ſeed is not formed in ſuch plenty, or ripened in ſuch perfection on any other. This is the reaſon that marſhy and fenny lands, when properly fitted for that purpoſe, anſwer ſo well with coleſeed: This black deep mellow earth is the natural ſoil in theſe places, one ſcarce ſees any other on breaking the turf in any of them. This is of all others the beſt ſoil for coleſeed; but we have ſhewn it is not limited to this only; any deep ſoil that is mellow, and properly ſituated, will do.

The ſoil we have recommended as moſt proper for coleſeed, is one of thoſe that does not require any great labour in tilling; nor does the coleſeed demand any particularly to its own management. The black mellow earth whereon this crop ſhould be raiſed, cuts eaſily, and turns freely under the plough; and when it is in

a proper

a proper degree of drynefs, breaks freely and finely in the working. All that is particularly neceffary to fit it for colefeed, is to make it very fine; and this, unlefs the feafon prove quite unfavourable, or the hufbandman be very unfkilful, is a condition whereinto it is brought eafily.

In May the land intended for colefeed is commonly fallowed; in June it is twy-fallowed; and in the latter end of that month, or the firft week in July, the colefeed is fown.

After the laft ploughing, a fine-toothed harrow fhould be drawn over the field; after this, if the weather be dry, let there be a light roller carried over it; then let it be very gently and tenderly harrowed again. This laft harrowing, after the roller has crufhed and broke the lumps, ufually makes it as even as the flower-border in a garden, and this is the proper condition wherein it is to receive the feed.

If the weather prove too wet, let the rolling be deferred; and afterwards let it be performed with great caution; for though the roller may do great good in this cafe, it may alfo do much harm. In fome lands the foil is naturally fo loofe, but once harrowing divides it fufficiently.

Colefeed is to be ordered much in the fame manner as turnips. When it is got to fome fmall height, hoers are to be fent into the ground, whofe work ferves very well to cut down the weeds; and they may alfo thin the plants where they happen to have rifen too thick, as they will always do in fome places from this irregular manner of fowing. To thrive well in this way, they fhould be fuffered to ftand at about ten inches diftance.

In the fame manner, when the hufbandman fhall think proper to raife this crop by the drill and horfe-hoeing method; they muft be hoed when they have got a little ftrength. In this refpect we need not tedioufly repeat the particulars, the fame management fhould be obferved as in hoeing of turnips, raifed by this hufbandry.

The weeds in the partitions between the double rows, are to be cut up with the broad hand-hoe; and the plants fhould be at the fame time thinned till they ftand but one every foot and a half, and thefe not oppofite in the two feries, but one in each row oppofite to the middle of the fpace between two in the other.

When the plants are thus cleaned out and thinned, let the horfe-hoe or hoe-plough be fent in as foon as any weeds appear in the intervals. This will thoroughly deftroy them, and well break the ground.

This is to be repeated as often as the weeds rife, only obferving this caution, that at firft the plough tears up only the middle of each interval; and afterwards that it come nearer the edges.

When the colefeed is fown, there are only two things neceffary, the fingling out the plants to a proper diftance, and the keeping them clear of weeds while young; for afterwards they will need no care on that head, the plants are fo ftrong, and draw fo much nourifhment, that nothing can live among them.

Which ever method of raifing the crop be ufed, it is to be thus prepared for a good growth; and this done, the owner is to confider that it has more ufes than one. Though the feed be the principal confideration, it is not the only one; and the more regard is to be fhewn to another, becaufe it comes in order of time before it.

We have obferved that this plant is of the eatable kind. As it does not grow fo much into root as the turnip, its leaves are more delicate. Sheep are very fond of them, and they afford a rich and wholefome nourifhment. This, properly managed, is a great article. The fheep are fupplied at a time when they extremely want nourifhment, and the crop is far from being injured; on the contrary, it is improved by it. This, therefore, is to be confidered as a very effential part in the management of a colefeed crop, and we fhall give the practical hufbandman the method of ordering it to the beft advantage.

Colefeed having been fown in the beginning of July, fhoots with fome ftrength; after a few weeks keeps itfelf up during the droughts of autumn, and getting new ftrength and fize in the

the leaves from the rains, which introduce the winter, becomes in a condition to resist the strongest frosts. It stands well, and on every open day or two, grows during the depth of winter; so that in January, February, and March, the ground is well-covered.

The leaves which now rise are of no real use to the plant in perfecting its seed, which is to be done the succeeding summer. If they grow very rank they rather are injurious, swallowing up too much of the nourishment that should go to the forming of the young stalk, therefore they may be spared without injury. Here is then a great supply of food for sheep, at a season when grass is low, and it is extremely wanted; and the sheep are to be turned in to eat it without any damage to the succeeding crop of seed.

There are those who sow coleseed in some parts of Northamptonshire for this use alone; and it answers the intent very well. They use the poorest land for this purpose, and on that, although the plant would never grow vigorous and strong so as to yield any profitable quantity of seed, it shoots up very well in leaves.

In the proper lands for this growth, the leaves at this season are much finer and stronger, and they may be eaten without damage to the crop.

There are those who prefer the cole plant on these poor lands for food for sheep, to the young growth on such as is richer, and they say it is more wholesome; they are not without reason; but their experience on this head should not have led them to discard the use of coleseed for feeding on rich ground, but to use it with discretion.

The disadvantage that attends the feeding of sheep on the rank growth of coleseed in rich ground is, that it makes them swell. This is the same consequence that happens from feeding them on clover, but it is easily remedied. It is only at first that this rich food takes so ill an effect, and this may be prevented by proper regulations. When the sheep are first turned in, let it be towards the middle of the day; and an hour before sunset let them be driven out again into a common pasture. The next day let them be turned in earlier, and driven out later; and so the third, fourth, and fifth; after this, let them be just driven out at night for two or three days more, and let in again as soon as they will in the morning. This will prevent the effect of the coleseed at first, and being now hardened to it by a little custom, they may be left in the fields of it altogether, and will thrive upon it excellently, without the least damage.

Under this article of the effect of coleseed on sheep, it is proper to mention, that the first shoots are not all that serve this purpose. There is another growth of them that is less rank, and that the sheep love better; and which not being liable to affect them with any disorder, is to be trusted to them at their discretion.

The shoots of the coleseed after gathering the stalks for seed, are also a mild, sweet, and wholesome food we have been naming. These grow very strong when there has been rain, but they are never rank, or over-rich. Every one knows the difference there is between the cabbage and coleworts; full-grown leaves first cut for the pot, and the sprouts that grow on the stumps and stalks after cutting; the difference is just the same between the first growth of large leaves from the coleseed plant, and the shoots that rise after the cutting down the full-grown stalks for seed.

Towards the end of June the coleseed plant in whatever way it has been raised, will be fit to cut. The husbandman must therefore keep his eye upon his field very carefully toward that period; for it is of the utmost importance to him to seize it when it comes. No day of the month, or other precise time, can be named for the gathering this crop, because the differences of soils and seasons promote and retard its ripening; and even the variety of management, or the age of the plant, may make ten days or a fortnight difference in the ripening in two fields of the same soil in the same year. We have told the husbandman about what time he is to expect it; and shall add the signs by which he shall know that it is fit for harvest. One caution we must give him withal, that as the soil and method of of culture may make a very great alteration in the time of ripening, he must be upon the watch accordingly, expecting it earlier by a fortnight in rich soils and the most careful conduct, than he need in poor land in the common way. It will be in vain that we lay down the signs of its ripening, if he slips the time.

We have observed that the colesed plant has small flowers on the tops of the stalks and branches, which when the leaves fall off are succeeded by pods. As the flowers that opened first are thus followed by the seed-vessels, other flowers open upon the tops, which shoot up continually higher and higher. Thus, when the plant begins to flower, nothing is seen but a little button or tuft of buds at the top of the stalk, and of every branch, with one or two flowers opened or opening upon it; but when it has been some time flowering, the aspect differs, for then the branches having lengthened from the time of their beginning to flower, all that part of them which was the top, and where successively the former flowers appeared, is covered with seed-vessels; thus each branch terminates in a spike of seed-vessels, a foot or more in length, with a few flowers at its top.

The quantity of seed is the riches of the crop, therefore it would appear at first sight, that the longer the plant stood, so long as it continued flowering, the more advantageous would be the growth, but there are limits to this increase, beyond which all is waste.

The course of nature is to ripen these seeds, and then shed them upon the ground for producing the plant again; therefore when ripe the pods open of themselves, and the seeds are lost. This no art can prevent; and for that reason the time is to be watched when any of them begin to open, and that is the exact period for gathering.

When some of the pods approach towards ripeness they change colour, and the greenness is only seen at top; when, upon a cursory view, there are some found to grow brownish at the bottom, and those in the middle are yellowish or pale, those at the top only being green, then the time of gathering is at hand. It is the interest of the owner to let them stand so long as all are safe, but no longer. He is therefore now to look into the field once or twice every day, in a more strict manner. He must examine the bottom pods of the ripest spikes; so long as these are close all is safe; but as soon as some of them begin to open, the time of gathering the crop is come, for after this every hour's standing will be attended with loss.

The best method of cutting coleseed is with a strong sickle, in the same manner as wheat is reaped; but this must be done carefully. There is no part of the farmer's occupation that requires more expert and honest labourers than this. The stalks are pretty thick, and by that time the seed is ripened thus far, they have lost their juicy condition, and are grown hard and sticky. They are not easy to be cut, and yet that must be done evenly and with little shaking. A great deal of care is to be taken that the sickle goes easily through them, and when separated from the root they must be laid gently down in handfuls, that they may dry.

About one-third part of the seed is ripe at the time when the lowest pods are ready to open; in the lying exposed to the heat of the sun at this season, more than another third hardens, and becomes good; so that above two-thirds of the whole quantity of pods yield good seed, and this is all that can be expected; for if the farmer were to stay for the ripening of the other third, while growing, he would lose the seed from the lower pods, which is much more valuable; and the seed is of a sufficient growth to ripen or harden in the sun after the plant is cut down.

When the crop has been once laid on the ground it is not to be stirred till dry, for the seeds in the lower pods are so loose, that they will shake out with the least motion, and be lost. What is required from this exposure is, to dry and harden them, and they will get this sufficiently by lying tolerably thin, without being moved. If the weather be very hot, the business is done the sooner; if otherwise, somewhat more time is required; generally from ten days to a fortnight proves sufficient. The proof that they are dried enough is, when the pods toward the upper part of the spikes open easily, and the seeds in them are hard.

When the whole is in this condition, nothing is required but to get it to the barn, and thrash it. In Lincolnshire, they save themselves a part of this trouble, by thrashing it in the field; they spread a large sheet upon a level part of the ground, and lay a quantity of the herb on it. A little thrashing does to dislodge the seeds, which are already loose and most of them in danger of falling out of their own accord; but it is an irregular method; it leaves the farmer's produce, after all his toil, very much at the mercy of the winds, and cannot be performed so well as in doors.

The method we would therefore recommend to the husbandman, if the ground be any thing near home, is this: Let a parcel of large sheets be spread in the field, and the dried stalks carefully taken up in their bundles, and laid on them. Each sheet will hold a great deal this way; for though the parcels must be very gently moved to the sheet, they may be pressed hard, and handled roughly there; for what seeds fall out will be saved.

When the sheets have as much in them as they will hold, the edges and corners are to be gathered in and fastened, and the several parcels are to be carried to the barn, and there thrashed with a careful but light hand, that all the seed may be got out, and as little of it as possible bruised, for it is tender and easily hurt, especially when fresh.

After it is separated from the refuse that was mixed among it in the thrashing, it must be spread on a floor pretty thin, and turned often till it is thoroughly dry and hardened; for otherwise, when put up, it will quickly grow damp and mouldy.

The use of the coleseed is not over when the oil has been pressed from it. The cakes that remain are a large quantity, and as the fresh leaves feed sheep, these, in a proper method of giving them, turn to a very good account for feeding of cows. In winter this is an excellent food for them, for keeping them in heart and strength, at a time when other good food is scarce.

Calves are also to be fed with coleseed cakes very profitably, but that in a particular manner. After the oil is pressed out as clean as the common practice can obtain it, there still remains so much of it in the cakes, that when they are beat to powder, and mixed with hot water, they make it white and milky, in the same manner as sweet almonds beat up with water make an emulsion. This is the way of giving it to calves, and it proves a very rich, wholesome, and strengthening food. Calves may be fed with this from three days old, till they are fit to eat grass or hay.

Wild RAPE. Charlock.

RASPBERRY. [*Rubus Idæus.*] This plant grows naturally in the woods in the northern parts of England, but is cultivated in gardens for its fruit, which supplies the table at the season when they are ripe. There are two or three varieties of this, one with a red, and the other a white fruit, and the third generally produces two crops of fruit annually; the first ripens in July, and the second in October, but those of the latter season have seldom much flavour. These are accidental varieties, but the fourth sort we believe to be a distinct species, for the leaves are trifoliate, larger than those of the common sort, woolly on their under side, and the branches and stalks have no thorns. This produces but few fruit, and those are small, which has occasioned its being neglected.

The raspberry is generally propagated by suckers, though we should prefer such plants as are raised by layers, because they will be better rooted, and not so liable to send out suckers as the other, which generally produce such quantities of suckers from their roots as to fill the ground in a year or two; and where they are not carefully taken off or thinned, will cause the fruit to be small, and in less quantities, especially when the plants are placed near each other; which is too often the case, for there are few persons who allow these plants sufficient room.

In preparing these plants, their fibres should be shortened; but the buds, which are placed at a small distance from the stem of the plant, must

not

not be cut off, because those produce the new shoots the following summer. These plants should be planted about two feet asunder in the rows, and four or five feet distant row from row; for if they are planted too close, their fruit is never so fair, nor will ripen so kindly, as when they have room for the air to pass between the rows. The soil in which they thrive best, is a fresh strong loam, for in warm light ground they do not produce so great plenty of fruit, for they naturally grow in cold land, and in shade; therefore when they are planted in a warm situation and a light soil, they do not succeed.

The season for dressing of them is in October, at which time all the old wood that produced fruit the preceding summer, should be cut down below the surface of the ground, and the young shoots of the same year must be shortened to above two feet in length; then the spaces between the rows should be well dug, to encourage their roots; and if you bury a very little rotten dung therein, it will make them shoot vigorously the following summer, and their fruit will be much fairer. During the summer season, they should be kept clear from weeds, which, with the before-mentioned culture, is all the management they will require; but it is proper to make new plantations once in three or four years, because when the plants are suffered to remain long, they will produce few and small fruit.

The Virginian Flowering RASPBERRY is commonly propagated in the nurseries as a flowering shrub. The flowers of this sort are as large as small roses, and there is a succession of them for two months or more, so that they make an agreeable variety during their continuance. This sort frequently produces fruit in England, which are not so large as those of the common sort, and have little flavour. These ripen in September, or the beginning of October.

RAT, the name of a well-known animal, very troublesome to the farmer, &c.

We shall here give the two following receipts, as they are said to be effectual, for destroying rats.

The first has the sanction of the Dublin society, who on the 10th of November 1762, ordered a premium of five guineas to one Lawrence O'Hara, for this discovery; which is, "one quart of oatmeal, four drops of rhodium, one grain of musk, and two nuts of nux vomica finely rasped." This mixture is to be made up in pellets, and laid in the holes and places which the rats frequent.

The other receipt is thus: "Take of the seeds of staves-acre, or louse-worth, powdered, one fourth part, and of oatmeal three parts; mix them well and make them up into a paste with honey. Lay pieces of it in the holes, and on the places frequented by rats or mice, and it will kill such vermin as eat thereof."

The first step taken by rat-catchers, in order to clear a house, &c. of those vermin, is to allure them all together to one proper place, before they attempt to destroy them; for there is such an instinctive caution in these animals, accompanied with a surprising sagacity in discovering any cause of danger, that, if any of them be hurt, or pursued, in an unusual manner, the rest take the alarm, and become so shy and wary, that they elude all the devices and stratagems of their pursuers for some time after. This place, where the rats are to be assembled, should be some closet, or small room, into which all the openings but one or two may be secured; and this place should be, as near as may be, in the middle of the house, or buildings. It is the practice, therefore, to attempt to bring them all together to some such place, before any attempt be made to take them; and, even then, to avoid any violence, hurt, or fright to them, before the whole be in the power of the operator.

The means used to allure them to one place are various: one of those most easily and efficaciously practised is, the trailing some piece of their most favourite food, which should be of the kind that has the strongest scent, such as toasted cheese, or broiled red herring, from the holes or entrances to their recesses in every part of the house, or contiguous building, whence it is intended to allure them. At the extremities, and in different parts of the course of this trailed tract, small quantities

quantities of meal, or any other kind of their food, should be laid to bring the greater number into the tracks, and to encourage them to pursue it to the center place, where they are intended to be taken; at that place, where time admits of it, a more plentiful repast is laid for them, and the trailing repeated for two or three nights.

Besides this trailing and way-baiting, some of the most expert of the rat-catchers have a shorter, and perhaps more effectual method of bringing them together; which is, the calling them, by making such a kind of whistling noise as resembles their own call; and by this means, with the assistance of the way-baits, they call them out of their holes, and lead them to the repast prepared for them at the place designed for taking them. But this is much more difficult to be practised than the art of trailing; for the learning the exact notes, or cries, of any kind of beasts or birds, so as to deceive them, is a peculiar talent, not easily attained to in other cases.

In the practising either of these methods of trailing or calling, great caution must be used by the operator, to suppress and prevent the scent of his feet and body from being perceived; which is done by overpowering that scent by others of a stronger nature. In order to this, the feet are to be covered with cloths rubbed over with assa-fœtida, or other strong smelling substances; and even oil of rhodium is sometimes used for this purpose, but sparingly, on account of its dearness, though it has a very alluring, as well as disguising effect, as will be observed below. If this caution of avoiding the scent of the operator's feet near the track, and in the place where the rats are proposed to be collected be not properly observed, it will very much obstruct the success of the attempt to take them; for they are very shy of coming where the scent of human feet lies very fresh, and intimates to their sagacious instinct, the presence of human creatures, whom they naturally dread. To the abovementioned means of alluring by trailing, way-baiting, and calling, is added another of very material efficacy, which is, the use of oil of rhodium, which, like the marum syriacum in the case of cats, has a very extraordinary fascinating power on these animals. This oil is extremely dear, and therefore sparingly used. It is exhaled in a small quantity in the place, and at the entrance of it, where the rats are intended to be taken, particularly at the time when they are to be last brought together, in order to their destruction; and it is used also, by smearing it on the surface of some of the implements used in taking them by the method below described: and the effect it has in taking off their caution and dread, by the delight they appear to have in it, is very extraordinary.

It is usual, likewise, for the operator to disguise his figure as well as scent; which is done by putting on a sort of gown or cloak, of one colour, that hides the natural form, and makes him appear like a post, or such inanimate thing; which habit must likewise be scented as above, to overpower the smell of his person; and besides this, he is to avoid all motion, till he has secured his point of having all the rats in his power.

When the rats are thus enticed and collected, where time is afforded, and the whole in any house and out-buildings are intended to be cleared away, they are suffered to regale on what they most like, which is ready prepared for them, and then to go away quietly for two or three nights; by which means those, which are not allured the first night, are brought afterwards, either by their fellows, or the effects of the trailing, &c. and will not fail to come duly again, if they are not disturbed or molested. But many of the rat-catchers make shorter work, and content themselves with what can be brought together in one night or two; but this is never effectual, unless where the building is small and entire, and the rats but few in number.

The means of taking them, when they are brought together, are various. Some entice them into a very large bag, the mouth of which is sufficiently capacious to cover nearly the whole floor of the place where they are collected; which is done by smearing some vessel placed in the middle of the bag with oil of rhodium, and laying in the bag baits of food. This bag, which

which before lay flat on the ground with the mouth spread open, is to be suddenly closed when the rats are all in it. Others drive, or fright them, by slight noises or motions, into a bag of a long form, the mouth of which, after all the rats are come in, is drawn up to the opening of the place by which they entered, all other ways of retreat being secured. Others, again, intoxicate or poison them, by mixing with the repast prepared for them, the coculus Indicus, or the nux vomica. A receipt for this purpose has appeared, which directed four ounces of the coculus Indicus, with twelve ounces of oatmeal, and two ounces of treacle or honey, made up into a moist paste with strong beer; but if the nux vomica be used, a much less proportion will serve than is here given of the coculus. Any similar composition of these drugs, with that kind of food the rats are most fond of, and which has a strong flavour, to hide that of the drugs, will equally well answer the end. If, indeed, the coculus Indicus be well powdered, and infused in the beer for some time, at least half the quantity here directed will serve as well as the quantity before-mentioned. When the rats appear to be thoroughly intoxicated with the coculus, or sick with the nux vomica, they may be taken with the hand, and put into a bag or cage, the door of the place being first drawn too, lest those which have strength and sense remaining escape.

By these methods, well conducted, a very considerable part of the rats in any farm, or other house, and the contiguous buildings, may be taken.

RATTLE-GRASS. [*Rhinanthus.*] This is a very troublesome weed growing among grass, and spreading itself over the whole ground.

RATTLESNAKE-*Root.* [*Senecka.*] The root of a species of polygala, which grows spontaneously in Virginia, and bears the winters of our own climate. This root is usually about the thickness of the little finger, variously bent and contorted, and appears as if composed of joints, whence it is supposed to resemble the tail of the animal whose name it bears: A kind of membranous margin runs on each side, the whole length of the root. Its taste is at first acid, afterwards very hot and pungent.

This root is not at present much known in the shops. The Senegaro Indians are said to prevent the fatal effects which follow from the bite of the rattle snake, by giving it internally, and applying it externally to the wound. It has of late been strongly recommended in pleurisies, peripneumonies, and other inflammatory distempers; in these cases, Lemery, du Hamel, and Jussieu, experienced its good success (see the French memoirs for the years 1738, 1739.) Its more immediate effects are those of a diuretic, diaphoretic, and cathartic; sometimes it proves emetic: the two last operations may be occasionally prevented, by giving the root in small doses, along with aromatic simple waters, as that of cinnamon. The usual dose of the powder is thirty grains or more.

Some have likewise employed this root in hydropic cases, and not without success: Bouvart (in the memoirs above-mentioned, 1744) relates examples of its occasioning a plentiful evacuation by stool, urine, and perspiration, and by this means removing the disease, after the common diuretics and hydragogues had failed: Where this medicine operates as a cathartic, it generally proves successful: if it acts by liquifying the blood and juices, without occasioning a due discharge, it should either be abstained from, or assisted by proper additions.

RAT-TAILS, Excrescences which creep from the pastern to the middle of the shanks of a horse, and are so called from the resemblance they bear to the tail of a rat. Some are moist, others dry; the former may be treated with drying ointment and washes, the latter with mercurial ointment. If the hardness does not submit to the last medicine, it should be pared off with a knife, and dressed with turpentine, tar, and honey, to which verdigrease or white vitriol may occasionally be added; but before the use of the knife you may apply this ointment.

> Take black soap four ounces, quicklime two ounces, vinegar enough to make an ointment.

RED-LAND, a term much used by husbandmen

Rawen. See Tore. Aftermath.

huſbandmen to expreſe a ſandy ſoil of a reddiſh hue, interſperſed for the moſt part with pieces of ſand-ſtone of the ſame colour, or ſomewhat deeper.

There are ſeveral varieties of this ſoil, one of which is almoſt entirely made up of ſand; another with an admixture of clay with the ſand, the whole making a looſe loamy earth; and a third, full of fragments, of a poor ſandy iron ore, and often containing ſhining ſpecks of ſelenitæ.

REDWEED. Wild Poppy.

REDWOOD. [*Ceanothus Arboreſcens*] This plant grows naturally wild in the American iſlands; it riſes with a ſhrubby ſtalk eighteen or twenty feet high, ſending out ſeveral horizontal branches, which are garniſhed with oval veined leaves; the flowers come out at the wings of the leaves, with very ſhort foot-ſtalks; they are of a white herbaceous colour, and are ſucceeded by dry capſules, ſhaped like thoſe of the firſt ſort.

This plant requires to be placed in a warm ſtove, otherwiſe it will not thrive in England; it is propagated by ſeeds, which muſt be ſown upon a hot-bed in the ſpring; and when the plants are fit to remove, they ſhould be each planted into a ſeparate ſmall pot, filled with light ſandy earth, and plunged into a hot-bed of tanners bark, obſerving to ſhade them till they have taken root; then they muſt be treated in the ſame manner as other tender exotic plants. In the autumn they muſt be placed in the bark-ſtove, and during the winter muſt be watered with great caution, for too much moiſture at that ſeaſon will deſtroy them.

RED-WORM, the name of an inſect very deſtructive to young corn.

"I have often (ſays Mr. Baker, in his report to the Dublin Society) heard of the havock which red-worms make in young wheat, barley, and oats; and in ſome few writers upon huſbandry have read of them; but never ſaw them till May 1764; when, to my great mortification, in a few days, they deſtroyed, almoſt totally, nine acres of my wheat, for I did not reap above half a barrel per acre. This miſfortune induced me to propoſe to the conſideration of the Dublin Society, whether the offer of a premium might not probably produce a diſcovery of ſome effectual method for deſtroying ſo injurious an inſect, to the infinite advantage of the public: and the ſociety were pleaſed to offer a premium accordingly.

"I now have the honour to lay before them, what has occurred to me upon that ſubject.

"The moſt ingenious M. de Chateauvieux ſpeaks of an inſect, which is certainly the ſame kind, if it be not the very inſect which I have now under conſideration. This gentleman, after ſaying, "our wheat, in the month of May 1755, ſuſtained a loſs, which even that cultivated according to the New Huſbandry, did not eſcape, deſcribes the worm thus: We found in it many little white worms, which afterwards became of a cheſnut colour. They poſt themſelves between the blades and eat the ſtems. They are uſually found between the firſt joints of the roots; every ſtalk which they attacked grew no more, but became yellow, and withered. The ſame misfortune happened to us in the year 1732. The inſects appeared about the middle of May, and made ſuch havock, that the crops were almoſt deſtroyed."

"It perhaps might be expected, that this great man ſhould have made the very enquiry which we are now upon, as the loſs appears to have been very great in Geneva, at the two periods which he mentions; but when we conſider, how much the high office which he held in the city and republic of Geneva, muſt have engaged his attention, it is rather aſtoniſhing that he could oblige the world ſo much as he hath done by his repeated experiments in huſbandry, and his judicious obſervations upon them: It is therefore leſs to be wondered at, that this circumſtance eſcaped him.

"The ingenious Mr. Benjamin Stillingfleet alſo, in the ſecond edition of his miſcellaneous tracts, in a note, p. 175-6, ſpeaks of an inſect, which is probably the ſame as that we are ſeeking to deſtroy. His words are,

"Thus in Suffolk, and in ſome parts of Norfolk, the farmers find it their intereſt to encourage the breed of rooks, as the only means to free their grounds from the grub, from which the

the tree or blind beetle comes, and which in its grub ſtate deſtroys the roots of corn and graſs to ſuch a degree, that I myſelf have ſeen a piece of paſture-land, where you might turn up the turf with your feet.

" Mr. Matthews, a very obſerving and excellent farmer of Wargrave in Berkſhire, told me, that the rooks one year, whilſt his men were hoeing a turnip field, ſat down in part of it, where they were not at work, and that the crop was very fine in that parr, whereas in the other part there were no turnips that year.

" We ſee, that M. de Chateauvieux deſcribes this worm as being firſt white, and afterwards becoming of a cheſnut colour. I have carefully ſought them at different periods during the paſt year, but always found them of the ſame cheſnut colour, never varying in any particular, except that of ſize, which I find to be the caſe at all ſeaſons in which I have ſeen them.

" The inſect which Mr. Stillingfleet ſpeaks of, he calls a grub, which, he ſays, deſtroys corn and graſs: This induces me to believe that it is the ſame inſect (though the report which he relates from Mr. Matthews ſeems to contradict it) becauſe I have obſerved, that the red or cheſnut worm never appears voluntarily upon the ſurface; but when the earth is turned up, either with plough or ſpade, the rooks and crows are very bold in their approach to pick them up; a circumſtance which I own has in ſome degree abated my enmity to theſe birds; I therefore never deſtroy nor frighten them off my land whilſt I am ploughing it; but when I ſow, when the corn riſes, and when it is ripe, I deſtroy or baniſh them as well as I can, becauſe the miſchief which they do at thoſe times is intolerable.

" A member of the Dublin Society informed me laſt ſummer, that ſome of his turnips were deſtroyed by the worm; I had ſome few which decayed in their leaves, and became of a lemon colour, preceding the putrefaction which followed and deſtroyed the turnips: I examined their roots, but could not diſcover any inſect which had injured them, and therefore I cannot pronounce that it is the red-worm which deſtroyed this gentleman's turnips; but I ſhall be very watchful with reſpect to this circumſtance upon every opportunity that may preſent itſelf.

" I have obſerved my lucerne to decay in its tops ſoon after it has been up, and upon examining the roots, I have found the red-worm which had cut them off.

" This inſect ſeems to be every where in Ireland called the red-worm; by ſome of the Engliſh writers who have ſpoken of an inſect which deſtroys corn in the manner already mentioned, which I think is undoubtedly the ſame, it is called a grub; by others the large maggot, and the rook worm, becauſe the rooks eat it; but as none of the writers have given any other deſcription of it, than the name by which they reſpectively call it, I ſhall endeavour to deſcribe it.

" Red-worms are about half an inch long, and about one tenth of an inch in diameter; they are jointed in their ſkins, and are of a very firm texture; they have many ſhort legs, two ſmall black ſpecks, which appear to be their eyes, and two ſmall points ſpringing from their heads, with which I believe they cut the corn, and which, in that work, I apprehend, act like forceps: and all I have ſeen of this ſpecies are of a bright cheſnut colour. For this reaſon, I ſhould conceive it would be more deſcriptive to call them the cheſnut worms.

" When they are expoſed to the air, by turning up the earth which is infeſted with them, they will very ſoon cover themſelves again in the ſoil, which they are very capable of doing, by the ſtrength which their make gives them, although they appear to be a ſluggiſh inſect, and have not the advantage of a ſlimineſs upon their ſkins which the common large creeping worm has, which enables that inoffenſive worm to penetrate the earth, and get under timber and ſtones with eaſe.

" The red-worm immediately endeavouring to cover itſelf from the air, is certainly from natural inſtinct, as it will ſoon die when expoſed to the air, as will appear by the experiment Numb. 10, hereafter-mentioned.

" Theſe worms deſtroy wheat, barley, oats, and lucerne, whilſt in an infant ſtate, in the months of March, April, and May. Late-ſown barley and oats they will deſtroy as late as June. I have not yet experienced that they will deſtroy any other crops.

" The miſchief done by them is in dry weather. Rain ſufficient to penetrate the ground, makes them deſiſt from deſtroying the corn; and, I ſuppoſe, every thing elſe which they at any time injure.

" They cut wheat off juſt above the crown of the roots; barley and oats in the ſame place, and alſo higher up, upon any part of the ſtem, which is below the ſurface of the earth.

" Theſe worms ſeem to abound more in ground which is lightly tilled, than in ſuch as hath been well tilled; but, in lay ground, they ſeem to be more numerous than any where elſe; and the fields upon my farm, in which I have found them, are wetter than other fields where they are not; whether that circumſtance contributes to their increaſe, I cannot ſay, but the following experiments prove that they will live longer in water than they can when expoſed to the open air.

Experiments on Red-worms.

" Numb. 1. I put ten red-worms into a wine glaſs with common ſalt in it. They were all dead in twenty-four hours.

" Numb. 2. Into a glaſs with brine in it I put ten red-worms. They were all dead in ſix hours.

" Numb. 3. Into a glaſs with lime in it, which had been ſlaked for a long time, and expoſed to the weather, I put the like number. They were all dead in forty-four hours.

" Numb. 4. Into a glaſs with the above lime, and ſome water in it, I put the like number. They were dead in twenty hours.

" Numb. 5. Into a glaſs with lime newly ſlaked, and when cold, I put the like number. They were dead in fourteen hours.

" Numb. 6. Into lime-water, made with cold water, I put the like number. They were dead in ten hours.

" Numb. 7. Into a glaſs with ſoot in it, I put the like number. They were dead in four hours.

" Numb. 8. Into ſoot and water I put the like number. They were dead in four hours.

" Numb. 9. Into fair water I put the like number. They were dead in fifty-two hours.

" Numb. 10. Into a glaſs without any thing in it, I put the like number. They were dead in thirty-two hours.

" By theſe experiments we ſee all the articles uſed will kill this inſect in a ſhort time, particularly the ſalt and ſoot. I thought it neceſſary to conſider different articles, the better to ſuit different parts of the kingdom.

" Where lime can be conveniently had, and that it is uſed as a manure, I am apt to believe from the experiments, that no injury can be ſuſtained from theſe worms, but I am afraid a ſmall quantity will not effectually deſtroy them; beſides, I ſhould fear, if it were not put on before the ſowing of the corn, that it might ſinge the blades of the corn; for, from the experiments, it appears, that lime newly ſlaked, is more ſuddenly deſtructive to them than old lime, and therefore it is to be preferred.

" Where lime is uſed for no other purpoſe than to deſtroy this worm, I ſhould conceive that about eight barrels regularly ſown by hand on an acre of ground might be ſufficient; it muſt be firſt ſlaked and cold before a man can poſſibly caſt upon the ground with his hand, lime being a very ſtrong cauſtic; and even when it is cold, the man ſhould have a thick glove upon his hand.

" Where ſalt ſhall be uſed to deſtroy this worm, it muſt always be ſown upon the ground before the intended crop; for, although corn will vegetate and receive benefit from ſalt as a manure when it is uſed antecedent to the ſowing the corn, yet, if it be added after the corn is growing, it will certainly deſtroy it; and therefore, it ſhould never be uſed for this purpoſe, but before the corn is ſown, or at leaſt before it vegetates.

" I conceive that where ſalt is uſed for this purpoſe only, about four hundred and a half to an acre will anſwer this purpoſe, which is a trifle more than one ounce to every ſquare yard.

" We ſee by the experiment, that ſoot kills this worm as ſoon as ſalt; and, as in moſt places it is to be had at a much leſs price than ſalt, I think there

there can be no doubt about preferring of it; besides which, it may be safely used after the corn is up.

"I had some parcels of barley under experiments, which these worms began to destroy; and in order to convey the soot as soon as possible to the roots of the plants, I mixed a little of it in water, and poured it on the plants with a garden watering-pot; the consequence was, that I did not lose one plant afterwards.

"It will hardly be imagined, that I mean that the same method is to be pursued upon a whole farm: No; the method I would recommend to the practice of the farmer is this, to spread or cast by hand, as he sows his corn, about six or eight barrels of soot on an acre, and let him be careful to choose a calm day for the work, otherwise, the wind will carry away great part of it, and as what remains cannot be regularly disposed, let him be careful to do it early enough in the spring, that the rain may wash the soot and convey it to the roots of the plants before the worm begins the mischief; if he does this, I am persuaded his crop will be preserved.

"We see by the experiments, that this worm will live longer in water by twenty hours than when exposed to the open air; but at length, i. e. in fifty-two hours, they died in the water; perhaps this might be from the effect of drowning, but if so, I might have expected they would have been totally destroyed in my two fields in the winter of 1763 and 1764, by the immoderate rains which fell at that season for a long continuance, by which the land was often flooded. But they survived that winter, as appeared by the great loss I afterwards sustained by their destroying my wheat; and therefore, whether water be an enemy to them or not, it seems not easy to determine: but if those which died in the glass of water were really drowned, yet, I think we may conclude, that water is necessary to their existence in the earth, and probably aids them in getting their food from it; and what seems to confirm this notion is, that when the land is wet, they do not touch the corn, but as soon as ever the land is dry, they begin their mischief. However, this speculation I must submit to the consideration of persons more capable of discussing it than I am.

"We see by the experiment, Numb. 10, that they cannot live in the open air; which seems to prove, that, where they abound in land, the oftener it is ploughed, particularly in the summer, when they cannot penetrate the ground so easily as when it is moist, they must be, by such ploughing, greatly diminished; besides which, the frequent ploughing gives the crows more opportunities of picking them up, in which, as I before said, they are very watchful.

"Frequent ploughing has been recommended by some writers, as the only means of destroying this worm; and they have recommended the plough's being stuck with nails, urging, that by those nails the worms are cut to pieces; others have recommended walnut leaves being soaked in water, to sprinkle the land; and steeping seed-corn in various liquors, as infallible remedies: But such methods as these are founded upon mistaken principles; they only mislead the farmer, and must disappoint him.

"Worlidge recommends a strong lye made of fixed salts, but that would be impracticable. Mortimer recommends sea-water for such lands as are near the sea-coast, which I believe would answer very well. He says he used soot once with success, but that it did not succeed with him afterward. I am persuaded he did not use the soot early enough to have it washed into the ground by rain, or perhaps he used too small a quantity.

"I would not be thought to arrogate any merit to myself on account of what I have offered on this subject, since it appears, that other persons have used the articles which I have recommended against this common enemy; but many persons have been disappointed in their expectations from these remedies, which must have arisen from their either having used too small a quantity, or not having observed the necessary precautions; if those which I have recommended shall be put in practice, and found to answer, I shall think myself amply rewarded."

REED. [*Arundo.*] The species are, 1. The common Marsh Reed. 2. The

manured

and placed into pans of water, which should be plunged into a hot-bed; and as the water wastes, so it must, from time to time, be renewed again. In July these plants may be set abroad in a warm situation, still preserving the water in the pans, otherwise they will not thrive; and towards the latter end of August they will produce their grain, which will ripen tolerably well, provided the autumn proves favourable.

RICK, A pile of corn, hay, straw, &c. regularly heaped up in the open air, and sheltered from wet.

RIDDER, or RIDDLE. A sieve to clean corn.

RIDGE, the rising ground left between the furrows in ploughing, &c.

RINCES *in a horse's mouth*, are wrinkles or risings of flesh in the roof of the mouth, running across from one side of the jaw to the other, with furrows between them.

RING-BONE, A hard swelling on the lower part of the pastern of a horse, that generally reaches half round the fore-part. It has its name from the resemblance to a ring.

It often arises from strains, &c. and when behind, from putting young horses too early upon their haunches; for in that attitude a horse throws his whole weight as much, if not more, upon his pasterns, than on his hocks.

When it appears distinctly round the pastern, and does not run downwards toward the coronet, so as to effect the coffin-joint, it is easily cured; but if it takes its origin from some strain or defect in the joint originally, or if a callosity is found under the round ligament that covers that joint, the cure is generally dubious, and sometimes impracticable; as it is apt to turn to a quittor, and in the end to form an ulcer upon the hoof.

The ring-bones that appear on colts and young horses will often insensibly wear off of themselves, without the help of any application; but when the substance remains, there needs no other remedy besides blistering, unless when by long continuance it is grown to an obstinate hardness, and then it may require both blistering and firing.

To fire a ring-bone successfully, let the operation be performed with a thinner instrument than the common one, and let the lines or razes be made not above a quarter of an inch distant, crossing them obliquely, somewhat like a chain; apply a mild blister over all, and when quite dried up, the rupture plaister; and then turn the horse to grass for some time.

RIPPLING *of Flax*, The operation of taking off the seed from the flax by drawing it through a ripple, or large comb. See FLAX.

ROCKET. [*Eruca.*] This was formerly much cultivated in gardens for medicinal use, and for sallads, but is at present less common. In appearance it resembles mustard, but is easily distinguishable by the smoothness of its leaves, and its disagreeable smell. The seeds have a pungent taste, of the mustard kind, but weaker; they have long been celebrated as aphrodisiacs, and may, probably, have in some cases a title to this virtue, in common with other acrid plants.

Garden ROCKET. Dame's violet.

ROCK-ROSE. *See* CISTUS.

ROD. A measure in length containing sixteen feet and a half. In land measure, sixteen feet and a half square.

Golden ROD. *See* GOLDEN ROD.

ROLLER, A large piece of wood turning on its axis, and drawn over the surface of the ground to break the small clods, and render it smooth and even.

ROOD, A quantity of land equal to forty square poles or perches, that is, a quarter of an acre.

ROOP. Hoarseness.

ROOT, The lower part of a plant, by which it adheres to the earth, and by which it draws its nourishment, and transmits the juices to the other parts.

ROSACEOUS, An epithet applied to such flowers as are composed of several petals or leaves, disposed in a sort of circular form, like those of the rose; of this kind are the flowers of the piony, ranunculus, &c.

ROSIL, or *Rossils*, Land neither light nor heavy, being a medium between sand and clay.

ROSE-TREE. [*Rosa.*] Of this plant are reckoned fourteen different species, the varieties of which are still more numerous.

1. The dog rose, or hip tree. 2. The

The white rose, and its varieties. 3. The red rose, and its varieties. 4. The hundred-leaved rose, and its varieties, which include the Moss, and Provence. 5. Cinnamon rose. 6. The Alpine rose, or virgin rose, without prickles. 7. Carolina, or Virginia rose. 8. Apple-bearing rose. 9. Burnet-leaved rose. 10. Scotch rose. 11. Musk rose. 12. Evergreen musk rose. 13. The Damask rose. 14. The sweet-briar.

All these are of the shrub kind, and all the fourteen kinds deciduous and hardy.

The propagation of all the sorts is by suckers, layers, budding, and some sorts by seeds; but suckers are the most common and expeditious method for propagating most of the species.

By suckers. Most of the roses send up many suckers annually from the root, attaining from one or two to three or four feet in height, or more, in one summer, and by these the shrubs may be expeditiously propagated in great plenty; they may be taken up in autumn, winter, or early in spring, with some fibres to their bottom; and the strongest may be planted out finally, and the weakest in nursery lines for a year or two, or longer; they will readily grow, and will most of them produce flowers the following summer.

When these shrubs have grown into large bunches, with many suckers grown up to stems from the root, the whole may be taken up and slipped, or divided into so many separate plants, and planted out, as above.

Observe, that as the moss rose, musk rose, apple-bearing rose, and some others, furnish suckers but sparingly, so in default thereof must have recourse to layers, or budding; particularly for the Moss Provence.

By Layers. All the sorts of these plants will grow by layers of the young shoots; and is an effectual method of propagation, for such sorts particularly as sparingly furnish suckers, as the Moss Provence, &c. and to obtian plenty of shoots for laying, a quantity of the plants should be planted for stools; which being headed down low, they will throw out plenty of shoots near the ground in summer, for laying in autumn or winter following, by slit or twist-laying, they will be rooted by next autumn, and fit for transplantation in nursery rows; though sometimes the Moss Rose, &c. require two years before they are tolerably well rooted; but of these sorts you may also try layers of the young tender shoots of the year, layed in summer, any time in June, they will probably root a little the same season. However, the layers of all sorts, after being properly rooted, should be taken up in autumn, and planted in the nursery, to have a one or two year's growth, or to remain till wanted.

By Budding. This is sometimes practised in propagating some choice sorts that seldom send up suckers, such as the Moss Provence, &c. also, when intended to have two, three, or more different sorts of roses upon the same tree, for curiosity; working upon the Frankfort, or any other strong shooting rose-stocks raised from suckers.

By Seeds. This is sometimes practised to try to obtain new varieties; also sometimes for raising some particular permanent species, such as the Canine Rose, Burnet-leaved Rose, Scotch Rose, Apple-bearing-rose, single Sweet-Briar, and such others as continue the same by seedlings; sowing them generally in autumn soon after they are ripe, and they will sometimes rise the following spring, as if not sowed till the spring season, most of the sorts are apt to remain till the second year before they rise freely; sow them however in any bed of light earth, either in shallow drills, or all over the surface, covering them half an inch deep; and when the seedlings are a year old, transplant them in nursery rows.

Observe, however, that the double kinds, and other particular varieties of the species in general, cannot be continued the same with certainty by seeds, so must always be propagated by suckers or layers, &c.

But remark, the common single Sweet Briar, when required in any considerable quantity should generally be raised from seed, sowing it in drills half an inch deep, either to remain, or for transplantation; though when designed to form a sort of hedge of this plant to produce a crop of shoots

to

to cut for the ſupply of markets during the ſummer, it is eligible to ſow the ſeed at once in a drill where the plants are to ſtand.

Hoffman ſtrongly recommends the flowers of the Damaſk Roſe as of ſingular efficacy for raiſing the ſtrength, chearing and recruiting the ſpirits, and allaying pain; which they perform without raiſing any heat in the conſtitution, rather abating it when inordinate. Damaſk roſes, beſides their cordial aromatic virtue, which reſides in their volatile parts, have a mildly purgative one, which remains entire in the decoction after the diſtillation: This, with a proper quantity of ſugar, forms an agreeable laxative ſyrup, which has long kept its place in the ſhops. The other officinal preparations of this flower are of ſolutive honey, and the diſtilled water, which laſt is an ingredient in the muſk-julep, the confection of kermes, and ſaponaceous lotion, and is uſed alſo in making the ſimple ointment called pomatum.

Rose-bay. See Oleander.

Dwarf Rose-bay. [*Rhododendron.*] There are five ſpecies of this plant, two of which are evergreens, all flowering in June. They are propagated by ſowing the ſeeds in autumn.

Rose Campion. [*Agroſtemma.*] The ſingle roſe campion has been long in the gardens, where ſometimes it becomes a troubleſome weed. The double ſort is now placed in its room, but is only cultivated by parting the roots.

China Rose. [*Hibiſcus Chinenſis.*] This grows naturally in the Eaſt Indies, from whence it has been carried to the Weſt-India iſlands, and obtained the name of Martinico roſe. The flowers of this plant at the firſt opening are white, then change to a bluſhing red, and at their decay turn purple; it is propagated by ſeeds, and muſt be treated tenderly.

Gelder Rose. See Gelder Rose.

Rose *of Jericho.* [*Anaſtatica.*] This plant grows naturally in the ſands near the borders of the Red Sea, and in many parts of Syria. It is a low annual plant, dividing into many irregular woody branches near the root; at each joint is placed a ſingle, oblong, hoary leaf, and at the ſame places come out ſmall ſingle flowers of a whitiſh green colour, compoſed of four ſmall leaves, placed in form of a croſs, like the other plants of this claſs. Theſe are ſucceeded by ſhort wrinkled pods, having four ſmall horns; theſe open into two cells, in each of which is lodged a ſingle brown ſeed.

It is propagated by ſeeds ſown the beginning of March on a moderate hot-bed.

South-Sea Rose. Oleander.

Rose-wort. [*Rhodiola.*] There are two ſorts, one growing in Wales, Yorkſhire, and Weſtmoreland; and another with ſmaller roots found on the Alps. They are preſerved in gardens for the ſake of variety, and are propagated by parting their roots about the beginning of September.

Rosewood. [*Rhodium.*] The writers on botany, and the materia medica, are much divided about the lignum rhodium, not only with regard to the plant which affords it, but likewiſe in their accounts of the drug itſelf, and have deſcribed under this name ſimples manifeſtly different. This confuſion ſeems to have ariſen from an opinion, that the rhodium and aſpalathus are the ſame; whence different woods brought into Europe for the unknown aſpalathus were ſold again by the name of rhodium.

The lignum rhodium of the ſhops is uſually in long crooked pieces full of knots, which when cut appear of a yellow colour like box, with a reddiſh caſt; the largeſt, ſmootheſt, moſt compact, and the deepeſt coloured pieces, ſhould be choſen; and the ſmall, thin, or pale ones, rejected. The taſte of this wood is lightly bitteriſh, and ſomewhat pungent; its ſmell very fragrant, reſembling that of roſes; long kept, it ſeems to loſe its ſmell; but on cutting, or rubbing one piece againſt another, it ſmells as well as at firſt. Diſtilled with water, it yields an odoriferous eſſential oil, in very ſmall quantity. Rhodium is at preſent in eſteem only upon account of its oil, which is employed as an high and agreeable perfume in ſcenting pomatums, and the like. But if we may reaſon from analogy, this odoriferous ſimple might be advantageouſly applied to nobler purpoſes: a tincture of it in rectified ſpirit of wine,

which

which contains in a small volume the virtue of a considerable deal of the wood, bids fair to prove a serviceable cordial, not inferior perhaps to any thing of this kind.

ROUGHNESS *of the Coat*. When a horse grows rough in a stable in spite of the usual care, and his heels swell, the following mixture is to be given him with all his food:

Take a pound of flower of brimstone, half a pound of turmerick, and a quarter of a pound of crude antimony in powder. Sift these together, by which means they will be thoroughly mixed, and strew a little of it over and among his victuals.

ROSEMARY. [*Rosmarinus.*] The name of an odoriferous plant very common in almost every garden.

Rosemary may be raised from seeds; but it is more commonly and more easily propagated by planting slips or cuttings of it in a spot of light fresh earth, in the spring of the year just before its buds begin to open. When these plants have taken root (till which they must be watered gently from time to time, and shaded if the sun be too powerful) they should be transplanted into the places where they are to remain. This should be done early in September, or the latter end of March; but in whatever season they are transplanted, it should not be during a cold drying easterly wind, because this would soon shrivel up their leaves and kill them. If a few warm showers fall soon after they are set, they will soon take root, and after that they will require no farther care than keeping them free from weeds. The distances between the plants should be full sufficient to allow for their utmost growth, so that they may not touch one another. The growth will be most luxuriant, especially in the summer, if they are set in a rich mould: but then they will be most subject to be injured by frosts; nor will their odour be near so strongly aromatic, as when raised on a poor gravelly soil.

Rosemary is a native of Spain, Italy, and the southern parts of France, where it grows in great abundance in dry gravelly soils. It has a fragrant smell, and a warm pungent bitterish taste; the leaves and tender tops are strongest; next to these the cup flower; the flowers themselves are considerably the weakest, but most pleasant. Aqueous liquors extract great share of its virtues by infusion, and elevate them in distillation; along with the water arises a considerable quantity of essential oil, of an agreeable strong penetrating smell. Pure spirit extracts in great perfection the whole aromatic flavour of the rosemary, and elevates very little of it in distillation; hence the resinous mass, left upon abstracting the spirit, proves an elegant aromatic, very rich in the peculiar qualities of the plant.

ROT. A disease incident to sheep, arising frequently from wet seasons, and too moist pasture.

"But the rot in sheep," says an ingenious and practical writer, "does not always proceed either from moisture alone, or the nature of the soil alone; for all moist grounds do not cause the rot in sheep, and there are some lands which rot sheep in wet years only.

"The rot, in fact, arises from a certain putrefaction, both in the air, and in the grass or herbs that usually grow in such moist years: these, together with their moist food, corrupt their livers, and bring on the disease.

"It is indeed very difficult to cure this disorder, unless it is attempted before the liver is too much wasted: where there is a convenience of doing it, the best remedy is an immediate removal to salt-marshes; but this not being in every farmer's power, I shall endeavour, from my own experience, to supply the deficiency.

"In such cases as these, a prevention of the evil is to be recommended to the practice of every rational farmer.

"Some grounds naturally yield a soft, spungy grass, which is, more than any other, subject to breed the rot in sheep; I would therefore advise, that other cattle be fed in these grounds, and the sheep kept in the driest, hardest, and healthiest pastures.

"I have known land that has kept sheep in health for many successive years, yet afterwards, when the months of May and June have proved wet, a frim and frothy grass has suddenly sprung up, which, together with the bad air that must of course follow, has caused a rot in the sheep that were then on it; the evil was observed in time, the sheep were removed to a

 dry

dry and almoſt barren heath, and in the ſucceeding winter they were foddered with good, dry, ſweet hay, and a great loſs was prevented.

" This unwholeſome graſs is moſt apt to grow in cold land, and in the ſummer-time; and it is a general opinion, and well founded on experience, that if the ſummer does not rot ſheep, the winter will not, the power of the winter alone not being ſtrong enough to begin a rot.

" A very ſenſible writer, whoſe book I have juſt turned to, I mean Mr. Liſle, ſays, that broom is very good for the rot; and indeed I have often experienced it, for in a farm I occupied ſome years ago there were ſeveral broom-fields, and I have often obſerved that ſuch of my ſheep as were part of the year fed in them were never infected with the rot, whilſt others in my poſſeſſion had it to a great degree. I profited however by experience, for I took care thenceforward that all my ſheep ſhould, by turns, enjoy the advantages to be derived from their feeding on the young ſhoots of the broom.

" As to what Mr. Liſle ſays, on the authority of Mr. Ray, that the marſh-trefoil will cure the rot, I cannot, from experience, corroborate it: I have heard its efficacy in this diſorder often mentioned, but never yet heard any particular fact related ſo circumſtantially as to induce me to depend on its effects.

" That ſalt is good, I agree with the above gentleman, and Mr. Boyle; and this gives me an opportunity of communicating a receipt which I know to be a good one.

" When you perceive by the colour of your ſheep's eyes, that the rot has taken them, drive your flock into a barn, a covered fold, or ſome ſuch convenient place; around this place let there be wooden troughs, like mangers, in which you ſhould feed your ſheep with good, dry, clean oats, for forty-eight hours; then have ready ſome bay ſalt finely powdered and ſearced, of which you are to ſprinkle a little among the oats, increaſing the quantity till it diſguſts the ſheep, and you perceive they fall off their appetites; afterwards, for the two following days, give them again clean oats; and then mix your ſalt with them as before, continuing this proceſs till their eyes have recovered their natural colour, when you will find them perfectly cured; and to be convinced, it will only be neceſſary to kill one or two out of the flock.

" To this I ſhall add a receipt for the rot in ſheep, which was communicated to me by a friend, a man of credit and veracity, who ſays he has often tried it with ſucceſs.

> " Steep ſome regulus of antimony in ale, adding thereto ſome grains of paradiſe, and a little ſugar to ſweeten it. Of this infuſion ſomewhat leſs than a gill is to be given to every one of your affected ſheep; they are to have two or three doſes, according as they are more or leſs affected by the diſtemper, allowing two days intermiſſion between each doſe."

" This is ſaid, as I have already obſerved, to be a cure almoſt certain.

" I juſt now take notice, that when rain falls in the months of May and June it is apt to cauſe the rot in ſheep; it will be neceſſary to add, that folding them in the above months increaſes the diſorder; for after having been deprived of their liberty during the whole night, they bite the noxious graſs the more greedily in the morning, having leſs ceremony in their choice of herbs than if they were not folded. This is a matter of ſome conſequence, therefore worthy of being attended to.

" One thing more I muſt, on the authority of Mr. Liſle, communicate to your readers, viz. an obſervation of a Leiceſterſhire farmer, that ſheep, when firſt touched with the rot, will thrive mightily in fatting for ten weeks, but if they are not diſpoſed of when they are come up to a pitch, they will, in ſeven or eight days time, fall away to nothing but ſkin and bone. The ſame farmer obſerved, that he had often had them die in the height of their pitch, in half an hour's time, with twenty-ſeven pounds of tallow in their bellies." *Muſeum Ruſticum*, vol. i. page 434.

To this account we ſhall add a receipt communicated to Mr. Mills by a gentleman of Lincolnſhire.

" Steep

" Steep a handful of rue in a pail of water all night, and at morning put in as much salt as will make it bear an egg. Give each sheep half a pint of this liquor, and repeat it thrice, every other morning.

" A farmer who kept four hundred sheep tried this receipt in the last general rot (about fourteen years ago) and did not lose any, though his neighbours lost almost all theirs. For the sake of the experiment, he set apart about twenty, and did not give them this drink. Many of these were rotten."

ROUP. The name of a filthy disease in poultry, consisting of a boil or swelling upon the rump, and is known by the staring or turning back of the feathers.

The roup, if not soon remedied, will corrupt the whole body of the fowl; to prevent which, the feathers should be plucked away, the swelling laid open, and the matter pressed out; after which, the part is to be washed with brine, or salt and water.

ROWEL. A kind of issue made in horses for the cure of various disorders, as inward strains, hard swellings, &c.

The operation is performed in the following manner:

A little slit being made through the skin, about a hand-breadth below the part aggrieved, big enough to put a swan's quill in, the skin is raised from the flesh, the end of the quill put in, and the skin blowed from the flesh upwards, and all over the shoulder; then the hole being stopped with the finger, the part blown is beat with a hazle-stick, and the wind spread with the hand all over, and then let go; this done, a skain of horse-hair, or red sarsenet, half the thickness of the little finger, is put in a rowelling needle, seven or eight inches long, and the needle is put into the hole, and drawn through again, six or seven inches higher; then the needle is drawn out, and the two ends of the rowel tied together, anointing it every day, as well as before the putting it in, with sweet butter, and hog's grease, and drawing it backwards and forwards in the skin, to make the putrid matter discharge itself more plentifully.

Rowen – [illegible] [illegible] Tore.

RUE. [*Ruta.*] This is a small shrubby plant, met with in gardens, where it flowers in June, and holds its green leaves all the winter: we frequently find in the markets a narrow-leaved sort, which is cultivated by some in preference to the other, on account of its leaves appearing variegated during the winter, with white streaks.

Rue has a strong ungrateful smell, and a bitterish, penetrating taste; the leaves, when in full vigour, are extremely acrid, insomuch as to inflame and blister the skin, if much handled. With regard to their medicinal virtues, they are powerfully stimulating, attenuating, and detergent; and hence, in cold phlegmatic habits, they quicken the circulation, dissolve tenacious juices, open obstructions of the excretory glands, and promote the fluid secretions. The writers on the materia medica in general have entertained a very high opinion of the virtues of this plant. Boerhaave is full of its praises, particularly of the essential oil, and the distilled water cohobated, or re-distilled several times from fresh parcels of the herb: After somewhat extravagantly commending other waters prepared in this manner, he adds, with regard to that of rue, that the greatest commendations he can bestow upon it fall short of its merit. " What medicine (says he) can be more efficacious for promoting sweat and perspiration, for the cure of the hysteric passion, and of epilepsies, and for expelling poison?" Whatever service rue may be of in the two last cases, it undoubtedly has its use in the others; the cohobated water, however, is not the most efficacious preparation of it. An extract made by rectified spirit contains, in a small compass, the whole virtues of the rue; this menstruum taking up by infusion all the pungency and flavour of the plant, and elevating nothing in distillation. With water, its peculiar flavour and warmth arise; the bitterness, and a considerable share of the pungency remaining behind.

Dog's RUE. There are several species of this plant cultivated in gardens for variety, all propagated by seeds, or by planting slips or cuttings.

Dog's RUE, Figwort.

Goat's Rue. See Goat's Rue.

Meadow Rue. See Meadow Rue.

Wall Rue. See White Maiden Hair.

Syrian Rue. [*Peganum.*] This plant is a native of Syria and Spain, and the stalks decay every autumn, but the roots are perennial. It is propagated by seeds sown the beginning of April, requires a warm situation, and dry soil.

RUPTURE-WORT. [*Herniaria.*] This is a low herb growing wild in sandy and gravelly grounds. It is a very mild restringent, and may, in some degree, be serviceable in disorders proceeding from a weak flaccid state of the viscera: The virtue which it has been most celebrated for, it has little title to, that of curing hernias.

RUSH. [*Juncus.*] Rushes grow on moist, strong, uncultivated lands in most parts of England, and consume the herbage where they are suffered to remain. The best method of destroying these rushes is, to fork them up clean by the roots in July, and after having let them lie a fortnight or three weeks to dry, lay them in heaps and burn them gently, and the ashes which these afford will be tolerable manure for the land; but in order to prevent their growing again, and to make the pasture good, the land should be drained, otherwise there will be no destroying these rushes entirely; but after it is well drained, if the roots are annually drawn up, and the ground kept duly rolled, they may be subdued. Lime is a good manure for rushy land, as likewise wood-ashes from a lime-kiln. Also Cinders.

Flowering Rush. [*Butomus.*] There are two varieties of this plant, one with a rose-coloured flower, and the other with a white flower; but these are only accidental variations, therefore not to be enumerated as distinct species.

The rose-coloured sort is pretty common in standing waters in many parts of England; the other is a variety of this, though less common with us near London. These plants may be propagated in boggy places, or by planting them in cisterns, which should be kept filled with water, that should have about a foot thickness of earth in the bottom, into which the roots should be planted, or the seed sown as soon as they are ripe; these, though common plants, yet produce very pretty flowers, and are worth propagating for variety's sake, especially if in any part of the garden there should be conveniency for an artificial bog, or where there are ponds of standing water, as is many times the case, and persons are at a loss what to plant in such places that may appear beautiful.

Sweet-scented Rush. [*Juncus Odoratus.*] This is a dry smooth stalk, brought to us along with the leaves, and sometimes the flowers, from Turkey and Arabia, tied up in bundles about a foot long. The stalk, in shape and colour, somewhat resembles a barley-straw; it is full of a fungous pith, like those of our common rushes; the leaves are like those of wheat, and surround the stalk with several coats, as in the reed; the flowers are of a carnation colour, striped with a lighter purple. The whole plant, when in perfection, has a hot bitterish, not unpleasant, aromatic taste; and a very fragrant smell; by long keeping, it loses greatly of its aromatic flavour. Distilled with water, it yields a considerable quantity of essential oil. It was formerly often used as an aromatic, and in obstructions of the viscera, &c. but at present is scarce otherwise employed than as an ingredient in mithridate and theriaca.

RUST *in corn.* Mildew.

RYE. [*Secale.*] Rye has been generally thought the next best bread-corn to wheat, and accordingly was formerly very much used for that purpose, and is so still in some places; sometimes alone, but then it has a peculiar sweetness, which is generally disagreeable to those who are not used to it, and subjects many to cholicks and loosenesses, and the bread made of it is black and heavy.

But a small quantity of it was formerly, and still is in several places, mixed with wheat in the making of bread, on account of its keeping the bread moist, and then is attended with no ill consequences, but is rather thought to render the wheat more tender, fresh, and agreeable to the taste. And it was the more cultivated on account of its being the product of barren, gravelly, sandy land, which was then thought capable of producing

cing nothing else, or very little worth the farmer's care.

The common or winter rye requires a summer's fallow, and more expence and trouble in the management of it, than it is found to answer well; since the great improvements made of those dry sandy soils proper for it, by the advantages made of such sort of soils, by the sowing of turnips, and several artificial grasses, and the great profit made by them; and from the several species of corn, they give the farmer an opportunity of raising much more advantageous crops than rye; this must, of course, sink it in the husbandman's esteem, and make it in general to be much less regarded.

There are two sorts of rye.

First, The common or winter rye.

Second, The lesser or spring rye.

The first sort is what is usually propagated amongst us, and generally on such dry barren land as is above-mentioned, where better corn will not grow.

The second sort, or small rye, is to be sown in the spring, about the same time when oats are. It is apt to run into straw if it prove a wet season, and this sort is generally lighter than the other; however, it may be very conveniently used where wheat or other autumn crops have miscarried.

Two bushels are commonly allowed for seed to an acre, and four loads generally reckoned a middling crop; and it usually carries equal price with barley, and about one half the price of wheat

In several places they sow rye together with wheat on the same ground, and then it is called Maslen, that is, Miscellane, and will then bear a price in proportion to the quantity of wheat which is mixed with it.

The best judges think this sort of husbandry to be a very ill one, since as the rye is ripe before the wheat, and must stand till they are cut together, the consequence must necessarily be, that the rye will shed a good deal of its grain; and what is more, the grains when so mixed seldom make a bread that those persons can well bear, who have been used to wheat. But the rye producing a spirit, it is now said to be much used for that purpose, and so far may save the wheat; though we doubt such a use of it will prove of no advantage to our country.

Rye is a quick grower, and for that reason the common sort, as well as the other, sometimes is sowed in spring, when wheat miscarries, and has answered expectation; and the smaller rye (as before-mentioned) is very proper for this purpose, as it is usually ripe at the common times of harvest. The common sort is sometimes sowed so late, in order to be ploughed in to fertilize the ground for a better species of grain.

But there is another more beneficial prospect of sowing it in autumn, which is, in order to provide food for ewes and lambs in the spring, when turnips and coleseed are gone, or have failed, and before any other sorts of grasses are grown to support them; and it may be sowed for this purpose either on land prepared particularly for this end, or on the wheat land after the corn is carried off, or on other stubbles when ploughed up, or where turnips have failed, and will probably answer expectation whichever method of management is taken with it for this purpose.

It is certainly the best proof of a man's being a good farmer, when he is known to provide proper and sufficient food for his cattle and sheep for the whole year in general, and also has a further particular view for a second provision for his ewes and lambs, in case any of the former intended sorts should miscarry.

All this he may certainly generally do, if he will but carefully consider the several respective times. The common natural, and the several artificial grasses, or turnips, &c. will continue at the latter end of the year; and also when he may expect any of them to come in to his assistance in the spring; and then think of, and provide such other supports for them in the time. None of them are to be had in the usual course of things, by sowing either turnips, rye, or coleseed, by the help of one or other of which (with God's blessing) he need not much fear but he may have a plentiful provision for his flock all the year round.

It is for want of this knowledge and care to provide greens and grasses for their sheep in the winter and the spring, that in many places in the north they are obliged to prevent their ewes from having lambs, till they have natural graſs on the ground to help them to milk to ſupport them, which is often not till the end of April, and ſometimes not till the beginning of May; and then they are obliged to eat their beſt mowing grounds ſometimes to the twentieth of May, before they can turn their ſheep to the commons, and ſave their grounds for hay. If a dry time then ſucceeds, theſe grounds are burnt up, and their expected product of hay from their beſt land, wholly, or in a great meaſure, deſtroyed; to the exceeding diſadvantage of the farmers, and ſometimes to their ruin.

And why may not rye be ſowed for the purpoſes above-mentioned amongſt turnips, and anſwer the farmer's expectation, eſpecially as the ground on which turnips are commonly ſowed, is generally better prepared, and uſually of a better nature, and in much better heart than the land commonly allotted for the growth of rye; eſpecially where turnips are ſowed after the drill manner.

In plentiful years rye may be given to fowl, or hogs, which laſt delight in it, and will feed very well on it when ground, and made into a paſte, but then they ſhould always have water, and alſo a few beans or peaſe at the laſt, to harden their fat, which is commonly very beneficial in moſt methods of feeding them.

This grain is very ſubject to grow in the ear, if any wet comes to it; and it will be ſoon damaged if any green weeds are mixed with it, ſo that particular care muſt be taken of it in both theſe reſpects, to let it have time in the field, to prevent the weeds making it to give in the barn, which will make the corn muſty, and therefore it ſhould be houſed dry, and that as ſoon as ever you can get it ſo.

The keeping it in the chaff, on a dry floor, is adviſed for the preſerving it ſweet after it is thraſhed; the dry chaff imbibing any moiſture which may happen. This method has been mentioned for preſerving wheat, and is uſeful in ſeveral other grains.

Rye-grass. See Rey-grass.

S.

SAF-FLOWER. [*Carthamus.*] Baſtard ſaffron is cultivated for the ſake of the flower, as the ſaffron is; and probably the culture of ſaffron gave riſe to this article, for its flower is uſed to ſome of the ſame purpoſes, and is called for that reaſon baſtard ſaffron.

The plant however is utterly unlike ſaffron; it is a kind of thiſtle, and wherever it grows, whether wild or cultivated, it has very much the appearance of a weed.

It is an annual plant. The ſtalk is ſturdy, robuſt, and four feet high. The leaves are large and broad, not divided or indented, but beſet with prickles at the edges; the flowers grow at the tops of the branches, into which the main ſtalk divides towards its upper part; and are a kind of large ſcaly heads, ſomewhat reſembling thoſe of our thiſtles, with a great quantity of threads iſſuing out at their tops. Theſe threads are of a moſt bright and beautiful yellow, and have been ſuppoſed by ſome to reſemble the blades in the flower of ſaffron; but there is not much likeneſs. It is for the ſake of theſe the plant is cultivated principally, though the ſeeds are alſo an article in trade. The root is white and long, and it periſhes as ſoon as the ſeeds are ripened. Its firſt ſhoot when ſown, is in certain large broad leaves, but theſe periſh when the ſtalk riſes.

The flower of the Carthamus, examined more accurately, is found to be contained in a large common cup; this ſerves for the ſeveral flowers of which the whole tuft is compoſed, and forms what we call the head of the Carthamus. It is of an oval form, and is compoſed of a great number of ſcales placed like tiles one over another,

ther, and they have each the addition of a kind of little leaf of an oval form. The whole tuft is compofed of feveral tubelar flowers, each is formed of a fingle leaf, and has the hollow narroweft at the bafe, and wider all the way to the mouth, where it is dividad into five little, and nearly equal fegments.

In this flower rife five fhort filaments, and at the tops of them ftand fo many buttons, which are of a cylindrick form, and oblong.

In the bafe of the flower is depofited the rudiment of the fruit; this is very fmall and fhort; from its top there rifes a kind of filament longer than the others. This is the part to which the three blades grow in the flower of the right faffron; but in this it is terminated only by a plain little head, which ferves to receive the duft from the heads of the fhort filaments to impregnate the feed.

When the whole tender part of the flower is faded, the fcaly head remains, and contains the feeds. One follows every flower.

Several other fpecies have been added to this, and called by the fame name, one with blue flowers, and others with divided leaves; but the true and proper plant to be raifed for ufe is that here defcribed.

It is a native of Egypt, and feveral parts of the eaft; and is cultivated in many of the warmer parts of Europe; it thrives alfo very well in England.

The principal place where we have feen it in England, is in fome parts of Norfolk; but, if worth while, it might be raifed in any other part of the kingdom.

Thofe who fhall think it worth while to raife it, muft obferve the following directions: In the firft place, let the farmer take care to have the feeds from abroad; and as often as he fows it et him get frefh ones, for they do not ripen well in England. Thefe may be had at a very fmall expence, and with little trouble. The druggifts fell them, but theirs are not to be ufed, for they are commonly old. But fuch a quantity of it is raifed every year in Germany, that good feed may always be had.

When the feed is procured, the fecond care is the ground. The beft foil is a dry loam, and it does not require a rich piece of land of this kind, fo that the charge of this article is not great, nor indeed in any other.

The feeds are to be fown by hand in a fparing manner on the land in fpring, and ro be harrowed in. When they have fhot, and the plants have fome ftrength, they are to be thinned. Hoers fhould be fent into the field for this purpofe, and they fhould have orders not only to cut up what weeds have rifen, but to thin the plants themfelves, leaving them about a foot diftant, and faving fuch as appear the ftrongeft and moft thriving. From this time no farther care need be taken of them; they will grow quick, and being ftrong plants, and thus near to one another, no weeds will be able to get nourifhment among them. Early in autumn they will begin to flower; and then the field will make a beautiful appearance; there is nothing can exceed the brightnefs and golden hue of the flowers, nor have we any thing of our own growth that comes near them. The plants branch out towards the top, and the upper part of every branch is loaded with flowers, fo that the whole field is covered, and as it were gilded with them.

The gathering of thefe flowers fo far refembles that of faffron, that they are to be taken as they open; for if left for feveral days together, they will lofe their colour, and that is in a manner their whole value.

For this reafon as foon as there is any number of them open, the pickers, who are in this article the gatherers alfo, are to be fent into the field. The flowers are not gathered there and picked afterwards, but the whole bufinefs is done at once. The whole tender part of the flower is to be taken, leaving the fcaly bud. When thofe which are open are thus carefully picked off, they are to be fpread upon a large floor in an airy place out of the fun to dry; and this is all that is to be done to them.

When they are dried in this manner, they look of as beautiful a colour as while growing, and they are ready for fale without farther care or trouble.

Every day or two the pickers are to be then fent into the field as at firft, to gather the flowers as they fhew themfelves,

felves, and this is to be the method till the whole quantity are blown; one parcel being put to dry after another. The whole parcel being thus prepared by a fimple and natural drying, is ready for the purchafer.

If the feafon has been favourable, and the crop have flowered early, fome feeds may ripen; but as this is fuch a great uncertainty, there is no dependence upon it; and the better method is to grub up the plants as foon as the flowers are gathered, that the land may be prepared for fome other crop.

The dyers are the people who purchafe the flowers; fome have idly fuppofed they were of the fame nature with faffron, becaufe they refembled that drug in fome degree in appearance; but it is fo far otherwife, that as faffron is a cordial and fweat, thefe flowers are a purge, and the feeds a vomit.

We have mentioned the only right and honeft ufe of the flowers of this plant; but there have been fome, when it was more cultivared than it is at prefent in England, who had a way of mixing it with faffron when they worked it in the drying.

How improper this was we may know from the difference of the virtues of one and the other; but there was another reafon why the farmer never fhould have done this, which is, that it reduces the price.

The thready part of the Carthamus is narrow, harfh, dry, and paler coloured than the blades of faffron; therefore no art can fo blend them together, as to make them capable of impofing upon any but the ignorant; it was the inferior fort of faffron made up from the laft gatherings that they mixed up in this manner, and it reduced the price of this ftill lower.

One reafon why the foreign faffron is held in fo much contempt in England is, that there is too often Carthamus among it.

SAFFRON. See CROCUS.

Meadow SAFFRON. See MEADOW SAFFRON.

SAGAPENUM. A concrete juice brought from Alexandria, either in diftinct tears, or run together in large maffes. It is outwardly of a yellowifh colour, internally fomewhat paler, and clear like horn, grows foft upon being handled, and fticks to the fingers; its tafte is hot and biting; the fmell difagreeable, by fome refembled to that of a leek, by others to a mixture of affafcetida and galbanum.

Sagapenum is an ufeful aperient and deobftruent; and frequently prefcribed either alone, or in conjunction with ammoniacum, or galbanum, for opening obftructions of the vifcera, and in hyfterical diforders arifing from a deficiency of the menftrual purgations. It likewife deterges the pulmonary veffels, and proves of confiderable fervice in fome kinds of afthmas, where the lungs are oppreffed by vifcid phlegm. It is moft commodioufly given in the form of pills; from two or three grains to half a dram, may be given every night or oftner, and continued for fome time. When fagapenum is fcarce, the druggifts ufually fupply its place with the larger and darker coloured maffes of bdellium, broken into pieces; which are not eafily diftinguifhed from it.

SAGE. [*Salvia*.] Officinal fage, the varieties of which are, The common broad-leaved green fage; the common culinary red fage; the broad-leaved hoary balfamic fage, having the broadeft leaves of all the forts, ftanding on long foot-ftalks; wormwood fage; narrow-leaved hoary fage, or fage of virtue; lavender-leaved fage; variegated green fage; and variegated red fage.

Sage is moft ufually propagated by flips, which fhould be planted about the middle of April in a fhady border, and watered if the weather be dry.

There are feveral other fpecies of fage cultivated in gardens for variety, fome of which want the affiftance of the ftove and green-houfe occafionally.

The writers on the materia medica are full of the virtues of fage, and derive its name from its fuppofed falutary qualities, (*Salvia falvatrix, naturæ conciliatrix—Cur moriatur homo, cui falvia crefcit in horto, &c.*) Its real effects are, to moderately warm and ftrengthen the veffels; and hence, in cold phlegmatic habits, it excites appetite, and proves ferviceable in debilities of the nervous fyftem. The beft preparation for thefe purpofes is an infufion of the dry leaves, drank as tea; or a tincture, or extract, made with rectified

rectified spirit, taken in proper doses; these contain the whole virtues of the sage; the distilled water and essential oil, only its warmth and aromatic quality, without any thing of its roughness or bitterishness. Aqueous infusions of the leaves, with the addition of a little lemon juice, prove an useful diluting drink in febrile disorders, of an elegant colour, and sufficiently acceptable to the palate.

SAGE *of Jerusalem*. Lungwort.

SAGE-TREE. [*Phlomis.*] A shrubby evergreen plant, of which there are many species; but four, chiefly cultivated in the English gardens. They are all propagated by layers and cuttings.

Wood SAGE. This grows wild in woods and hedges. In smell, taste, and medical virtues, it is more like scordium than sage.

SAGO. The medullary part of the tree is beaten with water, and made into cakes, which are used by the Indians as bread: These reduced into granules, and dried, are the sago brought to us. It is moderately nutritious, though not perhaps superior to our own grain.

SAINTFOIN, or SAINFOIN, the name given by the French, and continued by us, to a species of plant, frequently used for the food of cattle, either fresh or dried; it is called holyhay, or wholesome hay, from its excellent nutritive quality. The stalks of the plant are commonly about two feet long, but they grow sometimes to five or six feet, and it has tufts of red flowers of three, four, or five inches in length.

This plant will make a forty times greater increase in poor ground than the common turf; and this is owing to having a long perpendicular root, of that kind called tap root, which sinks to a great depth to attract its nourishment. The length of this root is scarce to be credited by any but those who have seen it; it is frequently drawn out of the ground to the length of twelve or fourteen feet, but it is said to be often thirty feet or more in length.

The farmers have a general opinion that this plant never succeeds well in any land where there is not an under stratum of stone, or chalk, or some other hard matter, to stop its running; but that otherwise it spends in root, and comes to nothing above ground. This is an error too gross to need much refutation. It is certain, that the roots being to plants what the stomach and guts are to animals, the more and larger roots any plant has, the more nourishment it receives, and the better it thrives.

Saintfoin always succeeds where its roots run deep, and the best crops of all are produced upon lands where there is no hard under soil to obstruct their passage. An under soil of clay may kill the plants by retaining the water, and chilling and rotting their roots.

The long root of saintfoin has, near the surface, many horizontal roots issuing from it, which extend themselves every way; there are of the same kind all the way down as the roots go, but they grow shorter and shorter all the way. Any dry land may be made to produce this valuable and useful plant, though it be ever so poor, but the richest and best land will produce the best crops of it. The best way of sowing it is by drilling, but the earth must be very well prepared, and the seed well ordered, or else very little of it will grow. The heads of these seeds are so large, and their necks so weak, that, if they be much more than half an inch deep, they are not able to rise through the incumbent mould; and, if they are not covered, they will be malted, as the farmers express it; that is, it will send out its root while it lies aboveground, and be killed by the air; and whether the farmer plants bad seed that will not grow, or good seed that is buried or malted, the event will be the same. The ground will be understocked with plants. A bushel of seed to an acre of land is full twenty seeds to each square foot of land; but as there is some difference in the largeness of the seeds, there is no absolute certainty as to this calculation. The worst seasons for planting it are the beginning of winter, and the drought of summer; the best is the beginning of the spring; and it is always strongest when planted alone, and is not sown together with corn, as is the practice of some farmers. If barley, oats,

St. Anthony's Fire. See Horse. Sow-worm.

oats, or any other corn, ſown with the ſaintfoin, happen to be lodged afterwards, it kills the young ſaintfoin. If it be planted with any other corn, it is beſt done by drilling in the horſe-hoeing way; in this caſe it is not much liable to be killed by the lodging of the corn, as the drilled corn ſeldom falls at all, and when it does, never falls ſo low as the ſown corn.

The quantity of ſeed to be drilled upon an acre of land will depend wholly upon the goodneſs of it; for there is ſome ſeed of which not one in ten will ſtrike, whereas in good ſeed not one in ten will fail. The method of knowing the goodneſs is, by ſowing a certain number of the ſeeds, and ſeeing how many plants are produced by them. The external ſigns of the ſeeds being good are, that the huſk is of a bright colour, and the kernel plump, of a light grey or blue colour, and ſometimes of a ſhining black. The ſeed may be good, though the huſk be black, as that is owing ſometimes to the letting it receive the wet in the field, not to its being half-rotted in the heap.

If the kernel be cut a-croſs, and appear greeniſh and freſh, it is a certain ſign that it is good. If it be of a yellowiſh colour, and friable, and look thin and pitted, they are bad ſigns. The quantity of ſeeds allowed to the acre in the drill way is much leſs than that by ſowing, and is to be computed according to the number of plants that are to be allowed in that ſpace, allowing for the common caſualties. It is not neceſſary to be exact in this calculation, or to ſay whether two, three, or four hundred plants are to be allowed to a ſquare perch; neither is it poſſible to know before-hand the preciſe number of plants that may live out of thoſe that come up; for ſometimes the grub takes them when they have only the two firſt leaves, and the crop is greatly diminiſhed by this means. Four gallons of good ſeed to an acre of land will cover it with plants, when judiciouſly managed.

Single plants of ſaintfoin make the greateſt crops; but the farmers in general plant them ſo cloſe, that they ſtarve one another. The ſingle plants always run the deepeſt, and thoſe which do ſo will always draw moſt nouriſhment. The plants which ſtand crowded ſtarve one another, and often die after a few years; but the ſingle ones grow to a vaſt bigneſs, and are every year better and better.

The beſt way to calculate how many plants are to be allowed to a perch, is to compute how much hay each ſingle large plant will produce; for if kept ſingle and well cultivated, they will all be large ones. Without culture, theſe plants never arrive at a fourth part of the ſize that they do with it. The hay of a large ſingle cultivated plant will weigh more than half a pound; a hundred and twelve plants upon a ſquare perch, weighing but a quarter of a pound a piece, one with another, amount to two tons to an acre. If ſaintfoin be planted on ſome ſorts of land early in the ſpring and hoed, it will ſometimes produce a crop the following ſummer; in a garden the ſeeds ſown in February will yield plants of two feet high that will flower in the month of June following; and though March be froſty, the young plants ſeldom ſuffer by it. This ſhews that this plant is naturally a quick grower; but the farmers uſually plant it on poor or cold land, and give it too little culture, which makes it backward, and ſlow of growth with them. The poor land, uſually allotted to this plant, alſo makes it generally yield but one crop a year, but on a rich land it will yield two very good crops annually, with a moderate ſhare of culture and management.

The farmer who expects to make a profit of this plant muſt not expect a good crop the firſt year. Nothing is ſo injurious to ſaintfoin as its ſtanding too thick: if it be ſo thick as to cover the ground the firſt ſummer, the plants will ſtarve one another for ever after; but if the owner will be content to place them ſo thinly as to have but a ſmall crop the firſt year, they will increaſe prodigiouſly, and every ſucceeding crop will be better and better. When ſaintfoin is well hoed, it will grow as much in a fortnight as it would otherwiſe do in ſix weeks; and this quick growing is of advantage to it every way, not only making the plants large, but of better nouriſhment to the cattle, whether they are eaten green or made into hay.

The

The proper distance to drill this plant for the horse-hoeing husbandry is at double rows with eight-inch partitions between them, and thirty-inch intervals between every two and two. These intervals need only be hoed alternately, leaving every other interval for making the hay on. This method of hoeing is of vast advantage, and poor land by means of it will always produce two crops a year. The land is always to be perfectly cleared of grass before the sowing the saintsoin, and the lumps of earth carefully broken. But no harrowing is to be allowed after it is drilled, for that would bury it; and it is not proper to roll it at all, unless for the sake of barley, when they are sown together; and when that is done, it should be with a light roller, and in dry weather. This should be done lengthwise of the rows, and as soon as it is drilled; if it is not done at this time it is best to stay three weeks before it is done, that the necks of the young saintsoin may not be broken.

No cattle are to be suffered to come in the first winter upon the saintsoin, after the corn is out among which it was sown. Their feet would injure it by treading the ground hard, as much as their mouths by cropping it, and it would never come to good. Sheep should not be suffered to come at it, even the following summer and winter. One acre of drilled saintsoin, considering the difference of the quantity and goodness of the crop, is worth two acres of sown saintsoin on the same land, though the expence of drilling be twenty times less than that of sowing. The first winter is the time to lay on manure after the corn is reaped off. Pot-ashes, or the like, are very proper, and a small quantity of them will do, as there are at this time no other plants to partake of the benefit, but the young crop has it all, and the young plants being thus made strong at first, will continue so, and be long the better for it.

It is observed, however, that in the drilling and horse-hoeing way, there is no necessity for any manure at all. Some farmers sow eight or ten bushels of the seed of saintsoin to an acre along with their corn, with intent that it should kill all the other weeds; but the consequence is, that the plants stand close, and starve one another, and are no bigger than where the plant grows wild on the hills in Calabria, where it is so small and seemingly despicable a plant, that it seems a wonder that any body should be tempted to think of cultivating it; yet, when rightly managed, it seems capable of being as useful a plant as any in the world. Where these plants stand so think they draw all the nourishment from the ground in a few years, and so die, though manured ever so carefully. Six or seven years seem their greatest duration; whereas, when the seed is drilled in, and the plants are horse-hoed, they will be as strong and vigorous as ever at 30 years standing.

Some people who have turned their thoughts to husbandry, have been of opinion, that the cytisus would succeed better with us than saintsoin; it is probable enough that it would grow well; but the labour of sheering it would, with us, where the pay of servants is so dear, run away with the profits of the crop.

Lucerne is another thing which many have thought of introducing among us in the place of saintsoin, but it requires so much care to suit it with a proper soil, that, whatever are the profits of it, it never can be so general as saintsoin.

Saintsoin, says Mr. Duhamel, deserves the farmer's utmost attention, as one of the most profitable plants he can cultivate. It will do on almost any land; and though it succeeds best in good soils, yet it will grow even on dry barren spots where scarce any other grass can live, provided its roots be not chilled by a cold clay, or other substance which retains water; and it has this farther advantage, that it may be mowed at different degrees of ripeness, with nearly the same profit.

1. It may be mowed before it is in bloom, for it is then admirable food for horned cattle; and when cut thus early, it yields a second crop, which makes ample amends for what was lost by not letting the first come to its full growth. This early cutting is likewise attended with another benefit, which is, that it purges cattle in the

beginning of the summer, and thereby frees them from disorders occasioned by the winter's cold, or dry food.

2. If the weather be rainy, the saintfoin may be left standing till it is in bloom; when it still is excellent fodder for cows. But care must be taken in making it into hay, that the flowers do not drop off, as they are very apt to do: for cattle are so fond of these flowers that they often induce them to eat the rest of the plant.

3. If the rain continues, the saintfoin may be left standing till some of its seeds are formed, and the crop will then be the more plentiful, not only because it will have attained its full growth, but likewise because its leaves being more substantial, diminish less in drying. It is not indeed, then, quite so sweet as before; but horses eat it readily, because they love to feel between their teeth the seeds, which now begin to be formed.

Mr. Tull says, this fodder is so excellent, that horses need no oats when they are fed with it. He affirms, that he kept a team of horses with it a whole year in good plight, without giving them any oats, though they were worked hard all the time. He adds, that he fattened sheep with it in less time than others which were fed with corn. But the hay of this plant can never be so good as when it is cultivated with the horse-hoe; for in the common husbandry, it blossoms almost as soon as it is out of the ground.

4. If the season continues rainy, it may be more adviseable to let the saintfoin remain standing, than to run the hazard of having it rot upon the ground; for then the seed will ripen, and nearly make up for the loss of the fodder; not only because it will fetch a good price, but also because two bushels of it will go as far in feeding of horses, as three bushels of oats; and cattle in general, as well as poultry, are extremely fond of it.

The first of these sorts of saintfoin hay, cut before the bloom, is Mr. Tull's virgin hay, which, he says, is the best beyond comparison, and has not its equal in the world except lucerne. He gives the next place to the second sort, cut whilst in bloom, and says that an acre of land, well cultivated, may yield three tons of this blossomed hay; and he esteems the third sort, which he calls the full-grown, many degrees inferior to either of the former; though it yields a greater crop, because it has grown to its full bulk, and shrinks but little in drying.

Even the saintfoin that has yielded its seed may be cut down and dried; and when other fodder is scarce, this will be better food for horses and large cattle, than the coarse hay of flowed meadows, or any kind of straw.

The manner of making saintfoin hay is thus directed by Mr. Duhamel.

In a day or two after the saintfoin has been mowed, it will be dry on the upper side if the weather be good. The swarths, or mowed rows, should then be turned, not singly, but two and two together; for by thus turning them in pairs, double the space of ground is left betwixt pair and pair, and this needs but once raking, whereas, if the swarths were turned singly, that is, all the same way, the ground would require as much raking again.

As soon as both sides of the swarths are a little dry, they should be made up into small cocks the same day they are turned, if possible; for when the saintfoin is in cock, a less part of it will be exposed to the injuries of the night, than when it lies scattered upon the field. The sun and dew would exhaust almost all its juices in this last case, in less than a week's time.

These little cocks of saintfoin may be safely made into larger ones, without waiting for their being so thoroughly dry as those of common hay ought to be before they are laid together; because common hay, by sinking down closer, excludes the air necessary for keeping it sweet; so that if the weather prevents its being frequently stirred and opened, it will heat, turn yellow, and be spoiled; whereas saintfoin, by admitting the air more freely, because its stalks are less flexible, will remain much longer without any danger of fermenting.

Saintfoin hay is never better than when it has been dried by the wind only, without the assistance of the sun. A little rain, or a mist, which will turn common hay or clover, and even lucerne black, will do no hurt to saintfoin, which is not really spoiled till it rots upon the ground. If the weather threatens rain, and the ſaintſoin is not yet dry, it may be laid in cocks, without fear of its heating, provided a large baſket, or buſhy tagget, be ſet up in the middle of each cock, where it will ſerve for a vent-hole, through which the ſuperfluous moiſture of the hay will tranſpire.

As ſoon as all danger of heating is over, theſe cocks ſhould be made into ricks, and thatched. That which is laid up quite dry, will come out of the rick of a green colour; that which has heated much in the rick, will look brown.

It requires ſome experience to know at what degree of ripeneſs it is beſt to cut the ſeeded ſaintſoin; becauſe all its ſeeds do not ripen at the ſame time. Some ears bloſſom before others; every ear begins bloſſoming at its lower part, and continues to blow gradually upward, for many days; ſo that before the flower is gone off at the top, the ſeeds are almoſt filled at the bottom. By this means, if the cutting be deferred till the top ſeeds are quite ripe, the lower, which are the beſt, would ſhed and be loſt. The beſt time, therefore, to cut it, is when the greateſt part of the ſeed is well filled, the firſt blown ripe, and the laſt blown beginning to be full. The unripe ſeeds will ripen after cutting, and be in all reſpects as good as thoſe that were ripe before. Some for want of obſerving this, have ſuffered their ſaintſoin ſeed to ſtand till all of it has ſhed, and been loſt in cutting.

Saintſoin ſhould never be cut in the heat of the day, while the ſun ſhines out; for then much, even of the unripe ſeed, will ſhed in mowing. The right time for this work is the morning or the evening, when the dew has rendered the plants ſupple.

If the weather is fine and clear, the ſaintſoin will ſoon dry ſufficiently in the ſwarths, without turning them; but if any rain has fallen, and there is a neceſſity for turning them, it ſhould be done very gently while they are moiſt, and not two ſwarthed together, as in the other hay made of ſaintſoin before it has ſeeded. If the ſwarths are turned with the handle of the rake, it is beſt to raiſe up the ear-ſides firſt, and let the ſtub-ſide reſt on the ground in turning; but if it is done with the teeth of the rake, let the ſtub-ſide be lifted up, and the ears reſted on the earth.

If ſaintſoin be cocked at all, the ſooner it is done the better, becauſe if the ſwarths are dry, much of the ſeed will be loſt in ſeparating them, the ears being entangled together. When moiſt, the ſeed ſticks faſt in the ear; but when dry, it drops out with the leaſt touch or ſhaking.

There are two ways of thraſhing it, the one in the field, the other in the barn. The firſt cannot be done but in very fine weather, and while the ſun ſhines in the middle of the day. The beſt manner of performing this is to have a large ſheet pegged down to the ground for two men to thraſh on with their flails, while two others bring them freſh ſupplies in a ſmaller ſheet, and two more clear away the hay that has been thraſhed. The ſeed is emptied out of the larger ſheet, and riddled through a large ſieve, to ſeparate it from the chaff and broken ſtalks; after which it is put into ſacks and carried into the barn to be winnowed. Care ſhould be taken not to let the hay get wet, becauſe it would then be ſpoiled.

A very important, and at the ſame time very difficult article is, the keeping of the ſeed that has been thraſhed in the field, without ever having been wetted. If it be winnowed immediately, and only a little of it laid amidſt a great heap, or put into a ſack, it will ferment to ſuch a degree in a few days, that the greateſt part of it will loſe its vegetative quality. During that fermentation, it will be very hot, and ſmell ſour. Spreading it upon a barn floor, though but ſeven or eight inches thick, will anſwer no end, unleſs it be frequently and regularly turned both day and night, until the heating is over; but even this will not make its colour keep ſo bright as that which is well houſed, well dried, and thraſhed in the winter. This laſt, laid up unthraſhed, will keep without any danger of ſpoiling, becauſe it does not lie cloſe enough to heat. The beſt way to preſerve the ſeed thraſhed in the field is, to lay a layer of ſtraw upon a barn floor, and upon that a thin layer of ſeed, then

another

another layer of ſtraw, and another layer of ſeed, and ſo on alternately. By this means the ſeed mixing with the ſtraw, will be kept cool, and come out in the ſpring with as green a colour as when it is put in.

SALEP, A celebrated reſtorative among the Turks, is probably the prepared root of certain plants of the orchis kind. This drug, as ſometimes brought to us, is in oval pieces, of a yellowiſh white colour, ſomewhat clear and pellucid, very hard, and almoſt horny, of little or no ſmell, and taſting like gum tragacanth. Satyrion root, boiled in water, freed from the ſkin, and afterwards ſuſpended in the air to dry, gains exactly the ſame appearance; the roots thus prepared, diſſolve in boiling water into a mucilage. Geoffrey, who firſt communicated this preparation of orchis, recommends it in conſumptions, in bilious dyſenteries, and diſorders of the breaſt proceeding from an acrimony of the juices.

SALLENDERS. A diſeaſe in horſes, conſiſting in cracks in the bending of the hough, and occaſion a lameneſs behind. This diſeaſe is cured in the ſame manner as the mallenders. *See* MALLENDERS.

SALT-MARSHES. Paſture-lands lying near the ſea, and ſometimes overflowed by the ſea-water.

"It has been obſerved," ſays an ingenious writer in the Muſeum Ruſticum, "that horſes and black cattle thrive better, and get fat ſooner, in ſalt-marſhes, than in freſh-water meadows or upland paſtures; yet I do not remember ever to have heard any good reaſon aſſigned for it.

"Some will tell you that the air of the ſea whets their appetites; that the paſture is rich and nouriſhing; and that the herbs produced by the lands near the ſea are more conducive to the health of herbaceous animals, than ſuch as grow on upland paſtures, whether natural or artificial.

"But may we not rather attribute the thriving of cattle on theſe marſhes, to the ſaline particles with which the earth as well as its produce is, when near the ſea, ſtrongly impregnated? Perhaps even the dews have their portion of ſalt; but of this I have made no experiment, therefore mention it only as a probable conjecture; for as they fall ſoon after they are exhaled from the ſea, without paſſing through the ſecretions neceſſary to ſeparate their ſaline parts, why ſhould not this be the caſe?

"But to return to my firſt ſubject: I am fully of opinion, that the ſaline particles only, with which the graſs is impregnated in the above-mentioned marſhes, cauſe cattle to thrive in them in the manner they are known to do. Theſe ſalts purge away the foul humours which the beaſts have contracted, either by idleneſs, or by being over-heated in labour; by which means they are better diſpoſed to be nouriſhed by the aliment they receive.

"It may perhaps be objected, that if the graſs of theſe marſhes is apt to purge cattle, this very purging, by being long continued, will be a means of preventing their growing fat. To this I anſwer, that the cattle take with their food every day nearly the ſame quantity of theſe purgative particles; but that the quantity of ſalt, which at their being firſt put into the marſh will have that effect, will ceaſe producing it when they are by cuſtom habituated to take a daily portion of it; this muſt be allowed, as we all know, that a few grains of rhubarb will operate as a cathartic to a perſon that is not accuſtomed to take it; yet it is as well known, that a man may take many grains daily, if he uſes himſelf to it, without its being ſenſibly purgative to him.

"It is not convenient to every one to ſend their cattle to a ſalt-marſh: would it not, therefore, be happy, if we could ſubſtitute a method that would nearly anſwer the ſame purpoſe? I do not think this impoſſible; perhaps if common ſalt-water were to be laid in the fields for horſes to lick as often as they pleaſed, they would thrive much better; were I to ſay I know it would have that effect, it would be no preſumption.

"Cattle are all naturally fond of ſalt, and if left at their liberty, will take no more of it than what will do them good. With this help, our freſh-water meadows, and natural and artificial paſtures, would yield us a greater profit, and of courſe be worth more to the land-holder and farmer.

"Some

"Some will not allow a thing to have merit, unleſs it is ſupported by what they call a proper authority; and they do not allow the experiments of a particular perſon to be ſufficient. To ſatisfy ſuch, I can aſſure you, that in the inland parts of Switzerland, when their horſes and cattle have endured the hardſhips of a long and ſevere winter, they turn them in the ſpring looſe into the mountains, laying ſalt here and there upon the rocks, for them to reſort to when they pleaſe; and of this they are ſo fond, that when the farmers want to catch their horſes, they take ſome ſalt in their hats, as we do oats in a ſieve, to allure them.

"Experience has long convinced them, that the ſalt thus laid in their way anſwers every good purpoſe; their cattle are more healthy in general than ours are in England, and almoſt to this alone do they attribute it.

"In the province of Munſter and Connaught, in Ireland, they very frequently lay ſalt on ſlates, for the benefit of their horſes when at graſs: this they find does the cattle great ſervice. and in this we ſhould imitate them, and not be too proud to learn of them, becauſe in Ireland Agriculture is not in ſo flouriſhing a ſtate as in England.

"Some few farmers have (to do them juſtice) practiſed this method in our own country; but, contenting themſelves with the profit reſulting from it, they have not propagated the knowledge or the many advantages they are ſenſible may be derived from this practice of giving ſalt to cattle.

"The farriers and horſe-jockeys know well the uſe of ſalt; they mix it often in their medicines, and find by experience, that nothing proves ſo powerful a ſtomachic to horſes, as a little ſalt thrown into their oats.

"I muſt farther obſerve, that the uſe of ſalt is very proper when cattle are turned into clover, lucerne, or coleſeed, to feed; it is well known, that on theſe occaſions they are very apt, unleſs great care is taken, to be ſurfeited; the ſalt would prevent this accident, and thereby greatly accelerate the fattening of the cattle, and make it much ſafer to the farmer.

"Salt has alſo been found to be of great ſervice in fattening hogs, by cauſing them to drink more plentifully than otherwiſe they would."

SALTWORT. Glaſſwort.

SALLOW. [*Salix.*] The ſorts are, 1. The common willow, with acute-pointed rough leaves. 2. The white willow. 3. Yellow, or golden willow. 4. The purple, or red willow. 5. The oſier willow. 6. Broad-leaved ſweet-ſcented willow, with five ſtamina. 7. Willow, with ſmooth ſaved leaves, and three ſtamina. 8. Almond leaved willow. 9. Crack willow. 10. Babylonian, or weeping willow; with ſeveral others, as Norfolk willow; the upland red willow; Dutch oſier; white oſier, &c. The flowers of all are katkins; from the ſides of the branches they are all eaſily propagated by cuttings or layers; the former when deſigned for pollards, and the latter when intended for trees.

SAMPHIRE. [*Crithmum.*] This plant grows wild on rocks, and in maritime places; the leaves are ſomewhat like thoſe of fennel, but the ſegments much thicker and ſhorter; their ſmell reſembles that of ſmallage; the taſte is warm, bitteriſh, not agreeable. They are ſaid to be ſtomachic, aperient, and diuretic.

SANICLE, [*Sanicula.*] This plant grows wild in woods and hedges, and flowers in May. The leaves have an herbaceous, roughiſh taſte; they have long been celebrated for *ſanative* virtues, both internally and externally: nevertheleſs, their effects, in any intention, are not conſiderable enough to gain them a place in the preſent practice.

Bear's Ear SANICLE. [*Cortuſa*] This plant grows naturally on the Alps, and the mountains of Auſtria, and Siberia; it is propagated by parting the roots as for the auricula.

SAND. A genus of foſſils found in minute concretions, forming together a kind of powder, the genuine particles of which are all of a tendency to one determinate ſhape, and appear regular, though more or leſs complete concretions; not to be diſſolved or diſ-united by water, or formed into a coherent maſs by means of it, but retaining their figure in it; tranſparent, vitrifiable by extreme heat, and

not

not diſſoluble in, nor effervefcing with acids.

Theſe are ſubject to be variouſly blended and intermixed either with homogene, or heterogene particles, particularly with flakes of talc; and according to theſe, and their different colours, are to be ſubdivided into ſeveral kinds, as red, white, &c.

Dr. Liſter divides the Engliſh ſands into two claſſes: The firſt, ſharp, or rag ſand, conſiſting of ſmall tranſparent pebbles, naturally found on the mountains, and not calcinable; theſe he farther divides into fine and coarſe, and ſubdivides each, according to the colours, into white, grey, reddiſh, brown, &c.

The ſecond, ſoft or ſmooth, which he ſubdivides into that with flat particles broken from lime-ſtones, that with ſilver-like particles, and that with gold like particles.

As to ſand, its uſe is to make the clayey earth fertile, and fit to feed vegetables, &c. for earth alone, we find, is liable to coaleſce, and gather into an hard coherent maſs, as is apparent in clay; and earth thus embodied, and as it were, glued together, is no-ways diſpoſed to nouriſh vegetables; but if with ſuch earth, ſand, &c. i. e. hard cryſtals, which are not diſſolvable in water, and ſtill retain their figure, be intermixed, they will keep the pores of the earth open, and the earth itſelf looſe and incompact, and by that means give room for the juices to aſcend, and for plants to be nouriſhed thereby.

Thus a vegetable, planted either in ſand alone, or in a fat glebe, or earth alone, receives no growth or increment at all, but is either ſtarved or ſuffocated; but mix the two, and the maſs becomes fertile. In effect, by means of ſand, the earth is rendered in ſome manner organical; pores and interſtices being hereby maintained, ſomething analogous to veſſels, by which the juices may be conveyed, prepared, digeſted, circulated, & at length excerned, and thrown off into the roots of plants.

Grounds that are ſandy and gravelly eaſily admit both of heat and moiſture; but then they are liable to theſe inconveniencies, that they let them paſs too ſoon, and ſo contract no ligature, or elſe retain it too long, eſpecially where there is a clay bottom; and by that means it either parches or chills too much, and produces nothing but moſs, and cankerous infirmities; but if the ſand happens to have a ſurface of good mould, and a bottom of gravel, or looſe ſtone, tho' it do not hold the water, it may produce a forward ſweet graſs; and tho' it may be ſubject to burn, yet it quickly recovers with the leaſt rain.

Sea ſand is accounted a very good compoſt for ſtiff ground, for it effects the two things following, viz. it makes way for the tree or ſeed to root in ſtiff ground, and makes a fume to feed it.

Sand, indeed, is apt to puſh the plants that grow upon it early in the ſpring, and makes them germinate near a month ſooner than thoſe that grow upon clay, becauſe the ſalts in the ſand are at full liberty to be raiſed and put into motion upon the leaſt approach of the warmth of the ſun; but then, as they are haſty, they are ſoon exhaled and loſt.

It is remarkable, that ſand, though it appear a very hard, denſe, and indiſſoluble body, yet is contained inviſibly in the brine, or ſalt water of our ſalt ſprings; and even on the ſhooting of the ſalt after evaporation, there ſtill remain the particles of it in the clear pellucid ſalt; and this, though wholly ſoluble in water, yet when a brine made by ſuch a ſolution is boiled, depoſits as much of the ſand as the common brine of the pits, or ſea-water.

Dr. Plot, who was very curious to know the true hiſtory of this ſingular effect, procured experiments to be made in the following manner: Eight folds of fine holland, and as many of finer cambrick, were put together, and a quantity of the brine of the Staffordſhire ſalt pits being ſtrained thro' this, there was nothing ſeparated from it but a ſmall quantity of black duſt, which ſeemed to have fallen in by accident, and which was not at all like ſand; yet, on evaporating this brine, it was found to contain no leſs than one fourth part as much ſand as ſalt; the quantity of brine, yielding a buſhel of ſalt, yielding alſo a peck of ſand.

Some have ſuppoſed from theſe, and the like obſervations, that the ſand was generated during the time of the boiling

boiling the liquor, but the more careful examiners think otherwise; it appearing to them that the particles of this sand may be seen in the brine by the help of a microscope, before the boiling, in form of rectangular oblong plates, some nearly square; these were so small as readily to pass the strainer with the water, and appearing as numerous in it after, as before the straining, shew that they are no more to be kept by such means than the salt.

The pores of the finest strainers, examined by the microscope, appear twenty times bigger than these plates, or particles of the sand, and therefore it is not to be wondered at, that they let them through. There requires, therefore, no more to the formation of the sand, than the coalescing of several of these particles into one larger granule, and so on; and this is very likely to be done by means of the evaporation of a part of the fluid which kept them separate, and of the motion given to them in boiling, which naturally and necessarily brought them into the spheres of their own mutual attractions, at a time when their attraction with the fluid they swam in was also much diminished with its quantity. This attraction seems even evidently to increase between the particles as the water becomes evaporated, and when finally the salt is drawn from it, and it is examined as it drops from the baskets in which the salt is put to drain, it is seen to contain more numerous particles of this sandy matter than before; and these are found to coalesce into yet larger concretions by degrees, as the remainder of the fluid evaporates from them on the glass.

The particles of this stony matter, when once thus united, are no more to be separated by water, nor is the matter any longer soluble in that fluid. The common spar found in form of stalactites and incrustations on the roofs, walls, and floors of old caverns, shews that it was once dissolved in water, and by that means brought to those places, and made into those forms; and it should seem that this sand, as it is called, was only this sort of spar, which is contained more or less in all water; and which, on the evaporating of that water, and separating the salt, which might help in making the water a menstruum proper for the retaining it, shoots out into its own natural concretions; for the figure of these thin plates is the true and natural thin parallellopiped or rhomboidal figure of the smaller concretions of that matter, and even of those pieces into which it falls on breaking.

Common sand is a very good addition by way of manure to all sorts of clay lands; it warms them, and makes them more open and loose. The best sand for the farmer's use is that which is washed by rains from roads or hills, or that which is taken from the beds of rivers; the common sand that is dug in pits never answers nearly so well. Sand mixed with dung is much better than laid on alone; and a very fine manure is made by covering the bottom of sheep-folds with several loads of sand every week, which are to be taken away and laid on cold stiff lands impregnated as they are with the dung and the urine of the sheep.

Besides clay land, there is another sort of ground very improveable by sand; this is that sort of black foggy land on which bushes and sedge grow naturally, and which they cut into turf in some places. Six hundred loads of sand being laid upon an acre of this land, according to the Cheshire measure, which is near double the statute acre, meliorate it so much, that without ploughing, it will yield good crops of oats or tares, though before it would have produced scarce any thing. If after this crop is taken off, the land be well dunged and laid down for grass, it will yield a large crop of sweet hay.

Once sanding this land will improve it for a vast number of years, and it will yield two crops of hay in the year, if there be weather to make it in. Some land in Cheshire has been by this means rendered of twelve times its former value to the owner. The bogs of Ireland, when drained, have been rendered very fruitful land, by mixing sand in this manner among the earth, of which they consist. Add to this, that in all the boggy lands, the burning them, or firing their own turf upon them, is also a great advantage.

The common peat, or turf ashes, mixed with the sand for these purposes, add greatly to its virtue.

Sea sand, which is thrown up in creeks and other places, is by much the richest of all sand for manuring the earth; partly its saltness, and partly the fat and unctuous filth that is mixed among it, give it this great virtue. In the western parts of England, that lie upon the sea-coasts, they make very great advantages of it. The fragments of sea-shells also, which are always in great abundance in this sand, add to its virtues; and it is always the more esteemed by the farmers the more of these fragments there are among it.

The sea sand used as manure in different parts of the kingdom is of three kinds: that about Plymouth, and on other parts of the southern coasts, is of a blue grey colour, like ashes, which is probably owing to the shells of muscles, and other fish of that or the like colour, being broken and mixed among it in great quantity. Westward, near the land's end, the sea sand is very white, and about the isles of Scilly it is very glistering, with small particles of talc; on the coast of the north sea the sand is yellowish, brown, or reddish, and contains so great a quantity of fragments of cockle-shells, that it seems to be chiefly composed of them. That sea sand is accounted the best which is of a reddish colour; the next in value to this is the bluish, and the white is the worst of all.

Sea sand is best when taken up from under the water, or from sand banks which are covered by every tide.

The small grained sand is most sudden in its operation, and is therefore best for the tenant who is only to take three or four crops; but the coarse or large-grained sand is much better for the landlord, as the good it does lasts many years.

Where the sand is dredged out of the sea, it is usually twice as dear as where it is taken from the sand banks.

When the land has been well manured with the large sand, they take four crops of corn from it, and then lay it down for pasture for six or seven years before they plough it again. The grass is so good, that they commonly mow it for hay the first year; it always abounds very much with the white-flowered clover. If the grass grows but short, it is the farmer's interest to feed his cattle upon it, and it will turn to as good account this way, being very sweet and rich, and making the cattle fat, and the cows yield a very large quantity of milk.

SAP. A juice furnished by the earth, and changed into the plant, consisting of fossil, saline, aërial, and other particles from putrified animals, vegetables, &c.

SARCOCOLLA. A concrete juice, brought from Persia and Arabia, in small, whitish, yellow grains, with a few of a reddish, and sometimes of a deep red colour, mixed with them; the whitest tears are preferred, as being the freshest: Its taste is bitter, accompanied with a dull kind of sweetness. This drug dissolves in watery liquors, and appears to be chiefly of the gummy kind, with a small admixture of resinous matter. It is principally celebrated for conglutinating wounds and ulcers, a quality which neither this, or any other drug, has a just title to. It is an ingredient in the *pulvis e cerussa compositus.*

SASSAFRAS. See BAY.

SATTINFLOWER. See HONESTY

SATYRION. See DOGSTONES.

SAUCE-ALONE. See HEDGE MUSTARD.

SAVIN. See JUNIPER. This is a warm irritating aperient medicine, capable of promoting sweat, urine, and all the glandular secretions. The distilled oil is one of the most powerful emmenagogues, and is found of good service in obstructions of the uterus, or other viscera, proceeding from a laxity and weakness of the vessels, or a cold sluggish indisposition of the juices.

SAVORY. [*Saturcia.*] A plant much cultivated in the kitchen-garden, and is of two sorts, viz. summer and winter savory, the uses of both which are nearly the same.

The former is an annual plant, raised only from its seed, which should be sown in the beginning of April, in a bed of loose and light earth. If the plants are not intended to be removed, their seeds should be scattered thinly; but if they are to be transplanted, they may be sown thicker. They must

must be kept clear from weeds, and are in other respects to be treated as marjoram.

Winter savory may be propagated from seeds sown at the same time as those of the summer sort; or by slips off its roots, for these are perennial, and will last several years; but as they do not put forth equally tender or well furnished shoots after they are grown old, the best way is to raise a supply of young plants every other year. The slips of the winter savory will soon take root and flourish; and they, as well as the plants of this species raised from seed, will endure the greatest cold of our winters, and have the most aromatic smell and taste, when they are planted in a poor and dry soil. Wet ground is very apt to render them mouldy, and consequently make them rot. Mr. Miller has noticed some of these plants growing upon the top of an old wall, where they were fully exposed to the cold, and they there survived such severe frosts as killed most of those of the same kind that were planted in the ground.

The winter savory flowers in June, and the summer savory in July; but the seed of both ripen in the autumn, and at no great distance of time from each other.

SANDERS. [*Santalum.*] There are three species of this wood, the white, the yellow, and the red. The first is of little value; the second has a pleasant smell, and a bitterish aromatic taste, and though but little regarded might be applied to valuable purposes. The red is principally used as a colouring drug.

SAW-WORT. [*Serratula.*] There are several species of this plant propagated in the gardens, and growing wild, some annual and some perennial; the former are propagated by seeds, and the latter by parting their roots.

SAXIFRAGE. [*Saxifraga.*] The common white saxifrage grows naturally in most parts of England. The roots of this plant are like grains of corn, of a reddish colour without, from which arise kidney-shaped hairy leaves, standing upon pretty long footstalks. The stalks are thick, a foot high, hairy, and furrowed; these branch out from the bottom, and have a few small leaves like those below, which sit close to the stalk; the flowers terminate the stalk, growing in small clusters: they have five small white petals, inclosing ten stamina and the two styles. The roots and leaves of this plant are used in medicine.

There are many species of this plant cultivated in the gardens, and growing naturally in England; among them is reckoned the None-so-pretty, or London-Pride. They are all cultivated by parting the roots, or by off-sets.

Burnt SAXIFRAGE. [*Pimpinella.*] There are three sorts principally noticed by medical writers. 1. The large or white saxifrage. 2. Two others smaller; but they all seem to be possessed of the same qualities, and to differ only in external appearance: and even in this, their difference is so inconsiderable, that Linnæus has joined them into one, under the general name of *pimpinella*. Our college, instead of the first, which has been generally understood as the officinal sort, allow either of the others (which are more common) to be used promiscuously.

The roots of pimpinella have a grateful, warm, very pungent taste, which is entirely extracted by rectified spirit; in distillation, the menstruum arises, leaving all that it had taken up from the root united into a pungent aromatic resin. This root promises, from its sensible qualities, to be a medicine of considerable utility, though little regarded in common practice; the only officinal composition in which it is an ingredient, is the *pulvis ari compositus*. Stahl, Hoffman, and other German physicians, are extremely fond of it, and recommend it as an excellent stomachic, resolvent, detergent, diuretic, diaphoretic, and alexipharmac. They frequently gave it, and not without success, in scorbutic and cutaneous disorders, foulness of the blood and juices, tumours and obstructions of the glands, and diseases proceeding from a deficiency of the fluid secretions in general. Boerhaave directs the use of this medicine in asthmatic and hydropic cases, where the strongest resolvents are indicated; the form he prefers is a watery infusion; but the spirituous tincture possesses the virtues of the root in much greater

 perfection,

perfection. There is another species of pimpinella called *nigra*, from its root being externally of a bright black colour, whilst those of the foregoing sorts are whitish; this is remarkable for its yielding an essential oil of a blue colour. It grows wild in some parts of Germany, Swisserland, &c. and is now and then met with in our gardens.

Golden SAXIFRAGE. [*Chrysosplenium*.] There are two sorts, one with alternate, and the other with opposite leaves. These two plants are found wild in several parts of England, but especially the first, upon marshy spils and bogs, as also in most shady woods, and are seldom propagated in gardens, where, if any person have curiosity to cultivate them, they must be planted in very moist shady places, otherwise they will not thrive. They flower in March and April.

Meadow SAXIFRAGE. See HOG'S FENNEL.

SCAB. A disease incident to sheep, chiefly occasioned by a tedious length of wet weather.

" I imagine," says Mr. Vesey, "your readers will not be displeased if I should, with your assistance, communicate to them a remedy for this disorder, which I have several times tried, and almost always found to answer extremely well.

" Some men, whom I have known to breed and feed a great number of sheep, have been grossly mistaken in their comprehension of the nature of this distemper, which they rashly judged to be merely cutaneous; whereas, when a sheep has the scab, the blood is always more or less affected by it; therefore the outward applications, which are in general alone resorted to for a cure, do for the most part more hurt than good, by driving in the eruption, and making it fix on the internals, thereby occasioning the death of the animal.

" Now the true way to treat this disorder is, first to give the animal something inwardly to drive out the eruption; then comes, with propriety, the outward application, which completes the cure by killing the scab.

" When a farmer has any of his flock afflicted with the scab, let him attend to the directions which follow:

" Take a gallon of soft well or pond water, which divide into two equal parts; in one of these parts dissolve eight ounces of old hard soap; to which, when it is dissolved, add two ounces of spirits of hartshorn, and seven ounces of common salt, with four ounces of roll brimstone, beat to a fine powder and sifted; then take the other part of the water, in which put two ounces of tobacco leaf, and one of white hellebore root; boil this second part till you have a strong infusion, after which strain it clear from the leaves and roots.

" When you have got thus far in the process, take that part of the water, first mentioned, and set it over the fire; let it boil for about half an hour, keeping it continually stirring with a wooden ladle during that time; in the mean time heat again the other part, in which the tobacco and hellebore were infused, and when it is hot, mix the two parts gradually together over the fire, keeping the mixture continually stirring till it is taken off the fire, which should be in about a quarter of an hour; when it is quite cold, let it be put into a stone bottle, in order to its being kept in a cool place for use.

" Then take four quarts of new ale or beer; put into it twelve ounces of common salt, two ounces of bay salt, and eight ounces of powdered nitre, together with twelve ounces of pounded roll brimstone; set them over a gentle fire, and when the ale boils, take off the scum; let it boil for about half an hour; after which set it by till it is cold, and put it into a stone bottle for use.

" When you are so far prepared, take one quart of ale, set it on the fire; mix into it by degrees, three ounces of flour of brimstone; when it is just ready to boil take it off the fire, and let it stand to cool; and when it is only blood-warm, give this quantity inwardly to three sheep, which is to be repeated every second day till they have had three doses. This will drive out the disorder, when the first mixture is to be rubbed on the distempered parts; and two days afterwards the second, and so alternately for about eight or ten days, till the cure is effected: Sometimes two

rubbings

rubbings will be sufficient. I must observe, that all these mixtures will be best boiled in well glazed earthen or iron pots."

"The two greatest enemies the sheep," says another ingenious gentleman, "or at least their wool (which is the most valuable part of them) have, are the scab and fly. I believe they destroy more wool than all the other diseases incident to that animal.

"Mr. Vesey has given us an approved remedy for the scab, and at the same time enters somewhat into the nature of the distemper. For my own part, I have not presumption enough to look into first causes; secondary ones are all I aim at; I always took nature to be a wise instructor, and the surest guide; but if we will hobble out of the way ourselves, she is not to blame.

"I agree with Mr. Vesey, that in this, and every other distemper a sheep labours under, the blood is more or less affected and disturbed; which disturbance, if I am not mistaken, the faculty call a fever; therefore it must be always considered, that a fever is no more than a struggle of nature to get rid of some enemy in the blood, by throwing it out by some of the outlets of the body, namely, by sweat, urine, or stool; or upon the surface of the skin; and then she seems to say, I have thrown the distemper out to your view, and there destroy it by proper applications.

"It surely is not scab until it is thrown out upon the skin; and when it is thrown out, what avails giving internal remedies, to do that which nature has done before? If it be out, there's your ailment; and I think, it is an axiom in physic, that when a distemper is once known, it is half cured; if it is only coming out, my advice would be, not to disturb nature, who is always acting for our good, in a wiser and better manner than we can do ourselves; she sometimes, indeed, is too weak for her office, and sometimes too strong; in the one case she is to be properly assisted, and in the other, prudently restrained; and when we do more or less, the effects are generally fatal. I hope this will satisfy Mr. Vesey, that he is not altogether in the right, any more than his neighbours.

"To cure an illness with a few medicines, is as commendable, as to say a great deal in a few words. One great obstacle to Mr. Vesey's treatment of sheep with scab, is its being too compound, troublesome, and laborious, setting aside the expence, and where there are a great number of sheep, hardly to be practised. I would have all remedies for the ailments of sheep be as simple as possible; and to be obtained and prepared with as little trouble; for certain I am, when it is otherwise, many will let their flocks go neglected, or at best leave them to a slovenly shepherd, who knows very little of the matter; and when clip-day comes, when the poor creatures are cut of their wool, (if they had any on before) what a sight presents itself to view! most part of their skins being one continued scab, and other parts eat quite through, and deep into the flesh, by the maggot: This I have seen at clip-day, and may speak it; but what must I alledge it was owing to? Sorry am I to say, to the over credulity of the master, who thought he had a shepherd who knew every thing; but the event proved the contrary.

"You must not be surprized when I say, what will destroy the fly will also cure the scab, with little or no alterations; mercury is a mortal foe to both; and the remedy for the fly is as follows:

"Take of corrosive sublimate, half an ounce; dissolve it in two quarts of rain water; to which add a gill of spirits of turpentine: This is the whole of it, which must be used in the following manner:

"When the sheep is struck, the shepherd must make a circle round the maggots with some of the water, by dropping it out of a bottle; this prevents them getting away, for they will not come near the water; then he must shred or open the wool within the circle, and drop a few drops of the water among them, and rub them about with his finger, and there leave them, for they will all die presently.

"I speak this from my own certain knowledge, and many others in this part

part of the country (Isle of Ely) can do the same.

"To a quart of the above water I add a pint of the simple lime-water of the London Dispensatory; and I declare it from experience, there is no more certain cure for the scab than it; I am sure it is the cleanest, the soonest prepared, and when so, the cheapest; which are an inducement, I think, sufficient to have every countryman make use of it." *Museum Rusticum*, vol. ii, p. 369.

SCABIOUS. The name of a flowering shrub cultivated in most pleasure gardens.

All the shrubby sorts of scabious may be propagated by cuttings, which may be taken off during any of the summer months, and should be planted in a shady border, and duly watered in dry weather, which will promote their taking root; and then they may be potted and placed in a shady situation, till they have taken new root, after which time they may be placed amongst other hardy exotic plants, in a sheltered situation, where they may remain until the end of October, when they must be moved into shelter. In some favourable seasons these plants will produce good seeds in England, so that the plants may be raised from these, by sowing them in an open border of light earth about the middle of March; and if the spring should prove very dry, it will be necessary to water the ground now-and-then, which will forward the vegetation of the seed, so that the plants will appear in about three weeks after the seeds are sown. When they come up, they must be kept clear from weeds, and in dry weather duly watered; and when they are strong enough to transplant, they should be planted in pots, and managed in the same manner as those plants which are propagated by cuttings.

All the sorts of scabious continue a long time in flower, for which they are regarded; for there is no very great beauty in many of their flowers; but as most of the hardy sorts produce flowers near three months successively, so they may be allowed a place in the borders of large gardens, because they require very little care to cultivate them. And as the shrubby kinds continue in flower most part of the year, so they make an agreeable variety amongst hardy exotic plants in the winter.

SCAMMONY, [*Scammonium.*] Scammony is a concrete juice extracted from the roots of a large climbing plant growing in the Asiatic Turkey. The best comes from Aleppo, in light, spongy masses, easily friable, of a shining ash colour verging to black; when powdered, of a light grey or whitish colour: An inferior sort is brought from Smyrna, in more compact ponderous pieces, of a darker colour, and full of sand and other impurities. This juice is chiefly of the resinous kind: rectified spirit dissolves five ounces out of six, the remainder is a mucilaginous substance mixed with dross: proof spirits totally dissolve it, the impurities only being left. It has a faint unpleasant smell; and a bitterish, somewhat acrimonious taste.

Scammony is an efficacious and strong purgative. Some have condemned it as unsafe, and laid sundry ill qualities to its charge; the principal of which is, that its operation is uncertain, a full dose proving sometimes ineffectual, whilst at others a much smaller one occasions dangerous hypercatharses This difference however is owing entirely to the different circumstances of the patient, and not to any ill quality, or irregularity of operation, of the medicine; where the intestines are lined with an excessive load of mucus, the scammony passes through, without exerting itself upon them; where the natural mucus is deficient, a small dose of this or any other resinous cathartic, irritates and inflames. Many have endeavoured to abate the force of this drug, and correct its imaginary virulence, by exposing it to the fume of sulphur, dissolving it in acid juices, and the like; but this could do no more than destroy as it were a part of the medicine, without making any alteration in the rest. Scammony in substance, judiciously managed, stands not in need of any corrector; if triturated with sugar or with almonds, as is frequently recommended for other resinous purgatives, it becomes sufficiently safe and mild in operation. It may likewise be conveniently dissolved, by trituration, in a strong decoction

coction of liquorice, and then poured off from the feces. The college of Wirtemberg assures us, that by this treatment it becomes mildly purgative, without being attended with gripes, or other inconveniencies; and that it likewise proves inoffensive to the palate. The common dose of scammony is from three to twelve grains.

SCORDIUM. *See Water* GERMANDER.

SCORPION-GRASS. *See* CATERPILLAR.

SCORZONERA. *See Vipers*-GRASS.

SCRATCHES, A distemper incident to the heels of horses.

It has so much affinity with the grease, and is so often a concomitant with that disease, that the method of curing the scratches may be selected from that article.

The parts affected should be first covered with the linseed and turnip poultice, having a little common turpentine added to relax the vessels; the green ointment may then be applied to promote the discharge, when the scratches may be dried up with the ointments and washes recommended in that article.

It is best afterwards to keep the heels supple, and softening with curriers dubbing, which is made of oil and tallow. This will keep the hide from cracking, and be as good a preservative as it is to leather; and by using it often before exercise, will prevent the scratches, if care be taken to wash the heels with warm water, when the horse comes in. When they prove obstinate, and the sores are deep, use the following; but if any cavities or hollow places are formed, they should first be laid open, for no foundation can be laid for healing, till you can dress to the bottom.

> Take Venice turpentine four ounces, quicksilver one ounce; incorporate well together by rubbing some time, and then add honey and sheep's suet, of each two ounces.

Anoint with this once or twice a day; and if the horse is full or fleshy, you must bleed and purge; and if the blood is in a bad state, the alteratives must be given to rectify it.

SCULL-CAP. [*Scutellaria.*] There are several species of this plant growing in different parts of Europe and America. They are all propagated by seeds.

SCURVY-GRASS. [*Cochlearia.*] Scurvy-grass is a pungent stimulating medicine; capable of dissolving viscid juices, opening obstructions of the viscera and the more distant glands, and promoting the fluid secretions: it is particularly celebrated in scurvies, and is the principal herb employed in these kinds of disorders in the northern countries. It is propagated by sowing seeds in July in a moist shady spot of ground. The Sea Scurvy-Grass is also used in medicine; but this grows in in the salt-marshes in Kent and Essex, where the salt water overflows it almost every tide, and can rarely be made to grow in a garden, or at least to last longer there than one year; but it being easily gathered in the places before mentioned, the markets are supplied from thence by the herb-women, who make it their business to gather herbs.

The little Welch scurvy-grass is a biennial plant, and may be preserved in a garden, if planted in a strong soil and shady situation. This plant grows plentifully in Muscovy, as also in Davis's Streights.

SCYTHE, SITHE, or SYTHE, The instrument used in mowing, being a crooked blade joined at right-angles to a long pole.

SEA BUCKTHORN. See *Sea* BUCKTHORN.

SEAGRIM. See RAGWORT.

SEAM. Tallow, grease, hog's-lard.

SEAM *of Corn.* A quarter, or eight bushels.

SEAM *of Wood.* A horse-load of wood.

SEARCHER. See BORER.

SEAVES. Rushes.

SEAVY *Ground.* Ground over-run with rushes.

SEED, the product of a plant, whereby the species is propagated.

The choice of the seed intended to be sowed is an object of greater importance than many farmers seem to imagine. It is not sufficient that the finest grains be chosen for this purpose, unless they are likewise very clean. Such wheat is not difficult to be had from land cultivated according to the principles of the new husbandry; but we seldom find corn entirely free from ſeeds of weeds when it had been raiſed in the common way.

It is natural to ſuppoſe, that the grains of ſtinted and ſickly corn neceſſarily partake of the weakly diſpoſition of the plant which produced them, and that their productions cannot be ſo fine as thoſe which grow from the ſeeds of ſtrong and healthy plants. For this reaſon Mr. Tull adviſes to take the ſeed corn from a richer ſoil than that in which it is to be ſowed, and rather from ground in perfect tilth, than from land which has been leſs carefully cultivated. This ſeems to be very right (tho' the contrary opinion is almoſt generally received) becauſe more may reaſonably be expected from the productions of a fine good ſeed, full of vigour and well conditioned, than from a poor weak plant.

M. de Chateauvieux, who often ſowed with no other intention than merely to try, for the benefit of mankind, at what time, in what manner, and what condition, it is beſt to ſow wheat, found that this grain ſprouted pretty well even when ſowed ſo green that it had not yet loſt its milky quality; but thinks it much more adviſeable to ſow none but what is thoroughly ripe; becauſe the ſeed has then attained its full perfection, from whence we may moſt certainly expect the beſt and ſtrongeſt plants.

" The wheat, ſays he, which has been reaped in a warm dry year, ſeems to me fitter for ſowing, than that which has been gathered in a cold wet ſeaſon: for in ſuch a time as this laſt, all the productions of the earth are leſs good; their taſte is leſs ſavoury; and as that corn in particular in which there is moſt moiſture, is moſt difficult to keep, I infer from thence that the formation of its grain muſt be leſs perfect. I ſhould therefore prefer wheat a year old, provided the year it was gathered in was warm and dry, to that which may have been juſt gathered in too rainy a ſeaſon; for the ſame reaſon, I always chooſe for ſowing, wheat of my high grounds, rather than that which has been produced in flats. The benefit accruing from all this care may, perhaps, not be extremely great; but at the ſame time it does not coſt any thing. Let us do in Agriculture what is done in all manufactures, where the very ſmalleſt profits, the very leaſt ſavings, are not neglected. Thoſe ſmall articles, often repeated, make large ſums in the long run, and are a real gain.

" Another thing of greater conſequence firſt made known to me by chance, but ſince confirmed by repeated experiments always attended with the ſame ſucceſs, I ſtrongly recommend as extremely ſerviceable to the firſt ſprouting of the ſeed. In my experimental ſowings, I commonly uſed wheat taken from the heap in the granary; and likewiſe frequently, corn picked out of the ears the moment before I ſowed it. I counted exactly the grains of both ſorts, and ſuppoſe that few will think there could be any difference in their productions. Yet I found a conſiderable one. What was picked out of the ears always roſe extremely well; ſcarce a grain of it ever miſſed; whereas numbers of thoſe which were taken from the heap, never ſprouted at all. I did not perceive this difference at firſt; but at laſt it ſtruck me. I relate the fact as it is, without pretending to account for the cauſe of this difference, which would lead me into too long a digreſſion. The experiment itſelf may be of real uſe, by ſhewing us, that inſtead of thraſhing the wheat intended for ſeed at any time, without diſtinction, it ought not to be thraſhed till a very few days, at moſt two or three, before it is ſowed. A few hands will be able to ſupply the ſeeds-men with as much as they will want: nor will this method, which may be a means of ſaving ſomewhat in the ſeed, be attended with any extraordinary expence.

" Perhaps too this practice may be attended with a very valuable advantage. I have not yet made the trials neceſſary to ſatisfy myſelf of what I imagine; but my deſire to be of ſervice to the public induces me to mention it, that the lovers of agriculture may reflect upon it, and try ſuch experiments as will clear up my conjectures.

" Thraſhing the ſeed only juſt before it is ſowed may poſſibly, in ſome meaſure, or perhaps entirely, prevent the cauſe of ſmut in wheat. By this I mean, that the ſeed which has not been mixed with ſmutty corn, or any way infected

mixed with smutty corn, or any way infected by its black powder, will be exempt from that distemper. Not that I take black powder to be absolutely the original cause of this distemper in corn; but I believe it is very capable of communicating it to grains which are sound.

"That nothing may be neglected which can be of any service to the seed, great care ought to be taken in thrashing the corn, especially in the manner that business is commonly performed, with flails, upon the barn floor: for a great number of grains are frequently so much bruised thereby, that it is impossible they should ever grow. If the wheat thus thrashed for seed is not thoroughly dry and hard, the mischief is still greater; much more of it being then absolutely crushed by the flail.

"As sowing in drills requires less seed than is used in the common method, it will be the easier to execute there an operation which might be too long and troublesome for so great a quantity as is used in the old way. The method which I advise, and which I have practised, is this. Let one or two beams, two feet and a half, or three feet thick, be laid across the barn floor: let the thrashers stand on each side of the beam, and take out of loose sheafs of wheat, one of which should be placed behind every man, a handful at a time, and give it two or three strokes against the beam. This will bring out a great deal of grain, which is to be reserved for seed. The ears thus shaken may be bundled up again, and afterwards thrashed out with the flail, for other uses. This method is not so tedious as some may imagine: we are sure that not a grain is bruised; and those are the most perfect which drop out thus. I think I may compare this operation with what is done in the making of wine, where the first running is always the highest flavoured and best."

Another excellent way to separate the fullest, and consequently heaviest grains, which are undoubtedly the fittest for seed, from those which are of less value for that purpose, and at the same time to clear them from many seeds of weeds, is, to make a stout man, with a broad wooden shovel, throw the corn with all his force towards an opposite corner of the barn, or rather a large boarded hall, which generally is fittest for this work. All the light, small, shrivelled grain, unfit for sowing, and the seeds of cockle, darnel, &c. not being so heavy as the sound solid corn, will fall short, and lie nearest to the man who throws them; while such as are large, plump, and weighty, out-flying all the rest, are separated widely, and may easily be gathered up. Experience will shew the vast advantages of sowing seed thus chosen.

The use of steeps was introduced very early into husbandry, not only as a means of preserving corn from several distempers to which it is subject, but also with a view to render the seed more fruitful. That some of them have sometimes answered the former of these intentions is undeniable: but with regard to the latter, much stronger and oftner repeated evidences than any that have yet been produced, are still wanted to confirm their boasted efficacy. We shall however give a concise account of some of the most famous of both kinds; with this previous observation, that even such of them as have not succeeded in some cases, through causes perhaps unknown to us, may possibly do well in others, when tried with proper judgment, and attention. Experiments of this kind should by all means be continued on a double account; first, to take off a prejudice which seems to gain ground, though it be not founded on any rational principle; and next, to be well assured whether these preparations do, or do not, produce any sensible effect. Experiments seldom prove useless to careful accurate observers. If they do not always answer the end proposed, they at least sometimes lead the way to other important discoveries.

The Romans had their lees of oil, decoction of cypress leaves, juice of house-leek, &c. on which they have bestowed full as much commendation as they merit. Lord Bacon seems to have been the first who paid any attention to this subject in England: but he has only pointed out the path to others: nor do I know any author who

who has yet given us a set of experiments with this view, long enough continued absolutely to determine what effects some kind of steeps may have towards rendering grain more fruitful.

With regard to the seeds of plants sown in the kitchen-garden, all of them should be gathered in dry weather, when there is not any moisture upon them; and the best way to preserve them is, to hang them up in bags, in a dry room, where vermin cannot come at them. The temperature of this place should be moderate; lest either too much warmth, or a too strong current of air, should make them dry, and consequently decay, sooner than they would otherwise do: and at the same time care must be taken not to exclude the air totally from them; it having been repeatedly experienced, that seeds kept long in bottles closely stopped have entirely lost the power of growing. They will keep longest in their pods, when they can be so laid up, because those coverings not only defend them from the injuries of the outward air, but, so long as they are not disjoined from them, continue to supply them with a degree of nourishment which helps to maintain them in a plump state, fit for vegetation. The seed of all soft fruits, such as cucumbers, melons, &c. are of course excepted from this general rule; for they must be well cleansed from their surrounding pulp, the rotting of which would otherwise soon corrupt them. Those of melons in particular, are so far benefited by being kept in a warmer state than would suit any others, that the plants produced from them are thereby rendered the less luxuriant, and therefore more fruitful: for which reason it is that many people carry them in an inner pocket of their breeches for six weeks or two months before they sow them, in order to exhale part of their moisture; and in effect, this will weaken them as much as two years keeping them in the common way.

Those seeds which swim upon the surface of water, when they are put to that trial of their goodness, should be rejected for sowing; because, though many of them will grow, they never produce so good plants, or so fine fruit, as the fuller, plumper, and more perfect ones, which sink to the bottom.

The age at which it is best to sow the seeds of the plants before treated of, and the time to which they will keep good, are thus ascertained by Mr. Miller, after many years experience and very accurate observation:—

The seeds of asparagus, basil, beans, beet, borage, capsicum, carrots, celeri, chervil, cresses, endive, fennel, finocchia, hyssop, kidney-beans, lavender, leeks, lentils, marjoram, marigolds, onions, parsley, parsneps, peas, purslain, radishes, savory, skirrets, spinnage, thyme, and turneps, are best sown the first spring after they have been saved; and indeed many of them will not grow if they are kept longer.

Those of cabbages, colliflowers, endive, lavender, lettuce, mustard, and sorrel, will not be the worse for keeping two years, if they are well preserved; though all of these are equally good for use the first year.

The seeds of cabbages, cucumbers, lettuces, melons, and savoys, will grow very well at the end of three years, if they have been properly saved and kept. Some of them, and particularly those of cucumbers and melons, are generally reckoned best when they are three years old; because, when they are new, the plants produced by them will grow too vigorous, and yield but a small quantity of fruit. However, none of these seeds should be kept longer than four or five years, though they will grow at the end of nine or ten: but then their plants will be weak, and their fruit small.

The seeds of fennel will frequently remain in the earth a whole year, especially if they are sown in the spring; so that whenever the plants do not come up the first year, the ground should be left undisturbed till the following spring, except only keeping it clear from weeds, and the plants will then appear.

SEEDLINGS. Young plants which have not been removed from the beds where they have been sown. It is also used to distinguish plants raised from seeds from those of the same kind which

which have been propagated by layers or cuttings.

SEED-LIP, SEED-LEAP, *or* SEED-LOP. A seed-basket, or the vessel in which the sower carries his seed, in order to sow it.

SEELING. A term used by horse-dealers to imply the time when a horse begins to have white eye-brows; that is, when there grows on that part about the breadth of a farthing, a parcel of white hair, mixed with those of his natural colour. This is a mark of old age, a horse never seeling before he is fourteen, and always before he is sixteen years old.

SELF-HEAL, [*Prunella.*] This plant grows wild in meadows and pasture grounds, and produces thick spikes of purplish flowers during the latter part of the summer. It has an herbaceous roughish taste: and hence stands recommended in hæmorrhages and alvine fluxes: it has been principally celebrated as a vulnerary, whence its name; and in gargarisms for aphthæ, and inflammations of the fauces.

It is easily propagated by seeds sown in autumn. There are several species brought from different parts of Europe and America, but all hardy enough to bear the open air of England.

SEGGRUM. Ragwort.

SEMBRADOR, an instrument used in Spain for sowing corn.

SEMIFISTULAR *Flowers*, are those whose upper part resembles a pipe cut off obliquely.

SEMIFLOSCULOUS *Flowers*, are those whose petals are hollow in their lower part; but in their upper flat, and continued in the shape of a tongue.

SEMINARY. A seed plat, or place allotted for raising plants from seed, and keeping them till they are fit to be removed into the garden or nursery.

SENA. The leaves of a shrubby plant cultivated in Persia, Syria, & Arabia; from whence they are brought, dried & picked from the stalks, to Alexandria in Egypt; and thence imported into Europe. They are of an oblong figure, sharp pointed at the ends, about a quarter of an inch broad, and not a full inch in length, of a lively yellowish green colour, a faint not very disagreeable smell, and a subacrid, bitterish, nauseous taste. Some inferior sorts are brought from Tripoli and other places: these may easily be distinguished by their being either narrower, longer, and sharper pointed; or larger, broader, and round pointed, with small prominent veins; or large and obtuse, of a fresh green colour, without any yellow cast.

Sena is a very useful cathartic, operating mildly, and yet effectually; and, if judiciosluy dosed and managed, rarely occasioning the ill consequences which too frequently follow the exhibition of the stronger purges. The only inconveniences complained of in this drug are, its being apt to gripe, and its nauseous flavour.

Bastard SENA. *See* CASSIA.

Bladder SENA. *See* BLADDER SENA.

Jointed Podded SENA, [*Coronilla.*] This is a shrubby plant of which there are several species differing in height, some rising about two feet from the ground, others trailing on the ground, and one rising to the height of five or six feet. Some are annuals, and others perennial, the latter as well as the former are propagated by seeds.

Scorpion SENA. *Jointed Podded Sena*.

SENGREEN. Houseleek.

SENEKA ROOT. Senecka, rattlesnake root; the root of a species of *polygala*, which grows spontaneously in Virginia, and bears the winters of our own climate. This root is usually about the thickness of the little finger, variously bent and contorted, and appears as if composed of joints, whence it is supposed to resemble the tail of the animal whose name it bears: a kind of membranous margin runs on each side, the whole length of the root. Its taste is at first acid, afterwards very hot and pungent.

This root is not at present much known in the shops. The Senegaro Indians are said to prevent the fatal effects which follow from the bite of the rattle-snake, by giving it internally; and applying it externally to the wound. It has of late been strongly recommended in pleurisies, peripneumonies, and other inflammatory distempers; in these cases, Lemery, du Hamel, and Jussieu, experienced its good success, (see the French memoirs for the years 1738, 1739.) Its more immediate effects are those of a diu-

 retic,

retic, diaphoretic, and cathartic; sometimes it proves emetic: the two last operations may be occasionally prevented, by giving the root in small doses, along with aromatic simple waters, as that of cinnamon. The usual dose of the powder is thirty grains or more.

Some have likewise employed this root in hydropic cases, and not without success: Bouvart (in the memoirs above-mentioned, 1744.) relates examples of its occasioning a plentiful evacuation by stool, urine, and perspiration, and by this means removing the disease, after the common diuretics and hydragogues had failed: where this medicine operates as a cathartic, it generally proves successful: if it acts by liquifying the blood and juices, without occasioning a due discharge, it should either be abstained from, or assisted by proper additions.

Gum SENECA. This is brought from the coast of Guinea, and usually mixed with, and commonly sold in the shops for Gum Arabic.

SENSITIVE PLANT, [*Mimosa.*] There are several kinds more or less irritable of this uncommon plant, natives of the West-India islands, and the warmer parts of America; some of them are annual, and others perennial. They require the same general management with other exotics of a warm climate; under this genus of plants are ranged the different species of Acacia.

SEPTEMBER. The ninth month of the year.

Products of the Kitchen-Garden.

Cabbages, carrots, artichokes, parsneps, potatoes, shallots, onions, leeks, garlick, cellery, endive, cabbage lettuce of several sorts, scorzonera, salsafy, mushrooms, cucumbers for pickling, melons, kidney-beans, rouncival peas, marrowfat pease, garden beans planted late, beets, turneps, radishes, large rooted parsley, black and white Spanish radishes, sprouts from the early cabbage stalks; and for soups, chervil, sorrel, tomatos, gourds, squashes, burnet, cardoon, chard beets, parsley, origanum: as also thyme, basil, marjoram, hyssop, winter-savory, and all sorts of young sallet herbs.

Fruits in Prime, or yet lasting.

Peaches; the nivette, Portugal peach, belle-garde or gallande, rossanna, pourpree tardive, purple alberge, old Newington, teton de Venus, pavy ropal, admirable, monstruous pavy of Pompone, Catharine, rambouillette, malacoton.

Plums; white pear plum, bonum magnum, green gage, reine claude, perdrigon, St. Catharine, and imperatrice, damsons, and bullace.

Pears; poir de Prince, autumn bergamot, swiss bergamot, brute bonne, beurre-rouge, Doyenne or St. Michael, verte-longue, mouille bouche d'automne, summer boncretien, rousselet de reins.

Grapes; the chasselas, white muscadine, red muscadine, black, red, and white morillon, currant or corinth grape. parsley-leaved grape, black, red, and white frontiniacs, Warner's red hamburgh, black hamburgh, St. Peter or Hesperian grape, orleans, malmsey, miller grape, damask grape, pearl grape, party-coloured grape, with some others.

Several sorts of figs, walnuts, filberts, hazle-nuts; and, against north walls, some currants and morella cherries, melons, quinces, medlars, lazaroles.

Apples; embroidered apple, pearmain, golden rennet, red calville, white calville, courpendu, aromatick pippin, rennet grise, catshead, quince apple, spice apple, with some others.

In the bark-bed, the ananas, or pine-apple.

Plants in Flower.

Annual stock-gilliflowers, scabiouses, sweet sultan, marvel of Peru, female balsamine, china pinks, Africans, French marigolds, hollyhocks, chrysanthemums, capsicums, lupines of several sorts, sweet-scented peas, Tangier peas, double ptarmica or sneezwort, true saffron, carthamus or bastard saffron, autumnal crocuses, cyclamens, colchicum, autumnal hyacinth, asters of several sorts, five or six sorts of golden-rod, double sopewort, double camomile, larkspurs, tree primrose, polyanthuses, spiderwort, auriculas, snap-dragon, Venus looking-glass, Venus navelwort, candy tuft, China starwort, ox-eye, helian-

themums;

themums, heliotropiums, lychniſes, campanulas, autumnal gentians, ſcarlet bean, oriental perſicaria, ſtramoniums, ſolanums, alkekengi with large blue flowers, ſantolinas, chryſocoma, chelone with white and red flowers, phlomis, amaranthoides, xeranthemums, jaceas, oriental mallow, lavatera, dwarf annual ſtock, ketmia veſicaria, ſeveral ſorts of ſun-flower, elichryſums, eupatoriums, hearts eaſe, red garden valerian, catanance quorundam, ruyſchiana, rudbeckia, ſilphium, large blue aconite, wholſome wolfſbane, cerinthe, alyſſon fruticoſum, alyſſoides, dianthera, hydrangea, tetragonotheca, monarda, ambroſia, old man's head pink, anemiſes two or three ſorts, ſea phularia, dodartia, coliums, bugloſs of three or four kinds, convolvulus of ſeveral ſorts, double and ſingle Indian naſturtium, with ſome others.

Hardy Trees and Shrubs now in Flower.

Jaſmine, monthly roſe, muſk roſe, paſſion-flower, arbutus, pomegranate with double flowers, ſhrub cinquefoil, mallow tree, althæ frutex, ketmia ſyriaca, lauruſtinus, honeyſuckle, ſcorpion ſena, agnus caſtus, rhus of ſeveral ſorts, celaſtrus, medicago fruteſcens, ſhrubby St. Johnſwort, Itea, clethra, kalmia, azalea, dwarf medlar from Crete, Spaniſh broom, Pocock's bladder ſena, hamamelis ſymphoricarpos, ciſtuſes, lucca broom, cytiſſus hirſutus, tamariſk with ſome others.

Medicinal Plants, which may now be gathered for Uſe.

Calamus aromaticus, winter cherry, arum or cuckow-pintle roots, wholſome wolfſbane roots, barberry fruit, hemp ſeed, capſicum or Indian pepper, baſtard ſaffron, cucumber ſeed, bitter vetch ſeed, fennel ſeed, fenugreek ſeed, aliſander ſeed, walnut fruit, lettuce ſeed, lentil ſeed, lovage ſeed, gromwell ſeed, flax ſeed, hops, millet ſeed, ſweet fern ſeed, garden creſs ſeed, macedonian parſley ſeed, candy carrot ſeed, common parſley ſeed, radiſh ſeed, elderberries, ſavin, ſeſeli ſeed, flixweed ſeed, muſtard ſeed, nightſhade, golden-rod.

Plants now in Flower in the Green-Houſe and Stove.

Oleanders with double and ſingle flowers, colutea Æthiopica, amomum Plinii, myrtles, tree candy tuft, ſcabious tree, houſeleek tree, ſeveral ſorts of ficoides, cotyledons, aloes, Indian fig, double naſturtium, Spaniſh jaſmine, azorian jaſmine, yellow Indian jaſmine, arabian jaſmine, polyanthuſes, Guernſey lily, belladonna lily, leonurus, cytiſus incanus, capers, granadillas, ſenſitive and humble plants, heliotropium arboreſcens, amber tree, apocynums, lantanas of ſeveral ſorts, abutilons, fritilaria craſſa, canna indica, bean caper, Indian arrow-root, African alcea, African groundſel tree, indigo, palma chriſti, ſpurges, euphorbium, phyſick nut, elichryſums, grewia, papaw, turnera, ſtramoniums, cleſmas, chironia, anemonoſpermoſes, ſolanums, ſpartiums, dorias, lotus hæmorrhoidalis, cardinal's flower, caſſias, ſena alexandrina, ſena ſpuria, ketmias, piercea, pancratiums, crinum two ſorts, hæmanthus, plumeria, bauhinia, martynia, milleria, ceſtrums, helleborine, rauvolfia, malpighia, convolvuluſes, baſſelia, alkekengi three or four ſorts, ſpigelia, oldenlandia, mauroceria, cliffortia, Lotus with black flowers, African wood ſorrel, ornithogalum luteum, kleinia, ſaururus, anthericums, ginger, coſtus, kempferia, volkhameria, galingale, d'ayena, ruellias, barleria, ſweet-ſcented heliotrope from Peru, phylica, commelina, rondelitia, upright torch thiſtle, clutia, geraniums of ſeveral ſorts, arums, tournefortia, with ſome others.

SEPTOIL. *See* TORMENTIL.

SERMOUNTAIN. *See* LASERWORT.

SERPENT's TONGUE. *See* ADDER's TONGUE.

SERVICE TREE, [*Sorbus.*] The right ſervice tree is a tall and beautiful tree, and very well worth planting for its timber. There are two or three other kinds which are called by the ſame general name, and they agree in the nature of the wood, as well as in the flowers, and the ſhape of the fruit; but they vary in the ſhape of the leaf, and the degree of goodneſs. Theſe other kinds are diſtinguiſhed by the names of, 1. The Service Tree, with the fruit red in the middle. 2. The ſhort fruited ſervice; and, 3. The wild ſervice or quick beam.

The firſt is the moſt valuable, and the

the two next come nearest its nature. The last differs more, and is not generally accounted of the service kind, but called by a distinct name. The flowers of the others are much alike; they appear early in spring, and the fruit is very rough to the taste till thoroughly mellow. All the summer it makes a beautiful appearance.

The best soil for the Service Tree is a tough and firm loam, with some rich earth among it. Such are very common toward the foot of hills, or on any gentle ascent, and these are the best situations also for this tree. When the soil is too light, the tree grows very slowly; and when it is too dry, the fruit ripens very poorly, neither do the leaves stand their time. When the service is judiciously planted, it grows quick, and answers very well to the husbandman; but when the plantation is made at random, none answers worse. Few know its value; because few have given it a fair trial; nor is its timber so much known, or so common to be had, as it ought to be, for this very reason. He who will fall into the method of raising these tres, will do a service to the public, as well as to himself; for there needs but a beginning to incite others, and the consequence would be a ready market for the timber, and it would prevent the importation of a great deal of foreign fine wood; which, however called by sounding names, is inferior to the service tree in beauty, and in value.

The service may be raised from seed, but the better way is by layers, which take root very freely, and are naturally produced in great abundance. Those who have a mind to raise them from seed, must sow them in shallow trenches, in a nursery, and keep them clear from weeds. At two years old they must be planted out at a yard distance, and three or four years after that, be set where they are to stand. Such as want only a few trees, may conveniently enough raise them from suckers, which grow about the old trees in great abundance. These are to be transplanted early in spring.

Which ever way the service tree be raised, it should be carefully trimmed up for the first eight or ten years, that it may not spread into branches till at a certain height, when there will be a handsome trunk for timber. After this it is best left to itself.

It is a very proper tree for avenues, clumps and hedge rows, and 'tis great pity that it is not more frequent. Its beauty should be an inducement to the gentleman, and its quick growth and valuable wood to the husbandman.

The Quick Beam, or, as some call it, the Quicken Tree, or according to others, the Wild Service, or Mountain Ash, for it has all these names, is properly a kind of service tree. It is a beautiful but a small tree, being one of the least of those that are accounted timber trees, or planted for that purpose.

The bark is pale and smooth, the leaves are beautifully formed, each being composed of many smaller, which are long, narrow, and finely dented at the edges. The flowers stand in great bunches at the end of the branches, and are whitish, large and handsome: and after these come beautiful berries red like coral.

This elegant little tree is a native of England, and is a great beauty and ornament to our coppices and hedgerows, in those counties where it is most frequent. Its fair appearance has occasioned its being taken also into gardens, where it makes a fine figure in the wilderness quarters.

The best soil for the quick beam is a light and dry loam; and it grows best on a somewhat rising situation. No tree is better suited to thrive in hedgerows, where the soil is light and dry. It roots itself very firmly; and shoots up in a moderate time to its full stature.

The best way of raising the quick beam is from seed. The berries are to be gathered when full ripe, and sown after they have been spread a fortnight in a dry airy garret. They shoot up very regularly and freely, and should be removed from their first bed to some other part of the nursery at two years growth, and planted at two foot distance. Three or four years after this, they are fit to be transplanted to the places where they are to stand; and a small nursery will thus, with little or no trouble, raise such a quantity as will stock a large piece of ground; where being set in hedges, or the banks of coppice woods, & other such places, they will quickly grow to some value.

Those

Those who would only raise a few trees, may take up suckers from about the old ones, for they rise in abundance, and grow freely.

The quick beam should have very little trimming or lopping; for, as it is not to be carried to a large tree, 'tis best left to nature, the branches of themselves growing with a pretty irregularity.

— HORN-BEAM, [*Carpinus*.] This by mistake in its alphabetical arrangement is referred to SERVICE, and accordingly we have on that account placed it here.

The horn-beam is a beautiful and regularly growing tree. Its bark is brown and tolerably smooth, and the wood firm. The leaves are short and indented at the edges, they are somewhat like those of the elm, but of a more beautiful green. The flowers are small and inconsiderable. They hang in catkins like those of the hazel; and the fruit, which is dry and light, grows on a different part of the tree.

There are four kinds of this tree raised in nurseries. 1. The common Horn-Beam. 2. The Hop Horn-Beam. 3. The flowering Horn-Beam; and, 4. The Horn-Beam with striped leaves: but the husbandman who would plant for advantage, has nothing to do with any of these except the common kind.

The horn-beam is an extreamly hardy tree, it will grow in the worst soil and bleakest situation. For this reason it is very proper to be planted on the tops of cold hills, and in places so exposed, that others will not grow on them. It will thrive very well in hedges, and in woods; and is excellent for clumps in the bleakest and worst parts of parks, and it every where engages the eye by its beauty.

The best way of propagating the horn-beam is by layers. It may also be raised from seeds, but this is a more tedious method, and the other does as well. If the seeds are preferred, they must be gathered in September, and sown three weeks or a month after, laying them in the mean time in a dry airy place. They will sometimes come up in five or six months, sometimes they will lie till the following spring. They are to be thinned soon after they appear, and kept clear of weeds, and at two years old to be removed to another part of the nursery, where they must be planted at a greater distance, and 3 or 4 years after they are to be finally removed, and set where they are to remain. But the method by layers is much more expeditious, and the trees grow as beautiful that way as the other.

SETTER. A kind of seton or issue, made by cutting a hole in the dewlap of an ox or cow, and putting into the wound a sort of tent formed out of the root of helleboraster; by which the ill humours vent themselves.

SETTERWORT. Bearsfoot.

SETWELL. Valerian.

To SEW, *or* Go SEW, to go dry; spoken of a cow.

SHADDOCK. *See* ORANGE TREE.

SHAKING. A disease incident to sheep, consisting of a weakness in their hinder quarters, so that they cannot rise up when they are down. No cure is yet known for it.

SHARE *of a Plough*. That part which cuts the ground, the extremity forward being covered with a sharp-pointed iron, called the point of the share; and the end of the wood behind, the tail of the share. *See the article* PLOUGH.

SHAVE GRASS. Horse tail.

SHAW. A wood that encompasses a close.

SHEAT *of a Plough*. That part of the plough which passes through the beam, and is fastened to the share.

The sheat, or as it is sometimes called the fore-sheat, there being another piece of timber behind it called the hinder-sheat, should be seven inches wide, and fastened to the beam by a retch (a piece of iron with two legs) and by a wedge driven by it into the hole of the beam. The angle contained between the sheat and the beam of the plough should be about forty-two degrees.

SHEAVES. Bundles of corn bound up in the field.

SHED. A slight temporary covering.

SHEEP. Next in value and consideration to the larger of the horned cattle comes the sheep; an article of vast concernment to the farmer: cheap in the purchase; easily fed; and returning

ing a great profit by many feveral ways: even its dung upon the land often paying for all it eats while fed upon it.

We have already advifed the farmer in the choice of his larger cattle, to proportion their kind to the degree of richnefs in his land: it is not the fortune of every hufbandman to labour upon a fruitful foil: but the worft is not without its ufes; and fheep are a ftock for fuch as will not fupport the larger kinds. We fee them thrive upon the moft barren downs; and the farmer will always find them ready to fatten upon fuch grounds as will not keep the other kinds alive.

As the oxen of England are of very different breeds, though all the fame in kind, fo it is with the fheep, which differ extreamly according to the feveral breeds in different places; and are therefore fuited one to one kind of land, and another to another.

We fhall advife the hufbandman to great caution, in the ftocking his farm with fheep: and this under two heads, firft, with refpect to the breed, and fecondly, for his choice of the creatures themfelves; for there are, in every breed, many that are much finer than others, and thefe he fhould chufe. Half the profit that might be made by this part of the hufbandman's ftock, is loft by careleffnefs in the firft choice, and in the following management: but an error in the firft choice is the moft fatal, becaufe it is irrecoverable, except by beginning over again. We fhall therefore firft confider that, and laying before the practical hufbandman the properties and particular ufes of the feveral different breed of fheep that we have in England, fhall advife him in his choice according to his main defign, his beft advantage, and the nature of the land he has to ftock with them.

With refpect to the finenefs of the wool, there is a fmall breed, diftinguifhed by their black face and thin coat, that exceed all others. They bear but a fmall quantity in comparifon of many, but the quality of it makes amends. Thefe are eafily known by fight. They were firft raifed in Herefordfhire and Worcefterfhire. And for that reafon are known in many places by the name of the Hereford fhire or the Worcefterfhire breed. A dry, barren, and expofed pafturage will very well feed this kind, for they are hardy; and the fhorter the grafs on which they feed, it is obferved the finer the wool. They are alfo excellent for the table, the joints being fmall and full of a fine gravy. We fee this kind kept in many parts of England, in gentlemen's parks and lawns, and they every where make a pretty appearance.

The kind moft oppofite to thefe are a large, tall, and heavy-loaded fheep: thefe have ftrong limbs, and a ftout gait in walking: they carry a great deal of wool, but it is coarfe. Thefe were firft bred in Lincolnfhire, and in fome of the adjoining counties; and are fond of living in falt marfhes. They have been taken into many parts of the kingdom, to other ground, where they do not keep entirely to their own nature: and yet are called, from the place whence they were brought, the Lincolnfhire breed.

The flefh of thefe is large grained, but moderately tafted, and no where very much efteemed. However, as they are obferved to fucceed better than the other breeds, in places toward the fea, it may be proper for the hufbandman who has land in fuch a fituation, to take fome of them: though not for his whole ftock in this kind.

Thirdly, there is a breed between thefe two kinds, which in general fhould be preferred to either. This is a large, tall, and ftrong fheep, of the beft fhape of any, & having the deepeft coat of wool. This was originally fed in feveral of our midland counties, and has thence been called by fome the Midland Breed; and by others, from fome particular counties famous for them, the Leicefterfhire or Northamptonfhire breed. The wool of this kind, though not altogether fo good as that of the fmall black-faced fheep, is greatly preferable to that of the Lincolnfhire breed; and the quantity is fo much greater than that of the fmaller kind, that it very well makes amends for its inferior quality.

The flefh of this fheep is the common mutton, not in any thing particular for goodnefs or badnefs: and it will do very well upon the common pasture grounds, and thrive upon every common kind of food. For these reasons it is fit that these sheep should be most generally bred.

When the husbandman has very poor pasture grounds, let him take the Herefordshire breed; and when he borders upon the sea-coast, or upon the shores of large salt-water rivers, let him prefer, in part at least, the Lincolnshire kind; but when he has none of these particular reasons to byass him, let him prefer this midland breed to any other.

To these three, which may be called the general breeds of sheep, we shall add a few words on two other kinds.

The sheep bred in the northern parts of this kingdom, are a large and big-boned sort; they approach to the Lincolnshire kind in shape; but their wool is harsh, rough, and hairy; these are called by some the Yorkshire breed.

Their flesh is inferior to that of several other kinds, as well as their wool; but they have an advantage over the others, in that they will stand the coldest weather, and take care of themselves where some of the tenderer breeds would be lost. This may recommend them to the husbandman whose lot has thrown him far north, where the other kinds will not thrive; but he should not introduce them into his farm in any other situation, for they are less profitable than any others.

The last kind, or breed, to be mentioned, is in a manner peculiar to mountainous countries; and is most frequent in Wales. It may therefore be called the Welch breed. This is a small, but well-shaped sheep; and so hardy that it will live any where. The flesh is excellent for the table. But the wool is not only small in quantity, but is the worst produced by any breed of sheep in this country.

The husbandman will see by this account, that it never can be his interest to admit this breed among his flock, unless compelled to it by the particularity of his situation. The little black-faced sheep of Herefordshire has the same advantage in the excellence of its flesh; and it has, into the bargain, the finest wool. Therefore it is highly to be preferred, where it will thrive: and it will do on very poor and very exposed ground. However, if at any time the farmer finds his pastures so poor, so exposed, and miserable, that they will not support this kind, all he has to do is to call in the other, or Welch breed, which will live any where.

Having laid before the husbandman this account of the three principal different breeds of sheep in England, and the two other kinds that are in a manner particular to certain places, the next part of our care must be, the instructing him in his choice, not only of the breed he shall fix upon, for the grounds of that choice have been laid down already, in their several characters; but of the particular creatures he shall fix upon in the breed that is most suited to his purpose.

But to this particular let us premise a few words upon his general choice, that is, as to the breed. He sees here five several kinds of sheep, some large, others smaller; and some yielding a greater, some a smaller quantity of wool, which is also on one breed fine, and on another coarser. He has his choice given him among all these, for we suppose him not yet to have begun stocking his farm with this article: it would be natural for him to prefer at once the finest kind as most profitable; but let him not only remember, but strictly observe what we have just laid down, that every breed will not suit every pasture.

He has now seen what are the kinds of sheep; let him examine what is the nature of his land; and when he has impartially considered this, let him fix upon that breed which will thrive best on that kind of pasturage he has at his command, for this we have expresly told him with respect to each; and let him then purchase for his farm that breed which he sees will be most suited to thrive on it.

This he may be assured of, and he may extend the rule farther than barely to his sheep, that he will have more profit from the very worst kind that shall thrive upon his land, than he possibly can from the very best that shall starve upon it.

One thing farther is to be noted before we come to the particular choice, that is, the difference of the land which he is to bring them to from that whence he purchased them: this must be in

tures, and finds that his lambs want milk, it is best to sell them at once to the butcher: for it is not the running by the ewe that will preserve them, she can be of no service against such an accident, if she wants milk for their full support.

Those he lambs that are intended to be bred as rams, should be separated from the rest, and the others gelt in time. The sooner this is done the better: for every creature bears this operation best while it is tender, and is with the dam. If this operation have been neglected at a proper time, it must be done toward the end of September, at which season it is best to separate the breed or this purpose, and see it be done sperfectly.

SHEEP'S FESCUE *Grass*, [*Festuca ovina*.] This grass is much esteemed for feeding of sheep in Sweden, where they have not such downs as we have.

Gmelin says, that the Tartars choose to fix, during the summer, in those places where there is the greatest plenty of this grass, because it affords a most wholsome nourishment to all kinds of cattle, but chiefly sheep: and he observes, that the sepulchral monuments of the ancient Tartars are mostly found in places which abound with this grass, which shews, adds he, that it has long been valued among them.

This grass abounds in many parts of England and Wales, and particularly on all the finest sheep pastures in Herefordshire, Oxfordshire, Norfolk, &c. Mr. Stillingfleet observes, that it is a very early grass, and that, contrary to what Linnæus says, either sheep, or some other animals do eat the flowering stems of this grass; for, when he searched for it upon Benstead downs, he could see no part of it but the radical leaves, except among bushes near the hedges, where it was guarded from the sheep.

SHEARING *of Sheep*. There are two articles in the condition of the wool which enhance its price. These are, fattyness and cleanness. And it is in the owner's power to give it these in a much greater degree than they otherwise would be, by his care and attention. The first will be increased by the time of shearing, the other by cleanliness.

The fattyness of the wool will never give it any value, unless it be at the same time clean; and the cleanness will discover its imperfection, instead of enhancing the price, if it be not fatty.

This fattyness of the wool is owing to the creature's sweating, and therefore there must be some hot weather past before it is sheared, that it may have sweated well: not once or twice, for that will answer no purpose: but several times for days together, that the moisture may have lodged itself about the wool, and in a manner oiled it so, that the necessary washing of the creature for cleanlyness, shall not be able to carry it off.

Unless the sheep have sweated well before the washing, that will do harm equal to its good, for as much as it increases the price by cleanness, it diminishes it by taking off the fatness. It is very necessary sheep should be well washed before they are sheared: but the farmer is to know at the same time, that unless they have well sweat in their wool first, this will hurt it.

Upon this foundation depends all the art of sheep-shearing. The best season of the year for doing it is toward midsummer. But let the weather determine, and let not the farmer be carried away by the name of any day, or month, against the use of his reason.

SHEPHERD'S *Needle*. See *Sweet* FERN.

SHEPHERD'S POUCH. } SHEPHERD'S PURSE. } [*Bursa Pastoris*.] This plant is common in waste places; and is found in flower all the summer. Shepherd's purse has long been celebrated as an astringent, and strongly recommended in diarrhœas, dysenteries, uterine fluors, and in general in all diseases where astringents of any kind can avail; but present practice pays little or no regard to it.

SHEPHERD'S STUFF. Teazel.

SHOODS. Oat hulls.

SHOULDER-WRENCH. To understand the nature of these infirmities, it will be necessary to remember, that the blade-bone of the shoulder is fixed to the body, not by articulation or jointing, but by apposition, being laid to the ribs, and fastened by the muscles which lie under and above it; so when a horse happens to receive a blow or strain in the shoulder, the tendons of these muscles are stretched and relaxed; and when

splait,

that is violent, it is called a *shoulder-splait*, and becomes more or less dangerous, as the horse is more or less hardy.

Every one sufficiently knows, that a slip, false step, or any undue position of a horse's leg, will strain and weaken the shoulder, by stretching those ligaments; and sometimes the shoulder is affected by a hurt or bruise on the withers, the reason of which may be easily enough conceived, by any one who will examine into the structure of these parts; but when the accident proves not so violent as to shew a looseness and swelling, it is not easily discerned whether the lameness be in the shoulder, in the foot, or any other joint. The best judges have therefore, in all such cases, thought it proper to examine all parts from the shoulder downwards, and even to unshoe the horse, that they may know certainly where to apply their remedies. But the infirmities of the shoulders may be distinguished from those of the feet, by having a horse put to exercise; for if the lameness be in the feet, he will halt most when he is ridden; but if it be in the shoulder, the warmer he grows, the less he will halt; and, if the wrench be violent, he will be apt to cast his leg outwards, forming a circle as he goes. But if none of these signs are perceivable in his gait, the surest way is to turn him short on the lame side, for that tries the muscles the most of any thing; so that if the grief be in the shoulder, he will set his foot on the ground hardily, and endeavour to favour his shoulder.

But in order to the cure, a distinction ought to be made between an old grief, and a hurt that is newly received; for, in a fresh strain, the first intention is to apply such things as are proper to allay the heat and inflammation, and prevent a too great afflux of matter to the part; whereas in an old grief, those things are chiefly made use of that attenuate and render the superfluous humours fit to pass thro' the pores; and therefore, as soon as you perceive your horse lamed in the shoulder, by a fall, or any other accident, after he has been bled on the opposite side, a cold restringent charge may be applied of vinegar, bole, and the whites of eggs. Verjuice may be used instead of vinegar upon the road, which may be had at any farm-house; for the sooner a cold application is made, the better. The part ought, in the beginning, to be refreshed 3 or 4 times a day, with a spunge dipt in vinegar and bole; and after that the following plaister may be applied:

'Take common pitch half a pound, 'de Minio plaister or diachylon six 'ounces, common turpentine 'four ounces: melt them altogether in a pipkin over hot embers, continually stirring; and 'when these are dissolved, add 'bole in fine powder four ounces, 'myrrh and aloes, of each an 'ounce. Spread this upon the 'horse's shoulder, before it grows 'cold, and put fine flocks of the 'colour of the horse all over it.'

But when the lameness happens to be of an old standing, the following ointment willl be of great service.

'Take of the soldiers ointment, or 'nerve ointment, half a pound, 'ointment of marshmallows six 'ounces, rectifyed oil of amber 'four ounces. Mix them all together, & with a hot bar of iron 'held as near as possible, chafe 'the part twice a day; and, at 'some intervals, with camphorated spirits.'

The soldiers ointment is made as follows:

'Take fresh bay-leaves three pounds, 'rue two pounds and a half, marjoram two pounds, mint one 'pound, sage, wormwood, costmary, basil, of each half a pound, 'oil olive twenty pounds, yellow 'wax four pounds, Malaga wine 'two pounds.'

Bruise all the leaves, and boil to the consistence of an ointment, and keep it for use. This may be made in a smaller quantity by those who keep but few horses.

Sollysell recommends the ointment of *Montpellier* as an excellent remedy in all strains in the shoulders, &c. It is composed of the ointment of roses, marshmallows, populeon and honey, of each equal quantities. The oils of turpentine, earth-worms, oil of *Petre*, St. *John's* wort, nerve oil, bear's grease, horse grease, mules grease, deers suet, badgers grease, and many such things, are also used in the same intention. But

But if the lameneſs does not yield to theſe things, recourſe may be had to roweſing, or to the fire; but the laſt is preferable, and leſs painful than the uſual method of roweling, by bruiſing and blowing up the ſhoulder.

And, therefore, with a hot iron, make a circle the breadth of a trencher round the joint, and within the whole circle pierce the ſkin, leaving about an inch between the holes, and to each apply yellow wax and roſin melted together, until the eſcars fall off, and then dreſs them every day with turpentine and honey, applying plaiſters as directed, until the ſores are dried up.

Some adviſe ſwimming a horſe for a ſhoulder-ſplait, from an opinion of the joint being out; but if it were really ſo, he muſt ſwim with three legs, which is almoſt as impoſſible as for a door to move without hinges. But yet ſwimming is not always unſucceſsful; and, in all old griefs, it becomes ſerviceable in the ſame manner as a cold bath, by helping perſpiration, and giving a more lively motion to the obſtructed matter; and therefore the morning is the propereſt time, becauſe the water is then the coldeſt, and it ſhould be a continued cuſtom for ſome time to do effectual ſervice.

But, in all other reſpects, the horſe ſhould be put to no kind of labour, neither ought any one to ride him, for a weight upon his back muſt needs add to the infirmity, as the greateſt ſtreſs lies upon the ſhoulders; but it will be very proper for him to be walked out every day, when the weather is favourable; and his exerciſe may be increaſed as his ſhoulder recovers ſtrength; a patten ſhoe may alſo be ſet upon the oppoſite foot, if he leans too much upon it.

SHOVEL. A well-known inſtrument, conſiſting of a long handle, and a broad blade, with raiſed edges.

SHOWEL. A blind for a cow's eyes.

SHROUD. A ſhelter, or harbour.

SHUCK. A huſk or ſhell.

SICKLE. A toothed hook, with which corn is reaped.

SIDE-SADDLE. A ſaddle for women to ride on horſeback.

SIDE-SADDLE *Flower*, [*Sarracena.*] There are two ſpecies; one growing in the bogs of moſt parts of North-America, which has a ſtrong fibrous root, which ſtrikes deep into the ſoft earth, from which ariſe five, ſix, or ſeven leaves, in proportion to the ſtrength of the plant; theſe are hollow like a pitcher, narrow at their baſe, but ſwell out large at the top; their outer ſides are rounded, but on their inner they are a little compreſſed, and have a broad leafy border running longitudinally the whole length of the tube; and to the rounded part of the leaf there is on the top a large appendage or ear ſtanding erect, of a browniſh colour; this ſurrounds the outſide of the leaves, about two-thirds of the top. From the center of the root, between the leaves, ariſes a ſtrong, round, naked foot-ſtalk about a foot high, ſuſtaining one nodding flower at the top, which has a double empalement; the outer one is of one leaf, divided into five parts to the bottom, where they are connected to the foot-ſtalks; theſe ſegments are obtuſe, and bend over the flower, ſo as to cover the inſide of it; they are of a purple colour on the outſide, but green within, having purple edges; the inner empalement, which is compoſed of three green leaves, falls off; within theſe are five oval petals of a purple colour, which are hollowed like a ſpoon; theſe cover the ſtamina and ſummits, with part of the ſtigma alſo. In the center is ſituated a large, roundiſh, channelled germen, ſupporting a ſhort ſtyle, crowned by a very broad five-cornered ſtigma, faſtened in the middle to the ſtyle, covering the ſtamina like a target; this is green, but the five corners, which are ſtretched out beyond the brim, are each cut into two points, and are purpliſh. Round the germen are ſituated a great number of ſhort ſtamina, joining the ſides of the germen cloſely, which are terminated by target-ſhaped furrowed ſummits, of a pale ſulphur colour. When the flower decays, the germen ſwells to a large roundiſh capſule with five cells, covered by the permanent ſtigma, filled with ſmall ſeeds.

The ſecond ſort grows naturally in Carolina, upon bogs and in ſtanding ſhallow waters. The leaves of this ſort grow near three feet high, ſmall at the bottom, but widening gradually to the top. They are hollow, and arched over at the mouth like a friar's cowl. The flowers of this grow on naked pedicles, rising from the root to the height of three feet; the flowers are green.

These plants are esteemed for the singular structure of their leaves and flowers, which are so different from all the known plants, as to have little resemblance of any yet discovered; but there is some difficulty in getting them to thrive in England, when they are obtained from abroad; for as they grow naturally on bogs, or in shallow standing waters, so unless they are constantly kept in wet they will not thrive; and although the winters are very sharp in the countries where the first sort naturally grows, yet being covered with water, and the remains of decayed plants, they are defended from frost.

SIEVE. Hair, lawn, or basket-work, strained on a hoop, for separating the flour from the bran, the dust from corn, &c. *See Sear—*

SIG. Urine, chamber-lie.

SIKE. A little rill, a water furrow, a gutter.

SILK GRASS. Dogsbane.

SILVER BUSH. Jupiter's beard.

SILVER TREE, [*Protea.*] This is a native of the Cape of Good Hope, of which there are no less than twenty species, but all require the assistance of a stove or green-house.

SILVER WEED, [*Potentila.*] Cinquefoil.

SIMAROUBA. A bark with pieces of the wood adhering to it, brought from Guiana, in long tough pieces, of a pale yellowish colour, and a pretty strong bitter taste. It has lately come into esteem in dysenteric fluxes: a decoction of half a dram is given for a dose, and repeated at intervals of three or four hours.

SIT-FAST. A part of a horse's hide turned horny, and which if it cannot be dissolved, and softened by rubbing with mercurial ointment, must be cut out, and afterwards healed as a fresh wound. It generally proceeds from a warble. *Hide-bound.*

SIZZING. Yeast, or barm.

SKID. The chain by which the wheel of a waggon is fastened, so as to prevent its turning round, upon descending a steep hill.

SKILLING. An isle, or bay of a barn.

SKIRRETS. A kind of parsnep, which thrive best in a light and moist soil. They are propagated either by seeds, or by slips from the root, which is composed of several fleshy fibres, about the thickness of a man's little finger, terminating in one head. This root, for which only the skirret is cultivated, is reckoned wholsome and nourishing: but it is flatulent, and too sweet tasted for many palates. The seeds of this plant, which generally produce larger roots than the slips, should be sown about the end of March or the beginning of April, and if they are good, the plants will appear in five or six weeks. When they have put out their leaves so as to be well distinguished from weeds, the ground should be carefully hoed; and this should be repeated three several times, in the same manner as is practised for carrots. In these hoeings, which should be performed in as dry weather as possible, the better to destroy the weeds, the skirrets, whether sown in broad-cast, or in drills, should be thinned the distance of at least three inches from each other. In autumn, when the leaves begin to decay, the roots will be fit for use. These may be preserved all the winter, and till they begin to shoot in the spring, when they will become hard and sticky. So will also those which run up to seed the first summer, and which should therefore be pulled up and thrown away.

The season for propagating skirrets by offsets is in the spring, before they begin to shoot. The old roots should be dug up then, and the side roots should be slipt off with an eye or bud to each. These should be planted four inches asunder, in rows sufficiently distant to leave room for digging between them.

SLAB. The out-side plank of a piece of timber when sawn into boards.

SLECKS. Small pit coal.

Ladies SLIPPER, [*Cypripedium.*] This plant must be taken in the place where it grows, and transplanted into the gardens.

SLOE TREE. *See* PLUM TREE *and* BLACKTHORN.

SMALLAGE, [*Apium graveolens.*] A plant growing naturally by the sides of brooks and ditches in many parts of England

England, and is rarely cultivated in gardens. Thoſe however, who are fond of it in their pottage, may raiſe it in a moiſt ſoil, either by ſlips, or from ſeeds ſown in March. This ſeed is reddiſh, and pretty big, of a roundiſh oval ſhape, a little more full and riſing on one ſide than on the other, and ſtreaked lengthwiſe.

SMUT. A diſeaſe in corn, which partially or totally deſtroys the grain in the ear. When it is in the full height of its miſchief, the whole inner ſubſtance of the corn is black as ink, of a faint, nauſeous taſte, a bad ſmell, and of offenſive qualities, occaſioning ſickneſs in thoſe who eat bread made of flour in which there was much of it. In this caſe, if the corn be bruiſed, and ſteeped in water, it preſently ſhews innumerable worms, like little eels, living in every part of it.

When the diſorder is not arrived to this full height, the inner ſubſtance of the corn is not then entirely hurt, but the outſide is ſpotted with black; and, in ſome corns, a part of the flour within. This makes a great change in the matter; for the firſt is wholly deſtroyed, whereas the other may ſometimes be recovered for certain uſes, though not for all ſervices.

England is more ſubject to this diſorder of corn than any other country we know; and this is owing to our wet ſummers: in the warm and naturally dry countries it is not known at all, or not in a degree worth notice.

In Egypt no age ever ſaw a black grain of any corn; for in Egypt they have no rain: and even in Italy it is little regarded now; and was ſo ſlighted in earlier time, that all the Roman writers have not a name for it. There is not a word of ſmut in the Latin language. The reader muſt not cenſure this aſſertion, if ſome modern writers, in that language, have attempted to name it: they uſe words which properly expreſs blight and mildew: to both theſe the old Roman fields were ſubject, therefore they have terms to expreſs them; but this was little known, and leſs regarded.

For the beſt known prevention of this diſeaſe, we recommend good tillage, with a due courſe of crops and fallows; and particularly change of ſeed. In fallows we include turnips, &c.

See also Barren Corn — Worms — Blight. — Burnt Grain — Abortive Corn

SNAIL TREFOIL. *See* BASTARD MEDIC.

SNAKE WEED. Butort.

SNAKE ROOT. Birthwort.

Virginian SNAKE ROOT, Is a ſmall, light, buſhy root, conſiſting of a number of ſtrings or fibres, matted together, iſſuing from one common head; of a browniſh colour on the outſide, and paler or yellowiſh within. It has an aromatic ſmell, like that of valerian, but more agreeable; and a warm, bitteriſh, pungent taſte. This root is a warm diaphoretic and diuretic: it has been greatly celebrated as an alexipharmac, and eſteemed one of the principal remedies in malignant fevers and epidemic diſeaſes. In theſe intentions, it is given in ſubſtance from ten to thirty grains, and in infuſion to a dram or two.

SNAIL-COD. A name given by Mr. Worlidge to a ſpecies of manure found at the bottom of deep rivers. It is a kind of mud or ſledge, very ſoft, full of wrinkles, and intermixed with many little ſhells and ſnails, to which it is thought to owe a great part of its fatneſs.

SNAPDRAGON. *See* CALVES SNOUT.

American SNAPDRAGON, [*Ruellia.*] This plant grows naturally in the Weſt-India Iſlands and Carolina, it is propagated by ſeeds, but requires the aſſiſtance of a bark ſtove.

SNAP-TREE, [*Juſticia.*] This plant is a native of India, riſing with a ſhrubby ſtalk to the height of three or four feet, & is propagated by cuttings.

SNATHE. The handle of a ſcythe.

SNEEZEWORT, [*Ptarmica.*] This grows wild upon heaths and in moiſt ſhady places; the flowers, which are of a white colour, come forth in June and July. The roots have an acrid ſmell, and a hot biting taſte: chewed, they occaſion a plentiful diſcharge of ſaliva; and when powdered and ſnuffed up the noſe, provoke ſneezing. Theſe are the only intentions to which they have been uſually applied.

SNOWDROP, [*Galanthus.*] This flower is valued for its early appearance in the ſpring, for it uſually blows in February when the ground is often covered with ſnow. The ſingle ſort comes out the firſt, and though the flowers are but ſmall, yet when the

roots

roots are in bunches they make a very pretty appearance; therefore these roots should not be planted single, as is sometimes practised by way of edging to borders; for when they are so disposed, they make very little appearance. But when there are twenty or more roots growing in a close bunch, the flowers have a very good effect; and as these flowers thrive well under trees or hedges, they are very proper to plant on the sides of wood-walks, and in wilderness quarters, where, if they are suffered to remain undisturbed, the roots will multiply exceedingly. The roots may be taken up the latter end of June, when their leaves decay, and may be kept out of the ground till the end of August; but they must not be removed oftner than every third or fourth year: these plants are got scarce in the gardens near London.

SNOWDROP-TREE. *See* FRINGE-TREE.

SOAP ASHES. *See* ASHES.

SOLDANEL, [*Soldanella.*] This plant is a native of the Alps, and the mountains of Germany, and may be propagated by parting the roots.

WATERSOLDIER, [*Stratiotes.*] Water Aloes, or Freshwater Soldier. This plant is like the aloes in shape, but the leaves are thinner and serrated on the edges very sharply. It grows naturally in standing waters of the Isle of Ely and other parts of England.

SOLOMON's SEAL, [*Polygonatum.*] This grows wild in woods, but is not very common: the root has several joints with some flat circular depressions, supposed to resemble the stamp of a seal. It has a sweetish mucilaginous taste. As to its virtues, practitioners do not now expect any considerable ones from it, and pay very little regard to the vulnerary qualities which it was formerly celebrated for.

SOOT. Soot is of two general kinds, the one, that which arises from wood, the other that of coal. These differ very much in many respects, but they are nearly the same in their effects and value to the farmer. The wood soot is solid and shining, the coal soot loofer, and of a deader colour. The wood soot sells in London at a great price, in comparison of the other, for the use of chymists and apothecaries, because it is scarcer, the fuel of London being, in general, coal: but in the country, where this is as common and cheap as the other, the farmers rather prefer coal soot.

Those who have written on husbandry, differ much in the kind to which they give the preference. Mortimer says sea-coal soot is by much the best, and Worlidge tells us, that soot is a good manure, especially such as is made of wood: these are both very honest and good writers; but experience is to be preferred to either. The truth is, that neither kind deserves a general preference, but that wood is better for some soils, and coal soot for others. Indeed the latter is best on the greatest number of soils, and therefore the farmer is right in valuing it the more. However, this difference is not so great, that any danger can arise from a mistake about it, for such land as will do well with one kind of soot, will also with another: all that the best choice can do gives only a little advantage.

As to the suiting the particular kinds of soot to the different soils, the rule is this. For all clayey, chalky, and mossy lands, the coal soot is best. And this is the reason why the coal soot is most in repute in London for this traffick, because the Hertfordshire farmers, who buy it almost entirely, have, for the most part, clayey or chalky soils to cultivate.

For gravelly, sandy, and loamy soils, the wood soot is preferable to that of coal; and in its nature indeed this kind is better and richer than the other, because, being made from a vegetable substance, it is richer and warmer than that other which comes from a mineral origin; but the great reason of the difference which suits one kind to one soil, and another to another, is the consistence. The wood soot is in firmer and harder lumps; the coal soot is crumbly; now in a clayey or a mossy soil, the lumps of the wood soot would lie a long time unbroken, whereas the coal soot breaks and mixes immediately. Experience shews also, that the wood soot will lie in large pieces a long time in a chalky land; whereas the gravelly sands, and sandy loams, cut and break it to pieces in two or three ploughings, and spread and mix it thoroughly.

SOPEBERRY-TREE, [*Sapindus.*] This plant grows naturally in the West-Indies, and rises with a woody stalk, to the height of 20 to 30 feet, bearing flowers in loose spikes at the end of its branches, succeeded by oval berries as large as middling cherries; the covering of these berries is sometimes used for soap to wash, when it is propagated by seeds.

SOPEWORT, [*Saponaria.*] This grows wild, though not very common, in low wet places, and by the sides of running waters; a double-flowered sort is frequent in our gardens. The leaves have a bitter, not agreeable taste; agitated with water, they raise a saponaceous froth, which is said to have nearly the same effects with solutions of soap itself in taking out spots from cloths, and the like. The roots taste sweetish and somewhat pungent; and have a light smell like those of liquorice: digested in rectified spirit they yield a strong tincture, which loses nothing of its taste or flavour in being inspissated to the consistence of an extract. This elegant root has not come much into practice among us, though it promises, from its sensible qualities, to be a medicine of considerable utility: it is greatly esteemed by the German physicians as an aperient, corroborant, and sudorific: and preferred by the college of Wirtemberg, Stahl, Neumann, and others, to sarsaparilla.

SORREL, [*Acetosa.*] Sorrel grows wild in fields and meadows throughout England. The leaves have a restringent acid taste, without any smell or particular flavour: their medical effects are, to cool, quench thirst, and promote the urinary discharge: a decoction of them in whey affords an useful and agreeable drink in frebile or inflammatory disorders: and is recommended by Boerhaave to be used in the spring as one of the most efficacious aperients and detergents. Some kinds of scurvies have yielded to the continued use of this medicine: the Greenlanders, who are very subject to this distemper, are said to employ, with good success, a mixture of the juices of sorrel and of scurvygrass. The only officinal preparation of this plant is an essential salt from the juice of the leaves.

Wood Sorrel, [*Lujula.*] This is a small plant, growing wild in woods. In taste and medical qualities, it is similar to the common sorrel, but considerably more grateful, and hence is preferred by the London college. Boiled with milk, it forms an agreeable whey; and beaten with sugar, a very elegant conserve, which has been for some time kept in the shops, and is now received in the dispensatory.

SOURSOP. See *Custard* Apple.

SOIL. A general name for all sorts of land. See Meadow-Pasture

SOURLAND. A cold, hungry, clayey soil.

SOUTHERNWOOD, [*Abrotanum Mas.*] This is a shrubby plant, clothed with very finely divided leaves, of a greyish green colour: the flowers, which are very small and yellowish, hang downwards, several together, from the middle of the branches to the top. It is a native of the warmer countries; in this it is cultivated in gardens: the leaves fall off every winter: the roots and stalks abide many years.

Southernwood has a strong, not very disagreeable smell; and a nauseous, pungent, bitter taste; which is totally extracted by rectified spirit, less perfectly by watery liquors. It is recommended as an anthelmintic; and in cold leucophlegmatic habits, as a stimulant, detergent, aperient, and sudorific. The present practice has almost entirely confined its use to external applications. The leaves are frequently employed in discutient and antiseptic fomentations; and have been recommended also in lotions and unguents for cutaneous eruptions, and the falling off of the hair.

SOW. The female of the swine.

SOWING. The act of distributing seed on the ground to produce a crop.

SOWBREAD, [*Cyclamen.*] This plant is met with in the gardens of the curious. The root has, when fresh, an extremely acrimonious burning taste, which it almost entirely loses on being dried. It is recommended as an errhine; in cataplasms for schirrous and scrophulous tumours; and internally as a cathartic, detergent, and aperient; it operates very slowly, but with great virulence, inflaming the fauces and intestines; and hence is deservedly rejected from the London dispensa-

dispensatory, though retained in that of Edinburgh.

SOWTHISTLE, [*Sonchus.*] This is a troublesome weed both in gardens and fields, and should be taken care of, that the seeds be not suffered to ripen, and be scattered by the wind.

SPANISH NUT. See FILBERT.

SPANISH ROSEMARY, [*Passerina.*] Sparrow-wort. This plant grows naturally at the Cape of Good Hope, rising with a shrubby stalk five or six feet high, and may be propagated by cuttings; sheltering the plants in the greenhouse during winter.

SPANISH BROOM, [*Spartium.*] This plant has long held a place in the English gardens, and is easily propagated by seeds. There are several species kept for variety.

SPANISH ELDER. See *Spanish* ELDER.

SPANISH PICKTOOTH, [*Visnaga.*] A species of carrot, growing naturally in Spain and Italy; the footstalks of the flowers are used as tooth-picks.

SPANISH MARJORAM, [*Urtica Dodartia.*] This is a species of nettle, growing naturally in Spain, and is easily propagated by seeds.

SPADE. A well-known instrument used in digging.

SPANCEL. A rope to tye a cow's hinder legs. Shackle.

SPATLING-POPPY. See CHICKWEED.

SPARSED-LEAVES. Are those which are placed irregularly about the several parts of a plant.

SPAVIN. A disease in horses, being a swelling in or near some of the joints, that causes a lameness.

There are two kinds of spavin, called a blood-spavin, and a bog-spavin.

A blood-spavin is a swelling and dilatation of the vein that runs along the inside of the hock, forming a little soft swelling in the hollow part, and is often attended with a weakness and lameness of the hock.

The cure should be first attempted with restringents and bandage, which will contribute greatly to strengthen all weaknesses of the joints, and frequently will remove this disorder, if early applied: but if by these means the vein is not reduced to its usual dimensions, the skin should be opened, and the vein tied with a crooked needle and wax thread passed underneath it, both above and below the swelling, and the turgid part suffered to digest away with the ligatures: for this purpose, the wound may be dressed with turpentine, honey, and spirit of wine, incorporated together.

A bog-spavin is an encysted tumour on the inside the hough, or, according to Dr. Bracken, a collection of brownish gelatinous matter, contained in a bag, or cyst, which he thinks to be the lubricating matter of the joint altered, the common membrane that incloses it forming the cyst: this case he has taken the pains to illustrate in a young colt of his own, where he says, when the spavin was pressed hard on the inside of the hough, there was a small tumour on the outside, which convinced him the fluid was withinside the joint: he accordingly cut into it, discharged a large quantity of this gelatinous matter, dressed the sore with dossils dipped in oil of turpentine, putting into it, once in three or four days, a powder made of calcined vitriol, allum and bole: by this method of dressing, the bag sloughed off, and came away, and the cure was successfully compleated without any visible scar.

This disorder, according to the above description, will scarcely submit to any other method, except firing, when the cyst ought to be penetrated to make it effectual; but in all obstinate cases that have resisted the above methods, both the cure of this, and the swellings called wind-galls, should, we think, be attempted in this manner. If, through the pain attending the operation or dressings, the joint should swell and inflame, foment it twice a day, and apply a poultice over the dressings till it is reduced.

SPAYING. The operation of castrating the females of several kinds of animals, as sows, bitches, &c. to prevent any farther conception, and promote their fattening.

It is performed by cutting them in the mid flank, on the left side, with a sharp knife or lancet, taking out the uterus and cutting it off, and so stitching up the wound, anointing the part with tar, and keeping the animal warm for two or three days. The usual way is to make the incision aslope two inches and a half long, that the fore finger may be put in towards the back to to feel for the ovaries, which are two kernels as big as acorns on both sides of the uterus, one of which is drawn to the wound, the string thereof cut, and thus both taken out.

Kings SPEAR. See ASPHODEL.

SPEAR MINT. See MINT.

SPEEDWELL, [*Veronica.*] There are several species of this plant growing wild in different parts of the kingdom, as also in other parts of Europe, the Female Speedwell is admitted into the Materia Medica, as is also the Male Speedwell. The Male Speedwell is a rough procumbent plant, not unfrequently met with on dry commons, and in sandy grounds. In taste, smell, and medical virtues, it is similar to the betonica, of which in its place: though the veronica is commonly supposed to have more of an aperient and pectoral virtue, and betony to be rather nervine and cephalic. Hoffman and Joh. Francus have written express treatises on this plant, recommending infusions of it, drank in the form of tea, as very salubrious in many disorders, particularly those of the breast. For Female Speedwell, see FLUELLIN.

SPELT. The name of a species of grain, which though commonly reckoned a summer corn, is sowed either in autumn or in the spring, at the same time as wheat and rye. This grain, of which there are two sorts, one with a single, and the other with a double chaff, though both have always two seeds in each husk, was formerly much esteemed in Italy and Egypt, and is now very common in Germany, where they make of it bread, which is very nourishing and well tasted, but hard to digest. They likewise brew beer from it in some places. It was of this grain that the ancients made their frumenty, of which they were very fond. Though commonly ranked as a species of wheat, which it is not unlike when growing, its grain is smaller and of a blackish hue, its stalk thinner and less firm, and its ear flat and bearded, with seeds only on each side. Some writers distinguish a third sort, by the name of white-rye, which they take to be the olyra of the Greeks and Latins; and seems to be what Mr. Mortimer calls taitico-speltum, a sort of naked barley, or wheat barley, cultivated in Staffordshire, shaped like barley, but with a grain like wheat. It is much sown at Rowley, Hamstal, and Redmore, where they call it French barley. It makes good bread and good malt, and yields a good increase; and therefore would do well to be tried in other places. It ripens early, does best in a dry soil, and is not apt to be much hurt by birds, from which its beard and double husk preserve it.

SPIDERWORT. See *African* ASPHODEL.

SPIGNEL, [*Athamanta.*] Spignel is an umbelliferous plant, found wild in Italy, and the warmer parts of Europe, and sometimes also in England. The roots have a pleasant aromatic smell, and a warm, pungent, bitterish taste: in virtue, they are similar to the Lovage, from which this root seems to differ only in being weaker, and somewhat more agreeable. It is an useful aromatic and carminative, tho' at present little regarded.

SPIKE. A large nail.

SPIKE, } See *Lavender.*
SPIKE LAVENDER. }

SPINACH, [*Spinacia.*] A well-known plant, cultivated in kitchen gardens.

It requires a rich, light, and well loosened soil. It is propagated by its seeds only, of which there are two sorts, namely, the rough and prickly, which produces the prickly spinach with arrow-pointed leaves, and the smooth, from which springs the spinach with oblong oval leaves.

The seeds of the first of these kinds, which is by much the hardiest, and therefore fittest to be cultivated for winter use, should be sown upon an open spot of ground, in August, just before a shower of rain, if it can luckily be so timed: for if the season should prove dry for a long while after the sowing, many of them will not sprout at all, and the plants of those that do grow will come up so irregularly, that half the crop will frequently be lost. It therefore is highly adviseable to water these seeds within two or three days after their being sown, if rain does not fall in the mean time.

When the plants begin to be strong, the ground on which they grow should be well hoed, to destroy the weeds, and to thin the plants to the distance of three or four inches asunderr. This, like

like all other hoeings, should always be performed in dry weather, the more effectually to kill the weeds: or, if it be rainy, they should be carried off the ground as soon as they are cut up, to prevent their taking fresh root: for if many of them spring up, and the season prove wet, they will stifle the plants of the spinach, and make them rot. A second careful hoeing is therefore necessary in about a month or five weeks after the first; and with the help of this the spinach will begin to be fit for use by the end of October. The best way of gathering it is, to crop off only the largest outer leaves, and to leave the middle ones to grow bigger: for by this means a regular supply may be had during the whole winter, and even till the subsequent spring sowing shall have produced plants large enough for use, which generally is in April. The winter spinach will also then be ready to run up, and should therefore be entirely cleared off, unless a parcel be left for seed, if wanted. But if early cabbages, which will want earthing up, have been planted among this spinach, as is the usual practice of the gardeners about London, a separate small spot of ground should be allotted purposely for sowing some of this spinach for seed, without any other plants among it, and to cut up all the remains of the other winter crop, as soon as the spring spinach is fit for use.

The oblong oval leaved spinach, commonly called plantain spinach, which has thicker leaves and more succulent stalks than the former sort, is sown in the spring, likewise upon an open spot of fine rich earth. The London gardeners, who always endeavour to have as many crops in a season as they possible can, generally mix radish seed with those of the spinach which they sow at this season: but the best way for those who have ground enough, is to sow their spinach seeds alone. This crop must be hoed, cleared from weeds, and thinned, in the manner before directed for the winter spinach; and when the plants, which were at first left three or four inches asunder, have grown so as to meet, it will be right to cut them out here and there for use, and to thin them in this manner, as they are wanted for the table, till those that are left stand eight or ten inches asunder. The thinnings in the mean time will give the remaining plants room to spread; and if, after this last, the ground between them is well stirred to a good depth, and kept perfectly clear from weeds, this sort of spinach will frequently produce leaves as large as those of the broad-leaved dock, and extremely fine.

A succession of spinach may be had throughout the whole season, by sowing it every three weeks, from about the middle of January to near the end of May; only observing, that the earliest sowings must be upon the naturally driest soils, and that the latest should be thinned most at their first hoeing, because the remains of the former crops will furnish a supply till these are full grown, and the plants will not be so apt to run up to seed when they stand at a distance from each other, as when they are close together.

In order to have good seeds of spinach, each particular sort should be sown by itself, in an open spot of rich and well dug ground. This sowing should be in February, as soon as the danger of the frost is over; and when the plants are come up, they should be thinned with a hoe till they are six or eight inches asunder every way. All weeds should at the same time be carefully cut up and carried off: and in about three weeks or a month after this, the plants should be hoed and thinned a second time. Their distance from each other should then be enlarged to at least twelve or fourteen inches: for they will cover the ground very sufficiently after they have shot out their side branches. Particular care is requisite at this time to keep them very clear from weeds; because these would make the plants of spinach run up weak, and thereby greatly injure them.

Mr. Miller is here extremely judicious in his directions for the farther management of spinach intended for seed. "When the plants, says he, have run up to flower, you will easily perceive two sorts among them, viz. male and female. The male will produce spikes of stamineous flowers, which contain the farina, and are absolutely

though it is a much lower plant than the common sort, but they esteem it a much better grass. The seeds of this kind are smaller and flatter than those of the common sort, and have a white border round each.

To SPRIT. To shoot or sprout, as seen in vegetation.

SPARREWAY. A horse-way through inclosed lands.

SPROUTHILL. Anthill.

SQUASH. See GOURD.

SQUILL, [*Scilla.*] There are two sorts, one with a red, and the other a white root, which are supposed to be accidental varieties, but the white are generally preferred for medicinal use. The roots are large, somewhat oval-shaped, composed of many coats, lying over each other like onions; at the bottom come out several fibres. From the middle of the root arise several shining leaves, which continue green all the winter, and decay in the spring; then the flower-stalk comes out, which rises two feet high, is naked half way, and terminated by a pyramidal thyrse of flowers, which are white, composed of six petals, which spread open like the points of a star. This grows naturally on the sea-shores, and in the ditches, where the salt water flows with the tide, in most of the warm parts of Europe, so cannot be propagated in gardens, the frost in winter always destroying the roots, and for want of salt water they do not thrive in summer. Sometimes the roots, which are brought for use, put out their stems, and produce flowers without being planted in earth, as they lie in the druggists shops.

The root for medicinal use should be chosen plump, sound, fresh, and full of a clammy juice; some have preferred the red sort, others the white, though neither deserves the preference to the other; the only difference perceivable betwixt them, is that of the colour; and hence the college allow both to be used promiscuously. This root is to the taste very nauseous, intensely bitter and acrimonious: much handled, it exulcerates the skin. With regard to its medical virtues, it powerfully stimulates the solids, and attenuates viscid juices; and by these qualities, promotes expectoration, urine, and (if the patient is kept warm) sweat: if the dose is considerable, it proves emetic, and sometimes purgative. The principal use of this medicine is where the primæ viæ abound with mucous matter, and the lungs are oppressed by tenacious phlegm. Dr. Wagner (in his clinical observations) recommends it given along with nitre, in hydropical swellings, and in the nephritis; and mentions several cures which he performed, by giving from four to ten grains of the powder for a dose, mixed with a double quantity of nitre: he says, that thus managed, it almost always operates as a diuretic, though sometimes it vomits or purges. The most commodious form for the taking of squills, unless when designed as an emetic, is that of a bolus or pill: liquid forms are to most people too offensive, though these may be rendered less disagreeable both to the palate and stomach, by the addition of aromatic distilled waters.

There are several species of squills, kept for the beauty of their flowers, besides those for medicinal purposes; among which are the flowers called the Starry Hyacinth, and the Hyacinth of Peru; they are all hardy, and propagated by seeds or offsets.

STABBING *of Cattle*. *See* HOVEN.

STAGGERS. *See* APOPLEXY.

STAFF *Tree*. *See* SPINDLE TREE.

STAGGERWORT. *See* Ragwort.

STAKE. A piece of wood, or a strong stick fixed in the ground.

STALE. Urine.

STALK. The stem or stock of a plant.

STALL. A crib at which an ox is fed, or where any horse is kept in a stable.

STALL-FED. Fed with dry feed, not with grass.

STALLION. A stone horse, designed for the covering of mares, in order to propagate the species.

STAMINA. Those fine threads or capillaments growing up within the flowers of tulips, lillies, and most other plants, around the style or pistil.

STAMINEOUS. An epithet applied to those flowers of plants which have no petals or flower-leaves, but consist only of a number of stamina and pistils placed in a cup.

STAMWOOD. The roots of trees grubbed up.

STANDARDS, *or* STANDRELS. Young trees reſerved at the felling of woods, for the growth of timber.

STANDARDS. Fruit-trees, intended to grow in an open expoſure, and not to be hacked and mangled with the knife, as the dwarf trees, and thoſe planted againſt walls are.

Theſe ſtocks ſhould not exceed two years growth from the bud or graft when they are planted. They ſhould be faſtened to ſtakes till they have acquired ſufficient ſtrength not to be in danger of being blown down.

STANK. A dam, or bank to ſtop water.

STAR APPLE, [*Chryſophillum.*] This tree grows naturally in the Weſt-Indies, riſing to the height of thirty or forty feet, bearing an auſtere fruit about the ſize of a golden pippin, which however becomes mellow and agreeable by keeping. It is propagated by ſeeds, but in England requires the general aſſiſtance of tender exotics.

STAR *of Bethlehem,* [*Ornithogalum.*] This plant grows naturally near Briſtol, and ſome other parts of England. It has a pretty large bulbous root, from which come out ſeveral long keel-ſhaped leaves, which ſpread on the ground. There are ſeveral other ſpecies growing naturally in Spain, Portugal, Africa, and Arabia.

STARCH. The fineſt parts of wheat flour, manufactured into cakes.

STAR HYACINTH. See SQUILL.

STARWORT. See ASTER.

Yellow STARWORT. Elecampane.

STAVES ACRE, [*Staphiſiſagria.*] This is a ſpecies of the larkſpur, growing naturally in the Levant and ſome parts of Italy. The ſeeds are large and rough, of an irregular triangular figure, of a blackiſh colour on the outſide, and yellowiſh or whitiſh within; they are uſually brought from Italy: the plant is not very common in this country, though it bears our ſevereſt colds. They have a diſagreeable ſmell, and a very nauſeous bitteriſh burning taſte. Staveſacre was employed by the ancients as a cathartic; but it operates with ſo much violence both upwards and downwards, that its internal uſe has been, among the generality of practitioners, for ſome time laid aſide. It is chiefly employed, in external applications, for ſome kind of cutaneous eruptions, and for deſtroying lice and other inſects; inſomuch, that it has from this virtue received its name in different languages, *herba pedicularis, herbe aux poux, lauſskraut, louſewort.*

STEE. A ladder.

STEM. That part of a plant ariſing from the root, and which ſuſtains the leaves, flowers, fruits, &c.

STEEPS. Certain preparations for ſteeping of corn intended to be ſown.

STELE. A ſtalk, a handle.

STEER. A young bullock.

STEG. A gander.

STERCORARY. A collection of dung properly ſecured from any injuries of the weather.

STERILE. Barren, unfruitful.

STEW. A ſmall kind of fiſh-pond, the peculiar intention of which is to maintain fiſh, and keep them for the daily uſes of a family.

STICKADORE. *See* CASSIDONY.

STOCK. The trunk or body of a fruit-tree, into which the graft, or bud is inſerted.

STOCK GILLIFLOWER. *See* GILLIFLOWER.

DWARF STOCK GILLIFLOWER. Dame's violet.

STONE. A certain quantity or weight of ſome commodities.

A ſtone of beef in London is the quantity of eight pounds; in Herefordſhire, twelve pounds; in the north 16 pounds; in other parts, 14 pounds.

A ſtone of wool, according to a ſtatute made in the eleventh year of the reign of Henry VII. is to weigh fourteen pounds, but in ſome places it is more, in others leſs; as in Glouceſterſhire fifteen pounds, in Herefordſhire twelve pounds.

A ſtone, among horſemen, is the weight of fourteen pounds.

STONE BREAK. A perennial plant common in paſture grounds. The root has a ſharpiſh and aromatic taſte. The ſtalks are round, ſtreaked, and reddiſh towards the bottom. The leaves are ſmooth, of a dark green, and divided twice into long, narrow, ſharp ſegments. The foot-ſtalks are membraneous at the baſe. The flowers grow in looſe umbels; and are of a pale yellow colour. The ſeeds are oval, ſtreaked, and red at the top.

STONY *Lands.* Such as are full of flints, pebbles, or ſmall fragments of free-ſtone. Theſe lands, in many places, yield good crops, and the general rule is, that in ſtiff and cold lands the ſtones ſhould be as carefully picked out as poſſible, but in light and dry grounds they ſhould be left. In Oxfordſhire they have great quantities of a lean earth, and a ſmall rubble ſtone, or a four ſort of land mixed with it; this is ſometimes very full of weeds, and ſometimes very clear of them. If they are weedy they fallow them late; but if they are ſcary, as they call it, that is, if they have a ſward upon them, they either ſold them in winter, and add ſome hay-ſeed to the ſheep's dung, to bring up the graſs; or elſe they lay old thatch or ſtraw, and dung upon it; for they reckon that if thoſe lands have no ſward upon them before they are fallowed, they will by no means be brought to bear a good crop, but a great deal of May-weed, and other uſeleſs weeds. In September, November, and December, they fallow as the ſward directs them; if this be done in either of the two laſt months, they call it a winter fallowing; and never ſtir it again, till they plow it, and ſow it with barley; and thoſe lands are reckoned to do better than if finely tilled. They will bear wheat and meſlin in a kindly year, and large crops of barley, if they are well managed, and kept in good heart.

They always fallow theſe lands every other year, unleſs they ſow peaſe upon them; ſometimes they ſow them with lentils, and when they are quite worn out, they lay them down for clover or rey-graſs. See - Gravel - Sand.

Stone Crop. Wall pepper.

Free Stone Crop. Gooſe foot.

STOOMING *of Wine*. Putting bags of herbs, or other ingredients into it.

STOOP. A poſt fixed in the earth.

STOT. A young bullock; a ſteer.

STOVES. Buildings erected in gardens for the preſervation of tender exotic plants, which will not live in theſe northern countries, without artificial warmth in winter. Theſe are built in different methods, according to the ingenuity of the artiſt, or the different purpoſes for which they are intended; but in England they are at preſent reducible to two.

The firſt is called a dry ſtove, being ſo contrived, that the flues through which the ſmoke paſſes are either carried under the pavement of the floor, or elſe are erected in the back part of the houſe, over each other, and are returned 6 or 8 times the whole length of the ſtove. In theſe ſtoves are commonly placed the tender ſorts of aloes, cereus's, euphorbiums, tithymals, and other ſucculent plants, which are impatient of moiſture in winter; and therefore require, for the moſt part, to be kept in a ſeparate ſtove, and not placed among trees, or herbaceous plants, which perſpire freely, and thereby often cauſe a damp air in the houſe, which is imbibed by the ſucculent plants, to their no ſmall prejudice.

Theſe ſtoves may be regulated by a thermometer, ſo as not to over-heat them, nor to let the plants ſuffer by cold; in order to which all ſuch plants as require nearly the ſame degree of heat, ſhould be placed by themſelves in a ſeparate houſe; for if in the ſame ſtove there are plants placed of many different countries, which require as many different heats, by making the houſe warm enough for ſome plants, others, by having too much heat, are drawn and ſpoiled.

The other ſorts of ſtoves are commonly called bark ſtoves, to diſtinguiſh them from the dry ſtoves already mentioned. Theſe have a large pit, nearly the length of the houſe, three feet deep, and ſix or ſeven feet wide, according to the breadth of the houſe; which pit is filled with freſh tanner's bark, to make an hot-bed; and in this bed the pots of the moſt tender exotic trees, and herbaceous plants, are plunged: the heat of this bed being moderate, the roots of the plants are always kept in action; and the moiſture, detained by the bark, keeps the fibres of their roots in a ductile ſtate, which, in the dry ſtove, where they are placed on ſhelves, are ſubject to dry too faſt, to the great injury of the plants. In theſe ſtoves, if they are rightly contrived, may be preſerved the moſt tender exotic trees and plants, which, before the uſe of the bark was introduced, were thought impoſſible to be kept in England; but, as there is ſome ſkill required in the ſtructure of both theſe ſtoves, we ſhall deſcribe them as intelligibly as poſſible, particularly the bark ſtove; by which it is hoped every curious perſon

person will be capable of directing his workmen in their structure.

The dimension of this stove should be proportioned to the number of plants intended to be preserved, or the particular fancy of the owner; but their length should not exceed forty feet, unless there are two fire-places; and in that case, it will be proper to make a partition of glass in the middle, and to have two tan-pits, that there may be two different heats for plants from different countries, for the reasons before given in the account of dry stoves; and a range of stoves, they should be all built in one, and only divided with glass partitions, at least the half way toward the front; which will be of great advantage to the plants, because they may have the air in each division shifted by sliding the glasses of the partitions, or by opening the glass-door, which should be made between each division, for the more easy passage from one to the other.

This stove should be raised above the level of the ground, in proportion to the dryness of the place; for, if it be built on a moist situation, the whole should be placed upon the top of the ground; so that the brick-work in the front must be raised three feet above the surface, which is the depth of the bark-bed, whereby none of the bark will be in danger of lying in water; but, if the soil be dry, the brick work in front need not be more than one foot above-ground, and the pit may be sunk two feet below the surface. Upon the top of this brick work, in front, must be laid the plate of timber, into which the wood work of the frame is to be mortifed; and the upper timber in front must be placed four feet asunder, or somewhat more, which is the proportion of the width of the glass-doors or sashes: these should be about six feet and a half, or seven feet long, and placed upright; but from the top of these should be sloping glasses, which should reach within three feet of the back of the stove, where there should be a strong crown-piece of timber placed, in which there should be a groove made for the glasses to slide into. The wall in the back part of the stove should be at least thirteen inches thick; but eighteen inches is still better; because, the thicker the outside wall is built, the more the heat of the flues will be kept in the house; and carried up, about nine feet above the surface of the bark-bed; and from the top of this wall, there should be a sloping roof to the crown-piece where the glasses slide in. This crown-piece should be about sixteen feet high from the surface of the bark-bed or floor, which will give a sufficient declivity to the sloping glasses to carry off the wet, and be of a reasonable height for containing many tall plants. The back roof may be slated, covered with lead, or tiled, according to the fancy of the owner: for the manner of this outside building is often very various, and differently built.

In the front of the house there should be a walk, about eighteen or twenty inches wide, for the conveniency of walking; next to which the bark pit must be placed, which should be in width proportioned to the breadth of the house: if the house is twelve feet wide, which is a due proportion, the pit may be seven feet wide; and behind the pit should be a walk eighteen inches wide, to pass in order to water the plants, &c. then there will be twenty-two inches left next the back wall, to erect the flues, which must be all raised above the top of the bark-bed; these flues ought to be one foot wide in the clear, that they may not be too soon stopped with the soot; and the lower flue, into which the smoke first enters from the fire, should be two feet deep in the clear; and this may be covered either with cast-iron plates, or broad tiles; over this the second flue must be returned back again, which may be eighteen inches deep, and covered on the top as before; and so, in like manner, the flues may be returned over each other three or four times, that the heat may be spent before the smoke passes off. The thickness of the wall in front of these flues need not be more than four inches; but it must be well jointed with mortar, and plaistered within side to prevent the smoke from getting into the house; and the outside should be faced with mortar, and covered with a coarse cloth, to keep the mortar from cracking, as is practised in setting up coppers. If this be carefully done there will be no danger of the ſmoke entering the houſe, which cannot be too carefully avoided; for there is nothing more injurious to plants than ſmoke, which will cauſe them to drop their leaves; and if it continue long in the houſe, will entirely deſtroy them.

The fire place may be made either at one end, or in the middle, according as there is moſt conveniency; for, wherever it is placed, it ſhould have a ſhed over it, and not be expoſed to the open air; for it will be impoſſible to make the fire burn equally, where the wind has full ingreſs to it; and it will be troubleſome to attend the fire in wet weather, where it is expoſed to the rain.

The contrivance of the furnace muſt be according to the fuel which is deſigned to burn; but as turf is the beſt firing for ſtoves, where it can be had, becauſe it burns more moderately, and laſts longer than any other ſort of fuel, and ſo requires leſs attendance, I ſhall deſcribe a proper ſort of furnace for that purpoſe.

The whole of this furnace ſhould be erected within the houſe, which will be a great addition to the heat; and the front wall on the outſide of the fire-place, next the ſhed, ſhould be three bricks thick, the better to prevent the heat from coming out that way. The door of the furnace, at which the fuel is put in, muſt be as ſmall as conveniently may be to admit of the fuel; and this door ſhould be placed near the upper part of the furnace, and made to ſhut as cloſe as poſſible; ſo that there may but little of the heat paſs off through it. This furnace ſhould be about twenty inches deep, and ſixteen inches ſquare at the bottom, but may be ſloped off on every ſide, ſo as to be two feet ſquare at the top; and under this furnace ſhould be a place for the aſhes to fall into, which ſhould be about a foot deep, and as wide as the bottom of the furnace: this ſhould alſo have an iron door to ſhut as cloſe as poſſible; but juſt over the aſh-hole, above the bars which ſupport the fuel, ſhould be a ſquare hole about four inches wide to let the air in to make the fire burn: this muſt alſo have an iron frame, and a door to ſhut cloſe when the fire is perfectly lighted, which will make the fuel laſt the longer, and the heat will be more moderate.

The top of this furnace ſhould be nearly equal to the top of the bark-bed, that the loweſt flue may be above the fire; ſo that there may be a greater draught for the ſmoke; and the furnace ſhould be covered with a large iron plate, cloſely cemented to the brick-work, to prevent the ſmoke from getting out; or it may be arched over with bricks; but you ſhould be very careful, wherever the fire is placed, that it be not too near the bark-bed; for the heat of the fire will, by its long continuance, dry the bark, ſo that it will loſe its virtue, and be in danger of taking fire; to prevent which, it will be the beſt method to continue an hollow between the brick-work of the fire and that of the pit, about eight inches wide; which will effectually prevent any damage ariſing from the heat of the fire; and there ſhould be no wood-work placed any where near the flues, or the fire-place, becauſe the continual heat of the ſtove may in time dry it ſo much, as to cauſe it to take fire; which ought to be very carefully guarded againſt.

The entrance into this ſtove ſhould be either from a green-houſe, the dry ſtove, or elſe through the ſhed where the fire is made, becauſe in cold weather, the front-glaſſes muſt not be opened.

The other ſort of ſtove, which is commonly called the dry ſtove, as was before ſaid, may be either built with upright and ſloping glaſſes at the top, in the ſame manner, and after the ſame model of the bark-ſtove; or elſe the front glaſſes, which ſhould run from the floor to the ceiling, may be laid ſloping, to an angle of forty-five degrees, the better to admit the rays of the ſun in ſpring and autumn: the latter method has been chiefly followed by moſt perſons who have built this ſort of ſtoves; but it is a better method to have it built after the model of the bark ſtove, with upright glaſſes in front, and ſloping glaſſes over them, becauſe this will more eaſily admit the ſun at all the different ſeaſons; for in ſummer, when the ſun is high, the top glaſſes will admit the rays to ſhine almoſt all over the houſe; and in winter, when the ſun is low, the front

front glasses will admit its rays; whereas, when the glasses are laid to any declivity in one direction, the rays of the sun will not fall directly thereon above a fortnight in autumn, and about the same time in spring; and, during the other parts of the year, they will fall obliquely thereon; and in summer, when the sun is high, the rays will not reach above five or six feet from the glasses.

Besides, the plants placed towards the back part of the house will not thrive in the summer season for want of air; whereas, when there are sloping glasses at the top, which run within four feet of the back of the house; these, by being drawn down in hot weather, will let in perpendicular air to all the plants; and, of how much service this is to all sort of plants, every one who has had opportunity of observing the growth of plants in a stove, will easily judge; for when plants are placed under cover of a ceiling, they always turn themselves towards the air and light, and thereby grow crooked; and if, in order to preserve them strait, they are turned every week, they will nevertheless grow weak, and look pale and sickly, like a person shut up in a dungeon; for which reasons, whoever has made trial of both sorts of stoves, will recommend the model of the bark-stove for every purpose. *Miller's Gardener's Dictionary.*

STOVER. Fodder for cattle.

STOUND. A wooden vessel to put small beer in.

STOWK. The handle of a pail; also a shock of twelve sheaves.

STOWRE. A round of a ladder; a hedge-stake; also the staves in the sides of a waggon, in which the everings are fastened.

STRAIN, *or* SPRAIN. A violent extension of the sinews or tendons of some muscle, whereby the tendinous fibres are over-stretched, and sometimes ruptured or broken.

As soon as a Horse is strained, we advise to turn the horse to grass immediately, external applications will then not be wanted, and if this be not done, applications will be of little or no use. Perhaps as good an embrocation as can be used is four ounces of good Vinegar and two ounces of Camphorated Spirit of Wine, with which the part may be bathed twice a day.

STRANGLES. A distemper to which colts and young horses are very subject; it begins with a swelling between the jaw-bones, which sometimes extend to the muscles of the tongue; and is attended with so great heat, pain, and inflammation, that sometimes till matter is formed, the horse swallows with the utmost dificulty.

Keep your horse tolerably warm, give him doses of nitre and sulphur twice a day, with meshes of bran and water barely warm.

STRANGURY. A disease in Cattle to be cured by giving decoctions of Marshmallow roots, in which a little Nitre and Gum Arabic is dissolved; keeping the body open with clysters.

STRAW the stalk of Corn.

STRAWBERRY [*Fragaria.*] The distinct species are, 1. the Wood-Strawberry; 2. the Virginian or scarlet Strawberry 3. the Hautboy; 4. the Chili Strawberry; with several other varieties.

An ingenious writer in the Museum Rusticum has obliged the world with the following method of cultivating strawberries.

" I have them, says he, of several kinds; and the fruit, in the season, is in great perfection, being large, and possessing a fine flavour. These I procure with no great trouble or difficulty in the cultivation.

" I plant them in regular rows on beds three feet wide. The soil I chuse for them is a good, natural, fresh, rich loam: the less it requires of manure the better, the fruit being the sweeter and finer.

" On each of these beds abovementioned, I plant three rows of plants, in quincunx order, at fifteen inches distance every way; and I rather chuse to plant them each on a little hillock, as it were, something in imitation of hops.

" Between the beds are intervals of the same width.

" My next care is, by frequent hoeing, to keep my plants as clear from weeds as possible, by which they are sure to be supplied with plenty of nourishment; a matter of great consequence, particularly when the fruit is set, as then they require most, and the weeds are also at that season most luxuriant;

luxuriant: I therefore then ſtir the earth with the hoe often, which anſwers as I have ſaid before, a double purpoſe.

" I obſerve to keep my plants as clear as poſſible from runners; by which means my fruit is larger, and ſooner ripe than it would otherwiſe be.

" When my ſtrawberry plants have borne fruit two ſucceſſive years on the beds, I get the alleys, or intervals, dug up and prepared, into which I tranſplant them in the ſame manner they were planted in the firſt-mentioned beds, which then become in their turn the intervals.

" Here they remain two years more, when I again remove them into freſh land prepared for the purpoſe, in this manner never letting them bear fruit more than two years in one ſpot.

" I cannot eaſily deſcribe to you the great benefit this method of management is of to the plants, which are thereby greatly invigorated, and the fruit prodigiouſly improved, both in point of ſize and flavour, inſomuch that they appear to be quite of a different nature from thoſe of my neighbours, who firſt furniſhed me with the plants." '

STRAWBERRY BLITE. *See* Blite.

STRAWBERRY SPINACH. *See* Blite.

STRAWBERRY TREE, [*Arbutus*.] The ſpecies are, 1. Strawberry-tree with ſmooth ſawed leaves, berries having many ſeeds, and an upright trunk. This ſort grows naturally in Italy, Spain, and alſo in Ireland, and is now very common in the Engliſh gardens. It produces the following varieties, viz. one with an oblong flower and oval fruit; another with a double flower; and a third with red flowers.

2. Strawberry tree with ſmooth entire leaves, berries full of ſeeds, and an erect woody ſtem. This kind grows in the eaſt, particularly about Magneſia, where it is ſo plenty, as to be the principal fuel uſed by the inhabitants of the country. This grows to a middle-ſized tree; the branches are irregular, and are garniſhed with large oval leaves, ſomewhat like thoſe of the Bay tree, but not quite ſo long; theſe are ſmooth and entire, having no ferratures on their edges; the flowers are ſhaped like thoſe of the common Arbutus, but grow thinly on the branches. The fruit is oval, and of the ſame colour and conſiſtence with the common ſort, but the ſeeds of this are flat, whereas thoſe of the common ſort are pointed and angular.

3. Arbutus with trailing ſtalks, oval leaves, ſomewhat indented, flowers growing looſely, and many ſeeds. This ſort grows naturally in Acadia, and other northern parts of America, upon ſwampy land, which is frequently overflowed with water; this is a low, buſhey ſhrub, with ſlender trailing branches, which are garniſhed with oval leaves, a little ſawed on their edges; the flowers come out from the wings of the leaves, growing in thin looſe bunches. The fruit of this ſort is never produced in England, and it is with great difficulty the plants are kept alive here.

4. Arbutus with trailing ſtalks and rough ſawed leaves. This grows naturally on the Alps and the Helvetian mountains. It never riſes high, but ſends out from the root many ſlender branches, which trail upon the ground, garniſhed with oblong rough leaves, of a pale green colour; the flowers are produced from the wings of the leaves, upon long ſlender foot-ſtalks, and are ſucceeded by berries abou tthe ſize of the common black Cherry, which are firſt green, afterwards red, and when ripe are black. Theſe are of a pleaſant taſte, ſo are frequently eaten by the inhabitants of thoſe countries where they grow naturally. This is a very difficult plant to keep alive in gardens, for it is an inhabitant of bogs, growing among moſs. Where the ground is never dry.

5. Arbutus with trailing ſtalks and entire leaves. This grows naturally upon the mountains in Spain, and in moſt of the northern parts of Europe. The branches trail on the ground, which are cloſely garniſhed with ſmooth thick leaves of an oval form, placed alternately; the flowers are produced in ſmall bunches towards the extremity of the branches, which are ſhaped like thoſe of the common ſort, but ſmaller; and are ſucceeded by berries, of the ſame ſize with thoſe of the former ſort, which are red when ripe.

The common Strawberry tree is well known, being at preſent in moſt

of

of the English gardens, and one of their greatest ornaments in the months of October and November, that being the seasen when the trees are in flower, and the fruit of the former year is ripe, for the fruit is a whole year growing to perfection; so that the fruit which is produced from the flowers of one year do not ripen till the blossoms of the succeeding year are fully blown; when there is plenty of fruit and flowers upon the trees they make a fine appearance, and at a season when most other trees are past their beauty.

Those trees which have large oval fruit make the greatest figure, their flowers being larger, and oblong. The sort with double flowers is a curiosity; but as the flowers have only two orders of leaves, so they make no great appearance; nor do the trees produce fruit in any plenty, therefore the other is preferable. The sort with red flowers makes a pretty variety, when intermixed with the other; for the outsides of them are of a fine red colour at their first appearance, and afterwards they change to purple before they fall off. The fruit of this is the same with the common sort. All these varieties are preserved by inarching or grafting them upon the common Arbutus, for the seeds of either do not produce the same kind; though from the seeds of the oval fruit, there are generally many more of the same produced than from the seeds of the common sort.

The best method to propagate the Arbutus is from seeds; therefore when the fruit is perfectly ripe, it should be gathered and mixed with dry sand, to preserve it till the time for sowing; the surest method of raising the plants is to sow the seeds in pots, which should be plunged into an old bed of tanner's bark, which has lost its heat, covering the bed with glasses, &c. to keep out the frost; this should be done in December; if the seeds are good, and as the spring advances the pots are refreshed with water, the plants will come up the beginning of April, when they should be frequently but sparingly watered, and constantly kept clean from weeds.

As the summer advances, if the plants are shaded in the heat of the day, it will greatly promote their growth; but in warm weather they must be open all night to receive the dew, so should only be covered in the middle of the day: with this management the plants will rise to the height of five or six inches the first summer.

STRICKLE. The whet-stone placed upon the extremity of the shaft of a scythe.

STRIKE. A bushel, or four pecks of corn.

STRINGHALT. A disease in horses, consisting in a twitching and snatching up of the hinder leg much higher than the other.

STUBBLE. The stalks of corn left in the field by the reaper.

STUM. The unfermented juice of the grape, after it has been several times racked off, and separated from its sediment.

STUMP. The part of any solid body, particularly of trees, &c. remaining after the rest are taken away.

STUMPY. Full of stumps; hard, stiff.

STURK. A young bullock.

STY. A cabbin or small building to keep hogs in.

SUCCORY. See Endive.

Gum Succory. See Gum Succory.

SACCHARUM. The sugar cane. This plant grows naturally in the West-Indies, Arabia, &c. where its juice is boiled, and made into sugar.

Sugar Maple. See Maple.

SUCKER. A young twig, or shoot from the root.

SUFFOLK GRASS. The same with meadow grass, or poa.

SUILLAGE. A drain of filth.

SULL. A plough.

SULL-PADDLE. A plough paddle.

SULPHURWORT. Hogs fennel.

SULTAN FLOWER, } A species of
Sweet Sultan, } centaury, which may be propagated by sowing the seeds, on a hot-bed in the spring, and then managing them as other annuals, not very hardy.

SUMACH, [*Rhus*.] This tree, or shrub, is cultivated in some places on account of the culinary uses of its fruits, and for the purposes of the dyers, &c. among us, it is met with only in the gardens of the curious. The seeds or berries are of a red colour, in shape round and flat. Both these and the

the leaves are moderately astringent, and have sometimes been exhibited in this intention, but are now become strangers to the shops.

There are several species, no less than 15, reckoned by Miller, which are kept in the gardens for variety or ornament; some of which, natives of Africa, are too tender to bear the open air of the winters in England. They are all propagated by cuttings or layers.

SUMMER. The season in which the sun arrives at the northern solstice, and the days are at the greatest length.

SUMMER, also implies the large piece of timber, or principal beam, of a floor.

To SUMMER-LAND, or *To* SUMMER-STIR. To fallow land in the summer.

SUNDEW. See ROS SOLIS.

SUN-FLOWER. The name of a well-known flower, much cultivated in large gardens.

The sun-flower is an annual plant, and the seeds should be sown every spring in a bed of good light earth. When the shoots are about three inches they should be transplanted into nursery beds, and set at eight inches distance every way; they should remain there till they are a foot high, and then be carefully taken up with a ball of earth at their roots, and planted in large borders, or intermixed with flowering shrubs, and other large plants; they must be frequently watered till they have taken root, after which they require no other care. The flowers appear in July, and stand a considerable time: the largest of them should be preserved for seed. The birds are very fond of the seed of the sun-flower, and must therefore be carefully guarded from them, and the head left on the plant till October, at which time it should be cut off, and hung up to dry in an airy place, and in a month more the seeds will be perfectly hardened.

Dwarf SUN-FLOWER, [*Rudbeckia.*] This is a native of North-America, but will bear sometimes in the open air of our English climate; there are several species, which are propagated by parting the roots.

SUN-SCORCHED. A term used in some parts of England to express a distemperature of fruit-trees, owing to the sun's affecting them too forcibly on a sudden; the consequence of which is the loss and withering of the fruit. Such trees only are subject to this, as are planted in places sheltered from the spring sun, and open to that of the summer; and may be always cured by proper waterings.

SUNSPURGE. Euphorbium.

SURBATING. A term used by farriers to signify the sole of a horse's foot being worn, bruised, or spoiled by beating the hoof against the ground in travelling without shoes, or going in hot sandy lands, or with a shoe that hurts the sole, or the like. It also sometimes happens by over riding a horse while young, before his feet are sufficiently hardened, or even by the hardness of the ground, and high lifting of his feet. The signs of this defect are his halting on both fore legs, going stiffly, and creeping as if foundered.

There is nothing better for surbated feet than tar melted into the foot, or vinegar boiled with soot to a proper consistence and poured into the foot boiling hot, with hurds over it, and splints to keep it in.

SURFEIT. A disease incident to horses and other cattle.

Surfeits arise from various causes; but are commonly the effects of some diseases not attended to, or that have been ill cured.

A horse is said to be surfeited, when his coat stares, and looks rusty and dirty, though proper means have not been wanting to keep him clean. The skin is full of scales and dander, that lays thick and mealy among the hair, and is constantly supplied with a fresh succession of the same, for want of due transpiration. Some horses have hurdles of various sizes like pease or tares: some have dry fixed scabs all over their limbs and bodies; others a moisture attended with heat and inflammation; the humours being so sharp, and violently itching, that the horses rub so incessantly, as to make themselves raw. Some have no eruptions at all, but an unwholsome look, and are dull, sluggish, and lazy: some appear only lean and hide bound: others have flying pains and lameness, resembling a rheumatism: so that in the surfeits of horses, we have almost all the different species of the scurvy, and other chronical distempers.

The

The following method is usually attended with success in the dry species. First take away about three or four pounds of blood; and then give the following mild purge, which will work as an alterative, and should be repeated once a week or ten days for some time.

Take Succotrine aloes six drams, or one ounce; gum guaiacum half an ounce; diaphoretic antimony, and powder of myrrh, of each two drams: make into a ball with syrup of buckthorn.

In the intermediate days, an ounce of the following powder should be given morning and evening in his feeds.

Take native cinnabar, or cinnabar of antimony, finely powdered, half a pound; crude antimony, in fine powder, four ounces; gum guaiacum, also in powder, four ounces: make into sixteen doses for eight days.

This medicine must be repeated till the horse coats well, and all the symptoms of surfeit disappear. If the horse is of small value, two or three common purges should be given, and half an ounce of antimony, with the same quantity of sulphur, twice a day, or the alterative balls with camphor and nitre.

If the little scabs on the skin do not peel off, anoint them with the mercurial ointment; during the time of using which, it will be proper to keep the horse dry, and to give him warm water. This ointment properly rubbed into the blood, with the assistance of purging physick, has frequently cured these kinds of surfeits, without any other assistance.

The wet surfeit, which is no more than a moist running scurvy, appears on different parts of the body of a horse, attended sometimes with great heat and inflammation; the neck oftentimes swells so in one night's time, that great quantities of a hot briny humour issue forth, which, if not allayed, will be apt to collect on the poll or withers, and produce the poll-evil or fistula. This disease also frequently attacks the limbs, where it proves obstinate, and hard to cure: and in some horses shews itself spring and fall.

In this case bleed plentifully, avoid externally all repellers, and give cooling physic twice a week; as, four ounces of lenitive electuary, with the same quantity of cream of tartar; or the latter, with four ounces of Glauber salts, quickened, if thought proper, with two or three drams of powder of jalap, dissolved in water-gruel, and given in a morning fasting.

After three or four of these purges, two ounces of nitre made into a ball with honey may be given every morning for a fortnight; and if attended with success, repeated for a fortnight longer.

The powders above-mentioned may also be given with the horse's corn; or a strong decoction of guaicum shavings, or logwood, may be given alone to the quantity of two quarts a day. These, and indeed all alterative medicines, must be continued for a long time, where the disorder proves obstinate.

The diet should be cool and opening, as scalded bran or barley; and if the horse is hide-bound, an ounce of fenugreek seeds should be given in his feeds for a month or longer; and as this disorder often proceeds from worms, give the mercurial physic too, and afterwards the cinnabar powders, as above directed; but as in general it is not an original disease, but a symptom only of many, in the cure, regard must be had to the first cause: thus, as it is an attendant on surfeits, fevers, worms, &c. the removal of this complaint must be variously effected.

In a mangy horse the skin is generally tawny, thick, and full of wrinkles, especially about the mane, the loins and tail, and the little hair that remains in those parts stands almost always strait out or bristly: the ears are commonly naked and without hair, the eye and eye-brows the same; and when it affects the limbs, it gives them the same aspect; yet the skin is nor raw, nor peels off, as in the hot inflamed surfeit.

Where this distemper is caught by infection, if taken in time it is very easily cured; and we would recommend a sulphur ointment as most effectual for that purpose, rubbed in every day. To purify and cleanse the blood, give antimony and sulphur for some weeks after. There are a great variety of external remedies for this purpose, such as train oil and gunpowder, tobacco steeped in chamberlye, &c. Solleysell recommends the following:

Take burnt allum and borax in fine powder, of each two ounces; white vitriol and verdigrease powdered, of each four ounces; put them into a clean pot, with two pounds of honey, stirring till they are incorporated; when cold, add two ounces of strong aquafortis.

But when this disorder is contracted by low feeding, and poverty of blood, the diet must be mended, and the horse properly indulged with hay and corn. The following ointments are effectually used for this disorder, rubbed into the parts affected every day:

Take powdered brimstone, train oil, and tar, of each equal quantities; to which may be added ginger, or white hellebore. Or,

Take sulphur vivum, half a pound, crude sal ammoniac one ounce; hogs lard, or oil, a sufficient quantity to form into an ointment.

Or this:

Take quicksilver, and oil of vitriol, of each one ounce; hogs lard, one pound, sulphur vivum four ounces, oil of turpentine one ounce and half.

These are both very powerful remedies for this disorder, and can scarce fail of success.

To the two first, occasionally, may be added a third part of mercurial ointment; but as sulphur is in general allowed to be the specific in the itch, and being found both more safe and efficacious than mercury; so we apprehend it will sufficiently answer the purpose here; for as this disorder seems best accounted for by Leuwenhoek, from certain small insects he discovered in the pustules by the microscope; so it seems as if they were destroyed by the steams of brimstone, though only raised by the heat of the body; for in the human body, the itch may be cured by partial sulphureous unctions on the legs only; but where the mange proves obstinate in horses, let the parts be washed with sublimate water before the application of the ointment, and subjoin the internal use of sulphur, in order to diffuse the steams more certainly through the skin; there being reason to believe, as in the itch, that the animalculæ may sometimes lie too deep to be thoroughly destroyed by external applications only.

SUGAR. The essential salt of the *arundo saccharifera*, a beautiful large cane growing spontaneously in the East-Indies, and some of the warmer parts of the West, and cultivated in great quantity in our American plantations. The expressed juice of the cane is clarified with the addition of lime water (without which it does not assume the form of a true sugar) and boiled down to a due consistence; when, being removed from the fire, the saccharine part concretes from the grosser unctuous matter, called treacle, or melasses. This, as yet impure or brown sugar, is farther purified, in conical moulds, by spreading moist clay on the upper broad surface: the watery moisture, slowly percolating through the mass, carries with it a considerable part of the remains of the treacly matter. This clayed sugar, imported from America, is by our refiners dissolved in water, the solution clarified by boiling with whites of eggs and despumation, and after due evaporation poured into moulds: as soon as the sugar has concreted, and the fluid part drained off, the surface is covered with moist clay as before. The sugar, thus once refined, by a repetition of the process, becomes the double-refined sugar of the shops. The candy, or crystals, are prepared by boiling down solutions of sugar to a certain pitch, and then removing them into a hot room, with sticks set across the vessel for the sugar to shoot upon: these crystals prove of a white or brown colour, according as the sugar was pure or impure.

The uses of sugar as a sweet, are sufficiently well known. The impure sorts contain an unctuous, or oily matter, in consequence of which they prove emollient and laxative. The crystals are most difficult of solution, and hence are properest where this soft lubricating sweet is wanted to dissolve slowly in the mouth.

SURVEYING. The art or act of measuring of lands; that is, of taking the

the dimensions of any field, parcel, or tract of land, laying down the same in a map or draught, and finding the area or content thereof.

SWALLOW WORT, [*Vincetoxicum*] Tame poison.

SWAMP. A hollow, watery place, in any part of a field; a bog. See BOG.

SWANG. A fresh piece of green sward lying in a bottom among arable or barren land.

SWARD. The surface of the ground.

SWARM. A large number of bees, seeking a proper settlement. See BEE.

SWATH, or *Swarth*. A line of grass, &c. cut down by the mower.

SWATH-BUCK. A swarth, or line of new-mown grass or corn.

SWATH-RAKE. A rake about two yards long, with iron teeth, and a bearer in the middle, to which a man fixes himself with a belt; and when he has gathered as much as his rake will hold, he raises it and begins again. This instrument is in some counties called a dow-rake, and much used in Essex for gathering barley after mowing.

SWEET APPLE. *See* Custard Apple.

SWEET PEA. *See* Everlasting Pea.

SWEET JOHN, } *See* CARNATION.
SWEET WILLIAM, }

SWEET WILLOW. Candleberry-tree.

SWEAL. To singe, or burn off the hair, &c.

SWILL. A vessel to wash in, standing on three feet. Hog-drink.

SWINE. See HOG.

SWINE-CRUE. A hog's-sty.

SWINE-HERD. A keeper of swine.

SWINHULL. A hog's-sty.

SWINE'S CRESS. Scurvy-grass.

Swolled or Swolled Neck. See Clush–

SYCAMORE, or *Wild Fig-Tree*, falsely so called, is our acer majus, or broad-leaved Mas, one of the maples, and is much more in reputation for its shade than it deserves; for the honey-dew leaves, which fall early, like those of the ash, turn to mucilage and noxious insects, and putrefy with the first moisture of the season, so as they contaminate and marr our walks; and are therefore, by my consent, to be banished from all curious gardens and avenues. It is raised of the keys in the husk, as soon as ripe, and they come up the first spring; also by roots and layers, in ground moist, not over wet or stiff, and must be governed as other nursery plants. There is in Germany a better sort of sycamore than ours (nor are ours indigenous) wherewith they make saddle-trees, and divers other things of use. Our own is excellent for trenchers, cart and plow-timber, being light, tough, and not much inferior to ash itself; and if the trees be very tall and handsome, they are the more tolerable for distant walks, especially where other better trees prosper not so well, or where a sudden shade is expected: Some commend them to thicken copses, especially in parks, as least apt to the spoil of deer, and that it is good fire-wood. This tree being wounded, bleeds a great part of the year; the liquor emulating that of the birch. The sap is sweet and wholesome, and in a short time yields sufficient quantity to brew with, so as with one bushel of malt is made as good ale as four bushels with ordinary water, upon Dr. Tongue's experience. Phil. Trans. vol. iv. fol. 917.—*Evelyn*.

SYRINGA. Lilac.

SYTHE. See SCYTHE.

T.

TABERN. A cellar.

TAGGE. A ſheep of the firſt year.

TAIL-SOAKED. A diſeaſe incident to cows, by which the joint of the tail near the rump, will, as it were, rot away. The cure is generally performed by cutting a deep gaſh into the part affected, then rubbing a handful of ſalt into the wound, and binding it with a rag. Others mix ſoot and a clove of garlick with the ſalt.

TACAMAHACCA-TREE. A ſpecies of the poplar.

TACAMAHACCA. A reſin obtained from a tall tree, which grows ſpontaneouſly on the continent of America, and in a ſheltered ſituation bears the winters of our own climate. Two ſorts of this reſin are ſometimes to be met with. The beſt, called (from its being collected in a kind of gourd-ſhells) tacamahacca in ſhells, is ſomewhat unctuous and ſoftiſh, of a pale yellowiſh or greeniſh colour, an aromatic taſte, and a fragrant delightful ſmell, approaching to that of lavender and ambergris. This ſort is very rare: that commonly found in the ſhops is in ſemitranſparent grains or glebes, of a whitiſh, yellowiſh, browniſh, or greeniſh colour, of a leſs grateful ſmell than the foregoing. The firſt is ſaid to exude from the fruit of the tree, the other from inciſions made in the trunk. This reſin is ſaid to be employed among the Indians, externally, for diſcuſſing and maturing tumours, and abating pains and aches of the limbs: it is an ingredient in the anodyne, hyſteric, cephalic, and ſtomachic plaſters of the Edinburgh pharmacopœia. The fragrance of the finer ſort ſufficiently points out its being applicable to other purpoſes.

TALCK. Talcky earth is ſcarcely alterable by a vehement fire. The maſſes of this earth are generally of a fibrous or leafy texture; more or leſs pellucid, bright or glittering; ſmooth and unctuous to the touch; too flexible and elaſtic to be eaſily pulverized; ſoft, ſo as to be cut with a knife. In theſe reſpects ſome of the gypſeous earths greatly reſemble them, but the difference is readily diſcovered by fire; a weak heat reducing the gypſeous to powder, while the ſtrongeſt makes no other alteration in the talcky, than ſomewhat diminiſhing their flexibility, brightneſs, and unctuoſity.

TAMARIND. This tree grows naturally in both Indies, and alſo in Egypt; but it has been ſuppoſed by ſome eminent botaniſts, that the tamarind which grew in the Eaſt-Indies was different from that of the Weſt, becauſe the pods of the firſt are almoſt double the length of thoſe of the latter. The pods which have been brought from the Eaſt-Indies have generally been ſo long as to contain five, ſix, and ſometimes ſeven ſeeds, whereas thoſe of the Weſt-Indies have very rarely more than four; but the plants raiſed from the ſeeds of both ſorts are ſo like as not to be diſtinguiſhed.

This tree grows to a very large ſize in thoſe countries where it is a native, but in England it will not thrive out of a ſtove, eſpecially in winter. The ſtem is very large, covered with a brown bark, and divides into many branches at the top, which ſpread wide every way, and are cloſely garniſhed with winged leaves, compoſed of ſixteen or eighteen pair of lobes, without a ſingle one at the end. The lobes are about half an inch long, and a ſixth part of an inch broad, of a bright green, a little hairy, and ſit cloſe to the midrib. The flowers come out from the ſide of the branches, five, ſix, or more together upon the ſame footſtalk in looſe bunches; theſe are compoſed of five reddiſh petals, one of which

which is reflexed upward like the ſtandard in ſome of the butterfly flowers, two others ſtand on each ſide like the wings, and the other two are turned downwards; theſe (in the countries where the plants grow naturally) are ſucceeded by thick compreſſed pods, two, three, four or five inches long, having a double ſkin or cover, and ſwell in every place where the ſeeds are lodged, full of an acid ſtringy pulp, which ſurrounds ſmooth, compreſſed, angular ſeeds.

The tamarinds which are brought from the Eaſt-Indies are darker and drier, but contain more pulp, being preſerved without ſugar, and are fitter to be put into medicines than thoſe from the Weſt-Indies, which are redder, have leſs pulp, and are preſerved with ſugar, ſo are pleaſanter to the palate.

The pulp of theſe fruits, taken in the quantity of two or three drams, or an ounce or more, proves gently laxative or purgative; and at the ſame time, by its acidity, quenches thirſt, and allays immoderate heat. It increaſes the action of the purgative ſweets, caſſia and manna, and weakens that of the reſinous cathartics. Some have ſuppoſed it capable of abating the virulence of antimonial preparations; but experience ſhews that it has a contrary effect, and that all vegetable acids augment their power. Tamarinds are an ingredient in the electuary of caſia, the lenitive electuary, and decoction of tamarinds with ſena.

The plants are preſerved in the gardens of thoſe who have conveniency to maintain rare exotic-trees and ſhrubs.

They are eaſily propagated by ſowing their ſeeds on a hot-bed in the ſpring; and when the plants are come up, they ſhould be planted each into a ſeparate ſmall pot, filled with light rich earth, and plunged into a hot-bed of tanner's bark to bring them forward, obſerving to water and ſhade them until they have taken root; and as the earth in the pots appear dry, they muſt be watered from time to time, and ſhould have air given to them in proportion to the warmth of the ſeaſon, and the bed in which they are placed. When the pots in which they are planted are filled with their roots, the plants ſhould be ſhifted into pots of a larger ſize, which muſt be filled up with rich light earth, and again plunged into the hot-bed, giving them air as before, according to the warmth of the ſeaſon. In very hot weather the glaſſes ſhould be ſhaded with mats in the heat of the day, otherwiſe the ſun will be too violent for them through the glaſſes, nor will the plants thrive if they are expoſed to the open air, even in the warmeſt ſeaſon; ſo that they muſt be conſtantly kept in the bark-ſtove both ſummer and winter, where if rightly managed, they will grow very faſt.

TAMARISK, [*Tamarix.*] There are two ſpecies of this tree; one with flowers having five ſtamina; the other whoſe flowers have ten ſtamina. The firſt grows naturally in the ſouth of France, in Spain and Italy, where it arrives to a tree of middling ſize; but in England is ſeldom more than fourteen or ſixteen feet high. The other grows naturally in Germany, in moiſt land: it is rather a ſhrub than a tree, having ſeveral ligneous ſtalks ariſing from the ſame root, which grow erect, ſending out many ſide-branches which are alſo erect.

Both theſe ſorts caſt their leaves in autumn, and it is pretty late in the ſpring before the young leaves puſh out, which renders them leſs valuable; they are now frequently planted in gardens for ornament, and when mixed with other ſhrubs, make a pretty variety.

The culture of both ſorts of tamariſk is very eaſy: every cutting will grow that is ſet in winter, and will be a good plant by the autumn following. The cuttings ſhould be of the laſt ſummer's ſhoot; and a moiſt part of the garden is moſt eligible for them to be planted in. In two years they will be good plants for the wilderneſs or ſhrubbery, and may then be planted out in almoſt any ſoil, though they beſt like a light moiſt earth, eſpecially the German ſort; for in countries where it grows naturally, it is generally found in low watery grounds.

The bark and leaves of this tree are moderately aſtringent; they are never met with in preſcription, and have long been entire ſtrangers to the ſhops.

TAME-POISON, [*Vincitoxicum.*] Swallow-wort. This is a native of the warmer climates: it is ſometimes

met

met with in our gardens, but rarely perfects its ſeeds. It is reckoned by botaniſts a ſpecies of apocynum, or dogſbane; from all the poiſonous ſorts of which it may be diſtinguiſhed, by yielding a limpid juice, whilſt that of the others is milky. The root has a ſtrong ſmell, eſpecially when freſh, approaching to that of valerian, or nard; the taſte is at firſt ſweetiſh and aromatic, but ſoon becomes bitteriſh, ſubacrid, and nauſeous. This root is eſteemed ſudorific, diuretic, and emmenagogue, and is frequently employed by the French and German phyſicians as an alexipharmac, ſometimes as a ſuccedaneum to contrayerva, whence it has received the name of contrayerva Germanorum. Among us, it is very rarely made uſe of: it appears from its ſenſible qualities, to be a medicine of much the ſame kind with valerian, which is indiſputably preferable to it.

TAN. The bark of oak, chopped and ground by a tanning mill into a coarſe powder, to be uſed in the tanning or dreſſing of ſkins.

Tan is of great uſe in gardening: firſt, by its fermentation, when laid in a body, which is always moderate and of long duration, which renders it of great ſervice to hot-beds: and ſecondly, after it is well rotted, it becomes excellent manure for all ſorts of cold ſtiff land; upon which one load of tan is better than two of rotten dung, and will continue longer in the ground.

The uſe of tan for hot-beds has not been many years known in England; the firſt hot-beds of this ſort, which were made in England, were at Blackheath, in Kent, about fifty-five years ago: theſe were deſigned for raiſing of orange-tees; but, the uſe of theſe hot-beds being but little known at that time, they were made but by two or three perſons, who had learned the uſe of them in Holland and Flanders, where the gardeners ſeldom make any other hot-beds: but in England there were very few hot-beds made of Tanner's bark, before the ananas were introduced into this country, which was in 1719, ſince which time the uſe of theſe hot-beds have been more general; and are now made in all thoſe gardens where the ananas plants are cultivated, or where there are collections of tender exotic plants preſerved.

Tank. See Stank.

TANSEY, [*Tanacetum.*] The name of a plant often cultivated in kitchen-gardens, and of which there are three varieties, that have all been produced accidentally from the ſeeds of the common tanſey. All the varieties are eaſily propagated by the creeping roots, which, if allowed to remain undiſturbed, will overſpread the ground where they are permitted to grow; ſo that wherever tanſey is planted in a garden, the ſlips ſhould be placed two feet aſunder, and in particular beds, where the paths round them may be often dug, to keep their roots within bounds. They may be tranſplanted either in ſpring or autumn, and will thrive in almoſt any ſoil or ſituation.

Conſidered as a medicine, it is a moderately warm bitter, accompanied with a ſtrong, not very diſagreeable flavour: ſome have had a great opinion of it in hyſteric diſorders, particularly thoſe proceeding from a deficiency, or ſuppreſſion of the uterine purgations. The leaves and ſeeds have been of conſiderable eſteem as anthelmintics: the ſeeds are leſs bitter, and more acrid and aromatic, than thoſe of rue, to which they are reckoned ſimilar: or of ſantonicum, for which they have been frequently ſubſtituted.

Wild TANSEY, [*Potentilla.*] Cinquefoil.

TARES. [*Vicia.*] Vetches. The Tare is a low climbing or drooping plant, reſembling the pea in its manner of growth, but ſmaller. The ſtalks are weak, and lean on the ground. The leaves are each compoſed of ſeveral pairs of ſmaller, of a pale green colour, and there are tendrils for climbing or hanging upon any thing. The flower reſembles that of the pea in ſhape, but is ſmaller, and of a mixed purple colour in the common kinds, tho' of various hues in others. The ſeeds are contained in ſlender pods, and are round and ſmall. The colour varies like that of the flowers.

There are two kinds of Tares, the white and the black. Theſe are named after the colour of the ſeeds, and have little other difference: they properly are only ſeminal varieties of the ſame ſpecies; the white Tare riſing originally from the ſeed of the black, as the common blue and red flowers of many kinds, in our gardens, will occaſionally

casionally yield such as are white. In the same manner the first variation in this kind of Tare is, that the flower is white, whereas it is purple in the other and the seeds afterwards are of the same colour. Either of these may be sown in fields, and they will answer the same purpose; but the common or black Tare is the hardier kind, and the best bearer.

There may be a great advantage in the sowing Tares properly, among the variety of articles with which the present practice of husbandry gives the farmer an opportunity of varying his crop. They excellently prepare the land for corn, and their produce is of a certain and not inconsiderable price, being the proper food of pigeons, and useful to many other purposes.

Wherever there are pigeons there must be Tares raised or bought; and this is not their only use, for the straw when when dried is an excellent food for cattle. So that upon the whole, the Tare, though greatly inferior to many other articles, is a very profitable, and very useful crop at proper seasons; as a very poor land will support it, and it demands little preparation.

It is a hardy product, approaching to the nature of a weed; and it will therefore grow either on land naturally poor or such as is exhausted: this is what makes the farmer find his principal advantage in its culture: for it not only thus stands in the place of barrenness, but prepares the ground for better crops.

The most favourable land for Tares is a good sandy loom. They will succeed excellently on mellow earth, if not too moist for them, which is a very common inconvenience in that sort of ground, that is not rich in any respect; and we see great crops of them in the lime-stone countries, and that frequently where there is very little depth of soil.

The worst ground for the Tare is a tough wet clayey soil. In Hertfordshire, where a great quantity is raised, they find them always succeed better on the hilly grounds than in the vales.

Though the field where they are to stand has been pretty well exhausted by the last crop of corn, no preparation by manure, or repeated tillage, is wanted: all that is needful is to plough in the stubble; and let this lie to rot; and in spring to open the ground for the seed: these kind of crops are so far from demanding manure, that they serve as manure to the land themselves; and of them all none more than this species.

In his choice of the seed, the Husbandman should not be negligent: a little care costs nothing, and it ensures a profitable crop. Let the seed Tares be bought or purchased by exchange from some farmer, at ten or twelve miles distance, and let the farmer who is to sow them take care to purchase such as have grown on a different kind of soil from his own.

Thus, if his field be mellow earth, let him chuse the seed Tares from a loamy or sandy soil; and on the contrary, it his be sandy, let him chuse the seeds from one that is not.

These Tares are in general best for sowing that are of a middling size, round, full, and plump of a smooth and bright surface, and heavy. There is reason the husbandman be careful in this choice, because few seeds are so apt to spoil; and all pains are thrown away upon land where there is a defect in the seed.

In sowing, five pecks are generally allowed to the acre, but a bushel is fully sufficient: three pecks will be very well. The best time for sowing them is in the middle of February. Very little trouble need be taken about them, for the most slight stirring of the ground is sufficient; but there must never be more sown in a day than can be well covered before evening; for if they lie exposed to the dews of the night, they contract a damp that decays a great part of them; and the rest grow poorly.

In general, a poorer is better than a more rich land for Tares. In the former they pod well; in the latter, they are to run into stalks and leaf with less bearing. There is also another misfortune attending the sowing of Tares on rich ground, especially if it be a little moist, which is, they are more apt to lie upon the ground, because of the weight of the stalk, and then they rot. There is an old custom among the farmers of Essex, and some other

other counties, of sowing tares and horse-beans together, they thrive tolerably well in this way, but they do better singly. There is no difficulty attending the reaping of them, for they may be very well cut together, when ripe, as they will be about the same time; and the different sizes of the bean and tare make them easily separated in the barn by a riddle.

There are two seasons of cutting them, the one for the straw, as it is called; that is, for the green plant for the food of cattle, the other for seed. The first may be continued at different times for several weeks, and it is a very wholesome and profitable food; the other is only to be done at one time, that is, when the tares are ripe in the pods; and for the knowing the exact period for this, the tare is to be watched in the same manner as the pea.

The cutting them for fodder is often the most important service they can be put to; as to the letting them stand for ripening, it is for seed, or for food for pigeons; and they must be left to dry in the field in little heaps, before they are carried home for getting out the seed.

The farmer has seen how easily tares are damaged by wet, the consequence of which is, their growing mouldy, or musty: after this they never recover their right condition, look, or value: but, beside this, there is another accident to which they are very liable, that is, the being infected with worms, mites, and other little vermin. Now in this case the pulpy part is eaten, and they become light, dusty, imperfect, and of little value.

The preservation of tares from both these accidents depends principally on the drying of them; for, as it is damp that moulds them, the same makes way for those little mischievous vermin, which are always found in damp tares, but rarely in such as have been properly dried.

If the air be very warm and dry, the spreading and turning them on a floor for some days will answer the purpose; if otherwise, they should be laid upon a kiln: but, in this case, the heat must be very gentle, and well moderated, otherwise it may do more harm than the damp, destroying the vegetative power in the seed, and injuring it in its nourishing quality.

When the tares are thus properly ordered, they must be kept in a dry place, and properly secured from vermin. The thorough drying is very essential, for otherwise they will breed disorders in the pigeons that are fed with them; and, when used as seed, not one in ten will grow.

When they are to be kept any long time, the best way is to put them up in large barrels; then setting them in a dry, cool place, they will be out of all danger whatsoever, and keep good for all purposes for many years.

TAR. A thick, black, unctuous substance; obtained from old pines and fir-trees, by burning them with a close smothering heat. It differs from the native resinous juice of the trees in having received a disagreeable impression from the fire, and containing a portion of the saline and other juices united with the resinous and oily; by the mediation of these, a part of the terebinthinate oil proves dissoluble in aqueous liquors, which extract little or nothing from the purer turpentines. Water impregnated with the more soluble parts of tar proves, in consequence of this hot pungent oil, warm and stimulating: it sensibly raises the pulse, and quickens the circulation: by these qualities, in cold languid phlegmatic habits, it strengthens the solids, attenuates viscid juices, opens obstructions of the minuter vessels, and promotes perspiration and the fluid secretions in general; whilst in hot bilious temperaments, it disposes to inflammation, and aggravates the complaints which it has been employed to remove.

TAR PILLS. Take any quantity of tar, and mix with it as much powdered elecampane root as will reduce it to a proper thickness for being formed into pills.

The powder here mixed with the tar, though of no great virtue, is nevertheless a very useful addition, not only for procuring it a due consistence for taking, but likewise as it divides the resinous texture of the tar, and thus contributes to promote its solution by the animal juices. In the Edinburgh infirmary, half a drachm of the mass, made into middle-sized pills, is given every morning and evening, in disorders of the breast, scurvies, &c.

TAR WATER. Take of tar, two pounds; water, one gallon. Stir them ſtrongly together with a wooden rod; and after ſtanding to ſettle for two days, pour off the water for uſe.

Tar water has lately been recommended to the world as a certain and ſafe medicine in almoſt all diſeaſes; a ſlow yet effectual alterative in cachexies, ſcurvies, chlorotic, hyſterical, hypochondriacal, and other chronical complaints; and a ſudden remedy in acute diſtempers which demand immediate relief, as pleuriſies, peripneumonies, the ſmall-pox, and all kinds of fevers in general. The medicine, though certainly far inferior to the character that has been given of it, is doubtleſs in many caſes of conſiderable utility: it ſenſibly raiſes the pulſe, and occaſions ſome conſiderable evacuation, generally by perſpiration or urine, though ſometimes by ſtool or vomit: hence it is ſuppoſed to act by increaſing the vis vitæ, and enabling nature to expel the morbific humours.

We ſhall here inſert, from the firſt public recommender of this liquor (Biſhop Berkeley) ſome obſervations on the manner of uſing it:—

"Tar water, when right, is not paler than French, nor deeper-coloured than Spaniſh white-wine, and full as clear; if there be not a ſpirit very ſenſibly perceived in drinking, you may conclude the tar water is not good. It may be drank either cold or warm: In cholics, I take it to be beſt warm. As to the quantity, in common chronical indiſpoſitions, a pint a day may ſuffice, taken on an empty ſtomach, at two or four times, to wit, night and morning, and about two hours after dinner and breakfaſt; more may be taken by ſtrong ſtomachs. But thoſe who labour under great and inveterate maladies, muſt drink a greater quantity, at leaſt a quart every twenty-four hours: all of this claſs muſt have much patience and perſeverance in the uſe of this, as well as of all other medicines, which, though ſure, muſt yet in the nature of things be ſlow in the cure of inveterate chronical diſorders. In acute caſes, fevers of all kinds, it muſt be drank in bed, warm, and in great quantity (the fever ſtill enabling the patient to drink) perhaps a pint every hour, which I have known to work ſurprizing cures. But it works ſo quick, and gives ſuch ſpirits, that the patients often think themſelves cured before the fever hath quite left them."

TARRAGON. The name of a ſpicy plant, often cultivated in kitchen gardens.

It is propagated by ſeeds, ſlips, or cuttings. March or April is the proper time for ſetting them, and they may be tranſplanted again in the ſummer. The plants ſhould ſtand at leaſt a foot aſunder every way, and they ſhould be kept clean from weeds. They will endure great cold; and even extraordinary drought will not hurt them, if they are but a little watered, or if the earth about them is kept looſe and well ſtirred. A very few of their leaves mixed with a ſallad, particularly of lettuces, give it a high aromatic flavour. The tendereſt and freſheſt are the beſt for this purpoſe.

TARTAR, [*Tartarum.*] Tartar is a ſaline ſubſtance, thrown off from wines, after fermentation, to the ſides and bottom of the caſk: it proves of a red or white colour, and more or leſs foul or droſſy, according to the colour and quality of the wine; the white is generally looked upon as the pureſt: of either ſort, ſuch as is clean, ſolid, ſomewhat tranſparent, and has its outſide covered over with ſmall ſhining chryſtals, is preferable to ſuch as appears porous, droſſy, opake, and leſs bright. This ſubſtance, though truly ſaline, is ſcarce acted upon by cold water; the pureſt ſort, or ſuch as has been purified by art, requires twenty-four times its weight of boiling water to diſſolve in: the ſolutions of both the tartars paſs the filter colourleſs, and ſhoot, in the cold, into ſmall, white, ſemitranſparent chryſtals. All ſuch earths as are ſoluble in vinegar, and alkaline ſalts, render tartar more eaſily ſoluble in water; hence the refiners at Montpellier are ſaid to employ a certain earth for promoting its ſolutions with ſome particular managements for making it ſhoot into large chryſtals. This addition may occaſion a conſiderable alteration in the ſalt, inſomuch that the finer ſorts of white tartar are perhaps preferable on many occaſions to the common chryſtals. The virtues of tartar are thoſe of a mild,

 cooling,

cooling, aperient, laxative medicine. Taken from half an ounce to an ounce, it proves a gentle, though an effectual purgative.

TEA, [*Thea.*] The leaves of a ſhrub cultivated in China.

The ſeveral ſorts of tea met with among us, are the leaves of the ſame plant, collected at different times, and cured in a ſomewhat different manner: the ſmall young leaves very carefully dried, are the finer green: the older afford the ordinary green and bohea. The two firſt have a ſenſible flavour of violets; the other of roſes: the former is the natural odour of the plant; the latter, as Neumann obſerves, is probably introduced by art. Some of the dealers in this commodity in Europe, are not ignorant that bohea tea is imitable by the leaves of certain common plants, artificially tinctured and impregnated with the roſe flavour. The taſte of both ſorts is lightly bitteriſh, ſubaſtringent, and ſomewhat aromatic. The medical virtues attributed to theſe leaves are ſufficiently numerous, though few of them have any juſt foundation: little more can be expected from the common infuſions, than that of a diluent, acceptable to the ſtomach: the diuretic, diaphoretic, and other virtues which they have been celebrated for, depend more on the quantity of warm fluid, than any particular qualities which it gains from the tea. Nothing ariſes in diſtillation from either ſort of tea with rectified ſpirit; water elevates the whole of their flavour.

South-Sea TEA. Caſſioberry.

TEAZLE, [*Dipſacus.*] The Fuller's Teazle is the only kind cultivated for uſe. Teazle is not one of thoſe univerſal commodities for which there is every where a market. It may be raiſed in any place, and it is of cumberſome carriage; therefore he muſt be very imprudent, who ſets about to cultivate it at a diſtance from the parts of the kingdom where it is uſed, becauſe nothing need prevent theſe from doing it who are upon the ſpot; but to ſuch as are, it proves on many occaſions a very profitable growth.

The teazle is propagated by ſowing the ſeeds in March, upon a dry ſoil. About one peck of the ſeed will ſow an acre, for the plants ſhould have room to grow; otherwiſe the heads will no be ſo large, nor in ſo great quantity. When the plants are come up, you muſt hoe them in the ſame manner as is practiſed for turneps, cutting down all the weeds, and ſingling out the plants to about ſix or eight inches diſtance; and as the plants advance, and the weeds grow again, you muſt hoe them a ſecond time, cutting out the plants to a wider diſtance; for they ſhould be at laſt left a foot aſunder; and you ſhould be particularly careful to clear them from weeds, eſpecially the firſt ſummer; for when the plants have ſpread ſo as to cover the ſurface of the ground, the weeds will not ſo readily grow between them. The ſecond year after ſowing, the plants will ſhoot up heads, which will be fit to cut about the beginning of Auguſt; at which time they ſhould be cut and tied up in bunches, ſetting them in the ſun, if the weather be fair; but if not, they muſt be ſet in rooms to dry. The common produce is about 160 bundles or ſtaves upon an acre, and they will ſell for about one ſhilling a ſtave.

TEAM. A number of horſes or oxen drawing at once.

To TEAM. To pour or lade out of one veſſel into another.

To TED. To ſpread abroad new-mown graſs, which is the firſt thing done in order to its being dried, and made into hay.

TEDDER *or* TETHER. A rope with which a horſe is tied in the field, that he may not paſture too wide.

To TEEM. To be pregnant; to engender young.

TENDRIL. The claſper of a vine, or other climbing plant.

TENEMENT. Any thing held by a tenant, as a houſe, &c.

TENURE. The manner in which tenants hold their lands, &c. of their lord.

THATCH. Straw laid on the top of a building, rick, &c. to keep out the weather.

THEAVE. An ewe of the firſt year.

THETCHES. *See* VETCHES.

THICKET. A cloſe knot or tuft of trees; a cloſe wood.

THILL-HORSE. The laſt horſe in a team; the horſe that goes between the thills or ſhafts.

THISTLE, [*Carduus.*] A prickly weed, growing among corn, &c.

The

The following observations on thistles is selected from the papers of the Bath Agriculture Society :—

" *Some observations on Thistles as injurious to agriculture, more particularly the Seratula Arvensis of Linnæus. By* William Curtis, *Author of the Flora Londinensis.*

" Gentlemen,

" While some of your correspondents are laudably engaged in enriching agriculture, by discovering and promoting the cultivation of new plants, permit one whom you have been pleased to elect an honorary member of your Society, to lay before you a few observations on some of the plants which are more particularly noxious to the farmer. Should they be considered as contributing to advance even in the smallest degree the design of your institution, he may be again excited to trouble you on other subjects, as information may arise from a cultivation of most of the British plants on a small scale.

" There are no plants over which the œconomical farmer ought to keep a more watchful eye than the thistle tribe. He is sensible that they are not only useless, as resisting the bite of most animals, the hardy ass excepted, but that they occupy much ground; and being furnished with downy seeds, are capable of being multiplied to almost any distance. Hence in many parts of the kingdom, the farmers whose lands are contiguous unite in preventing the increase, by cutting them down before they seed; but this operation, though destructive to some species, will only palliate the bad effects of others.

" To be acquainted with the qualities of each kind, we must observe them with much attention, and view them in a botanical and philosophical light: this alone will enable us to judge with certainty how far and by what means their destruction may be effected.

" The English thistles meriting notice, as more or less noxious, are,

1. Carduus Lanceolatus, or *Spear Thistle*
2. Carduus Nutans, — *Musk Thistle*
3. Carduus Palustris, — *Marsh Thistle*
4. Carduus Marianus, — *Milk Thistle*
5. Carduus Acanthoides, *Welted Thistle*
6. Carduus Crispus, — *Curled Thistle*
7. Onoperdum Acanthium *Cotton Thistle*
8. Seratula Arvensis, — *Cursed Thistle*

" The *Spear Thistle* is a large strong plant, about four feet high, the extremity of each leaf running out into a long point; its heads are large, and it grows very commonly by the sides of roads, near dunghills, and not unfrequently in fields and pastures.

" The *Musk Thistle* grows to the height of two or three feet, the heads hang down, and the flowers smell somewhat like musk; it is often found occupying whole fields, particularly on chalky or barren land.

The *Marsh Thistle* is very tall and prickly; its heads are numerous, small, and of a red colour; it grows abundantly in wet meadows, also in woods.

" The *Milk Thistle* has very large leaves, which are most commonly beautifully marbled with white. Near London it appears frequently on banks by road sides; in which situation we also meet with the *Curled* and *Welted Thistles*. These three seldom intrude into fields or pastures.

The *Cotton Thistle* is distinguished by its size, (being perhaps the largest of the British herbaceous plants) and its white woolly leaves. It grows in the same situation as the three last-mentioned.

" The *Cursed Thistle* is more general in its growth than any of the others, being found not only by the sides of roads universally, but also in arable land, and is not uncommon in meadows, even in such as are yearly mown. It is remarkably prickly, grows about three feet high; its heads are small, the flowers purple, and frequently white. The scales of the heads are smooth, and may in a particular manner be distinguished from all the others before mentioned, by having a perennial root about the size of a goose-quill, which runs deep into the earth, and afterwards creeps along horizontally.

" Of these thistles, all except the last are either annual or biennial; that is, remain in the ground not more than one or two years, unless renewed by seed. The last, having a perennial root, continues in the earth, increasing, and throwing up new shoots every year.

" Hence it will appear obvious, that if the first seven species of thistles are cut down before they perfect their seed, the ground will be entirely cleared of them; and that the last-mentioned can no otherwise be destroyed, than by rooting it out, a process which the following experiments will sorrowfully convince the rural œconomist to be impracticable in large fields, and scarce to be performed even in an inclosed garden.

" Experiment 1. *To ascertain the effects of mowing the Seratula Arvensis.*

" The Hon. Daines Barrington, who is ever anxious to promote useful enquiries, desired me to try whether this kind of thistle could not be destroyed by mowing. A small patch of them, about two feet square, was accordingly planted in a good garden, in the year 1777. In the course of the summer they were mown three several times, but without any other good effect than that of preventing their seeding; for instead of being destroyed, the next spring they came up extremely vigorous, not only on the bed where they were first planted, but all around it to the distance of six feet.

" Experiment 2. *To ascertain the annual increase of the root of the Seratula Arvensis.*

" April 1, 1778, I planted in a garden a piece of the root of this thistle, about the size of a goose-quill, and two inches long, with a small head of leaves, cut off the main-root, just as it was springing out of the ground. By the 2d of November 1778, this small root had thrown out shoots, several of which had extended themselves to the distance of eight feet; some had even thrown up leaves six feet from the original root. Most of these shoots which had thus far extended themselves were about six inches under ground—others had penetrated to the depth of two feet and a half; the whole together, when dug up and washed from the earth, weighed four pounds.

" In the spring of 1779, contrary to my expectation, this thistle again made its appearance on and about the spot where the small piece was originally planted. There were between fifty and sixty young heads, which must have sprung from those roots, which had penetrated deeper than the gardener was aware of, although he was particularly careful in extracting them.

" From these experiments it appears deducible, that no plants are more easily destroyed than the generality of thistles, or with more difficulty than this one; there being no soil, however poor, in which it will not vegetate, nor earth so stiff but it will penetrate; in proportion, however, as the soil is rich, will be its increase.

" It were much to be wished, that an investigation of this evil had afforded a remedy; at present, none appears. It is, therefore, to be feared, that spudding, or cutting them down close to the ground, once or twice in the spring, is the only operation the farmer can perform to prevent their bad effects in destroying his crops on arable land, and rendering his pastures unseemly.

" As nature in the preservation of this plant seems to have exerted her greatest powers, it is possible that in some future period, uses may be discovered to which it has not yet been applied.

" To the ass it is the highest treat; and I have been credibly informed, that in some parts of Scotland, it is cut down as food for horses.

" It would be well, if a plant so noxious in some respects could be rendered beneficial in others.

" I am, &c. Wm. Curtis."

Blessed Thistle. See Carduus Benedictus.

Carline Thistle. See Carline Thistle.

Distaff Thistle. See Distaff Thistle.

Fuller's Thistle. See Teazle.

Globe Thistle. See Globe Thistle.

Melon or *Thorn* Thistle. See Melon Thistle.

Melancholy Thistle. See Melancholy Thistle.

THISTLING. The action of cutting or pulling up thistles.

Thorn Apple. See Thorn Apple.

Black Thorn. The Sloe tree.

Box Thorn. See Box Thorn.

Christ's Thorn. See Christ's Thorn.

Cockspur Thorn. Service.

Egyptian Thorn. Acacia.

Evergreen Thorn. See Evergreen Thorn.

Glastonbury Thorn. See Glastonbury Thorn.

Goat's

Goat's THORN. See TRAGACANTH.

Haw THORN. See HAWTHORN.

Purging THORN. See BUCKTHORN.

White THORN. See HAWTHORN.

THOROUGH WAX. Hare's ear.

THREE-LEAVED GRASS. Trefoil, Clover.

THRASHING. The action of getting the corn out of the straw.

THRASHING *Floor*. The floor on which the corn is thrashed.

THRAVE. A shock of corn, consisting of twenty-four sheaves.

THREAF. A handful, a bundle.

THRIFT, [*Statice.*] There are two or three kinds of this herb, natives of the Alps and salt-marshes of many parts of England; some years ago it was much esteemed for borders, but at present it is not much regarded. It may be propagated by parting the roots in autumn.

THROATWORT, [*Trachelium.*] This plant will grow on old walls, and is easily propagated by throwing the seeds on old walls where there is the least earth to hold them.

THYME, [*Thymus.*] A well-known aromatic plant propagated in kitchen gardens.

Botanists enumerate nine different species of thyme, besides several varieties; but they are all propagated either by seeds or parting the roots.

The most useful sort, either for culinary purposes, or for medicine, is the broad-leaved thyme, most commonly cultivated in the kitchen-garden; for the narrow-leaved kind never grow so large. Their culture is, however, exactly the same.

The seeds of thyme, if it be raised from thence, should be sown either in March or October, but the former of these months is best, in a well-dug bed of light earth: taking care, as they are very small, not to drop them too close together, nor to bury them deep, for this last would make them rot. When the plants are come up, they should be carefully over-looked and cleared from weeds, and if the season be dry, their growth will be greatly promoted by watering them twice a week, for some time. In June, if it be a spring sowing, the plants should be thinned to the distance of six inches asunder every way, that they may have room to spread: and those which are drawn out may be set in other beds, at the same distance from each other. They must be watered till they have taken root, and will then require no farther care, except weeding them, till the winter, when they may be pulled up, and laid by in a dry place, for use. The autumnal sowing should be thinned as before, early the next spring, if it be let stand till then; for there will be little danger of its resisting the severest winter of this country, especially if the plants grow on a dry, poor, and stony land. In rich ground, indeed, where they grow luxuriantly, they are sometimes destroyed by severe frosts. Thyme will even flourish upon a stone wall.

If the plants are propagated by parting their roots, this should also be done in March or October. The old plants should be taken up, their roots should be slipt into as many parts as can be, and these slips should be set six or eight inches asunder every way, in beds of fresh light earth. If the season be dry, they must be watered there till they have taken root; and with only one weeding of them afterwards, they will soon be fit for use.

To save the seeds of thyme, some of the plants should be left unremoved till the next spring. They will then flower in June, and their seeds will ripen in July. These must be pulled up and beaten out as soon as they are ripe, for the first shower of rain would otherwise wash them all out of their husks.

Thyme is so great an impoverisher of the earth, that no crop will thrive well where that stood the year before, unless the ground be trenched deeper than the thyme rooted, and at the same time enriched with dung, or some other suitable manure.

Lemon THYME. A variety of the common thyme.

Mother of THYME, [*Serpillum.*] A species of thyme growing wild on heaths.

TICHING. Setting up turfs in such a manner as they may be dried by the sun, and fit for being burnt for their ashes upon the land.

TIKE. An insect found in dogs, sheep, cows, &c.

TILLABLE. Arable, fit for the plough.

TILLAGE. The act or practice of tilling, or cultivating land.

TILLER. A branch of corn.

To TILLER. To spread or shoot out.

TILLS. Tares or vetches.

TILTH. The condition of the earth after ploughing, &c.

TIMOTHY-GRASS. The name of a grass now cultivated in England, of which it is a native, though the seeds of it were carried from Virginia, by one Mr. Timothy Hanson, to North Carolina, where it is now cultivated by the inhabitants; and from this circumstance it received the name it now bears.

It thrives most in low, damp, marshy grounds; for in such soil and situation it will produce a fine turf in three weeks from the time of sowing the seed. It is very luxuriant, grows to a considerable height, and has in some sort the appearance of wheat or rye, having a broad blade or leaf.

All sorts of cattle are very fond of this herb whilst in a green growing state; and it will not be improper to add, that they are nearly, if not quite, as fond of it, when dried and made into hay; but when it is intended for this use, it should always be mown when it is in full sap, just before it flowers, for if it is left longer before it is cut, being so luxuriant and quick a grower, it becomes harsh, and is much dryer and more chirky food, than when it is cut in its prime.

TINE. A tooth or spike. And hence the common phrase of giving two or three tinings, signifies to draw the harrows twice or thrice over the same spot of ground.

TIT. A small horse.

TOAD-FLAX. See TOAD-FLAX.

TOBACCO, [*Nicotiana.*] There are many species of this plant, but they are in general supposed too tender to grow from seeds in the full ground, to any degree of perfection in this country, so require to be raised in a hot-bed, after the following manner:

The seeds must be sown upon a moderate hot-bed in March, and when the plants are come up fit to remove, they should be transplanted into a new hot-bed of a moderate warmth, about four inches asunder each way, observing to water and shade them until they have taken root; after which you must let them have air in proportion to the warmth of the season, otherwise they will draw up very weak, and be thereby less capable of enduring the open air: you must also observe to water them frequently, but while they are very young it should not be given them in too great quantities; though when they are pretty strong, they will require to have it often, and in plenty.

In this bed the plants should remain until the beginning of May, by which time (if they have succeeded well) they will touch each other, therefore they should be inured to bear the open air gradually; after which they must be taken up carefully, preserving a large ball of earth to each root, and planted into a rich light soil, in rows four feet asunder, and the plants three feet distance in the rows, observing to water them until they have taken root; after which they will require no farther care, but only to keep them clear from weeds, until the plants begin to shew their flower-stems; at which time you should cut off the tops of them, that their leaves may be better nourished, whereby they will be rendered larger, and of a thicker substance. In August they will be full grown, when they should be cut for use; for if they are permitted to stand longer, their under leaves will begin to decay. This is to be understood for such plants as are propagated for use, but those plants which are designed for ornament should be planted in the borders of the pleasure-garden, and permitted to grow their full height, where they will continue flowering from July till the frost puts a stop to them.

TOLU. See BALSAM OF TOLU.

TOOTH-PICK. See SPANISH TOOTH-PICK.

TOOTHWORT, [*Dentaria.*] There are three species, the five-leaved, the seven-leaved, and the three-leaved. The second sort is found growing naturally in some parts of England, the others are natives of the mountains of Italy and Austria. They are cultivated by seeds, or by parting the roots in October.

TORMENTIL, [*Tormentilla.*] The species are, 1. Tormentil with an erect stalk. 2. Creeping Tormentil.

The first sort grows wild on dry pastures and commons in most parts of England,

England, ſo is never cultivated in gardens; this is ſo commonly known as to need no deſcription. The roots of this plant have been frequently uſed for tanning of leather, in places where oak-bark is ſcarce. This root is alſo much uſed in medicine, and is accounted the beſt aſtringent in the whole vegetable kingdom.

The ſecond ſort is found in ſome particular places of England growing wild, but particularly in Oxfordſhire. The ſtalks of this ſort ſpread on the ground, and emit roots from their joints, whereby they propagate very faſt: this is rarely preſerved, unleſs in ſome botanic gardens for the ſake of variety. It requires no care to propagate theſe plants, ſince, if their roots are once planted in almoſt any ſoil or ſituation, the plants will flouriſh without any other care but to prevent their being over-run with great weeds.

TORE. Rowen, rowet, or winter graſs.

TOSET *or* TOVET. Half a buſhel.

TOUCH ME NOT. Yellow balſamine. See BALSAMINE.

TOWER MUSTARD, [*Turritis.*] This plant is kept in botanic gardens for variety, and is eaſily propagated by ſowing the ſeeds on old walls in autumn.

Ladies TRACES. Dogſtones.

TRAMEL. An inſtrument or device, made ſometimes of leather, but more uſually of ropes, fitted to a horſe's legs, to regulate his motion, and teach him to amble.

Tramel alſo ſignifies an iron inſtrument hanging in the chimney, whereon to hang pots or kettles over the fire.

TRANSPLANTING. The act of removing trees or plants from the places where they are ſowed, or raiſed, and planting them in others.

TRAGACANTH, [*Tragacantha.*] There are four ſpecies of this plant, natives of Italy, Spain, and the iſlands of the Archipelago. Theſe plants may be propagated by ſeeds, when they can be procured from the countries where the plants grow naturally, which ſhould be ſown on a bed of freſh earth in April; and when the plants come up, they ſhould be carefully kept clean from weeds. They may alſo be propagated by ſlips; the moſt proper time for which is April.

The gum tragacanth of the ſhops is the produce of this ſhrub.

TRAVELLER'S JOY. Climbers.

TREE. The firſt and largeſt of the vegetable kind, conſiſting of a ſingle trunk, out of which ſpring forth branches and leaves.

Standard trees are ſuch as naturally riſe to a great height and are not topt. For the choice of trees of this kind, to be tranſplanted out of a nurſery, Quintiney recommends us to ſuch as are ſtrait, ſix feet high at leaſt, and five or ſix inches thick at bottom, and three or four at top; the bark pretty ſmooth and ſhining, as a token of their youth, and the good ſoil they grew in.

Dwarf trees are ſuch as are kept low, and never ſuffered to have above half a foot of ſtem.

TREE GERMANDER. See TREE GERMANDER.

TREE *of Life*. See ARBOR VITÆ.

TREFOIL. See CLOVER.

Bean TREFOIL. See BEAN Trefoil.

Bird's-Foot TREFOIL. See BIRD'S-FOOT Trefoil.

Marſh TREFOIL. Buckbean.

Moon TREFOIL. Lucern.

Shrub TREFOIL, [*Ptelea.*] This plant is a native of North America, and riſes with an upright ſtem to the height of twelve or fourteen feet; there is another ſpecies, a native of the Weſt-India iſlands. They are both propagated by ſeeds; the latter requires the aſſiſtance of a ſtove in winter.

Snail TREFOIL. See BASTARD MEDICA.

TREACLE MUSTARD. See *Treacle* MUSTARD.

TRELLISES. A contrivance for ſupporting the branches of fruit trees, conſiſting of laths of wood croſſing each other in the form of a lattice.

Some perſons who are very curious in their fruit, and who do not mind a little extraordinary expence, erect trelliſes againſt their walls, extending from the inſide of one pier to the neareſt inſide of the next; where the walls are built with piers, as they muſt be for this purpoſe. This frame-work is conſtructed in the ſame manner as that for eſpaliers, like which it need not be ſet up till the trees are well ſpread, and begin to bear fruit plentifully; for they may be trained till then againſt any ordinary low eſpalier

lier of ash-poles or other slender sticks, in order not needlesly to expose the trellises to the injuries of the weather; because these, being generally made of regularly cut yellow-deal, or oak, and run up higher, cost more. Every fourth upright rail or post of the trellis should be much stronger than the rest, and fastened to the wall with iron hooks, which it is best to fix in the wall at the time of building it. These strongest upright posts should be about three, but by no means more than four feet from each other. The cross rails may be slight, as for common espaliers, but they must be laid much closer together. For peach, nectarine, and apricot trees, for example, which, for the most part, produce their fruit on the young wood, the squares of the trellis frame should not exceed three or four inches; but for trees which continue to bear on the old wood, they may be five or six inches wide, and for vines, eight or nine inches. The shoots of the trees are fastened to this frame with osier twigs, rope yarn, or any other soft bandage, in the same manner as they are to espaliers: for they must not be nailed to either, because that would injure the wood-work.

These trellises, which should project about two inches from the wall, are thought to contribute greatly to preserve the beauty of the fruit, by preventing its lying too close to the wall, whilst it has at the same time all the advantages of the heat reflected therefrom: nor are the walls where these are used hurt by driving nails into their joints, and drawing them out again every year, at the hazard of pulling out some of the mortar with them, and consequently of weakening the wall, and making holes in which snails and other vermin take shelter and breed.

TRENCH. A furrow cut in the earth for draining land.

TRENDLE. Any thing that turns round.

To TREFALLOW. To plough land the third time before sowing.

TROUGH. A long vessel for holding water, &c.

TRUG *or* TRUGG. A hod for mortar.

TRUNDLE. A sort of carriage with low wheels, for carrying heavy and cumbersome loads. Trundel.

TRUNK. The stem or body of a tree; or the part between the ground and the place where it divides into branches.

TRUSS. A bundle of hay, straw, &c. A truss of hay must contain 56 pounds, or half a hundred weight; 36 trusses make a load. In June, July, and August, a truss of new hay must weigh 60 pounds.

TRUSS *of Flowers*. Signifies many flowers growing together on the head of a stalk, as in the cowslip, auricula, &c. &c.

TRUELOVE. One berry.

TRUMPET FLOWER. Scarlet Jasmine.

TRUMPET *Honeysuckle*. See HONEYSUCKLE.

TUBEROSE, [*Polianthes*.] The varieties of this plant are the tuberose with a double flower, the striped-leaved tuberose, and the tuberose with a smaller flower; the last is mentioned by several authors as a distinct species, but is certainly a variety.

This sort is frequent in the south of France, from whence the roots have been often brought to England early in the spring, before those roots have arrived from Italy which are annually imported; the stalks of this are weaker, and do not rise so high, and the flowers are smaller than those of the common tubrrose, but in other respects is the same.

The tuberose grows naturally in India, from whence it was first brought to Europe, where it now thrives in the warmer parts, as well as in its native soil. The Genoese are the people who cultivate this plant, to furnish all the other countries where the roots cannot be propagated without great trouble and care, and from thence the roots are annually sent to England, Holland, and Germany. In most parts of Italy, Sicily, and Spain, the roots thrive and propagate without care, where they are once planted.

This plant has been long cultivated in the English gardens, for the exceeding beauty and fragrancy of its flowers; the roots of this are annually brought from Genoa, by the persons who import orange-trees; for as these roots are too tender to thrive in the full ground in England, so there are few persons who care to take the trouble

ble of nursing up their offsets till they become blowing roots, because it will be two or three years before they arrive to a proper size for producing flowers; and as they must be protected from the frost in winter, the trouble and expence of covers is greater than the roots are worth, for they are generally sold pretty reasonable by those who import them from Italy.

TUBULATED FLOWERS. A term used to express those smaller flowers, a great number of which go to compose one large compound flower. These are called tubulated in distinction from another kind of them, which are from their shape called ligulated. The tubulated floscules generally compose the disk, and the ligulated ones the radius of the compound flowers. The tubulated ones are formed into a hollow cylinder, which expands into a mouth at the top, and is divided into five equal segments, which stand expanded, and in some measure bent backwards.

TULIP, [*Tulipa.*] The distinct species are two, 1. The tulip with a nodding flower, or Italian tulip. 2. The tulip with an erect flower. But the varieties are innumerable. The properties of a good tulip as distinguished by Miller, are, 1. It should have tall strong stem. 2. The flower should consist of six leaves, three within, and three without; the former ought to be larger than the latter. 3. Their bottom should be proportioned to their top, and their upper part should be rounded off, and not terminate in a point. 4. These leaves, when opened, should neither turn inward, nor bend outward, but rather stand erect, and the flower should be of a middling size, neither over large, nor too small. 5. The stripes should be small and regular, arising from the bottom of the flower, for if there are any remains of the former self-coloured bottom, the flower is in danger of losing its stripes again. The chives should not be yellow, but of a brown colour. When a flower has all these properties, it is esteemed a good one.

Tulips are generally divided into three classes, according to their seasons of flowering; as præcoces, or early blowers, medias, or middling blowers, and serotines, or late blowers; but there is no occasion for making any more distinctions than two, viz. early and late flowers.

The early-blowing tulips are not near so fair, nor rise half so high, as the late ones, but are chiefly valued for appearing so early in the spring; some of which will flower the middle of March in mild seasons, if planted in a warm border near a wall, pale, hedge, or other shelter, and a month after the others will succeed them; so that they keep flowering until the general season for the late flowers to blow, which is toward the end of April.

The roots of the early-blowing tulips should be planted the beginning of September in a warm border, near a wall, pale, or hedge, because if they are put into an open spot of ground, their buds are in danger of suffering by morning frosts in the spring. The soil for these should be renewed every year, where people intend to have them fair. The best soil for this purpose is that which is taken from a light loamy pasture, with the turf rotted amongst it; and to this should be added a fourth part of sea-sand. This mixture may be laid about eighteen inches deep, which will be sufficient, for these need not be planted more than four or five inches deep at most. The offsets should not be planted amongst the blowing roots, but in a border by themselves, where they may be planted pretty close together, especially if they are small; but these should be taken up when their leaves decay, in the same manner as the blowing roots, otherwise they would rot; for these are not so hardy as the late blowers, nor do they increase half so fast as those, so that a greater care is required to preserve the offsets of them.

When the tulips come up in the spring, the earth upon the surface of the borders should be gently stirred and cleared from weeds; and as the buds appear, if the season should prove severe, it will be of great service to cover them with mats, for want of which many times they are blighted, and their flower-buds decay before they blow, which is often injurious to the roots, as is also the cropping of the flowers, so soon as they are blown, because their roots, which are formed new every year, are not at that time arrived to their full magnitude, and are hereby deprived of proper nourishment.

If, when these flowers are blown, the season should prove very warm, it will be proper to shade them with mats, &c. in the heat of the day; as also if the nights are frosty, they should be in like manner covered, whereby they may be preserved a long time in beauty; but, when their flowers are decayed, and their seed-vessels begin to swell, they should be broken off just at the top of the stalks, because if they are permitted to seed, it will injure the roots.

When the leaves of these flowers are decayed (which will be before the late blowers are out of flower,) their roots should be taken up, and spread upon mats in a shady place, to dry; after which they should be cleared from their filth, and put up in a dry place, where vermin cannot come to them, until the season for planting them again, being very careful to preserve every sort separate, that you may know how to dispose of them at the time for planting them again, because it is the better way to plant all the roots of each sort together and not to intermix them, as is commonly practised in most other kinds of flowers; for as there are few of them which blow at the same time, so, when the several roots of one sort are scattered through a whole border, they make but an indifferent appearance; whereas, when twenty or thirty roots of the same sort are placed together, they will all flower at the same time, and have a better effect.

When the flowers are faded, the heads of all the fine sorts should be broken off to prevent their seeding; for if this be not observed, they will not flower near so well the following year, nor will their stripes continue so perfect; this will also cause their stems to decay sooner than otherwise they would do, so that their roots may be taken up in June; for they should not remain in the ground [illegible] ir leaves are decayed [illegible]

upon mats in a shady place to dry; after which they should be put up in a dry place, where vermin cannot get to them, observing to keep every sort separated; but they should not be kept too close from the air, nor suffered to lie in heaps together, lest they should grow mouldy, for if any of the roots once take the mould, they commonly rot when they are planted again.

The offsets of these roots, which are not large enough to produce flowers the succeeding year, should be also put by themselves, keeping each sort distinct; these should be planted about a month earlier in autumn than the blowing roots, in particular beds by themselves in the flower nursery, where they may not be exposed to public view; but the earth of the beds should be prepared for them in the same manner as for larger roots; these should not be planted above five inches deep, because they are not strong enough to push through so great covering of the earth as the old roots; they may also be placed much nearer together than those which are to flower, and in one year most of them will become strong enough to flower, when they may be removed into the flower-garden, and placed in the beds amongst those of the same kinds.

African TULIP. Bloodflower.

TULIP TREE, [*Tulipifera.*] The tulip-tree is a native of North-America; it is a tree of the first magnitude, and is generally known through all the English settlements by the title of poplar. Of late years there have been great numbers of these trees raised from seeds in the English gardens, so that now they are become common in the nurseries about London; and there are many of them in several parts of England which do annually produce flowers. The first tree of this kind which flowered here, was in the gardens of the late Earl of Peterborough, at Parsons [illegible] near Fulham, which was [illegible] dernefs among ot[illegible] [illegible] pots and tubs increased slowly in their growth; so that afterward there were many others planted in the full ground, which are now arrived to a large size, especially those which are planted in a moist soil. One of the handsomest tree of this kind, near London, is in the garden of Waltham Abbey; and at Wilton, the seat of the Earl of Pembroke, there are some trees of great bulk; but the old tree at Parsons Green is quite destroyed by the other trees which were suffered to over-hang it, and rob it of its nourishment, from the fear of taking them down, lest, by admitting the cold air, the tulip-tree might be injured. The young shoots of this tree are covered with a smooth purplish bark; they are garnished with large leaves, whose foot-stalks are four inches long; they are ranged alternate; the leaves are of a singular form, being divided into three lobes; the middle lobe is blunt and hollowed at the point, appearing as if it had been cut with scissars. The two side lobes are rounded, and end in blunt points. The leaves are from four to five inches broad near their base, and about four inches long from the foot-stalk to the point, having a strong mid-rib, which is formed by the prolongation of the foot-stalk. From the mid-rib run many transverse veins to the borders, which ramify into several smaller. The upper surface of the leaves is smooth, and of a lucid green, the under is of a pale green. The flowers are produced at the end of the branches; they are composed of six petals, three without and three within; which form a sort of bell-shaped flower, from whence the inhabitants of North-America give it the title of tulip. These petals are marked with green, yellow, and red spots, so make a fine appearance when the trees are well charged with flowers. The time of this tree's flowering is in July, and when the flowers drop, the germen swells and forms a kind of cone, but these seldom ripen in England.

Mr. Catesby, in his Natural History of Carolina, says, "There are some of these trees in America which are thirty feet in circumference; the boughs are unequal and irregular, making several bends or elbows, which render the trees distinguishable at a great distance, even when they have no leaves upon them. They are found in most parts of the northern continent of America, from the Cape of Florida to New-England, where the timber is of great use, the trunk being frequently hollowed, and made into boats big enough to carry a number of men."

This tree is propagated by seeds, brought from North-America.

Laurel-leaved Tulip Tree, [*Magnolia.*] There are four species of this tree, growing in North-America, some growing to the height of twenty feet, others to eighty feet. They are cultivated in England and are beautiful evergreens. They are propagated by seed, which must be procured from the place of their natural growth.

TUMBREL. A dung-cart. See Trundle.

TUPP. A ram.

Tupping Time. Ramming time.

TURBITH, [*Turpethum.*] The cortical part of the root of an Indian convolvulus, brought to us in oblong pieces, of a brown or ash colour on the outside, and whitish within: the best is ponderous, not wrinkled, easy to break, and discovers a large quantity of resinous matter to the eye: its taste is at first sweetish; chewed for a little time, it becomes acrid, pungent, and nauseous. This root is a cathartic, not of the safest or most certain kind.

TURF. A blackish sulphureous earth, used in several parts of England, Holland, and Flanders, as fuel.

In Flanders, their turf is dry or pared from off the surface of the earth, and cut in form of bricks. The sedge, or species of grass growing very thick on the turf earth, contributes greatly, when dry, to the maintenance of the fire.

TURKEY. The turkey is a very large and fine bird, and exceedingly well worth the regard of the prudent husbandman. There are advantages and disadvantages attending upon the raising of this, as other kinds of fowl; but all being weighed together, the former far outweigh the latter, and the interest of the farmer will lead him to think very seriously of receiving them as a part of his stock.

There is also this farther encouragement to his industry, that a great many of the disadvantages attending the keeping of this fowl, may be remedied or prevented by prudent management: and that there is no kind among all the poultry which will afford so many opportunities of improvement. There are several breeds of the turkey, much more different than those among the cock and hen kinds; and the properly choosing among these, will greatly add to the profit and ease of keeping them.

Among the advantages of the turkey may be reckoned his size, the price he fetches at market when in good condition, and the quantity of his dung, which is as valuable as any other kind whatsoever. He is fit for sale also in the common condition at a good price; and his feathers are not to be neglected, in counting up these benefits.

Among the disadvantages of turkeys are to be reckoned their straggling disposition, their being liable to many accidents, the difficulty of raising them, and the frequent destruction of them by vermin; as also the quantity of corn they devour. If fed altogether with this, they will eat more than they can ever be worth; but to this it may be answered, that the feeding them with corn is not necessary, for they will in general provide very well for themselves; and in the same manner we shall shew that every other objection made against them may be removed: and that it will be greatly to the farmer's advantage to raise them in most places.

This kind of bird always succeeds best for the owner in open countries, because these are not so much infested with vermin; and they are subject to ramble and be destroyed more than any kind, as observed already. This may be a very reasonable caution for the husbandman not to keep them in improper places; but we have counties enough in England that are not at all liable to that objection.

The first article to be considered in respect of the breeding of turkeys is the age of the cock and hen. The cock must be young, for the brood is never good unless he be in the vigour of his life; the hen may be older, for her care in sitting and leading them is all that is required of her, and in the latter article the cock often assists her, when he is of a kindly sort.

The turkey cock for breeding should be about two years old; and the best time for the hen is at about four years; she may be employed in breeding till she is six, but when she is too young, she is most apt to neglect the brood; and when the cock is at all declined from his strength, they are weakly.

Turkeys are not natural to our kingdom, and there is therefore always a wildness about them. The female of this kind does not lay familiarly and conveniently about houses as the common hen, but rambles to a distance, and makes her nest among thickets: for this reason her brood is from the beginning more liable to accidents. The farmer must therefore be watchful about the time of her laying, and take care to get her into the hen-house, and compel her to lay there; for this is the first precaution, and it is a very essential one about the brood.

It is a custom with some, if there be convenience of thickets, or a little wood near the house, to let them take their own way, and lay and sit there; and in the hardier breeds, with a little care of the young when new hatched, this will do very well; but there is never any harm in the other method, whatever be the breed; and there is a much greater certainty of success.

The turkey naturally begins to lay in the month of March, and will sit in April. The eggs are very large, and are excellent in the way of food, particularly they have a restorative virtue.

The proper number of eggs to let the hen sit upon is eleven, some advise thirteen, but commonly there is less success in that avaritious method, for they cannot all be well covered.

The turkey sits about seven or eight and twenty days. Some of the eggs will sometimes be hatched at five or six and twenty, and some will lie till thirty, but the middle time is the most natural.

The hatching of the brood is the time when the great care is required in their management. The turkey being naturally a bird of a warmer climate, is chilly in this; and particularly the tender young. They must be kept very carefully at first, especially such as happen to hatch before others of the same brood; the best way is to put them into a basket with wool in it, and set them before the fire, at such a distance as to be gently warmed.

From

From this time the farmer is to depute somebody to act as a parent for them, for the hen is not to be expected to do much; they will follow her, and should be permitted to do so in the warm part of the day, and she should be managed to take care of them. The cock also will often watch over them, keep them together, and defend them better than the hen; but neither are to be trusted without careful looking after. The proper method of managing them is this. They are to be kept in a warm and close place altogether, while they are very young; and when they have got some strength, they are to be let out two hours after the sun is up in the morning, and taken in again before he sets in the evening; and in the mean time they should only be let into some walled place, or some inclosure so secure that they cannot stray.

At first they are to be fed in the house, and afterwards in this open place; and at all times they must be allowed a sufficient supply of food, for their parents take at best but little care to help them to any. The very best food for them is green fresh cheese, and while they are young, their drink should be only new milk; afterwards milk and water, making it weaker and weaker till they come to water alone, which they will then drink wherever they can find it. Curds are a very good food for them, but not so well as cheese. A very wholesome food also is a kind of thick hasty pudding made of oatmeal, water, and a little new milk among it.

As the tenderness of the young is one great article in the disadvantage of the turkey, indeed the greatest, care must be taken that the hen do not set herself at too early a season. If the young are hatched in cold weather, it is scarce possible to rear them without considerable loss; but if they be produced toward the latter end of May, which indeed is the most natural time, as well as the best, they will have a much better chance.

It is only while young that this bird is so exceedingly tender; for, when grown up, they are not only strong enough to defend themselves; but they always love to keep in flocks together.

"Most of our housewives, says a Swedish author on husbandry, have long despaired of success in rearing turkeys, and complained that the profit rarely indemnifies them for their trouble and loss of time; whereas, continues he, little more is to be done than to plunge the chick into a vessel of cold water, the very hour, or if that cannot be, the day it is hatched, forcing it to swallow one whole peppercorn, and then restoring it to its mother. From that time it will become hardy, and fear the cold no more than a hen's chick. After which it must be remembered that these useful creatures are subject to one particular malady whilst they are young, which carries them off in a few days. When they begin to droop, examine carefully the feathers on their rump, and you will find two or three, whose quill part is filled with blood. Upon drawing these the chick recovers, and after that requires no other care than what is commonly bestowed on poultry that range the court-yard.

"These articles are too true to be denied; and in proof of the success, three parishes in Sweden have, for many years, gained several hundred pounds by rearing and selling turkeys."

TURNIP, [*Rapa.*] Miller reckons three distinct species of turnips, the round, the oblong, and the French turnip; the first is the common field turnip, and of this there are several varieties, but the large green topped is chiefly preferred above all the rest.

Perhaps there has never been a greater improvement in husbandry than sowing turnips, not only for the advantage of keeping a larger quantity of stock than could otherwise be done, but also the great advantage which the ground will receive from the turnips themselves, especially if they are eaten off the land by sheep. Turnips will grow on strong land as well as on light land, but light land will best bear the foot of the sheep, when feeding off.

Turnips should be sown according as they may be wanted, from Midsummer to a fortnight following, and will require a winter and summer fallow of the land thoroughly to clean it; dung will be proper where it can be afforded, as the turnips will grow the faster, and be sooner out of the reach of the fly. About a pint of seed is enough for an acre; and soon after they put forth the first leaf, they should be hoed and thoroughly thinned, and soon after they should be hoed again with a six or seven inch hoe; this will keep down all annual weeds, and wonderfully assist the vegetation and growth of the turnips, by drawing the earth to the roots and leaving them sufficient room to spread.

We would advise the farmer to be very careful to obtain his seed of a good sort, and at a distance, from a person on whom he can rely.

If the fly should attack the turnips, we advise him to sow some lime-kiln wood-ashes which have never been wetted over the turnips, while the dew is on them, as from our own experience we can warrant it successful.

There has been another method practised in the turnip husbandry, and that is by drilling, which by those who have tried it, is much recommended, but still, we fancy the broad-cast will outlive the other. Farmers are a prudent set of men, and not easily misled into the schemes of uncertainty; whenever they find the practice is really good they will follow it, but they must have better evidence than is generally given.

When caterpillars attack the turnips, Mr. Miller recommends to turn in hungry poultry.

When the turnips are all off, Mr. Miller says one ploughing will do for barley;—it may be so, but we will take upon ourselves to say that three will do better; nor would we chuse to trust to one ploughing for barley. Indeed when the season ran backward, we might venture to trust white oats to one ploughing, but nothing but necessity should induce us to do that.

Turnip-rooted *Cabbage*. See Cabbage.

TURNSOLE. See Heliotrope.

TURPENTINE, [*Terebinthia.*] The species of turpentines kept in the druggists shops are, the Chian or cypress turpentine, the Venice turpentine, the Strasburg turpentine, and the common turpentine.

The Chian or cypress turpentine is generally about the consistence of thick honey, very tenacious, clear, and almost transparent, of a white colour, with a cast of yellow, and frequently of blue; it has a warm, pungent, bitterish taste, and a fragrant smell, more agreeable than any of the other turpentines.

This juice is the produce of the common terebinth, an evergreen tree or shrub, which grows spontaneously in the warmer climates, and endures the colds of our own. The turpentine brought to us, is extracted in the islands whose names it bears, by wounding the trunk and branches a little after the buds have come forth; the juice issues limpid, and clear as water, and by degrees thickens into the consistence in which we meet with it. A like juice exuding from this tree in the eastern countries, inspissated by a slow fire, is of frequent use, as a masticatory, among the Persian ladies, who (as Kœmpfer informs us) are continually chewing it, in order to fasten and whiten the teeth, sweeten the breath, and promote appetite.

Venice turpentine is usually thinner than any of the other sorts, of a clear, whitish, or pale yellowish colour, a hot, pungent, bitterish, disagreeable taste, and a strong smell, without any thing of the fine aromatic flavour of the Chian kind.

The true Venice turpentine is obtained from the larch, a large tree growing in great abundance upon the Alps and Pyrenean mountains, and not uncommon in the English gardens. What is usually met with in the shops, under the name of Venice turpentine, comes from New England; of what tree it is the produce, we have no certain account: the finer kinds of it are in appearance and quality not considerably different from the true sort above described.

Strasburgh turpentine is, as we generally meet with it, of a middle consistence betwixt the two foregoing, more transparent, and less tenacious than either; its colour a yellowish brown. Its smell is very fragrant, and more agreeable than that of any of the other turpentines, except the Chian; in taste it is the bitterest, yet the least acrid.

Common turpentine is the coarsest, heaviest, in taste and smell the most disagreeable, of all the sorts; it is about the consistence of honey, of an opake brownish white colour.

This is obtained from the wild pine, a low unhandsome tree, common in different

different parts of Europe: this tree is extremely resinous, and remarkably subject to a disease from a redundance and extravasation of its resin, insomuch that, without due evacuation, it swells and bursts. The juice, as it issues from the tree, is received in trenches made in the earth, and afterwards freed from the grosser impurities by colature through wicker baskets.

All these juices yield in distillation with water, an highly penetrating essential oil, a brittle insipid resin remaining behind. With regard to their medical virtues, they promote urine, cleanse the parts concerned in the evacuation thereof, and deterge internal ulcers in general; and at the same time, like other bitter hot substances, strengthen the tone of the vessels: they have an advantage above most other acrid diuretics, that they gently loosen the belly. They are principally recommended in gleets, the fluor albus, and the like; and by some in calculous complaints: where these last proceed from sand or gravel, formed into a mass by viscid mucous matter, the turpentines, by dissolving the mucus, promote the expulsion of the sand; but where a calculus is formed, they can do no service, and only ineffectually irritate or inflame the parts. In all cases accompanied with inflammation, these juices ought to be abstained from, as this symptom is increased, and not unfrequently occasioned by them. It is observable, that the turpentines impart, soon after taking them, a violet smell to the urine; and have this effect, though applied only externally to remote parts; particularly the Venice sort. This is accounted the most powerful as a diuretic and detergent; and the Chian and Strasburgh as corroborants: the Strasburgh is an ingredient in the mercurial pills and Locatellus's balsam, and the Chian in mithridate and theriaca. The common turpentine, as being the most offensive, is rarely given internally. Its principal use is in plaisters and ointments, among farriers, and for the distillation of the oil or spirit, as it is called. The dose of these juices is from a scruple to a dram and a half: they are most commodiously taken in the form of a bolus, or dissolved in watery liquors by the mediation of the yolk of an egg or mucilage. Of the distilled oil, a few drops are a sufficient dose: this is a most potent, stimulating, detergent diuretic, oftentimes greatly heats the constitution, and requires the utmost caution in its exhibition.

TURPENTINE *Tree*. See MASTIC TREE.

Venice TURPENTINE *Tree*. The Larch tree.

TUTSAN. St. John's Wort.

TWIFALLOWING. Ploughing the ground a second time.

HERB TWOPENCE, [*Nummularia.*] This grows spontaneously in moist watery places, and creeps on the ground, with two little roundish leaves at each joint. Their taste is subastringent, and very lightly acid; hence they stand recommended by Boerhaave in the hot scurvy, and in uterine and other hæmorrhages. But their effects are so inconsiderable, that common practice takes no notice of them.

TWYBLADE. See BIFOIL.

Twitch-grass. See Couch-grass.

Twin cow-calf never breeds. See Freemartin.

— [illegible] — is [illegible] to breed &c.

V.

VALE. Low ground; a valley.

VALERIAN, [*Valeriana.*] There are many species of this plant, but that chiefly esteemed, is the mountain, or wild valerian, the roots of which are much used in medicine.

This root consists of a number of strings or fibres matted together, issuing from one common head; of a whitish or pale brownish colour: its smell is strong, like a mixture of aromatics with fœtids; the taste unpleasantly warm, bitterish, and subacrid. There is another wild valerian, with broader leaves, of a deeper and shining green colour, met with in watery places. Both sorts have hitherto been used indiscriminately, and Linnæus has joined them into one species, under the name of *valeriana foliis omnibus pinnatis*. Our college have restrained the shops to the first, which is considerably the strongest, and loses of its quality, if transplanted into such soils as the other naturally delights in. The roots, produced in low watery grounds, have a remarkably faint smell in comparison of the others, and sometimes scarce any at all. Wild valerian is a medicine of great use in nervous disorders, and is particularly serviceable in epilepsies proceeding from a debility of the nervous system. It was first brought into esteem in these cases by Fabius Columna, who by taking the powdered root, in the dose of half a spoonful, was cured of an inveterate epilepsy after many other medicines had been tried in vain. Repeated experience has since confirmed its efficacy in this disorder; and the present practice lays considerable stress upon it. The common dose is from a scruple to a dram, in infusion from one to two drams. Its unpleasant flavour is most effectually concealed by a suitable addition of mace.

Greek VALERIAN. See GREEK VALERIAN.

VAN. An instrument to winnow corn.

VASCULIFEROUS *Plants*. Such whose seeds are contained in vessels divided into cells.

VAT. A vessel for holding wine, ale, beer, cyder, &c. in the time of their preparation. Also Cheese Vat

UDDER. That part of a cow, mare, ewe, &c. where the milk is prepared, answering to the breasts in women.

VEGETABLE. A term applied to all plants, considered as capable of growth, i. e. all natural bodies which have parts organically formed for generation and accretion, but not sensation.

Vegetables, according to the analyses made of them by chemistry, are distinguishable into two grand tribes, the acid and the alkaline; the first affording a volatile acid, and the second a volotile alkali, upon a dry distillation; thus guaiacum, cedar, box, cinnamon, cloves, sorrel, mint, balm, &c. afford an acid; but garlic, onions, horse-radish, scurvy-grass, mustard, &c. afford an alkali, which rectified, is hardly distinguishable from that of animal substances, so as nearly to resemble the spirit and salt of hartshorn.

VEGETATION. The act whereby plants receive their nourishment and growths; of which, three principal functions are understood, viz. nutrition, increase, and generation.

From Scripture we learn, that the earth has been endued, from the beginning, with a certain seminal virtue to produce plants; which virtue, proceeding from God, was not confined to the first production of things, but extends likewise to all future consequences of times; and this faculty which the earth has of producing plants,

plants, is from this commandment of the Almighty: "Let the earth bring forth grass, the herb yielding seed, and the fruit-tree yielding fruit after his kind, whose seed is in itself upon the earth; and it was so."

VELLING. Ploughing, or cutting up the turf, or upper surface of the ground, in order to its being burnt.

VENTILATOR. A machine by which the noxious air of any close place (as an hospital, jail, ship, chamber, granary, &c.) may be changed for fresh air.

VENUS' COMB. See *Sweet* FERN.

VENUS' LOOKING GLASS. Corn Violet.

VENUS' NAVELWORT. See *Venus'* NAVELWORT.

VERJUICE. A liquor obtained from grapes or apples too acid for wine or cyder. It is generally made in England from the juice of the crab, or wild apple.

VERMIN. A collective name including all kinds of small animals, that are troublesome to men, beasts, corn, fruits, &c.

VERNAL. Something belonging to the spring season.

VERTICULATE *Plants*. Such as produce their flowers round the joints of the stalks in whorles; as hyssop, mint, thyme, &c.

VERVAIN, [*Verbena*.] This plant is very common on the sides of roads, foot-paths, and farm-yards, near habitations; for although there is scarce any part of England, in which this is not found in plenty, yet it is never found above a quarter of a mile from a house; which occasioned its being called Simpler's Joy, because wherever this plant is found growing, it is a sure token of a house being near; this is a certain fact, but not easy to be accounted for. It is rarely cultivated in gardens, but is the sort directed by the College of Physicians for medicinal use, and is brought to the markets by those who gather it in the fields.

There are many other species of vervain, natives of different counties, some of which are too tender to bear the cold of our climate, and require the assistance of the green-house and stove.

VERVAIN MALLOW. Hollyhock.

VETCH. See TARE.

Bitter VETCH. See BITTER VETCH.

Chicklin VETCH. See CHICKLIN VETCH.

Crimson Grass VETCH. Chicklin Vetch.

Hatchet VETCH, [*Securidaca*.] This plant grows naturally in the corn-fields in Spain and Italy; it is annual, and hath trailing herbaceous stalks, which grow a foot and a half long, dividing into many branches, which spread on the ground, garnished with winged leaves, composed of seven or eight pair of oval obtuse lobes terminated by an odd one, of a deep green and smooth.

It is propagated by sowing the seeds in borders of light earth in the spring, in the places where the plants are to abide, for they seldom succeed well if they are transplanted; they should be allowed at least two feet distance, because their branches trail upon the ground. When the plants come up, they will require no other care but to thin them where they are too close, and keep them clean from weeds. A few of these plants may be admitted into every good garden for variety, though there is no great beauty in their flowers.

Horse-shoe VETCH. See HORSE VETCH.

Liquorice VETCH. See WILD LIQUORICE.

Milk VETCH. Liquorice Vetch.

VETCHLING, [*Apaca*.] This plant is found wild in divers parts of England on arable land, but is seldom preserved in gardens. It is an annual plant, which perishes soon after the seeds are perfected.

VINE, [*Vitis*.] There are a great number of grapes cultivated in the gardens, and are all propagated either from layers or cuttings, the latter of which is the more preferable method; for the roots of vines do not grow strong and woody, as in most sorts of trees, but are long, slender, and pliable; therefore when they are taken out of the ground they seldom strike out any fibres from the weak roots, which generally shrivel and dry; so that they rather retard than help the plants in their growth, by preventing the new fibres from pushing out; for which reason it is betteer to plant a good cutting than a rooted plant, provided it be well chosen,

chosen, for there is little danger of its growing.

But as there are few persons who make choice of proper cuttings, or at least that form their cuttings rightly in England, so it will be proper to give directions for this in the first place. You should always make choice of such shoots as are strong and well ripened of the last year's growth; these should be cut from the old vine, just below the place where they were produced, taking a knot or piece of the two-years wood to each, which should be pruned smooth; then you should cut off the upper part of the shoots, so as to leave the cutting about sixteen inches long. When the piece or knot of old wood is cut at both ends near the young shoot, the cuttings will resemble a little mallet; from whence Columella gives the title of malleolus to the vine-cutting. In making the cuttings after this manner, there can be but one taken from each shoot; whereas most persons cut them into lengths of about a foot, and plant them all, which is very wrong, for the upper part of the shoots are never so well ripened as the lower, which was produced early in the spring, and has had the whole summer to harden; so that if they take root, they never make so good plants, for the wood of those cuttings being spongy and soft, admits the moisture too freely, whereby the plants will be luxuriant in growth, but never so fruitful as such whose wood is closer and more compact.

When the cuttings are thus prepared, if they are not then planted, they should be placed with their lower part in the ground in a dry soil, laying some litter upon their upper parts to prevent them from drying: in this situation they may remain till the beginning of April, (which is the best time for planting them) when you should take them out, and wash them from the filth they have contracted; and if you find them very dry, you should let them stand with their lower parts in water six or eight hours, which will distend their vessels, and dispose them for taking root. Then the ground being before prepared where the plants are designed to remain (whether against walls or for standards, for they should not be removed again) the cuttings should be planted; but in preparing the ground you should consider the nature of the soil, which, if strong, and inclinable to wet, is by no means proper for grapes; therefore where it so happens, you should open a trench where the cuttings are to be planted, which should be filled with lime rubbish, the better to drain off the moisture; then raise the border with fresh light earth about two feet thick, so that it may be at least a foot above the level of the ground; then you should open the holes at about six feet distance from each other, putting one good strong cutting into each hole, which should be laid a little sloping, that their tops may incline to the wall: but it must [illegible] the uppermost eye may be level with the surface of [illegible] for when any part of the cutting is left above ground, as is the [illegible] used by the English ga[illegible] most of the buds attempt to [illegible] the strength of the cutting [illegible] divided to nourish so many shoots, which must of course be weaker than if one only of them grew; whereas, on the contrary, by burying the whole cutting in the ground, the sap is all employed on one single shoot, which consequently will be much stronger; besides, the sun and air are apt to dry that part of the cutting which remains above ground, and so often prevents their buds from shooting.

Then having placed the cutting into the ground, you should fill up the hole gently, pressing down the earth with your foot close about it, and raise a little hill just upon the top of the cutting, to cover the upper eye quite over, which will prevent it from drying; this being done, there is nothing more necessary but to keep the ground clear from weeds until the cuttings begin to shoot; at which time you should look over them carefully, to rub off any small shoots, if such are produced, fastening the first main shoot to the wall, which should be constantly trained up, as it is extended in length, to prevent its breaking or hanging down; you must continue to look over these once in about three weeks during the summer season, constantly rubbing off all lateral shoots which are produced; and be sure to keep the ground constantly clear from weeds, which, if suffered to grow, will exhaust the goodness of the soil and starve the cuttings.

The

The Michaelmas following, if your cuttings have produced strong ſhoots, you ſhould prune them down to two eyes.

In the ſpring, after the cold weather is paſt, you muſt gently dig up the borders, to looſen the earth; but you muſt be very careful in doing this, not to injure the roots of the vines; you ſhould alſo raiſe the earth up to the ſtems of the plants, ſo as to cover the old wood, but not ſo deep as to cover either of the eyes of the laſt years wood. After this they will require no farther care until they begin to ſhoot, when you ſhould look over them carefully, to rub off all weak dangling ſhoots, leaving no more than the two ſhoots, which are produced from the two eyes of the laſt year's wood, which ſhould be faſtened to the wall; and ſo from this, until the vines have done ſhooting, you ſhould look them over once in three weeks or a month, to rub off all lateral ſhoots as they are produced, and to faſten the main ſhoots to the wall as they are extended in length, which muſt not be ſhortened before the middle or latter end of July, when it will be proper to nip off their tops, which will ſtrengthen the lower eyes, and during the ſummer ſeaſon you muſt conſtantly keep the ground clear from weeds; nor ſhould you permit any ſort of plants to grow near the vines, which would not only rob them of nouriſhment, but ſhade the lower parts of the ſhoots, and thereby prevent their ripening; which will not only cauſe their wood to be ſpongy and luxuriant, but render it leſs fruitful.

As ſoon as the leaves begin to drop in autumn, you ſhould prune theſe young vines again, leaving three buds to each of the ſhoots, provided they are ſtrong; otherwiſe it is better to ſhorten them down to two eyes if they are good, for it is a very wrong practice to leave much wood upon young vines, or to leave their ſhoots too long, which greatly weakens the roots; then you ſhould faſten them to the wall, ſpreading them out horizontally each way, that there may be room to train the new ſhoots the following ſummer, and in the ſpring the borders muſt be digged as before.

The third ſeaſon you muſt go over the vines again, as ſoon as they begin to ſhoot, to rub off all danglers as before, and train the ſtrong ſhoots in their proper places, which this year may be ſuppoſed to be two from each ſhoot of laſt year's wood; but if they attempt to produce two ſhoots from one eye, the weakeſt of them muſt be rubbed off, for there ſhould never be more than one allowed to come out of each eye. If any of them produce fruit, as many times they will the third year, you ſhould not ſtop them ſo ſoon as is generally practiſed upon the bearing ſhoots of old vines, but permit them to ſhoot forward till a month after Midſummer, at which time you may pinch off the tops of the ſhoots; for if this were done too ſoon, it would ſpoil the buds for the next year's wood, which in young vines muſt be more carefully preſerved than on older plants, becauſe there are no other to be laid in for a ſupply of wood, as is commonly practiſed on old vines.

During the ſummer you muſt conſtantly go over your vines, and diſplace all weak lateral ſhoots as they are produced, and carefully keep the ground clear from weeds, as was before directed, that the ſhoots may ripen well, which is a material thing to be obſerved in moſt ſorts of fruit-trees, but eſpecially in vines, which ſeldom produce any fruit from immature branches. Theſe things being duly obſerved, are all that is neceſſary in the management of young vines.

Spaniſh Arbor VINE. Bindweed.

White VINE. } Briony.
Wild VINE. }

VINEGAR, [*Acetum.*] An acid penetrating liquor, prepared from wine, cyder, beer, &c. of conſiderable uſe both as a medicine and ſauce.

The proceſs of turning vegetable matters to vinegar, is thus delivered by Dr. Shaw: Take the ſkins of raiſins, after they have been uſed in making wine, and pour three or four times their own quantity of boiling water upon them, ſo as to make a thin aqueous mixture. Then ſet the containing caſk, looſely covered, in a warmer place than is uſed for vinous fermentation; and the liquor in a few weeks time will become a clear and ſound vinegar; which being drawn off from its ſediment, and preſerved in another caſk, well ſtopped down, will continue perfect, and fit for uſe.

 This

This experiment shews us a cheap and ready way of making vinegar from refuse materials; such as the husks of grapes, decayed raisins, the lees of wine, grounds of ale, beer, &c. which are frequently thrown away as useless. Thus, in many wine countries, the marc, rape, or dry pressing of grapes, are thrown in heaps, and suffered to putrify unregarded, though capable of affording as good vinegar as the wine itself. In some places they bury copper plates in these husks, in order to make verdigrease; but this practice seems chiefly confined to the southern parts of France. Our present experiment shews us how to convert them to another use; and the direction extends to all the matters that have once undergone, or are fit to undergo a vinous fermentation, for that all such matters will afford vinegar. Thus all our summer-fruits in England, even blackberries; all the refuse washings of a sugar-house, cyder-pressings, or the like, will make vinegar, by means of water, the open air, and warmth.

The whole process, whereby this change is effected, deserves to be attentively considered; and first, the liquor to be thus changed, being kept warmer than in vinous fermentation, it begins in a few days to grow thick or turbid; and without throwing up bubbles, or making any considerable tumult, as happens in vinous fermentation, deposits a copious sediment.

The effect of this separation begins to appear first on the surface of the liquor, which gathers a white skin, that daily increases in thickness, till at length it becomes like leather; and now, if continued longer in this state, the skin turns blue, or green, and would at last grow solid, and putrify; therefore, in keeping down this skin as it grows, and thrusting it gently down to the bottom of the vessel, consists much of the art of vinegar-making, especially from malt.

Method of making Cyder Vinegar. The cyder (the meanest of which will serve the purpose) is first to be drawn off fine into another vessel, and a quantity of must, or pouz of apples, to be added; the whole is to be set in the sun, if there be a conveniency for the purpose; and at a week or nine days end, it may be drawn off.

Method of making Beer Vinegar. Take a middling sort of beer, indifferently well hopped; into which, when it has worked well, and is grown fine, put some rape, or husk of grapes, usually brought home for that purpose; mash them together in a tub, then, letting the rape settle, draw off the liquid part, put it into a cask, and set it in the sun as hot as may be (the bung only covered with a tile or slate-stone) and in about thirty or forty days, it will become a good vinegar, and may pass in use as well as that made of wine, if it be refined, and kept from turning musty.

Or thus: to every gallon of spring-water, add three pounds of Malaga-raisins; which put into an earthen jar, and place them where they may have the hottest sun from May till Michaelmas; then pressing all well, tun the liquor up in a very strong iron-hooped vessel, to prevent its bursting; it will appear very thick and muddy, when newly pressed; but will refine in the vessel, and be as clear as wine.

Thus let it remain untouched for three months, before it be drawn off, and it will prove excellent vinegar.

Method of making Wine Vinegar. Any sort of vinous liquor, being mixed with its own fæces, flowers, or ferment, and its tartar, first reduced to powder; or else with the acid and austere stalks of the vegetable from whence the wine was obtained, which hold a large proportion of tartar; and the whole being kept frequently stirring in a vessel which has formerly held vinegar, or set in a warm place full of the steams of the same, will begin to ferment anew, conceive heat, grow sour by degrees, and soon turn into vinegar.

The remote subjects of acetous fermentation are the same with those of vinous; but the immediate subjects of it are all kinds of vegetable juices, after they have once undergone that fermentation which reduces them to wine; for it is absolutely impossible to make vinegar of must, the crude juice of grapes, or other ripe fruits, without the previous assistance of vinous fermentation.

The proper ferments for this operation, whereby vinegar is prepared, are, 1. The fæces of all acid wines. 2. The leys of vinegar. 3. Pulverised tartar;

tartar; especially that of Rhenish wine, or the cream, or chrystals thereof. 4. Vinegar itself. 5. A wooden vessel well drenched with vinegar, or one that has been long employed to contain it. 6. Wine that has often been mixed with its own fæces. 7. The twigs of vines, and the stalks of grapes, currants, cherries, and other vegetables of an acid austere taste. 8. Baker's leaven, after it is turned acid. 9. All manner of ferments, compounded of those already mentioned.

The French use a method of making vinegar different from that above described. They take two large oaken vessels, the larger the better, open at top; in each of which they place a wooden grate, within a foot of the bottom; upon these grates they first lay twigs, or cuttings of vines, and afterwards the stalks of the bunches without the grapes themselves, or their stones; till the whole pile reaches within a foot of the brim of the vessels; then they fill one of these vessels with wine to the very top, and half fill the other; and with liquor drawn out of the full vessel, fill up that which was only half full before; daily repeating the same operation, and pouring the liquor back from one vessel into another; so that each of them is full, and half full, by turns.

When this process has been continued for two or three days, a degree of heat will arise in the vessel, which is then but half full, and increase for several days successively, without any appearance of the like in the vessel which happens to be full; during those days; the liquor whereof will still remain cool; and as soon as the heat ceases in the vessel that is half full, the vinegar is prepared: which, in the summer, happens on the fourteenth or fifteenth day from the beginning; but in the winter, the fermentation proceeds much slower, so that they are obliged to forward it by artificial warmth, or the use of stoves.

When the weather is exceeding hot, the liquor ought to be poured off from the full vessel into the other twice a day; otherwise the liquor will be over-heated, and the fermentation prove too strong; whence the spirituous parts will fly away, and leave a vapid wine, instead of a vinegar behind.

The full vessel is always to be left open at the top, but the mouth of the other must be closed with a cover of wood, in order the better to keep down and fix the spirit in the body of the liquor; otherwise, it might easily fly off in the heat of fermentation. The vessel that is only half full seems to grow hot rather than the other, because it contains a much greater quantity of the vine-twigs and stalks, than that, in proportion to the liquor; above which, the pile rising to a considerable height, conceives heat the more, and so conveys it to the wine below.

Vinegar is a medicine of excellent use in all kinds of inflammatory and putrid disorders, either internal or external; in ardent bilious fevers, pestilential and other malignant distempers, it is recommended by Boerhaave as one of the most certain sudorifics. Weakness, fainting, vomiting, hysterical and hypochondriacal complaints have also been frequently relieved by vinegar applied to the mouth or nose, or received into the stomach. Distilled vinegar has the same virtues, only in a stronger degree.

There are also medicated vinegars; as vinegar of antimony, of elder, litharge, roses, squills, treacle, &c. which derive their chief virtues from the vinegar.

VINEYARD. A plantation of vines without the assistance of walls.

VINOUS. Something that relates to wine, or that hath the taste and smell of it.

VINTAGE. A crop of grapes, or the produce of a vineyard each season.

VIOLET, [*Viola*.] This is often found wild in hedges and shady places, and flowers in March; the shops are generally supplied from the gardens. In our markets we meet with the flowers of a different species; these may be distinguished from the foregoing by their being larger, of a pale colour, and of no smell. The officinal flowers have a very pleasant smell, and a deep purplish blue colour, denominated from them violet. They impart their colour and flavour to aqueous liquors: a syrup made from this infusion has long maintained a place in the shops, and proves an agreeable and useful laxative for children.

Dame's

Dame's VIOLET. See DAME's VIOLET.

Bulbous VIOLET. Snowdrop.

Dog's Tooth VIOLET. See DOG's TOOTH.

Corn VIOLET. See CORN VIOLET.

VIPER. The name of a well-known ferpent, common in many parts of England.

The bathing the part bit by a viper with olive oil, is faid to effectually prevent the fatal confequences that would otherwife attend it.

VIPER's BUGLOSS, [*Echium.*] This plant grows naturally on chalky lands in moft parts of England. There are feveral fpecies brought into the Englifh gardens, from Germany, France, Portugal, and other countries, fome of which are annual, and fome biennial plants. They are propagated by feeds.

VIPER's GRASS, [*Scorzonera.*] This plant is cultivated in the Englifh gardens for food and phyfic; it grows naturally in Spain. The root is carrot-fhaped, about the thicknefs of a finger, covered with a dark brown fkin, is white within, and has a milky juice; the lower leaves are long, ending with a long acute point; they are waved and finuated at their edges. The ftalk rifes three feet high, is fmooth, branching at the top, and garnifhed with a few narrow leaves, whofe bafe half embrace the ftalk. The flowers terminate the ftalks in fcaly empalements, compofed of many narrow, tongue-fhaped hermaphrodite florets, lying imbricatim over each other like the fcales on fifh; they are of a bright yellow colour. After thefe are decayed, the germen which fits in the common empalement turns to oblong cornered feeds, having a roundifh ball of feathery down at the top. There are feveral fpecies kept in the gardens, all propagated by feeds.

VIRGIN's BOWER. See CLIMBERS.

VIRGINIAN SILK, [*Periploca.*] This plant grows naturally in Syria, but is hardy enough to thrive in the open air in England. It hath twining fhrubby ftalks, covered with a dark bark, which twift round any neighbouring fupport, and will rife more than forty feet high, fending out flender branches from the fides, which twine round each other, and are garnifhed with oval fpear-fhaped leaves near four inches long, and two broad in the middle, of a lucid green on their upper fide, but pale on their under, ftanding by pairs upon fhort footftalks.

This is hardy enough to thrive in this country with a little protection from the froft of the winter. Another fort brought from Vera Cruz requires the affiftance of a warm ftove.

VIRGINIAN ACACIA. See ACACIA.

VITRIOL. A faline chryftalline concrete, compofed of metal, and an acid, fimilar to thofe of fulphur and allum. There are but three metallic bodies, which this acid is capable of perfectly diffolving or being united with i to a chryftalline appearance, zinc, copper, and iron; with the firft it forms a white, with the fecond a blue and with the third a green falt.

White VITRIOL. Found in the mines of Goflar, fometimes in tranfparent pieces, but more commonly in form of white efflorefcences, which are diffolved in water, and afterwards reduced by evaporation and chryftallization into large maffes.

Blue VITRIOL. Greateft part of the blue vitriol at prefent met with in the fhops, is faid to be artificially prepared by uniting copper with the vitriolic acid.

Green VITRIOL. This is prepared in large quantity at Deptford, by diffolving iron in the acid liquor, which runs from certain fulphureous pyrites expofed for a length of time.

ULIGINOUS. An appellation given to a moift, moorifh, and fenny foil.

UMBEL. The extremity of a ftalk or branch of a plant, divided into feveral peduncles, or rays, beginning from the fame point, and opening in fuch a manner, as to form an inverted cone.

UMBELLIFEROUS *Plants.* Thefe whofe flowers are produced in an umbel, on the top of the ftalks, fomewhat refembling an umbrella. Of this kind are the fennel, parfley, parfnip, carrot, hemlock, &c.

UNDERWOOD. Coppice, or any wood not accounted timber.

VOOR. Fallow land.

URE. The udder of a cow, fheep, or other animal.

URITH.

URITH. Etherings, or windings of hedges.

URRY. A sort of blue or black clay, lying near a vein of coal.

URINE. A serous and saline matter separated from the blood of animals, and emitted by the canal of the urethra.

It is of excellent use as a manure, when deprived of its hot fiery particles by time, which will so alter its nature as to render it an extraordinary fertilizer of every kind of soil. Columella certifies that old urine is excellent for the roots of trees. Mr. Hartlib commends the Dutch for preserving the urine of cows as carefully as they do the dung, to enrich their lands; and instances a woman he knew near Canterbury, who saved in a pail all the urine she could, and when the pail was full, sprinkled it on her meadow, the grass of which looked yellow at first, but afterwards grew surprisingly. Similar to this is what Mr. Bradley relates, as of his own knowledge. Human urine was thrown into a little pit constantly every day, for three or four years. Two years after, some earth was taken out of this pit, and mixed with twice as much other earth, to fill up a hollow place in a grass walk. The turf which was laid upon this spot grew so largely and vigorously, besides being much greener than the rest, that by the best computation he could make, its grass, in a month's time, was above four times as much in quantity as that of any other spot of the same size, though the whole walk was laid on very rich ground. The author of the English Improver is therefore very right in saying, that human urine is of greater worth, and will fatten land more, than is generally imagined by our farmers, whom he advises to take all opportunities of preserving this, and every sort of urine, for their ground, as carefully as is done in Holland.

USTILAGO. The same with burnt grain.

UTENSIL. A domestic moveable of any kind.

W.

WAD, black lead.

WAGGON, a vehicle or carriage, of which there are various forms, accommodated to the different uses they are intended for. *See the article* WHEEL.

WAIF, an estray, which for want of the owner's appearance after it has been cried and published in the neighbouring markets, is forfeited to the lord of the manor.

WAKE ROBIN. See ARUM.

WALKS are made either of gravel, sand, or grass; these three sorts of walks are the most common in England; but where gravel or sand cannot be procured, they are sometimes laid with powdered coal, sea-coal ashes, and sometimes of powdered brick, but these are rarely used, when either gravel or sand can be procured; however, where sea coal ashes can be had, it is preferable to the powdered coal or bricks, because they bind very hard, and never stick to the feet in frosty weather, which is a good quality, but the darkness of its colour has been an objection to the use of it in gardens; however, for wilderness-walks we think it is preferable to most other materials; but we shall proceed to give directions for the making of the several sorts of walks, and first of the gravel-walks.

In order to the laying of walks in gardens, when they are marked out, the earth should be taken away to a certain depth, that the bottom of them may be filled with some lime-rubbish, or coarse gravel, flint stones, or other rocky materials, which will be serviceable to prevent weeds from growing through the gravel, and also to keep away worm-casts. This bottom should be laid ten inches or a foot thick, over which the coat of gravel should be six or eight inches; which gravel should

be

be fine, but yet not ſkreened, becauſe that ſpoils it. This ſhould be laid on a heap, rounding, that the larger rough ſtones may run down on the ſides, which being every now and then raked off, the gravel by that means will be ſufficiently fine.

After the gravel has been laid to the thickneſs above-mentioned, then the walks muſt be exactly levelled, and raked true from all great drips, as well as little holes. By this means moſt of the ſtones of the walks will be raked under your feet, which ſhould rather be gently ſprinkled back again, over the laſt length that is raked, than buried, (as is the practice of many gardeners) for by this means the walk will lie much harder, and the coarſeſt ſtones will very much contribute to its firmneſs.

There is alſo a great fault committed frequently, in laying walks too round, and ſome to that degree, that they cannot be walked on with that eaſe and pleaſure that ought to be.

The common allowance for a gravel-walk of five feet breadth, is an inch riſe in the crown; ſo that if a walk be twenty feet wide, according to this proportion, it will be four inches higher in the middle than on each ſide, and a walk of twenty-five feet will be five inches, one of thirty feet ſix inches, and ſo on.

When a walk has been thus carefully laid, trodden down, and raked, or rather, after every length or part of it, (which commonly is about fifteen feet each) then it ſhould be rolled well both in length, and alſo croſs-ways. The perſon who rolls it ſhould wear ſhoes with flat heels, that he may not make holes in the walks, for when theſe are once made in a new walk, it will not be eaſy to roll them out again.

In order to lay gravel-walks firm, it will be neceſſary to give them three or four water-rollings, that is, they muſt be rolled when it rains ſo very faſt, that the walks ſwim with water; this will cauſe the gravel to bind, ſo that when the walks come to be dry, they will be as hard as terrace.

Iron-mould gravel is accounted the beſt for binding, or gravel with a little binding loam in it; which latter, tho' it be apt to ſtick to the heels of ſhoes in wet weather, yet nothing binds better in dry weather.

When the gravel is over ſandy, ſome ſharp loam is frequently mixed with it, which, if they be caſt together in heaps, and well mixed, will bind like a rock; whereas, looſe gravel is as uncomfortable and uneaſy to walk on as any other fault in a walk can render it.

The beſt gravel for walks is ſuch as abounds with ſmooth pebbles (as is that dug at Blackheath) which being mixed with a due proportion of loam, will bind like a rock, and is never injured by wet or dry weather, and the pebbles being ſmooth, are not ſo liable to be turned up and looſened by the feet in walking, as are thoſe which are angular and rough; for where walks are laid with ſuch gravel as is full of irregular ſtones, they appear unſightly in a day's time after rolling, becauſe the ſtones will riſe upon the ſurface whenever they are walked upon, but the ſmooth pebbles will remain handſome two or three days without rolling.

Gravel-walks are not only very neceſſary near the houſe, but there ſhould always be one carried quite round the garden, becauſe, being ſoon dry after rain, they are proper for walking on in all ſeaſons; but then theſe ſhould be narrow, and thoſe adjoining to the houſe ought to be large and magnificent, proportionable to the grandeur of the houſe and garden. The principal of theſe walks ſhould be elevated, and carried parallel with the houſe, ſo as to form a terrace; this ſhould extend itſelf each way, in proportion to the width of the garden; ſo that from this there may be a communication with the ſide-walks, without going on the graſs, that there may be a dry walk continued quite through the gardens; but there is not a more ridiculous ſight, than that of a ſtrait gravel-walk leading to the front of a houſe, interſecting the graſs, ſo as to make it appear like the ſtiff formal graſs-plats frequently made in little court-yards by perſons of low taſte.

Graſs-walks in gardens were formerly in great eſteem, and looked upon as neceſſary ornaments to a garden; but of late years they have juſtly been baniſhed by every perſon of true taſte.

Having given directions for the making

king of gravel-walks, we come next to treat of sand-walks, which are now very frequently made in gardens, as being less expensive in the making, and also in the keeping, than the former; and in very irregular gardens, which are such as most persons esteem, this is a very great article; for as the greatest part of the walks which are made in gardens are carried about in an irregular manner, it would be very difficult to keep them handsome if they were laid with gravel, especially where they are shaded by trees; for the dripping of the water from their branches in hard rains, is apt to wash the gravel in holes, and render the walks very unsightly; and when these wood-walks are of grass, they do not appear sightly, nor are they very proper to be walked on; for after rain they continue so long damp as to render them unfit for use, and the grass generally grows spiry and weak for want of air, and by the dropping of the trees, will by degrees be destroyed; therefore it is much better to lay these walks with sand, which will be dry and wholsome; and whenever they appear mossy, or any weeds begin to grow on them, if they are scuffled over with a Dutch hoe in dry weather, and then raked smooth, it will destroy the weeds and moss, and make the walks appear as fresh and handsome as if they had been new laid.

In the modern way of laying out gardens the walks are carried through woods and plantations, so that these are shady and convenient for walking in the middle of the day. These are usually carried about, winding as much as the ground will admit of, so as to leave a sufficient thickness of wood to make the walks private; and that the persons who are walking in one part of them may not be seen by those who are walking in any of the other parts.

Where these walks are contrived with judgment, a small extent of ground will admit of a great many turns, so that a person may walk some miles in a small garden. But these turns should be made as natural as possible, so as not to appear too much like a work of art, which will never please so long as the former.

The breadth of these walks must be proportioned to the size of the ground, which in a large extent may be eight or ten feet wide, but in small gardens five or six feet will be sufficient. As the walks are designed to wind as much as the ground will allow, so this width will be sufficient; because the wider they are, the greater must be the turns, otherwise the walks will not be private for any distance. Besides, as it will be proper to line the sides of these walks with honeysuckles, sweet-briar, roses, and many other sweet-flowering shrubs, so the tall trees should be placed at least five or six feet from the walk, to allow room for these.

When the ground is traced out in the manner as the walks are designed, the earth should be taken out of the walks and laid in the quarters. The depth of this must be proportioned to the nature of the soil, for where the ground is dry, the walks need not be elevated much above the quarters, so the earth should be taken out four or five inches deep in such places; but where the ground is wet, the bottom of the walks need not be more than two inches below the surface, that the walks may be raised so high as to throw off the wet into the quarters, which will render them more dry and healthy to walk on.

After the earth is taken out to the intended depth, the bottom of the walks should be laid with rubbish, coarse gravel, or whatever of the like nature can be most readily procured. This should be four, five, or six inches thick, and beaten down as close as possible, to prevent the worms from working through it, then the sand should be laid upon this about 3 inches thick, and after treading it down as close as possible, it should be raked over to level and smooth the surface. In doing this, the whole should be laid a little rounding to throw off the wet, but there will be no necessity of observing any exactness therein; for as the whole ground is to have as little appearance of art as possible, the rounding of these walks should be as natural, and only so contrived as that the water may have free passage from them.

The sand with which these walks are laid should be such as will bind, otherwise it will be very troublesome to walk on them in dry weather; for if the sand be of a loose nature, it will be moved with strong gales of wind, and in dry weather will ſlide from under the feet. If, after theſe walks are laid, they are well rolled two or three times, it will ſettle them, and cauſe them to be firm. If the ſand is too much inclinable to loam, it will alſo be attended with as ill conſequence as that which is too looſe, for this will ſtick to the feet after every rain; ſo that where ſand can be obtained of a middle nature, it ſhould always be preferred.

In ſome countries where ſand cannot be eaſily procured, theſe walks may be laid with ſea-ſhells well pounded, ſo as to reduce them to a powder, which will bind extremely well, provided they are rolled now and then; but where none of theſe can be eaſily procured, ſea-coal aſhes, or whatever elſe can be gotten, which will bind and be dry to the feet, may be uſed for this purpoſe; and where any of theſe can only be had in ſmall quantities, the walks ſhould have a greater ſhare of rubbiſh laid in their bottom, and theſe ſpread thinly over them; and in moſt places rubbiſh, rough ſtones, or coarſe gravel, may be eaſily procured.

WALLS, are abſolutely neceſſary in gardens, for the ripening of all ſuch fruits as are too delicate to be perfected in this country without ſuch aſſiſtance. Theſe are built with different materials; in ſome countries they are built of ſtone, in others with brick, according as the materials can be procured beſt and cheapeſt.

Of all materials proper for building walls for fruit-trees, brick is the beſt, in that it is not only the handſomeſt, but the warmeſt and kindeſt for the ripening of fruit; beſides that, it affords the beſt conveniency of nailing, for ſmaller nails will ſerve in them than in ſtone walls, eſpecially if the joints are not too large; and brick walls with copings of free-ſtone, and ſtone pilaſters or columns at proper diſtances, to ſeparate the trees, and break off the force of the winds, make not only the moſt beautiful, but the moſt durable walls.

In ſome parts of England there are walls built both of brick and ſtone, which have been very commodious. The bricks of ſome places are not of themſelves ſubſtantial enough for walls, nor are they any where ſo durable as ſtone; and therefore ſome perſons, that they might have walls both ſubſtantial and wholeſome, have built double ones, the outſide being of ſtone and the inſide brick, or a ſtone wall lined with brick; but when theſe are built, there muſt be great care taken to bind the bricks well into the ſtone, otherwiſe they are very apt to ſeparate one from the other, eſpecially when hard froſt comes after much wet; which ſwells the mortar, and frequently throws down the bricks, when the walls are only faced with them, and not well tied into the ſtone.

Where the walls are built entirely of ſtone, there ſhould be trelliſſes fixed up againſt them, for the more convenient faſtening the branches of the trees; the timbers of theſe eſpaliers need not be more than an inch and a half thick, and about two inches and a half broad; theſe ſhould be fixed croſs each other, at about four inches diſtance: for if they are at a much greater diſtance, it will be difficult to faſten the ſhoots of the trees properly. As this trellis will be laid cloſe to the wall, the branches of the trees will lie about two inches from the wall, in which poſition the fruit will ripen better than when it lies cloſe to the wall; ſo that there ſhould always be theſe eſpaliers framed againſt them, which will render theſe walls very good for fruit-trees, which, without the eſpaliers, ſeldom are found to anſwer the purpoſe of ripening the fruits well, beſides the inconvenienee of having no good faſtening for the branches of the trees.

There have been ſeveral trials made of walls built in different forms; ſome of them having been built ſemicircular, others in angles of various forms, and projecting more towards the north, to ſkreen off the cold winds; but there has not been any method as yet, which has ſucceeded near ſo well, as that of making the walls ſtrait and building them upright.

The faireſt trial Mr. Miller ſays, he has ſeen made of circular walls was at Good wood in Suſſex, the ſeat of the Duke of Richmond, where in the middle of two ſouth walls, there were two large ſegments of circles, in which there were the ſame ſorts of fruit-trees planted, as againſt the ſtrait parts of the walls; but there never was any fruit upon the trees of the circular part

part of the walls which came to maturity, nor were the trees of long continuance, being blighted every ſpring, and in a few years were totally deſtroyed; and when the branches of theſe trees which grew upon the ſtrait part of the walls, had extended themſelves ſo far as to admit of their being led into the circular parts of the walls, they were conſtantly blighted & killed.

When the trees which had been planted in the circular parts were deſtroyed, the walls were filled with vines; but the grapes of the ſame ſort were full a month later than thoſe growing againſt the ſtrait part of walls; ſo that they rarely ripened, which occaſioned their being rooted out, and figs were afterwards planted, but the fruit of theſe ſucceeded little better; nor can it be ſuppoſed that any trees or plants will thrive ſo well in theſe circles where there is a conſtant draught of air round them, which renders the ſituation much colder than the open free air.

WALL-*Flower*. See GILLIFLOWER.

WALLWORT. Dwarf Elder.

WALNUT, [*Juglans*.] The ſpecies are, 1. The common walnut. Of the common walnut there are ſeveral varieties, which are diſtinguiſhed by the following titles: the large walnut, the thin-ſhelled walnut, the French walnut, the late-ripe walnut, and the double walnut; but theſe do all of them vary when raiſed by the ſeed, ſo that the nuts from the ſame tree will produce plants whoſe fruit will differ; therefore there can be no dependance upon the trees which are raiſed from nuts, till they have produced fruit; ſo that thoſe perſons who plant the trees for their fruit, ſhould make choice of them in the nurſeries when they have their fruit upon them, otherwiſe they may be deceived, by having ſuch as they would not chooſe.

2. Black Virginia Walnut. This grows to a large ſize in North-America. The leaves are compoſed of five or ſix pair of ſpear-ſhaped lobes, which end in acute points, and are ſawed on their edges; the lower pair of lobes are the leaſt, the other gradually increaſe in their ſize to the top, where the pair at the top, and the ſingle lobe which terminates the leaf, are ſmaller; theſe leaves, when bruiſed, emit a ſtrong aromatic flavour, as do alſo the outer cover of the nuts, which are rough, and rounder than thoſe of the common walnut. The ſhell of the nut is very hard and thick, and the kernel ſmall, but very ſweet.

3. Black Virginia Walnut, with an oblong fruit very deeply furrowed. This ſort grows naturally in North-America, where the trees grow to a large ſize. The leaves are compoſed of ſeven or eight pair of long heart-ſhaped lobes, broad at their baſe, where they are divided into two round ears, but terminate in acute points; they are rougher and of a deeper green than thoſe of the ſecond ſort, and have nothing of the aromatic ſcent which they have. The fruit is very long; the ſhell is deeply furrowed, and very hard; the kernel is ſmall, but well flavoured.

4. White Virginia Walnut, called Hickery Nut. This is very common in moſt parts of North-America, where it is called Hickery Nut. The leaves are compoſed of two or three pair of oblong lobes, terminated by an odd one; theſe are of a light green, and ſawed on their edges; the lower pair of lobes are the ſmalleſt, and the upper the largeſt. The fruit is ſhaped like the common walnut; but the ſhell is not furrowed, and is of a light colour.

5. White Walnut, with a ſmaller fruit, and a ſmooth bark. This ſort is not ſo large as the laſt. The leaves are compoſed of two pair of lobes, terminated by an odd one; theſe are narrow at their baſe, but broad and rounded at their ends; they are ſawed on their edges, and are of a light green. The nuts are ſmall, have a ſmooth ſhell, and are very hard and white.

6. White Walnut, with an oval compreſſed fruit, a ſweet kernel, and a ſcaly bark, commonly called Shag-bark in America. This kind grows naturally in North-America, where it riſes to a middling ſtature. The leaves are compoſed of three pair of ſmooth ſpear-ſhaped lobes, of a dark green colour, ſawed on their edges, and ending in acute points. The fruit is oval, the ſhell white, hard, and ſmooth, the kernel ſmall, but very ſweet. The young ſhoots are covered with a very ſmooth browniſh bark, but the ſtems and older branches have a rough ſcaly bark, whence it is called ſhag-bark.

 The

The walnut, in the Linnæan ſyſtem, belongs to the claſs and order *Monoecia Polyandria*. The flowers begin to open about the middle of April, and are in full blow by the middle of May, before which time the leaves are fully diſplayed.

Theſe trees are propagated by planting their nuts, which ſeldom produce the ſame ſort of fruit as ſown; ſo that the only way to have the deſired ſort is to ſow the nuts of the beſt kinds; and if this is done in a nurſery, the trees ſhould be tranſplanted out when they have had three or four years growth, to the place where they are deſigned to remain; for theſe trees do not bear tranſplanting when they are of a large ſize, therefore there ſhould be a good number of trees planted, which need not be put at more than ſix feet apart, which will be diſtance enough for them to grow till they produce fruit; when thoſe, whoſe fruit are of the deſired kind, may remain, and the others cut up, to allow them room to grow.

But as many people do not care to wait ſo long for the fruit, the next beſt method is to make choice of ſome young trees in the nurſeries, when they have their fruit upon them. But though theſe trees will grow and bear fruit, yet they will never be ſo large or long-lived, as thoſe which are planted young.

All the ſorts of walnut which are intended for timber, ſhould be ſown in the places where they are to remain; for the roots of theſe trees always incline downward, which being ſtopped or broken, prevent their aſpiring upward, ſo that they afterwards divaricate into branches, and become low ſpreading trees; but ſuch as are propagated for fruit, are greatly mended by tranſplanting; for hereby they are rendered more fruitful, and their fruit is generally larger and fairer; it being a common obſervation, that downright roots greatly encourage the luxuriant growth of timber in all ſorts of trees; but ſuch trees as have their roots ſpreading near the ſurface of the ground, always produce the greateſt quantity and beſt-flavoured fruit.

In tranſplanting theſe trees, you ſhould obſerve never to prune either their roots or large branches, both which operations are very injurious to them; nor ſhould you be too buſy in lopping or pruning the branches of theſe trees when grown to a large ſize, for it often cauſes them to decay; but when there is a neceſſity for cutting any of their branches off, it ſhould be done early in September, (for at that ſeaſon the trees are not ſo ſubject to bleed) that the wound may heal over before the cold increaſes; the branches ſhould always be cut off quite cloſe to the trunk, otherwiſe the ſtump which is left will decay, and rot the body of the tree.

The beſt ſeaſon for tranſplanting theſe trees is as ſoon as the leaves begin to decay, at which time if they are carefully taken up, and their branches preſerved entire, there will be little danger of their ſucceeding.

The diſtance theſe trees ſhould be placed, ought not to be leſs than forty feet, eſpecially if regard be had to their fruit; though when they are only deſigned for timber, if they ſtand nearer, it promotes their upright growth. The black Virginia walnut is much more inclinable to grow upright than the common ſort, and the wood is generally of a more beautiful grain.

WANG-TOOTH, a jaw tooth.

WANT, a mole. See MOLE.

WANTY, a broad girth of leather, by which the load is bound upon a horſe.

WAPENTAKE, the ſame with what is called a hundred, and is the term generally uſed in the northern counties beyond the Trent.

WARBLES, ſmall hard tumours on the ſaddle part of a horſe's back, occaſioned by the heat of the ſaddle in travelling, or its uneaſy ſituation. see Sit-fast

A hot greaſy diſh-clout, at firſt frequently applied, will ſometimes remove them. Camphorated ſpirits of wine are alſo very effectual for this purpoſe to diſperſe them, eſpecially if a little ſpirit of ſal ammoniac be added to the camphorated ſpirit. If there be a neceſſity for working the horſe, care ſhould be taken to have the ſaddle nicely chambered.

WARREN, a franchiſe, or place privileged, either by preſcription or grant from the king, to keep beaſts and fowl of warren in; as rabbits, hares, partridges, &c.

WARP,

Wart or pimples in Mouth of Horse &c. The Cause & Cure - See Camory or

WARP, miscarry, slink her calf.

WARTWORT. Euphorbium.

WASTE, a name given to such lands as are in no man's possession, but lie common.

WATER is one of the most considerable requisites belonging to a garden; if a garden be without it, it brings a certain mortality upon whatsoever is planted. By waterings the great droughts in summer are allayed, which would infallibly burn up most plants; besides as to noble seats, the beauty that water will add, in making cascades.

Water not only acts as a vehicle to the nourishment of plants, but carries with it many particles which enrich the soil; especially after heavy rains. It then deposits a fertilising sediment, which turns the mould to a blackish colour. Watering likewise promotes the putrefaction of every vegetable and animal substance found in the earth, and thereby contributes greatly to meliorate the soil underneath the sward.

Plants which grow on dry pastures contain richer and more nourishing juices, than those which grow in moist places. Care should therefore be taken, that the quantity of moisture brought upon the pasture, be only such as shall give vigour to the plants, without over-charging their vessels.

Extreme heat should also be avoided in watering; because heat draws the moisture too hastily up into the plant, which is thereby filled with a watery juice, and rendered of so tender a texture, as easily to be killed afterwards by drought or cold.

Water CALAMINT. Horsemint.

WATER-CRESS. See *Water*-Cress.

WATER DROPWORT. See *Water* DROPWORT.

Water FLAG. [*Gladiolus Luteus.*] Yellow water-flag, Iris, bastard acorus, or water flower-de-luce. This plant grows common by the brinks of rivers and in other watery places. The root has a very acrid taste, and proves when fresh a strong cathartic: its expressed juice, given to the quantity of eighty drops every hour or two, and occasionally increased, has occasioned a plentiful evacuation, after jalap, gamboge, &c. had proved ineffectual. By drying, it loses its acrimony and purgative virtue. The *pulvis ari* of our dispensatory contains about one-fifth of the dry root.

Water GERMANDER. See *Water* GERMANDER.

Water HEMP AGRIMONY. See *Water* AGRIMONY.

Water HOREHOUND. See *Water* HOREHOUND.

Water LILY. See *Water* LILY.

Water PARSNEP. Skirret.

Water PEPPER. Biting Arsmart.

WATTLE. A kind of hurdle formed with split wood, and used for making folds for sheep.

WAX, or BEES-WAX. A substance formed by bees from the farina of flowers. See BEE.

WAY-BREAD. Plantain.

WAYFARING-TREE. [*Libinum.*] This tree grows naturally in many parts of Europe and America, and is either propagated from seeds or layers.

WEANEL. An animal newly weaned.

WELD. Dyer's Weed. See WOAD.

WEED. Any plant growing in a field different from what the farmer intended.

WHEAT. [*Triticum.*] The sorts of wheat cultivated in England now, and to answer all purposes, are known to the farmer under the names of red wheat, white wheat, and cone wheat; there are abundance of varieties, but when every thing is considered, these are enough, and distinction enough to make. We cannot with the greatest precision, perhaps, point out where each is particularly cultivated; but the red is much found in Bedfordshire, the white about Taunton, in Somersetshire, and the country about London, and the cone in Staffordshire, Herefordshire, &c.

Whatever distinctions might have been made of each grain to different sorts of land, we believe that each will grow on each, not that cone wheat is so well adapted to light land as white wheat, or as white wheat is to strong land.

It has been very justly observed by ancients, as well as moderns, that wheat will grow in almost any part of the world, and that, as it is the plant most necessary to mankind, so it is the most general, and the most fruitful. It thrives not only in temperate climates, but also in very hot and very cold

cold regions; and, when ſown in places where it never grew ſpontaneouſly, ſucceeds as well as where it has been always common. The ſucceſs of the crops of wheat in America plainly prove this: and, in Peru and Chili in particular, where this grain was not known till the Europeans introduced it there, it now produces as large crops as in moſt parts of Europe.

Wheat ſhould be ſowed in autumn, and always when the ground is moiſt. In the downs of Hampſhire, Wiltſhire, and Dorſetſhire, farmers begin to ſow their wheat in Auguſt, if any rain has fallen; and even employ their people to ſow one place, while they reap another, if wet weather interrupts them in the harveſt; for if the corn be not forward in autumn, ſo as to cover the ground before winter, it ſeldom does well on thoſe high dry lands, eſpecially if the enſuing ſpring proves likewiſe dry. In low ſtrong lands, ſome huſbandmen think they are in good ſeaſon, if they get their wheat into the ground by the middle of November; nay, it is ſometimes Chriſtmas, or even later, before all their wheat is ſown. But this late ſown wheat, beſides being apt to run too much to ſtraw, eſpecially if the ſpring be moiſt, is liable to be thrown out of the ground by froſts.

Some gentlemen have been curious enough to procure their ſeed wheat from Sicily, and it has ſucceeded very well as to the growth; but the grain of this ſpecies has proved too hard for our Engliſh mills to grind.

The beſt time for ſowing wheat is about the beginning of September, eſpecially if any rain has fallen; a circumſtance ſo eſſential, that if the earth be very dry, the farmer had better ſtay till friendly ſhowers have moiſtened his ſoil, than put his corn in ground where it will not grow before it has been wet, let the time be ever ſo long. Mr. Mortimer ſays, he has known wheat to be ſo muſtied and ſpoiled by laying long in the ground before rain has come, that it has never grown at all; to which he adds, that he has likewiſe ſeen very good crops grow from ſeed ſown in July. At all events, the huſbandman ſhould certainly have his wheat ſowing finiſhed by the middle of October. Whoever neglects this, ſhews in ſo doing a want of proper œconomy in his affairs, and will have cauſe to repent his delay.

Early ſowings require leſs ſeed than late ones, becauſe the plants then riſe better, and acquire ſtrength to reſiſt the winter's cold. More ſeed ſhould always be allowed for poor lands than for rich, becauſe a greater number of plants will periſh on the former. Rich lands, ſowed early, require the leaſt ſeed of any.

Another circumſtance which the huſbandman ſhould carefully attend to in ſowing is, that his eſtimate of ſeed be formed, not from the capacity of any particular meaſure, but from the number of grains which that meaſure will contain; becauſe the grains of ſome growths of wheat are much larger than thoſe from off other lands, though of the ſame ſpecies, and perhaps equally good. By not conſidering this, the ground will of courſe frequently be ſown too thick, or too thin; though we believe, farmers are ſeldom apt to run into this laſt extreme. That they too often commit the former error, ſo manifeſtly contrary to their intereſt in every reſpect, is demonſtrated by reaſon, and by daily experience:—but neither of theſe is ſufficient to make them deviate from the beaten track. Inſtead of the uſual allowance of three buſhels of ſeed wheat to an acre of land, repeated trials have ſhewn that half or two-thirds of that quantity is generally more than ſufficient; conſequently a great deal of corn is actually thrown away; for the expence of purchaſing ſeed, which moſt ſkilful huſbandmen generally do, at leaſt every other year, amounts to a conſiderable article in large farms, and in a whole country, merits the attention of the public, eſpecially in ſcarce years; beſides which, the future plants, crowded together by being thus ſown too thick, and not having a ſufficient ſpace allowed them for a ſuſtenance, cannot yield near ſo fine and plentiful a crop as they would otherwiſe produce. A fair trial, made with proper care, would ſoon convince farmers of their error in this reſpect; for if they but examine a field of corn ſown in the common way, they will find few plants with more than two or three ſtalks, unleſs by chance, where ſome of them ſtand ſo as to have room to ſpread.

These

Theſe will have ſix, eight, or ten ſtalks, and frequently many more; but a field of wheat ſown with only a buſhel of corn, has been known to be well covered with healthy vigorous plants, each of which has had from ſix to fourteen or more ſtalks, crowned with long well-nouriſhed ears, full of fine plump grain, of which it has yielded a much greater quantity than any of the neighbouring grounds, ſown with the common allowance. If the land be good, and the plants ſtand at a proper diſtance from each other, few of them will produce leſs than the above number of ſtalks and ears. But farmers think they ſhall have no crops if the ground be not covered with the blades of corn by the ſpring: whereas if they would have patience to wait till the plants put out all their ſtems, they would be amply convinced of the contrary. Every one muſt have obſerved, in places where foot-paths are made through corn fields, that, by the ſides of thoſe paths, where the corn is thin, and has been trodden down in winter and ſpring, the plants have ſtood erect, when moſt of the corn in the ſame field has been laid flat upon the ground; and advantage which can ariſe from no other cauſe, than that their ſtalks are ſtronger from their having more room: for theſe of the other plants are drawn up tall and ſlender, by being too cloſe together.

Cow WHEAT. See COW WHEAT.

Indian WHEAT. See GUINEA *Wheat*.

WHEE *or* WHEY. A heifer.

WHICKEN TREE. Service tree.

WHINS. Furze.

WHISKET. A baſket.

WHITE-CLOVER. A well known plant, and reckoned the ſweeteſt feed of any of the ſown graſſes; and it is of moſt advantage to the farmer, becauſe it is perennial, or laſts a great number of years on the land.

This plant ſends forth roots at every joint, ſo that it thickens, and ſoon makes a thick ſward. When land is to be laid down for paſture, the farmer will reap great profit, if, with about four buſhels of clean-ſifted hay-ſeed to an acre, he ſows eight pounds of this clover, but it is to be remarked, that it is never to be ſown with corn.

It may be ſown either in ſpring or autumn; if in ſpring, it may be cut about the latter end of July; if ſown in autmun; the crop will be much earlier. As ſoon as ever the hay is off the land, it ſhould be rolled with a heavy roller. In laying down land with theſe graſſes, it will be proper for the farmer to be very careful that he cleans the land of all ſorts of weeds; and the hay-ſeeds are to be ſown firſt, immediately after which the clover is to be regularly ſcattered. After ſowing, the land ſhould be lightly harrowed, with a ſhort tined harrow, to bury the ſeed; and a few days after-if the weather be dry, it ſhould be rolled, to break the clods, and cloſe it.

It will be good huſbandry, if, after the plants are come up, the farmer ſhould ſend in ſome weeders, to pull up all the tall rampant weeds which might injure the crop, for, if they are ſuffered to ſeed, they will ſoon ſtock the land.

It will be proper to take the advantage of dry weather, and roll the land three or four times, after the plants have attained ſome ſize; for the clover taking root at every joint, the ſward will thereby be greatly thicken'd.

If a farmer knows his own intereſt, he will ſow ſome of this white clover-ſeed by itſelf, in order to ſupply himſelf with what feed he may want, for it is ſometimes very dear. The beſt ſeaſon for ſowing is autumn, upon dry lands, about the beginning or middle of September; but in open, cold lands, much expoſed, a month ſooner is better: all the caution required in this autumnal ſowing is to let the land be very well rolled in the month of October, before the froſts come on, and again in March.

WHITE-SCORE. A diſeaſe with which ſheep are too often affected and by which great numbers of them die.

The following medicine has been often given with ſucceſs, provided the ſheep are at the ſame time removed into a dry paſture.

Take a pint of old verjuice, half a pound of common or bay ſalt, dried well before the fire, pounded, and ſifted through a ſieve. Then mix the verjuice with the ſalt by degrees; and add half a pint of common gin, and bottle it up for uſe. When any of your ſheep are ſeized with this diſorder,

ſeparate

ſeparate them from the flock, and give each of them three large table ſpoonfuls of the mixture for a doſe, repeating it two days after if they are not better.

WHITE-LANDS. Chalky lands.

WILDS. A term uſed by our farmers to expreſs that part of a plough by which the whole is drawn forward.

WILDERNESS. A kind of grove of large trees, in a ſpacious garden, in which the walks are made either to interſect each other in angles, or have the appearance of meanders and labyrinths.

WHORTLEBERRY. Bilberry.

WIDOWWAIL. [*Cneorum.*] This is a low evergreen ſhrub, and might form an agreeable variety in wilderneſſes, &c. It is eaſily propagated by ſcattering the ſeeds.

WILLOW. See SALLOW.

Dutch or *Sweet* WILLOW. Candle-berry-tree.

French WILLOW. See French *Willow.*

Sweet WILLIAM. See Carnation.

WINDFLOWER. See ANEMONE.

To WINNOW. To clear corn of the chaff.

WITHERS. The part of a horſe where the ſhoulder-bones join at the bottom of the neck and mane.

WITHWIND. Bindweed.

WINTER *Aconite.* Hellebore.

WINTER *Cherry.* See *Winter* Cherry.

WINTER *Green.* See *Winter* Green.

WINTER *Creſs.* Water-Creſs.

WINTER's BARK. [*Cortex Winteranus.*] The produce of a tree growing in Jamaica, Barbadoes, &c. called by Sir Hans Sloane *periclymenum rectum, foliis laurinis, cortice acri aromatico.* It was firſt diſcovered on the coaſt of Magellan, by Captain Winter, in the year 1567; the ſailors then employed the bark as a ſpice, and afterwards found it ſerviceable in the ſcurvy; for which purpoſe it is at preſent alſo ſometimes made uſe of in diet-drinks. The true winter's bark is not often met with in the ſhops, canella alba being generally ſubſtituted for it, and by many reckoned to be the ſame; there is, nevertheleſs, a conſiderable difference betwixt them in appearance, and a greater in quality; the winter's bark is in larger pieces, of a more cinnamon-colour than the canella; and taſtes much warmer and more pungent.

WITCH HAZEL, [*Hamamelis.*] This plant grows naturally in North-America, from whence the ſeeds have been brought to Europe, and many of the plants have been raiſed in the Engliſh gardens, where they are propagated for ſale by the nurſery gardeners. It hath a woody ſtem from two to three feet high, ſending out many ſlender branches, garniſhed with oval leaves, indented on their edges, having great reſemblance to thoſe of the hazel; they fall away in autumn, and when the plants are deſtitute of leaves, the flowers come out in cluſters from the joints of the branches; theſe ſometimes appear the latter end of October, and often not till December, but are not ſucceeded by ſeeds in this country.

As the flowers of this ſhrub make very little appearance, ſo it is only preſerved in the gardens of the curious, for the ſake of variety.

It is propagated by laying down the young branches in autumn, which will take root in one year, and may then be taken from the old plants, and planted where they are to remain. The ſeeds of this plant always remain a whole year in the ground, ſo they ſhould be ſown in pots.

WOAD. Weld, or Dyer's Weed. The Engliſh plant, called by botaniſts *Iſatis ſativa, vel latifolia.*

A light, black, kindly, and rich ſoil, or a meadow newly broken up, is choſen for the cultivation of Woad; but it muſt not by any means be ſown on ſtony or ſhallow land. It thrives well in plains, but ſtill better on the ſouth ſide of a hill; the eſſential point is, that the ſoil be good, and that it have the above-mentioned qualities.

Though the land which is intended for Woad be never ſo good, it muſt be dunged a year before it is ſown with this plant, and be made firſt to bear a crop of wheat, or of onions, &c. After theſe are taken off, three deep ſtirrings ſhould be given with the plough, or, which is much better, with the ſpade: the firſt ſtirring ſhould be in November, and the other two in February, March, or April. If the land which is intended for woad lies flat, and has not ſlope enough to carry off the wet, channels muſt be cut of a greater or leſs ſize, according as the ground is more or leſs diſpoſed to retain the water.

In warm climates, Woad is sown so early as the beginning of April, unless the weather chance then to be too cold, in which case this sowing is deferred till the beginning of May; but for countries like ours, where the spring is attended with frosts, particularly in the night, Mr. Miller is certainly right in advising to lay the land up in narrow high ridges just before winter, that the frost may mellow it: to cross plough it in the spring, laying it again in narrow ridges, and between this time and the ensuing month of June to harrow it well twice at different intervals, in order to root up whatever [illegible] may have appeared; then, in June, to give the ground a third ploughing as deep as the plough will go, making the furrows narrow; after this, to harrow it again when any new weeds are come up; and finally, towards the end of July, or the beginning of August, to plough it for the last time, laying it as smooth as possible. A good harrowing after this will fit it completely to receive the seeds, which if rain falls soon after their being sown, or if they are steeped in water during the night before their sowing, as Mr. Miller advises, will appear in a fortnight, if the season be favourable. They should be but lightly covered, and should be sowed so thin as that the plants may stand six inches asunder. Some strew pigeon's dung on the land just after having sown it with Woad, and the plants become much the finer for this manure.

When the Woad is grown large enough to be distinguished, it should be carefully cleared of all weeds, for these would hurt it greatly; and at the same time the plants should be thinned wherever they stand too close: without this precaution, the Woad would produce but very few leaves, and would remain extremely stinted in its growth.

Woad generally affords two crops in the same year, and sometimes, when the season has been favourable, it has yielded even four. The two first are the best, and these are commonly mixed together in the manufacturing of this plant; but the after-crops are always kept separate; for if these are mixed with the other, the whole will be spoiled.

The first crop should be gathered towards the end of August, and the last at the end of October, or in the beginning of November: but this last crop must be got in before the first frosts come on; for the leaves that might be gathered afterwards would not be worth any thing. When the plant is ripe, which is known by its first leaves beginning to dry, all the leaves are cut off by a man who grasps the plant by handfuls, and they are then laid in a heap to wither. Whilst they are in this situation, they must be sheltered from the sun and rain, and they must be frequently turned, in order that they may heat equally: they are then carried to a mill somewhat like that which is used for pressing the oil out of linseed, and are there ground till they are reduced into a paste, which is afterwards formed into cakes of about a pound weight, and these are laid to dry in a covered place where neither the sun nor rain can come at them. This paste is dried thus for about a fortnight, that is to say till it has acquired consistence enough to be formed into small roundish lumps, by means of little wooden moulds into which it is put for that purpose. As fast as these lumps are taken out of the moulds, they are laid upon wicker hurdles loosely woven, so as not to touch one another, and in such manner that the air may come at every part of them, as is practised in the drying of starch. These lumps become very hard, and in this condition it is that they are sold. When they are to be used, they must be steeped a long while in water before they can be broken.

The Woad thus prepared yields an excellent blue dye, very lasting, and with which all the degrees of this colour may be made. It is not long since this plant was preferred to indigo; afterwards, through a kind of toleration, the dyers were allowed to put a small quantity of indigo into their vats of Woad; but now, that the making and manner of using indigo have been greatly improved, it is looked upon as a matter of indifference whether that or Woad be used for dying blue.

WOLFSBANE, [*Aconitum.*] The plants, of which there are severa cies, grow naturally on the Alps, and on the mountains of Auſtria and Tartary. Moſt if not all are hurtful in a greater or leſs degree, ſo care ſhould be taken where they are planted.

Wholeſome WOLFSBANE, [*Anthora.*] This plant may be diſtinguiſhed from the poiſonous aconites by its leaves being more finely divided, and not at all bright or ſhining: it grows wild on the Alps. The root has been ſuppoſed uſeful againſt poiſons, particularly that of the *thora*, (whence its name.) Some nevertheleſs look upon this pretended antidote itſelf as unſafe.

WOOD. A large plantation of trees.

WOODCOCK *Soil.* Ground whoſe ſoil under the turf is of the colour of a woodcock, and is not good.

WOODLAND. Ground covered with woods. It is alſo a term uſed by the farmers of many counties in England, for a ſort of ſoil, from its conſtant humidity and dark colour, reſembling the ſoil in woods, which, of whatever nature it originally is, will always be made to appear thus from the continual dropping of trees, and the want of a free air and ſun, together with the fall of leaves, deſtroyed and waſhed to pieces by the wet.

WOODY. Abounding with wood.

WOODBINE. See HONEYSUCKLE.

WOODROOF. Petty Madder.

WOOD-SAGE. Tree Germander.

WOOD-SORREL. See WOOD *Sorrel.*

WOOL. The covering of ſheep. Each fleece conſiſts of wool of ſeveral qualities and degrees of fineneſs, which the dealers therein take care to ſeparate.

The Engliſh and French uſually ſeparate each fleece into three principal ſorts, viz. 1. Mother-wool, which is that of the back and neck. 2. The wool of the tails and legs. 3. That of the breaſt and under the belly. The Engliſh wool moſt eſteemed is, chiefly that about Leominſter, Coltſwold, and the Iſle of Wight; the Spaniſh, principally that about Vegovia; and the French, about Berry.

Both wool, and woollen rags, make an excellent manure. The rags ſhould be chopped ſmall, about an inch or two ſquare, and ſcattered on the earth at the ſecond ploughing; for being thereby covered, they will begin to rot by ſeed-time. They imbibe the moiſture of dews and rain, retain it long, and, as Dr. Home obſerves, thereby keep looſe ſoils in a moiſt ſtate. They coſt about four-pence a buſhel at London, from whence many loads are ſent every year to Dunſtable (which is 30 miles) where they are laid even on ſtiff lands, juſt after the ſowing of the corn, allowing to the acre four ſacks of ſix buſhels each.

WORMS, are very prejudicial to corn fields, eating up the roots of the young corn, and deſtroying great quantities of the crop. Sea-ſalt is the beſt of all things for deſtroying them. Sea water is proper to ſprinkle on the land where it can be had; where the ſalt-ſprings are, their water will ſerve, and were neither are at hand, a little common or bay-ſalt does as well. Soot will deſtroy them in ſome lands, but is not to be depended upon, for it does not always ſucceed. Some farmers ſtrew on their lands a mixture of chalk and lime; and others truſt wholly to their winter-fallowing to do it, if this is done in a wet ſeaſon, when they come up to the ſurface of the ground, and ſome nails with ſharp heads be driven into the bottom of the plough. If they are troubleſome in gardens, the refuſe brine of ſalted meat will ſerve the purpoſe, or ſome walnut leaves ſteeped in a ciſtern of water for a fortnight or three weeks, will give it ſuch a bitterneſs that it will be a certain poiſon to them. A decoction of wood-aſhes, ſprinkled on the ground, will anſwer the ſame purpoſe; and any particular plant may be ſecured both from worms and ſnails by ſtrewing a mixture of lime and aſhes about its roots. It is a general caution among the farmers to ſow their corn as ſhallow as they can, where the field is very ſubject to worms.

WORMWOOD, [*Abſinthium vulgare.*] Common wormwood. The leaves of this ſort of wormwood are divided into roundiſh ſegments, of a dull green colour above, and whitiſh underneath. It grows wild in ſeveral parts of England; about London, large quantities are cultivated for medicinal uſe: it flowers in June and July, and after having ripened its ſeeds, dies down to the ground, excepting a tuft of the lower leaves, which generally abides the winter.

Sea Wormwood. The leaves of sea wormwood are much smaller than those of the common, and hoary on the upper side as well as the lower; the stalks also are hoary all over. It grows wild about our salt marshes, and in several parts about the sea coasts. In taste and smell, it is weaker and less unpleasant than the common wormwood. The virtues of both are supposed to be of the same kind, and differ only in degree.

Roman Wormwood. This species is very different in appearance from the two foregoing: it is in all its parts smaller than either; the leaves are divided into fine filaments, and hoary on the lower side; the stalks, either entirely or in part, of a purplish hue. It is a native of the warmer countries, and at present difficultly procurable in this, though as hardy and as easily raised as any of the other sorts.

Roman wormwood appears to be the most eligible of the three as a stomachic; and is likewise recommended by some in dropsies.

WOUNDWORT. Golden Rod.

Woundwort *of Achilles*. Milfoil.

Y.

Yard Disease in [illegible] See Colt-Evil. Yeast. See Barm

YARD-LAND. A quantity of land, in some countries fifteen acres, in some twenty, and in others twenty-four, thirty, and thirty-four acres.

YARROW. Milfoil.

Water Yarrow. This plant grows naturally in standing waters in many parts of England; the leaves which are for the most part immersed in the water, are finely winged and flat, like most of the sea plants, and at the bottom have long fibrous roots, which strike into the mud: the flower-stalks rise five or six inches above the water; they are naked, and toward the top have two or three whorls of purple flowers, terminated by a small cluster of the same. These flowers have the appearance of those of the stock-gilliflower, so make a pretty appearance on the surface of the water.

YELLOWS. See Jaundice.

YEW. [*Taxus.*] This tree grows naturally in England, and also in most of the Northern Counties of Europe, and in North-America. If suffered to grow, it will rise to a good height, with a very large stem. It naturally sends out branches on every side, which spread out, and are almost horizontal; these are closely garnished with narrow, stiff, blunted pointed leaves, of a very dark green. The flowers come out from the side of the branches in clusters; the male flowers having many stamina, are more conspicuous than the female; these for the most part are upon different trees, but sometimes are upon the same tree; they appear the latter end of May, and the berries ripen in autumn.

The Yew tree has been generally cultivated for the pleasure-garden, both to clip into the figures of beasts, birds, &c. and also for hedges. Whoever is pleased with such figures in his garden, can raise no tree more proper for his purpose, as the branches and leaves may be clipped and fashioned into almost any form or shape. But as this method is justly exploded, and as every one who has the least pretension to taste must always prefer a tree in its natural growth to those monstrous figures, the Yew is now chiefly planted for wilderness quarters, as also for hedges, for which service it is excellently well adapted, as no tree bears clipping so well.

These trees may be easily propagated by sowing their berries in autumn, as ſoon as they are ripe, (without clearing them from the pulp which ſurrounds them, as hath been frequently directed) upon a ſhady bed of freſh undunged ſoil, covering them over about half an inch thick with the ſame earth.

In the ſpring the bed muſt be carefully cleared from weeds, and if the ſeaſon proves dry, it will be proper to refreſh the bed with water now and then, which will promote the growth of the ſeeds, many of which will come up the ſame ſpring, but others will remain in the ground until autumn or the ſpring following; but where the ſeeds are preſerved above ground till ſpring before they are ſown, the plants never come up till the year after; ſo that by ſowing the ſeeds as ſoon as they are ripe, there is often a whole year ſaved.

Theſe plants, when they come up, ſhould be conſtantly cleared from weds, which, if permitted to grow amongſt them, will cauſe their bottoms to be naked, and frequently deſtroy the plants when they continue long undiſturbed.

In this bed the plants may remain two years; after which, in autumn, there ſhould be a ſpot of freſh undunged ſoil prepared, into which they ſhould be remov'd the beginning of October, planting them in beds about four or five feet wide, in rows about a foot aſunder, and the ſame diſtance from each other in the rows, obſerving to lay a little mulch upon the ſurface of the ground about their roots, as alſo to water them in dry weather until they have taken root; after which they will require no farther care, but to keep them clear from weeds in ſummer, and to trim them according to the purpoſe for which they are deſigned.

In theſe beds they may remain two or three years, according as they have grown, when they ſhould again be removed into a nurſery, placing them in rows at three feet diſtance, and the plants eighteen inches aſunder in the rows; obſerve to do it in autumn, as was before directed, and continue to trim them in the ſummer ſeaſon, according to the deſign for which they were intended; and after they have continued three or four years in this nurſery, they may be tranſplanted where they are to remain; always obſerving to remove them in autumn where the ground is very dry, but on cold moiſt land it is better in the ſpring.

Theſe trees, though of ſlow growth, do ſometimes arrive at a conſiderable ſize. Mr. Pennant mentions one in Fontingal church-yard, in the Highlands of Scotland, whoſe ruins meaſured fifty-ſix feet and a half in circumference.

Of the Yew there is a variety with ſhort leaves, which appear very ornamental in plantations. There is alſo another with ſtriped leaves of great value amongſt the variegated tribes. Theſe are increaſed by layers, but the ſtriped ſort muſt be planted upon a barren ſoil, otherwiſe it will become plain.

YEOMAN. The firſt, or higheſt degree of the plebeians of England. The yeomen are properly freeholders, who cultivate their own lands.

YOAK, or YOKE. A frame of wood, fitted over the necks of oxen, whereby they are coupled together, and harneſſed to the plough.

Yoak *of Land.* The quantity of land which a yoak of oxen might plough in a day.

F I N I S.

www.ingramcontent.com/pod-product-compliance
Lightning Source LLC
Chambersburg PA
CBHW030916270326
41929CB00008B/712